METAL TECHNIQUES FOR CRAFTSMEN

By the same author

ENAMELING ON METAL
JEWELRY CONCEPTS AND TECHNOLOGY

OPPOSITE: Copper water pot with repoussé decoration
from New Delhi, India, 12″ high, collection of Mr.
and Mrs. Leonard Gang. *Photo by Oppi.*

METAL TECHNIQUES FOR CRAFTSMEN

A Basic Manual for Craftsmen

on the Methods of Forming and Decorating Metals

By OPPI UNTRACHT

ROBERT HALE · LONDON

First published in Great Britain 1969

Reprinted 1974
Reprinted 1975
Reprinted 1977
Reprinted 1978
Reprinted 1979
Reprinted 1980
Reprinted 1985
Reprinted 2001
Reprinted 2002
Reprinted 2005

ISBN 0-7091-0723-4

Robert Hale Limited
Clerkenwell House
Clerkenwell Green
London EC1R OHT

ACKNOWLEDGMENTS

Line drawings by Saara Hopea Untracht, a dutiful wife.

The craftsman's tools on the endpapers were photographed by the author at the Allcraft Tool and Supply Co., Inc., New York.

Tool drawings are from the catalogs of the following companies, to whom many thanks are given for their kind permission to allow their reproduction: Allcraft Tool and Supply Co., Inc., Anchor Tool Co., Craftools, Inc., William Dixon, Inc., Gamzon Bros., Paul H. Gesswein and Co., Inc., Alexander Saunders and Co., Inc., I. Schor Co., Inc., S. S. White and Co.

Thanks are also due to the many individual craftsmen and the companies and organizations who cooperated by responding to requests for photos and information. They are too numerous to mention individually here, but credits are given along with the photos used and in the text. Although every effort was made to obtain permissions for the use of photographs, some permissions might have been unobtainable by the time the book went to press. If the owner of reproduction rights will advise the author of failure to credit them properly, corrections will be made in a second printing. Apologies are hereby extended.

A great debt of gratitude is acknowledged to the cooperation of the museums both in America and abroad whose photo files were rapaciously ransacked. They are all credited, but the one that was perhaps the most useful is the Museum of Contemporary Crafts in New York City, which does not yet have a large permanent collection but does have an excellent photo file of the work of contemporary craftsmen and an extremely agreeable and cooperative staff.

To Mr. Thomas O'Connor Sloane III, thanks for a careful and constructive job editing.

O.A.J.U.

To Saara

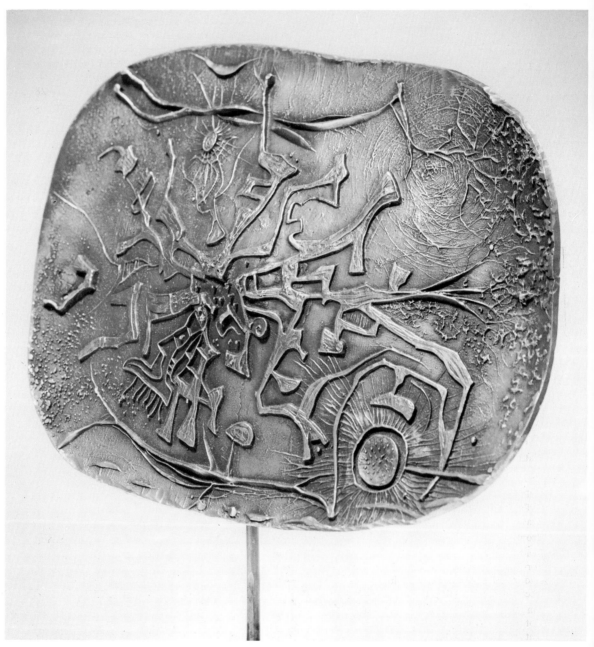

Cast pewter panel, by John Prip. The design was
created by carving directly into the mold and then
pouring the metal.

Contents

Silver bottle, Lower Egypt (Ptolemaic Period), about
90 B.C. Height with cover: 11¼ inches. The finely
ridged fluting emphasizes the ripeness of the form.

*Metropolitan Museum of Art, New York. Rogers
Fund, 1938.*

Introduction

With his first knowledge of metals, and the eventual skill he acquired in handling them, man launched himself into civilization. Starting with the copper ax of prehistoric, primitive man, technology has progressed in the use of metals to the creation of a metal container in which contemporary man will undoubtedly launch himself into an exploration of other planets.

Though today we are looking outward beyond the confines of mere Earth, we have spent several thousand years delving into its surface, exploring its properties, analyzing, extracting, and combining metals to create not only objects of purely functional purpose but objects to delight the eye. A look back at the products of almost all cultures made for personal adornment and use and for the most meaningful rituals shows an ingenuity of craftsmanship that is staggering in the variety of form, decoration, and skills.

Such objects, even on a primitive level, would not have been possible without the development of the science of *metallurgy*—the art of extracting metal from ores, purifying and alloying them, and working them to satisfy man's needs and imagination.

Geologists tell us the earth's crust contains, among other elements, the following approximate percentages of metals:

Silicon	27.720	Zinc	.004
Aluminum	8.130	Lead	.002
Iron	5.010	Tin	.0001
Magnesium	2.090	Mercury	.00001
Chromium	.037	Silver	.000001
Nickel	.020	Gold	.0000001
Copper	.010		

From these estimates we can understand why gold, for instance, for its rarity alone, not to mention its beauty and desirable working qualities, has always been considered a valuable metal and a symbol of wealth.

We can see too, if these estimates be correct, that metals exist in the earth in finite quantities. Our world would be quite impossible to imagine without metals, yet at the rate that man is consuming metals, in the not too distant future we may be forced to turn to other materials to replace this important element of our material culture. In our lifetime, the depletion of prime supplies of some metals has caused the development of improved technology to extract metal from low-quality ores once considered not worth the trouble to work. The need to conserve our present supplies has created a great industry, the collection and processing of scrap metals. The realization that *primary* metals, produced directly from ores, are not inexhaustible has made *secondary* metals, reclaimed from scrap, an important supplement to mined ores.

This is true of precious as well as ordinary metals. Companies exist that collect a metal workshop's floor sweepings (called *sweeps*), filings (called *lemel* or *limail*), rags, and drain deposits. These are processed, purified, and assayed, and the owner is paid almost as much for the reclaimed metal as the price of these metals sold pure on the market. (A minimum of twenty-five ounces is acceptable.) The gradual withdrawal of silver used in the metal coinage of many countries and the substitution of less expensive metals is another indication of an increasing shortage of precious metals, as is the increase in the price of precious metals in the market. As craftsmen, we simply cannot afford to be careless with our metal resources.

Metal objects can endure beyond the range of man's short life and become both an inheritance and a contribution to culture. They can be made to do jobs that man is too frail to accomplish unaided. Metals are intrinsically beautiful. When polished, they brilliantly *reflect light*. They exist in a *variety of colors* ranging from the pure white of silver to the yellows, reds, and greens of gold and the pink of copper. In some metals, the natural color changes slowly with exposure to the atmosphere due to *oxidation,* but the color range can be infinitely extended by the use of chemicals to artificially create *patinas* or surface colors. It is possible to create *alloys,* or combinations of metals in measured proportions, that have their own color character and working qualities. The forms into which metal can be manipulated in wire and sheet form and by casting makes practically any shape possible. Metal can be bent, twisted, pierced, poured, stretched, compressed, mixed, and combined with other materials. To all these characteristics add the many ways in which metals can be joined, and its attraction to craftsmen is understandable.

Craftsmen have evolved ways of using metals which through the course of history have become known to the world by special names derived from their *place of origin,* or the *method of fabrication. Damascene* (a form of metal decoration in which one metal is inlaid with a contrasting metal) is commonly supposed to have originated in Damascus, Syria. *Repoussé* (from the French repousser—to push, the metal being thrust back by hammering, usually from the reverse side) is an example of a name derived from a technique.

Most decorative techniques have remained relatively unchanged *technically* for hundreds of years, though stylistic changes have occurred. Some have fallen into disuse, not through lack of merit but mainly because the *time* spent in working on a piece has become almost more valuable than the object, and few can afford it. New work methods made possible by new tools might become the means for a revival of neglected decorative processes. Contemporary aesthetic concepts applied to traditional techniques have shown the enduring possibilities inherent in them. A revival of interest in surface enrichment of decorative objects seems imminent as the ever-changing cycle of taste seems to be moving away from pure, "unblemished" form. It is hoped that this book will be of help to those craftsmen who choose to follow this direction.

Throughout the book, besides contemporary work, photographs of historic pieces will be found illustrating techniques where applicable. That some are astonishingly contemporary in feeling is not so surprising when one understands the reason: *the designs and treatments are suitable to the material and the manner of construction.* This *basic concept,* sensed by craftsmen of all ages, cannot be overemphasized. A study of the work of the past is rewarding as an inspiration, a lesson in problem solving, and as a means of developing that most desirable quality in craftsmen: humility. Today's craftsmen do not spring fullborn and independent into the world, nor are their creations always unique. We have ties with the past and are as much its products as we are the foundations of the future.

OPPI UNTRACHT
Roaring Brook Lake,
New York, 1966

Silver teapot, designed by Johan Rohde in 1906. The surface shows the characteristic planishing hammer texture found on early Jensen pieces. *Georg Jensen Silversmiths, Ltd.*

Part One

METALS: BASIC INFORMATION

Native platinum nuggets.

Native gold nugget, Hungary.

Crystallized native copper from Upper Peninsula, Michigan.

Native silver formation partially embedded in the matrix rock in which it was found in Kongsberg, Norway.

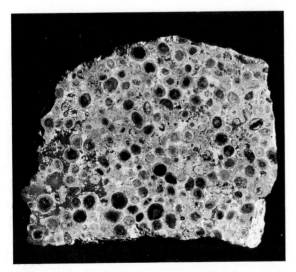

Bauxite, Aluminum ore. *All these specimens courtesy American Museum of Natural History, New York.*

OPPOSITE: *Copper Mining.* One of the largest open pit copper mines in the United States is Bingham Canyon, near Salt Lake City, Utah. The distance across this vast mining pit is approximately one mile. *Copper and Brass Research Association.*

Metals: Origin, Behavior, and Manufacture

Origin

Man's first knowledge of metals is thought to have occurred when he built a fire over a natural outcropping of copper and observed the effect of the heat on the substance. Once he made the cause-and-effect connection, he put metal to use. Since then, more than fifty metals have been discovered, their properties observed, recorded, and utilized.

Metals occur in the earth in a state called *ores,* which are usually natural compounds containing metal constituents in varying percentages. *Native* ores are those that can be found in a pure state, and the most common are silver, gold, platinum, and copper. These metals are also found in combination with others. *Oxide* ores are a group consisting of oxides, carbonates, and silicates of common metals. *Sulphide* ores are those in which metals are combined with sulphur. Metals can be found on the earth's surface, as is alluvial gold; in pit mines, as is copper; and in mines many feet below the surface. These metals, to be brought to a working state of purity, must be processed to extract the ores and remove the *gangue* or worthless material.

Metallurgy

The science of metallurgy, which is the economical extraction of metals from ores, has three main branches today: pyrometallurgy, hydrometallurgy, and electrometallurgy. *Pyrometallurgy,* or smelting, is concerned with the use of heat to reduce the metal from the ore by the burning of a fuel. *Hydrometallurgy,* or leaching, depends on aqueous solutions for the extraction of metal from ores; the metal can then be recovered by electrolysis and cementation, or precipitation from a solution. *Electrometallurgy* calls upon electric current to provide heat and also to electrolyze igneous (molten rock) and aqueous (liquid) solutions. The result is *primary* metals, or metals produced directly from ores. In this process of reduction or concentration, the valuable constituent of the ore is collected in the form of metal called *matte,* a sulphide; or *speiss,* an arsenide. The almost worthless remnant is known as *slag. Secondary* metals produced from scrap are in most cases no different from primary metals.

There are two main groups of metals: *ferrous* and *nonferrous.* Ferrous metals are iron

and alloys containing iron; all others are non-ferrous. A subgroup of the nonferrous metals is called the *noble* metals. These metals have surfaces that are relatively unchanging in air, such as pure gold, silver, platinum, and the platinum family group. Metals in descending order of susceptibility to atmospheric or chemical corrosion are aluminum, zinc, iron, nickel, tin, lead, copper, mercury, silver, platinum, and gold.

Characteristic Physical Properties of Metals

All elements are divided into metals and non-metals. An element is a substance that cannot be separated from itself into substances different from itself by ordinary chemical processes. Every element has its *atomic weight,* which is the relative weight of its atom as referred to a standard element. Most chemists prefer the atomic weight of oxygen, which is 16, as the standard.

Metals constitute over three-fourths of the known pure elements on Earth. All metals are *opaque* and *crystalline* in structure. If they are submitted to sufficiently high temperatures, they will become liquids. This occurs at temperatures that vary with the metal, and each metal has its own *melting point,* or solidus temperature. As it cools, the metal becomes solid at a specific temperature called the *freezing point;* the molecules arrange themselves in positions that are relatively fixed. The *liquidus* temperature is the metal's boiling point.

All metals are *fusible,* that is, they can be brought to a liquid state by the application of heat and can therefore be united to other metals. This quality, not confined to metals, allows them to be *smelted* or separated from their impurities and combined with other metals to create *alloys.* It also allows metals to be cast and to be joined by soldering, brazing, and welding.

Metals expand in length, width, and thickness when heated and contract upon cooling. The actual increase of a solid when heated one degree is called its *coefficient of linear expansion.*

Many metals are good *conductors of electricity;* they do not resist the passage of an electrical current through them. Silver is the best conductor of all, followed by copper, gold, and aluminum, in that order. This is an important factor in the plating of metals. At the other extreme, metals that have high electrical resistance are used for heating by electrical means. Nichrome wire, an alloy of nickel, for example, is used for the heating-element wire in electric kilns, as it has high electrical resistance.

Most metals, with the notable exception of mercury, which is liquid at normal temperatures, are relatively dense. They are heavier than water (lithium is an exception), and each has its *specific gravity* (also called specific density), which is the ratio of the weight of a given volume of a substance to an equal volume of water, whose specific gravity is 1. Thus a metal can be compared in density with other elements. The standard is water for solids and oxygen for gases. Thus the specific gravity of gold, which is 19.3, tells us that the density of gold, bulk for bulk, is 19.3 times that of water.

All metals have a characteristic *color* in their pure state, and certain standard alloys also have their particular color or surface

Sheet brass magnified 75 times showing the appearance of the crystalline structure of the metal as it was originally, after cold working, and after annealing.

Cold working compresses the structure, while annealing restores it almost to its original form. *Copper and Brass Research Association.*

 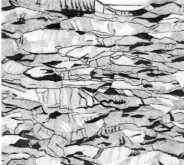 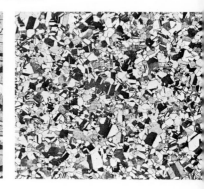

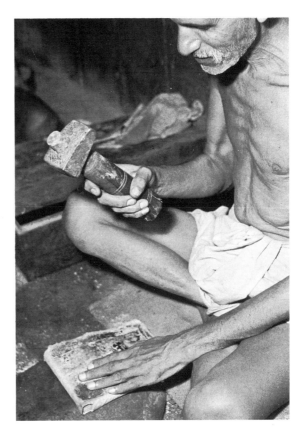

Making gold foil and leaf by hand: Because of the extreme malleability and compressibility of gold, it can be hammered into extremely thin sheets called foil, or, if thinner, leaf. Gold foil and leaf are still made today in India, Japan, and other places, in the same manner as the ancients. A small amount of pure gold is placed on a smooth anvil or steel slab and hammered out carefully, allowing no break. Single, square pieces (about 1½ inches across) that result from the hammering are then placed, each on a separate page, in a goldbeater's book. The square leaves of the book, which are parchment made from the membranes of various animals' parts, are sewn together along one edge. *Photo by Oppi.*

ABOVE: The cover, made of leather, projects beyond the pages on three sides. When the book has been filled with gold squares, the projecting parts of the cover are folded over the three open ends of the book and tied. The book is then placed on a large, smooth stone and hammered lightly with spiraling blows with a heavy, squat-handled hammer. The process is continued with occasional inspections until foil or leaf of the desired thickness is achieved. Should the gold extend beyond the pages during the process, it is cut off with a special shears. *Photo by Oppi.*

quality. Metals can be polished to a high *luster,* or ability to reflect light. The harder metals take a higher polish and retain it longer, unless the metal is exposed to atmospheric gases that *oxidize* or *corrode* it.

The Behavior of Metals: Their Mechanical Properties

HARDNESS

The hardness of metals is expressed in terms of the system by which it is measured. There are several standard testing methods, devised by various people after whom they are named. A mineralogist called Mohs originated a system that measures the ability of one metal to be scratched by being rubbed against another.

The Mohs table of hardness is relative and not as exact as others. The Brinell test consists of forcing a steel ball one centimeter in diameter, under standard pressure, into the surface of the metal. The resulting impression is measured and the hardness calculated. Other hardness tests, calculated by different methods of measuring metal indentation, were devised by Rockwell, Vickers, and others.

MALLEABILITY

A metal's malleability (from Latin *malleare,* to hammer) is its ability to be extended or shaped by being beaten or rolled in all directions without breaking or cracking, since the molecules adhere in the process. The most malleable of metals is gold, which can be beaten to a thickness of 0.000005 of an inch; at this point it is a foil, which when held up to the light is greenish and almost transparent. Metals in descending order of malleability by hammering are gold, silver, aluminum, copper, tin, platinum, lead, zinc (when hot), wrought iron, and soft steel. Cast iron and hard steel are not malleable. Metals in descending order of malleability by rolling are lead, tin, gold, silver, aluminum, copper, and platinum. The similarity in the malleability characteristics of copper and silver accounts for the success of Sheffield Plate, a form of cladding (covering one metal with another in fairly thick slabs) of silver on copper which after being rolled in the mills retained the same *ratio* of thickness after rolling.

DUCTILITY

The ductility of metal is its ability to be drawn into fine wire. Though it is related to malleability, not all malleable metals are ductile. Lead, for instance, is extremely malleable, but very difficult to draw into wire. In wire form such as lead solder, it is *extruded* (forced through dies by pressure). Gold is extremely ductile, and can be drawn into the fineness of hair. The most ductile metals in descending order of ductility are gold, silver, platinum, iron, copper, aluminum, and nickel.

TENSILE STRENGTH

Tenacity is the measure of the greatest longitudinal stress a metal can take without breaking. A metal's ability to resist elongation before finally breaking is called its tensile strength. This is usually stated in pounds per square inch, or kilograms per square centimeter. It is measured on a machine that pulls a sample of a certain cross section till it elongates and breaks while the machine records the necessary power for this to occur. The tenacity of metals is extremely important in relation to their use as construction materials and is one of the basic tests for metals. The relative tensile strengths of some metals, for the sake of comparison, are lead: 1; tin: 1.3; zinc: 2; aluminum: 10; worked copper: 12–20; wrought iron: 20–40; steel: 40–100.

COMPRESSION

Compression is the opposite of tension. It refers to the ability of a metal to be squeezed or reduced in volume and its resistance to cracking or buckling while so compressed.

SHEAR

Shear refers to the ability of metal to resist the perpendicular action of two parallel forces acting toward each other to penetrate and sever the metal, as in the action of a pair of shears or a shearing machine. *Shear, tension,* and *compression* are thought to be the three basic stresses to which metal can be subjected, and they describe the strength of a metal.

TOUGHNESS

The resistance to forces under the strains of twisting, bending, and shock before breaking is described as a metal's toughness. Under the heading of toughness can be considered elasticity, torsion, brittleness, and impact resistance.

ELASTICITY

Elasticity is a metal's recovery to normal size and shape after it has been subjected to forces of compression, bending, or stretching. The range of elasticity of a metal is between its limits of compression and tension. If the elastic limit of compression is raised, the elastic limit of tension is lowered by an equal amount.

TORSION

The ability of a metal to return to its original state after being twisted is its torsion resistance.

BRITTLENESS

The characteristic in metals of being easily fractured or snapped without warning deformation is called brittleness. Such metals are lacking in tenacity, ductility, and malleability. Cast iron is an example of a brittle metal.

IMPACT RESISTANCE

A metal's resistance to sudden shock, measurable mechanically, is its impact resistance.

RIGIDITY

The opposite of ductility, malleability, and flexibility, the characteristic of showing resistance to change of form is a metal's tendency to remain stiff or rigid.

Classification of Metals

As already mentioned, metals are generally divided into two main groups: ferrous and nonferrous (from Latin *ferrum,* iron). The most important metals in the ferrous group are iron and steel, of which there are many types. The nonferrous group can be divided into three main subgroups: precious metals, base metals, and alloys. The precious metals most likely to be used by craftsmen are gold, silver, and platinum. The base metals are copper, aluminum, lead, tin, nickel, and zinc. Some base metals and precious metals are used to create such alloys as brass, bronze, pewter, nickel silver, solder, sterling silver, karat gold, Monel Metal, and Nichrome. A *binary* alloy contains two metals, and a *ternary* alloy contains three.

Nonferrous Precious Metals

GOLD Au 79

Properties (fine)
Atomic weight   197.2
Specific gravity   19.32
Melting point   1063° C 1945.4° F
Boiling point   2970° C 5380° F

Gold, a bright-yellow metal very widely disseminated in nature, is probably one of the earliest metals to be known by man, perhaps second after copper. Because it is one of the few metals found in a native state, it is easily recognizable by its natural color and weight. In one of its forms as *placer* gold, it is found in the alluvial soil in riverbeds where it has been deposited after the rock in which it was contained had weathered and worn away. Placer gold ranges in size from small flakes or grains to nuggets weighing several thousand ounces. It is also found in a combined form called *reef* gold, in which the metal is embedded in a solid matrix of quartz or other rock. The gold occurs in veins of the rock in

the earth from which it is mined, and is usually combined with silver, copper, lead, and sometimes zinc. Of all the metals used in decorative work, gold is exceeded in heaviness only by lead and mercury.

It is extracted from ores by one of several processes: amalgamation with mercury, cyanidation, a combination of amalgamation and gravity concentration, oil flotation, roasting and cyanidation, or smelting with lead and copper ores.

No other metal surpasses gold in malleability and ductility. In its pure state as *fine* gold, it can be hammered into foil .000005 of an inch in thickness and drawn into wire several miles in length from one ounce of pure metal. It is highly resistant to ordinary solvents. It is resistant to corrosion and is chemically inactive. This accounts for the excellent state of preservation of ancient articles of gold discovered in the tombs of Egypt, Etruria, Colombia, Mexico, and many other places.

In a pure state (99.95 per cent pure as used in the arts), gold resists oxidation even after *annealing* (subjecting it to heat to soften it after it has been worked). Gold in an alloy form, as it is always used in jewelry, oxidizes after annealing because of the alloy it contains, but this oxidation can be removed by *pickling* (submerging it in a bath of dilute sulphuric or nitric acid).

Gold Alloys As gold in its pure or fine state is considered too soft for ordinary jewelry and dental work, its most common uses, it is generally alloyed with other metals such as copper, silver, nickel, and zinc. Each of these other metals produces a gold of a particular character and color. Its melting point, hardness, and malleability also vary with the particular alloy.

White gold contains 25 per cent platinum or 12 per cent palladium and has a higher melt-

South Indian gold wire-work decorated pendant, set with stones. *Museum of Fine Arts, Boston.*

Lost-wax bracelet of 18-karat gold with baroque pearls, by Irena Brynner. *Photo by Tommy Yee.*

Cast 18-karat gold engagement and wedding ring with diamond, by Irena Brynner, New York, designed so that they may be worn separately or as a unit. The textured surface is heat oxidized. *Photo by Tommy Yee.*

Cast gold pendant, Chibcha Indian, Colombia. Height: 16.5 cm. *American Museum of Natural History, New York.*

ing point than pure gold. It is whiter than platinum and darker than sterling. Tough, but malleable, it must be worked all over evenly between stages of annealing, or the stresses left in the metal will cause it to crack either during annealing or afterward on resumption of work. *Green gold,* made by the addition of 30–40 per cent silver or silver plus cadmium and zinc, is soft and malleable and has good working properties. *Yellow gold* is made with the addition of silver and copper, with higher copper percentages producing a gold of reddish cast. Yellow gold is an excellent all-purpose gold, as is red gold; the working qualities of both vary with the percentages of the alloy.

Karat Gold Although pure gold is too soft for most uses, the best grade of gold foil for decorative purposes is 23 karat, or almost pure. Certain forms of damascene employ pure gold wire which, because of its purity, stays bright indefinitely. For articles to be handled or worn, such as jewelry, it is common to use *karat* or alloyed gold. Generally speaking, the properties of the alloys are similar to those of gold itself, and karat gold is not popularly thought of as an alloy but as a different "grade" of gold.

The word *karat* should not be confused with *carat,* which is a unit of measurement for precious stones. The term karat refers specifically to the relative purity of gold. Pure gold is expressed as 24 karat, and gold alloys contain percentages of gold content, the remaining percentage being the alloying metal.

PERCENTAGE OF GOLD IN KARAT GOLD ALLOYS

Karat	Percentage	Karat	Percentage
24	100	12	50.00
23	95.83	11	45.83
22	91.67	10	41.67
21	87.50	9	37.50
20	83.33	8	33.33
19	79.17	7	29.17
18	75.00	6	25.00
17	70.83	5	20.83
16	66.67	4	16.67
15	62.50	3	12.50
14	58.33	2	8.33
13	54.17	1	4.17

The stamping of gold in the United States with a mark declaring its quality is governed by the *U. S. Stamping Law,* controlled by the National Bureau of Standards (see Stamping: For Metal Identification and Hallmark, page 85). Any metal article declared by the stamp as being of a specific quality (example: 18K) must not be lower, if *assayed* or tested, than one-half karat below the stated mark; with the solder, the whole article may not be less than one karat different from the stated mark. European gold and silver articles must contain *more* precious metal than the stated mark. In America, the limit is drawn at gold below 10 karat; this cannot be stamped, because the gold percentage is so low and it is, in effect, more alloy than gold. The most commonly used karats in the West are 18 and 14. Craftsmen in the Far East often use 22 karat gold, which, though soft and easily worn, is favored for its characteristics bright-yellow color and because of traditional taboos against alloying the purity of gold.

The terms "gold filled" and "gold rolled" mean that a layer of karat gold has been soldered, brazed, or welded by mechanical means to one or both sides of a base metal. The combination is then rolled or drawn to specific thinner dimensions. For example, "1⁄10 12 kt. gold filled" means the base metal has been covered with a 12 karat gold on one or more surfaces, and that this gold alloy consists of one-tenth of the total weight of the object. When a sheet of this metal is cut, the base metal core is exposed.

Karat Gold Solders The art of soldering is believed to have originated in the soldering of gold. Generally speaking, a solder of lower karat gold than the one used for the article is employed, and is designed to flow at a lower melting point than the metal being soldered. Gold solders are manufactured today with temperature control and with the solder alloys designed to match the color of the gold being soldered. Solders for 18K, 14K, and 10K colored and white golds are available from reliable companies such as Handy and Harman. Some craftsmen simply employ gold of a lower karat when soldering; this procedure can be reliable if one is certain the melting point of the karat gold solder is below that of the gold of the article.

Gold solders are sold in half pennyweight and pennyweight pieces. A pennyweight of 30 B. & S. (Brown & Sharpe) gauge is approximately 1⁄2″ × 1 1⁄2″ standard.

Purchasing Gold The sale of gold is controlled by the U. S. Bureau of the Mint. The weight of gold and other precious metals is measured by *Troy Weight,* which takes its name from Troyes, France, where it originated. It is a system of weights commonly used in the U.S. and England. In this system the weights are as follows:

1 pound=12 ounces=240 pennyweights=5760 grains
1 pound is abbreviated: (lb. t.)
1 ounce=20 pennyweights=480 grains
1 ounce is abbreviated: (oz. t.)
1 pennyweight=24 grains (gr.)
1 pennyweight is abbreviated: (dwt.)

Gold is usually sold by the pennyweight but can also be purchased by the square inch and square foot. It is furnished annealed unless otherwise requested. Gold is manufactured in sheet and wire form of various gauges. The Brown & Sharpe Standard sheet and wire gauge is used in the United States. Decimal equivalents may be found in the tables (page 451). As a basic example, 1 millimeter=18 B. & S.=.039 inches.

Sheet gold is manufactured in a variety of gauges, and many karat fine. Gold wire is made in round, half round, square, rectangular, and special shapes. When ordering sheet, you should specify karat, color, length, width, and thickness (gauge). When purchasing wire, specify length (or weight), shape, and gauge. For the table of approximate weight of gold in sheet per square inch, and wire weight in pennyweights or ounces per foot, see the tables on pages 452 and 453.

Apart from purely aesthetic considerations, the choice of one kind of gold over another depends mainly on the use to which it will be put. Some gold alloys, for instance, are unsuited to enameling, which requires a zinc-free composition. Other considerations, such as the need for fine detail, good casting properties, scratch resistance, and color retention after annealing can be satisfied by the choice of the proper alloy for the specific requirement.

Using Karat Gold: General Considerations
Gold is suited to forming by all methods. A basic consideration in the use of gold, especially for those who are accustomed to working in silver, is the fact that gold, having a specific gravity almost twice that of silver, weighs more, bulk for bulk. This may be a factor in the creation of a design (especially in jewelry) or in the method of manufacture.

In soldering, the proper solder should be chosen for the function. In articles requiring several solderings, work should start with the hardest solder and proceed down the scale to the softest or lowest-melting-point solder so that previously soldered joints are protected. A liquid or paste flux can be used, and fluxes specifically designed for use on gold are recommended. Liquid fluxes are used for solderings of short duration, and the heavier paste flux for prolonged soldering. Solder gauges should be thinner than the article being soldered.

In the annealing of gold, care should be taken not to overheat the metal, or it will become misshapen and collapse suddenly. Overheating also causes a change in molecular structure, which may cause difficulties in forming. It also brings the alloying metal to the surface, causing a change in surface color and a stubborn deposit of oxide.

To enable the temperature to be judged better during annealing, the practice of coating the object with a flux that becomes fluid at a known temperature is a good one. Yellow, red, and green golds are heated to about 1200° F, or a dull red, to render them soft. Red gold should be quenched hot, or it will harden, while green and yellow gold may be either quenched hot or air cooled. White gold will take a higher annealing temperature (about 1400° F or bright red), and can be hot quenched or air cooled. The casting temperature for gold is 1100–1300° C (2000–2370° F).

Testing for Gold with Acid A general method of relative accuracy for testing gold requires a set of testing needles marked with karat numbers, a black testing stone, nitric acid (used for testing up to 10 karat gold), and aqua regia (used for testing above 10 karat gold).

A notch of sufficient depth to reveal the inner metal of the piece being tested is made with a file in an inconspicuous area. A drop of nitric acid is applied. If the reaction is bright green in color, this indicates the article is gold-plated on a brass or copper base. A pink cream reaction indicates silver, gold-plated. A slight reaction indicates at least ten karat gold, and above that, gold will not react to nitric acid.

Gold above ten karat is tested by rubbing it, sufficiently to make a visible deposit, on a *touchstone*—a black, siliceous stone related to

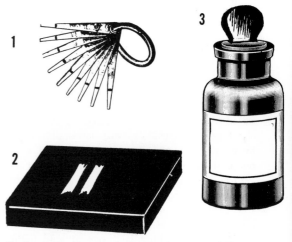

Testing gold with acid: 1. Gold testing needles 2. Black touchstone with a rubbing from the needle and the object 3. Glass bottle with ground glass stopper for acid solutions.

flint, or basanite, used to test the purity of gold and silver. (The word "touch" also refers to the determined quality of the metal so tested, and also to the official stamp placed on an article of a tested, standard quality.) Next to this rubbing, but allowing some space, a test needle is selected and rubbed. Aqua regia is applied simultaneously over both marks and the reaction is observed. Should the mark from the testing needle react first, this indicates the gold is of a higher karat than supposed. The next higher karat needle is selected, the stone wiped dry, and the same procedure is followed till the reactions match. If the test needle rubbing is slower than the other, this indicates a lower karat test needle is needed.

Small glass containers, one with nitric acid

and the other with aqua regia, made with ground glass stoppers with attached glass applicators, are available for this purpose.

SILVER Ag 47

Properties (fine)

Atomic weight	107.88	
Specific gravity	10.50	
Melting point	960.5° C	1760.9° F
Boiling point	2210° C	4010° F
Melting point (sterling)	893° C	1640° F

Silver is found in nature in both native and combined forms: in flakes, forms like wire, and in massed forms, one such find having weighed 1500 pounds. The native form is not frequent, but when it is discovered it is between 900–980 out of 1000 parts fine. Today, for the most part, silver is a by-product in the refinement of gold, lead, copper, or zinc ores, with which it is most frequently associated in nature. It is recovered from these metals in the refining process. It is also extracted from ores by direct smelting, amalgamation, cyanidation (similar to the process for refining gold ore), and other hydrometallurgical processes. A primitive method of refining gold or silver, called *cupellation,* was to place the ore in a cupel or small, shallow, porous cup made of bone ash, and then expose the cup to a high temperature and air blast. The base metals oxidized and sank into the porous cupel, and the precious metals could be poured off.

RIGHT: Silver pins in the form of "Southern Crosses" made in Algiers, Algeria. Filigree wire on pierced metal bases, with domes and shot. *Photo by Oppi.*

Silver bowl, designed by Henning Koppel for Georg Jensen. The irregular form is supported by a sculptured solid silver base. Diameter: approximately 16 inches. *Georg Jenson Silversmiths, Ltd., Copenhagen.*

In its pure state, silver is second in malleability and ductility only to gold. It is the whitest of metals and can be polished to a luster of high reflectivity. Pure silver is about half as heavy as gold and platinum and four times as heavy as aluminum. Fine silver, so called in commerce, is 999.0 parts per thousand fine; *high fine* silver, 999.5 fine or higher, is also available at a premium price.

As with gold, the discovery of silver in native form and its attractive working properties caused it to be valued at an early time. Besides its ornamental use in the form of jewels today, silver is used in coinage, photography, and dentistry and in the form of silver or hard solders. Silver was the metal used in the first commercially important electroplating processes, more than one hundred years ago. Besides the attractiveness of the metal, its resistance to corrosion by foods and organic acids (but not those containing sulphur) is still a factor in its popularity for use in holloware.

Silver Alloys In its pure form, silver, like gold, is too soft for most decorative objects, and it is usually alloyed with other metals to harden it and increase its durability. The most common of these alloys is *sterling silver,* so called as it was the standard of British silver

coinage before 1920. Sterling silver consists of 925 parts silver and 75 parts copper. In the United States, to be so stamped it must assay at least .921 or .915 with soldered parts, according to regulations set by the U. S. Government Bureau of Standards (see Stamping: For Metal Identification and Hallmark, page 85). Articles less than 90 parts silver cannot be stamped silver. In Europe, the standard requires a *higher* percentage of silver content than that which is stamped.

Silver, unlike gold, is usually not alloyed beyond 80 per cent in the West when used for decorative purposes, though it may be further alloyed in the Far East, "coin" silver being as low as 800 parts silver or lower. Alloys are made for other uses, however, with gold, tin, lead, and zinc. Electrum was a pale yellow gold-and-silver alloy used by the ancient Greeks and Romans. American silver coins were 90 per cent silver and 10 per cent copper. A typical dental amalgam is a silver alloy consisting of 65–70 per cent silver, 3–6 per cent copper, 25–29 per cent tin, and a maximum of .2 per cent zinc.

Silver solder, an important silver alloy, is discussed on page 159.

Purchasing Silver Sterling (and fine silver on special request) may be purchased in sheet, wire, foil, in special forms such as grain (irregular shot made by pouring molten silver into water), hollow tubing that may be rectangular, round, or square in section, and in circles of various diameters. It is sold by the troy ounce, as is gold, but may be ordered by giving all dimensions of length, width, and thickness B. & S. gauge. Orders made by the ounce must also include width and gauge of the metal. Wire is purchased by B. & S. wire gauge, which is the same as the thickness of corresponding sheet gauge. Wire is also available in square form (6–18 B. & S.), flat (10–20 B. & S.), round (6–22 B. & S.), half round (5⁄16″–15 B. & S.), oval (4×8–14×18 B. & S.), half oval (3⁄16×14–13×21 B. & S.), triangular (1⁄8″, 3⁄16″ and 1⁄4″ base), hexagonal (5–9 B. & S.), ball wire, half ball wire, pearl bead wire, sterling and fine bezel wire (for setting cabochon-shaped stones), and spring-hardened tie bar stock. All silver (except the tie bar stock) is furnished annealed or soft unless the customer specifies otherwise.

Sterling findings are available in many different forms for use in jewelry and in the form of hollow beads, many types of chain, and special decorated gallery wire used for

Sterling silver comb with rock crystal drops by Torun Bülow-Hube, Biot, France, uses both sheet metal and wire. *Photo by Paolo Monti.*

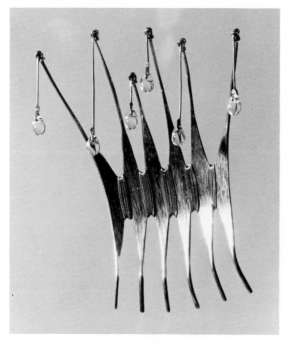

bezels in stone setting or for the edges of traditionally styled holloware pieces. *Many companies that furnish precious metals require a minimum order.*

General Considerations in the Use of Silver
During the working of silver (the reference is to sterling unless stated otherwise, as this is the most common form of silver used by craftsmen), *rolling* to flatten sheet uniformly, *drawing* through a drawplate to change the diameter or cross section of wire, *hammering* to shape or raise a form, or *stamping* with dies or a dapping block, all result in the eventual hardening of the metal, as the molecules become compressed from the action of the tool on the metal. Stresses are also created in the metal that may make it difficult to work or cause cracks in the surface or structure. It then becomes necessary to bring the metal to a soft, malleable state if the working is to continue. This is done by *annealing,* or subjecting the metal to heat. The best annealing temperature for sterling is 1100–1200° F (593–649° C). The metal can be air cooled or quenched in water or dilute acid, and it will retain its softness. Lower temperatures may be used, but they require a prolonged heating. Higher temperatures will cause overheating, a change in the structure of the metal with possible scarring of the surface unless it is filed smooth again, and a thick "fire" or firescale of copper oxide, which forms just under the surface of silver-copper alloys when annealed in air. Firescale becomes evident during polishing as a dark cloud and is due to the appearance of the copper oxides from the sterling copper content. It can be removed by dissolving in a cold solution of 50 per cent nitric acid, care being taken to watch the surface and remove the metal immediately after areas that do *not* contain firescale turn gray, while those that *do* contain it turn black. After thorough washing, the sterling should be free of firescale, but if any traces remain the process can be repeated.

Sterling can be protected from the formation of firescale by coating it with a solution of borax, boric acid, or both, and washing it after heating. Much firescale can be avoided by not overheating the metal from the start.

Large pieces in sterling can be given a final *age hardening,* which will increase its strength and minimize denting. Low-temperature heating at 280° C (536° F) for 2½ hours, after quenching, is effective.

Sulphur will attack silver and tarnish it,
forming a sulphide on the surface that decreases its reflectivity. Advantage can be taken of this characteristic of the metal to deliberately color it or "antique" it. This is done by subjecting the metal to a solution of mixed potassium sulphides known commonly as liver of sulphur. (See section on the coloring of metals, page 415.) Tarnish-resistant, high-silver-content alloys have been developed by the addition of noble metals (palladium or gold). Plating silver with a thin nickel plating and rhodium is pleasing in appearance and highly tarnish-resistant.

Testing for Silver A simple method which gives a *general* indication of the presence of silver is as follows. With a file, make a deep notch in the metal (in an unobtrusive place on finished articles). Apply a drop of pure nitric acid to the notched area, and observe the results. Pure silver produces a white, creamy bubbling of the acid, sterling makes a cloudy cream, coin silver becomes dark or blackish. Silver-plated articles on a copper base turn green, and nickel silver also turns green. Acid traces should be washed away with water.

Cleaning Silverware by Electrolytic Action
Flatware and other pieces made of silver can be made free of sulphide tarnish quickly by immersing the articles in an aluminum pot containing a dilute solution of baking soda (sodium bicarbonate) and table salt (sodium chloride, NaCl), plus some soap, brought to a boil and allowed to stand for a few minutes. Remove, rinse in water, and dry.

PLATINUM Pt 78

Properties

Atomic weight	195.23	
Specific gravity	21.45	
Melting point	1773.5° C	3224.3° F
Boiling point	4330° C	8185° F

Platinum was discovered in the sixteenth century (about 1538) in Colombia, South America, where it received the name "platina del Pinto" (little silver from the Pinto, a riverbed where it was found). Platinum was quite rare till 1822 when large deposits were found in the Ural Mountains in Russia. A group of related rare metals or noble metals are residues of platinum ore. *Osmium* and *iridium* were discovered in 1804, as were *palladium* and *rhodium. Ruthenium,* also in this group,

Necklace, by Cartier, New York, in a platinum setting containing diamonds and an unusual collection of emeralds that match in both color and size. The entire setting, except for the prongs of the emeralds, is platinum, which is utilized with precious stones because of its durability and non-tarnishing qualities. Yellow gold is used for prongs holding emeralds and rubies, as it is felt that this creates softness in appearance. The baguette diamonds in the inner ring are set in channel settings, with several stones resting next to each other without separations; they are held only on the sides of the group. All other stones of this older Cartier necklace are in platinum prong settings. *Cartier, New York.*

OPPOSITE: Platinum necklace and oval pendant with diamonds, designed by Gilbert Albert for Patek Philippe, Geneva, Switzerland. The use of platinum for jewelry, which became more widespread around 1906, revolutionized jewelry design because it allowed lighter, and yet safe, construction employing precious stones than had been possible with gold. Settings, such as in this necklace, could be almost invisible, thus allowing the maximum display of stones. *Worshipful Company of Goldsmiths, London. Photo by James Mortimer.*

was discovered in 1845. There are two main platinum groups of related metals, the *light* platinum group: rhodium, ruthenium, and palladium, whose specific gravity is about 12; and the *heavy* platinum group: osmium, iridium, and platinum, whose specific gravities are over 21.

Platinum can be found in nature as a native metal, alloyed with one or more of its allied

metals, and in the form of very fine grains or nuggets in alluvial material. Considerable quantities of platinum are found in nickel ores, from which it is refined as a by-product. The largest source of platinum today is in the copper-nickel ores of Canada.

Platinum is the least rare and the best known of the group of platinum metals and has the widest range of uses. It is ductile, resists cor-

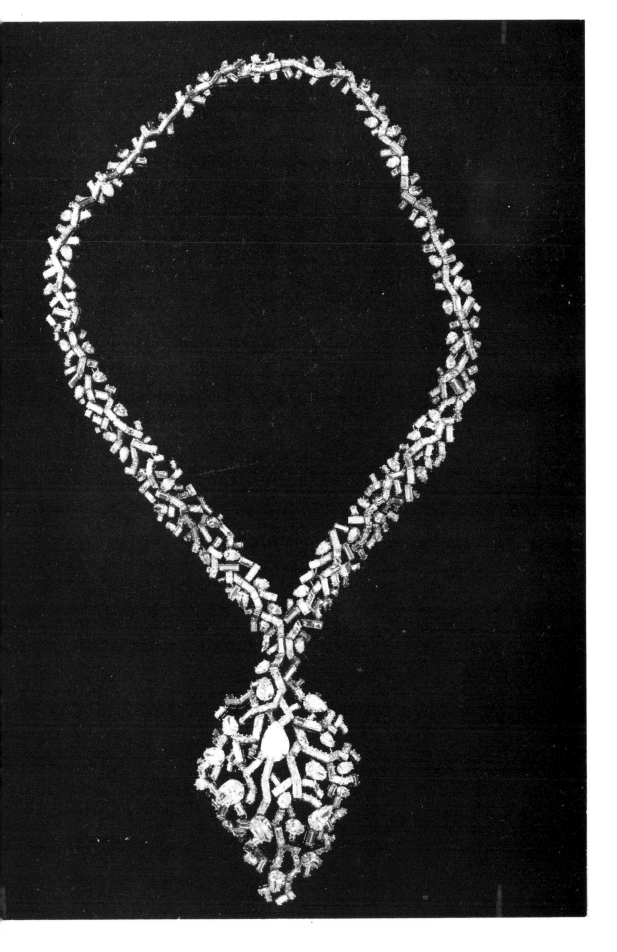

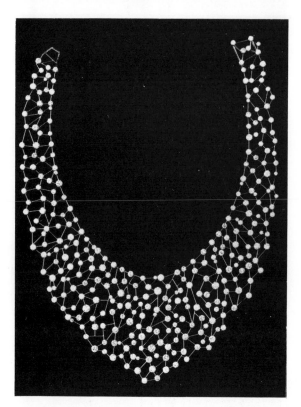

Flexible platinum wire necklace set with diamonds, designed by Gilbert Albert for Patek Philippe, Geneva, Switzerland. The strength and ductility of platinum make possible this light, delicate system of construction and insure the retention of the diamonds. *Worshipful Company of Goldsmiths, London. Photo by James Mortimer.*

rosion (dissolves slowly in aqua regia), has a high melting point, expands only slightly on heating, and is malleable and attractive. It can be cast or forged, and soldered with special platinum alloys. Its hardness makes it widely used in the jewelry industry for articles containing expensive cut stones. Its high ductility and strength insure the holding of precious jewels. The jewelry industry consumes 50 per cent of the total production of this metal. Diamonds look whiter when mounted in platinum than when mounted in yellow gold.

Platinum-palladium alloys have a lower density than pure platinum and allow the construction of large articles of jewelry of lighter weight. Alloys containing 5 and 10 per cent ruthenium or iridium are called medium hard and hard platinum, and are used especially for jewelry as they are even harder than pure platinum.

Its high ductility allows it to be manufactured in the form of platinum leaf for decorative purposes. As platinum is resistant to corrosion and practically does not tarnish in the normal urban atmosphere with its sulphur con-

tent, which oxidizes silver in this form, platinum is preferred in decorations requiring silver-colored leaf. In the processing of platinum, dry soap powder is used as a lubricant when drawing wire. It is important for maintaining purity to assure conditions of oxidation in the flame used when soldering or heating. Platinum has a thermoelectric attraction for such other metals as iron, silicon, and manganese, which may diffuse into the metal if they are nearby and a reducing flame is used. After working and *before* annealing, it is essential to pickle platinum in hot hydrochloric acid to remove whatever iron may have combined with it from the tools used. This is particularly necessary in maintaining high purity in sheet and wire. When used for lost-wax casting, if a high-silica crucible is used, an oxidizing atmosphere must be maintained to avoid the reduction of silica from the crucible, and its contamination of the platinum.

An alloy of 50 per cent palladium, 10 per cent platinum, and 40 per cent silver is suitable for jewelry. It may be used as a solid or in *cladding,* a process in which one metal is covered with another in fairly thick slabs, in a definite ratio, and is then subjected to co-rolling through a mill, resulting in a clad composition.

The National Bureau of Standards states in its Commercial Standard booklet CS66-38, *Marking of Articles Made Wholly or in Part of Platinum,* that articles of platinum, iridium, palladium, ruthenium, rhodium, and osmium, including alloys of these metals, may have the quality mark for the particular metals stamped on them (Plat., Irid., Pall., Ruth., Rh., Osmi.) if the articles contain at least 985 parts per thousand of the metals where solder is not used and 950 parts per thousand where solder is used. For regulations on articles containing alloys of platinum and other metals, the reader is referred to the above-mentioned booklet, which is available from the Superintendent of Documents, Washington, D.C.

Base Metals

COPPER   Cu 29

Properties

Atomic weight	63.54	
Specific gravity	8.96	
Melting point	1083° C	1981.4° F
Boiling point	2595° C	4703° F

The discovery of copper, the *first* metal known to man, is thought to have occurred

Copper chief's collar, with chased designs, Teke tribe. Diameter: 335 mm. *Musée Royal de L'Afrique Centrale, Tervuren, Belgium.*

Traditional tin-lined copper coffee pot, which is commonly used in Finland today. Hand-raised with dovetailed, brazed joints and rivets holding the handle. Its largest diameter is 8 inches. *Photo by Oppi.*

about 8000 B.C. in the Tigris-Euphrates River valleys, the sites of the oldest known civilizations. From there its use spread shortly to Egypt.

The reducing action of a cooking fire's heat on copper-bearing rock is thought to have been the origin of the discovery. From this accident, man discovered that the "rock" or ore could be transformed into nuggets of tough, red metal and eventually that this substance could

be melted and cast into shapes. With the knowledge that metal could be obtained by reducing ore through heat, the birth of metallurgy occurred.

Stone Age man was precipitated into the transitional Copper-Stone Age, and about 5000 B.C. into the age of alloys, the Bronze Age. Early Egyptians were making weapons and knives from copper about 6000 B.C. and pipes and tubes about 2750 B.C. The *controlled* alloying of copper with tin to make bronze is thought to have occurred about 3800 B.C. in Egypt.

Among the first widely known sources of copper were the mines of the island of Cyprus, which were fought over by many civilizations. The Latin for copper, *cuprum,* is derived from *Cyprium aes* (Cyprian metal), corrupted to *cuprum.* The first two letters of *cuprum* are used for the chemical symbol for copper: Cu.

Today copper is one of the most important and widely used metals. It is obtained by open pit mining, vein mining, or block caving, the method depending on the form and location in which the ores are found in the earth's crust. It is extracted from ores by heat (concentration, smelting, and refining), the most widely used method, and wet-extraction (flotation and leaching), used for low-grade ores, which supply a smaller percentage of the world's copper.

Copper is high in electrical and thermal conductivity, is easily fabricated, good in joining and soldering characteristics, high in ductility, and good in tensile strength. It can be electroplated and has good polishing qualities. It is soluble in oxidizing acids such as nitric and sulphuric. It is hardened by cold working, as in raising a shape in copper, but, as it has no critical temperature that would change its crystalline grain structure, it can be formed hot or cold. When hardened by working, it can be annealed to restore softness by heating to the proper annealing temperature, between 700° F and 1200° F.

Copper is manufactured by electrolytic and furnace-fire refining methods in many forms, each having inclusions of small amounts of various other metals which change its character and make it suitable for special applications or methods of working.

Tough pitch copper is produced in largest quantities by the electrolytic method and is the copper used for most general purposes. It contains varying amounts of oxygen, which increases its tensile strength and reduces its ductility in direct relation to the increase of oxygen content. *Deoxidized copper,* a tougher copper containing high residual phosphorus, is used in processes requiring hot working, annealing, brazing, and welding. *Oxygen-free copper* retains its high residual ductility in hard temper form.

Copper-Based Alloys Copper has been widely used in the arts, both in its pure form and in alloys. As copper has the natural ability to combine with other metals, several hundred copper alloys are available commercially today. Their color range is wide, ranging from silver to yellow, gold, and bronze. The main types of copper alloys are low-zinc brasses, high-zinc brasses, leaded brasses, free-cutting brass, forging brass, tin brasses, nickel silvers, phosphor bronzes, silicon bronzes, aluminum bronzes and brasses, and other special alloys. The category of alloy is determined by the alloying metal that is in *largest* quantity.

BRASS

The brass alloys are the most important among the copper alloys, and consist essentially of alloys of *copper and zinc*. Brasses containing up to 36 per cent zinc, termed single-phase alloys, are called *Alpha* brasses and have excellent cold-working qualities. Beyond 37 per cent zinc, a second-phase group comprises the *Beta* brasses, excellent in hot-working qualities.

In the low-zinc brass group (containing 5 to 20 per cent zinc) are alloys especially suited

Contemporary cast brass six-spouted oil lamp, used by the Santhals, a tribal group in Bihar, India. The top is unscrewed and the inside filled with oil; then a wick is inserted in each spout and burned. Diameter: about 8 inches. *Photo by Oppi.*

for use in costume jewelry and tube manufacture. *Gilding metal* (copper 95 per cent, zinc 5 per cent) is golden in color and is used for jewelry, emblems, and novelties that are to be gold-plated. It is very malleable, resists corrosion, and works well. *Pinchbeck metal* (88 per cent copper, 12 per cent zinc) was used by Victorian jewelers as a gold substitute, as it strongly resembles gold. *Red brass* (copper 85 per cent, zinc 15 per cent) is the closest contemporary alloy to pinchbeck and is also used for costume jewelry.

Yellow brass (copper 65 per cent, zinc 35 per cent; melting point: 1660° F; annealing temperature: 800–1300° F) is especially suited to wire drawing, beads, chains, rivets, architectural grillwork, stamping, and spinning. *Muntz brass* (copper 60 per cent, zinc 40 per cent; melting point: 1650° F; annealing temperature: 800–1100° F) is used for brazing rods and hot forging and in maritime and decorative architectural situations where high corrosion resistance is a factor. *Leaded brasses* contain ½ to 3 per cent lead which, when added to the copper-zinc alloys, makes them desirable for machining, as the particles form small chips when pared off and thus prevent tools from fouling and dulling. *Naval brass* (copper 60 per cent, zinc 39.25 per cent, tin 0.75 per cent; melting point: 1630° F) is used for welding rods, among other uses.

BRONZE

Bronzes are basically *copper-tin* alloys, but there are bronzelike alloys that contain no tin. Descended from the ancient bronzes are the modern *phosphor bronzes* of today. The tin content varies from 1.25 to 10 per cent, with the 5 per cent tin, maximum 0.35 per cent phosphorus being the most common. The phosphor bronzes have great resiliency, hardness, and fatigue endurance, plus superior resistance to corrosion. Their melting points range from 1550° F to 1900° F. These alloys can be soft soldered, silver soldered, brazed, and oxyacetylene welded, but they are *hot-short,* or brittle when heated beyond a red heat.

There are special alloys for *casting,* some of which are cast-leaded tin bronzes, cast-leaded brasses, cast nickel silver, and cast aluminum bronzes. Nickel silver and Monel Metal, both copper alloys, are discussed under nickel and its alloys (pages 29–30). Still other alloys of copper are made with percentages of cadmium, silicon, beryllium, and tellurium, each having its special purposes.

Persian bronze incense burner, thirteenth century, inlaid with silver wire. *Museum of Fine Arts, Boston.*

LEAD   Pb 82

Properties

Atomic weight	207.22	
Specific gravity	11.3437	
Melting point	327.35° C	621.3° F
Boiling point	1740° C	3160° F

Lead is one of the oldest metals known to man. Thousands of years ago, man discovered that it could be easily reduced by carbon and carbon monoxide. Lead was used in ancient times for glaze on pottery by the Egyptians and for plumbing pipes by the Romans. The Latin word *plumbum,* meaning lead, is the origin of our modern words plumber and plumbing. A plumber was originally a worker in lead, and Roman plumbing in the form of lead pipes was made in fifteen standard sizes of ten-foot lengths at least two thousand years ago. The Phoenicians worked Spanish lead deposits in 2000 B.C. Lead was used for orna-

ments in Assyrian and Babylonian times. Lead spires, statues, cisterns, and gargoyles made in Medieval times have been almost perfectly preserved.

Lead is a unique metal having many uses. Its softness, extreme workability without becoming hard at ordinary temperatures, its ductility, forgeability, and weldability make it a metal easily worked. It alloys well with other metals, has a low melting point and a high boiling point, high anti-friction properties, resistance to atmospheric corrosion and to corrosion underground, in salt water, and in contact with a long list of everyday corrosive chemicals. Its resistance to sulphuric acids and compounds have caused it to have many applications. It is low in cost and high in reclamation value. Its tensile strength and fatigue strength are low, but the addition of 1 to 14 per cent antimony results in a metal of almost double strength and greater hardness.

The main source of the metal is from the mineral *galena,* the sulphide of lead which, when pure, contains 86 per cent lead and almost always some gold and silver. To separate the gold and silver from the lead in the refining process, small amounts of zinc are added. The precious metals immediately leave the lead and combine with the zinc, as they have a greater affinity for zinc than for lead. The zinc compound is lighter than lead and rises

An important historical application of the use of lead is seen in these almost perfectly preserved, excavated lead pipes used by the ancient Romans for conducting water almost nineteen hundred years ago. The Romans made pipe in fifteen standard sizes in ten-foot lengths. The Latin word for lead, *plumbum,* was used to denote spouts or water conductors. Its counterpart in contemporary English is the word "plumber." *Lead Industries Association, Inc.*

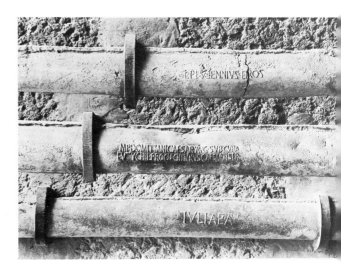

Cast lead cistern, English, dated 1713. *Victoria and Albert Museum, London.*

LEFT: Lead form, made by melting lead in a ladle and then pouring it directly into cold water. This custom is observed in Finland on New Year's Eve; the resulting form is interpreted as a divination for the New Year. *Photo by Oppi.*

OPPOSITE: "Harvest," by Alistair Bevington. Construction in colored glass and lead, approximately 18 inches high. Brass wires are used vertically both as supporting members and to make frames around each piece of glass. The frames are covered with lead solder to hold the glass. Lead solder is also used to join the frames to the supporting wires. *Collection of the Museum of Contemporary Crafts, New York. Photo by Bevington.*

to the surface, where it is allowed to form a skin at a lower temperature. The skin is then removed and refined further to recover the precious metals.

Forms of Lead Sheet lead has been used as a decorative metal for repoussé work and casting by artists for hundreds of years. Today, sheet is rolled in lengths up to 11¾ feet and standard widths of eight feet in almost any thickness desired. A common use of lead is in an alloyed form for lead or soft solders (see pages 159 and 178). It is sold in bulk for casting.

Casting Lead Lead is an excellent casting metal because its castings are dense and rapidly made. The low melting point of the metal allows it to be melted by almost any fuel in

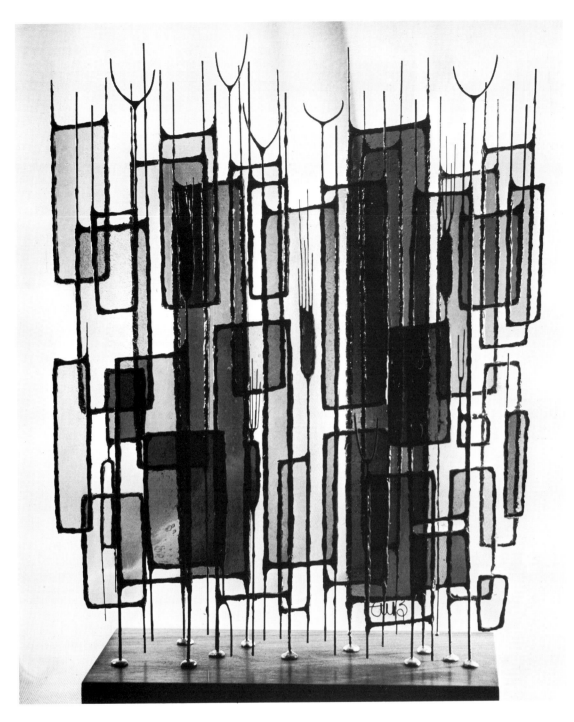

ladles of cast iron or steel or in welded or spun-steel pots with wrought-iron or cast-iron handles. No special coating is normally necessary to prevent the molten lead from adhering to the container. To reduce the metal content of the dross that forms on the surface, a flux such as a small amount of ammonium chloride (sal ammoniac) is sprinkled on the surface. An exhaust hood should be used for fume protection.

The pouring temperature of most lead alloys is not critical beyond 150° F above the melting point. Many kinds of molds are used, made of a variety of materials: paper, wood, plaster, rubber, and sand. They may be semi-permanent or permanent in nature. Lead-alloy molds are used to make plastic and rubber articles. For ornamental work, gravity-casting techniques are employed.

Soldering Lead The most common methods of joining lead are welding and soldering. Good joints must be well fitting, and after joining they will be stronger than the metal itself. All surfaces should be thoroughly cleaned with an emery scratch cloth or wire brush. Immediately after cleaning, a flux of salt-free mutton tallow or a liquid flux of rosin melted in alcohol is applied to all surfaces to be joined. For soldering procedure see page 179.

Lead Welding Lead welding, also known as *lead burning,* is the joining of two pieces of lead with torch heat and no flux. Additional lead in the form of a rod of the same composition as the lead being joined and approximately 1½ times as thick—is used to make the joint. All surfaces must be thoroughly clean, and the flame on the torch should be non-oxidizing. Oxygen and hydrogen, oxygen and acetylene, or oxygen and other hydrocarbon gases may be used. Small tips on the torch (00, 0, and 1) are suitable for lead weighing up to six pounds per square foot, and larger torch tips (2 or 3) for lead six to ten pounds

Tin wall lantern, Mexico, nineteenth century. The faceted pattern on the back is meant to heighten the reflection of light. *Museum of Popular Regional Art, Patzcuaro, Michoacan, Mexico. Photo by Oppi.*

per square foot and over. The main precaution in welding lead is to avoid burning through the metal or appreciably reducing its thickness.

Lead Wiping Wiping as a method of joining lead consists of repeatedly pouring the molten solder over the surfaces to be joined. While the solder is still in a semi-molten state, it is worked into shape (gloves being worn) with a cloth pad. The same flux is used as for soldering with coppers. A solder that has a composition of 37–40 per cent tin is preferred in this method because of its plastic range. A coating of plumber's soil, paper, or library paste should be applied to the lead at the points beyond which the solder should not extend. This prevents the solder from adhering where it is not wanted.

Decorative Patina Finishes for Lead When exposed to the atmosphere, lead loses its metallic luster and develops a gray coating or patina that is strongly adherent. A microscopically thin film, it protects the metal underneath from further corrosion. Special artificially created colored patinas such as green and jet black are possible with the use of chemicals. (See the section on the coloring of lead, page 418.)

TIN Sn 50

Properties

Atomic weight	118.70	
Specific gravity at 15° C (59° F)		7.2984
Melting point	231.90° C	449.4° F
Boiling point	2270° C	4120° F

Tin is produced from cassiterite, a tin oxide 78.6 per cent pure, widely distributed in the world but mined today mainly in Bolivia, the Malay Peninsula, Indonesia, and the Congo. Tin was produced for centuries in Cornwall, England, by the Romans. Mines were in operation there as early as 1500 B.C., and the metal was used as an ingredient in bronze casting alloys, as it still is today. Bronze was probably discovered by the accidental mixing of tin and copper in smelting.

Because tin is highly resistant to organic acids, the early Romans coated copper and bronze utensils and vessels with it to make containers suitable for holding foods. This practice is still followed. Tin is also used for plating steel containers intended for food. The common "tin" can is plated tin on steel.

Tin is white, soft, malleable, and shiny. Though it is not strong by itself and is low in

Decorative tin mask, Taxco, Mexico. *Photo by Oppi.*

RIGHT: Candlestick holder, Mexico, nineteenth century. It is made of tin patterned by scoring with a steel-pointed tool. *Museum of Popular Regional Art, Patzcuaro, Michoacan, Mexico.*

Articles made of tin can be joined by soldering with a low-melting-point solder such as the eutectic tin-lead solder (63% tin). Care should be taken not to overheat the pieces joined, because the fusion point of the tin or alloy is only a little higher than that of the solder being used.

Hot-Tinning Nonferrous Metals Copper, brass, and bronze may be hot tinned, as is often done with cooking or food-containing objects which might otherwise be toxic. The piece must be cleaned first to free it from grease by immersion in cold 15 per cent nitric acid for about 2 to 5 minutes, followed by rinsing under cold running water. The piece is then preheated to a point somewhat above the melting point of tin, and the surface sprinkled with a flux of finely powdered ammonium chloride.

The entire surface of the piece is then rubbed with a solid piece of pure tin, which coats the metal. This process can be followed up by pouring a small amount of molten tin on the object and wiping it with a cloth wiping pad to distribute the tin over the sur-

tensile strength, it can be rolled into very thin foil (88 parts tin, 4 copper, 5 antimony, 7.5 lead). It will not tarnish in air or humidity or lose its brightness, since the tarnish film is transparent, does not affect the luster, and can be easily removed by light polishing. When polished, tin is pleasing in appearance and quite similar to silver.

Its main uses are as an alloying metal with copper in the production of bronzes, as plating for steel in the canned food industry, and in combination with lead to make solders. Combined with antimony, copper, and lead, it is used for making a casting alloy that expands on cooling and has excellent definition, as in type metal used in printing. Tin is also used to produce the alloy known as britannia metal, the contemporary pewter.

When dies of cold rolled steel are used for casting tin, a lubricant such as lard oil should be distributed over the new die until in time the die metal forms a natural oxide.

Tin does not harden during cold working, and it anneals in room temperature. In fact, it softens after cold working, and its original hardness may be restored by annealing at 437° F, but it becomes brittle if overheated.

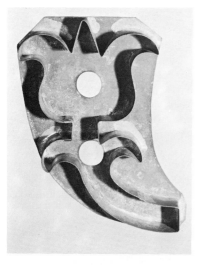  

Tin cookie cutters, large tulip design, American eagle design, deer design, edge joined with soft solder. Pennsylvania Dutch, nineteenth century. *Titus C. Geesey Collection, Philadelphia Museum of Art.*
BELOW: Copper serving tray, tin-washed, designed by Zahara Schatz and executed by craftsmen in Israel for Israel Creations, New York. Length: approximately 20 inches. *Photo by Oppi.*
OPPOSITE: Bidri zinc-alloy plate inlaid with silver, Hyderabad, Deccan, India. *Photo by Oppi.*

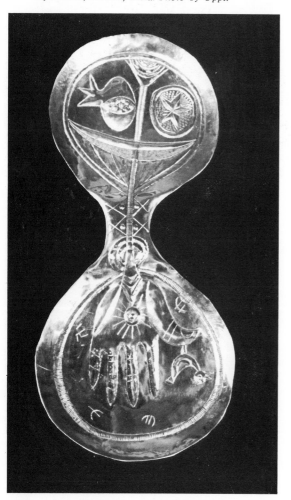

face. The same pad can be used to remove the excess tin, or the piece can be shaken to make the excess metal drop off. It is sometimes necessary to reheat the piece with a gas flame after wiping, to smooth the surface. The piece must not be heated beyond 545° F during the wiping, or a yellowish cast and dark streaks may develop from the pad.

To coat an entire plate of copper with tin, the reverse surface may be painted with slaked lime or whitewash to resist the tin, the sheet placed on a sloping heated metal surface or table to allow drainage, and the molten tin poured over the surface.

Antimonial Tin Solder High-tin solder is used in situations where lead-content solder may create a hazard, as in contact with foodstuffs. It consists of 95 per cent tin and 5 per cent antimony and melts at 233° C (452° F). The thinner the layer of solder, the stronger the joint will be. Rosin fluxes are suitable for high-tin-lead alloys but not for antimony solders. For joining copper, copper alloys, low-alloy steels, stainless steel, and cast iron, a flux of zinc-ammonium chloride, stannous chloride, and free hydrochloric acid is satisfactory, but as the residue is corrosive, excess flux should be removed.

WHITE METAL

White metal (92 per cent tin, 8 per cent antimony) is an alloy used in the casting of inexpensive costume jewelry. It melts at 246° C (475° F). Annealing at 200–225° C (392–437° F) will make severely worked metal harden slightly. Sheet and extruded wire are both made in this metal.

For a discussion of the tin alloy known as britannia metal or pewter, see page 264.

ZINC Zn 30

Properties

Atomic weight	65.38	
Specific gravity at 25° C (77° F)	7.131	
Melting point	419.4° C	787° F
Boiling point	906° C	1663° F

Zinc is a bluish-white crystalline metallic element that occurs abundantly in nature but never in the native state. The chief ores are the sulphide sphalerite or blende, smithsonite, and calamine, and the oxides willemite and franklinite (formerly found only in Franklin, New Jersey, where mining was terminated in 1954 because of the depletion of commercial grade ore). Though the commercial smelting of zinc did not begin in Europe till the middle of the eighteenth century, it was used by the ancient Greeks and Romans even before it was known to them to be a separate metal element. This separation occurred in the preparation of brasses through cementation of copper and calamine (zinc carbonate). The metal was produced in India long before it was in Europe; the description of its manufacture by the roasting and reduction of calamine was described in papers dating from the reign of a king who ruled in India about A.D. 1100. Portuguese traders brought the metal to Europe from India, where it was used in the manufacture of brass. For several centuries a zinc-based alloy known as *bidri,* from the town Bidar in Hyderabad Deccan, India, has been used to make decorative objects inlaid with silver (see page 138).

Uses of Zinc The main use of zinc today is as a corrosive-preventing agent over iron and steel, where it provides the best and cheapest protection. A zincking process known as *galvanizing* was based on the discovery by the Italian eighteenth-century scientist Galvani that there is a flow of electrical current between dissimilar metals in contact. Semiautomatic or hand-hot dipping of a steel object in molten zinc results in the freezing of a uniform, spangled coating of zinc on the object. For the same corrosion-resistant reason, galvanized nails do not rust and therefore do not rot the wood around them.

Die casting of zinc for automobile parts and the parts of other machines is the second main use of zinc, and the production of brass alloys is the third. The most important by-product of the purifying process for zinc is the production of sulphuric acid, the most widely used chemical, made from sulphur trioxide (the by-product) combined with water. Zinc oxide is used in the manufacture of pigment having high corrosion resistance. Zinc is also used for terrazzo strip, in dust form in the refining of gold and silver, in fireworks manufacture, and as one of the alloying ingredients in silver solder.

ALUMINUM Al 13

Properties

Atomic weight	26.97	
Specific gravity at 20° C	(68° F)	2.703
Melting point	660.2° C	1220.4° F
Boiling point	2060° C	3740° F

Aluminum was identified as a metal in 1709 by Marggraf, but it was not produced in sufficient quantities to determine its qualities till 1824, when the Danish electromagnetist Oersted studied its properties. At first, the cost of production was so high that it was treated as a rare metal and used as an oddity in pieces of jewelry. Today, its production has increased more rapidly than any other metal except magnesium, and its uses have expanded accordingly.

The principal mineral ore for the extraction of aluminum is bauxite, which occurs in abundance in many places in the world, and is mined if it contains between 50 and 65 per cent alumina. Bauxite contains hydrated oxides of aluminum, from which aluminum or its salts can be extracted with little difficulty by an electrolytic process that requires high electrical energy. Cheap electric power is essential to commercial production.

Aluminum weighs about one-third as much

as other commonly used metals (except for magnesium and beryllium) and is the lightest-weight metal used structurally. Besides being light in weight, it is malleable, resists corrosion, has high thermal and electrical conductivity (it is used for electric wire and cooking pots for this reason), can be polished to a high silvery luster, and is used to reflect light and heat.

Aluminum can be worked by almost all the usual methods: stamping, rolling, spinning, extruding, forging, and sand and die casting. Joining processes such as riveting, welding, and brazing are all possible. Soldering is also possible with the use of ordinary "coppers," but special fluxes suitable for aluminum are necessary.

When aluminum is exposed to humid air, it develops a thin, impervious film of oxide, which prevents further attack. It can also be *electrolytically* oxidized to create a harder, more resistant oxide film. The process of coloring this film by the introduction of dyes or inorganic mineral pigments through absorption or impregnation is called *anodizing*.

Anodizing aluminum is similar in method to electroplating; it consists of immersing the aluminum in a 15 to 25 per cent sulphuric or chromatic acid bath which produces an almost colorless, anodic aluminum oxide coating. After immediate washing, the oxide film absorbs the dye when the metal is submerged in a dyeing vat because of the film's submicroscopic porosity. Submersion is followed by hydration, or washing in boiling water for one-half hour. The surface is then sealed with lanolin dissolved in gasoline. Oils can be used to act as a "stop off" to create designs and patterns with dyes. The colors are usually not sunproof (though advances in color durability have recently been made) but are permanent in most indoor conditions. Anodized aluminum should be cleaned with plain water or mild soap; many alkaline cleaners attack and dissolve the coating oxides.

Aluminum Alloys Aluminum will alloy readily with other metals. Aluminum alloys can be divided into two main groups: those used for *casting* and those used in the *wrought* condition. The choice of alloy depends on the method of forming and the mechanical properties desired.

Aluminum alloys are made with copper, silicon, magnesium, and other metals. Some are designed for sand casting, some for permanent mold casting, and others for die casting. Still others are made for their good machining qualities, stamping qualities, or high tensile strength. Aluminum-magnesium alloys 214 and 218 tend to retain a whiter appearance under exposure to atmospheric conditions and are often used for ornamental exterior work, because their corrosion resistance is also high.

Soldering Aluminum (For full details on soldering techniques, see page 159.) To solder aluminum, an ordinary soldering iron (copper) is heated by a gas flame, torch, or electricity, in much the same way that copper is soldered. The copper tip of the soldering iron is first tinned with an ordinary lead-tin solder, and then an aluminum solder is used. If soldering is done with a flame, this should always be directed at the part *away* from the joint (not directly on the flux or the solder), so that the solder is melted by *conduction*.

It is sometimes advisable to secure a good joint by applying abrasion or friction with a tool such as a scraper, soldering iron, steel wool, wire brush, or solder stick, *under the molten solder,* to remove the oxide film that may form and insure the adherence of the solder to the surface of the metal. This can also be done *prior* to the joining of the pieces. Once the solder has set, the parts to be joined can then be assembled, with heat and, if necessary, more solder.

Alloys containing relatively large amounts of magnesium are difficult to solder. It is possible to solder other metals to aluminum with the proper solders and fluxes. Common wrought-aluminum alloys that present no soldering difficulties with a torch are alloy 2S (99.0 per cent pure aluminum), 3S (containing 1.2 per cent manganese), 61S, 53S, and A51S. All can be soft soldered with Alcoa ≹800 solder and Alcoa ≹61 flux.

Aluminum such as 2SO and 3SO can be soldered with an aluminum-alloy fusion solder called A-500. The edges to be joined should be cleaned with steel wool and liberally coated with the fusion solder, which contains flux, cleaning agent, and soldering metal in combination. Heat is applied with a torch to the metal but not yet concentrated on the joint. It must be moved constantly to avoid melting the metal. When the solder starts to boil and bubble and white smoke appears, the flame is directed at the joint itself, and the solder will flow. The metal is cleaned when cool with a stiff brush or steel wool and water.

Brazing Aluminum In brazing aluminum, special filler rods and fluxes having a lower melting point than the aluminum alloy being joined are used. The weld is also an aluminum alloy, matching the object in color and strength, and can be treated uniformly in processes such as anodizing and plating. Three types of brazing are commercially practiced: torch brazing, flux bath or dip brazing, and furnace brazing, but only the first is of interest to the hand craftsman. A welding torch employing oxyacetylene or oxy-natural gas can be used, and the heat is applied to the joint directly, with a reducing flame.

Aluminum brazing sheet is made of an aluminum-alloy core, coated on one or both surfaces with a thin layer of aluminum brazing alloy. It is heated to a point higher than the coating alloy's melting point but lower than the core's melting point. With the assistance of flux, the coating melts and flows into the joint by capillary attraction. The brazing-temperature range is from $1060°$ F to $1185°$ F. On aluminum alloys 2S, 3S, and 406, 43S wire and ≹33 flux can be used in torch brazing. On aluminum alloy 53S, ≹717 brazing wire, and ≹33 flux are used ($1060–1090°$ F brazing temperature).

Casting Aluminum Aluminum and its alloys can be cast in sand molds, plaster molds, and die castings. The selection of the method of casting depends on the size and shape of the piece, section thickness, and surface finish desired.

Sand Casting of Aluminum Sand casting is the best-known and most frequently used casting process. (For a procedural discussion, see page 325.) The method used for aluminum is the same as that used for other nonferrous metals, with care taken for temperature control. In small sand castings, a section of $\frac{3}{16}$ of an inch is considered the minimum possible. The surface of sand castings depends for its character on the fineness of the sand used. For large castings, coarser sand is advisable. Aluminum sand castings generally have smoother surfaces than other sand cast metals, partly because of the lower melting point required of the metal, and partly because the sand does not burn into the surface of the casting.

The best alloys for sand casting are alloys ≹43, 108, 355, and 356. These alloys have the lowest shrinkage tendency, are good in hot shortness (not brittle when hot), and pressure

Cast aluminum door pull, by Don Drumm. Diameter: 20 inches.

tightness (the casting is free of porosity). *Permanent steel molds* produce castings of fine surface grain and reduced porosity because of the chilling action of the metal mold on the poured metal. Thinner sections are possible owing to the nature of the process. Alloys ✕ 13 and 360 are best for die casting, because they are low in hot shortness and high in mold-filling capacity.

Plaster-Mold Casting of Aluminum Plaster-mold casting is a refinement of the sand-casting process. (See page 330 for a procedural discussion.) Gypsum plasters are used, and they produce greater accuracy and surface smoothness than sand. The mold is generally usable for only one casting, and castings weighing two pounds and larger are possible. The metal is poured under gravity conditions, and its solidification is slower than sand castings, because of the refractory nature of the plaster.

"Architectural Landscape," panel in cast aluminum, Jan de Swart. Dimensions: 2 feet by 5 feet. *Museum of Contemporary Crafts.*

The most suitable alloys for this process are ✕ 43 and 355, both aluminum-silicon alloys.

Other Casting Procedures with Aluminum Aluminum alloys may also be used in investment casting in the lost-wax process (page 338) and in centrifugal casting (page 351). There is a shrinkage in cast aluminum of approximately 3.5 to 8.5 per cent. Preheating the aluminum for casting to about 900° F before submerging or combining it with other molten material helps to eliminate gases, which are the result of hydrogen-forming materials on the metal's surface that might cause porosity. A minimum of agitation of the molten metal and avoidance of holding the molten metal at melting point for long periods before pouring will result in greater casting success. Melting pots made of graphite or other refractory material are suitable for casting, as are cast-iron pots if they are coated with a protective wash.

It is possible to have copper, brass, or cast-iron inserts or inclusions in aluminum alloys when casting, as these metals have a higher melting point than aluminum.

Aluminum is finished after casting by scratch brushing, wire brushing, sand blasting, wheel buffing, and all the usual polishing methods.

Aluminum is sold in ingots, sheets, wire, powder, and in various structural or extruded forms.

NICKEL   Ni 28

Properties

Atomic weight	58.69	
Specific gravity	8.9	
Melting point	1445° C	2651° F
Boiling point	2730° C	4950° F

Nickel was discovered at an early time but was not recognized as an elemental metal till 1751 by Axel F. Cronstedt of Sweden. Before that, prehistoric man in his search after stronger "stones" for use as tools had found nickel in the form of meteoric metal, which

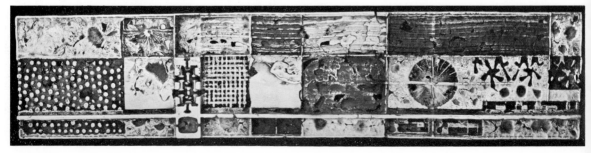

often contains a high nickel content. The Chinese of Yunan Province, where the metal exists, used it to make the copper-nickel alloy they called paktong, "white copper," which was used for money and household utensils (copper 45 per cent, nickel 30 per cent, zinc 24 per cent, pure iron 1 per cent).

The nickel industry of today began with the discovery of deposits in New Caledonia, in western Canada, and Sudbury, Ontario, in 1866. Nickel is found in nature as sulphide, oxided, and arsenical ores, combined with iron, copper, and silicon. The importance of nickel has grown in the past fifty years as an alloying metal, though about one-quarter of its production is used in the pure state. It is most important as an alloying element in steel, where it increases hardness (as it does in *all* its alloys) without reducing ductility. It is also a component in nickel silver, nickel-copper alloys, and Monel Metal, and is widely employed as an undercoating in electroplating for producing a brilliant chromium finish.

Nickel is hard, malleable, ductile, and nearly silvery white but varies in color with the percentage in alloys from warm gray to pink. It is highly resistant to oxidation and corrosion, can be cast, forged, machined, welded, brazed, or soldered, and its strength is not affected by quite high and low temperatures.

Considerations in Working Nickel Nickel can be worked by all methods. When it becomes work hardened and must be annealed, the metal should be heated gradually at first until enough preheating has been done to prevent cracking from the sudden release of tensions. After annealing, it can be allowed to cool gradually, or quenched. K Monel and Z nickel *must,* however, be quenched or they may develop cracks on slow cooling. To bright-anneal nickel and its alloys, it should be quenched in a 2 per cent by volume solution of denatured alcohol. This eliminates the oxide flash that otherwise occurs from the oxygen in the air. The annealing temperature range is 1100–1500° F.

Soldering and Joining Nickel All oxides and dirt must be removed from nickel and its alloys. In general, any joining process can be used. Phosphorus-free silver solders used with a fluoride flux and a reducing flame at temperatures lower than 1400° F are advisable. In soft soldering, the same acid fluxes as those used for copper are used. In oxyacetylene welding, nickel welding rods are used without flux, with a reducing flame. Nickel and its alloys can be joined to other metals by soft soldering and silver soldering.

Polishing Nickel and its Alloys In polishing, abrasives and polishing agents of all kinds can be used except lime compounds and rouge, as these do not have sufficient cutting characteristics. Canton-flannel buffs charged with chromic oxide compound will give nickel a high mirror finish. For a satin finish, a high-count-muslin loose disc wheel should be used, charged with a greaseless compound such as Lea's Compound. Rubbing with a clean, soft rag and whiting should follow. The mirror finish is also finally polished with a clean flannel rag and whiting.

NICKEL ALLOYS

Nickel Silver Nickel silver is basically a copper and nickel alloy (Alloy A: copper 62 per cent, nickel 33 per cent, zinc 5 per cent; melting point: 1960° F; used for jewelry). There are several nickel-silver alloys, *none of them containing silver.* Their close resemblance to silver, and the name "German" silver sometimes used for them, plus the uses to which they are put, account for the name. Nickel silver resists oxidation at high temperatures, resists corrosion, and can be formed by a variety of means and joined by any method. Its pleasing white color and receptivity to high-luster finishes have made it popular for use in architectural ornamentation, such as trim.

Pin of gold cast around Monel Metal wire cloth, by Bob Winston.

Tibetan gilded bronze statue, eighteenth century. Gilding done by the mercury gilding process. This is a representation of the Green Tara or Sgrol-Yan, a manifestation of Sgrol-Ma (Dolma), the goddess who saves man from transmigratory existence. *Museum of Fine Arts, Boston.*

Other uses include costume jewelry, holloware, and eating utensils; these are usually silver- or chrome-plated, though they may of course be used alone.

Monel Metal A nickel alloy, Monel consists of 67 per cent nickel, 30 per cent copper, and small percentages of iron, manganese, carbon, silicon, and sulphur. Its melting temperature range is 1300–1350° C (2370–2460° F). Monel is highly resistant to corrosion from acids, alkalies, brines, water, and food products in moist and dry atmospheres. It can be soft and silver soldered, welded, and brazed. In soft soldering, an acid flux is used, not a rosin flux. If Monel is in contact with iron in an acid dip, a copper flash plating will occur that can be removed by immersion in a 4–5 per cent ammonia solution (approximately 1 pint commercial aqua ammonia to a gallon of water) for one minute at room temperature. Monel can be polished to a soft, lustrous, yellowish-gray color.

Nichrome Wire Nichrome alloy consists of 80 per cent nickel and 20 per cent chromium. Because of its suitability to cold drawing, high resistance to electricity, oxidation resistance up to 2200° F, and high melting point (1400° C, or 2550° F), it is used for electrical resistance heating elements in kilns and furnaces. The wire retains its strength at high temperatures. Another nickel alloy (60 per cent nickel, 24 per cent iron, 16 per cent chromium) is used for enameling racks and trivets because of its low oxidation under heat.

Invar Consisting of 36 per cent nickel, 63 per cent iron, and 1 per cent of small portions of manganese, silicon, and carbon, invar alloy has a coefficient of thermal expansion of almost zero at ordinary temperature changes. The name invar arose because of its invariability. It is used for absolute standards of length, rods and tapes for geodetic work, pendulums and balances in clocks and watches, and automobile pistons.

MERCURY Hg 80

Properties

Atomic weight	200.61
Specific gravity	13.55
Melting point	−38.85° C −37.97° F
Boiling point	357.25° C 675° F

Mercury, a liquid metal at normal temperatures, has been called quicksilver because of the ease with which the ore is reduced. It occurs in nature as a mineral of brilliant red crystals or brownish masses, which are mercuric sulphide, also known as cinnabar. It is prepared by roasting the crystals or masses and condensing the vapors.

Mercury has been known and used as a red pigment since before written history. Any alloy of mercury with another metal is called an *amalgam*. In an amalgamated form with gold, mercury has been used as a gilding medium on base metals, as in the Limoges enameled reliquaries, on armor, and on silver, which often was partly (parcel-gilt) gold-plated. Its use in gold plating predates the electroplating of gold by many centuries.

Alchemists from A.D. 700 to 1100 and even later assigned magical properties to this mysterious substance in their ceremonies. Their main objective was to transform base metals into gold. They did not recognize mercury as a metal, and, indeed, it was not till about 1760 that Braune of St. Petersburg recognized mercury as a true metal and succeeded in solidifying it at −40° C (approximately).

Besides its uses today for measuring devices such as thermometers and barometers, as a pigment in special paints that prevent the fouling of ships' bottoms, and in the ceramics, cosmetics, and pharmaceutical industries, mercury is also used to form dental amalgams for filling teeth. Its greatest use occurs in the gold and silver refining process, in which finely divided raw ores containing gold or silver are suspended in water, which passes over a surface of liquid mercury. A large percentage of the gold and silver unites with the mercury and forms an amalgam. The amalgam is collected and the precious metals are separated from the mercury by further processing.

Italy is the world's largest producer of mercury, and the next largest are Spain, Mexico, and the United States. Mercury is sold in flasks from chemical supply houses.

Amalgam Gold Plating Though the process of gold plating has been almost completely superseded by electroplating, the old process of using an amalgam of gold and mercury is interesting. The result is even more durable, as is witnessed by the many ancient articles seen in museums today still brightly and freshly plated. This form of gilding can be done on silver, copper, bronze, brass, and copper-plated iron.

Mercury amalgam gold plating is still practical in Tibet, Nepal, Bhutan, and India for the gilding of images of deities and jewelry.

Mercury vapors are poisonous, and any handling of the material should be done with utmost care. Good ventilation and avoidance of contact with the skin are important.

Preparing Gold Amalgam Several methods of preparing gold amalgam are found in old books. One calls for the proportion of eight parts of gold to one part of mercury. Thin gold plates are made red hot and inserted into boiling mercury, which is held in an iron ladle. The ladle was previously lined with whiting and water and dried. The gold immediately combines with the mercury, and the amalgam is poured into cold water. The greater part of the fluidity of the amalgam is lost. It is placed in a chamois leather bag, the bag is squeezed, and the free mercury escapes through the pores of the leather, while the rest of the

Forged and carved steel "Rocking Horse," by L. Brent Kington, Carbondale, Illinois. Length: 52 inches.

amalgam remains as a mass of about the consistency of stiff clay. It is then ready for use.

Applying the Amalgam The article or area to be gilded must be absolutely clean, or the amalgam will not adhere. Cleaning can be done by washing the metal surface with dilute nitric acid or a combination of potash of lye and prepared chalk.*

The piece is then heated, and while it is hot the amalgam is applied as evenly as possible with a brush. The article is then placed with the gilded surface up (to allow the fumes to escape) on a grate in an open iron pan over a charcoal fire, or in an oven, and heated to a low red heat to volatilize the mercury in the amalgam. The gold remains behind and, at this point, looks dull. It is then polished by covering it with a coat of equal parts of alum and pulverized niter mixed into a paste with water. The article is heated again till this paste

---

* For surfaces that do not seem to have a chemical affinity for the amalgam when it is applied, the following is suggested by an ancient source. Make a solution by pouring a tablespoon of mercury into a quart of nitric acid. The mercury rapidly unites with the acid. Red fumes form instantly, along with the production of considerable heat. The article is brought into contact with the solution and its surface immediately becomes an amalgam. Gold and mercury amalgams will readily adhere to this surface by molecular attraction.

melts, and is then plunged into water. The gilt surface is burnished with a steel, agate, or bloodstone burnisher, or with a finely powdered abrasive rubbed over the surface with the fingers.

Mercury can be tried as a means of removing a gold ring from a swollen finger. A drop of absolute alcohol is put on the ring, and the ring and finger are brought into contact with liquid mercury held in a bowl. In some circumstances, the ring will snap because of stresses in the gold, which may react in this manner on contact with mercury.

Ferrous Metals

Ferrous metals are metals that contain a percentage of iron.

IRON Fe 26

Properties

Atomic weight	55.85
Specific gravity	7.87
Melting point	1539° C 2802° F
Boiling point	2740° C 4960° F

It is estimated that about 5 per cent of the earth's crust is iron. Aluminum (over 8 per cent) and silicon (over 27 per cent) are the only other metals found in larger quantities. Iron is a hard, gray metal, both malleable and ductile, is strongly attracted by magnets, readily oxidized (rusted) in moist air, and attacked by many corrosive agents. As a basic ingredient in steel and in its other forms, cast iron, wrought iron, and ingot iron, it is the world's most widely used and important metal.

Iron is rarely found native except in meteorites but is combined with other elements in rock in widely distributed areas in the world. Unless at least one-fifth of the rock content is iron, it is not profitable for mining, because of the high cost of recovery from low-grade ores. As iron ore occurs most frequently near the surface of the earth, the greater part is mined in open pit mining, though underground iron mines exist where the quality of the ore makes it economically feasible in this more expensive mining operation.

The main ores from which iron is derived are hematite, magnetite, limonite, and siderite. Most iron ores contain more than two minerals but are classified according to which one is dominant. Hematite, brownish-red in color, is the main iron ore, containing 70 per cent iron when pure, but it is usually mined 50 to 60 per cent pure and contains little phosphorus or sulphur, both of which must be eliminated to produce iron of good quality. Magnetite, a hard, black stone, contains between 60 and 70 per cent iron, is free of sulphur, contains

little phosphorus, and is one of the richest iron ores. It is found mainly in northern Sweden, where the smelting process using charcoal results in the famous high-quality Swedish soft iron. Limonite consists of hematite combined with water, is yellowish-brown, and contains 30 to 50 per cent iron, and as much as 1 per cent phosphorus. Siderite is a low-quality ore containing between 20 and 35 per cent iron, and about ½ per cent phosphorus.

Cast iron is relatively inexpensive to produce, easily fusible, fluid when pouring, and used where strength is not a deciding factor. It contains between 2.75 and 3.75 per cent carbon, is hard and brittle, and cannot be hammered, bent, or formed after casting without breaking. A type of cast iron called *malleable iron,* containing 2.50 per cent carbon, is of less brittleness because of the extensive annealing process, which takes a few days. Heat treatments called *aging* are designed to relieve cast iron of residual stresses. The cast iron is heated to 800 to 1100° F, and held at this temperature for thirty minutes to five hours, then cooled slowly in a furnace. Malleable iron is stronger, more elastic, and tougher than ordinary iron castings, and can be worked to a limited extent. Some of the many items made from malleable cast iron are automobile parts, hardware and small tools, household appliances, machine tools (lathes, planers, grinders, drills), pipe fittings, toys, and manhole covers.

Two fish formed in silver by hand processes to create their basic shapes, then completed with hand-formed additional units (spines, fins, and scales) and textured by engraving. Gilding the entire article is the final process. Produced by Tiffany & Co., where they are known as articles in *vermeil. Tiffany & Co., New York.*

OPPOSITE: Silver rosebowl, gilded inside by electroplating, designed and executed by Gerald Benney, London. *Worshipful Company of Goldsmiths, London.*

Chilled cast iron has a surface of white iron while its interior is gray, due to the rapid cooling of its surface in the mold.

Wrought iron is an almost carbon-free iron, containing less than 0.3 per cent carbon. It is fibrous in structure as can be seen when it is fractured, and contains uniformly distrib- uted, very fine streaks of slag (1 to 2 per cent) which is mechanically mixed with it. Relatively soft, it is malleable and ductile and withstands shock because of its inherent toughness. It has remarkable resistance to cor- rosion, forges well, can be shaped at red heat, welds easily when cold, and cannot be hard-

OPPOSITE: Cast iron necklace, bracelets, pin and earrings. Made about 1820 by the Berliner Königlichen Eisengiesserei, Germany, who created a fashion for this kind of jewelry. *Museum of Decorative Arts, Copenhagen.*

ABOVE LEFT: Franklin stove made of cast iron with brass decorations, America, nineteenth century. Height: 53½ inches; width: 35 inches. *Metropolitan Museum of Art, New York. Gift of Mrs. J. Insley Blair, 1948.*
ABOVE RIGHT: Contemporary American cast iron trivet, utilizing a traditional design. Diameter: 6¾ inches. *Photo by Oppi.*
RIGHT: Cast iron waffle iron, Pennsylvania Dutch, early nineteenth century, made to be placed on a coal or wood stove for use. *Philadelphia Museum of Art.*

ened by sudden cooling or quenching. All these properties were known to early craftsmen and smiths, who used the metal to create many decorative objects (see Forging, page 271).

STEEL

Steel is an alloy of iron and up to 1.7 per cent carbon. The presence of carbon increases the hardness of the steel, its tensile strength, and its brittleness, though brittleness can be overcome by tempering. There are two main types of steel: plain carbon steel, and alloy steel. Both types are widely produced. Alloy steel contains small amounts of other metals plus carbon to produce steel of special qualities. Steel, unlike cast iron, can be both cast and wrought.

Carbon Steel Carbon steels are classified according to their carbon content. *Low-carbon steel,* also called mild or soft steel, contains between 0.15 and 0.30 per cent carbon, and is available in black iron sheet, rods, and bars.

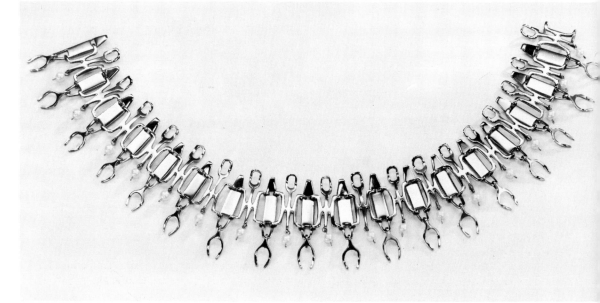

Necklace with pearls, executed in stainless steel by Mary Ann Scherr, who is a pioneer in the use of this tough metal for jewelry.

BELOW: Sterling silver pin employing stainless steel screen, by Margaret De Patta, California. The design was dictated by the need to protect the wearer from the cut edges of the screen without enclosing the material. *Photo by Charles Uht.*

It is easily welded, machined, and formed by other means and is used for rivets, wire, and structural sections. *Medium carbon steel* containing 0.30 to 0.50 per cent carbon is used for machine parts. *High-carbon steel,* containing 0.50 to 1.60 per cent carbon, is hard steel used for springs and tools which must be tempered. A special *tool steel* containing 0.90 to 1.50 per cent carbon is made for use in very hard steel tools and is relatively difficult to weld.

Alloy Steel Steel containing certain small amounts of various metals each of which imparts special characteristics to the steel alloy is widely used. Low-alloy steels have superior mechanical properties to mild carbon steels, and are more resistant to atmospheric corrosion. They are readily welded by most welding processes, and the welding metal added does not have to be of the same composition as the steel, provided it has similar properties. Alloyed steels have a small percentage of the alloying element in addition to carbon, silicon, sulphur, and phosphorus.

Alloying metals used in steel, and the qualities imparted, are as follows:

Aluminum restricts the growth of grain by forming dispersed oxides or nitrides.

Chromium, a widely used element in plain and complex steels, creates outstanding resistance to corrosion, oxidation, and wear, increases hardenability, adds strength at high temperatures, and with high carbon resists abrasion and wear. It is used in stainless steels, 10 to 20 per cent.

Cobalt contributes to red hardness by hardening ferrite, and strengthens magnetic properties.

Copper is widely used in structural and sheet steel because it resists atmospheric corrosion, increases fluidity in the melt, and increases machineability.

Manganese counteracts brittleness from sulphur, and inexpensively increases hardenability and tensile strength, reduces hot shortness, and allows the metal to be hot worked. It is used in many steels.

Molybdenum counteracts a tendency toward temper brittleness, deepens hardening, raises red hardness, increases strength at elevated temperatures, and is therefore used in high-speed steels. It enhances corrosion resistance in stainless steel, forms abrasion-resisting particles, and has free sealing characteristics.

Nickel strengthens unquenched or annealed steels, forms solid solutions with iron, resists embrittlement at low temperatures, and heightens corrosion resistance. It is used in stainless steel from 1.25 to 22 per cent.

Phosphorus strengthens low-carbon steel, increases resistance to corrosion, and improves machineability in free-cutting steels.

Silicon strengthens low-alloy steels, improves oxidation and corrosion resistance, and when added to chromium, chromium-tungsten, and chromium-nickel steels, increases resistance to high-temperature oxidation. It also increases magnetic permeability.

Tungsten was the first alloying element used in tool steels. It forms hard, abrasion-resistant particles in this metal, promotes hardness and strength at elevated temperatures, and is therefore used for cutting tools which generate high heat due to friction. It decreases the extent of softening during tempering. Tungsten carbide, an extremely hard steel, is used for cutting *tips* for tools, brazed onto a body of plain carbon steel.

Vanadium promotes fine grain structure, increases hardenability, and resists tempering. It is used in springs operating at high temperatures, is added to tool steels to increase serviceability, and resists wear at high and low operating temperatures.

Contemporary Japanese cast iron ashtray and cigarette box. *Bonniers, New York. Photo by Lee Michael.*

The Manufacture of Metals

Most metalworkers purchase their material in the exact basic form, size, and shape necessary for their immediate needs. The metal industry is prepared to go even farther and supply the user with special products to suit particular needs. This has not always been the case, as those craftsmen who must fabricate their sheet metal, wire, and other forms of metal for lack of availability of finished materials well realize. Before we take the convenience of ever-ready materials completely for granted, and better to understand and appreciate our fortunate state of affairs, the following description of the processing of sterling silver as prepared by Handy and Harman, which roughly approximates the procedures employed in the manufacture of many metals, might be of value.

Manufacture of Sterling Silver Sheet Metal

Careful attention is given to the preparation and melting of this alloyed form in which silver is most usually produced. Maximum purity, satisfactory crystalline structure, and other mechanical properties are factors to be considered for a standardized, uniform product.

The melt room contains several large electric furnaces which are each capable of melting approximately fourteen thousand troy ounces of metal in about forty-five minutes. Oil-fired furnaces having a capacity of eight thousand troy ounces require one to two hours, and are also used. Electric furnaces have the advantage of clean heat and shorten the time necessary to reach high temperatures. Each furnace has three men assigned to it: a feeder, a melter or pourer, and a mold man.

The metal to be melted consists of a percentage of scrap, bullion bars, and bullion brick, plus new metal. Scrap may consist of milling chips, turnings, trimmings, punchings, coils, cast bar ends, and reclaimed metal from customers (sweeps, filings, etc. after they have been refined). The metals to be melted are weighed before and after melting and the records of melt loss are carefully kept.

Every bar cast must meet legal standards and assay requirements. In addition, it must be "sound" so that it will withstand the stress and strain of future processing such as cold rolling, forging, and drawing. If the metal is improperly cast and therefore defective, it cannot be corrected later, but must be remelted, a highly uneconomical and wasteful procedure. Thus proper melting procedures, including the cleanliness of the metal, thorough melting and mixing, temperature control during the melting and at the time of pouring, and correct mold temperature are important and carefully regulated.

The proper pouring temperature of metal is generally just above its melting point. Silver is poured at $1100°$ C ($2012°$ F), $170°$ C ($252°$ F) above liquidus (melting point). Control of this temperature is necessary or metal of poor crystalline structure may occur which will result in unusable sterling. While melting, the metal is held in a crucible made of conventional clay, graphite, or other refractory material. The surface of the metal while melting is covered with charcoal or borax to prevent excessive oxidation. Excessive oxidation would create undesirable blowholes or pinholes in the solidified metal, and these trapped holes would produce blisters in rolled and annealed sheet metal.

A sample of the melt is taken prior to pouring the ingot, while the metal is still molten—the best way to get an accurate sampling. This sample is sent to the laboratory for analysis and approval before the metal can be released into production.

Prior to pouring, the mold is preheated with a large gas torch and is then prepared with a mold oil dressing to prevent automatic ejection during pouring, to eliminate sticking, and

1

2

PROCESSES IN THE MANUFACTURE OF STERLING SILVER. At the Handy and Harman plant, El Monte, California. *Photos by Nick Lazarnick. Courtesy Handy and Harman.*

1. Pouring molten sterling silver into an ingot mold.
2. Sterling silver ingots ready for further processing.
3. Rolling sterling silver in a finishing mill capable of rolling down to 0.0005 inch with tolerances of + or − 0.0001 inch.
4. Coils of strip sterling silver entering a box furnace for annealing. These furnaces, which are timed by automatic devices, are loaded and unloaded mechanically.
5. Sterling silver being processed on a slitting machine into required widths.

3

5

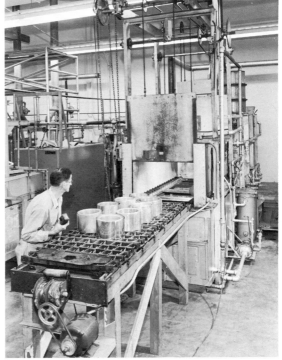

4

Copper and copper-base coils of wire designed for a wide variety of purposes. Extruded cold heading wire is fabricated for characteristics of strength, ductility, hardness, color, and electrical conductivity. *Copper and Brass Research Association.*

The principal forms in which many metals are fabricated include sheet, strip, rod, wire, bar, pipe, tube, and other special shapes. This photograph shows copper and copper-base alloys. *Copper and Brass Research Association.*

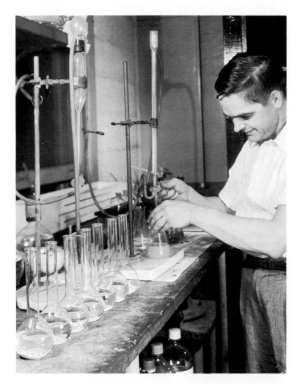

A metal-assaying laboratory at Handy and Harman, in which the purity of metals is tested to maintain a reliable standard and to fulfill specific requirements. *Handy and Harman. Photo by Nick Lazarnick.*

RIGHT: Scrap metal ready to be smelted and reclaimed. *Handy and Harman. Photo by Nick Lazarnick.*

"Structure 14B," sheet metal sculpture, by Stephen Gilbert, England. *American Federation of Arts.*

to produce a smooth surface on the ingot. The iron mold is held in an upright position, and in a method known as "end" pouring, the furnace is tipped, and the metal is poured in a steady flow which the experienced pourer knows is neither too fast nor too slow. A gas torch is played against the furnace lip and the pouring box through which the metal passes into the mold to prevent excessive oxidation during the pouring.

The rate of cooling of the ingot depends on the particular metal. Some metals demand instant quenching to preserve their structure, and others need slow cooling at a normal or slow rate. As most metals contract upon solidification, shrinkage occurs in the upper part of the ingot while in the mold, and there a longitudinal cavity develops which is called the "gate-end" of the bar. This end is later cut off with

a large shears. Upon cooling and extraction from the mold, the ingot is wire-brushed, washed, and stamped with the number of the melt, and its metal identification. After assaying is favorably completed, the cast bar is released for further fabrication.

Silver is sometimes sold in bar form when intended for casting, but sheet, wire, rod, tubing, and grain are also used and must then be manufactured from ingots. Ingots to be used for sheet metal are flat, and about one and a half inches thick. They are passed through rolling mills in various stages of thickness, and given intermediate temperature controlled anneals in molten salt at 1200° F for 8–10 minutes, after which the sheet is rolled again till it reaches the desired thickness.

The metal is then "scalped," to mill off approximately .025 inches. This process directly

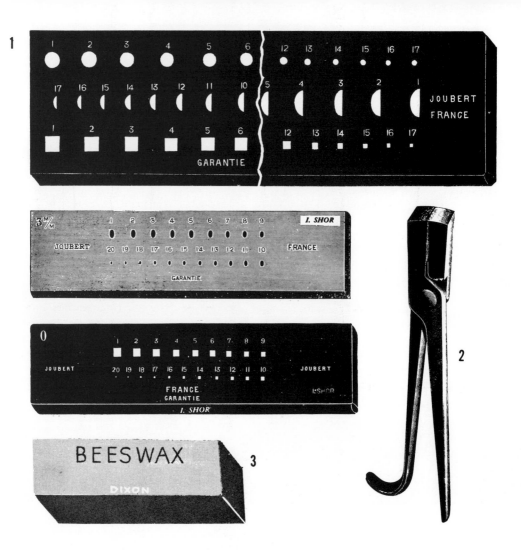

Wire-drawing equipment: 1. Drawplates 2. Drawtongs 3. Beeswax

affects the luster of the final product. To produce the proper finish, gauge, and thickness tolerance, the metal is fed through polished steel rolls. It is then trimmed to the desired width and length and given a final anneal for maximum work softness. This is done by passing it for several hours through a conveyer-type, atmosphere-controlled furnace held at one temperature. Prior to shipment, it is finally checked for gauge, width, and surface condition, then weighed and wrapped in paper packages.

Wire Drawing

Wire is solid metal of uniform cross section when round, which may range in thickness from a thread or filament to a slender bar or rod. Wire used as a decorative element in jewelry and ornamental work has a history of more than three thousand years. Its decorative possibilities for filigree work, and in heavier form for metal sculpture cover a wide range of treatments.

Though wire may be purchased in various forms and gauges, it is sometimes necessary for the metalworker to reduce a wire size or to change its cross-section shape. This can easily be done with a hardened steel wire drawplate which can be purchased with graduated holes tapered to reduce the wire cross section and numbered in specific B. & S. gauge thicknesses. Drawplates are made with round, half round, oval, square, rectangular, flat, hexagonal, octagonal, and other shapes, and are available in a single shape per plate or with a variety of shapes in one plate.

The necessary tools are few: a drawplate, drawplate tongs, and beeswax, oil, soap, or tallow as a lubricant. The drawtongs are specially designed for this purpose, and have heavy, square, serrated jaws to facilitate gripping the wire as it emerges from the drawplate hole, and a hooked handle for easy gripping while pulling the wire through the plate.

PROCEDURE FOR HAND DRAWING WIRE

If the wire being drawn is known to be previously annealed, the drawing procedure may begin at once. If the wire is hard and springy, it must be annealed before drawing. If the reduction of wire size makes it necessary to pass the wire several times through the drawplate, it should be annealed when it shows signs of excessive hardness, or the wire may break in the process of drawing.

Annealing the Wire To anneal wire, form the entire length into a compact coil with the ends tucked in, as they will melt if exposed. Wrap the coil with a length of the same wire being annealed so that the whole coil may be treated in the same manner during the subsequent pickling in acid. If it were of a different metal, the wrapping wire would have to be removed.

Annealing may be done with a torch, or in a temperature-controlled kiln. To prevent excessive oxidation, and to indicate the approach of correct annealing temperature, paint the entire wire mass with a flux that melts at a temperature known to be close to the annealing temperature. If you are using a torch, place the coil on a charcoal block when heating from above, or an open wire mesh when heating from below.

Heat the coil gradually, passing a soft flame over the wire so that all parts are evenly annealed. Once the metal shows a red glow, it can be immediately quenched in water or pickling acid. Do not overheat, as prolonged heat

The process of hand-drawing precious metal into fine wire has been known for many centuries. In India and other places, wire for decorative purposes is still, to a certain extent, drawn by hand. The wire is drawn through increasingly smaller dies, which are usually made of a hard, precious stone such as diamond. The wire is reeled from spool to die to receiving drum. A smaller die is put in place to decrease the wire diameter. The wire is then returned to the spool. The process continues until wire of the desired cross-section diameter is achieved. *Photo by Oppi.*

Wire, in this case silver, is reduced to the required cross-section diameter (gauge) by drawing it through a series of dies with graduated, diminishing openings (the disc shapes on the tray to the left and those mounted on the machine) and liquid lubricant in the tank, until the required dimension is achieved. The finished wire is automatically wound around the vertical drum or spool at the upper right. *Handy and Harman. Photo by Nick Lazarnick.*

will cause weakness in the wire. When using a kiln preheat it to annealing temperature, place the coil on a wire mesh trivet, and insert the whole with long-handled tongs. Take care to watch the coil through a peephole or by opening the kiln door slightly. Remove the wire coil as soon as it shows the first signs of redness, and pickle. (See page 122.)

Using the Drawplate Before placing the wire in the drawplate, the holes to be used should be checked to see that they are clear of foreign matter. They are then filled with a lubricant. This facilitates the drawing and prevents excessive friction, which causes heating and wearing of the holes. The end of the wire should be tapered, either by filing, grinding, or hammering so that sufficient wire projects through the hole opening to allow the end to be securely gripped by the drawtongs. Do not begin with too small a hole, which would offer great resistance, but plan on reducing the wire by stages to the desired size. The size of hole should be the one which is first to resist the easy passage of the wire. The wire should be clean and *dry* to prevent rusting of the drawplate.

The wire should be pulled through the plate in as even and continuous a movement as possible. It should emerge from the hole in a position perpendicular to the plate face. Once the entire length has passed through the drawplate, proceed to the next smaller holes in succession, not skipping any intermediate holes till the desired gauge is reached. Remember to anneal the wire should it become hard and springy. This is less necessary with *fine* silver and gold. After the final drawing, anneal again to facilitate bending the wire in use.

If only a round holed drawplate is available and half round wire is needed, it can be made by folding the wire in half, or using two lengths, and following the same procedure as for round wire. Flatten and taper the two ends before inserting them in the first hole, and draw the wire through the drawplate perpendicularly to the face of the plate, making sure it is being fed into the plate hole *straight,* to avoid twisting, a situation hard to correct later.

The drawplate can also be used to form tubing, though the diameter of the tube is limited to the size of the openings. Thin-gauge metals are commonly used, but this depends on the desired wall thickness. A general rule is to cut metal three times the diameter of the required tube.

Use a true edge of the metal and be certain

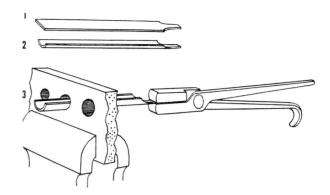

Forming a tube with a drawplate: 1. Flat metal with tapered end for threading through the drawplate and grasping with the drawplate tongs 2. Shaped metal ready to go through the drawplate 3. Drawplate anchored in a vise, with the metal being drawn through with drawplate tongs

the cut edges are also true. A blunt point is made at one end which will provide a gripping place for the tongs and allow the metal to enter the hole. First the metal is placed in a grooved forming block such as a swage block. It is hammered with a thin-faced collet hammer into the groove with the pointed edge or face, the metal being rolled slightly to make the edges curve toward each other, thus partly forming the tube. Another method for this preliminary shaping is to place a steel rod of suitable thickness on top of the metal which is held over the groove and hammer the rod, thus forcing the metal into shape. Beeswax is then applied to the tube strip, the point is inserted in the drawplate, and it is pulled through with the drawtongs. To keep the seam straight, a knife blade held in the seam as it passes through the plate will help. The seam can then be soldered, if it is desired. A tube with an accurate *inside* dimension can be formed around a steel wire of the proper size. To be able to remove the wire from the tube after drawing, it should be lubricated *before* use. After drawing, the tube is placed against the first hole in the drawplate that will resist its passage, and the projecting steel wire is pulled through leaving the tube free.

Double-strand wire which is first twisted and then drawn through a drawplate is sometimes used for filigree work when small wire is used and for decorative wire bangles made of heavy-gauge wire. Different combinations of wire result in a variety of effects, and several strands can be twisted and used together. It is possible to later *untwist* these wire strands completely or partly, removing one of several wires, and to use them in that manner.

Hand rolling mills must have hard steel, accurately polished rolls. This model has rolls that are 3⅜ inches long, with a 2-inch diameter and a maximum opening of ¼ inch. The rolls are interchangeable from the standard flat (left) to the smooth and square groove (top right), all-square groove (middle right), ring rolling (half round and flat; lower right) and others.

MECHANICAL WIRE DRAWING

The mechanical process of drawing wire is essentially the same as the hand procedure described. Great care must be taken to clean the wire or it may be scratched, and the die life reduced. The dies are made of tungsten carbide, a very hard steel, and diamond dies are used for very fine wire. The lubricant—tallow, pulverized soap, or a mixture of oil and flour— is used in so-called dry drawing, and liquid soap or a soluble oil in wet drawing. The lubricant is placed in a box before the die hole, and the wire passes through the lubricant as it is automatically drawn in a continuous motion through the die. The die is mounted in a wire-drawing block. After the wire passes through the die, it is gathered onto a reel. The wire is processed till the desired gauge is reached. A large quantity, often several hundred pounds, accumulates on the reel. As in hand drawing, annealing is often necessary.

THE FLAT ROLLING MILL

The hand rolling mill is used primarily to reduce the thickness or gauge of sheet metal. It can also be used to roll out cast ingots into sheet and strips, to flatten braided or twisted wire as a hammer substitute, and to change the cross-section shape of wire. It is well to remember that the rolling mill *increases the dimension of the metal in the direction in which it passes through the rolls.* If an increase in *width* is desired, the metal must be fed through the rolls *widthwise,* if this is possible, or at an angle.

Adjusting the Rolling Mill There are several models of flat rolling mills available which accommodate widths from 2¼″ to 5″ in width. On some models, the rolls are completely flat, on others they are grooved in graduated widths for reducing wire, and on still others, they are grooved on one side and flat on the other. The rolls are made of polished steel, and should be wiped clean before use. After use, they should be kept lubricated with a light oil to prevent rust.

During use, the rolls must be *kept parallel* to maintain an even thickness in the rolled metal. This is the first step in preparing them for use. On some models, the top center adjusting gear is removable, allowing the right and left gear to be turned to adjust the rolls till they are parallel. The center gear is then replaced and can be used from then on to decrease or increase the opening between the rolls.

Using the Rolling Mill The metal is placed between the rolls, and the rolls adjusted so that the metal readily passes through. It is then removed and the center adjusting gear is turned about a quarter turn to reduce the opening. The metal is then passed through the rolls, which are turned by a detachable handle. The process is continued, the opening each time being decreased till the desired gauge thickness of metal is reached. To help keep the metal flat, it can be reversed (inserting one end and then the other) and turned over for each passage through the rolls. If the metal becomes rigid and hard, it should be annealed before further rolling or it may crack. Pass the metal through the *center area* of the rolls to keep the pressure even and prevent unequal wearing of the rolls.

The rolling mill can be used as a device for impressing a texture or line pattern deliberately on a metal surface for decorative effect. This can be done by placing a soft iron wire mesh on top of a sheet and running them through the rolls simultaneously. Other hard materials can be used to impart textural patterns on metal similarly.

When using the rolling mill to reduce wire size, start with the largest opening first and feed the wire through the graduated grooves in order, till the wire reaches the desired thickness. Repeat the passage of the wire through each groove at least twice. If further reduction in diameter is desired, the wire can then be passed through a drawplate. Heavy round wire can be made into flat strip by running it through the rolling mill.

Micrometers for measuring metal sheet and wire thicknesses, capacity: 0 to 1″, accuracy: .0001″, marked in tenth readings

Metal wire and sheet gauge, Brown & Sharpe

Sheet and Wire Gauge Measuring Systems

A gauge is a tool used for measuring the thickness of sheet metal and the diameter of wire. The gauge is either circular or rectangular. Its edges are notched with a series of graduated, marked notches in thousandths of an inch. Several different standards for wire gauges exist, varying with the country and the metal being measured.

In the United States, the Brown & Sharpe (B. & S.) gauge is standard for nonferrous sheet metal and wire. This is also known as the American Standard gauge, or the American Wire Gauge (A. W. G.). The United States Standard (U. S. S.) is used for measuring iron and steel plate and wire. The Stubbs steel wire gauge is used for measuring drawn steel wire

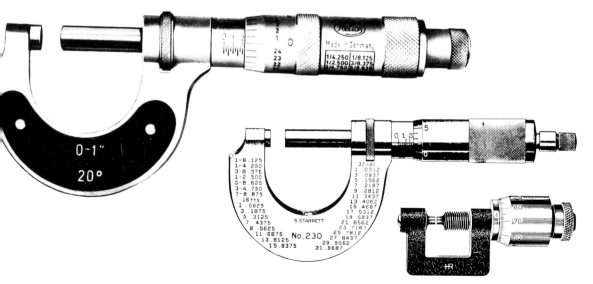

and drill rods both in the United States and Great Britain.

The Birmingham Wire Gauge (B. W. G.) or Stubbs iron wire gauge is generally used in Britain for iron, copper, or brass wire. The Birmingham Metal Gauge is used for measuring sheet gold, silver, copper, brass, etc. The Imperial Standard Wire Gauge (S. W. G.) is standard for all wire in Great Britain and Canada.

When measuring sheet metal, test for the size by inserting the sheet into the smallest notch which it will fit tightly. Insert the sheet as far as it will go to get an accurate measurement, as edges are often misshaped by cutting and handling. When measuring wire, insert the wire into the first groove only. The markings on one side of the B. & S. gauge give the B. & S. number, and the reverse side shows the decimal equivalent.

A micrometer measuring in ten-thousandths of an inch supersedes the need for most gauges, as it gives measurements in decimals of fractions of one inch, the measurements most metal suppliers use first. There are several types of micrometers made for measuring inside, outside, depth and screw sizes. The most commonly used is the 0–1 inch, outside micrometer. Detailed instructions are supplied with purchase. See pages 423 and 424 for other measuring tools used in metalwork.

Extruded Metals

Extruded metals are formed by forcing the metal to flow in a molten state through a die of a special shape, forming one continuous piece. It is one of the basic forming methods for metals used today. The craftsman who purchases prepared tubing, rods, bars, or a shape such as angle iron is using a form of

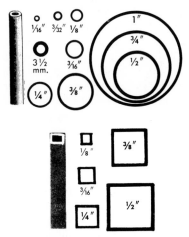

Extruded silver tubing in commercially available sizes, round and square, also called joint wire

Cross sections of some of the forms fabricated in copper, brass, and copper-base alloys by the process of extrusion. *Copper and Brass Research Association.*

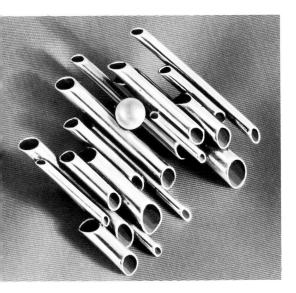

Silver pin, by Florence Nach. Length: 2¼ inches. Made with tubing of various diameters, this pin illustrates the utilization of an extruded metal form for design inspiration. *Warsaw Studios. Photo by Nach.*

Fine silver grains as they are supplied by the manufacturer. They are produced by the "shotting" method. They are intended primarily for melting to form mold cast pieces. *Photo by Oppi.*

Silver ring, designed and executed by Saara Hopea Untracht for Kultasepänliike Ossian Hopea, Porvoo, Finland. The ring uses silver grains for decoration. The grains are in the exact form in which they are supplied to the silversmith. *Photo by Pietinen.*

extruded metal. The dies are made of a hard steel alloy designed to be resistant to flow at elevated temperatures, and are able to stand high thermal shock. They are lubricated with a mixture of graphite and cylinder oil. Producing extruded metals is technically difficult and complicated, and some metals are more suited to extrusion than others.

Extruded forms are available in copper, brass, bronze, nickel, silver, gold, platinum, aluminum, steel, and special alloys.

Shotting

Shotting is a basic method of preparing metal for use, ordinarily for casting. Drops of molten metal are poured from a crucible held at a height into a tank or pail of water. As the metal falls, it forms round pellets, called "shot" or "grain," which freeze into shape before hitting the water at the end of the fall. Shot pieces are irregular in shape, and have their own particular appeal. They can be used for decorative purposes, after selection, without any change in form.

Annealing

Annealing is a process of heating and cooling metals to render them more workable, or to remove internal stresses which may occur during the working of the metal. After the metal is heated to a predetermined temperature for a particular length of time, there is usually a slow cooling period. For some metals, such as steel, the cooling process may be slow, for others, such as copper or nickel, it may be rapid or slow, and for other metals, it must be rapid.

Quenching is the process of rapidly cooling metals which have been heated to an elevated temperature by contact with liquids, gases, or solids. Some metals which are overheated and have been made "hot short," may crack if they are rapidly quenched, because of thermal stresses which occur. Brass and gilding metal should be cooled slowly, because the zinc content may cause the metal to crack if quenched immediately after annealing.

Soft Annealing is applied to metals which have become hardened during cold working as in rolling, deep drawing, spinning, and severe bending, and which will be worked on after annealing.

Temper Annealing or partial annealing is applied to work-hardened metals to soften them only partially.

Stress Equalizing Annealing is applied to work-hardened metals which are heated to a temperature too low to effect softening, but high enough to equalize or homogenize stresses in the metal and increase its mechanical properties. Stress-relieving temperatures range from 300° F to 400° F.

(See Annealing Temperatures of Some Metals, page 246.)

Brass water pot from India, showing decorative planishing marks. *Photo by Oppi.*

Texture of Metal Surfaces

Textural variety on metal surfaces is a means of increasing richness of appearance, tactile appeal, and heightened decorative effect. Texture is achieved in various ways:

1) By the use of tools involved normally in a process, such as planishing hammers, or tools used in a method of construction such as raising hammers.

2) By the use of tools applied *after forming,* for purely decorative effect, such as matting tools, chasing tools, engraving tools, stamping and punching tools. These may be tools designed for a special purpose, or tools such as nails and center punches which are improvised to create textures.

3) By additive methods such as granulation, the soldering of small units such as bits of wire, cuttings, coarse filings, or molten scrap, and the application of shot.

4) By subtractive methods such as the use of acid to etch or to texture surfaces; drills of various sizes to form depressions or to pierce the surface with holes completely; a flexible shaft in conjunction with variously shaped grinding heads, burrs, rotating files, or abrasives; and coarse hand files.

5) By the use of certain *materials* used in the construction of an object, such as wax in making a model in preparation for casting, and the form of the metal such as wire, sheet metal, and strips.

Individual methods are discussed in various sections of the book.

Additive method. "Olga," sterling silver bracelet with milky fire opals, by Ruth S. Roach. Surface of granulated units was created by fusing filings and shot by heat. Mounted on a leather thong. *Photo by Elden.*

Subtractive method: Drilling. "Minerva," sterling silver bracelet, by Ruth S. Roach, 1960. Double level construction with "legs" supporting the upper surface. Moss agates with fused metal texture and background spotted with drilled depressions. Width: 1¾ inches. *Photo by Elden.*

Gold watch bracelet with grooved texture and set with diamonds, emeralds, and sapphires, designed by Gilbert Albert for Patek Philippe, Geneva, Switzerland. *Worshipful Company of Goldsmiths, London. Photo by James Mortimer.*

Cigarette box in 18-karat gold, designed and made by John Donald. The textural interest in the surface is created by the method of utilizing the wax from which the box was cast. *Worshipful Company of Goldsmiths, London.*

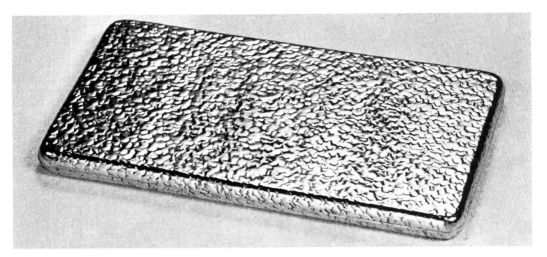

Toxicity of Metals

Though illness from contact with metals is rare among craftsmen using metals, there have been occasional cases where a lack of precautionary measures have led to ill effects. The toxicity of metals is more commonly encountered in industries dealing with the smelting, refining, and fabrication of metals, and elaborate precautions are usually taken to avoid health hazards. Reactions to metals arise mainly from the inhalation, skin absorption, or ingestion of metal fumes or dusts. The main precautions consist in providing good ventilation when dealing with metal fumes, probably in the form of an efficient exhaust fan, and installing dust catchers where this is called for.

Metals and their possible toxic effects are listed below. If there is any question of your health being affected after contact with metals, you should consult a physician immediately.

Aluminum is very low in toxicity.

Cadmium-plated steel is a source of poisonous vapors in welding, or where the cadmium is heated to a vapor-forming degree. Continued exposure results in severe illness with nausea, vomiting, and cramps. Cadmium vapors from solders containing this metal can also be dangerous. Work in a well-ventilated area.

Chromium is nontoxic ordinarily, but in certain forms, as in fumes produced in plating, it causes skin ulcers after prolonged exposure.

Copper is not an industrial health hazard. In the form of copper sulphate, it can cause irritation to the skin, and a thorough rinsing of the hands should follow contact. Copper as a food container can render the food toxic, unless the copper is tin-lined.

Lead in almost all forms is potentially toxic. The main source of poisoning, however, comes from the inhalation of dusts and fumes. Welding with lead must be carefully controlled to avoid the volatilization of the metal and subsequent breathing of the fumes.

The nervous system, blood, kidneys, and muscles are affected by the absorption of lead fumes, which is more dangerous than its ingestion. Lead is excreted in the feces and urine, but a certain amount is stored in the bones' mineral structure. Poisoning does not become evident till a considerable amount has been absorbed, and the symptom is a general sense of not feeling well. Blood tests and urine analysis

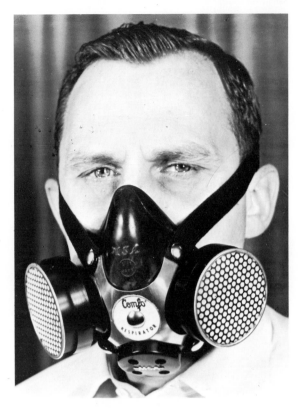

There are many situations in working with metals when the use of a respirator-type mask is advisable. A wide variety of models is available, designed for different functions. Some conditions requiring mask protection are those in which one is exposed to nuisance, fibrosis-producing, or toxic dusts, mists, metal fumes, smoke, toxic particles, or extra finely divided particles, as well as light concentrations of organic vapors and acid gases. The model shown here is manufactured by the Mine Safety Appliances Company and is approved by the U. S. Bureau of Mines.

should be made regularly by those who know they are possibly being exposed to lead fumes. Recovery from lead poisoning is usually complete if proper treatment is followed.

Manganese poisoning is rare and confined to industry.

Mercury poisoning is possible when the metal is carelessly overheated, or improperly handled and stored. Poisoning by mercury causes inflammation of the mouth and loosening of the teeth, shaking muscular tremors, saliva flow in excess of normal, irritability, and depression. Mercury when stored and used should be handled carefully, as it can be absorbed through the skin.

Nickel is not an important source of toxic poisoning, whether in the form of pure metal or salts.

The Precious Metals (Gold, Silver, Platinum, and Palladium) have no toxicity except when used as medicine by people who have a primitive belief in their efficacy as therapy and ingest the metal.

Tin is completely harmless.

Zinc poisoning comes mainly from the inhalation of zinc oxide fumes and from acid foods which become contaminated when stored in zinc containers. It is not cumulative, as is lead. Metal fume fever, known as the "zinc shakes," is accompanied by a rise in temperature and a cough, an increase in white blood cell count, and later, chills. The fever subsides and leaves a resistance but not an immunity to an immediate second attack. The oxide fumes occur mainly in the smelting of zinc or metals containing a high percentage of zinc such as some brasses. Metal fume fever can also occur when inhaling gases during the welding of galvanized iron which is coated with zinc, or in casting zinc without proper ventilation.

Dust collector drums of various capacities may be utilized by attaching the flexible tube to any polishing or dust-creating situation where dust collection may be required for economic or health reasons. *Craftool, Inc.*

Part Two

METAL DECORATIVE TECHNIQUES

Metal Techniques That Do Not Require Soldering

When using sheet metal to form articles such as jewelry and larger three-dimensional objects, the ultimate appearance depends mainly on the tools used. Each tool has certain potentialities and limitations, and a large part of the skill of the craftsman consists in selecting the proper tool for the job.

Basic cutting techniques can be easily accomplished with a *shears* when the shapes are simple. When they are complex, a saw frame and blade may have to be used. To add the element of dimension in *depth* or *relief,* a technique known as repoussé (page 93) can be employed, using repoussé tools. Texture and richness of surface are achieved by hammers, chasing tools, and liners.

Many tools and techniques available to the craftsman have been developed over the centuries. It is the purpose of this section to explore the possibilities in the fabrication and decoration of objects, from the simple to the complex.

Preparing the Metal for Outline Cutting

Once a design has been planned for execution, mentally or by a detailed drawing on paper, it must be transferred to the metal. There are several methods by which this can be done, depending on the shape to be cut. If all the lines are straight, accurate measurements can be taken from the paper design if it is drawn to size, transferred to the metal with a straight-edge ruler, and marked on the metal with a scriber ready for cutting. If any of the lines made are not actual cutting lines but are meant *for reference,* do not press on the marking tool too hard, as deeply embedded scratches are difficult to remove later.

If the design consists of curves or more complex shapes, other methods of transfer can be used. A simple method is to place a sheet of

Silver hairpiece, by Merry Renk. Made of one sheet of 32-gauge metal in a 2-inch module laid out with a scriber; it also has an additional ⅛-inch edge that is folded under for rigidity and to eliminate the sharp edge. The folds are then pressed lightly and repeatedly with a burnisher over dampened paper until the desired depth is reached. During the pressure of working the metal, it becomes rigidized. To preserve rigidity, which would be lost in the heat of soldering, the form is joined by rivets. *Photo by Paul Hassel.*

The hairpiece in use.

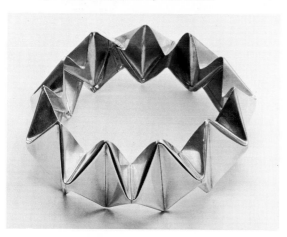

carbon paper between the metal and the original outline design drawn on paper. After the outline is traced, the carbon outline left on the metal can be made permanent by going over it with a scriber or pointed tool. It is possible to coat the back of a design on paper with a carbon deposit made with a soft lead pencil, and the same procedure followed as with carbon paper.

The metal can also be dyed temporarily with water-soluble dye and the pattern scratched through the dye to expose bright lines of metal to be followed for cutting. After cutting, the dye is washed away. Such a dye, called "layout dye," can be made by adding copper sulphate crystals (blue vitriol) to four ounces of water while stirring, till no more crystals dissolve. To this solution, add ten drops of sulphuric acid, making certain to *add the acid to the mixture.* Apply and allow to dry.

Another method is to clean the metal with acetone, carbon tetrachloride, or another grease-removing agent or detergent, and allow it to dry. White or colored tempera paint, which is water-soluble, or Chinese white can then be applied in a thin coat and dried. The outline can then be drawn directly with pencil, scratched through the paint with a scriber, or transferred with carbon paper as described. Black India ink can also be used for this purpose. The metal can then be cut. For cutting with metal snips or shears, see the section on Hand Tools, page 423 and illustrations page 241.

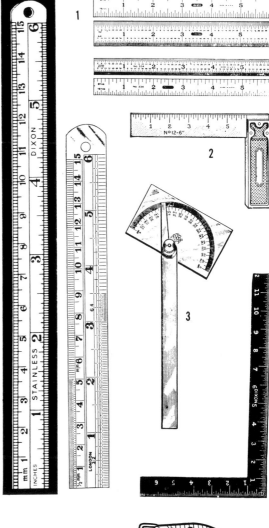

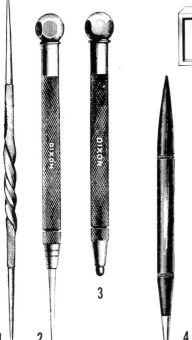

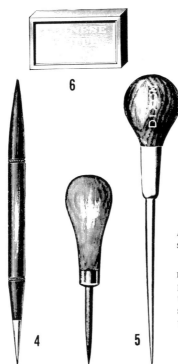

ABOVE: Measuring devices: 1. Steel rules 2. Steel square 3. Protractor 4. Cloth tapemeasure

LEFT: 1. Double ended scriber, 6″ long 2. Needle point scriber 3. Needle point scriber with retractable tip 4. Duplex tracer (rubber tip for carbon tracing, steel point for scribing) 5. Scratch awls 6. Chinese white cake paint

THE USE OF BASIC TOOLS IN METALWORK

Saara Hopea Untracht creates a silver pendant in these photos by Oppi.

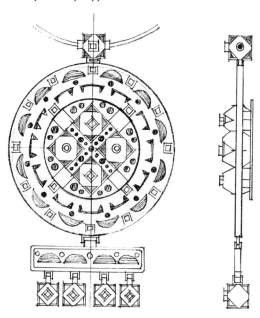

Working drawing for the silver pendant demonstrating basic metalworking procedures, by Saara Hopea Untracht

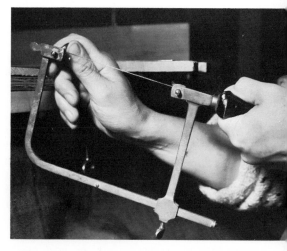

1. When preparing to use the jeweler's saw, the frame is first adjusted to the size of the blade length, and the back thumbscrew is tightened. The blade is inserted in the lower jaw, with the teeth pointing *down* toward the handle and *out* away from the back of the frame, and the lower thumbscrew is tightened. The frame is then pressed against a firmly resisting surface. The blade is inserted in the top jaws, and the top thumbscrew is tightened while frame is in tension.

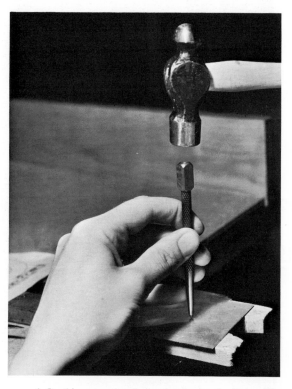

4. In this case, the design is circular in form. The center is found with a ruler and marked with a center punch and hammer. The center mark is a useful reference for future measurements.

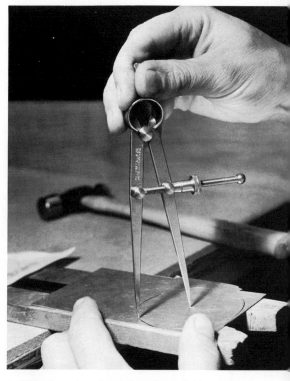

5. With the point of one leg of the dividers pressing in the center punch mark, the dividers is twirled in the fingers while the second leg scores the surface to enscribe the circle in the sheet of silver.

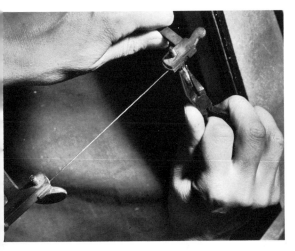

2. Before beginning to saw, all thumbscrews are tightened with an old pliers to make sure the blade is held securely.

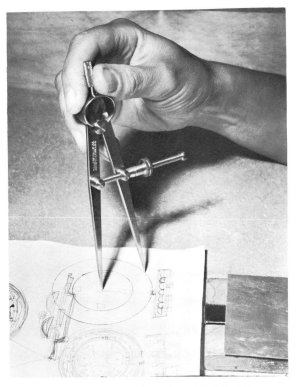

3. Measurements are taken from the original drawing of the design with a dividers.

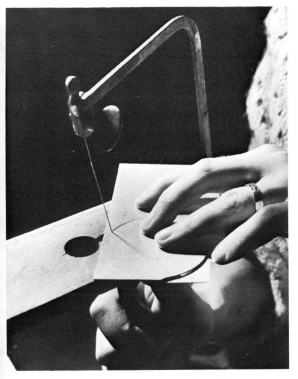

6. To begin the sawing action, the blade is drawn *upward* a few times at a convenient entry position in the metal. This creates a small groove in which the blade can begin to cut. During the sawing, the metal is held pressed firmly on the V board while the blade is guided along the *outside* of the curve to allow metal for trimming with files later.

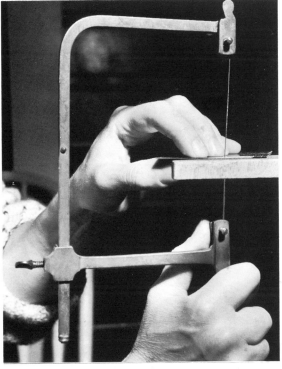

7. In any sawing operation, the frame should be held (as illustrated) in as nearly a vertical position as possible in relation to the metal being cut. This exposes a minimum of metal to the action of the blade and assures greater accuracy. Very little forward pressure is necessary, though slightly more pressure is exerted in the *downward* or cutting thrust of the blade.

METAL TECHNIQUES THAT DO NOT REQUIRE SOLDERING 57

8. Once the disc is cut out, the form is trued by using a medium double-cut file and removing any excess metal up to the enscribed dividers mark. All filing action occurs in the *forward* stroke of the file, which should be lifted on the return stroke.

9. If any burr remains after edge filing, it can be removed by moving the file along the edge of the metal while holding it at an angle.

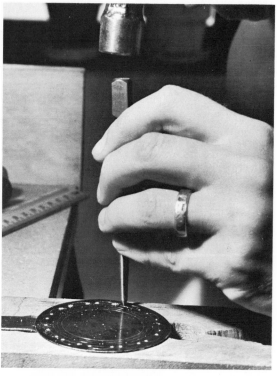

12. The design calls for many pierced openings. In preparation for sawing them, a center punch is used to establish an exact spot for drilling holes in the metal, the first step in piercing.

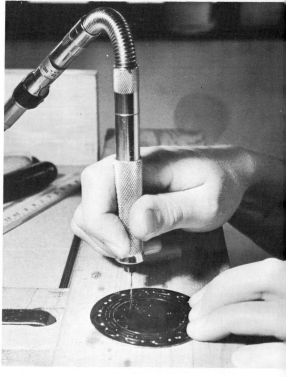

13. A small twist drill, which will make a hole large enough to allow the insertion of the saw blade, is tightened into the adapter collet of the handpiece of a flexible shaft. The point is placed vertically in the marked position and, with the metal held firmly in place, a hole is drilled. An ordinary hand drill could also have been used.

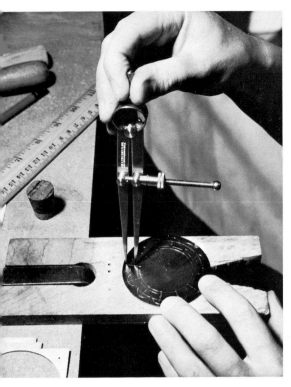

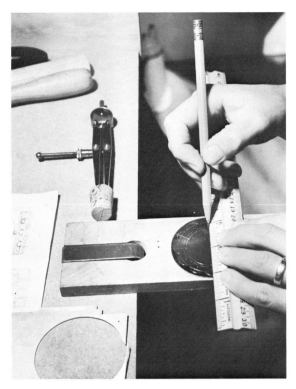

10. To make further markings and measurements of the design more easily visible, the silver is colored. The metal is cleaned with a greaseless detergent and water, rubbed with fine steel wool and pumice, rinsed, and dried. Ordinary black India ink is then painted over the surface with a brush and dried by holding the disc over heat with tweezers. Any marks subsequently drawn on the metal with either a tool or a pencil can be seen easily. Other methods of coloring can be used. (See page 55.)

11. The ruler is used for any straight line measurements. A sharp pointed pencil should be used. When not in use, the legs of the dividers are inserted into a cork to preserve the sharpness of their points.

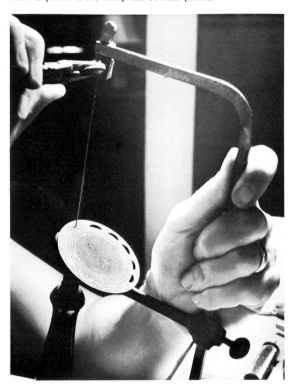

14. The saw blade is loosened at the top of the saw frame. The blade is then threaded through one of the drilled holes.

15. To avoid the possibility of the blade breaking, the metal is moved to rest on the bottom jaws of the frame. The loose blade end is then replaced in the top jaws while the frame is held in tension, and the thumbscrew is tightened.

METAL TECHNIQUES THAT DO NOT REQUIRE SOLDERING   59

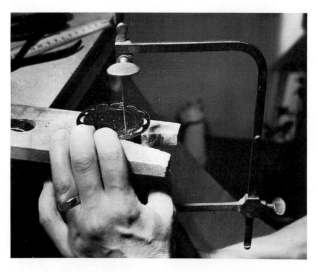

16. The pierced openings are then cut, this time staying on the *inside* of the line to allow for later filing.

17. This photograph shows the pendant with the outer row of semicircles pierced and a second series of cuts that are a part of the design. A hole was drilled in both cases at the beginning and terminating positions of the cut to assure accuracy.

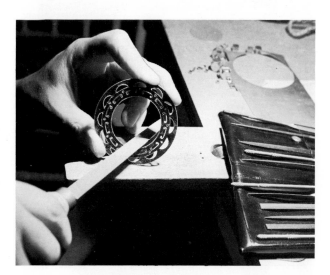

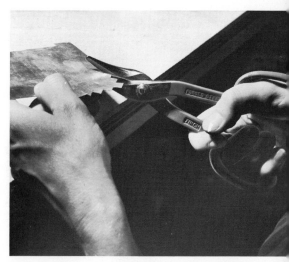

20. For larger openings or surfaces, larger files can be used. In this case, a double-cut, half-round file is being used to file the inside curve of the frame.

21. A curved-bladed universal shears can be used for cutting metal up to 18 gauge with ease. It is used here to cut out the cubed units of the pendant.

18. The outer frame of the pendant with the inner circle cut out with a jeweler's saw blade. Large openings such as these can then be filed smooth with a large, half-round file.

19. Small openings can be filed with needle files of appropriate cross-section shape. In this case, a half-round file is used. A set of needle files is seen on the right.

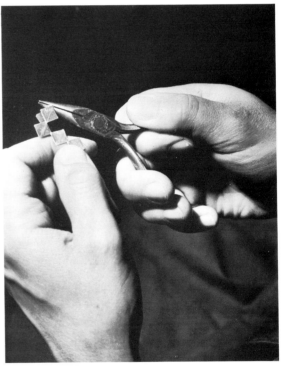

22. A small jeweler's anvil is a useful tool for working with small metal parts. It serves the function of helping to flatten and otherwise shape metal.

23. Pliers of various cross-section shapes have a number of different functions. Shown here bending metal at a sharp right angle, they are also used in shaping curves, twisting, making fits, etc.

METAL TECHNIQUES THAT DO NOT REQUIRE SOLDERING 61

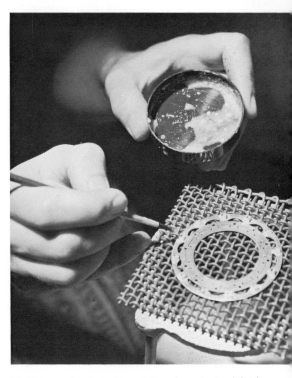

24. The central units of the pendant are arranged prior to soldering. They consist of cross sections of square tubing and cubes with their corners removed, the latter to be used in another part of the design. Tweezers are a convenient tool for handling or controlling the movement of small metal parts.

25. Before soldering, the metal surfaces to be joined must be *absolutely clean*. A flux is painted on these parts. In this case, powdered borax mixed with water is being used. (See section on soldering.)

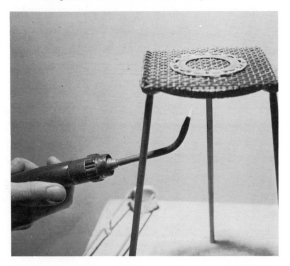

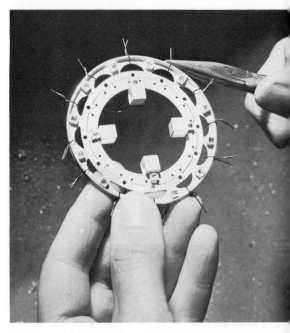

28. In certain situations, applying the heat of the torch from below is preferable to direct heat on the object. With an iron heating frame such as the one shown, in conjunction with a tripod, the torch can be applied from below.

29. An outer wire frame is being fixed in position before soldering. To insure uniform contact of the frame with the base so that the solder will flow evenly and not be confronted with gaps it cannot leap, iron binding wire is twisted all around the frame. A flat-nosed pliers is used for this procedure. After soldering, all such binding wire must be *removed before pickling* or the acid solution will be contaminated.

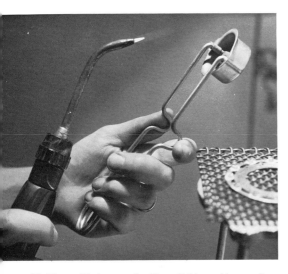

26. The soldering torch (Prest-O-Lite with acetylene gas) is lighted with a flint friction lighter, the safest and quickest method.

27. The entire soldering setup is seen here. From upper left: the torch, the pendant resting on an iron wire heating frame, a tripod resting on a sheet of asbestos or soldering block, the borax, borax brush, flint hand friction lighter, tweezers for placing solder snippets and adjusting the movement of parts being soldered should this occur during soldering, and the Prest-O-Lite acetylene tank showing the valve wrench and the regulator.

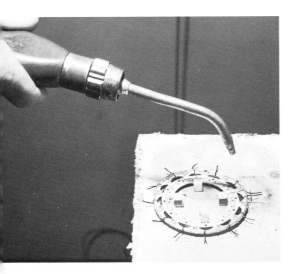

30. When soldering an entire article such as this, the heat should be applied first over the whole surface to avoid uneven heating that might cause warpage.

31. After each soldering operation, the metal will become oxidized because of the heat. To clean the surface and prepare it for the next soldering, the article is placed in a copper pickling pan filled with an acid solution (see section on pickling) and the solution is heated. To avoid contamination of the pickle, the article is handled with a copper tongs.

32. After pickling, the pendant is washed in cold running water and emerges with the silver appearing a dead white color.

33. When, in certain situations, a prolonged heating is undesirable, the article can be soldered on a charcoal block that retains the heat. Every soldering job has its unique problems and they must be met with ingenuity. A part of the pendant being soldered here is supported during the soldering by a coil of binding wire.

35. Before coloring, the pendant was hand polished to prepare it for the coloring solution and to increase the effectiveness of the coloring solution's action on the metal. A special "oxidizing fluid" is used here; it is applied only to those areas of the dry pendant on which coloring is desired.

36. The coloring is removed from areas on which it is not wanted by mixing a fine pumice with some water and applying it lightly on the pendant with a cloth. Fingers could also be used.

34. The finished pendant after its final emergence from the pickle and prior to polishing, coloring, and final polishing. It is dead white at this point.

37. The completed pendant by Saara Hopea Untracht, after hand polishing with rouge and a polishing cloth.

The Jeweler's Saw

The jeweler's saw consists of a frame made of spring steel which is designed to hold a blade. It is used mainly to saw soft, nonferrous metals, but thin gauges of ferrous metals may also be cut with this easily manipulated and versatile tool. Both rigid and adjustable frames are made, but the adjustable frame can be used for saw blades of various lengths, and fractions of blades, and is therefore preferable. The jaws which hold the blade should be clamped firmly together with the thumb screws to hold the blade securely. A frame depth of three to four inches is suitable for most purposes, but frames of greater depth for special situations are also made. The depth of the frame, from the blade to the back of the frame, determines how far into the metal the blade can penetrate.

Blades for the jeweler's saw frame are made in many sizes, designated by numbers, such as 8/0, 0, 1, up to 14. The smallest number (8/0) has the finest teeth and the narrowest blade thickness, and the largest (14) has the coarsest teeth and the widest blade. The width of the blade is sometimes important, as it determines the amount of metal actually removed in the cutting groove.

Selection of blade depends first of all on the thickness of the metal to be cut. Heavy gauge metals require coarser blades. Those numbered 2, 1, 0, and 2/0 are the ones most commonly used to cut 16–20 B. & S. gauge metal. For greatly curved cutting, and where it is desirable to remove a minimum of metal, narrow blades are used. Greater care is needed in the manipulation of the finer blades, as they break easily. Portions of broken blades can be used if more than two-thirds of the original length remains.

INSERTING THE SAW BLADE IN THE FRAME

The teeth of a blade are oriented *downward;* running the finger over the teeth in both directions will immediately reveal the direction in which they point. The teeth must *always* point *downward toward the handle of the frame,* and *away* from the back of the frame.

To insert the blade in the frame, loosen both thumbscrews, insert the blade about one-half inch into the *top* jaw, teeth out and pointing down, and then tighten the thumbscrew. Adjust the saw frame with the thumbscrew at the *back* of the frame to the length of the blade and tighten it. The bottom of the

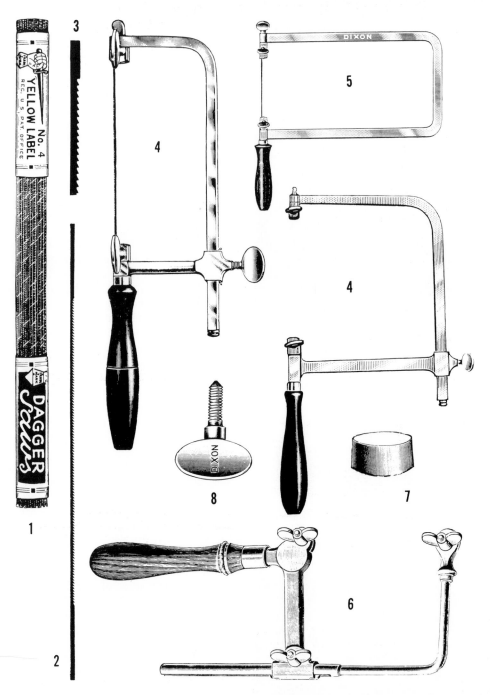

1. One gross package of jeweler's saw blades 2. Single blade 3. Enlargement showing the tooth direction 4. Jeweler's saw frame, adjustable, 4″ depth, 6″ depth

5. Non-adjustable, flat frame, 8″ depth 6. Round frame, adjustable, 6″ depth 7. Cake of lubricating beeswax 8. Thumbscrew

blade should barely touch the jaw near the handle. Place the top of the frame against the workbench or against the "V" board or bench pin with the back of the frame hanging down, and the saw blade teeth pointing up. Press the handle against the body to compress the frame which now acts as a spring, and allow the bottom of the blade to enter about one-half inch between the lower jaw. While the frame is under compression, tighten the

bottom thumbscrew. Release the pressure slowly or the blade may break from the sudden tension. If the blade should slip out, reinsert it in the same manner, tightening the thumbscrew more than before. It is rarely necessary to use more than hand pressure, but an old pliers may be used to tighten the screws if necessary.

Test the tightness of the blade by plucking it with the fingernail. This will produce a high

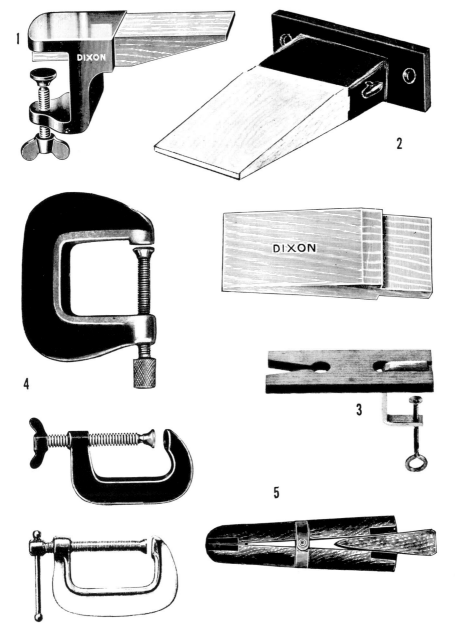

Holding and supporting devices: 1. Bench pin with anvil 2. Wood bench pins, mounted, unmounted 3. V-board with clamp 4. C-clamps 5. Double end ring clamp

note if the tension is sufficient. A loose or slack blade makes a dull sound. Blades should not be used loose, as they are inefficient and break easily. If keeping the blade in the jaw seems difficult, open the jaw and search for the remnant of a broken blade, the most common cause of such a situation.

Saw frames are used in conjunction with a "V" board or wood bench pin, either permanently attached to the workbench, or held there with a small "C" clamp. The bench pin is used to support the metal being worked during sawing, filing, and other operations.

OUTLINE CUTTING WITH THE JEWELER'S SAW

Before sawing begins, the blade must be lubricated to facilitate its movement. A cake of beeswax is generally used for this purpose. Running the blade through the wax *once* is sufficient for the operation. Too much wax may interfere with the efficiency of the blade's cutting action. Excess wax can be removed with a stiff brush. On extended use of the same blade, an occasional reapplication of wax may be necessary when the blade seems to be sticking.

To start a groove when beginning the sawing action, run the teeth *upward* at the edge of the metal where the sawing begins. This

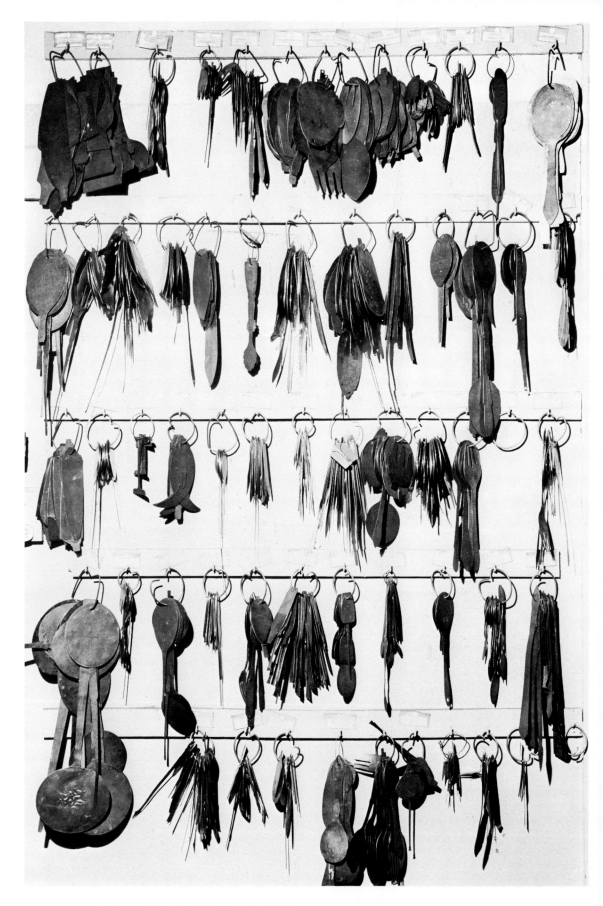

Ring in 18-karat gold, by Jean Claude Champagnat, Paris, France. Made of crumpled thin-gauge metal soldered to the ring shank. *Photo by Del Bocca.*

Silver necklace, designed by Nanna and Jørgen Ditzel for Georg Jensen Silversmiths, Ltd., Copenhagen, 1957. *Photo by Junior.*

OPPOSITE PAGE: Metal patterns for standard stock items of flatware. *Photographed in the Georg Jensen factory in Copenhagen by Oppi.*

Sterling silver necklace, designed by Nanna and Jørgen Ditzel for Georg Jensen Silversmiths, Ltd., Copenhagen, 1961. *Photo by Junior.*

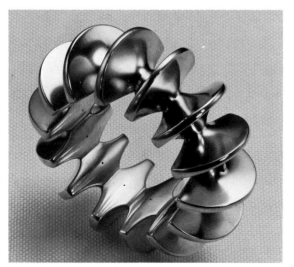

Silver bracelet, designed by Nanna and Jørgen Ditzel for Georg Jensen Silversmiths, Ltd., Copenhagen, 1960. *Photo by Jonals Co.*

will create a shallow groove which is sufficient for a start.

In operating a saw frame, keep in mind that the saw blade must be held in as vertical a position as possible. This brings the blade into *minimal contact* with the metal and therefore gives it less work to do. Cutting at an angle to the metal is equivalent to cutting a much thicker sheet of metal. Remember too that the actual cutting action of the blade takes place on the *downward stroke,* as the teeth cant downward. Long, rhythmic, even strokes are more efficient than short, quick, jerky ones, and prevent the teeth from quickly wearing out at one point, or overheating and possibly breaking from concentrated friction in a small area. A *slight* increase in pressure at the downward stroke, plus a *slight* forward pressure is all that is necessary. An excess of forward or downward pressure will cause sticking, jamming, or breaking of the blade. Working slowly and evenly is preferable to sudden spurts of speed, which in the long run are inefficient.

Pre-Columbian Inca silver Alpaca, Peru. It is formed of sheet metal and ridged by inscribing a tool across the metal. *American Museum of Natural History, New York.*

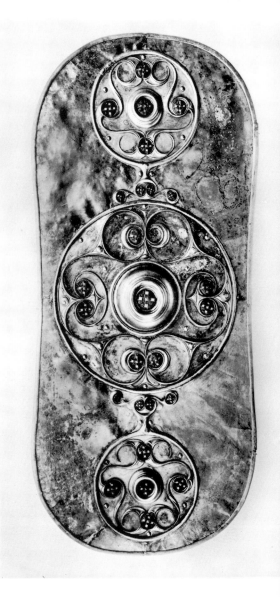

Bronze shield recovered from the Thames River at Battersea, England, first century B.C. or early first century A.D. Length: 2 feet 6½ inches. The embossed ornament is in a mature La Tene style and is enriched with studs set with red glass. *British Museum, London.*

One of a pair of white metal anklets, Bombay, India, c. 1872. Collection, Victoria and Albert Museum, London. *The Museum of Modern Art, New York. Photo by Soichi Sunami.*

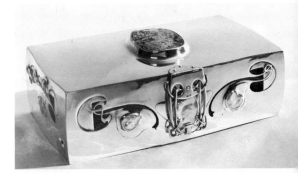

Silver jewel box, set with mother-of-pearl, turquoise, and enamel, c. 1900. Designed by Charles Knox, England, and executed by William Craythorne for Liberty and Co. 11¼ inches × 6 inches × 3¼ inches. *The Museum of Modern Art, New York. Gift of the family of Mrs. John D. Rockefeller, Jr. Photo by Soichi Sunami.*

"Io," bracelet, by Ruth S. Roach, 1961. The bracelet is 14-karat gold with aquamarines and pink and green tourmalines. Units are held on a flexible leather thong. Each unit is made of a flat piece of metal, bent dimensionally. *Photo by Elden.*

When curves are being cut, the saw frame should be kept in the same position as far as possible while the *metal* is turned to keep the blade pointing in the direction of the cut. If the design calls for a sharp right-angle turn, bring the blade to the point of direction change, and keep it operating *in one spot,* without moving forward. Gradually rotate the metal till a small hole, whose diameter is the depth of the blade, is created. The blade can then proceed in the right-angle direction.

With a little care, any line can be followed, no matter how complex, and few blades will be broken. Should it be necessary, however, to remove a blade (broken or not) from a cut, this can be done by keeping the blade in motion and slowly backing out of the cut, if the distance is not too great. If this is not practical, the top thumbscrew of the saw frame can be loosened, and the blade gently withdrawn by pulling it directly downward.

PIERCED WORK:
USING A SAW FRAME AND BLADE

The design possibilities of sheet metal can be greatly expanded by introducing another element—openings or holes in the sheet to create pierced work. Whether the work is simply or intricately pierced, the method is the same.

Transfer the design to the metal. Set the metal on a hard surface to resist deforming. With a *center punch* and a hammer, make a small dent at a point *just inside* the line outlining the area to be cut out. The purpose of the dent is to establish an accurate starting point for the *drill* and *bit,* which is

then used to make a hole at that point. Loosen the chuck jaws of the drill, insert the bit deeply, and tighten the jaws, making sure that the bit is grasped exactly in the center and is held straight, or it will wobble during drilling. Do not allow small bits to protrude too far from the drill chuck jaws or there will be a risk of their breaking. Carbon steel drills break less easily than high-speed drills and are recommended for hand-drilling operations. Dip the bit in a light machine oil to act as a lubricant while drilling and keep it cool. Be sure that the metal being drilled is

Pierced work brass lantern, Delhi, India. Length: 2 feet. The pierced openings were made with small, sharp chisels applied from the outside while the interior of the form was filled with asphaltum so that the holes are indented and the sharp edges point inward. *Photo by Oppi.*

1. Center punch 2. Automatic center punch 3. Ball peen hammer 4. Steel surface plate 5. Small jeweler's horn anvil

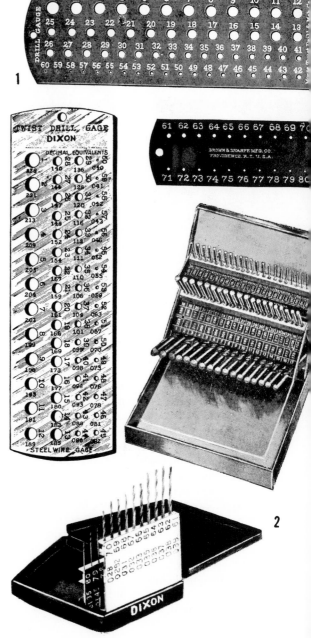

1. Twist drill gauges 2. Sets of twist drills

placed over a wood block or board so that when the bit emerges through the metal it does not become dulled as it would if it struck a metal surface. The time when it emerges is the most common time for breakage to occur, so proceed slowly at that point.

The hole should be large enough to easily admit the saw blade to be used to cut out the metal area being removed. The blade is entered by loosening the top thumbscrew of the saw frame, threading the blade through the hole, moving the metal down toward the handle and allowing it to rest there to avoid

breaking the blade, and tightening the top thumb screw while the frame is under pressure as in the original blade-setting procedure. The metal is then placed and held on the "V" board or bench pin, and the opening sawed out. The cutting line should be followed on the *inside*, in the area of the waste piece to be removed. This avoids the risk of removing too much metal; excess metal can be eliminated later with files. When the blade arrives at the starting point, the pierced piece will fall out. The blade is removed by again loosening the top thumbscrew of the saw frame,

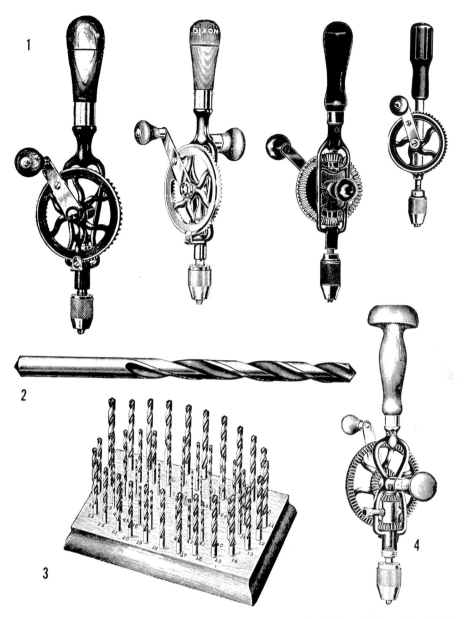

1. Hand drills 2. Twist drill 3. Twist drill set 4. Breast hand drill

and pulling it downward through the opening in the metal.

PIERCED WORK: USING CHISELS

In the Far East, particularly in India, craftsmen produce complicated pierced objects such as lanterns with sharp, small steel chisels and no saw. The openings are left in the exact condition produced by the tool and not filed.

The method is as follows, the example being a pierced-work cylindrical lantern of sheet brass, as shown on page 71.

The seam-soldered cylinder to be pierced with the design marked on its surface is secured in a bed of asphaltum (see repoussé work, page 93, for formulas). The asphaltum is applied to a board or metal tray just large enough to contain the diameter of the cylinder. A torch is passed over the asphaltum, and while it is soft the cylinder is pressed into the surface in a vertical position. The asphaltum is allowed to cool and harden, holding the cylinder in position. Additional asphaltum is poured into the cylinder to a depth of about one inch. To economize on the use of asphal-

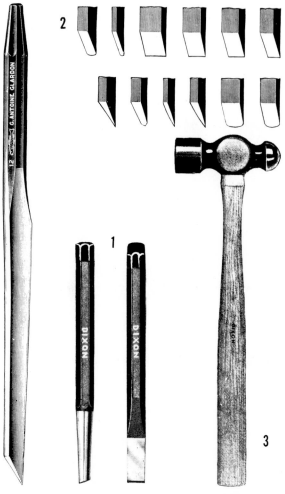

1. Cold chisels 2. Chisel point shapes 3. Ball peen hammer

tum, a metal cylinder of some inexpensive sheet metal such as galvanized iron, or a can that will fit into the cylinder and leave a space of about one inch between it and the brass, is placed in position. The edge of the metal (if a cylinder is used) or the bottom of the can is heated and pressed into the asphaltum. Additional asphaltum is poured into the remaining space *between* the can and the brass and allowed to cool and harden.

The cylinder is turned on its side, and with small sharp chisels and a lightweight hammer the holes or openings are cut out. The sharp edges formed by the chisel project inward, are never touched, and are no hazard.

When the design is completed, the asphaltum is removed by first heating the inside of the metal cylinder or can with a torch, and while the asphaltum is soft the can is pulled out with a pair of tongs. The remaining asphaltum is also removed by heat and stored for future use.

OPPOSITE ABOVE: Steel boot scrapers designed by Jean Ames, Oaxaca, Mexico. In these three articles the pattern was cut by cold chisels from the sheet metal. *Photos by Russell Ames.*

OPPOSITE BELOW: Egyptian gold pierced and engraved pectoral of Amenemhet III, XII Dynasty (1850–1800 B.C.). Height: 3 inches. The gold side seen is the *reverse* of the ornament. The front side is decorated with an inlay of carnelian, lapis lazuli, and turquoise. Collection, The Cairo Museum. *Archives Photographiques, Caisse Nationale des Monuments Historiques, Paris, France.*

BELOW: Brass and copper "alams." They are ceremonial spearheads that are mounted on wood shafts and carried in Moharram celebration parades by Muslim communities in Lucknow, India. The largest "alam" here is 1½ feet high. The "alams" are pierced work done entirely with small, sharp chisels. *Photo by Oppi.*

RIGHT: Contemporary brass pierced work lantern from Kairouan, Tunisia (Office National de l'Artisanat). *Tunisian Trade Center, New York. Photo by Oppi.*

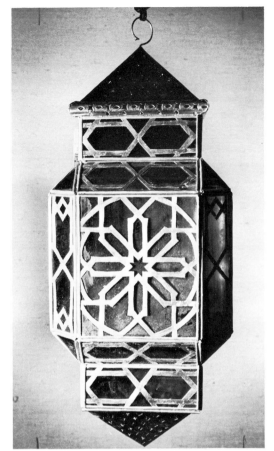

Silver pierced-work brooch, made by Georges Glaser, Paris, France. The design is inspired by the tracery of the rose window of the Cathedral of Notre Dame de Paris. *Photo by Oppi.*

Byzantine silver bracelet, sixth–seventh century. Length: 7 inches; width at clasp: 1⁵⁄₁₆ inches. Pierced units with stamped pattern. *Metropolitan Museum of Art, New York, Gift of Alastair Bradley Martin, 1952.*

Pierced and engraved steel lock and key, German, made in 1610. Lock: 12½ inches × 9 inches; key: 5¾ inches × 1¾ inches. *Victoria and Albert Museum, London.*

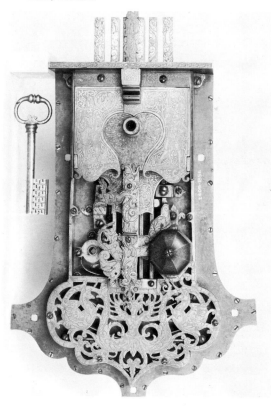

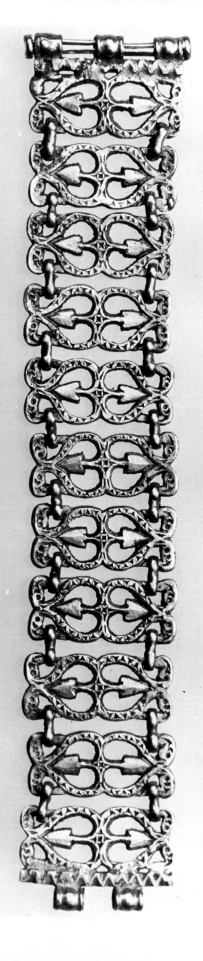

T'ang Dynasty Chinese mirror back. Gold pierced
work mounted on bronze with lions and phoenixes.
Victoria and Albert Museum, London.

Silver and gold bracelet with diamonds, by Ilya Schor. Front view. Mr. Schor's method consisted of engraving and chasing the design on the flat sheet metal and *then* cutting out and piercing the pattern, followed by repoussé and shaping processes and ending with assembling. The backs of his pieces are frequently decorated with equal attention to detail. Partly because

of a distain for overly finishing pieces, his work was always characterized by a direct and fresh use of materials, leaving the impact of tools and processes clearly evident. *Collection of the Metropolitan Museum of Art, New York. Courtesy Mrs. Schor. Photo by J. J. Breit.*

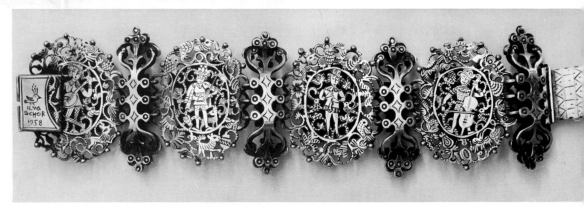

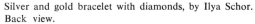

Silver Sabbath candlesticks, by Ilya Schor, New York. Pierced, chased, and repoussé work, showing great freshness in the chasing technique with folk art quality. *Courtesy Mrs. Schor. Photo by J. J. Breit.*

Silver and gold bracelet with diamonds, by Ilya Schor. Back view.

OPPOSITE: Pierced silver olive spoon, made by Charles Girard, master silversmith, 1759. Length: 11¼ inches. *Metropolitan Museum of Art, Bequest of Catherine D. Wentworth, 1948.*

PIERCED WORK: USING STAMPING DIES

Holes or openings can be cut in sheet metal with a stamping die. This can be a hand process or can be done with the aid of a die-stamping press, which supplies the pressure to cut through the metal. Die stamping involves a positive and a negative unit, called a *punch* and a *matrix* respectively. Each is designed to fit perfectly into the other to produce a sharp outline. The metal is held over the matrix, a perforated block into which the punched portion of metal enters, and the punch is driven into the metal with a hammer or by the press. An even pressure is exerted simultaneously over the entire surface of the metal that is forced into the matrix. The metal part freed from the sheet is called a *blank*. The kind of die described here contains no moving part and is known as a single-action die. Single-action dies can be purchased or, with skill, can be fashioned from tool steel.

Some punches are made for use with a matrix, and others can be applied directly to the metal. (See doming, page 83.)

Stamping dies are sometimes used to produce blanks intended for further processing (such as those used in the manufacture of flatware). This is a common procedure in forming mass-produced jewelry and in cases where many identical repeats of ornament are needed (see Swami work under metal encrustation, page 134).

Hanging Altar Cross, pierced Monel Metal. Height: 7 feet. Designed and executed by Ronald Hayes Pearson, 1959, for the Church of the Redeemer, Baltimore, Maryland. *Photo by M. E. Warren.*

METAL TECHNIQUES THAT DO NOT REQUIRE SOLDERING   79

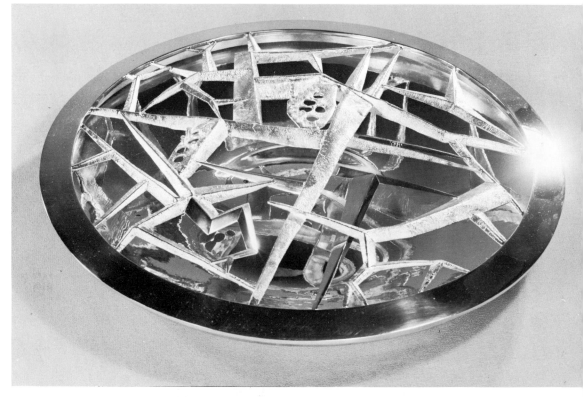

Rosebowl in silver, parcel-gilt. Openwork grill designed to hold flower stems. Presented to Leicester University by the Chancellor, Lord Adrian, 1958.

Designed and executed by Gerald Benney, London. *Worshipful Company of Goldsmiths, London.*

PRODUCTION AND ASSEMBLY OF A STAMPED-UNIT RING. *Handy and Harman.* *Photos by Steve Stillman.*

1. Stamping machine, manually fed with a gold sheet, preparing units to be assembled into mass-produced wedding bands. Dies of any shape can be used.

2. The units are placed with tweezers, on the strips that will later be bands, on an asbestos soldering block.

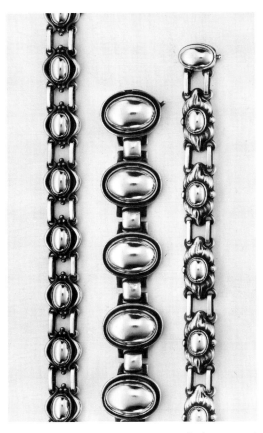

Silver bracelets from Georg Jensen employing repeated units of oval-shaped domes. *Georg Jensen Silversmiths, Ltd.*

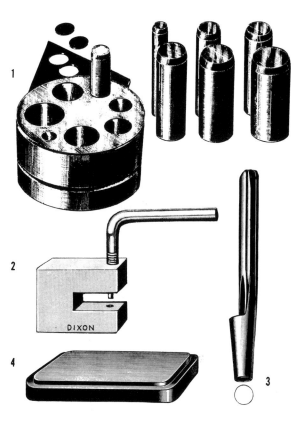

1. Disc punch set with hardened steel punches and matrix, cuts up to 14 gauge 2. Screw punch 3. Disc punching die 4. Lead block

3. The series or "gang" is soldered one after the other. The steel-pointed rod is ready to push back any unit that moves out of place during the soldering. (See section on soldering.)

4. From lower left to upper right: the stamped units; the units gold-soldered to the band; additional ornament of wire and shot added; the finished ring with all waste sawed away, shaped to size, and soldered at the seam.

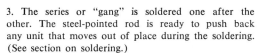

Bronze intaglio die used by goldsmiths in Egypt, Ptolemaic Period. Size: 227 mm by 135 mm. Left: the die; right: the brass impression taken from it. *Metropolitan Museum of Art, New York, Rogers Fund, 1920.*
BELOW LEFT: Mold impressions taken from brass dies to create small ikons or *murti* in silver, copper, and brass. The ikons are used in home worship in India. The annealed sheet of metal is placed over the intaglio die and a folded sheet of lead is placed on top. The lead is then hammered, forcing the sheet metal into the die cavity to make an impression from the die. The *murti* may be left as it comes from the die or it may then be chased for detail. *Photo by Oppi.*

BELOW RIGHT: Relief modeling stones used by the Chibcha Indians in Colombia for stamping or forming sheet gold ornaments. Specimens in the Berlin Ethnographic Museum. *Museum of the American Indian, Heye Foundation, New York.*

OPPOSITE BELOW: Gold plaque, made by the Chibcha Indians of Colombia, with stamped edge made with a punch. *American Museum of Natural History, New York.*

ABOVE: Gold double-strand necklace, Mochica, Peru. Length: 49 inches. Each unit was composed by forming and joining two half-domes, which seem to have been made by forcing the soft gold into a depression, and spinning the half-domes under pressure. *Museum of Primitive Art, New York. Photo by Charles Uht.*

Doming: Using Punched Discs

As previously mentioned, dies are used to make blanks or forms that can then be processed further. One such process is called *doming*. Circular sheets or discs of metal (formed with a die, cut out by hand, or purchased already punched) are shaped into hemispheres called *domes*. As a decorative device, domes have been used since ancient times. They may be applied to flat surfaces or used in pairs of hemispheres joined to each other to form beads or round balls (see left).

A round steel punch with a sharp edge may be used without any matrix to make a disc. A sheet of annealed brass is placed under the metal to be cut, to prevent the edge of the die from becoming dull when it pierces the metal. Both metals are placed on a flat steel stake or block. Using a heavy hammer (1½ pounds or over), hit the punch firmly with a sharp blow, and if this does not cut through the metal immediately, hold the punch securely in the *same position* and strike a few easier taps while slightly rocking the punch from side to side. Metal discs can also be cut directly on a lead block if the block surface is smooth. A disc loses diameter when domed. Choose a disc size larger than the dome size desired. When making a full hemisphere, about one-third of the diameter is lost.

FORMING THE DOME

To dome the disc, *dapping punches* and a *dapping die* or *block* are used. The dapping die is a square block of steel or brass which has a series of hemispherical hollows or depressions of many sizes on each of the six sides of the square. For each hollow there is a dapping punch of corresponding size. The punch is a steel shaft with an almost complete ball at one end.

To make a dome, the annealed disc is placed in the first depression into which it will fit slightly below the surface and which will hold it in position. The dapping punch is placed exactly in the center of the disc, and the disc is hammered till it touches the bottom of the depression. If the dome is not of the desired depth, put the disc into the next smaller depression and using the corresponding punch, hammer it again. This procedure can be followed till the desired shape is formed, with intermediate annealing if necessary. To make a hemisphere, the dome is passed from one depression to the next smaller one till the

83

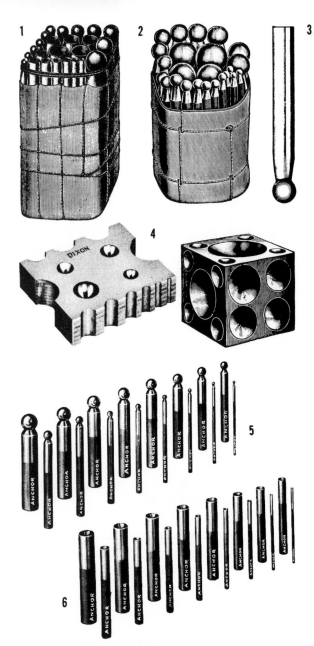

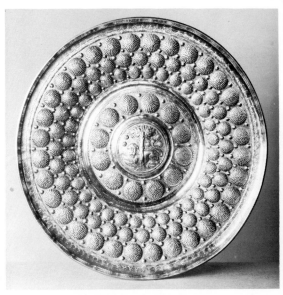

Spanish platter, silver-gilt, c. 1500. Diameter: 11¾ inches. The embossed decoration, mainly of half-domes, is further embellished with small raised "dots" made by hammering a pointed tool from the back. *Victoria and Albert Museum, London.*

1. Set of dapping punches and disc cutters 2. Set of dapping punches 3. Single dapping punch 4. Dapping blocks or dies 5. Set of dapping punches 6. Set of disc dies or cutters

desired size is achieved. Should the edge become irregular, the dome can be held in one of the depressions of the dapping die and filed even. When joining two hemispheres to make a bead, the hole is first punched or drilled from the inside of each half before soldering them together. The holes allow the expansion and contraction of air and gases, thus preventing the collapse of the ball. If a full sphere is formed at least one hole must be made, or its formation will not be possible.

If no dapping block is available, a *lead block* can be used in conjunction with dapping punches. First form a depression in the block with a dapping punch. One precaution: place a piece of paper between the disc and the lead block when hammering, to help prevent contamination of the metal by the lead. If traces of the lead remain on the surface of the metal, the surface will become pitted during annealing or soldering.

Punching Tools

Punches are tools made of rod steel or brass, shaped according to their function, and known by the name of the function they perform. Dapping punches used for doming have already been described. There are several other types of punches. A *tracer punch* is used to outline a pattern, shape, or design, as when chasing or starting repoussé work. A *planisher punch* is used to smooth or harden a surface too small for a planishing hammer. An *embosser punch* is used to raise metal into relief or to depress it. The above-mentioned tools are forms of repoussé tools. A *perloir* is a half-bead-form punch made for modeling balls on metal. A *beader* is a punching tool used in the setting of precious, usually faceted, stones; it raises a bead of metal to hold the stone in place. There are still other punches made for a variety of functions. *Matting tools* classified under chasing tools are really a kind of punch. Like *grounder punches* they are used to create an all-over pattern in an area, and are traditionally used for the background of designs for textural effect.

Punchwork Decoration

Two kinds of punchwork decoration are used in metalwork. The first employs smooth, polished punches that have a definite shape, such as round, square, oval, diamond. These punches usually are worked from the *back* of the metal, though they can also be worked from the front. The metal being punched rests on a soft material such as a lead or zinc block, a piece of hardwood, or a pitch block. When worked from the rear, the pattern appears on the front of the metal as a raised shape or *"boss,"* from which the word *em-*

Byzantine gold necklace, sixth–seventh century. Length: 12⅜ inches. Dot pattern stamped on pieces after casting. *Metropolitan Museum of Art, New York. Gift of J. Pierpont Morgan, 1917.*

bossing comes. In a sense, this is a species of repoussé work.

The second kind of punchwork involves the imprinting of a design which is engraved at the end of the punch onto a metal surface. The design may be a single unit, used as a unit, or as a repeat pattern. It is always seen from the *front* of the metal. The design usually is sharply enough engraved on the punch to impart the pattern with *one well-registered blow*. This kind of punching is done on a hard, solid bed, usually a stake, an iron block, or a bench block, as these surfaces offer resistance to the punch impact and the result is a sharply defined imprint of the pattern. Navajo American Indian jewelry often employs punched symbolic designs. One solid strike of the hammer should do the work, as a second strike runs the risk of movement of the punch, with a blurred result.

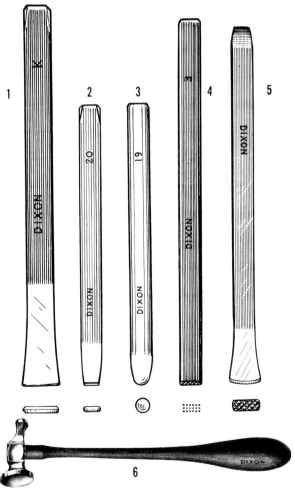

Chasing tools (a form of punch): 1. Tracer 2. Planisher 3. Embosser 4. Grounder 5. Matting tool 6. Chasing hammer

Stamping: For Metal Identification and Hallmark

The marking or stamping of articles made of *precious metals* to signify both the quality of the metal and the symbol or hallmark of the maker is an old tradition dating back to the

Tin coffee pot with punchwork design in the form of a tulip. Pennsylvania Dutch-German. *Titus C. Geesey Collection, Philadelphia Museum of Art.*

Etruscan bronze pail, approximately eighth century B.C. Height: 6⅜ inches; diameter: 7¾ inches. Embossed half-dome and stamped design. *Metropolitan Museum of Art, New York. Gift of J. Pierpont Morgan, 1917.*

medieval guilds of Europe. The practice is still carried out in many European countries, which model their systems after that of the oldest European metalworkers' guild, the Worshipful Company of Goldsmiths, of Goldsmiths' Hall, London, established in 1300. The word "hall-mark" originated in the place name of this guild and meant the mark of Goldsmiths' Hall.

The government of England strictly enforces the stamping of every article made of precious metal, thereby assuring its standard of quality and protecting the public. Every article made of precious metals must be sent to Goldsmiths' Hall, London, or to another branch in the country, where it is assayed and stamped and then returned to the maker. Articles not coming up to the standard are refused the stamp, and should the maker repeat this offense, the article is destroyed.

Four marks are used in England: the King's or Queen's mark (a leopard or a crowned lion's head, which tells where the piece was assayed), the maker's mark (an individual, registered symbol), the assayer's mark (testifying to the purity of the metal determined by specific testing standards), and the date letter, universally established, which tells when the article was made. (See page 90.)

In the United States, regulations concerning the quality marking of articles made of precious metals are controlled by the Federal Stamping Law (U. S. Code, Title 15, Chapter 8, Sections 294–300). A violation of this act is punishable by a fine of five hundred dollars, imprisonment for three months, or both. The U. S. Department of Commerce, in conjunction with the National Bureau of Standards, publishes several booklets called *Commercial Standards* which state the regulations concerning the stamping of precious metals. These booklets, listed below, are available from the Superintendent of Documents, U. S. Government Printing Office, Washington 25, D.C., for ten cents each.

CS66-38, *Marking of Articles Made Wholly or in Part of Platinum*
(Effective: June 20, 1938)

CS67-38, *Marking of Articles Made of Karat Gold*
(Effective: November 25, 1938)

CS118-44, *Marking of Jewelry and Novelties of Silver*
(Effective: August 15, 1944)

CS51-35, *Marking of Articles Made of Silver in Combination with Gold*
(Effective: July 1, 1935)

CS47-34, *Marking of Gold Filled and Rolled Gold Plate Articles*
(Effective: January 1, 1934)

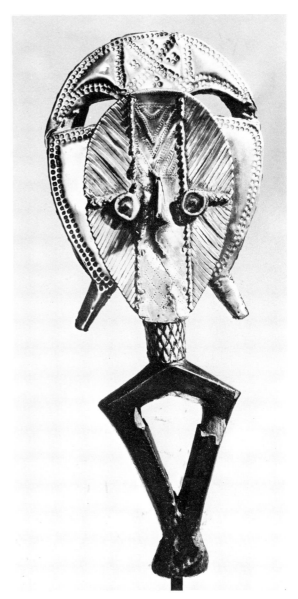

ABOVE: Funerary figure made of wood and decorated with stamped brass plates, Bakota tribe, Gabon Republic, Africa. Height: 16⅝ inches. *Museum of Primitive Art, New York. Photo by Charles Uht.*

OPPOSITE: Algerian copper and brass chessmen, eighteenth century. Height of king: 2¹⁵⁄₁₆ inches. Simple decoration of dots made by a pointed punch tool. *Metropolitan Museum of Art, New York. Gift of Gustavus A. Pfeiffer, 1953.*

The Jewelers Vigilance Committee, Inc., 41 East 42nd Street, New York City, a private organization established in 1913, has taken an active part in sponsoring or co-sponsoring every commercial standard now in use by the industry. It also has sponsored *Trade Practice Rules,* promulgated by the *Federal Trade*

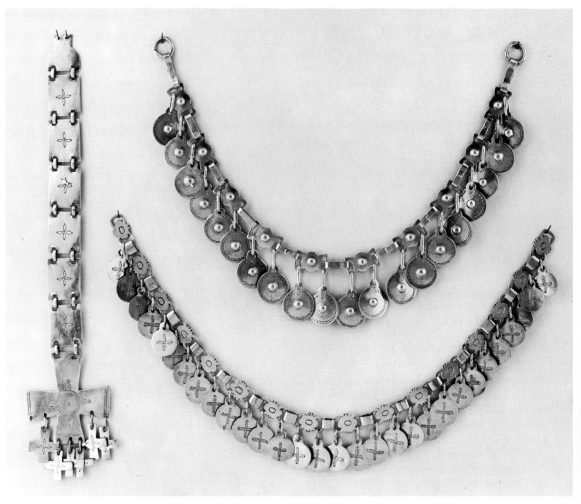

Two silver headbands and a silver pendant, Araucanian, South America. The simple, geometric forms are decorated with stamping tools. *Museum of Fine Arts, Boston.*

Navajo American Indian "concha" belt with turquoise-decorated or plain silver units strung on a leather belt. These belts are frequently decorated with symbolic stamped designs. *Clay Lockett Collection. Photo by Western Ways Features, Tucson, Arizona.*

Commission, which are designed to promote honesty in quality markings and advertising. Every reputable manufacturer and craftsman complies with these standards and regulations.

Some states have their own laws concerning the stamping of precious metals.

The standards and laws are always under revision. Public Law 87-354, passed October 4, 1961, states that any "person, firm, [or] corporation" must apply a *registered trademark* to an article *"by the same means as that used in applying the quality mark or stamp appearing thereon, in type or lettering at least as large as that used in such a quality mark or stamp, and in a position as close as possible to that quality mark or stamp."* This mark must be registered within thirty days of the appearance of an article bearing the trademark. *"Initials shall not be used in lieu of a name unless registered as a trademark."*

Gold regulations issued by the U. S. Treasury Department, effective July 14, 1954, Section 54.21, limit the amount of gold that can be held by an individual at any one time without a license to *50 fine troy ounces.* The amount of gold that may be acquired and used without a license during any calendar month is limited to *350 fine troy ounces.*

APPLYING THE STAMP

In the United States, the quality stamp may be applied by the maker. The piece to be stamped should be placed on a polished steel surface, the metals in contact with each other so that the stamp will mark the reverse side of the metal minimally. The stamp should be placed carefully and the mark made with *one,* well-placed blow with a hammer on the stamp. Should it be insufficiently deep, the stamp must be replaced *exactly* as before or the result will appear blurred. If you have not done this before, practicing on a piece of scrap of the same metal as is being stamped is advisable to acquire the "feel" of the correct amount of pressure needed. Gold requires more pressure than silver. The "blemish" that may appear on the side of the metal opposite the stamp can usually be removed by rubbing with a worn emery cloth.

If the article to be stamped is small, it is sometimes difficult to stamp it with the quality mark. In the case of jewelry where the position best suited to the placement of the mark may become inaccessible later during construction, a good procedure is to apply the mark *before assembling* the parts. Stamps made of case-hardened tool steel (the surface is substantially harder than the core) are sold by jewelers' supply houses and can be ordered with letters of various sizes.

On old pieces, the stamps were often deliberately exposed for decorative effect. Some metalworkers today have appreciated the decorative aspect of stamped markings and have used them where they can be readily seen.

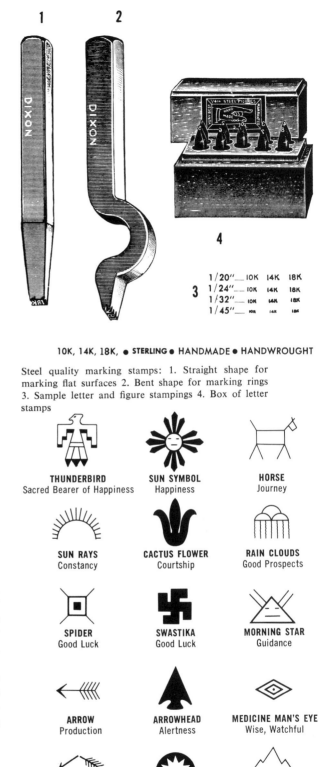

Steel quality marking stamps: 1. Straight shape for marking flat surfaces 2. Bent shape for marking rings 3. Sample letter and figure stampings 4. Box of letter stamps

THUNDERBIRD
Sacred Bearer of Happiness

SUN SYMBOL
Happiness

HORSE
Journey

SUN RAYS
Constancy

CACTUS FLOWER
Courtship

RAIN CLOUDS
Good Prospects

SPIDER
Good Luck

SWASTIKA
Good Luck

MORNING STAR
Guidance

ARROW
Production

ARROWHEAD
Alertness

MEDICINE MAN'S EYE
Wise, Watchful

BROKEN ARROW
Peace

RATTLESNAKE JAW
Strength

BIG MOUNTAIN
Abundance

CROSSED ARROWS
Peace

HOGAN
Permanent Home

THUNDERBIRD TRACK
Bright Prospects

Navajo American Indian stamping die designs, each having a symbolic meaning

METAL TECHNIQUES THAT DO NOT REQUIRE SOLDERING 89

The London hallmark for sterling silver 1964–5. Usually a piece of British sterling bears four punches. First, the maker's mark, usually his initials; second, the standard mark showing the quality of the metal, here the lion passant for sterling silver; third, the town mark showing where the piece was assayed, in this case the leopard for Goldsmiths' Hall, London; and last the date letter—when the piece was assayed and marked. *Worshipful Company of Goldsmiths, London.*

RIGHT: Silver decanter with ivory stopper, designed and made by John Grenville, 1959. The quality marks stamped here are required on every article of precious metal made in England; although most commonly hidden, they are placed as they are on this decanter for their decorative appeal. *Worshipful Company of Goldsmiths, London.*

OPPOSITE: Indian gold necklace (*Champa-kali*), eighteenth–nineteenth century. The central medallion, oval units, and round beads are made by stamping in a brass jeweler's mold. *Collection, Metropolitan Museum of Art, New York.*

BELOW: Egyptian broad, gold collar made entirely of stamped units, with inlay of carnelian and feldspar. Reign of Thutmose III, XVIII Dynasty, (1501–1447 B.C.), Thebes. *Metropolitan Museum of Art, New York, purchase 1926.*

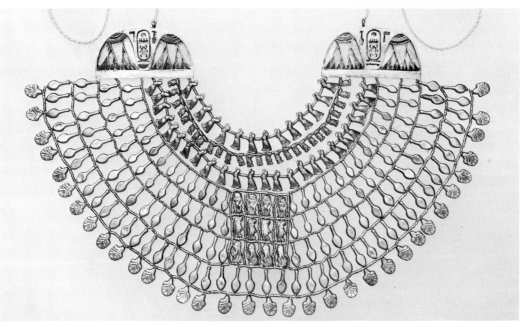

ered surfaces catch the light and cast shadows. Repoussé work is often done in combination with chasing, which, strictly speaking, is any modeling done from the *front* of the metal. Repoussé tools and chasing tools are therefore often used on the same piece of work.

During the working of the metal, the entire surface must be supported on a material resilient enough to give in to the hammer blows on the tools which form the metal and to hold it in place while it is being tooled. Traditionally, the material used for this purpose is *pitch,* which, combined with other materials, retains the necessary amount of plasticity and adheres to the metal when cool, thereby anchoring it firmly in place during the work. Pitch can be heated to allow the metal to be removed from the surface should it be necessary to anneal it or to allow its position to be changed for work on another area or direction (reversed).

OPPOSITE ABOVE: Silver bridal headgear, decorated with carnelians and embossed units stamped with a die, Turcoman style, Persia, c. 1750. The linked arrangement was worn over the bride's face. The movement of the headgear was enhanced by the sound of terminal bells. *Jewish Museum, New York. Photo by Frank J. Darmstaedter.*
OPPOSITE BELOW LEFT: Pair of matched silver bracelets, called "chud," worn by women in Porbandar, Saurashtra, India. The decoration is mainly of stamping processes on wire, crimped ridges, and small flower and bird medallions. *Photo by Oppi.*
OPPOSITE BELOW RIGHT: Contemporary silver bracelet, Cairo, Egypt. All of the applied units were stamped from a mold. *Photo by Oppi.*

ABOVE: Tibetan (Dongtsé Monastery) butter lamp (*chokún*), eighteenth or nineteenth century monastic manufacture. The repoussé and chased form is made of silver. Small stamped units are used to decorate the edges and central portion of the lamp. The decorative medallions represent the "Eight Glorious Emblems" (*asta mangala*), synonymous with the Chinese emblems of "Happy Augury." The base is in the form of a conventional lotus-petal motif. This kind of lamp, filled with yak butter that burns with a cotton wick, is used on a Lamaist altar. *Victoria and Albert Museum, London.*

Repoussé materials: 1. Cast iron pitch bowl with wood ring 2. Leather ring pad 3. Shellac stick 4. Felt ring pad 5. Sealing wax stick 6. Lump pitch 7. Lead block 8. Metal tray for pitch 9. Steel block 10. Linoleum mounted on plywood 11. Sandbag

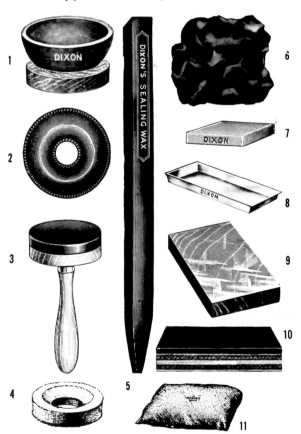

Repoussé

Repoussé consists of using variously shaped punches and a hammer to bring portions of sheet metal into relief and to push back other portions into concavity. The parts brought into relief are worked from the *back* of the metal, and the parts that are concave or depressed are worked from the *front*. Much of the appeal of repoussé work consists in the knowledge that the entire object is made of one piece of metal, whose raised and low-

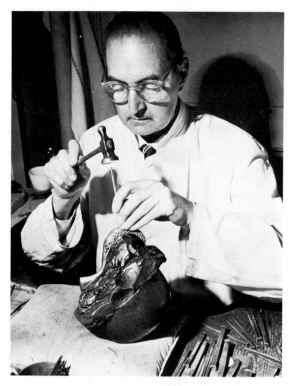

Craftsman of the Georg Jensen company in Copenhagen who specializes in repoussé and chasing work. He is shown here working on a pitcher handle that is mounted on a pitch block in an iron bowl. The bowl rests on a sandbag both to allow the article to be rotated easily and to absorb the shock of the hammer blows. *Photo by Oppi.*

Several small articles can be worked on simultaneously. In this photograph, silver spoons are being chased with a design by a craftsman in Kalimpong, India. A large refugee Tibetan community here creates a demand for articles originally used only in Tibet, such as these spoons, called *thuma*, which are hung by a leather thong from the waistband by women. *Photo by Oppi.*

Other containers for chaser's pitch may be improvised, such as this old brass bowl into which a tray has been fixed while the design is chased. *Photo by Oppi.*

PREPARATION OF PITCH

Depending on the size and shape of the article being worked, pitch can be used in variously shaped containers. For work up to approximately eight inches in diameter, a *pitch bowl* can be used. Made of cast iron, the bowl is hemispherical in shape and held in a wood base with a concave depression to allow the bowl's position to be easily shifted to accommodate a change in the angle of the work. Pitch bowls can also be placed on sand-filled, doughnut-shaped leather pads, circular felt ring pads, or rope rings. Cast-iron bowls have weight which allows work without too much movement.

For larger work, such as trays or plaques, a pitch bowl is obviously inadequate. But pitch can be placed in a pan big enough to ac-

Repoussé metalworker working on a large copper plaque that is mounted on boards spread with pitch, V. Ashwhatharamachar establishment, Bangalore, India. Articles of sheet copper and brass are made for use in worship in the temples of South India. Both bas-relief and completely three-dimensional forms are created. *Photo by Oppi.*

commodate the metal; or a hard, close-grained board can be spread with pitch and used for large pieces. If the pitch used is especially viscous, it may be necessary to fix an edge to the board to retain the pitch.

Pitch for repoussé and chasing work can be purchased already prepared, but the ingredients for its preparation are readily available and the process relatively simple. There are several workable formulas for pitch. Used alone, it is too brittle.

Chaser's Pitch ⎫
Burgundy Pitch ⎬ Six parts of any *one* of these three
Swedish Pitch ⎭
Plaster of Paris or Brickdust Eight parts
Linseed Oil or Tallow One part

The pitch is melted in an iron pan—over a medium flame to avoid burning. When it is quite liquid, the plaster or brickdust is added in handfuls and stirred in thoroughly; then the linseed oil or tallow is added. In warm seasons,

it may be necessary to reduce the amount of oil, and in cold seasons, increase it to maintain the proper firmness. The pitch is then poured into the container, mounded slightly toward the center, and set aside to cool and harden.

This same pitch mixture is used to *fill* a hollow object such as a vase, teapot, or sculptural piece which is to be worked from the outside with chasing tools, as it offers the proper resistance to malformation. Broken pieces of brick are sometimes used to fill the bottom of a deep pitch bowl prior to pouring, to economize on the amount of pitch used.

Though pitch is the most versatile material used in repoussé work, especially because of its adhesion to the metal, other materials such as a wood block, linoleum mounted on a wood block, or lead or zinc blocks are sometimes used. These materials offer the proper resilience but do not hold the metal in position without nails. They are therefore suited to the

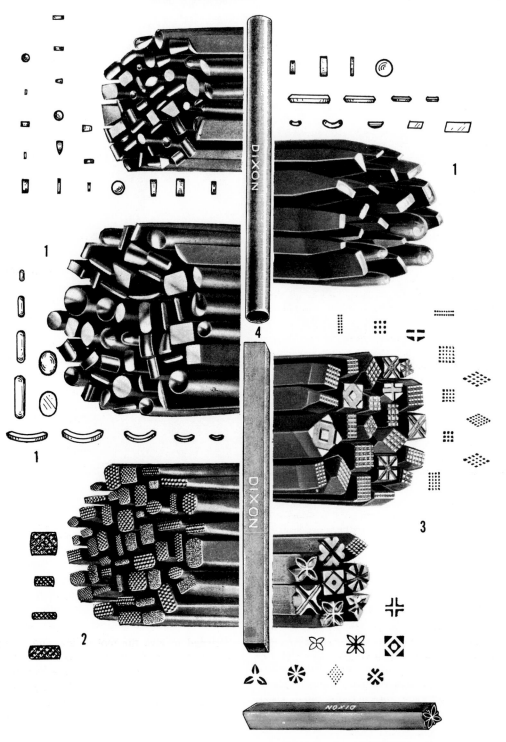

1. Repoussé tools 2. Matting tools and grounders 3. Design stamps 4. Blank round and square stock of hardened and tempered tool steel from which craftsmen can make their own tools

working of *small* pieces. After using a lead or zinc block (both metals having a low melting point), examine the metal being worked on for traces of the soft metals. These must be *removed* with steel wool, an abrasive cloth, or a file if necessary. If the traces are not removed, they will sink into the surface of the metal when it is heated and scar it permanently.

The adhesive nature of pitch permitted it to be used by the Mesopotamians and the Egyptians, who coated wood-carved objects such as animals and figures with it and then covered the entire surface with thin gold foil plates. The foil adhered to the pitch without any other joining means and has remained intact for more than three millennia.

REPOUSSÉ AND CHASING TOOLS AND THEIR USES

Repoussé and chasing tools are basically the same and are often interchangeable. Generally speaking, repoussé tools are more blunt and rounded at the ends, while chasing tools are flatter, with only the corners rounded off. Another difference is the manner in which they are worked: repoussé tools are held nearly upright for the most part, and chasing tools are held at an angle to the work. Both are worked with hammer blows.

Repoussé tools are blunt, polished steel punches—or chisels, as they are sometimes called—made of rectangular hardened-steel stock and about five inches long. The word "chisels" is a misnomer; these are *not cutting,* but *shaping,* tools. (Cuts made through the metal by accident can be mended later by hard soldering.) About fifty tools comprise a set, though specialists have need for even more shapes. The average craftsman can do with fewer. Many craftsmen prefer to make their own tools by forging them from round, square, or oblong blanks of tempered and hardened tool steel. Each tool has a specific function, and the proper selection of a tool depends mainly on its appropriateness to the particular effect or shape called for in the design. The most commonly used shapes can be classified into four main categories: tracers, bossing tools, modeling tools, and specially shaped tools.

REPOUSSÉ TOOLS

Tracers, which are narrow-edged tools very much like blunted chisels with corners rounded, are used to create a line which may be fine or broad, depending on the width of the edge. *Bossing* or, as they are sometimes called, *cushion* tools are used to create convex surfaces or areas and ordinarily are worked from the *back* of the metal. They can, of course, also be used in the opposite direction, pushing the metal back from the front. *Modeling* tools are of various shapes depending on the demands of the situation. *Specially shaped* tools are those made to create such effects as "V" marks, ring tools which create circles of various diameters, and tools leaving a curved mark. They generally are hammered with one blow and may be used from either side of the metal.

Chasing Tools Chasing tools are used mainly from the *front* of the metal, to give sharpness, definition, and textural richness to the design, and create more contrast in light and shadow.

Modeling tools are used to create concave surfaces when worked from the front, but are sometimes used from the back as well. They are round, oval, square, or oblong. *Matting* tools are surfaced on their working end with a variety of small repeats or hatched patterns, and are hammered into the metal to create textural effects. Texture may be used to offset smooth areas, and to create visual contrast. Matting tools are made in many sizes and shapes to fit any conceivable space requirement.

Making Your Own Tools Unfinished tools called *blanks* made of the same forged stock as finished ones may be purchased and finished by the metalworker in any shape to suit his needs. If necessary, the stock can be tapered by filing or forging. The working face can be shaped with a coarse file, and then by finer ones, and finished with an abrasive such as emery cloth, with a final polishing on a buffer with tripoli and rouge. The working face must then be *tempered* or hardened for greatest efficiency. (See page 444 for tempering and work-hardening tools.)

Repoussé or chasing hammers are made with steel heads of various diameters with polished faces up to 1¼ inches across, and have thinly tapered wood handles ten inches long, ending with oval, pistol, or round grip. The face is hardened so that when properly used with tools, being hit lightly and squarely at the repoussé or chasing tool end, it should not become dented. The tapered wood handle is designed to give the tool spring, and its light weight and form allow the tool to be applied rapidly. The broad face of the hammer is designed to provide a relatively large striking area so that this part of the work need not be watched. Vision is concentrated on the action of the tool on the metal.

Chasing hammers are designed to have a large striking surface, a springy handle, and a comfortable grip

Ornamental gold plaque from Colombia. Height: 4⅝ inches. The lines were created with the simplest tools in an elementary repoussé process. *Museum of Primitive Art, New York. Photo by Charles Uht.*

The pitch that will be used to anchor the metal is heated with a soft torch flame to soften and level the surface. While soft, the slightly heated metal, which has been lightly oiled on the part that is to make contact with the pitch to facilitate removal later, is pressed into the pitch with the handle of a hammer. When the pitch is nearly set, a little oil is put on the fingers, and a small amount of pitch is pressed over the edges of the metal to help *key* it in place. The metal should not be pressed too deeply into the pitch or it will become even more deeply embedded during working and will be difficult to remove. Be certain that all parts of the metal are backed with pitch. Should a hollow sound develop during working, the metal must be pushed farther into the heated pitch, as the risk of malforming or breaking is increased since it is unsupported.

When the pitch is cool (this can be hastened by placing it under cold water) the outline of the design can be traced with a tracer. Hold the repoussé punch in the *left* hand, between the thumb and the first two fingers, allowing the third and fourth finger to rest on the metal and support and guide the position of the tool and prevent it from slipping. (This is the position for holding all repoussé and chasing tools, though the angle varies slightly.) The position of the *tracer* should be nearly perpendicular, allowing it to lean slightly *back* from the direction in which it will move. With the front corner lifted slightly clear of the metal, the top of the tool is hammered, with the hammer in the *right* hand, while the back corner digs into the metal and progresses forward slightly with each blow. The eye should be kept fixed on the line being followed on the work and *not* on the end of the tool. Since the rapid blows are short and the face of the hammer is broad, there is little chance of missing the tool with the hammer strokes once the range has been established. The direction of the hammer blows should be in line with the axis of the tool. A little practice on a

The Repoussé Process

The design is transferred *in reverse* to the cleaned reverse side of the metal with carbon paper or a pencil while the metal is flat. The metal is then lightly scratched (the reason for working in reverse), so that the design will be visible after handling and permanent. If the design is applied to a convex surface such as a bowl, the scratched lines done with a scriber will have to be visible, and should therefore be scratched lightly so that they may later be obliterated.

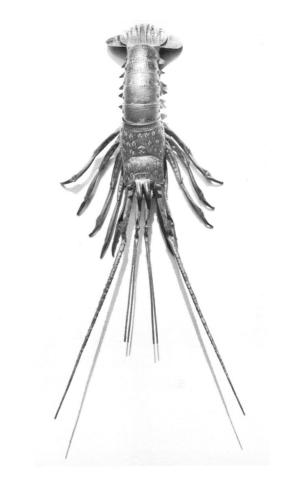

American copper aspic mold in the form of a lobster, constructed by the repoussé process. *The Cooper Union Museum for the Arts of Decoration, New York.*

ABOVE RIGHT: Copper crayfish, made in Kyoto, Japan. The creature is completely articulated at every joint and moves much like its living counterpart. The construction is all of sheet metal that is shaped with repoussé tools, stamped with details, and given a subtle, natural-appearing reddish patina. Japanese metal craftsmen are extremely skilled in the creation of a variety of patinas on metal. *Photo by Oppi.*

RIGHT: Traditional, repoussé decorated gold earrings worn by Lepcha women in Nepal and Darjeeling, West Bengal, India. *Photo by Oppi.*

piece of scrap metal will soon establish the proper angle for holding the particular tool, as each may vary slightly. If the groove progresses as it should, the line will move slowly enough, without skipping, so that the result looks continuous and not sketchy.

Modeling tools are held slightly straighter, as their progress is slower. *Matting* tools are used from the front and should be held vertically just above the surface of the metal so that they can move freely. Their position should be carefully considered, as the pattern is not easily changed once it is impressed on the metal. Changing the direction of the tool

as the work progresses and allowing some overlapping will result in a less mechanical look in the repeat of the pattern texture.

REMOVING THE WORK FROM THE PITCH,
AND THE PITCH FROM THE WORK

Once the work done from the *back* is completed, the metal must be reversed so that it can be worked from the *front* with chasing or modeling tools. This may be necessary several times in the course of the work's progress. The metal is removed from the pitch by warming it with a torch and prying it away with a dull tool. If the pitch is very hard, a tool driven under the metal might free it with a few lifting motions. For small pieces, the bottom of the pitch bowl or the block can be struck with a hammer, and in most cases the metal will come free.

To remove traces of the pitch from the metal, a cloth or brush dipped in hot paraffin and applied to the pitch will dissolve it, but the metal must be kept warm.

If the work is in need of annealing, which should be done as soon as it shows signs of work hardening, plunging it into water after annealing will remove the remnants of pitch; this is probably the best way. Pickling in acid should *never* be attempted till *all* traces of pitch are removed; pitch will act as an acid resist and leave the metal surface scarred.

A cloth impregnated with turpentine or benzine will also remove soft pitch if rubbed over the pitch till it dissolves. Take care to avoid overheating the pitch at any time, as this renders it useless. Burned pitch becomes brittle and hard and is more difficult to remove.

OPPOSITE PAGE: Gold soul washer's badge from Ashanti, West Africa, with repoussé decoration. Diameter, seven inches. *University of Pennsylvania Museum, Philadelphia.*

LEFT: Gold crown, Sambayeque, Peru. One sheet almost entirely covered with repoussé work. *Museum of the American Indian, Heye Foundation, New York.*

ABOVE: Chased and engraved silver bracelet representing a raven, Haida Indians, Queen Charlotte Islands, British Columbia. Width: 1½ inches. *Museum of the American Indian, Heye Foundation, New York.*

BELOW LEFT: Portable shrine, called a *gau,* made of silver, copper, and brass by Tibetan craftsmen of the large resident Tibetan community in Kalimpong, West Bengal, India. This type of shrine contains an image of Buddha or another deity, a prayer scarf, and writings from sacred scriptures; it is carried by pilgrims or traveling Tibetans. The *gau* shown here is about 8 inches high. Its elaborately repousséd and chased silver face is ornamented with the eight sacred Buddhist symbols of good fortune which are made of brass and joined by simple split rivets. Riveting is a method of construction widely used in Tibetan metalwork. *Photo by Oppi.*

BELOW: Late Chou Dynasty Chinese iron "sleeve-weight" plaque. Overlaid with sheet gold repoussé in medium and high relief and inlaid with jade. Size: 2¾ inches by 2⁹⁄₁₆ inches. *Freer Gallery of Art, Washington, D.C.*

METAL TECHNIQUES THAT DO NOT REQUIRE SOLDERING   101

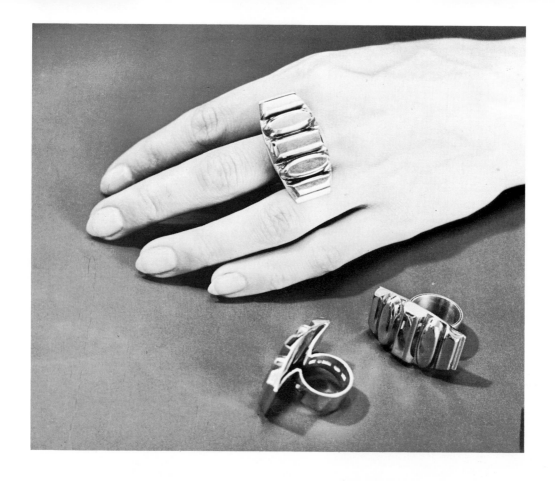

102 METAL DECORATIVE TECHNIQUES

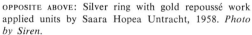

OPPOSITE ABOVE: Silver ring with gold repoussé work applied units by Saara Hopea Untracht, 1958. *Photo by Siren.*

BELOW LEFT: Gilded copper funerary mask, Limoges, France, thirteenth century. Constructed from flat sheet metal by the repoussé process with minor engraved details. *Le Louvre, Paris. Service Photographique, Caisse Nationale des Monuments Historiques, Paris.*

BELOW RIGHT: "Head of Girl," by Harry Hall. Made by the repoussé process from one sheet of lead. *Photo by Oppi.*

ABOVE RIGHT: Repoussé silver, parcel-gilt Armlet of Honor, Abyssinia, nineteenth century. Length: 6⅛ inches. *Victoria and Albert Museum, London.*

ABOVE: Silver Tibetan hand prayer wheel, called a *mani,* with repoussé work inscription, eighteenth or nineteenth century. Weighted to facilitate its rotation in use. *Museum of Fine Arts, Boston.*

RIGHT: Ceremonial gold vase from the Burmese Royal Regalia. Made of several units mounted by rivets on a wood core. The surface is decorated with repoussé and stamped designs accented with rows of rubies. *Victoria and Albert Museum, London.*

The Chasing Process

The metal is now annealed, quenched in water, freed of traces of pitch, possibly pickled in acid, washed and dried, and oiled slightly on the surface that is next to make contact with the pitch. It is ready to be returned to the pitch bowl or surface to be worked further from the *front*. This is usually done with chasing tools. The purpose of chasing is to refine and define the forms of the design, and to bring them to the height of relief desired. Modeling tools, liners, and matting tools are all used, much in the same manner as the repoussé tools but held at a *greater angle* as already mentioned. The tool can be lubricated with a light oil to facilitate its movement. It is held with the top tipped *away* from the worker, so that the tool is hammered *toward* him. This allows the line of the design that is being followed to be seen easily as the tool progresses. Angling the tool makes the heel of the tool do the work, and results in a smoother line. In the chasing of *large* pieces, the work should be done from the center out toward the edge. In the texturing of a background with matting tools, the work should be done from the tracer line, defining the forms of the design toward the open areas that are to be textured so that the background remains flat.

We have been assuming so far that the work is of some dimension and is not in one general plane. If, however, the work is flat, such as a large tray or plaque, and the design is to be carried out mainly in line, texture, and low relief, the chasing can be carried out almost completely upon a hardwood board of close grain, without pitch. In this case, the metal must be fixed to the wood by nailing it in place with headless, *oval* nails, which can easily be bent over the metal. They are spaced about a quarter of an inch from the edge of the metal to allow for expansion of large pieces, and proportionately less space for smaller pieces. Small pieces can also be worked on a lead, zinc, or steel block, or on a piece of rough, wet leather, though the problems of holding the work in place are greater. The main advantages of working small pieces on a pitch bowl is that the work is held securely, and it can easily be angled to a convenient working position by shifting the bowl in the supporting ring.

OPPOSITE: Polish silver and parcel-gilt Torah crown, Lemberg, 1809. Surmounted by a cast bird and decorated with cast bells and griffins. Mainly repoussé work chased with inscriptions and signs of the zodiac, it is enriched with semi-precious stones. *Jewish Museum, New York. Photo by Frank J. Darmstaedter.*

BELOW: Handmade chasing tools of tempered steel stock, forged and shaped to suit the craftsman's needs, by Adda Husted-Andersen, New York.

Chasing, an ancient form of decoration for metal objects, is being executed here on a large brass vase that was first formed by casting in sections and then joined by soldering. The method of manipulating the chasing tool with a broad, hardwood stick is typical of the craftsmen of Moradabad, India, where hundreds of workers, from children to old men, are skilled chasers. Large objects, such as this vase, are simply laid on an adjustable wooden frame that securely cradles the work. *Photo by Oppi.*

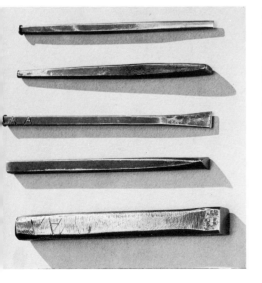

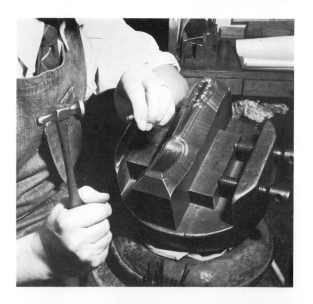

RIGHT: Chasing a cast bronze image of Krishna after casting. This bronze was made at the Sri Chamarajendra Technical Institute in Mysore, India. The image is held in position while it is worked upon by placing it in a chasing box. Since the force of the work is not great, the weight of the casting is sufficient to keep the casting in place. *Photo by Oppi.*

LEFT: Chasing a mold for detail on a flatware pattern. For ease in manipulation, the work is secured in an engraver's ball resting on a leather pad. *American Craftsmen's Council.*

BELOW: Craftsman in the Jensen factory in Copenhagen chasing a design on a series of cake knives. The work is secured to a pitch block that rests on a sandbag so that the block can be easily rotated during the process. *Photo by Oppi.*

BELOW: Cast bronze Krishna, made in Mysore, India. Height: 16 inches. Indian casters depend a great deal on chasing techniques after casting to create the small details in their castings. *Photo by Oppi.*

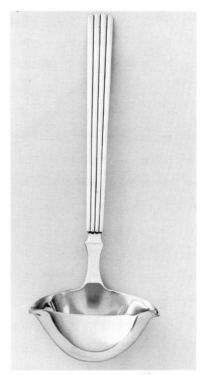

Gravy ladle with chased handle, designed by Sigvard Bernadotte. *Georg Jensen Silversmiths, Ltd., Copenhagen.*

Copper footprint representing Vishnu, from Gaya, Bihar, India. Length: 18 inches. Chased decoration of symbols of the firmament, the conch shell, the fish, the club, the male organ, the female organ, the lotus, and the banner. All of these symbols have significance in worship. The entire design is chased with one tool. *Photo by Oppi.*

Greek silver Ikon of St. George, mounted on wood,
1774. Height: 5½ inches. Chasing, stamping, and repoussé techniques were used to create a rich surface.
Victoria and Albert Museum, London.

Chased silver Torah Case from Meshed, Persia, 1764. Back view. Calligraphy is an important element in Hebraic design. *Jewish Museum, New York. Photo by Frank J. Darmstaedter.*

Brass tray that was first chased and engraved. The engraved areas were then inlaid with black lac, a a form of decoration known as "siah qalam" work in Moradabad, India, where it was made. The lac, in stick form, is melted into the depressed areas; then the surface is scraped level and polished. Diameter: 2 feet. *Photo by Oppi.*

Etruscan bronze mirror, fourth–third century B.C. Length: 10⅝ inches; diameter: 5³⁄₁₆ inches. The backs of these formerly polished mirrors were usually engraved with scenes from contemporary life and mythology. *Metropolitan Museum of Art, New York.*

Engraved and chased bronze aquamanile in the form of a lion, Mohammedan, eleventh century. Louvre, Paris. *Archives Photographiques, Caisse Nationale des Monuments Historiques, Paris.*

Repoussé and Chasing on Deep Pieces

When working in repoussé or chasing on articles such as deep vases or teapots, the inner surface is inaccessible to the tools. The entire work must be carried out from the *exterior* of the piece, with the exception of the following process. After a design has been lightly inscribed on the surface, a *snarling iron* is employed. This is a form of anvil with a long arm ending in a small, polished ball. It is operated by allowing the arm to enter the shape and positioning the ball *directly under* an area of the design that is to be generally raised. The *exposed* remaining part of the snarling iron arm is then hammered, with the result that the ball end *inside* the piece *kicks* the metal upward in reaction. This action can be controlled with a little practice. The resulting raised areas can then be worked from the *outside*. Some chasing in this case can be done "in air," that is, without the metal being supported by pitch, if the design does not call for any great depth. If there is deep relief or an undercut in the design, the procedure after using the snarling iron would be to fill the entire object with pitch and then work it in the usual way. The pitch is removed by heating the piece and pouring out the pitch after all work is finished.

Small hollow jewelry made of sheet metal may be worked in the same manner with miniature snarling irons and lightweight hammers.

Gold and silver wedding cup, by Ilya Schor. The elaborate pierced work with chased and engraved linear pattern is typical of the late Ilya Schor's work. *Collection of Mr. and Mrs. Nathaniel Hess. Photo by J. J. Breit.*

Brass "pandan" or box used for holding the ingredients for making "pan" (spices wrapped in a betel leaf and chewed, usually after meals). Made in Lucknow, Uttar Pradesh, India. The decoration was executed by the repoussé process with floral and crescent moon motifs, indicating that it was intended for use by Muslims. *Collection of Jay Gang. Photo by Oppi.*

Silver-gilt bowl and cover with repoussé work, chased and stamped ornament. Siam (Thailand), eighteenth century. *Victoria and Albert Museum, London.*

Contemporary Burmese silver bowl. Diameter: about 7 inches. The design units in high relief are worked almost completely from the outside with chasing tools after the main forms have been brought out with repoussé tools from the inside. *Photo by Oppi.*

Engraving

The use of engraving as a means of decorating metal surfaces predates the use of etchants, or acids. Metal engraving originated in Europe in the early Renaissance when it was used to decorate armor, and reached a peak of elaboration in the fifteenth century. The connection between engraving, intaglio printing, and etching is interesting, and is mentioned under the niello process (page 186).

Engraving is the process of incising lines with a tool called a *graver* or *burin* on gold, silver, brass, steel, and some other metals. The process can be done completely by hand, partly with the aid of mechanical devices, or entirely by machine. The mechanical process produces an engraved pattern called *engine turning,* which is done by means of a rose engine, a lathe attachment that makes curved lines in a relative eccentric movement, of the kind seen printed on paper currency and decorated watch cases. Engraving machines are available which can mechanically reproduce letters, monograms, and font type.

The decorative possibilities of hand engraving are great, though as a process it has fallen into disuse. The skills involved may very well suit the contemporary metalworker who enjoys working with meticulous skill and control, and is interested in refined, smaller effects. As in all highly controlled processes, practice is necessary to acquire the skill, and practice is easily had on scrap metal.

ENGRAVING TOOLS

The engraving tool, known variously as a *graver, burin,* or *scorper,* is a tool-steel rod in a variety of cross-section shapes, with a removable or permanent wood handle. A great many kinds of lines are possible, depending on the cross-section shape of the stock and the shape of the cutting edge. Flat, square, diamond, point or onglette, round, oval, knife, bevel-edge, lozenge, and lining gravers are available, and still others of special shape. Depending on the kind of surface being worked, the shaft of the tool may be straight (for flat or convex surfaces), angled (for flat or concave surfaces), or bent to accommodate special cases such as engraving spoons and the inside of rings.

The wood handles are also varied to accommodate individual preferences for comfort in work and to meet special situations. They are made round, oval, hemispherical, tapered, etc., and in several cases can be removed and interchanged, though this is probably not desirable, by forcing them off the *tang* end of the tool (the end opposite the pointed, cutting end) and hammering them on another tool. Setting a new handle on a tool is done by first drilling a hole in it of a size smaller than the tang end. The tool is placed tang end upright in a vise, the handle is placed on the tang and hammered tightly in place.

The metal that is being worked on must be

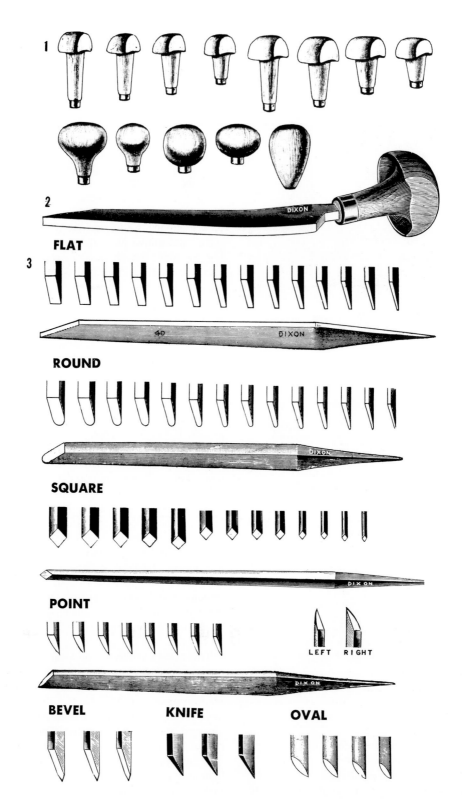

FLAT

ROUND

SQUARE

POINT

LEFT   RIGHT

BEVEL   **KNIFE**   **OVAL**

Engraving tools: 1. Wood engraving tool handles 2. Engraving tool mounted with handle 3. Types of engraving tool shapes

OPPOSITE: 1. Engraver's block and attachments 2. Leather block pad 3. Set of attachments 4. Key 5. set of four 6. set of four 7. set of four 8. set of two 9. set of four 10. set of four 11. set of two 12. set of four 13. set of four 14. set of four 15. set of four 16. set of four

112   METAL DECORATIVE TECHNIQUES

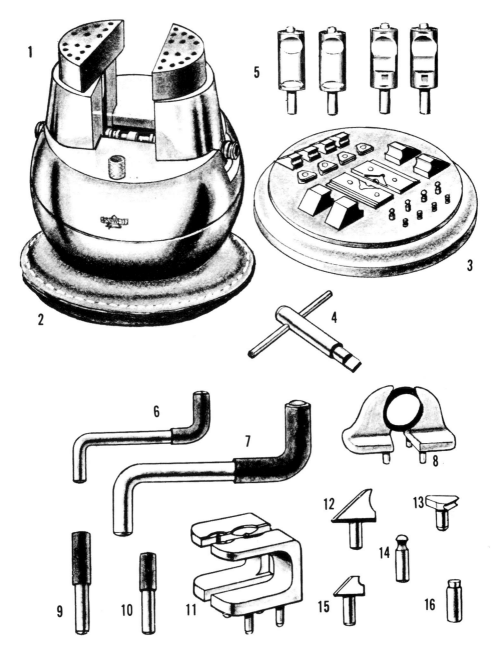

fixed firmly in position during the entire engraving process. A pitch bowl made of heavy cast iron may be used for this purpose if the size of the work allows. Large pieces can be fixed to a board spread with pitch or sealing wax, and the board then held in a vise or fixed to a table with clamps. For small work, a specially made engraving block or ball vise (see description of holding tools, page 438) is used. The engraver's block is a weighted ball with adjustable jaws (to hold the work), which are mounted on ball bearings within the ball to allow it to turn easily while engraving. It is set on a circular leather or felt pad which allows

the whole ball to be moved easily and angled for the needs of the work. Large, three-dimensional objects such as bowls and vases can be held securely in vises or cushioned on sandbags or pads easily shaped to accommodate them, also allowing mobility during working.

TOOL PREPARATION AND MAINTENANCE

Gravers can be purchased already sharpened for immediate use, but sometimes it is necessary to reshape or sharpen them. Like all tools that depend on sharpness to function efficiently, they must be resharpened when their cutting

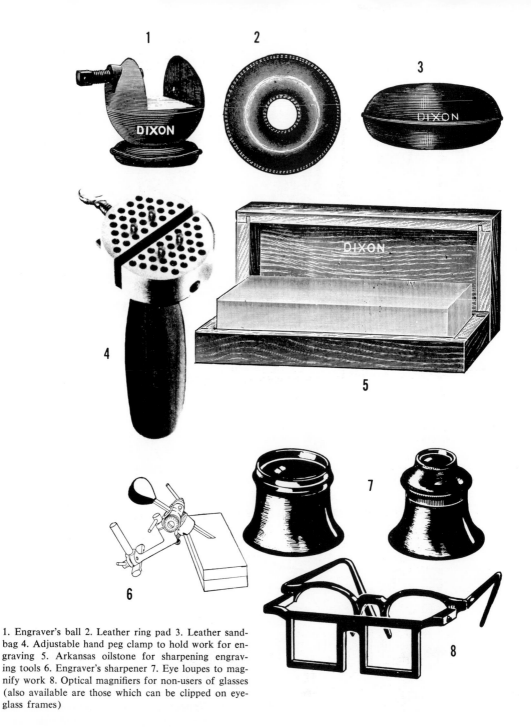

1. Engraver's ball 2. Leather ring pad 3. Leather sand-bag 4. Adjustable hand peg clamp to hold work for engraving 5. Arkansas oilstone for sharpening engraving tools 6. Engraver's sharpener 7. Eye loupes to magnify work 8. Optical magnifiers for non-users of glasses (also available are those which can be clipped on eyeglass frames)

edges become dull or when they break. The best angle for most cutting edges is at forty-five degrees to the stock. An angle of more than forty-five degrees produces a shallow cut and may cause the point to break; an angle of less than this produces a deep cut, but does not subject the cutting edge to breakage as readily.

The preparation of the cutting edge may be started on a grinder or by filing, and finished by being worked on a sharpening stone with oil. Arkansas oilstone (a natural stone quar-ried in the Ozark Mountains) gives a fine edge to all steel cutting tools. India oilstones (arti-ficial stones made of an aluminum oxide abra-sive) are available in three coarsenesses: fine, for polishing, and medium and coarse for cut-ting. They are already impregnated with oil, and only a small additional amount is necessary to prevent glazing, or impregnating the pores of the stone with fine metal particles, which would reduce its efficiency. A clear, thin, light oil should be used in sufficient quantity to float the minute particles of metal during honing or sharpening. The tool is moved in a rotating motion over the stone surface. From time to time, the old oil should be washed off the surface with a hot soap-and-water solution.

During the sharpening process, it is extremely important for maximum sharpness to maintain a constant, proper angle of the tool in relation to the stone, so that the polished surface is in one flat plane. The final polishing of the tool is done on a piece of fine emery paper placed on an *absolutely flat surface* such as plate glass. For those who find it difficult to maintain a constant angle, an *adjustable graver sharpening* tool which holds the engraving tool at any angle can be used. (See ⚒6 opposite.)

Traditionally, the sharpness of a tool is tested by pushing it lightly against a fingernail while holding it at a shallow angle. If it catches and shaves the nail, it is sharp, and if it does not shave it easily, it must be processed further.

If it is necessary to change the angle of the *shaft* of a tool so that it can be used on a different-shaped surface (advisable only in dire necessity), heat the shaft till it is red hot, bend it with gripping pliers (maintaining its shape otherwise), and quench it immediately in cold water. To restore the *temper* or hardness of the point, first polish the end of the tool, and then heat the polished end with a blue flame held one inch from the point. When the point turns a yellow straw color, quench it immediately in oil.

APPLYING THE DESIGN

If the design is to be engraved on a shaped metal surface, it can be drawn directly on the metal with India ink or lead pencil, and then *lightly* scratched with an *engraver's marker, scratch awl,* or *scriber.* To transfer a design from paper to flat metal, cover the metal with a thin coat of Chinese white paint by rubbing wet fingers on the solid cake and daubing the metal surface evenly, then letting it dry. Yellow ochre paste can also be used for this purpose, and both can be removed later with plain water. Place a carbon paper face down on the white paint, lay the design drawing on top, and trace it. Remove the design and carbon paper and scratch the design into the metal as above. If the work being engraved is not handled too much, just going over it with a pencil is sufficient.

A transfer pad made of rubber is available, and is used when repeats of identical patterns such as monograms are needed. The finished

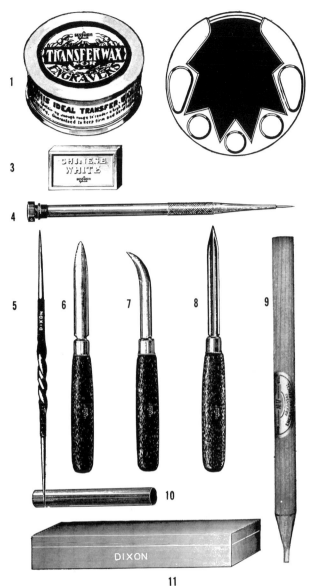

1. Engraver's wax 2. Engraver's transfer pad 3. Chinese white paint cake 4. Engraver's needle point marker 5. Engraver's scriber 6. Straight burnisher 7. Curved burnisher 8. Hollow steel scraper 9. Engraver's Arkansas stone pencil 10. Shellac stick 11. India oilstone sharpener

engraving is dusted with talc powder and pressed onto the transfer pad, leaving a talc impression. The new work to be engraved is pressed over the impression, which transfers to the metal and can then be engraved.

Complicated engraving designs can be transferred by placing a paper over the design and rubbing it with a burnisher, forcing the paper into the design so that it appears raised at the back. The metal is prepared with a thin coat of transfer wax, Chinese white or yellow ochre. Printer's ink is applied to the raised pattern on the paper with a brayer, and the design is placed on the metal and rubbed to produce an impression. It can then be engraved.

USING ENGRAVING TOOLS

The metal being engraved is held firmly in the pitch, sealing wax, or engraver's ball, or is braced on a sandbag. The tip of the graver can be lubricated with a small cotton ball saturated with wintergreen oil. Hold the graver in the *right* hand with the handle against the palm of the hand, toward the ball of the small finger. Use the thumb and the first two fingers to hold the blade or shaft of the tool. Depending on the kind of line being engraved, the thumb can act as an anchor for rotating a curve. The point of the graver should move along smoothly, just below the metal surface. The metal may be moved against the stationary tool when the engraving ball vise is used, or when no ball is used, by just resting on the thumb and fingers. A line varying in width may be cut by turning the tool on its axis slightly in the same cutting motion. This brings a larger part of the point in contact with the metal. A zigzag line can be made by rocking the graver from side to side during the cutting action. Lines may be deepened by repeating them in the same groove.

A line is terminated by releasing the forward pressure while digging in slightly with the tool. Bringing up the tool too quickly may cause it to break, when repolishing will be necessary. Should a cut terminate in a raised burr, this can be removed by using a graver and joining the line from the *opposite* direction, or by cutting it off with a scraper, taking care not to dig into the metal below the burr.

CORRECTING ENGRAVING ERRORS

If the cut of the engraver's tool is not too deep, minor errors can be eliminated by applying a steel burnisher or a stone engraver's pencil to the area and carefully smoothing it level. In the case of an error when engraving a monogram, if the mistake is irreparable, there is no other course but to remove the entire engraved metal area (if the metal thickness allows) and start again.

FLORENTINE FINISH WITH LINERS

Besides being used to create line designs, gravers can be used for the creation of all-over textural surfaces, such as the type now

THE ENGRAVING PROCESS

In this series of photographs taken by the author in the workshop of Kultasepänliike Ossian Hopea in Porvoo, Finland, a traditional form of engraving—the monogram—is being applied to flatware and to a coffee pot in silver.

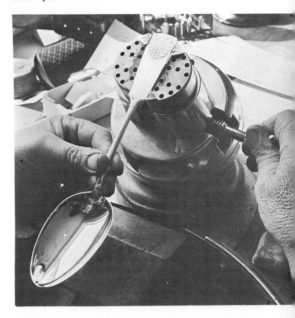

1. The spoon handle is secured in the engraver's block or ball vise. The movable jaws, in conjunction with a variety of attachment holding devices, can accommodate practically any shape. The jaws are then locked with a key.

4. Objects of a size or shape that cannot be held by an engraver's block can be made to rest against a leather pad or sandbag.

2. A paste mixture of yellow ochre and water is spread, with the finger, on the area that is to receive the engraved design. After the mixture has dried, the design is drawn on the metal with a pencil.

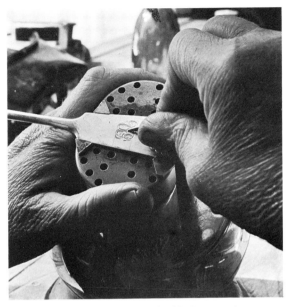

3. Since the polished engraver's block rests in a leather engraver's pad, it can be rotated easily to accommodate the direction of the engraving. The left hand rests on the revolving table, while the right hand, holding the graver, performs the engraving operation.

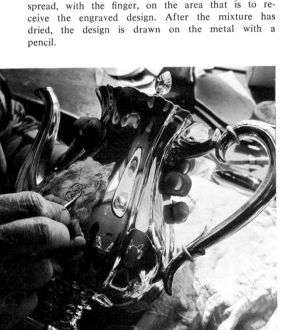

5. In this case, the left hand grips the object securely and rotates it while the right hand works the graver.

6. A convenient way of protecting the sharpness of engraving tools when they are not being used is to place their points in holes cut in a large cork.

METAL TECHNIQUES THAT DO NOT REQUIRE SOLDERING   117

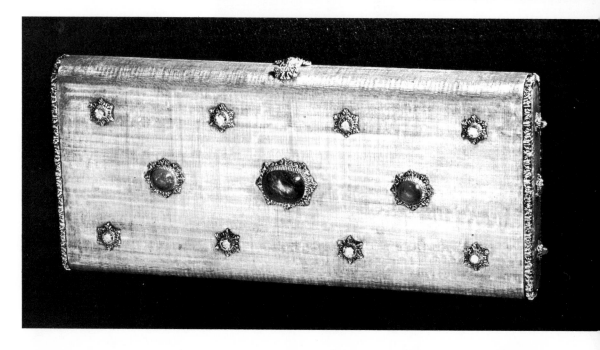

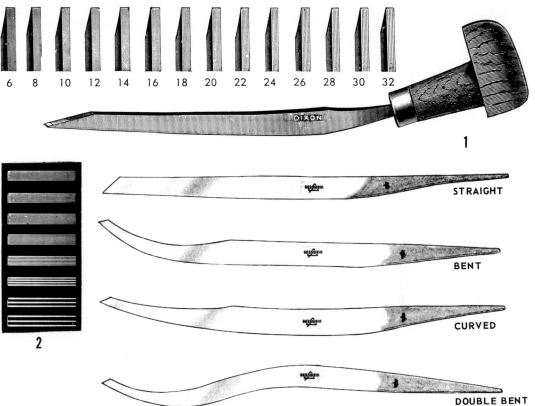

popularly known as "Florentine Finish." The engraved metal treatment was originated by Mario Buccellati of Milan, Italy, and has been imitated by Florentine craftsmen, from where it gets its name.

Some textures are made with the ordinary engraver's burin, but most of them are made with three- or five-grooved *liners*. *Liners* are tools which have several grooves or shallow lines across the face, and are used to create patterns of parallel lines. Partial or entire areas are covered completely with parallel or cross-hatched lines. Liners are made in various grades from fine to coarse, and with

Gold cuff links and tie clip with "Florentine" texture produced by liner tools. *Georg Jensen, Inc.*

ABOVE LEFT: Engraved silver teapot, designed and executed by Paul Revere, c. 1770–1818, Boston. Height: 6⅛ inches; length: 11⅞ inches. *Metropolitan Museum of Art, New York. Bequest of A. T. Clearwater, 1933.*

BELOW: Silver parcel-gilt beaker, made by Swedish silversmith Matthias Forswall, 1776. Height: 8½ inches; diameter: 6¼ inches. The engraved hunting scenes have a fresh, candid quality. *Metropolitan Museum of Art, New York. Gift of Frances and Stephen Markoe, 1943.*

varying numbers or groups of lines on their face. The numbering system mentions the *type* of graver, *grade,* and the *number of lines.* Example: Bent liner 8/4 means a liner of bent shaft, grade 8 coarseness, having four lines.

In the texture called "rigato," all the lines are cut in the same direction. "Telato" is a linen-like texture that consists of lines cut in perpendicular directions. "Ornato" is a lace-like pattern and "segrinato" is a velvety texture. The word "modelato" is used for three-dimensional details carved with engraving tools.

Liners may also be used to "key" the surface of metal to receive niello or enamel to provide a better gripping surface. Engraving tools (as well as chisels) can be used to make a line in damascene and inlay work, into which another, contrasting metal wire can then be hammered. Engraved lines can be used to add details or further enrich castings, repoussé, chased, and etched work. Engraving is an adjunct to many other techniques.

OPPOSITE ABOVE: Silver carry-all, designed by Mario Buccellati and executed in his workshops in Milan, Italy. Borders, clasp, and bezels are of 18-karat gold; the central sapphire is flanked by emeralds and diamonds. The *telato,* linenlike surface was done with engraving liners. *Mario Buccellati, Milan and New York. Photo by Peter Custer.*
OPPOSITE BELOW: 1. Engraver's lining tools (liners), made in various gradings, (18/10 recommended for Florentine finish), in various widths and number of lines per inch 2. Sample liner toolings and liner tool ends

Silver sugar castor with engraved pattern, designed and executed by Ronald Stevens, London, 1959. *Worshipful Company of Goldsmiths, London.*

Brass, gilded engraved clock case, signed "Francoy Nowe. Fecit a London Ao. Dm. 1588." *Victoria and Albert Museum, London.*

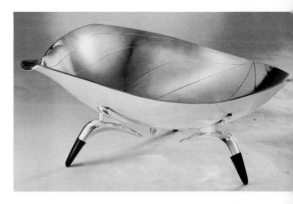

Silver bowl with ebony tipped feet, by Frederick Miller. The interior is engraved with a line pattern. *Photo by John Paul Miller.*

Splitting

Splitting as a method of achieving openings or of dividing metal at the edge *without the loss of any metal* has long been used by blacksmiths in decorative, forged, and wrought-iron work. The same technique used for precious metals produces a fresh effect. Different chisels are used for hot and cold splitting.

When splitting, apply sharp chisels to the metal while the metal is red hot. On a smaller scale, well-annealed silver, copper, and other metals may be split while cold. When splitting an edge, start from the edge and proceed *inward,* or the metal may crack. In splitting the inner part of the metal, start from the center and work alternately toward the extremes.

Silver brooch with engraved lines and smoky quartz stone, by Bertel Gardberg, Finland. *Photo by Studio Wendt, Helsinki.*

Silver candlestick constructed by forging and splitting processes, designed and executed by Ronald Hayes Pearson. *Photo by Charles Arnold.*

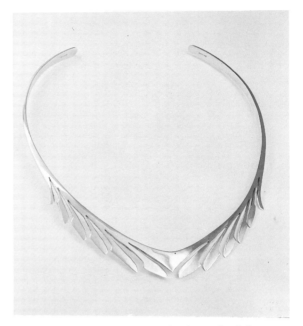

Sterling silver necklace made by forging and splitting processes, designed and executed by Ronald Hayes Pearson, 1961. *Photo by Charles Arnold.*

Carving

Designs may be developed on the surfaces of relatively thick pieces of metal with sharp cold chisels, which cut into and chip away the metal, leaving it bright as the tools progress. This is done frequently in India, where the metal is often cut into facets like those of a precious stone. Left that way without further treatment, it gives off flashing reflections. (See illustration, page 122.)

Filing

Designs can be developed on thick stock by first removing large amounts with heavy files followed by refinement in shape with small jeweler's files called *needle files* (see page 125). These fine-cut files are made in varying cross-section shapes, each capable of making a special kind of cut. The American Indians often use this technique in decorating bracelets and other types of jewelry. (See pages 123–25.)

Pickling

The use of acids for pickling metal to clean it and to remove oxide scale which forms on the surface during the heating, annealing, and soldering of alloyed metals, especially those containing copper, has been practiced since ancient

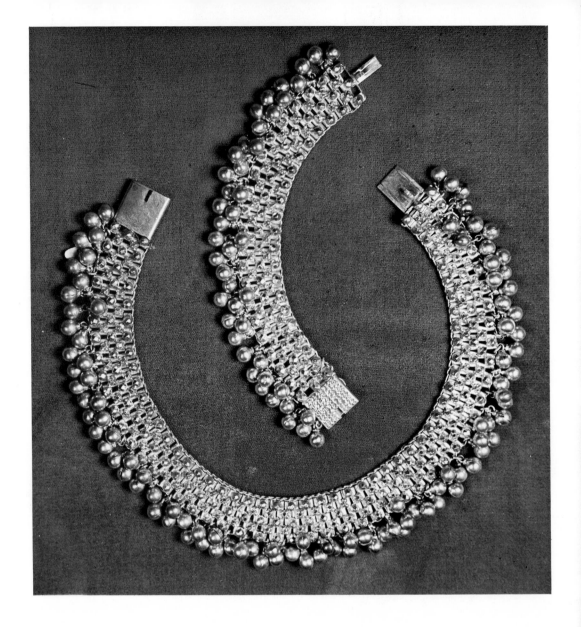

times. Since surface oxide or firescale does not permit the flow of solder when soldering, it must be removed. To accomplish this, the article is placed in a dilute acid solution and allowed to remain there till the oxide dissolves. Some metalworkers place metal pieces just after soldering, while they are still hot, directly into a cold pickle solution. Pickle also dissolves fused borax glaze (see soldering fluxes, page 163).

COMMON PICKLING BATH
(for gold, silver, and copper)

10 parts water
1 part sulphuric acid

For a more efficient gold pickling bath, a little sodium bichromate can be added. If sulphuric acid is not available, nitric acid may be substituted, using an eight part water to one part acid solution.

When preparing the pickle solution, remember to **always pour the acid slowly into the water,** and **NOT** the reverse or a spattering and fuming might occur which would be a hazard. (Should the skin come in contact with acid, wash immediately under running water using soap to alkalize it, or apply some bicarbonate of soda after washing with water.) A stronger solution may be used to hasten the action. Heating the bath also makes it work more quickly, and agitating the bath or moving the piece also helps. Always handle pieces in acid with copper tongs to avoid contamination.

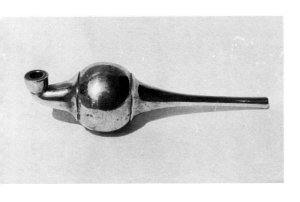
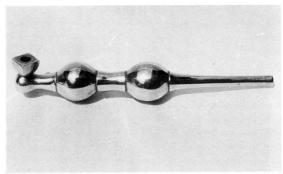
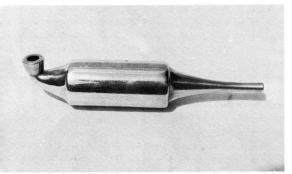
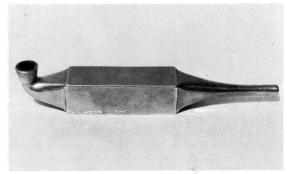
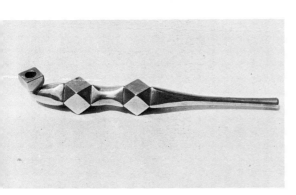
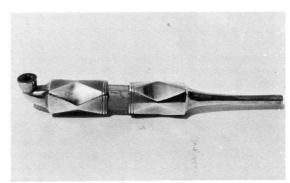
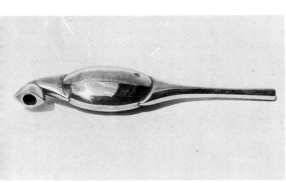
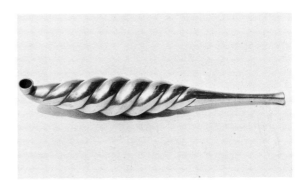

OPPOSITE: Contemporary gold bracelet and matching necklace, made in West Bengal, India. The faceted "stones" are the gold itself cut in facets with small, sharp chisels and not otherwise finished, so that they catch the light. *Photo by Oppi.*

ABOVE: Eight brass smoking pipes, designed by the late Kanjiro Kawai of Kyoto, Japan, a great craftsman and humanitarian. They were executed by craftsmen in Yasugi, near Matsué, Japan. The pipes are made in units, which are joined by soldering and finished by filing and polishing. *Photos by Hiroshi Kawai.*

METAL TECHNIQUES THAT DO NOT REQUIRE SOLDERING   123

Silver necklace utilizing ball and socket joints, designed and executed by Ronald Hayes Pearson. The necklace was formed mainly by filing from solid stock metal. *American Craftsmen's Council.*

PICKLE CONTAINERS

Pickling solution can be placed in a thick copper pickle pan when cleaning small work. The pickle solution after use in a copper pickle pan should be returned to a storage container, and the pan rinsed with water. For larger work, a Pyrex glass beaker or pan can be used. If provided with a cover, the acid bath may be stored in the same glass container. For even larger work, a stoneware ceramic crock with a cover can be used, and the acid stored in the same container. Large stainless steel vats are also used for pickling baths. All these containers can be heated to warm the pickle bath. Containers used for storage should be clearly marked as to their contents.

For production work, electric pickling containers are available holding 13 ounces or 1½ quarts of solution. They have a removable stainless-steel colander or sieve, with a handle, into which work is placed, and are provided with a safety pilot light, an on-off switch, and

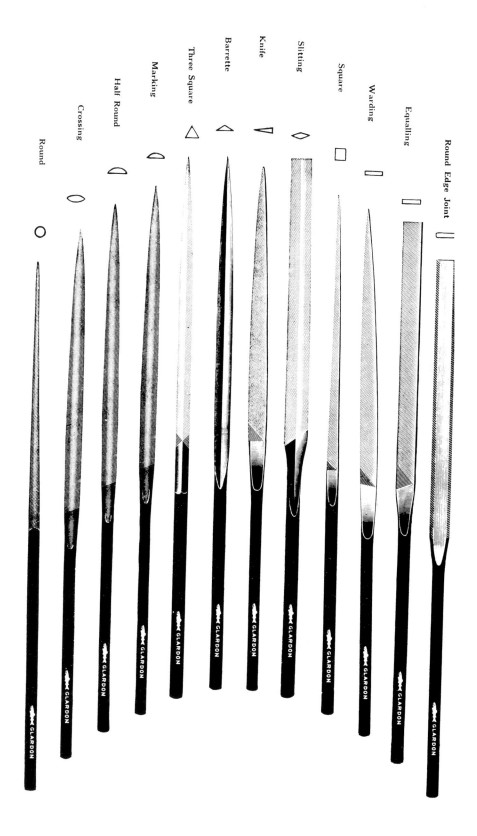

Round

Crossing

Half Round

Marking

Three Square

Barrette

Knife

Slitting

Square

Warding

Equalling

Round Edge Joint

A set of needle files

operate on AC-DC, 110 volts, 30 watts. They can be used for sulphuric acid or Sparex solutions.

Polyethylene plastic containers with covers, holding two gallons, can be used for pickling bath storage as the plastic is inert and does not react to acids.

Sparex No. 2, a dry commercial preparation available in one-pound, 2½-pound, and larger quantities, is an acid substitute which is mixed with water according to directions supplied. It is slower than sulphuric acid and less corrosive, but is more efficient when heated.

When pickling, all iron binding wire should be removed from the article before placing it in the bath or a copper flashing will be deposited on the metal surface and is difficult to remove. The article should be handled with copper tongs when placing it into and removing it from the bath. After pickling, the article should be washed under running cold water.

The pickling bath can be stored and reused for some time, but after prolonged use, its efficiency is reduced. This occurs because large amounts of metal have become deposited in the solution, usually indicated by its dark green color and the solution saturated. It should then be discarded and a fresh solution made. When discarding pickle, as when disposing of all acid solutions, allow quantities of running water to accompany the solution down the drain, and pour it away slowly to allow maximum dissolution in order to avoid damage to metal drains.

Stripping

Stripping is an electrochemical method of cleaning and brightening platinum, gold, silver, and copper articles after pickling and before polishing. This step is commonly practiced by production jewelers.

Stripping is the opposite of plating as the metal is *removed* rather than deposited as in plating (see pages 383–91). The article is placed in the solution attached to a copper wire and the source of current at the *positive* or *anode* bar, while the stainless steel container in which the electrolyte is placed becomes the *negative* or cathode by attaching a wire with a clip to it. When the current is applied, the metal which is removed dissolves into the electrolyte, and if separate containers are maintained for each metal used, they can ulti-

mately be collected and reclaimed as they accumulate at the bottom of the solution.

Stripping leaves the metal bright and makes finishing simpler. A used solution is more efficient than a new one.

STRIPPING SOLUTION

¼ pound sodium cyanide
1 teaspoon sodium carbonate
added to 1 gallon of boiling water

Additional water and small amounts of cyanide are added when replenishing is necessary. *Remember that these chemicals are highly poisonous and should be handled with care.* Breathing their fumes should be avoided, and stripping should be done in the presence of an exhaust fan. Commercially prepared stripping solutions are available.

Place the stainless steel container on an electric hotplate and bring it to a boil. The suggested voltage is 6 to 12 volts. Allow the piece to remain for a few seconds and remove it for observation. When it has reached the desired condition, rinse thoroughly with running water, touching the surface as little as possible. Dry in corn cob husk or sawdust and polish.

Etching

Etching metals with acids for decorative effect did not occur in Europe till the fifteenth century, when it was done extensively in the decoration of armor and weapons.

Basically, etching is a method of creating a design on metal by covering parts of the metal which are to be *protected* from the action of the acid with an *acid-resisting material,* while the exposed parts of the metal are eaten away or corroded by the action of the acid (or *mordant,* as the acid is also called). There are two main types of etching: *relief* and *intaglio.* In relief etching, the design is applied to the metal with the resist material; after etching, it appears in *relief,* or is positive, and the background is below the surface, having been eaten away. In intaglio etching, the entire metal surface is covered with the resist, and the design is scratched through the resist with tools varying in thickness from a fine needle point to a broader line. After etching, the *line* which was exposed metal appears *sunken,* or is negative. Combinations of the two methods are of course possible.

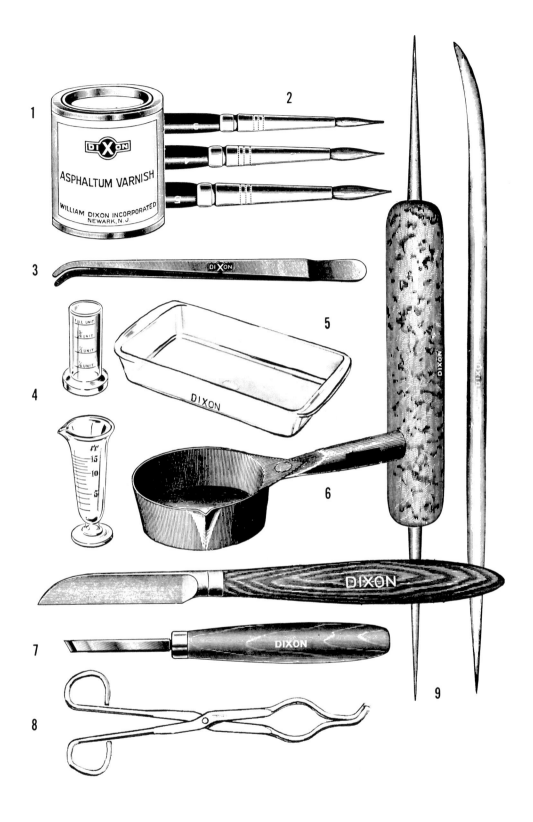

Etching and pickling tools and equipment: 1. Asphaltum varnish 2. Brushes to apply asphaltum 3. Copper pickle tongs 4. Graduated glass measuring containers 5. Pyrex glass tray for etching fluids 6. Copper pickle pan 7. Scrapers 8. Copper forceps for removing articles from the pickle bath 9. Etching needles

METAL TECHNIQUES THAT DO NOT REQUIRE SOLDERING   127

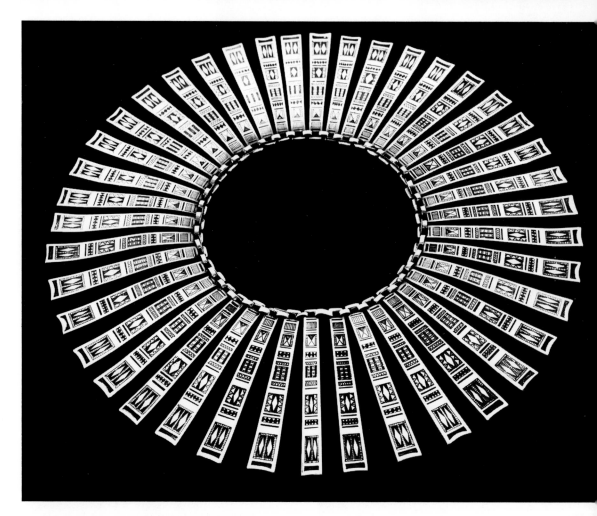

Sterling silver necklace utilizing 18-gauge metal, by
Mary Ann Scherr. Length: 16½ inches; each unit:
3½ inches by ½ inch. The intaglio pattern was
created with an etching solution of half nitric acid
and half water and was then oxidized.
BELOW: Etched bronze necklace with intaglio design,
by Clifford Herrold. *Photo by Elden.*

ACID RESISTS OR COVERING AGENTS

Before applying any acid resist the metal
surface must be cleaned thoroughly; dirt, especially grease, might in itself act as a resist.
Cleaning can normally be accomplished by using a detergent and hot water or with a soft
cloth and alcohol. If more drastic measures are
necessary, a torch flame passed over the surface will generally burn off or volatilize
greases. The metal can then be pickled and
washed. A paste made of whiting or fine pumice and water can also be rubbed over the
surface with a soft cloth and washed off under
running water.

In preparation for etching, the edges and
back of the metal to be etched must first be
protected with a resist. This resist may be the
same as the one used to create the design, or
a different one. As a resist, *beeswax* or paraffin is simple to prepare and apply, and it sets
quickly, allowing the work to proceed almost
immediately. Heat the beeswax in a pan to
melt it, but do not overheat, as it will smoke,

Contemporary relief-etched steel-bladed hunting knives, made by Aragon, Oaxaca, Mexico. *Photo by Oppi.*

German steel and iron coffer with relief-etched and engraved design representing "Charity and Temperance." Late sixteenth century. Height: 10⅝ inches; length: 18⅜ inches; width: 11¼ inches. *Metropolitan Museum of Art, New York. Rogers Fund, 1923.*

arrive at its flash point, and burn. Apply the wax with an old brush to the *warmed* metal. Warming allows the wax to be applied evenly. The design itself can be created with the wax for relief etching in which the background is etched and the design is in relief. For intaglio etching, the entire piece can be warmed and submerged in melted wax, and then withdrawn to allow the wax to cool. An even coating of wax will result. The surface can then be smoked with a candle to blacken it with a coating of carbon, which makes the design scratched into the wax more visible. The scratched areas of unprotected metal will then be etched, and the design appears in intaglio.

After etching, the wax can be melted off with hot water, or the metal can be heated and the wax wiped away with a cloth. Any remains of wax can be eliminated with a paste made of whiting and ammonia which is rubbed on the metal with a cloth, or carbon tetrachloride or acetone may be used.

The traditional resist for etching is *asphaltum*. Supply houses offer ready-made prepara-.tions called asphaltum varnish. It is quite black and can be easily applied with a brush and, if necessary, thinned with turpentine, its solvent. When applied, it should not "skip" over the metal but should flow easily from the brush.

Asphaltum must be allowed to dry thoroughly, perhaps up to twelve hours, depending on weather conditions; the drying can be hastened by exposure to an infrared heating lamp. Take care not to place the lamp too close to the metal: the metal will overheat, causing the asphaltum to run or buckle and the design to be destroyed. If, after drying, light brown areas appear, the asphaltum there is too thin, and there is a risk of the acid's lifting off these areas or causing undercutting. It is necessary to reapply asphaltum to these places and allow more drying. Whole sheets of metal can be covered with asphaltum varnish and allowed to dry, followed by scratching the design into the metal. After etching, the asphaltum can be removed with turpentine and a soft cloth.

Another traditional resist, called *hard ground,* used by graphic artists, can be made according to the following recipes:

#1 Asphaltum   2 parts
      Yellow Beeswax   2 parts
      Burgundy Pitch   1 part

#2 Asphaltum   1 part
      Yellow Beeswax   1 part
      Powdered white rosin   ½ part

(Burgundy pitch is a resin obtained from the Norway spruce. Rosin is the brittle material remaining after the distillation of volatile oil of turpentine prepared from extractions from pine or fir trees.) Either recipe can be used. Combine the ingredients in a double boiler under low heat. Use benzine as a thinner if necessary, *but add it when the boiler is away from the heat.* The preparation can be applied with a brush, rolled on the flat metal surface with a brayer, or daubed on after it has been enclosed in a small bag made of several layers of a closely woven cotton cloth, called a *dauber.* In this last case, the metal must be heated so that the hard ground seeps through the dauber as it touches the hot metal and becomes deposited evenly over the surface. The heating can be accomplished by placing the metal on a hotplate kept as its lowest heat while the metal is being coated. The advantage of the hard ground resist is that it allows the development of a design with very fine lines, and when allowed to dry properly it offers tough resistance to the acid. The protecting edge and backing wax would be applied *after* the hard ground is finished.

"Stopout" lacquers or varnishes are available as a resist. They dry very quickly and must be handled carefully, as they are subject to peeling or chipping in stronger acid etching solutions.

Resists can be used in a variety of ways. They can be spattered, stippled, dripped, or applied in other ways for interesting textural effects, in whatever manner suits the material and the method of application.

Etching can be combined with other methods of decoration. Whole metal surfaces can be prepared with an etched pattern and then used for engraving and metal inlay, or cut out, and soldered as is. Any method that preserves the character of the etched surface and then enriches it further is suitable in this combination.

ETCHING FLUIDS OR ACID SOLUTIONS

Many solutions are used to etch metals, most of them containing one or more acids, and some no acid. When preparing etchants containing acid, it is *extremely important* to remember that the ACID MUST BE POURED INTO THE WATER, and NEVER the opposite; the latter would cause a dangerous spattering and fuming, and possible injury to the user. Antidotes for acid should always be nearby when it is in use. Solutions should be carefully measured in a clearly marked beaker or measuring pitcher, preferably of glass. Etching should be done in a well-ventilated room, preferably in the presence of an exhaust fan. Containers for stored acids should be plainly marked as to contents, and kept in a safe place which is cool and dry. Acid burns the skin. Should any acid come in contact with the skin, wash immediately under running water, and neutralize with soap or bicarbonate of soda.

CONTAINERS FOR ACID IN USE

The container used for acid etchants *should be nonporous.* Pyrex glass trays and bowls are suitable for smaller pieces; for large work, a deep stoneware ceramic crock (whose composition is vitrified and therefore almost non-absorbent) is suitable. Pyrex glass has the advantage of being heat resistant, and this is important if it should be necessary to heat the solution to hasten the acid action.

ETCHING PROCEDURE

All edges and surfaces that must be protected from the acid should be covered with a resist. The work to be etched is immersed in the solution. Flat metal pieces are immersed *slowly* to avoid splashing the acid and should be covered to a depth of at least one-half inch. To prevent the hand from coming in contact with the etchant, the piece can be inserted with a soft string looped under the metal or with a *wood* or *bamboo tongs. Copper tongs* are also usable for most metals, but *iron* and *steel tongs should be avoided,* as they contaminate the solution and make it necessary to discard the preparation. (Iron tongs cause the surface of sterling to become flash-plated with a copper deposit that is difficult to remove.) Small articles can be handled with rubber gloves, which should be thoroughly washed after contact with the acid. Some objects to be etched, such as shallow bowls, can be etched by pouring the acid into the objects themselves.

The speed of the etching action may be hastened by agitating the acid or moving the article. While the etching progresses, a sludge forms on the surface of the metal. The action will be quicker if this sludge is removed by swabbing the metal surface with a feather, or a stick wrapped in a cloth. If the sludge is allowed to remain, it will retard the acid's action.

The speed of the etch depends mainly on the strength of the acid solution, but too strong a solution should be avoided, as the accelerated action may cause the resist on the metal to be lifted away or altered, and the formerly protected areas will then be attacked. Weaker solutions have a tendency to etch straight down, while stronger ones may have an undercutting action. The rate at which the bubbles of gas form where the acid is attacking the metal is usually an indication of the strength of the solution.

It is advisable to remove the metal from the acid during the etching process from time to time to test the depth of the etch and to inspect the condition of the resist. The depth of the etch can be judged by observing the depression formed where the resist ends and the metal begins, or by probing with a steel-pointed pin. Should it be necessary to repair the resist, wash the metal thoroughly in running water, dry it, and then apply the same resist or a more quickly setting one such as beeswax, or stopout varnish. Stopout varnish can also be used to halt the acid's action on one part of the design, while the remaining parts are allowed to be eaten to a greater depth.

ACID ETCHING SOLUTIONS
FOR PARTICULAR METALS

All etching and acid solutions should be used under conditions of good ventilation.

Gold

Nitric Acid	4 parts
Hydrochloric Acid	8 parts
Perchloride of Iron	1 part
Water	40–50 parts

Aqua regia or "royal water" is so called as it is used to dissolve gold and platinum. These are dissolved by the action of the chlorine liberated. These metals are insoluble in either of the component acids alone. Aqua regia, highly corrosive and fuming, is made as follows:

Nitric Acid	1 part
Hydrochloric Acid	3 parts

It can be used diluted with water to half strength, but the action is slower. Sulphuric acid may be used in place of hydrochloric acid. Add one acid to the other slowly and with caution, as the combination generates heat. *Reminder: always add acid to water.*

Silver

Nitric Acid	1 part
Water	3–4 parts

Copper, Brass

Nitric Acid	1 part
Water	2 parts

Iron and Steel
(ordinary etch)

Hydrochloric Acid	2 parts
Water	1 part

Iron and Steel
(light etch)

Nitric Acid	1 part
Water	4–8 parts

Copper, Brass, Steel
(slow etch, even, no odor)

Potassium Bichromate	15 parts
Sulphuric Acid	20 parts
Water	80 parts

Zinc #1

Sulphuric Acid	1 part
Water	16 parts

Zinc #2

Nitric Acid	1 part
Water	8 parts

Pewter, Tin, and Lead

Nitric Acid	1 part
Water	4 parts

Aluminum

Hydrochloric Acid	Diluted highly

Fused silver pendant by Katia Kamesar, San Francisco, 1¼ inches in diameter. *Photo by Ellen Ross Gibson.*

Etching solutions are generally much stronger than pickling solutions, as their functions are different. Etching solutions are meant to eat deeply into the metal, while pickling solutions are meant to clean the metal surface, mainly by dissolving oxides formed by heating processes.

Acids can also be used to produce a final appearance on the metal surface of an article, such as the solutions used for a *bright dip* or a *matte dip*.

BRIGHT DIP

Concentrated Nitric Acid
  (HNO_3, sp gr 1.40) 25% by volume
Concentrated Sulphuric Acid
  (H_2SO_4, sp gr 1.83) 60% by volume
Concentrated Hydrochloric Acid
  (HCl, sp gr 1.16) 2% by volume
Water   Balance

Use at room temperature. Immerse the metal and rinse immediately under running water. Hydrochloric acid increases luster, but an excess causes spotty surfaces. The metal should be pickled clean before dipping.

MATTE DIP

Used after the bright dip has been rinsed and dried.

Concentrated Nitric Acid
  (HNO_3, sp gr 1.40) 65% by volume
Concentrated Sulphuric Acid
  (H_2SO_4, sp gr 1.83) 35% by volume
Zinc Sulphate
  ($ZnSO_4$ Commercial) 1 pound per gallon
                              of solution

Dip, rinse, and dry. Agitate occasionally.

The use of a matte dip on jewelry is sometimes known as "blooming," an innovation of the Victorian era, especially in the creation of gold jewelry.

Parts of an object can be left bright by protecting them with a resist while the remaining exposed parts are made matte. The resist is then removed.

When an acid solution is worn out, it should be replaced. Old solutions saturated with dissolved metal will cause discoloration, as dissolved metal is redeposited on the clean metal.

When discarding old acid solutions by pouring them down a drain, allow a quantity of running water to dilute them and flush away the acid to avoid harming drain pipes.

Metal Fusing

A form of joining metal that actually does not require solder, but in effect joins metal to metal, is called *fusing*. Pellets, wires, and scrap or shaped metal forms can be joined to each other with heat. They are first coated with flux to prevent oxidation, and placed in contact with each other. Heat is applied equally on all parts to be fused, till the *surface* of the metal is actually in a molten state, when the molecules interpenetrate on contacting parts, and the metals become fused to each other. The moment when this occurs requires judgment, as if the metal is overheated it will melt and collapse. The heat must be withdrawn at the proper moment and this requires some experience. Fusing wire is more difficult, as the metal is more exposed and there is more risk of melting and collapse. The result when successful is unique in appearance.

Fused 14-karat gold necklace, by Ed Wiener, New York, 5½ inches in diameter, set with diamonds of ⅓ carat to 2 point, totaling 1.7 carat aggregate. *Photo by Ferdinand Boesch.*

Decorative Techniques Employing Contrasting Metals

The attractive contrast in color and texture of metals has been the basis for the development of many decorative metal techniques that have developed over the centuries. Techniques that employ overlaid or appliquéd metals (swami work), inlaid metals (damascene work), and metals of differing colors joined by soldering (married metals, mokume), fusion (niello), and, most recently, braze welding, have each produced distinctive results.

Metal Encrustation or Appliqué

There are two main methods of metal appliqué. One requires the soldering of cut-out or shaped units onto a base metal. The second method consists of joining units to a base by a form of inlay without solder. The latter will be described here in a method practiced in India today.

Tanjore Swami Work

A form of encrustation or appliqué known as *swami* work is practiced today in the South Indian city of Tanjore, where a group of metalworkers produce a variety of objects decorated in this manner. It is also known locally as *nagas* or embossed work.

Generally, this technique consists of applying embossed or repousséd medallions and flat-cut shapes on a metal background. The work is usually done on a brass shape such as a bowl, box, or plate, and the applied ornaments are made of silver and copper. This work displays a purely Hindu character, both because of the ornate style of design, full of small detail, and because the subjects of the medallions are mainly religious in nature, often depicting Hindu deities and sacred animals. Almost the entire background metal is covered in a carefully arranged pattern, always geometrically placed, of half domes, stamped pieces, engraved and stamped patterns, inlaid wire, and repoussé medallions. One piece is almost a dictionary of decorative metal techniques. In India there is often a division of work among craftsmen, who specialize in various stages, so that one piece is often a composite of the skills of several craftsmen. This is the case with swami work. The object to be decorated is made by one set of craftsmen, and another group decorates it.

PROCEDURE FOR SWAMI WORK

We will follow the process of decorating a tray. The metal surface to be decorated is first cleaned and polished. The polished finish can be retained, as there is no soldering process involved and it is not, therefore, subjected to heat, which would discolor it. The surface is then coated with a mixture of a paste of lime and water, and allowed to dry. The mixture is applied to allow the design to be marked on the surface and easily seen. When it is dry, a scriber and rule are used to mark the lines and divisions indicating the placement of the units to be applied. The lime is then washed away, and the enscribed lines remain.

Half domes are prepared in the sizes and numbers needed with a dapping punch and block. Wire is drawn to the desired cross section or is purchased already made. Both round and square wire can be used. We now will describe how the domes, the wires, and decorative medallions are inlaid in the tray.

A craftsman of Tanjore, India, securing an encrusted silver ornamental medallion on a brass plate in the "nagas" or "swami" process of metal decoration. *Photo by Oppi.*

POSITIVE AND NEGATIVE MOLD STAMPING

The procedure for the preparation of the *medallion*s of deities, bird, animal, and flower motifs is as follows. The metal used is thin, either 24-gauge silver or copper and must be annealed first for maximum softness. Lighter-gauge foils are also usable, but must be handled carefully. The metal is placed between a matching positive and negative lead alloy mold which is shaped to impart the *general shape* of the medallion, but not in great detail. With the thin metal sandwiched between the two parts of the mold, a cloth folded several times into a pad is laid across the top of the upper

mold. A wood mallet is then struck against the mold pad, but not too vigorously, as the soft mold metal might become deformed or even break. Since the metal sheet is thin and the metal soft, it does not require much pressure to form an impression.

When both parts of the mold seem to be as close together as they can get, they are separated and the metal with the impression is removed. The main depressions on the back surface of the sheet are filled with pitch, which is allowed to set. The unit is then fixed on a pitch board or bowl and is ready for the details, which are then added. These are worked out with repoussé, chasing, and modeling tools. Lines for small details are then engraved.

Another feature characteristic of swami medallions is the use of pierced areas between the figures and the outer frame which encloses

the medallion shape. The openings are easily made with small, sharp-pointed chisels while the metal is still mounted on the pitch. The openings are not finished in any way, but are left as the chisels make them, with the edges projecting inward.

Once all the units have been applied, those in high relief must be permanently filled with a supporting material to prevent their becoming dented or misshapen. They are taken from the pitch block and the chasing pitch is removed. They are then filled with a harder pitch or a composition made for this purpose. In India, the following preparation is used: 3 parts dry fish or animal glue, ¾ part powdered brick dust, 1¼ parts gingeli oil (squeegee oil can be substituted). These constituents are mixed in a pot over heat till they are liquid, when they are poured into the depressions in the back of the medallions and allowed to harden.

INLAYING OR ENCRUSTING THE MEDALLIONS

We will take a medallion as an example for the inlay technique, which is the same for all pieces, whether raised or flat. To give the medallion more thickness and rigidity, the entire edge is bent back uniformly for a fraction of an inch, and then hammered all around on a steel block to thicken the edge and flatten it into one plane. Each individual unit is then held in position on the tray, and the outline is scratched sharply around it with a scriber. (This must be done with each individual piece to be mounted, as the pieces inevitably will vary in shape.) The enscribed line is then followed with a small, sharp, beveled chisel and hammer. The tool is always held on the *inside* of the line shape, and slanted so as to cut away from the center of the shape. The groove that is made is actually an undercut "frame" into which the medallion will later fit.

Brass plate illustrating *Krishna Fluting*, water jug depicting Siva Nataraj and Ganesh, and bowl showing Sawaswati. "Nagas" or "swami" work, done in Tanjore, India, consists of encrustations of contrasting metals, usually copper and silver on a brass article. *Government of India Trade Center, New York.*

The tray is then placed on a flat steel surface. (If the article is a bowl being decorated from the outside with appliqués, it is placed on a curved stake that will accommodate the particular curvature.) The medallion is placed in position, and hammered into place with the rounded or peen end of a small chasing hammer. The undercut raised burr is hammered down first at the cardinal points to secure the medallion in place, and then the entire undercut "frame" is hammered. Thus the appliqué is held in place permanently, without solder. The practice is then to insure a good joint further by going around the outer edge of the medallion with a small beading punch and hammer. A border both decorative and functional is thus formed. Half domes are placed in the same way, without the beaded borders.

The method of inlaying *lines* with *wire* is the same as that employed on conventional damascene work. Following the enscribed line, a small, sharp chisel is used to raise two cuts along the entire line length, slanted in opposite directions, forming a single groove with two parallel undercuts the width of the wire apart into which the wire is hammered. In other words, two burrs are raised, and the wire placed between the burrs, then wire and burrs are hammered down. The wire is held in place by the burrs which, by being hammered down, are folded over onto it. It is sometimes worthwhile using a pointed chisel or graver to raise a burr about every half inch between the engraved lines (a procedure called *plinking*). When the metal is forced into the groove, the plinked burr provides an additional grip on the wire.

In traditional swami work, inlaid lines of wire are not left plain, but are patterned after they are set into the groove. This is done with stamping or chasing tools, and the designs are placed regularly over the entire surface of

Norwegian (Bergen) silver-gilt tankard decorated with applied coins, 1760. *Museum of Fine Arts, Boston.*

the line. Between medallions and lines of inlaid wire, small, shaped inserts are often added, and treated in the same way. If the piece inlaid is of any appreciable thickness, beveling the edge will help to hold it in place when hammered in.

After all the inlaid units and designs have been placed, the entire article is cleaned in diluted sulphuric acid and water, and scrubbed with a bristle hand brush charged with brick dust and tamarind paste. A final rubbing with a fine wire hand brush and soap leaves the surface with a pleasant, soft finish.

Bidri Work

Bidri work is a kind of decorative metalwork that originated in India. It is named for the town of Bidar, near Hyderabad City in the state of Andhra Pradesh. Today there are about a hundred workers practicing this craft in Bidar, and smaller groups in nearby localities. Bidri is the inlaying of pure silver, in wire and sheet form, into cast objects of a nonferrous zinc alloy. The process consists of first casting the object and then decorating it. The silver inlay is placed in grooves flush with the surface.

The elegance and richness of objects in bidri, in which the whiteness of the silver inlay con-

trasts strongly with the blackened alloy background, satisfied the taste of the rulers of India and their courts. Endless numbers of water pitchers, goblets, spice and cosmetic boxes, candelabra, couch legs, and water pipe bases (*hukkas*) were made. The best of these are intricately ornamented with Persian floral and geometrical motifs. Today, items better suited to contemporary needs such as vases, covered boxes, and ashtrays are produced in exactly the same manner, with extremely simple tools and equipment, as objects produced a few hundred years ago.

The process as described here is modified slightly from that practiced in India, to conform to Western working conditions.

CASTING THE BIDRI BASE

Zinc, the basic metal in the bidri alloy, was discovered in India, where it was first reduced from calamine. To create the bidri alloy (whose composition is said in India to be secret), the following formula is used:

Zinc	12,360 grains
Copper	460 grains
Lead	414 grains

(One pound [tr.] equals 5760 grains)

The metals are combined in crucibles which should first be coated inside with a refractory clay to act as a buffer between the crucible and the molten metal. The greater part of the zinc is placed in the larger of two crucibles, and the lead, copper, and a small amount of zinc are placed in a smaller crucible, which is covered with a lid punctured to allow the escape of gases. Both crucibles are placed in a previously prepared pit in the earth and packed around with hot charcoal embers. Fresh charcoal is added to cover the crucibles and the embers brought to white heat with a bellows. (A melting furnace could also be used.) When the metals in both crucibles are melted, they are combined, the contents of the smaller crucible being added to the larger. To prevent calcination, a mixture of rosin and beeswax is then thrown into the crucible, and after further heating to a temperature of about 725° F, the molten metal is poured into the mold.

OPPOSITE: The function of the bidri bowl decorated with silver has dictated its form. It is meant to be used for ritual hand washing in conjunction with the bidri water pitcher shown. While water is poured over the hands from the pitcher, waste is caught in the wide flange of this bowl and filtered through the pierced openings in the removable lid. *Photo by Oppi.*

Old water pitcher decorated by the bidri process with silver. Made in Bidar, Hyderabad, India, the town in which bidri work originated. The parts of the pitcher—lid, neck, body, base, handle, and spout—were all cast separately and then joined by soldering before being decorated. *Photo by Oppi.*

East Tibetan (Chamdo) iron water ewer with gilded brass spout and handle, nineteenth century. Encrusted with silver, brass, and copper. *Victoria and Albert Museum, London.*

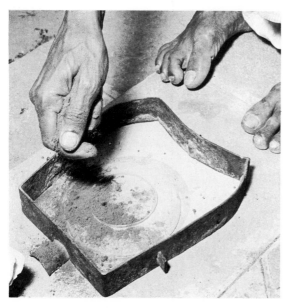

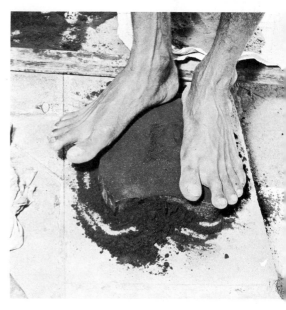

1. The bidri, zinc-alloyed object to be decorated must first be made by casting. The two-part sand mold shown here is similar to such molds used in many parts of the world. The bottom section, or drag, of the mold is placed upside down on a flat board. The pattern, in this case a finished bidri plate, is placed upside down on the board, toward the part of the mold flask that has the sprue opening. Prepared sand is riddled over the pattern until the drag is filled.

2. Once the drag is filled with sand, it is pressed to force the sand compactly against the pattern. In India, craftsmen use their feet for many functions, such as this one. In the West, the sand might be compressed by hammering it with a broad-faced mallet.

5. The pattern is lifted away from the sand, which is then dusted with parting powder.

6. The pattern is replaced in the drag and dusted with parting powder. The upper part of the mold, called the cope, is placed on top of the drag. The sprue is seen, as well as the projecting flange that keys the two parts of the mold together.

3. The excess sand in the drag is screed off with a straight edge; in this case, a board is used. The same board is placed on top of the drag, which is thereby sandwiched between two boards. Grasping both boards, the drag is turned over.

4. The drag is now in the parting-line-up position. The pattern is tapped lightly with a small piece of metal to free it from the sand.

BIDRI CASTING AND DECORATION.

This series of photos, taken by the author in Hyderabad, Andhra Pradesh, India, shows the process of casting and decorating a bidri plate with silver.

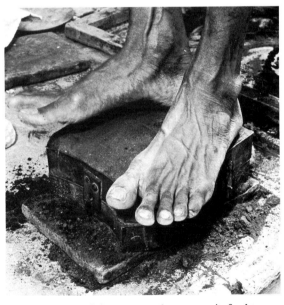

7. Additional sand is riddled into the cope until it is filled.

8. Again the sand is compressed to press it firmly against the pattern.

DECORATIVE TECHNIQUES EMPLOYING CONTRASTING METALS   141

9. The cope is scraped level and a molding board placed on top of it. The two parts of the mold are lifted away from each other.

10. The pattern is tapped gently with a lightweight hammer to dislodge it.

13. The temperature of the fire is brought up quickly with the help of a hand-operated blower.

14. The mold is placed with the sprue up and at an angle that will allow the easy escape of gases during the pour. Once the metal is judged ready for pouring, the crucible is grasped with a crucible tongs and the molten bidri alloy is poured into the mold through the previously made opening to the mold cavity by way of the sprue opening.

BIDRI SAND CASTING

The casting procedure is similar to methods employed elsewhere. The sand mold is prepared with the aid of a sample form or model which has a wall thickness of about $\frac{3}{16}$ of an inch. In the West, prepared casting sand is available from suppliers. In India, a fine-grained sand that has been filtered through a cloth is mixed with some vegetable oil to help give it contiguity and to produce a sharp mold impression. The preparation of the sand-casting mold is the same as described in the sand-casting section, and is illustrated here. Complex forms are

11. The two parts of the mold are seen here with the pattern removed. The cope is dusted with parting compound, and both cope and drag are reassembled and tied together with a molding board on each side.

12. The comparatively low-melting bidri alloy is heated in a crucible placed in a hole dug in the earth that is filled with a well-established charcoal fire. The metal is dusted with flux from time to time.

15. After allowing the metal to solidify and cool, the two parts of the mold are separated.

16. The bidri casting can then be grasped with a tongs, removed from the mold, and, after a further short cooling interval, doused with cold water. The casting can then be handled and finished.

made by dividing a casting into several units, which can then be joined to each other with soft solder made with an alloy of lead, tin, and zinc. (For further discussion of sand casting, see page 325.)

Once the metal is poured and sufficient time allowed for it to solidify in the mold, it is re-

moved and allowed to cool till it can be touched. As the mold material is sand, it can be used only once. The runner and sprues (see page 321 for definitions) are removed with a hacksaw. On simple forms there is often only one runner. The line indicating the place where the two parts of the mold separate,

17. The sprue is removed with a hacksaw. The fins that might form at the parting line can be filed away with a coarse file.

18. In bidri work, the inlay is of *fine* silver. A piece of silver sheet is flattened here in preparation.

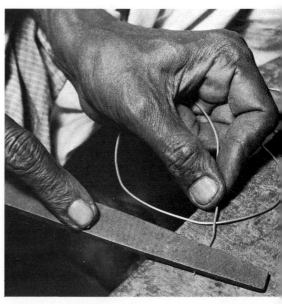

21. A small, sharp chisel is then used to cut out the shape in the silver.

22. Where it is necessary to inlay lines of wire in the design, wire of appropriate thickness or gauge is needed. If the diameter or gauge of the wire has to be reduced, the wire must be pulled through a drawplate. In preparation for this process, the end of the wire is being reduced with a file in order to facilitate its initial passing through the drawplate hole.

called the parting line, can be removed with a file or ground off with an abrasive wheel.

As most of the forms are circular, they can be finished further by mounting them on a lathe using a wood chuck and a shellac binder to hold the form to the chuck. The shape can be trued with lathe tools. The metal is

a relatively soft alloy, and does not need much pressure from the tool. A final sanding while on the lathe, and the bidri cast piece is ready for decoration. It is not absolutely necessary to finish the casting on a lathe, especially if the casting is done carefully and there is little finishing to be done.

19. Prior to inlaying the silver, the design must be traced on the form being decorated and then carefully cut out with small chisels. The outline is undercut to be sure that the inlay will remain in the base.

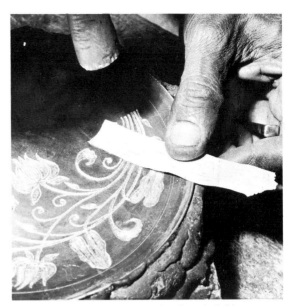

20. Before inlaying the silver, the sheet is held over the place where it is to be inserted. A light wood mallet is used to form on the silver an impression of the shape to be inlaid.

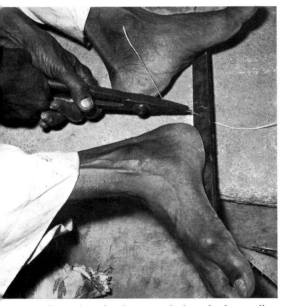

23. Once the wire has passed through the smallest possible opening, it is grasped with a drawplate tongs and pulled through the plate openings in diminishing order until it reaches the required dimension. Instead of holding the plate with the feet, as shown here, Western craftsmen would secure the drawplate in a bench vise before beginning this procedure.

24. The annealed wire can then be hammered into place with a flat hammer that forces the soft wire into the undercut grooves prepared to receive it.

BIDRI INLAY PROCESS

To prepare the form to receive the design, it is rubbed with a solution of blue vitriol (super sulphate of copper) and water. The alloy turns black, and the design can be scratched into the surface with a sharp-pointed steel tool. The bright line of the alloy is easily visible through the dye. The chemical is water soluble and can be readily removed by washing the object with water when it is no longer needed. The pattern can be laid out with the aid of compass and calipers if necessary.

The decorating metal is *fine silver,* in wire

25. After the silver inlay is completed, the ingredients for coloring the bidri alloy (see text) are prepared dry and crushed to combine them more easily.

26. With the addition of a small amount of water, the coloring ingredients are combined into a paste form.

29. A small cloth impregnated with the coloring paste is drawn across the heated plate to apply it evenly. The chemical composition of the paste acts on the bidri alloy, turning it a deep, permanent black color. Only the alloy is affected by the chemicals; the silver remains white.

30. To make the action of the coloring paste more effective, the plate is held over the hot charcoal. This applied heat will deepen the color. Should the bidri not take on an even coloring, the paste mixture can be reapplied and the article heated again. This can be repeated until the desired color is reached. The same procedure can be followed to restore color to an old or worn bidri piece.

and thin sheet form (approximately 24 gauge). With a sharp chisel and hammer, the lines and areas of the design are engraved into the rather soft bidri. Lines to receive silver wire should be *undercut* so that they will hold the inlay later when hammered in place. Small plates of metal can also be applied, according to the design requirement, by undercutting the border shape into which they will be inlaid, and removing with a chisel a thickness of metal equal to the thickness of the plate to be inserted, so that the resulting surface is *flush*.

27. The plate, with the silver inlay completed, is cleaned by scouring the surface with emery cloth to prepare it for coloring.

28. To hasten the action of the coloring paste, the plate is heated over charcoal embers that are fanned to increase the temperature.

31. After the desired color is established, the paste is washed away with cold water.

When plates are used, it is a good practice to roughen slightly the surface of the metal that is to receive the plate. The roughened surface provides a "key" for the metal to grip. The silver inlays are hammered lightly into the prepared grooves and spaces that hold them in place. The pieces and wire adhere without any need for other joining material. The completed surface can be finished by leveling it with a fine carborundum stick and rubbing with charcoal powder.

COLORING THE BIDRI ALLOY

In bidriware, the whole background, which is the zinc alloy, is permanently blackened to produce the handsome contrast between the silver inlay and the ground metal. This is the basis of the appeal of the technique. To produce the permanent color change, the finished surface must be covered with a chemical composition. The formula used is as follows:

Ammonium Chloride	1 part
Unrefined Potassium Nitrate	¼ part
Sodium Chloride (Table salt)	¼ part
Enough clay or mud to make a paste	

The cleaned metal surface is heated slightly over a charcoal bed, and the mixture is then smeared with a cloth over the entire surface.

DECORATIVE TECHNIQUES EMPLOYING CONTRASTING METALS   147

32. To create a deeper black and to preserve the color, a small amount of sweet oil is rubbed into the surface.

33. The silver is polished with a cloth dipped in oil mixed with a small amount of charcoal powder.

Contemporary cigarette box in bidri, decorated with gold and silver. Made in Hyderabad City, Andhra Pradesh, India. Today, the traditional bidri workers are making articles that are suited to contemporary needs. *Photo by Oppi.*

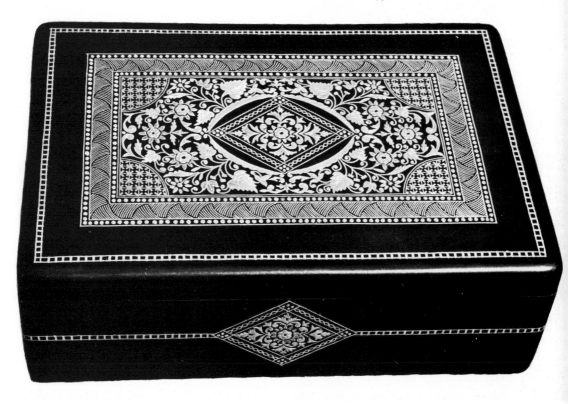

34. Any final, last-minute touches needed for completion of the bidri are then made. The lotus flower and plant motif are a frequent subject for decoration in India.

The zinc alloy will turn black almost immediately, but the silver will not be affected. Should the metal not be as black as desired after the paste has been washed off with water, the piece can be immediately heated again, and the process repeated. This will usually produce the desired depth of color.

After washing and drying, the surface is finished by finger-rubbing it completely with a little rape seed oil (or other mild oil) mixed with powdered charcoal. As the charcoal in this mixture is slightly abrasive, it polishes the silver, and the oil imparts a rich, black color to the zinc compound. The excess is wiped dry with a soft cloth.

The bidri alloy is nonferrous and not subject to rust. Old pieces in India have remained black for hundreds of years. The silver will oxidize, but less quickly than sterling, since it is pure. A soft polishing cloth is sufficient to restore the silver to brightness without affecting the alloy color. Should the zinc coloring fade *in time,* the same coloring procedure can be repeated, and the color restored.

Detail of the bidri cigarette box, showing the gold and silver wire inlay.

ABOVE: Chinese bronze covered urn, of the Chou Dynasty, inlaid with gold. *Freer Gallery of Art, Washington, D.C.*

Damascene Work

The inlaying of gold or silver wire into bronze, iron, or steel was practiced in ancient China and Egypt. It became a widely practiced art in Damascus (from which we get the name *damascene*). From there it spread to North Africa and Spain, and eastward as far as India. Divers forms of damascene are done today in Toledo, Spain; Tunis, Tunisia; and Kyoto, Japan, to mention a few places. It is also still practiced in a specialized form known as *kuftgari* by craftsmen in Trivandrum, Kerala, South India.

OPPOSITE BELOW RIGHT: Syrian canteen of brass (Damascus), Mosul School, mid-thirteenth century. Decorated with silver inlay with engraved details. The subjects of the design are of both Christian and Islamic origin, with inscriptions in Kufic and Nashi scripts. Height: 17⅝ inches; diameter: 14⅜ inches. *Freer Gallery of Art, Washington, D.C.*
OPPOSITE ABOVE: Detail showing a representation of the birth of Christ. The figures are of inlaid silver engraved with linear details.
OPPOSITE LEFT: Persian (Seljug Period) bronze candlestick, twelfth to thirteenth century. Height: 6⁷⁄₁₆ inches; diameter: 7¹⁄₁₆ inches. Inlaid on nine sides with silver medallions. Each medallion representing an enthroned ruler is followed by two medallions with scenes of a musician. *Freer Gallery of Art, Washington, D.C.*

DECORATIVE TECHNIQUES EMPLOYING CONTRASTING METALS　　151

Contemporary Tunisian brass tray. Inlaid with silver and copper inscriptions and border patterns, between which are engraved and stamped designs. *Photo by Oppi.*

BELOW: Detail of the Tunisian brass tray, showing both the silver and copper inlay held to the surface by undercutting and the stamped and engraved patterns.

Chinese bronze wine vessel, late Chou Dynasty (770–206 B.C.). "Hu" type, with ring handles; inlaid with gold and silver. Height: 19⅝ inches. *Victoria and Albert Museum, London.*

Cast brass Philippine Moro betel box inlaid with silver. The far-flung dispersion of both social and craft traditions is evident in this article, whose decorative technique originated in Syria and whose function originated in India. *American Museum of Natural History, New York.*

Early twentieth-century bronze vase with silver inlaid decoration, by Jean Dunand, Paris, France. Height: 10¼ inches. *Metropolitan Museum of Art, New York. Edward C. Moore, Jr. Gift, 1923.*

Kuftgari, A Form of Damascene

As in Renaissance Europe, damascene work was once practiced in India as a means of decorating arms and armor. Today it has been diverted to the decoration of objects such as picture frames, boxes, plates, and trays.

Like other forms of damascene, kuftgari is intended to enrich the surface of the metal of which the article is made. The base metal used is steel, and the decoration is done most frequently in finely drawn silver wire but sometimes in gold. The precious metals are used in their pure or fine state. The decorated article is made of 14–16 gauge steel, which has the body to withstand the necessary hammering that a thinner metal might not take without becoming misshapen.

THE KUFTGARI PROCESS

The article to be decorated must first be finished and ready to take the decoration. The simpler the form to be decorated, the better is the display of the design and the decoration. The method as described is modified to suit those employed in the West, though it is essentially the same as that practiced in India.

The following method is used on a flat steel tray with the edges turned up, as shown in the illustrations. Both the steel object and the wire are first annealed. To prepare the surface for

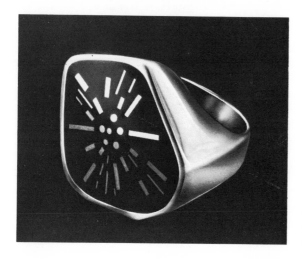

Contemporary damascene work plate, produced by the Castillo brothers in Taxco, Mexico, who have revived the process there. Diameter: about 10 inches. Brass wire inlaid in blued steel. The design depicts an Aztec jaguar from the Codices. *Photo by Oppi.*
LEFT: Ring in 14-karat gold, by Olaf Skoogfors. The face of the ring is made of dacron, which was cut to the approximate shape of the opening in the ring. The ring was heated to soften the dacron and then the dacron was pushed into the depression. Overheating was avoided or the dacron would burn and the surface become pitted. After cooling, the excess dacron was filed level. To create the design, pieces of sterling and 14-karat gold large enough to be gripped with a tweezer were heated and forced into the dacron. The metal, while hot, displaced the dacron under pressure. When the dacron cooled and hardened, the excess metal was cut off and then the whole face filed flush and polished. Nylon can also be used for this contemporary inlay process developed by Skoogfors. *American Craftsmen's Council.*

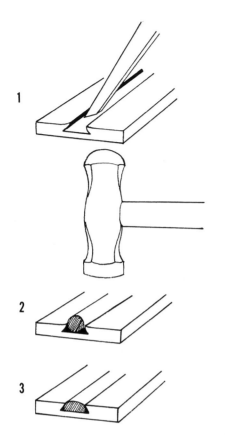

1

2

3

Damascene inlay: 1. Making the undercut groove 2. Hammering the wire in the groove 3. The finished inlay

receiving the metal inlay, the entire surface is given a "tooth." Instead of a single grooved line being made to receive the inlay, as in other forms of damascene, the wire used for the inlay can be freely placed *anywhere* on the surface in the manner to be described.

The "tooth" is made with a cold chisel, approximately ¾ of an inch wide, which is held *in the same position* throughout this part of the operation. The *top* of the chisel is canted *away* from the worker slightly, and after each rapidly applied stroke of the hammer, is moved slightly *toward* him. The chisel raises ridges very close to each other, perhaps fifty to the inch. This procedure is systematically followed until the *entire surface* is covered with evenly spaced ridges, all parallel with each other, and going in the same direction, so that it resembles a single-cut file.

The same process is performed again, and then a third time; each time, however, the direction of the cuts is *shifted* about thirty degrees horizontally from the direction of the first cutting. The slant of the cut should as nearly as possible follow the same direction,

so that after all three operations are completed, no direction is emphasized more than another. The length of time needed to create the surface tooth varies, of course, with the size of the article, but the process is fairly rapid.

The tray is fixed on a board spread with pitch to hold it securely in place for the entire operation of wire inlay.

The design is drawn on the prepared surface, first with a pencil, and then with a pointed steel scriber. If geometric elements are used they can be measured and marked with a steel rule and dividers.

Following the inscribed line design, an end of the light-gauge fine silver wire to be inlaid is tacked in position simply by hammering it into the grooved, toothed metal surface. The wire is "led" over the surface, constantly followed by the hammer, which fixes it in place with many rapid blows. The peen end of a chasing hammer is used, held in the right hand while the left-hand thumb and index finger maneuver the wire. Very fine silver wire is used, and since it is fine or pure, it is extremely malleable, and when hammered, it spreads to about twice its width. The action of the hammer forces the wire into the grooves and at the same time flattens the burrs on the steel, which hold the wire permanently in place. To cut the wire at any point in the design, a small, sharp chisel is placed at the ending point, and one easy blow from the hammer breaks the wire cleanly.

The description above is that of inlaying a single wire. If a line of greater thickness be desired, or if an area is to be covered entirely with silver, a series of wire lines are laid one *alongside* the other. Lines covering an *area* can be placed close enough so that no background metal appears.

Once the inlay wire application is completed, the tray is removed from the pitch board, the excess pitch is removed from the back, and the tray is annealed. The entire surface is then beaten with a planishing hammer; the hammering, besides smoothing the surface, gives the tray rigidity.

FINISHING KUFTGARI

Coloring the Steel A great part of the beauty of kuftgari work lies in the contrast in color between the steel and the silver inlaid wire design. The steel is made permanently bluish-black, while the silver remains white. To accomplish this effect, the tray's surface is rubbed

1

2

3

THE KUFTGARI INLAY PROCESS.

4

5

METAL DECORATIVE TECHNIQUES

Steel plate inlaid with silver damascene work. Centre
Régional D'Arts Tunisiens, Tunisia. Tunisian damascene work is done in exactly the same way as is
described for Indian kuftgari work. *Photo by Oppi.*

1. Kuftgari craftsman P. Mani in the S. M. S. M.
Institute, Trivandrum, Kerala, India, at work. *Photos
by Oppi.* Fine silver wire is inlaid on a steel plate,
which is held on a pitch spread board. The simple
tools needed are shown, including the charcoal-filled
ceramic dish used to heat the steel for coloring.

2. Close-up of the wire inlaying process for kuftgari
work, illustrating the method of leading the fine
silver wire while hammering it into the previously
prepared, grooved steel surface. The sharp, small
chisel, which is used to cut the ends of wire upon
completion of a line in the design, is held, ever
ready, in the hammer hand.

3. After the silver wire inlay is completed, the surface
is rubbed smooth with a steel, polished burnisher.

4. The final step in kuftgari work is coloring the
steel background. The decorated plate is held with a
tongs over a prepared charcoal-filled ceramic dish,
while the heat is brought up with a fan. The color
of the metal is observed, and when it reaches a
bluish-black, the tray is turned gradually so that the
entire article achieves the same color.

5. Kuftgari silver wire inlaid tray, showing the Das
Avatars (Ten Incarnations) of Vishnu. Diameter: 18
inches.

with fine sand and lemon juice to clean it, and then rinsed. A pickle dip in dilute nitric acid, followed by a thorough rinsing in water, can be used instead. In either case, the tray is next rubbed with charcoal, then with a polished steel burnisher and water, to smooth and compress the silver and any remaining burrs that may still exist in the steel. Fingers must be kept off the surface so that no greasy deposit is left to interfere with the even coloring process.

Charcoal Bluing of Steel A glowing-hot bed of charcoal is prepared, either in the ground, in a large, shallow ceramic container, or in a metal pan. The bed should be large enough to accommodate the diameter of the article being blued, if this is possible. The bed is ready when the lower layers of charcoal glow red hot and the upper layer is ash. The metal surface should be as highly polished as possible; the bluish color will then be most apparent.

The tray is held with one or two pairs of pliers or tongs over the heat and moved slowly so that the heat reaches all areas as evenly as possible. The method resembles that of tempering steel. The steel will begin to change color, and the change must be carefully observed so that the correct color can be arrested when it is reached. The color change begins with pale yellow and proceeds to full yellow, brown, and finally blue-purple black, at which point the process is stopped. When the blue color is reached, the metal has become heated to about 530–600° F. The tray can then be quenched in water, or oil-quenched by rubbing the surface quickly with waste cotton impregnated with raw sperm oil.

In this heating process the silver, being pure, does not oxidize and remains white. To preserve the color of the steel, and prevent rusting, a light coating of oil or paste wax is rubbed over the surface with a soft cloth. This can be repeated at intervals as necessary for maintenance. The *back* of the article may be lacquered.

Another Steel Bluing Method Near Puebla, Mexico, is a small town named Amozoc which is famous for its craftsmen who make blued steel saddle fittings, buckles, buttons, stirrups, spurs, and knife handles. The steel work is done in an iron foundry, and is then inlaid with silver or gold by a silversmith, after which it is blued to a color locally called *pavón* or peacock blue. The clean, finished, polished article is given a thin coat of oil and is plunged into a bath of hot nitre, then quenched in cold water, then dipped in boiling water, followed by a final dip in hot oil.

Metal Techniques
that Require Soldering

Up to this point, we have been discussing techniques which *in themselves* do *not* require the use of soldering, though the construction of the objects which are decorated may need soldering. We now turn to processes in which soldering plays an integral part.

The joining of two or more parts of the same metal or different metals through the fusion of heated alloys called *solders,* which melt at a *lower temperature* than the melting point of the metals being joined, is known as *soldering* (derived from the Latin *solidare,* to make solid).

The solder alloy melts, but there is no melting of the metals or alloys being joined. The solder flows *between* these parts, drawn by capillary attraction. The base metal is not fused, but the solder *diffuses into* the base, that is, it makes a surface alloy with the base.

Solders are classified according to the main constituent metal in their composition or according to the name of the metals they are intended to join. Platinum, gold, silver, copper, brass, nickel, aluminum, and lead are some of the metals that require their own solders or are major constituents in solders. Generally speaking, it is possible to join metals with solder alloys made of metals with which the metal being joined can be alloyed. For example, silver solder can be used to join not only silver, but copper, nonferrous alloys, steels, and iron—all metals with which silver can be alloyed.

For the craftsman, solders may be divided into two main types: *hard solder* (called *silver solder* in the most common form used by craftsmen, though there are other hard solders) and *soft solder,* a tin base or lead base alloy. Generally, hard solders melt at a temperature above 800° F, soft solders below that point. It would probably be more accurate to divide

the groups according to composition rather than melting point, though of course there is a relation between the two.

Silver Solders

Silver solder is a term used to classify solders in which a major ingredient is silver. Silver solder is called "silver *brazing* alloy" in industry, where it is also widely employed. Silver solders are alloys containing silver, copper, zinc, and sometimes small additions of other metals, with a melting range of between 627 and 880° C (1160 and 1616° F). Most silver solders are called *ternary alloys,* as they contain three metals.

Solders should have a working differential between their melting and flowing points to allow control of the flow and leeway in which their maximum efficiency is usable. In the solders commonly used by craftsmen, this differential ranges from zero in a eutectic to about 150° F in "IT" solder.

The *eutectic* alloy of any binary or ternary alloy contains components in such a proportion that *the melting point and the flowing point occur simultaneously, at the same temperature.* Most alloys have at least one and possibly more eutectic combinations. Usually the melting-flowing point of a eutectic is at a temperature *lower* than that possible with the two components if they were heated *separately.* The eutectic alloy of silver solder consists of 72 per cent silver and 28 per cent copper; it melts and flows at 779° C (1434° F). This alloy can be used in situations where any percentage in the solder of metals which volatilize at high temperatures, such as zinc, might be objectionable.

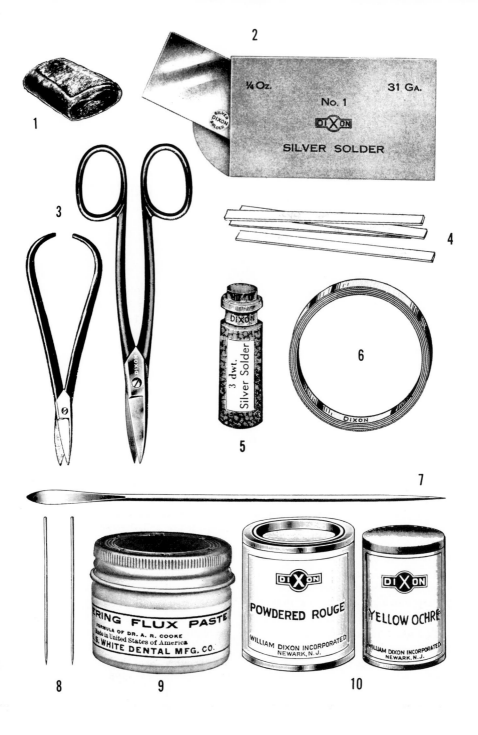

Silver or hard soldering tools and materials: 1. Pad of steel wool 2. Sheet of silver solder 3. Solder snips 4. Hard solder strips 5. Hard solder prepared in snippets 6. Roll of strip hard solder 7. Hard solder poker 8. Soldering needles made of tungsten, not affected by heat, remain rigid, can be mounted in a broach holder and used to push soldered parts to correct or change position during soldering 9. Hard solder flux paste, ½-ounce jar 10. Solder inhibitors: powdered rouge, yellow ochre

OPPOSITE: Solder is manufactured in various forms for both gold and silver soldering. They are illustrated here in sheet, strip, wire, pellets, and 40-mesh and 150-mesh powders. *Handy and Harman. Photo by Steve Stillman.*

Arranged according to the temperature in Fahrenheit of their flow points

Name	Silver	Copper	Zinc	Other	Melting Point	Flow Point
*Easy flo3 (H&H)† (used for poor fit)	50	15.5	15.5	16 Cadmium 3 Nickel	1170	1270
*Ready flo	56	22	17	5 Tin	1165	1200
Sil fos	15	80		5 Phosphorus	1190	1300
*Braze Easy (H&H)	65	20	15		1240	1305
Easy	60	25	15		1260	1325
ASM‡	45	30	25		1250	1370
*Medium (H&H)	70	20	10		1335	1390
*Hard (H&H)	76	22	3			
Eutectic	72	28			1435	1435
*Braze "IT" (H&H)	80	16	4		1340	1490
ASM	20	45	35		1430	1500
ASM	10	52	38		1450	1565 ·

* Silver Solders commonly used by craftsmen
† H&H   Handy and Harman
‡ ASM   American Society for Metals Standard

Silver solders having varying percentages of cadmium, phosphorus, tin, nickel, manganese, and zinc, besides the silver-copper content, flow at lower or higher temperatures, depending on the composition of the alloys. Each has its specific melting and flow points so that the soldering temperature for any given situation can be chosen accordingly, should the choice of solder be critical. (See the chart on page 161 for a sampling of alloy compositions along with their melting and flow points.)

CHOOSING A SOLDER

When choosing a solder, a general rule to follow is to use the solder that first of all has approximately the same strength and color as the metals to be joined. Use the solder that melts at the *lowest* melting point necessary for the job. A lower melting point reduces the likelihood of overheating or damaging the base metal, because with the lower temperature, the time needed for its fusion is less. Also it becomes a safety factor, as the time-temperature considerations in soldering are important.

Silver solders that flow at temperatures above 1500° F should not be used on sterling silver. The metal, when heated beyond that point, starts to break down; the crystalline structure grows and coarsens and the silver is rendered brittle and unsuitable for further working. It might also become uneven in surface and, if overheated enough, will suddenly collapse.

Silver solders are sold in various sheet gauges, strip, wire, rod, pellet, filed, or powdered forms. The choice of form depends on economy and convenience in use.

MELTING POINT AND FLOW POINT:
SOLIDUS AND LIQUIDUS

Solidus is the temperature at which melting begins during heating (or freezing finishes during cooling). *Liquidus* is the temperature at which melting is complete during heating (or at which freezing starts during cooling). The solidus is called the *melting point,* and the liquidus is called the *flow point.*

PREPARATION OF SOLDER

After sheet or strip solder is purchased, it should be marked *immediately* with a device that will identify it should it become wrongly placed. The appearance of hard or silver solders is the same, and the use of the wrong solder might cause difficulty. A system of marking solder should be decided upon and not changed. Marking strip or sheet solder by stamping it at intervals of about ½″ is convenient. Letter stamps can be used in a letter system such as "T" for IT, "H" for hard, "M" for medium, "E" for easy, and "EF" for easy flo; or a code of dots made with a center punch: one for easy flo, two for easy, three for medium, four for hard, and five for IT.

In the preparation of solder for use, the surface must be cleaned by rubbing it with clean steel wool or emery cloth just prior to cutting. It should be handled with a piece of paper to prevent the deposit of grease from fingerprints. A *jeweler's shears* or *lightweight snips* are used to cut the solder. For the sake of economy and ease in handling, the metal is cut into small squares called *snippets*. A series of parallel cuts are made into the solder, about ⅟₃₂ of an inch apart, with a shears. The shears are then used to cut *across* the cuts, making small squares of about ⅟₃₂ of an inch. Smaller pieces can be cut for small work, and larger pieces when necessary. To prevent the snippets from flying in all directions, they can be cut close to a piece of paper on a table or into a shallow cardboard box, the index finger placed *alongside* the shears. The snippets should go immediately into a marked container.

Preparing solder snippets in advance is sometimes worthwhile if they are going to be used within a reasonable length of time; otherwise they might become oxidized or tarnished and not flow properly.

PREPARING THE METAL FOR SOLDERING

All metal surfaces to be joined by soldering must be *chemically clean* before soldering. They must be greaseless, free of oxidation (solder will not flow where the surface is oxidized, but will "ball up" or freeze in place), and free of any other foreign matter such as graphite or carbon (pencil markings will inhibit the flow of solder). Besides cleaning by pickling, metal surfaces can be cleaned with abrasive, file, wire brush, scraper, crocus cloth, steel wool, emery paper, or polishing buff, depending on circumstances.

For best results, the metal surfaces to be joined should be *as close-fitting as possible* before heating. A clearance of four thousandths

Hard soldering materials: 1. Borax slate 2. Solder brushes 3. Liquid hard soldering flux 4. Powdered borax 5. Compressed borax cone 6. Tripod 7. Soldering tongs, 9" long 8. Charcoal block 9. Heavy iron heating frame 10. Large tripod to hold a heating frame and allow the torch to play on the work from below

of an inch makes the most successful joint. Solder will not leap across a big gap, but it will flow easily by capillary attraction along a close-fitting joint. It is sometimes possible to compensate for an imperfect joint by exerting a little pressure on the parts to be joined when the solder is ready to flow, using a tool such as a pointer, tongs, or old file, but do not depend on such devices. The best and easiest joints are those that fit properly to begin with. Mechanical devices called *jigs* can assist in making a good contact between parts to be joined. Binding wire, cotter pins, straight steel pins, clamps, or tweezers can be used to help make a successful joint.

Fluxes and Their Application

Silver soldering cannot be accomplished without the use of a *flux*. The flux is applied to the area of the metal to be joined and has several purposes. Areas covered with flux will not form oxides that occur when the metal is heated. Oxides inhibit the flow of solder and must be controlled. Some fluxes have the ability to *dissolve* existing oxides. Flux also serves to indicate the approach of mature soldering temperature, forming a glassy surface, or fusing, *before* the temperature necessary to melt the solder is reached.

Fluxes used in hard soldering are prepared in solid, powdered, paste, and liquid form. The most commonly used flux for most nonferrous and ferrous metals and alloys is *borax* in some form.

Borax is a crystalline salt (sodium tetraborate) which, when heated, loses water, forms a white porous mass, and finally fuses into a transparent glass called *borax glass*. This glass aids in the soldering operation by covering the metal and preventing its oxidation. In many cases it absorbs or dissolves oxides which are formed by the high heat necessary for soldering. This provides a condition in which the solder will flow easily. Borax dissolves the oxides of silver, copper, iron, tin, zinc, nickel, and their alloys, but not aluminum or lead and its alloys, which require other solders and fluxes.

Common borax in solid form such as com-

THE APPEARANCE OF HARD SOLDER-
ING FLUX IN VARIOUS CONDITIONS.
Handy and Harman. Photos by Steve Stillman.

1. On the right side, flux as it appears when applied to a cleaned surface; on the left, as it appears
with surface break because of the undesirable presence of grease.

2. When flux is applied to a properly cleaned surface and then subjected to heat, it evolves through
several steps.

pressed cones or sticks is prepared for use in
soldering by rubbing it in a *borax slate,* a
shallow slate dish filled with a little water, until
a milky paste is formed. Borax powder poured
into a slate and combined with some water
makes an inexpensive paste flux but has a
tendency to crystallize and solidify. *Fused
borax* which may be used instead of common
borax does not bubble as much as common
borax, but when used as a paste it should not
be mixed with water, as this will cause it to
return to common crystalline borax again. Instead, it is made into a paste by mixing it with
a little alcohol. Firescale oxides can also be
prevented by dipping the entire work in a
supersaturated solution of boric acid and denatured alcohol which when dry forms a protective coat, and then placing the solder. Prepared borax paste fluxes are sold in jars ready
for use.

A liquid flux for medium- and high-melting
solders can be made by first combining 75
per cent powdered borax and 25 per cent
powdered boric acid and dissolving these in
boiling water in excessive amounts. After cool,

one ounce of ammonium phosphate dibasic is
added to one quart of the above solution. This
mixture approximates the liquid commercial
flux available without the dye for color. This
type of liquid flux is more suited to solderings
of *short duration* as they do not offer the protection given by borax when a *prolonged* soldering must be done. In some situations it is
possible to mix solder filings with borax powder, applying them in combined dry form, as
when doing filigree work.

Prior to soldering, all surfaces and edges to
be joined, and the pieces of solder themselves,
should be covered with flux. Ordinarily flux is
painted on these areas with a brush. Pieces of
solder can be held with a tweezer and dipped
into the liquid or paste flux before placing
them. At this point, an indication of the cleanliness of the metal can be noticed. If the flux
rolls away and does not adhere to the metal
surface, causing a "water break," there is
grease present, and since the flux cannot remain in place, it will not offer the proper
protection for a successful soldering. The
grease will carbonize, and the metal must

3. The water with which the flux is combined first bubbles and then evaporates as steam. Without careful heating, the bubbling action will cause solder pieces to move out of position.

4. The surface will settle down smoothly. At this point, the flux condition indicates the proximity of correct soldering heat needed for solder flow.

5. RIGHT: The flux is then "spent" and no longer has the properties that will allow it to assist in the flow of solder. This can be due to an insufficient amount of flux or to an overly prolonged heating.

be recleaned. It is well to make the simple test of running water over the metal surface to be joined to see if it remains in an even coat without water break before applying flux.

REMOVING FLUX AFTER SOLDERING

Flux or borax glass should be easily removable after soldering by washing in hot water (180° or hotter). If the flux does not dissolve easily, it may be interpreted that too little flux was used, the metal was overheated, or the heating was too prolonged. Stubborn flux can be removed by soaking in water, pickling in heated acid, or mechanical abrasion.

PLACING THE SOLDER

If the work requires more than one soldering operation, it is standard practice to begin with the solder requiring the *highest* temperature to flow, followed by solders with lower flowing temperatures. A typical example would be hard solder followed by medium and, finally, easy flo solder. Now, while this is theoretically correct, in practice it often is possible to use perhaps two solders in multiple soldering, and ways to protect soldered joints are discussed under "Controlling the Flow of Solder" (page 176).

Good soldering practice requires the use of solder that is thinner in gauge than the metal being soldered. If thinner sheet solder is not available, solder-sheet thickness may be reduced by using a planishing hammer or a rolling mill. *Do not use an excess of solder* but only the amount necessary to do the job. Solder flows by capillary attraction, and larger distances in joints and contiguous sheet can be soldered with less solder than the inexperienced imagine possible. Excessive solder is always difficult to remove and can be a disadvantage when it becomes visible. Since it is a different alloy from the parent body, it may react differently in later coloring operations and become even more obvious.

Solder snippets are placed by means of a small brush dipped in paste or liquid flux. The brush is touched to the piece of solder, which can then be picked up and carried to the desired position. The solder thus becomes automatically coated with flux if it has not been in contact with flux before. Solder can also be placed with tweezers, each piece lifted separately and dipped in flux before placement. Generally speaking, *solder should be so placed that the snippets are touching both of the parts being joined.* When the solder flows it is drawn by capillary attraction into the joint.

Any trace of solder remaining after the solder has melted in ordinary slow heating is called a *skull,* or skeletal residue. The skull consists of a fraction of the higher melting metal in the solder alloy, and it remains because the lower melting portion has flowed away in the time needed to bring the heat to flow point. The skull can be removed by abrasives in finishing the piece when visible.

A commercially developed jet flux tank to be used in combination with a Prest-O-Lite fuel tank has been adapted for use by craftsmen. The two tanks are coupled with a Y-valve so that the Prest-O-Lite tank can also be used separately. When used for hard-soldering precious metal alloys, the formation of firescale is eliminated, and when melting casting metals, the continuous supply of flux through the torch eliminates metal oxidation.

Simple Heat Devices Heat for soldering can be created with various fuel sources in combination with several air arrangements. Air or oxygen combined with the flame produces the combustion and high heat necessary. The simplest method of producing heat is with a *bed of glowing charcoal embers* on which the article is placed while the embers are being *fanned* to raise the temperature. This method is still practiced in the Far East today to produce complicated articles of jewelry.

The next step in the increasingly complex progression of heating mechanisms is the use of a *brass mouth blowpipe* in combination with almost any fuel that will create a flame, such as an oil lamp, alcohol lamp, or Bunsen burner. The flame is pointed and fine but intense enough to solder small pieces of jewelry, and it can be directed easily.

Gas torches can be used with a city supply of gas such as a stove to which a rubber tube is attached. A *mouth-blowing torch* is placed at the tube end, and the gas is turned on and lighted. A steady pressure of air is then applied. With a little practice, air can be taken in through the nose and expelled with the cheeks. Air can also be supplied by a foot bellows, compressor, or motor-driven blower.

Torches for Separate Gas and Air or Oxygen Supplies A variety of *gas-air torches* are made for use with natural or manufactured gas (not all torches are good for both, and the proper torch for the specific gas supply should be used). Several different-sized tips for small and large flames, depending on the size needed, are available for interchange on torches. These torches have two adjustable valves, one for air and one for gas. A variety of flame types can be obtained.

In a shop situation where oxygen is piped to a bench or comes from a tank, and gas comes from a separate supply source, an oxygen-gas torch may be used. Compressed air can be used in place of oxygen but may require a separate tip. By the interchanging of tip sizes, a flame from pinpoint size to large annealing size is possible.

Single Unit Heat Sources Small torches made with tanks containing a combination of propane gas and propellant are made with disposable tanks which can be used for as long as fifteen hours. The tip is adjustable in fine-

The simplest of all soldering devices, the torch made of a blowpipe used along with an oil lamp, has been used by many cultures for centuries to solder the most intricate types of metalwork. An Indian jeweler is shown here using the pipette and oil lamp, which burns with a cotton wick, to solder a gold chain. The flame is easily directed and is intense enough to make any hard solder flow on small work. In the background are drawings of earrings from which the customers may choose, since the village jeweler does not usually carry a wide selection of stock. *Photo by Oppi.*

Heat sources for soldering: 1. Alcohol lamps for use with blowpipe, wind up wick and pull up wick 2. Bunsen burners 3. Rubber hose to carry gas to bunsen burners 4. Bernz-o-matic propane gas torch, bantam unit, disposable tank, which burns 15 hours at 2300° F 5. Plumber's torch
BELOW: Prest-O-Lite torches with interchangeable, graduated nozzles, soldering copper attachment, and tank gauge. *Craftool, Inc.*

ness and works at any angle. This torch is limited to use on small articles such as jewelry.

For a metalworker who wants mobility in a heating unit or who does not have a gas supply available, an *acetylene torch* with a tank of acetylene gas is very adaptable. Only torches designed for use with acetylene can be used. The gas is stored in the tank under pressure, dissolved in a liquid solvent (see oxyacetylene welding, page 288). The gas is released from solution when the tank valve is opened. The flame size is easily controlled by the use of interchangeable tips or torch stems. Number 1 is used for small work such as jewelry, and the tips progress in size up to number 5, which is suitable for annealing large work. Oxygen combines automatically with the flame at the torch head as the gas burns, and the flame is intensely hot (over 6000° F), as the fuel is close to pure liquid carbon. Though the initial cost is relatively high for a unit such as a Prest-O-Lite system, tank replacements are relatively inexpensive and are available almost everywhere.

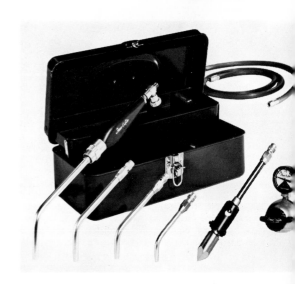

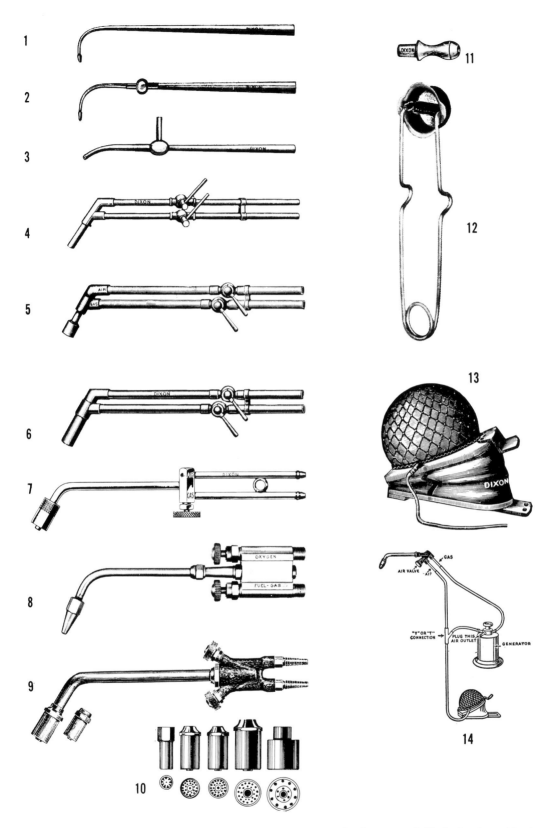

Soldering torches: 1. Mouth blowpipe 2. Mouth blowpipe with removable ball to collect saliva 3. Mouth blowpipe for use with a gas tube and natural gas 4 and 5. Air and gas torch, small work 6. For use with natural gas on large work 7. Air and gas torch 8. Oxygen and gas 9. Hi-heat torch, air and natural gas 10. Changeable torch tips for producing different sized flames ranging from one suitable for jewelry making to silversmithing 11. Wood mouthpiece for blowpipe 12. Friction flint hand lighter or striker 13. Foot bellows for creating 1–1½ pounds of pressure per square inch to heighten flame heat from a gas source 14. Setup showing a torch used with a gasoline-air arrangement and a foot bellows to create air pressure

Plumber's Torches The point of the flame produced with a plumber's torch cannot be regulated easily. The flame is broad and hot and suited to heating large areas (see Mexican Married Metals, page 184).

Lighting the Flame When gas-air, propane, or acetylene torches are used, the flame can be lighted with a pilot flame such as an alcohol lamp or with a *friction flint spark lighter*. Matches can be used, of course, but the friction lighter allows a one-hand operation while holding the torch in the other and is more convenient. In lighting gas-air torches, a small amount of gas should be allowed to escape before the flint lighter, held in the hand *before opening the gas,* is struck. Once the gas is ignited, the flame can be increased and the air slowly turned on to regulate the flame. When propane or acetylene gas is used, the torch should be turned on only enough to allow the flame to be lighted, and then should be adjusted for flame size. When an *air-gas* flame is turned off, *the air should be turned off first, and then the gas.* With the others, the torch should be turned off slowly to avoid backflash.

Regulating the Flame The size and condition of the flame used depends on the circumstances. On most torches, the size of the tip of the torch can be changed easily. Soldering small pieces of jewelry requires a small pointed flame. Annealing requires a large, soft flame with a slightly yellow tip. With an *air-gas* torch, a soft all-yellow flame indicates the presence of too much gas and not enough air. This kind of flame will deposit on the metal unconsumed carbon from the fuel in the form of soot. Such a flame cannot be used for soldering, as it hinders the flow of solder and the metal cannot be brought to the necessary heat for the solder to flow. A flame that is very pointed and intensely blue probably has too much air or oxygen and not enough gas. This kind of flame is extremely hot, might cause melting of the metal, and heats the metal locally in hot spots. The excess of oxygen causes the formation of oxides on the surface of the metal which hinders the flow of solder. Soldering is best performed with a *neutral* or *slightly reducing* flame. (A reducing flame is one in which there is an excess of gas over oxygen.) This prevents excessive oxidation of the metal surface. An oxidizing flame is undesirable in silver soldering but is used in some circumstances in welding. In cases where the flame is not easily controlled, a simulated reducing-flame atmosphere can be created by coating the *entire assembly* with flux. This will prevent oxides from forming on the metal surface, and the flux can be removed after soldering by washing with hot water or with a stiff brush.

The hottest part of a flame is the part from the tip to a point before the tip of the inner cone, and this is the area which should play on the metal. A rather soft flame that heats the whole area around the joint till the joint becomes dull red, then is concentrated on joint and solder, is best for most soldering operations.

SOLDERING SURFACES

A variety of surfaces on which to solder are available, the choice depending on circumstances. The most common surface is a *charcoal block*. Charcoal retains the heat of the flame and helps to build up the necessary soldering temperature quickly, thereby speeding up the soldering process, a desirable factor in the reduction of oxidation formation and solder flow. Tying a new charcoal block with binding wire will help to keep it from disintegrating too quickly. Work can be pinned easily to a charcoal block to hold parts in place during soldering.

Magnesium soldering blocks, made of carbonate of magnesium and asbestos fiber, are longer-lasting than charcoal. This composition also is porous enough to permit work to be pinned to it during soldering.

Coiled asbestos soldering blocks are made of asbestos strips coiled and held in a metal frame. Work can also be pinned easily to this surface.

Asbestos board soldering blocks are made in various thicknesses and may be used alone, or in conjunction with any of the blocks mentioned above.

Asbestos board can be used to cover and protect tables meant for soldering. Thin, small sheets of asbestos can be used in place of charcoal to support work being soldered.

Transite board, an asbestos composition board made in four-by-eight-foot sheets, can be used to cover large working areas to be used for heating functions. It can be cut to specifications, comes in several thicknesses, and is relatively inexpensive.

Asbestos soldering ring sticks are tapered to hold all sizes of rings during soldering and repairing.

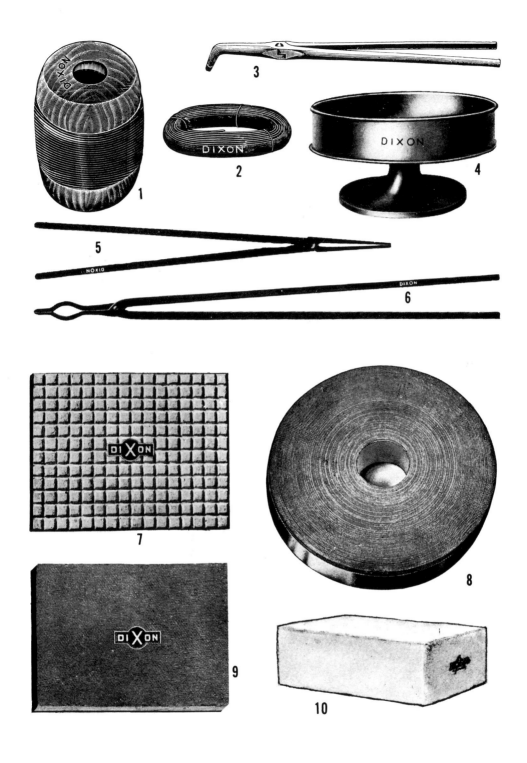

Soldering tools and materials: 1. Spool of iron binding wire 2. Heavy gauge coil of iron binding wire 3. Bent-nose annealing tongs, cast iron, 17″ long 4. Annealing pan which revolves on ball bearings, used with lump pumice, or No. 6 carborundum grains, available in 12″ and 18″ diameter 5 and 6. Long handled, 17″ cast iron annealing tongs, straight nose, curved nose, for use with large work 7. Corrugated asbestos sol-dering block for soldering large work. Corrugations allow the heat to pass around and beneath the work 8. Coiled asbestos soldering block, 5½″ diameter, 1″ depth, permitting the pinning of work in place during soldering 9. Asbestos soldering block, available in many sizes and thicknesses from ⅛″ to 1″ 10. Magnesium soldering block (made of asbestos fiber and carbonate of magnesium) suited to pinning work during soldering

Metal wire heating frames or trivets are used in situations which require heating the work from below. In the long run, the most economical kind is made of Nichrome wire, which does not disintegrate from oxidation or form excessive, flaking firescale as do iron-wire trivets. The trivet in this case must be elevated so that the torch flame can be directed at the work from below. The simplest way to do this is to support it on charcoal blocks or bricks or on a *tripod ring stand*.

A *soldering nest* (also called a wig or mop), made by twisting iron binding wire over a heavy wire frame, is useful in situations when small pieces must be held in place for soldering. This is done with binding wire, which easily pierces the wire mesh.

Annealing pans twelve or eighteen inches in diameter are made with raised bases constructed with built-in ball bearings that allow the work in the pan to be rotated while being heated. Such pans are suitable for soldering large pieces such as bowls and holloware. They can also be used for annealing. The tray is filled with refractory material which helps to retain the heat. Small lump pumice, carborundum grains, or coke may be used.

A *refractory brick* is used in soldering platinum, which requires intense, white heat.

GENERAL SOLDERING CONSIDERATIONS

Regardless of the soldering situation, certain general considerations in hard soldering are universally true.

1. Solder will not compensate for a poorly fitting joint.
2. All parts to be joined must be chemically clean.
3. Except in rare cases, the torch flame should be moved constantly during soldering to reduce the risk of scorching, melting, or collapsing the metal.
4. The flow of solder can best be judged by observing the effect of the heat on the solder and the metal being joined. Heat judgment depends on the appearance and color of the metal. It is therefore *a prime consideration* that all soldering should be done in a shaded or darkened place, away from bright light, so that *color observation* of the metal and *solder flow observation* are facilitated. Do not place your soldering table under a bright bulb. If you must have light in the beginning, once the work is ready for heating turn off or shield nearby lights.
5. The metals being soldered should be brought to solder flowing temperature as *rapidly* as possible. *The solder will not flow till the adjacent metal being joined has reached the temperature needed for flowing.* Therefore, when soldering, concentrate the heat first on the surrounding metal and *not* on the solder itself till the fusion of flux indicates the approach of solder-flowing temperature.

6. In this preheating stage, if the flux contains moisture the excess must first be driven off. As the sudden heat may cause the water to steam and the flux to foam, some of the pieces of solder may be caused to move. To avoid this movement or reduce it to a minimum, a few quick passes of the flame over the fluxed area first will help to dry the moisture. If it is necessary to replace moved solder snippets which have moved, they can usually be pushed back in place with a metal instrument. If the flux has frozen the solder in place, it can usually be picked up with a pair of tweezers or pried loose with a pointed tool.

7. Watch the pieces of solder or, if they are not visible, the joint where the solder will flow. As soon as the bright, silvery line of molten solder is visible (better seen in a subdued light), and the solder flows all along the joint, the flame should be removed. There is danger in overheating solder, because zinc, the low-melting component in most hard-solder alloys, will volatilize, pass off in gases, and leave the solder brittle and porous. This may reduce the strength of the joint. In soldering large pieces or long joints, it may be well to fuse all the solder snippets first and then pass over the entire joint with the flame one last time, to allow the solder to flow evenly along the entire joint.

8. When two metals of uneven thickness are being soldered, the heat must be concentrated first on the *thicker* metal, which takes longer to heat. The torch is then brought to bear on both parts so that, at the time of solder flow, they are equally hot.

SOLDERING GOLD

The procedures for soldering gold are the same as those for soldering silver. A few additional points may be mentioned.

Use solder that is *thinner* than the pieces to be joined. The solder chosen should match the color of the gold being used. Several solders are designed to be used with specific colors of gold and to flow at temperatures within the range needed for the karat purity of the gold being soldered. Choose a solder with a lower melting point than the metal being soldered

(*See below*) These gold solders are designed for specific flow points, and for use with the gold alloys mentioned above. This information is based on Handy and Harman Tables. Gold solders for karat gold are sold in pennyweight and half pennyweight pieces. The standard thickness for gold solders is 30 B. & S. (.010″), and the size of a pennyweight piece is approximately ½″×1½″.

Karat golds melt at a temperature lower than that of fine gold. Color appears first at the edges of sheet silver, and at the ends of wire.

VISUAL JUDGING OF APPROXIMATE TEMPERATURES DURING THE SOLDERING OF SILVER AND GOLD

	Fahrenheit	Centigrade
First faint redness:	900°	482°
Dull Red:	1200°	649°
Cherry red:	1400°	760°
Orange red:	1500°	816°
Bright salmon orange:	1600°	871°
Brilliant orange:	1640°	893°

(This is the liquidus temperature for *sterling silver*.)

Liquidus for fine silver	1760.9°	960.5°
Liquidus for fine gold	1945.4°	1063°

Karat Golds and Their Melting Points

Golds

	Fahrenheit	Centigrade
18K Yellow	1700°	926.6°
18K Green	1810°	987.7°
18K Red	1655°	901°
18K White	1730°	943.3°

	Fahrenheit	Centigrade
14K Yellow #29	1615°	879°
14K Yellow #2	1580°	860°
14K Green	1765°	963°
14K Light Yellow #245	1540°	837.7°
14K Dark Yellow #165	1545°	841°
14K Red	1715°	935°
14K White	1767°	964°

	Fahrenheit	Centigrade
10K Yellow	1665°	907°
10K Yellow	1625°	885°
10K Red	1760°	960°
10K White	1900°	1037.8°

Gold Solders and Their Flow Points

Solders

		Fahrenheit	Centigrade
18K Colored Golds			
Easy	14K	1390°	754.4°
Medium	12K	1485°	807°
Hard	16K	1520°	826.6°
18K White			
Easy	14K	1375°	746°
Hard	16K	1490°	810°
Extra Hard	19K	1640°	893.3°

		Fahrenheit	Centigrade
14K Colored Golds			
Extra Easy #2460	10K	1290°	698.8°
Regular Easy	10K	1380°	748.8°
Medium	10K	1415°	768°
Easy	14K	1390°	754.4°
Medium	12K	1485°	807°
14K White Gold			
Easy	10K	1350°	732.2°
Hard	12K	1440°	782.2°

Same solders listed under 18 K. White Gold can also be used on 14K White Gold.

10K Colored Golds
Same solders as 14K Colored Golds.
10K White Golds
Same solders as 14K White Golds.

within a safe range of about 150° F, or over-heating and collapse of the metal is risked. When ordering solder, state the color and karat of the gold to be soldered. Usually, the solder used is of a lower karat than the gold being soldered, but this will vary according to the alloy of the solder and gold and their melting points. It is important to know the melting point of the solder and of the gold being used.

ANNEALING AND PICKLING GOLD

When gold is worked, it is extremely malleable and ductile, but, like most metals, it hardens, and annealing is necessary. Judging the annealing temperature of gold may be more difficult than that of silver, as the color change may not be as easily apparent. It is therefore important to anneal gold in a darkened environment to observe the color change better. Color begins to become marked when the gold has nearly reached the desired annealing temperature of 1200° F. An added safety precaution is to cover the entire piece with a flux that becomes fluid at a temperature known to be near the annealing temperature. This is especially true in the case of red golds, where the color will tend to burn out unless the surface is entirely covered with a protecting flux during annealing and soldering.

Red golds should be quenched hot to avoid hardening. Green and yellow golds can either be quenched hot or air cooled. White gold should be annealed to 1400° F, a bright cherry red, and quenched hot or air cooled. White gold has to be worked evenly before annealing, or inner strains and stresses created by uneven working may cause cracking during the annealing or, later, during the working of the metal.

Firescale created on gold alloy surfaces when heated can be prevented by coating the entire surface with borax, boric acid mixed with alcohol into which the piece is dipped, or a prepared paste flux. Most fluxes can be removed after the metal has been heated by washing in hot water (180° F). Should firescale form, however, it can be removed by pickling the metal in a boiling solution of nitric acid (8 to 1), or sulphuric acid (10 to 1) heated to 180° F. High-karat golds, having less alloying metal, have less tendency to develop firescale. See the section on the coloring of gold (page 418).

BASIC SOLDERING SITUATIONS

The four most common basic soldering situations are (1) joining flat surfaces, (2) joining perpendicular surfaces, (3) joining edges (butt joints), and (4) joining wire to other surfaces.

Joining Flat Surfaces The parts of metals to be joined must be held in contact with each other during the soldering process. The simplest means for accomplishing this is by *gravity*. Wherever possible, gravity should be used as a soldering ally. When flat surfaces are to be joined, the surfaces in contact are cleaned and coated with flux. The solder snippets are placed on the *upper* part while it is fluxed surface up and allowed to dry. This procedure fixes the solder in place and assures proper placement. The upper part is then placed with the solder between it and the lower surface, and heat is then applied. The work should be placed *level* on the heating surface, an insurance against later movement. When the solder flows, the upper part, which has been resting on the solder particles, will suddenly drop. This is an indication of the completion of the solder flow, and the heat is then removed.

Flat pieces can be "sweat soldered" together by first fusing solder to each surface *separately*. Additional flux is painted on each surface and they are then put in position in contact with each other. Heat is applied till the solder melts again and joins the parts.

Perpendicular Joints Surfaces to be joined perpendicularly to each other present a more difficult problem. Ordinarily they must be held in contact by some mechanical means if the parts are not self-supporting.

The Use of Soldering Jigs A soldering jig is any device which is fastened to, or enclosed around, or which supports, an assembly while it is being joined by soldering. Binding wire, clamps, pins, and tweezers technically are soldering jigs when used for this purpose.

When a base is joined to a bowl, for example, the parts are held together with binding wire, ordinarily made of soft iron. This wire is available in various gauges, but for most purposes a fine wire (22 gauge) and a heavy wire (10 gauge) are suitable. Should an intermediate wire be needed, several strands of the thin wire can be twisted together for additional strength.

The wire is wound in at least two opposite directions around the parts to be held together, so that there is no movement of the parts. To tighten the wire the ends are twisted together with pliers. To allow for additional tightness,

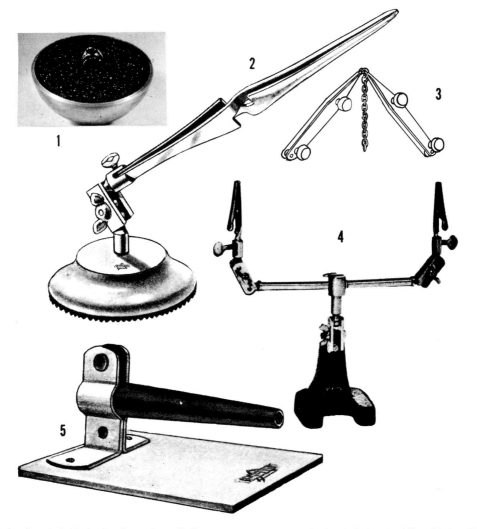

Soldering jigs: 1. Soldering bowl, cast iron, 4″ diameter, containing No. 24 carborundum grains used to hold work during soldering 2, 3, 4. Mounted tweezer and clamp arrangements designed to hold small work in any position on the jeweler's bench while soldering. Tweezers and clamps are replaceable 5. Carbon ring stick, transite base, used to solder ring shanks, tubing, and round formed articles

a kink is put into the wire with flat-nosed pliers. The kink has the additional function of allowing for the inevitable expansion of the metal which occurs when it is heated. *Before pickling the metal, always remove iron binding wire.* If this is not done, the acid solution will become contaminated and will coat the metal with a flashing that is a bother to remove.

Supports of various kinds can be improvised to hold parts together using Nichrome wire which maintains its shape and strength during heating. Findings (see glossary) which are otherwise difficult to support can be held by such wires, either vertically or at an angle. In some circumstances, heavy binding wire can be cut and bent to form hooks to support

pieces. Sometimes it is possible to prop parts up with bits of firebrick, other refractory material, or charcoal. Steel pins can be forced into charcoal to support perpendicular work. Other devices have been mentioned under soldering surfaces (page 170). The ingenuity of the metalworker must be brought to bear on any problem. All problems have a solution, no matter how unique. When making a decision as to which system to use, if there are alternative choices, take the simplest one.

A recent development which is of much help in difficult soldering situations involving jewelry, is the use of an iron bowl filled with carborundum grains. The parts to be joined are sunk into the grains which hold them in place and act as an insulator during soldering.

Butt Joints Joining two parts that come squarely together without scarfing (overlapping) or chamfering at the edges is known as making a butt joint. Butt joints with sheet metal must fit perfectly along the entire length of the seam, or the solder will not flow successfully. Wire can also be butt joined. When butt joining cylindrical objects, try to place the object so that gravity can assist the flow of solder. If possible, bind objects with wire to keep the joint in contact during soldering; the heat may tend to draw seams apart.

Soldering Wire to Sheet When soldering wire to sheet metal, a few general points should be kept in mind. Application of heat directly to wire generally presents the risk of melting the wire. Since solder will not flow till the whole area of the metal is heated to the necessary temperature, the risk of overheating the wire while this is done is great. It is therefore better practice to solder wire by *induction* of heat, that is, by *heating the adjoining metal*. Heat control can be used as a means of joining wire, on the principle that *solder will flow toward the direction of the heat source,* which can be utilized to this end.

The placement of solder is important. A more successful joining is accomplished by placing the solder pieces either *on top* of the wire or *leaning against* and making contact with the side of the wire as well as with the base metal. The metal is heated *from below,* and when the melting temperature is reached, the solder is drawn toward the heat source and flows the length of the wire where it comes into contact with the sheet metal.

Another method is to place the solder snippets at both ends of the wire and heat the area midway between them from below. The solder will melt and be drawn toward the center, where the heat is concentrated. A minimum of solder is needed in soldering wire, as one piece will flow for quite a long distance as long as the wire is in contact with the base metal. Too much solder results in a clogged look and destroys the contour definition of the wire.

CONTROLLING THE FLOW OF SOLDER

The fact that solder will always flow *toward* the direction of the heat source can be used to advantage to draw solder into otherwise difficult situations. For instance, if the solder seems to be flowing opposite to the direction desired, quickly reversing the flame to the side toward which you wish the solder to flow often works. Heat control can be used to help avoid a skull (solder remains). For example, when a bottom is being soldered to a deep cylindrical form such as a vase, or the walls to the bottom of a box, the solder snippets should be placed *inside* the cylinder or box. The heat, applied from the outside, will draw the molten solder into the seam, and no traces of solder are seen.

Another solution when soldering a bottom to a foot is to place the solder snippets beneath the edge of the cylinder wall, whose weight will then hold the solder in place. This procedure also eliminates the possibility of movement of the solder during the boiling of the flux, and rapid heating is possible. It sometimes helps to apply pressure on the top of the cylinder at the moment of solder flow with iron tongs or an old file, thus making better contact between the parts. Should solder form a ball and not flow, this indicates insufficient heat, dirt in the joint, or insufficient flux.

A small ball of solder, deliberately made, can be used in small solder work. It is picked up at the end of a pointed tool to which it adheres, held in place, and heated till it runs.

Solder-Inhibiting Pastes Several materials can be used in solder control to prevent the flow of solder to areas where it is not wanted. Pastes can be made by mixing any of several materials with water and applying it to the metal. Powdered *rouge* (a fine red powder of ferric oxide, prepared by gently calcining ferrous sulphate), *yellow ochre* (an impure iron ore, also called *limonite* or *loam*), and *whiting* (an impalpable powder of pulverized chalk or calcium carbonate) can each be used. They are mixed with water or, if necessary, mixed with some organic gum, such as gum tragacanth. The paste mixture can be painted along a joint so that solder will not flow beyond that point, or all over a finding such as a pin catch, to prevent the solder from flowing into the catch, clogging it, and making it inoperative. Whenever there is danger of a joint becoming *unsoldered* during heating, one of these pastes can be applied. Care should be taken not to allow the paste to contaminate any place where the solder is wanted. If yellow ochre combines with liquid flux, for instance, it will stop the flow of solder or cause it to flow unevenly along that joint.

Though it is possible to remove solder-inhibiting pastes after soldering by putting the hot metal directly into a pickle solution, this practice quickly contaminates and weakens the solution. It is better to remove pastes (which, incidentally, become hardened after being subjected to heat) with a small, stiff brush under hot water, and then removing any stubborn remainder with the pickle solution.

Solder-inhibiting pastes can also be used to protect exposed fine wires that might otherwise melt during a soldering operation.

THE USE OF STICK SOLDER

A method of applying solder in working large pieces, making long joints, or soldering strip ornaments or wire to the edge of a bowl to thicken the edge is by the use of *stick solder*. In this process, once the flux has been applied, *fast heating* is used on the work to *quickly bring the temperature of the metal above the flow point of the solder*. When the solder is then hand fed into the joint, no time is needed for the solder to reach the point of liquidation, and it flows *immediately* into the joint, leaving no residue or skull (except perhaps at the point of contact).

The joint to be soldered should be cleaned, coated with flux, and bound with wire or clamps. The solder stick itself should be cleaned; it may also be coated with flux and allowed to dry. The whole piece is then heated with a large flame till the flux fuses and becomes glassy, indicating that the temperature for applying the solder stick is near. Once the temperature passes the flow point of the solder, the stick is touched to the joint while the flame continues to play on the joint. Some of the solder will flow immediately. Do not continue to feed more solder, but watch the solder flow, and draw it along with the flame till it seems to stop. This is an indication that more solder is needed, and you should apply more. Continue the process till the entire seam is soldered.

For example, when soldering a wire edge to a bowl, place the bowl, with the wire bound or clamped in place, into a rotating annealing pan or on an asbestos sheet mounted on a turntable. Once the metal temperature is correct, rotate the bowl clockwise and apply the solder toward the direction in which the flame of the torch is pointing, that is, against the turning direction.

Solder sticks are available in ⅛"×20", 20 gauge. When ordering, specify the type of solder, gauge, and dimension.

UNSOLDERING

Soldering is a process that requires care, thought, and planning. The entire soldering sequence in the construction of an object should be so planned that important structural problems are not encountered while the work is in progress.

It may be necessary, however, because of unforeseen changes or accident, to *unsolder* work or separate parts already joined. If there are other joints *not* to be unsoldered, these should be protected with a solder-inhibiting paste. To protect surfaces that might become damaged, cover them with flux. Joints to be separated or unsoldered should also be painted with flux. To help in the separation of parts, anchor the most convenient part to a charcoal block or other heating surface with pins, allowing the part that is to be removed to be exposed. Heat the piece till the joint to be unsoldered shows the solder line bright and molten. Do not prolong the heat. Depending on how the part to be removed is joined to the other parts, it can then be lifted away with pliers or tweezers (for edge-soldered, perpendicular joints), pried or pushed loose with an old file or dull instrument (flat pieces, sweat soldered), or pulled apart with pliers or small tongs (butt joints).

SPELTER SOLDERS

Spelter solders, also known as brazing solders or alloys, are copper-zinc alloys which have relatively low melting points (from 1304° F to 2050° F). They are, in effect, a form of brass with the copper and zinc in approximately equal amounts, sometimes with the addition of small amounts of nickel and tin (which changes the color to a white metal), lead and phosphorus.

Several kinds are used in conjunction with a welding torch, such as spelter bronze, white spelter solder, phos-copper, white brazing rod, yellow bronze, and copper, each with its characteristic color and melting point. Those having a low enough melting point can be used with an ordinary torch. A general, all-purpose yellow bronze spelter which could be so used contains 42 parts zinc, 0.5 tin, and 67.5 parts copper. It melts at a temperature range of 1595° F to 1625° F. This could be used on steel, copper, brass, and bronze and has the advantage of matching these metals (except for steel) more closely in color than silver solder. This consideration may sometimes be a factor in its choice.

Spelters are available in rod, lump, and fine to coarse powders. They are used with borax as a flux. Fine powdered spelter is sometimes mixed with flux and water-free alcohol into a paste and applied with a brush, so that both solder and flux are applied simultaneously.

Soft Solders

Tin and lead alloys, commonly called *soft solders,* are fusible at temperatures below 700° F (371° C). They are considerably less strong than silver solders but are used in the construction of articles where strength is not a primary consideration, and in repair work. Soft solder should not be used on articles of precious metal where its use is avoidable. In England, its use on precious metals eliminates the possibility of the article being hallmarked for quality.

Soft solders can be used to join gold, silver, copper, brass, bronze, nickel, zinc, lead, pewter, mild steel, and wrought iron. They are made with varying percentages of tin and lead content:

70 tin, 30 lead

62 tin, 38 lead
  (eutectic soft-solder alloy)

50 tin, 50 lead
  (called "half and half," an all-purpose solder)

60 tin, 40 lead
  (widely used, called "fine solder")

All these alloys melt at 361° F (183° C) but have varying liquidus points. Low-tin-content alloys do not have good flow characteristics and are porous and weak. So-called "wiping solders" used by plumbers for pipe joints have a 38–40 per cent tin content. Tin is the major metal in these alloys. It is the "wetting" ingredient, which means it alloys readily with the metal surface to which the solder is applied.

Tin solders are made by extrusion in solid or hollow-cored wire form (hollow cores contain flux), in angular shapes, ribbon form, bars, cakes, slabs, foil, powder, and paste. The paste form of solder is called a "fusion solder" and combines the metals, flux, and cleaning agents. In one operation this form of solder cleans, fluxes, and solders when heat is applied.

Soft soldering materials: 1. Spool of soft solder 2. Nokorode soft solder flux paste 3. Solderall, a paste form of solder and flux combined, 2 ounce tube 4, 5, 6. Wire, bar, and sheet forms of soft solder 7. Soft soldering liquid flux 8. Liquid flux for soldering pewter

SOFT-SOLDER FLUXES

Soft-solder fluxes are used on metal for the same purposes as fluxes used in silver soldering. Flux functions as an active agent to speed up the wetting of metals by molten solder. This is accomplished in three ways: it removes oxides from metals by dissolving them, it prevents the formation of oxide during the heating of metal to soldering temperatures, and it lowers the surface tension of the molten solder, allowing it to spread evenly over the soldered area. Fluxes promote contact between solder atoms and the atoms of the metal being joined. There are four basic types of flux:

Acid or chloride fluxes contain zinc chloride, ammonium, and other ingredients. Since they are corrosive, a residue remover must be used after soldering. Corrosive fluxes are removed by a thorough washing with hot water or a water and soda solution. *Sal ammoniac* (ammonium chloride) is a corrosive flux commonly used in soft soldering. Iron, steel, stainless steel, zinc, and galvanized iron require corrosive fluxes. A good flux can be made by dissolving small pieces of zinc in muriatic acid (hydrochloric acid) held in a glass container. Pieces are added till the boiling action has stopped, when the solution becomes what is known as "killed acid." It is then left to settle, a little water is added, and it is stored in a ground-glass stoppered container. As a substitute for this preparation, six ounces of fused zinc chloride dissolved in a pint of water is satisfactory.

Organic base fluxes are intermediate between corrosive acid and noncorrosive rosin fluxes.

Pure rosin fluxes are noncorrosive and require no residue removal. Noncorrosive fluxes are not as efficient as corrosive fluxes in the removal of oxide, but they do prevent most formation of oxide during the heating. They are therefore used on *cleaned* copper, brass, and other metals. Rosin, tallow, olive oil, stearin (used for lead and lead alloys) are all noncorrosive fluxes. Prepared noncorrosive paste fluxes are available (Nokorode soldering paste and others). A typical paste flux contains 75 per cent petroleum jelly, 20 per cent zinc chloride, and 5 per cent NH_4Cl, with some water to act as an emulsifying agent.

Activated rosin fluxes are pure rosin fluxes, noncorrosive, and "accelerated" to make them almost as active as acid fluxes, without having their corrosive disadvantages.

SOFT-SOLDERING PROCEDURE

Soft soldering should be completed in as short a time as possible; extended heating of the molten metal is not considered desirable. The joint must be well fitting. Both the metal to be soldered and the solder itself should be clean. Metal can be cleaned with a file (for edges) or steel wool or abrasive cloth (for surfaces). Flux is then applied to the place to be soldered, with a stick for *paste* flux and a brush for *liquid* flux. Flux in excessive amounts will flow under the heat and take the solder along.

When a torch is used, the procedure is very much like that of hard soldering, except that a *much lower* temperature is needed to melt the solder. Small snippets of solder are cut and placed along the joint, evenly spaced. If the situation demands it, they can first be flattened with a hammer. The torch is used to bring the temperature of the metal just thirty to forty degrees above the melting point of the solder, as this is enough to control the flow. A soft flame is used, swept over the metal but not on the flux if possible. The solder first becomes a ball, then melts and flows freely along the fluxed joint. Once the solder starts to flow, the flame should be removed to avoid overheating. Excess solder can be wiped away with a cloth pad before the solder solidifies. Once the solder in the joint loses its brightness, the piece can be handled with tongs. If there is any doubt as to whether it has cooled sufficiently, the work may be left to stand till it can be touched comfortably. All remains of flux should be washed away with hot water and soap or detergent applied with a stiff brush.

SOLDERING COPPERS OR IRONS

Soldering "irons" are more properly called *soldering coppers,* because the point, which conducts the heat to the metal and melts the solder, is made of copper, a good heat conductor. There are two kinds. One is made with the copper tip attached to a steel rod, which is held by a wood handle. This kind must be *heated externally* by a torch, gas flame, Bunsen burner, charcoal fire, or gas-heated soldering stove which accommodates two or more coppers (while one is being used, the other or others are being heated in preparation for use so that the operation can continue uninterrupted).

The second kind of iron is *heated internally* by electric current conducted to the tip by a wire that leads from the tip through the handle to the electric outlet. Both types are used in essentially the same way.

TINNING THE SOLDERING COPPER

Soldering coppers are made with tips of various weights from 7/8 of an ounce to 2 pounds. The choice of size depends on the job to be done. For ordinary use by craftsmen, coppers under six ounces are satisfactory. A copper large enough to hold the heat needed for the job is the proper one to use. This, of course, is not a problem with electrically heated coppers, which get a continuous supply of heat.

To make the solder flow easily when "led" by the soldering copper, the *tip* must be cleaned. It is first filed or rubbed bright with abrasives. Then it is coated with flux by being dipped into liquid flux or spread with paste flux. The next step is to heat it to solder-melting temperature. Solder is applied to the tip and the sides either by rubbing the tip over a cake of solder or by applying solder in stick form to the tip up to a distance of about one-half to three-quarters of an inch from the tip end. Another method is to heat the copper, but short of redness. While hot, the tip is dipped into liquid flux or rubbed over a solid cake of sal ammoniac (a flux). It is then coated with solder as described above. Soldering coppers must be kept clean to operate efficiently.

Using the Tinned Soldering Copper The hot soldering copper, loaded with as much solder as it will hold, is held at the beginning of the seam being soldered till enough heat has been conducted to the metal and the placed solder bits begin to melt. The soldering copper is drawn slowly along the seam, moving as the solder melts and flows into the seam. More solder can be added to the tip, as long as the tip remains hot enough to operate, by dipping the tip in the flux and touching it with a solder stick or wire as it is drawn along. Once it has cooled below the solder's melting point, it must be returned to the heat. A second copper, if ready, can quickly replace the one being heated, and the operation can continue.

When large parts are being soft soldered with coppers, it is better, because of the speed with which the heat is conducted away, to pre-tin the parts to be joined and assemble, clamp, and solder them. Warming or preheating the entire object to a temperature below the flow point of the solder also helps to make the solder flow.

SWEAT SOLDERING

Joining two sheets of metal flush along their entire surface, thereby doubling the thickness, is sometimes necessary. To do this efficiently,

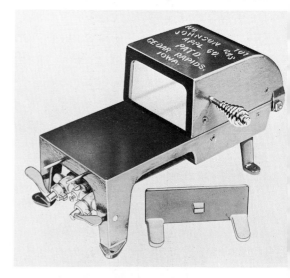

Bench soldering furnace #101, designed to hold two soldering coppers and other heat-treating functions. *Johnson Gas Appliance Co.*

the metal is cleaned and coated with flux. Solder snippets are placed, equally spaced, over the entire surface. The metal is heated with a torch having a soft flame till the entire surface is covered with a thin film of solder. The covering metal sheet is cleaned on the surface that is to make contact with the first sheet. It is placed on top of the first sheet, the layer of solder between the two. The sheets are clamped together with cotter pins, clamps, wire, pliers, or other means. The torch is played evenly over the entire surface. At the proper temperature, the solder will flow and become visible along the seam as a bright, silvery line. The heat is removed and the metal is allowed to cool. Excess flux is removed.

Thin, flat sheets of soft solder are available for sweat soldering. The solder is sandwiched between the two layers of metal being joined after all contacting surfaces have been coated with a thin flux application. All surfaces should be clean. The heat is applied, and the solder flows, joining the two layers evenly.

Always avoid overheating metals that have been joined by soft solder, as the lead content in soft solder will eat into the metal and cause pitting.

SOFT-SOLDER REMOVAL

Excessive exposed soft solder can be filed away with a *float file,* meant exclusively for use on soft metals. To avoid the clogging of files with metal, a recommended procedure is to rub the entire file with ordinary white chalk

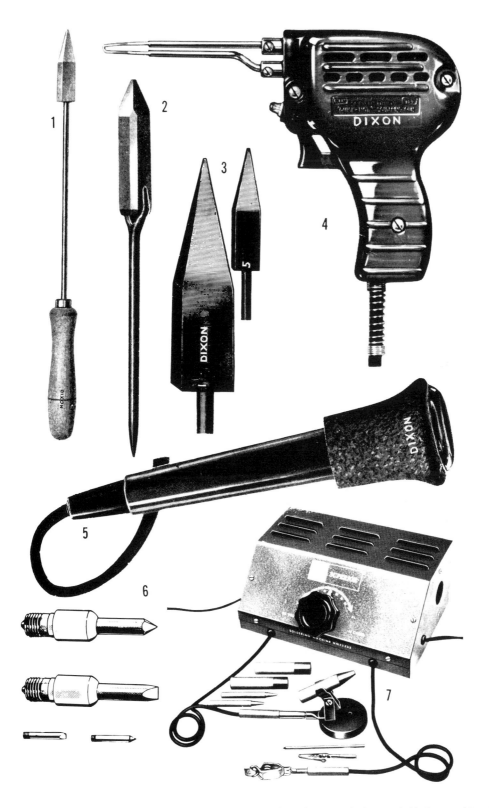

Soldering irons and coppers: 1, 2, 3. Soldering irons for external heating, in various sizes and weights 4. Electronic soldering gun, 120 volts, AC, 60 cycle, 1.1 amp, 5″ overall length without tip, hot in 2¼ seconds, with removable and interchangeable tips 5. Electric soldering pencil with tellurium tips 6. Tellurium tips of various shapes and sizes 7. Soldering machine, hard solders and soft solders on all metals, 115 volts, 60 cycle, AC. A carbon electrode is touched to the work and heats the object locally in seconds, to the required heat set on the dial. Many accessories especially suited to repair work before use. This also allows easier cleaning of the file after use. Any remaining traces of solder on the metal can be removed with a hollow ground *hand scraper* followed by an abrasive cloth to eliminate the last remains. Abrasive cloths may also be used, depending on the accessibility of the solder.

Soft-Solder Stripping Solution Should it be necessary to remove soft solder by chemical action, the following solution may be used.

Fluoboric Acid 42 per cent, one quart
Hydrogen Peroxide 30 per cent, 6.5 fluid ounces
Water including wetting agent sufficient, including the above, to make one gallon.
Immerse in a fresh solution for five to fifteen minutes, at room temperature. Agitate. Works best for copper and copper alloys.

On open, flat areas where solder is exposed, its removal is affected by heating the metal to the melting point of the solder, then brushing the solder away with steel wool while it is in a molten state. Most of the solder can be removed, and the rest by abrasive cloth or files.

Mokume

Japanese swords of the past and even the ornamental ones made today are masterpieces of the iron forger's art, brought to the ultimate in refinement. Equally skillful and fascinating are the metal ornaments used to decorate the sword scabbard and pommel. Especially interesting are the sword guards, or *tsuba,* upon which encyclopedic knowledge and metalcraft skills were lavished.

One of the many techniques employed on tsuba is known as *mokume,* or "wood grain." In the early pieces this technique consisted of welding together layers of iron of varying compositions, sometimes interlacing the layers with washes of various metal oxides, all of which were forged into a solid sheet on the anvil. Sometimes the metal was cut into pieces or folded over, and joined again by forge welding. Finally it was shaped, and the finished piece was subjected to an acid bath for etching. Because of the differences in composition of the layers of metal, the acid attacked the exposed strata in varying degrees, in some places eating deeply, in others less deeply. The result was a pattern of raised ridges exposing the metal structure, which closely resembled wood grain or bark. This rough appearance

Necklace made by the author in the mokume process, using silver, copper, and brass. These metals were soldered in a "sandwich," then sliced in cross section, hammered and run through the hand mill, and joined by soldering and riveting. *Photo by Oppi.*

was greatly admired and was often used as a foil against which precious-metal decorations were applied. Delicate inlays of insects, flowers, or leaves in gold or silver are common.

A later variation of mokume substituted nonferrous metals for iron. The interest shifted from the etching effect to the differences in color of the metals employed. The metal surface is *level.* Uniformly thick or varied thicknesses of layers or sheets of silver, copper, and special Japanese alloys were used. We can substitute brass, bronze, and nickel for additional color. The following is a description modified for use today.

Before starting the metal sandwich which is mokume, the selection of metals, their sequence and thickness is decided upon. The successive *contrast of colors* is kept in mind. All sheets of metal should be the same size, to avoid waste. The size of the sheet depends on how the metal is to be used later. For jewelry, a piece 3″ × 5″ might be sufficient; for making larger pieces such as boxes, more metal is needed. It is probably a good idea to prepare more metal than one plans to use.

All metal surfaces that are to be brought into contact are cleaned completely by pickling and are thoroughly washed. They should be handled by the *edges only,* as any greasy deposit from fingerprints might hinder the later flow of solder and leave an air space between layers. Each layer that is to come in contact with another layer is painted with a mixture of borax flux and hard solder filings or solder powder. It can also be painted with borax flux and then sprinkled with solder in filings or powder form. The flux is allowed to dry. The dried sheets are placed one on top of the other in any desired order of color to the requisite thickness. The whole assembly is then bound together with wire or clamped with cotter pins, and placed on a flat sheet of asbestos or charcoal. It might be a good suggestion to have either a copper layer or a brass layer on top, as silver is in danger of collapsing first in the heating process if overheating occurs.

The entire sheet is heated uniformly with a large, soft torch flame. As the solder is concealed, the only way of judging the flow is to watch the edge of the layers to see when the bright thin line of flowing solder appears along the entire length of seams. It helps in the joining of the sheets to press them together with a pair of iron tongs when the solder begins to flow. If there is any reason to suspect that the joining of the sheets was not complete, the whole sheet should be hammered after cooling with a planishing hammer or a flat mallet on a truly flat steel sheet or flat anvil surface. Paint all the edges with flux and heat the metal again, being careful not to overheat. Keep the flame in motion, and watch the metal edge again for signs of solder fusion.

Two silver rings with gold encrustation leveled to one plane, somewhat resembling mokume, by Bertel Gardberg, Finland. *Photo by Studio Wendt, Helsinki.*

The result so far is a lamination of several metals. There are several ways of using this laminate. The simplest way is, first, to cut slices of at least ³⁄₁₆″. This is best done with a hacksaw, but if an automatic jigsaw capable of cutting metal of this thickness is available, the work is considerably diminished. A jeweler's saw is not suitable for the thickness of metal to be dealt with here at this time. Cutting thinner slices results in great loss of metal, and, as will be seen later, the thickness is to be further reduced with a rolling mill.

It is possible to use these slices after rolling, as they are. Also, a completely new pattern can be created. The pieces can be arranged, before or after rolling, in patterns resembling a wood parquet floor or in any other arrangement. They are then joined to each other by soldering. Once joined, they are run through the rolling mill (if this has not yet been done), to reduce thickness. This is now the raw material, a variegated sheet of several metals which can be used for many purposes, such as jewelry, box tops, or belt buckles.

Another approach produces an irregular pattern unlike the above-mentioned process, where the repeats of pattern and colors are more regular. In this procedure, the surface of the laminate is deliberately distorted. It can be filed in a groove, either partially or completely across, exposing under layers of metal, with a triangular or "V"-shaped file. Holes can be drilled partly through. The surface can be domed in places, and the tops of the domes filed to produce concentric circles. The whole purpose is to expose various levels of metal and allow the differences in metal colors to be seen in the final sheet; the resulting pattern can be utilized in a design.

The next step is to reduce the thickness of the metal and at the same time to expose further the color differences of the metals. This can be done manually by hammering the surface systematically with a planishing hammer, reversing the metal, and working both sides (suitable for small pieces), or the process can be greatly facilitated by the use of a rolling mill. The metal should be annealed at the first signs of work hardening. Should any holes occur, they can be filled with hard solder if small. If they are large, a patch of any metal can be made, soldered carefully, or a complete insert can be added and soldered, and the rolling procedure continued.

The resulting mokume metal is a sheet of varicolored metal in one plane, which can be handled in a variety of ways. Once the article

THE "MARRIED METALS" PROCESS.
Photos by Oppi.

1. The original drawing and traced design separates the areas into silver, copper, and brass. The presenta-

tion cigar box was made for President Kennedy by the Castillo brothers workshop in Taxco, Mexico, in the "married metals" technique they have developed. The subject chosen was the Aztec tobacco god with his pipe.

is finished, the composition, consisting as it does of different metals, can be treated with a patina or oxidating coloring process. This treatment will dramatically emphasize the differences in the metals, which will take the coloring treatment in different ways.

When soldering *parts* of this composition sheet together, use medium or *easy* solder to avoid separating the layers.

Mexican Married Metals
(*Metales Casados*)

An old process which was in use in Pre-Hispanic Mexico, but recently revived, is the process of making objects from a combination of separate pieces of silver, copper, brass, and a nickel alloy which are soldered together. The

name *metales casados* or "married metals" was given to this technique by the revivers of this kind of work, Los Castillo, a family of silversmiths who work in Taxco, Mexico. All sorts of objects in this technique are made in their workshop—jewelry, boxes, coffee sets, and other pieces.

In this work, the metal is *not* a laminate as in mokume; rather, the various metals are joined in *butt* joints, next to each other, by their edges. This means that the pieces in the design must be very carefully cut out and matched so that they fit together exactly like a jigsaw puzzle to make a total, continuous surface, and the solder joining the parts is almost invisible. After cleaning, the parts of the units in the design are placed together on a flat asbestos sheet for soldering. Most of the articles made are first made flat and can be

2. The cleaned units of the various metals used in the design are cut out and placed in position. Then the surface is painted with borax flux and the large particles of solder are placed on or near the junctures of the pieces.

3. BELOW: Two compressed air plumber's torches are brought to bear on the solder. Once the solder has started to flow, it is "led" with pointed steel rods into joints where it seems reluctant to go.

shaped somewhat later after soldering, if so desired. The joining edges are painted with borax flux, and snippets of solder are distributed along the joints. The solder is then melted with a torch. In the Castillo workshop, a plumber's torch is frequently used for large work. On the larger pieces, a solder stick is used during the flowing of the solder where additional solder seems to be needed. This means that sometimes the surface can become flooded with solder, and the metal and the design underneath becomes covered. A thick gauge metal is used, however, so that, after soldering, the surface can be finished by metal removal or scalping.

Once all the joints are made, the entire surface is filed or gone over with an abrasive applied mechanically to remove surface solder and create a uniformly smooth surface level. If the metal is to be shaped, the shaping is the next step. The metal is handled as if it were one sheet, and the shape is kept simple so that maximum surface is seen.

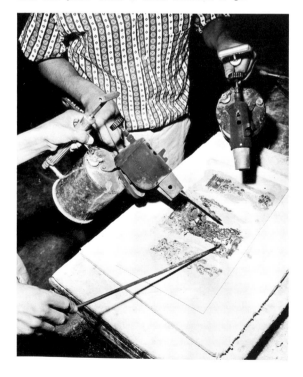

Married metals (silver, copper, and brass) coffee set with tray, designed by Los Castillo and executed in their factory-workshop in Taxco, Mexico. *Photo by Oppi.*

The surface can be polished in the same way as any other metals, but a high luster produces a surface which is too light-reflective to allow the difference in the colors of the metals to be seen. A finish created by a wire brush buff revolving at slow speed is therefore recommended. The matte surface so produced better displays the color differences.

The difference in the rate of oxidation of various metals is readily observable in married metals pieces. After polishing, copper oxidizes more rapidly than the others, and the contrast between metal colors becomes more evident. Repolishing the surface by hand is a simple matter with a piece of fine steel wool which most closely approximates the effect of a wire brush.

Niello

The word *niello* is the Italian form of the Latin word *nigellum,* the diminutive of *niger,* meaning *black*. Niello is a form of metal-on-metal decoration that takes full advantage of the contrast between the base metal color on which it is applied and the black, lustrous quality of the niello alloy. It was used by the ancient Egyptians, Greeks, Romans, and Persians and is still widely practiced in the Far East, especially in Thailand, where it is called *krueng tome*. Craftsmen of the West have shown a revival of interest in its use, especially in jewelry.

Niello as a decorative treatment for armor during the fifteenth century was directly responsible for the development of *intaglio printing,* a basic method of printing used to make etchings and engravings. In the niello process, the base metal is engraved or etched with a design, the low areas are filled with a powdered or granular mixture, approximately eutectic, of the sulphides of silver, copper, and lead, and the mixture is fused into the grooves under heat.

The armorers, at intervals during the engraving of their design, filled the engraved design with ink and took an impression of the design on paper to see more easily what the final appearance of the armor would be after the application of niello. From these "proofs" the design was altered and developed. Making proofs developed into the separate art of etching and engraving. Armorers sold engravings as a part-time occupation, and soon graphic artists, quick to realize the technique's possibilities, took over the process as a natural means of expression.

PREPARING METAL FOR NIELLO

The metals on which niello can be applied are gold, silver, bronze, and steel, among others, with silver the most commonly employed base in use today. As niello is the *final* treatment employed on any article so decorated,

Niello tools and materials: 1. Crucibles with stirring rod tongs holding graphite stirring rods 2. Crucible pouring tongs 3. Ball peen hammer for crushing niello 4. Steel plate to receive the pouring out of niello 5. Mortar and pestle, agate mortar and pestle, mounted agate pestle for grinding niello into powder 6. Tripod and heating frames for firing niello with a torch from below 7. Spatulas for loading niello and prodding it into place 8. Sifter for grading powdered niello 9. Glass bottle, 1½ ounce, with ground glass stopper for the storage of niello 10. Carborundum stick for grinding and levelling the surface of fired niello

Man's silver belt buckle, called a *pinding,* decorated with niello. From Perak or Panang, Malaya. *Photo by Oppi.*

The reverse side of the belt buckle, which shows the repoussé process used to create the depressions into which the niello was placed. The design on the front was refined and sharpened with chasing tools after the repoussé work was completed. *Photo by Oppi.*

the article must be completed in every other way. Its preparation and application are similar in several respects to the wet inlay technique in enamel in the method known as champlevé.

The design or the areas to receive the niello can be produced by engraving, etching, punching, working with repoussé tools or chasing tools, or by any means which will result in a depressed area into which the niello can be placed. The spaces do not have to be large—even finely engraved lines can be filled with niello. In larger areas, the metal should be removed to a uniform depth so that, later, in the leveling process, the niello will not become too thin or the base metal exposed. As too thick an application of niello may result in bubbles or pitting, the depth of the depression should be shallow, between ⅟₃₂″ and ⅟₆₄″. Undercutting is not necessary, as the fusion between the niello and the base metal is complete.

PREPARING NIELLO FOR METAL

Most preparations for niello require silver, copper, lead, and sulphur, with some recipes calling for other metals. Equipment consists of two crucibles, a torch, crucible tongs, a hammer, a steel plate, mortar and pestle, an 80-mesh sifter, and, if available, a small kiln capable of reaching and maintaining a temperature of 1000° F. The *cleaned* metals are weighed out according to the recipe being followed. They can be melted in one crucible in a kiln, or with a blowtorch, in the following sequence: silver, the metal with the highest melting point, is melted, and when this has liquefied, copper, with the next highest, is added, and finally lead, with the lowest melting point. The entire contents are stirred with a stout charcoal stick which, besides mixing the metals, introduces a small amount of carbon into the alloy. Should any slag form at the top, it should be removed with an iron ladle, or a graphite pencil or rod. Graphite rods, made in eight-inch lengths, are used to stir precious molten metals. They last a long time, do not melt, are not affected by violent temperature changes, and do not contaminate the metal. No metal will stick to the rods, and while the end touching the metal may be red hot, the other end remains cool and can be handled.

When all the metals are thoroughly combined, they are poured into the second crucible, which contains the sulphur. This crucible is prepared in advance by heating, sometime after the copper is melted, and before the lead has been included in the first crucible. When the molten metal has been poured into the sulphur crucible, some additional sulphur is added. The whole mixture is again brought to a molten state to insure complete fusion of the elements.

Some craftsmen use only one crucible for the entire process, putting the sulphur directly into the first and only crucible after the metals have fused. Covering the entire surface of the metals in the crucible with a half-inch layer of powdered charcoal has been found to aid considerably in complete fusion, and prevents surface oxidation.

The molten metal is poured onto a slightly oiled steel slab (a thick, polished stone slab can also be used), and while it cools, it is hammered out into a sheet of some thickness. If it cools too quickly, it becomes too brittle for hammering, and a torch can be applied intermittently to keep it hot while the hammering continues. It is then allowed to cool, and once cool, it is easily broken up with a hammer. The pieces are placed in a mortar and pestle and ground till all the particles can pass through an 80-mesh sieve. Heavier particles that do not pass through are returned to the mortar and ground till they do.

Niello can be ground finer than 80 mesh when it is intended for use over fine lines. Like hand-ground enamel, it should be washed before use to get rid of charcoal particles, ground mortar particles, and other foreign matter. To do this, place the ground niello in a glass jar, cover the niello with water, stir, allow the particles to settle, then pour off the liquid, which will carry the lighter waste with it. Repeat the process. To dry, spread the powder over a metal plate and heat from below till all traces of moisture vapor disappear. Dry niello can be stored for future use in a closed, airtight container, but it will deteriorate in time. The length of time it can be stored depends on climatic conditions, especially humidity, which hastens the disintegration of the alloy. It is a better idea, if the using of prepared niello is to be delayed, to store it in lump form, which is less susceptible to deterioration, and grind only the amounts needed just prior to use.

CHARGING THE NIELLO

Before applying or charging the metal with niello, the metal must be thoroughly cleaned by pickling, washing, and, if necessary, wire brushing. Prepare a borax mixture on a nearly water-filled, clean borax slate, grinding enough of the solid or cake borax to make a milky mixture. Paint the areas to receive the niello with this mixture. Charge the depressions with wet niello, using a small spatula such as that used to load wet enamel. Apply more than a level amount of niello, as it will shrink in volume during the heating and this loss in bulk must be compensated for. Experience will indicate how much more is needed.

The nature of the niello alloy allows it to fuse at a lower temperature than the base metal and to spread and sink into all the depressions. The surface is later filed and polished so that the niello remains only in the depressions of the design, while the entire surface is made uniformly flush. With fine-line designs, it may therefore be necessary to cover the *area* with niello, keeping the spread within the smallest possible limits, and later to expose the lines by filing away the excess. Because niello has a tendency to flow and spread when it fuses, use the minimum amount necessary.

FUSING THE NIELLO

Once the niello is charged, the moisture in the borax and niello should be allowed to dry by slowly heating the object till all traces of rising water vapors have disappeared. If a kiln is employed to fuse the niello, drying can be done by inserting the piece, mounted and ready for firing on a trivet, quickly into the kiln and out. Niello can be fused with a torch with careful heating, especially if the piece has niello applied on only one surface, so that the torch can be applied from underneath. A kiln heated to about 1000° F is the best heat source, as the heat is clean and even and the danger of uneven heating or of possible carbon deposit from a torch is eliminated.

Depending on the size and shape of the piece and the manner in which the niello is distributed, it should be mounted for firing on a trivet or supported with refractory material such as rods, small bricks, or stilts, or Nichrome-wire heating frames or wires that can be improvised for the occasion. The niello should not be allowed to come in contact with any support or firing device.

To achieve a smooth surface, it sometimes helps to sprinkle a small amount of powdered borax on the niello before firing. This fluxes the surface of the niello and prevents oxidation, which might cause the surface to be uneven. Flat pieces present no problem in keeping the niello in place, but shaped pieces sometimes create difficulties. A small amount of diluted gum tragacanth mixed with the powdered niello before loading it on the metal will help to hold it in place.

To fire the niello, the dried piece is inserted into the preheated kiln by opening the door and placing the mounted piece on its trivet on the kiln floor. It is handled with a long-armed spatula, firing fork, or tongs such as those used in enameling. Place the trivet gently so as to avoid jarring the niello out of place. Allow enough time for the niello to fuse smoothly, taking a peek into the kiln occasionally to observe the niello surface. Once the niello is smooth, remove the article *immediately*. Overheating, especially on shaped pieces, may cause the niello to run out of the depressions and no longer to be level, or cause the niello to eat into the base metal. Allow the piece to cool slowly *in air. Do not quench.*

When pieces are fired in the open with a torch applied from below, the article, probably flat with the niello on one surface, can be watched during the firing process. If necessary, in this situation the niello can be worked into recesses where it seems reluctant to flow by prodding it with a steel-pointed spatula while it is still molten and plastic.

Silver necklace with niello, *Taza, Morocco,* 17.55″ long.
Collection Musee de l'Homme, Paris.

It is best to fire the niello *once* if this is possible or, if not, then certainly to aim for a *minimum* number of firings. Repeated firings may cause the niello to form internal bubbles which, after leveling, will become exposed and necessitate refilling the hole and refiring. With each additional firing there is the risk that the lead content in the niello may eat into and corrode the base metal, or burn out and scar the niello.

If repairing is made necessary by the exposure of a hidden hole after leveling, or by shrinkage because of too little niello in the first application, flux the old niello with the borax solution, add more niello where needed, and fire again, following the same procedure as before.

FINISHING NIELLO

To finish the niello surface and make it flush with the base metal, the traditional treatment for niello, it must be filed. Use a flat, medium-coarse file, working carefully till nearly the whole base-metal surface is exposed. Then change to a Scotch stone (Water of Ayr or Tam O'Shanter) to expose the rest, and remove file marks. Keep the surface well moistened with water while working. A carborundum stick can be used instead of a file, followed by a Scotch stone. The surface is sometimes burnished by lightly heating it and going over it with an oiled burnisher. This compresses the surface and eliminates small air bubbles near the surface of the niello.

Once the level of the niello and the base metal has been reached, the final polishing can be done with a large-surfaced felt buffing wheel and tripoli, followed by rouge. If the niello design is delicate and the depth shallow, the only surfacing tool needed is a medium-coarse emery stick, which may take a while longer but is less risky, followed by a rouge buffing.

The ancient Egyptians practiced an interesting variation of niello not seen today, but easily tried. They inlaid pure gold or silver wire into the niello by shaping the wire and placing it in the groove where the niello was to go. The niello was then piled around and over the wire, and the article fired. After fusing, the niello was finished in the usual way; the leveling process exposed the wire, which appeared inlaid, much like cloison wire in cloisonné enameling. Grains, flattened or round, can be applied in the same way.

NIELLO FORMULAS

Many niello formulas are available in old source books. The monk Theophilus, who wrote a treatise on gold and silversmith's work in the eleventh century, includes a recipe and detailed description of niello work. Basically, the idea of all niello formulas is to convert the metals used into sulphides. These become plastic *below* the melting points of the metals when melted separately and turn the alloy into a dark color ranging from gray to black to blue-black, depending on the formula.

The various components and proportions thereof change the properties of the final product. Low lead content produces a more brittle niello, making it possible to grind it to a finer powder. An excess of sulphur produces a blacker niello. The niello worker is advised to try variations on given formulas to develop his own recipes.

Silver	3 parts
Copper	5 parts
Lead	7 parts
Sulphur	6 parts
Ammonium chloride	2 parts
Borax	24 parts

Silver	8	2	1	1	2	Russian	
Copper	18	5	6	2	1	Silver	1 part
Lead	13	7	10	4	0	Copper	2 parts
Sulphur	96	24	36	5	3	Lead	3 parts
						Sulphur	12 parts

Russian Tula (bluish niello)

Silver	9	
Copper	1	After melting, the
Lead	1	metals are saturated
Bismuth	1	with sulphur.

Gold buckle with niello inlay, 7th century A.D. Found in the ship burial at Sutton-Hoo, Suffolk, England. *British Museum, London.*

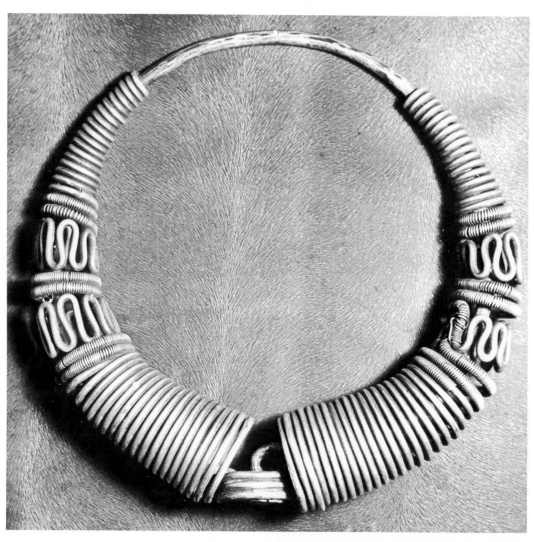

Contemporary silver wire necklace from Porbandar, Saurashtra, India. This necklace is made basically from five pieces of wire. The heaviest one supports the rest and forms the catch. The lighter ones spiral around it on either side and the finest wire, which adds interest, is wrapped around the outer wire on both sides. *Photo by Oppi.*

Wire

Wire is metal which is uniform in cross section and continuous. Wire can be in the form of a mere filament, as thin as hair, or a thin, flexible rod; beyond that point it might better be described as a bar. Wire is one of the basic forms of metal used by the craftsman. Ever since man discovered that metals have the quality of *ductility,* meaning they can be easily drawn into wire form, wire has been used for ornamental and practical purposes ranging

from the hairsbreadth wire used in weaving metallic brocades to the cables used for supporting suspension bridges.

The origin of wire is unknown, dating back thousands of years. Commercially produced drawn wire existed in France in the late thirteenth century and was made for the construction of chain-mail armor used by medieval knights. Wire drawing existed in other than European cultures before this time, and certainly wire was made by hammering metal

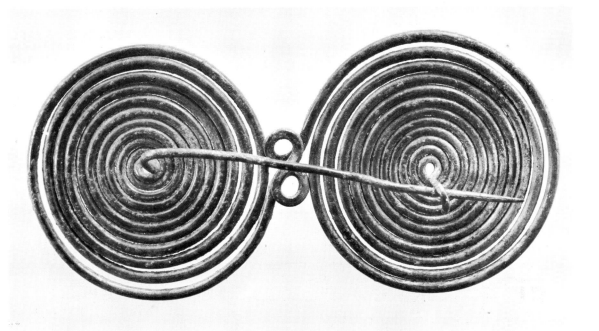

Greek bronze wire fibula, "spectacle type," tenth–eighth centuries B.C. (Geometrical Period). Back view. Length: 5⁵⁄₁₆ inches. This pin, including the pinstem and catch, is made entirely of one continuous piece of wire. *Metropolitan Museum of Art, New York. Fletcher Fund, 1937.*

Spiraled ribbon wire necklace of straight and twisted wire in 18-karat gold, with diamonds set in platinum. Designed and executed at Tiffany & Co., New York City. *Tiffany & Co.*

long before the idea of *drawing* wire occurred to anyone.

Today wire is available in hundreds of forms; the most common ones used by craftsmen are round, half round, oval, half oval, octagonal, hexagonal, rectangular, and square.

The process of wire drawing is described on page 42. A description of gold-plated hand-drawn silver-wire making as practiced in India today is given here.

HAND-DRAWN GOLD-PLATED SILVER WIRE

A bar of silver about three-quarters of an inch thick and a foot long, tapered at *both* ends, is gilded. This is done by wrapping the bar with two layers of pure gold leaf, applying some flux, and placing it in a furnace till the gold melts, fuses, and unites with the silver, after which it is immediately withdrawn, before the bar melts. The heating can also be done with a torch. The silver bar is then drawn through a drawplate to reduce its cross section in the usual way. The ends of the bar are entered into the drawplate *alternately*. The gold is so ductile that, no matter how many times it is drawn through the plate, a thin, even layer of gold remains to cover the silver wire underneath. The process is repeated till wire of the desired diameter section is achieved.

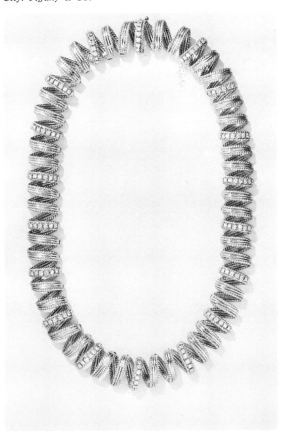

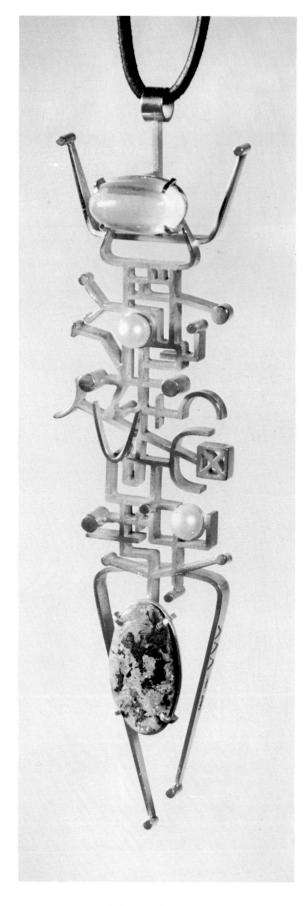

Silver wire bracelet or armlet from Balamun, Egypt, (Ptolemaic Period) (323–30 B.C.). The entire construction is made of twisted wires holding units together without any solder. Ornamented with five cobra heads bearing stamped, ridged patterns. *Metropolitan Museum of Art, New York. Carnarvon Collection, Gift of Edward S. Harkness, 1926.*

LEFT: Gold pendant set with black opal, moonstone, and pearls, designed and executed by John Prip. Made almost entirely in wire of rectangular cross section with round wire terminals.

Gold wire necklet, made by E. R. Nele, Munich, Germany. *Collection of the Victoria and Albert Museum, London. Worshipful Company of Goldsmiths, London. Photo by Peter Parkinson.*

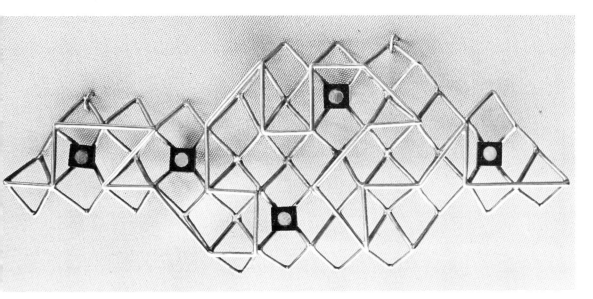

Pin made entirely of white gold wire and decorated with black onyx, jade, coral, jasper, and agate, by Margaret de Patta.

Necklace made entirely of gold wire set with diamonds, designed and executed by Louis Osman, 1961. *Collection of the Worshipful Company of Goldsmiths, London. Photo by Peter Parkinson.*

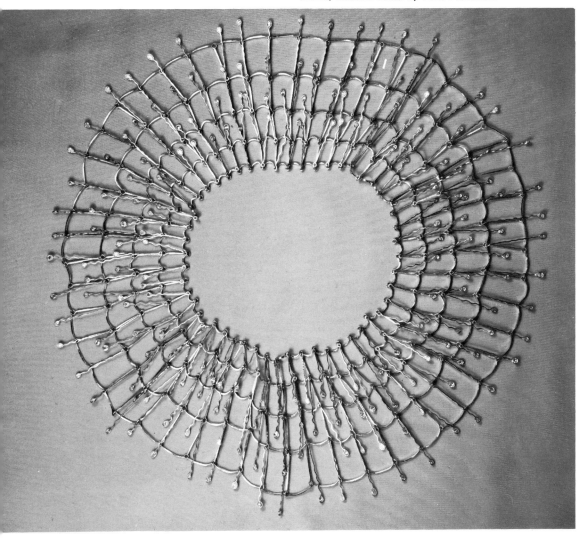

English Sheffield plate sugar bowl, with flaring rim forming a spoon rack, 1790. Height: 8 inches; width: 5⅜ inches. Sheffield plate owed its technical success to the similarity in malleability of silver and copper. After cladding the plate of copper with silver, the two metals remained in the same relative thicknesses, no matter how thinly the resulting sheet was rolled out. *Metropolitan Museum of Art, New York. Rogers Fund, 1912.*

Silver Torah Crown constructed almost entirely of wire of square and round cross section, made by Ludwig J. Wolpert, 1961. *Photo by Frank J. Darmstaedter.*

FILIGREE

Wire filigree has been used as a basic form of decoration on metal from earliest times in many cultures. It is still produced in quantity in Europe (Norway, Portugal, Yugoslavia, Hungary, Italy, and the U.S.S.R.), in Africa and the Middle East (Algeria, Iran, Turkey, Israel, and Yemen), and the Far East (India, China, and Japan), to mention the more productive places. Though stylistic differences exist in these areas, the method of creating filigree is basically the same.

Annealed, fine silver wire is often used for filigree, as it is the most pliable and easiest to shape, but in several places low-grade silver, copper, and white-metal wire is used and silver- or gold-plated afterward. Gold wire is also used, but not as often today as in the past. Silver or other metal wires can be gold-plated.

Though flat wire or braided or twisted wire that has been flattened is most commonly used, wire of other cross section is also employed (oval, triangular, half round, rectangular, etc.). If such wire is not available, it can readily be made by the use of a drawplate. (See wire drawing, page 42.) Twisted wire can be flattened with a hammer on a flat anvil or metal plate, or it can be run through a rolling mill. Braided or plaited wire is also used. All wire must be perfectly clean, or soldering will be difficult, and the wire should be annealed.

The method of making filigree described here is that employed in Cuttack, India, still an important filigree center today, producing work of great refinement, delicacy, and often virtuosic complexity.

When creating a *unit* of filigree for use as a *part* of an article of jewelry, or to be later incorporated into an object such as a tray, box, or other ornamental object, the heavier-wire, outer frame of the unit is made first. This is shaped with a pair of pointed pliers or heavy tweezers and soldered together with hard solder. Subdivisions in the design are then made with the same wire and soldered in place. The spaces are then filled with repeated shapes of finer wire, packed in tightly so that there is no movement in the unit. These filler shapes are made with pliers and fingers. Certain basic shapes are used constantly, in various combinations. Oval or completely round spirals, double-reverse spirals, comma shapes, angular shapes, and others to which wire can easily be formed are used. In India, each form has a special name.

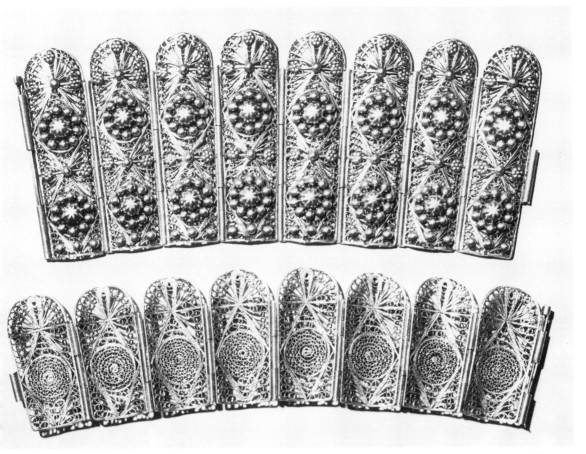

Contemporary filigree wire bracelets decorated with shot and stamped domes, from Cairo, Egypt. The bottom bracelet, similar in design and construction to the top one, shows the reverse side of the work. It reveals patterns that simply support the applied units and are never seen. *Photo by Oppi.*

BELOW: Silver wire filigree box, believed to be Turkish in origin. The filigree method of wire construction has been used to make objects serving a variety of purposes, despite its delicacy. (Its construction often consists of joining smaller units into larger frames.) *Photo by Oppi.*

Examples of contemporary silver wire filigree work done in Cuttack, Orissa, India, where many craftsmen work solely in this technique. Pictured here are bracelets, pins, hair ornaments, an evening purse, and a plate. Filigree work in Cuttack is always pickled a dead white after completion, and some parts of heavier wire and upper surfaces are burnished bright. *Photo by Oppi.*

BELOW: Contemporary plate of silver wire filigree, made in Cuttack, Orissa, India. About 10 inches square. A great variety of forms are joined into a larger framework, producing an effect of wire lace. *Photo by Oppi.*

Whenever wire must be cut, it is placed on a piece of soft brass and cut with a sharp chisel, which is simply pressed downward. End- or side-cutting nippers can also be used. It is important for the units to fit tightly in the outer frame of the unit so that they touch. Contact is an essential prerequisite to good soldering.

Fine particles of easy solder are prepared by filing clean solder sheet with a rough file and catching the lemel or filings on a clean paper. These particles are then mixed with about 10 per cent dry borax powder, and the combination is sprinkled over the whole piece. The flat unit being made ready for soldering is then lifted carefully with a spatula and placed either on a thin sheet of asbestos or on a sheet of mica. Asbestos is used if the soldering is done with a torch. Mica is used when the unit is to be soldered by placing it on a bed

The interesting method of filigree-like construction on this bracelet consists of wire and shot soldered to a shaped silver wire mesh that supports the wire decoration. The origin of the bracelet is China. *Photo by Oppi.*

BELOW: The same bracelet, reverse side, showing the wire mesh support.

of hot charcoal. The charcoal is brought to a higher temperature by fanning the coals or blowing them with a hand bellows. The unit is allowed to remain till the solder flows, and is then immediately removed to avoid melting the fine wire.

In the West, the charcoal fire can be simulated by heating the unit from *below* with a torch after placing it on its mica sheet on a ring stand. Heating from below is preferable to heating from above, because the whole unit heats more slowly and evenly. There is less chance of overheating the wire and melting it, as the soldering process is easier to watch. If the unit must be heated from above with a torch, use a soft flame with little air to avoid overheating.

The unit must be pickled after each soldering operation to remove oxide scale caused by the heat and to dissolve fused borax; both materials would impede the flow of solder, if not removed, when more soldering is necessary. Old soldered joints can be protected by mixing powdered rouge, yellow ochre, or whiting to make a solder-inhibiting paste. This paste

is painted on old joints with a brush to protect them. Do not allow the paste to come too near the joint about to be soldered. Remove the hardened paste under water, after soldering, with a stiff brush. This should be done before placing the unit in pickle to clean it, as inhibiting pastes can contaminate the acid. Pickling should be followed by a thorough rinsing in running water. It may be necessary to hold small units in place on the mica sheet with binding wire, cotter pins, or clips.

To flatten soldered filigree units, place them on a steel block and lightly tap them flat with a wood mallet. A soft wood block can also be placed on top of a unit and the wood lightly hammered to flatten the filigree. A filigree unit can also be shaped, after finishing, on a dapping block, in a wood mold of suitable shape, in a depression in a wood block, or on a sandbag, where it is hammered lightly with a wood mallet or a mallet of other soft material.

Filigree work can be left completely open, or the wire work can be mounted on a backing sheet of solid metal. This can be done by riveting units on the sheet or soldering them

in position. Large filigree pieces are made by joining smaller units.

In the East (India and China) filigree work is not mechanically polished. After the filigree has been placed for the last time in the pickle bath to clean it, it emerges dead white and matte. The wire is left this way. The top edges, however, are burnished *bright* by rubbing them with tapered and pointed steel or agate burnishers; the result is a nice contrast between dull and shining wire. The whole filigree unit can, of course, be oxidized to blacken the metal and then polished by hand with rouge only on its upper surfaces. This is followed by a scrubbing with a stiff brush and a solution of ammonia, soap, and water. A thorough rinsing in running water follows, and finally drying with a soft cloth.

BELOW: Mixtec Mexican Indian lost-wax cast gold, wirework ring. Discovered in a tomb in Monte Alban, in the state of Oaxaca, Mexico. Height: ⅞ inch. Although this ring looks like filigree work, the pattern was made with wax and then invested and cast. *Museum of the American Indian, Heye Foundation, New York.*

German silver-gilt knife and fork with filigree decorated handles, 1660–70. *Museum of Decorative Art, Copenhagen.*

Book cover, by Master J. M. Sandrat, Frankfurt-am-Main, c. 1710. The decoration is mainly cast openwork reproducing filigree wirework. *Jacob Michael Collection, Jewish Museum, New York. Photo by Frank J. Darmstaedter.*

BELOW: American wire birdcage, nineteenth century. *Cooper Union Museum for the Arts of Decoration, New York.*

RIGHT: Wire birdcage, from L'Art Tunisien des Cages, Sidi-Bou-Said, Tunisia. *Photo by Oppi.*

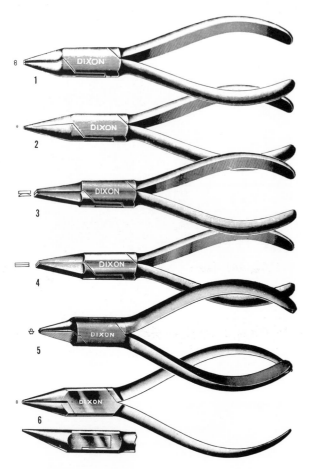

Hand pliers, forged steel, box joint, available in 3½",
4", 4½", 5", 5½", 6" lengths: 1. Round nose 2. Chain
nose 3. Half round 4. Flat nose 5. Forming 6. Offset
chain nose

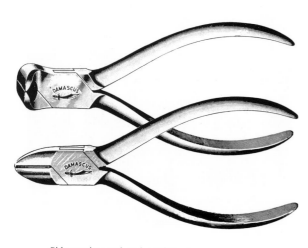

Side cutting and end cutting nippers

Granulation

Gold and silver granulation is a method of
decorating surfaces, usually on jewelry or
other small pieces because of the minuteness
of scale, with tiny full spheres of metal. These
"granules" are arranged in designed patterns,
or at random, and are joined to the base metal
without the use of solder. This method of decoration was found on ornaments discovered in
the tomb of the Egyptian Pharaoh Tutenkhamon (1350 B.C.), but the technique reached
a peak of perfection never quite equaled since
by the Etruscan goldsmiths of the eighth to
the second centuries B.C. The Greeks also were
masters of the process, often employing balls
of one hundredth of an inch in diameter. As
archaeological discoveries played an important
part in the influence of jewelry design and
metalwork of the Victorian Era, it was natural
that contemporary discoveries of Etruscan
granulated jewels should result in a revival and
find some expert practitioners.

Fortunato Pio Castellani, a goldsmith practicing in Rome, Italy, in 1814 discovered Um-
brian craftsmen still working in the ancient
style of gold *granaglia* and brought them to his
workshop to instruct his workers in the technique. At about the same time, discoveries
were being made in Pompeii and Hercula-
neum, and among them were gold-granulated
jewels. From these, Castellani developed the
"Etruscan style" of jewelry, which at first was
simply a reproduction of the original pieces
and later became a style using Etruscan
themes. The style became extremely popular,
and the technique spread to Paris with other
masters such as Fontenay in Paris and Robert
Phillips, John Brogen, and Carlo Giuliano in
London producing outstanding work. The
pieces of the nineteenth century can be identified by their use of gemstones, and colored
golds unknown in ancient times.

Though the technique has fallen into general
disuse in the West, granulation is still common
in the Far East, particularly in India, where
gold is used, and in Bali, where the work is
done with silver. There are a few outstanding
craftsmen in the West whose work concen-
trates on this specialty, among them Elisabeth
Treskow in Köln, West Germany, and John
Paul Miller in the United States.

Persian gold bracelet with quatrefoil hinge, (Seljug Period), eleventh century. Diameter: about 4¾₆ inches; weight: 73.6 grams. The decoration on the hinge is composed of four large and twelve small domes with granulation work and is embellished with four inlaid turquoises. The tubular ring part has a small pin lock and is covered with a wire spiral to imitate a torque. *Freer Gallery of Art, Washington, D.C.*

GRANULATION TECHNIQUE:
MAKING THE GRANULES

To make the granules of gold or silver, a graphite crucible or a steel box (4″×5″× 2½″) is prepared with a layer or bed of crushed, powdered, hardwood charcoal inside. Do not use charcoal which is crushed too fine or it will not support the metal, and the risk occurs of the metal sinking through it upon melting and forming a solid mass at the bottom. The metal used must be clean and oxide-free.

To make many balls of approximately the same size, several wires of the chosen metal are cut with a shears or nippers into uniform lengths or bits which are allowed to drop onto the charcoal bed inside the crucible or steel box. Sheet metal can also be used, rolled out thinly and cut into snippets exactly as one does in the preparation of solder. Very fine balls can be made by drawing a coarse file across

a bar or sheet of gold or silver and allowing the filings to drop directly into the charcoal-lined crucible or box. The cuttings or filings should be distributed separately, because if they touch, they will join one another and become larger balls nearer the size of shot. It is a good idea to make more granules than one expects to need, as there is bound to be a variation in size, and if one wants uniformity, sizes must be matched later by selection.

Once one layer is made, it is covered with about ½″ of powdered charcoal, and a second layer of cuttings is made, followed by as many layers as will fill the container. The crucible or steel box is then placed into a preheated kiln or furnace heated to about 1900° F, where it is kept at this temperature for at least one half hour. If a small crucible is used, two torches playing simultaneously on the crucible from opposite directions will probably be sufficient. While the container remains in the heat, the particles of metal melt and automatically form spheroid balls. The charcoal cover acts as a reducing agent and prevents the oxidation of the surface of the balls, and they remain bright.

After a slow cooling, the contents of the crucible are poured into a pan containing water and some detergent. The charcoal is floated off while the granules of metal remain at the bottom. These are dried and then can be sorted by passing them through sieves or screen mesh ranging from the finest first to the coarsest last, or by a more time-consuming manual selection with a pair of tweezers.

Granules can also be made on the surface of a charcoal block by first placing the metal, then playing a torch flame on it till the snippets melt and form a ball. Once the balls are formed, a red heat should be maintained for a few minutes before gradually removing the flame.

JOINING THE GRANULES

The base metal should be thoroughly cleaned first by heating and quenching it in a half and half solution of nitric acid and water, and then thoroughly rinsed. As previously mentioned, the granules are joined to the base metal without the aid of ordinary solder which, no matter how finely divided, would flood the granules on melting and destroy their round, spherical appearance. The joint is made instead by the exploitation of a metallurgical principle.

When pure gold is used, a copper salt such as finely divided powdered cupric hydroxide $[Cu(OH)_2]$ is mixed with an equal amount of an organic glue such as gum tragacanth, acacia or fish glue and water is added to make a thin paste. This mixture is used at the end of a fine brush, and the entire granule ball is coated with it, picked up, and placed in position. When all the granules are in place, the whole piece is allowed to dry thoroughly. (Some sources report using crushed Crysacolla stone, which has a copper content.)

A *reduced* flame from a torch is then applied, and the piece is heated *slowly*. The glue carbonizes, and at a certain temperature the cupric hydroxide becomes cupric oxide. The oxygen in the cupric oxide then combines with the carbon, and the carbon reduces the copper oxide to copper, while the rest is dissipated as carbon dioxide gas. A film of finely divided metallic copper forms and joins the grain to the base metal at the point of contact only.

"Starfish," by Dan Blumberg. Silver with granulation, gold-plated. Diameter: 2½ inches. *Photo by Blumberg.*

Contemporary 22-karat gold ring, with granulation decoration. Made for the author by the Nanubhai Jewelers in Bombay, India. The gold granulation technique is still practiced in many areas of India. *Photo by Lex Tice.*

This point is practically invisible, as the copper has become in effect an alloy with the adjacent gold at the point of contact and holds it firmly in place. When gold of a lower than fine karat is used, alloys already containing copper may form the joint without the addition of cupric hydroxide, but its use is an additional insurance toward a successful joint.

Gold ring with amethyst, by Toza Radakovich. Made in a combination of techniques, including lost wax, forging, granulation, and filing. *Photo by Lynn Fayman.*

LEFT: Part of an Etruscan gold granulation-decorated bracelet. The consummate skill with which the Etruscan goldsmiths practiced gold granulation has never been surpassed. *Victoria and Albert Museum, London.*

BELOW: Silver bead necklace, found in Finland. It is thought to have been made at the time of the Crusades. Almost every bead is decorated in a different manner, including granulation. *Finland's National Museum, Helsinki.*

Gold bead necklace decorated with granulation, by John Paul Miller. *Photo by Miller.*

RIGHT: Gold brooch with rectangular granulation, by John Paul Miller. *Photo by Miller.*

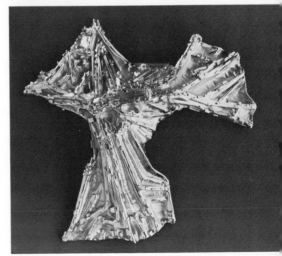

GENERAL CONSIDERATIONS

The main difficulty in granulation is in bringing the melting point of the metal surface and the granules to just the point when they will fuse without collapsing. This means a

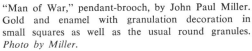

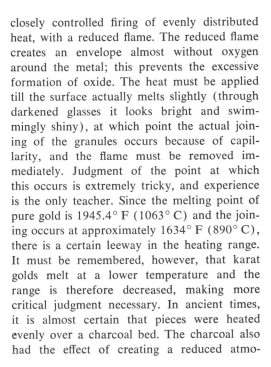

"Man of War," pendant-brooch, by John Paul Miller. Gold and enamel with granulation decoration in small squares as well as the usual round granules. *Photo by Miller.*

"Mollusk," pendant-brooch, by John Paul Miller. Gold and enamel with granulation. *Photo by Miller.*

closely controlled firing of evenly distributed heat, with a reduced flame. The reduced flame creates an envelope almost without oxygen around the metal; this prevents the excessive formation of oxide. The heat must be applied till the surface actually melts slightly (through darkened glasses it looks bright and swimmingly shiny), at which point the actual joining of the granules occurs because of capillarity, and the flame must be removed immediately. Judgment of the point at which this occurs is extremely tricky, and experience is the only teacher. Since the melting point of pure gold is 1945.4° F (1063° C) and the joining occurs at approximately 1634° F (890° C), there is a certain leeway in the heating range. It must be remembered, however, that karat golds melt at a lower temperature and the range is therefore decreased, making more critical judgment necessary. In ancient times, it is almost certain that pieces were heated evenly over a charcoal bed. The charcoal also had the effect of creating a reduced atmo-

sphere, essential in the joining of granules. This practice is still carried on in India and Bali, where granulation is done by only the most primitive means.

Some granulists claim that the best results occur when the thickness of the sheet upon which the joining of the granules is done is *less* than the diameter of the granules. In this case, it is claimed, there is less chance of the granules becoming overheated and melting while the sheet is absorbing the heat necessary for fusion. A prolonged and gradual cooling period after heating is essential.

Not only round granules but flattened granules, wire, and rectangular sections of wire can be joined in the same way. When placing granules on a dimensional surface, it is necessary to allow one area of glued granules to dry so that they will hold in place while the others are joined. If possible, all granules should be joined in one firing. Replacement of granules lost during firing is possible, but, of course, there is risk of injury unless great care is taken.

To finish granulated pieces, pickle them in a 20 per cent solution of sulphuric acid, and polish carefully with a slow-speed crimped nickel silver wire brush to which a soap solution is applied. After drying, the final bright finish can be done manually with a rouge cloth or by a very careful buffing with rouge on a soft cotton flannel buff. A bright-dip acid bath which eliminates mechanical buffing is also possible.

Two silver rings, by Saara Hopea Untracht. Shot has been used as the main decorative element. It is combined with turquoises on the left. Produced by Kultasepänliike Ossian Hopea, Porvoo, Finland. *Photo by Pietinen.*

Making Shot

It is difficult to say when a granule becomes a shot, but, generally speaking, granules are very small balls of gold or silver, and shot are larger spheres, perhaps, arbitrarily, larger than $\frac{1}{32}''$. As the method for the formation of shot is similar to that of making granules, and shot might be used in combination with granules, the procedure is discussed here. (Also see *Shotting,* page 49, one of the basic methods in which metals are formed, but resulting in large pieces of shot.)

Shot are balls of metal which take their name from the form in which balls of similar size are used in ammunition made for hunting. Shot balls are widely used as a form of decoration in metalwork, especially for jewelry, and their use dates back for centuries.

Shot balls are made by cutting pieces of wire or sheet metal (scrap can be used for this purpose) and placing them in, preferably, a round depression made in a charcoal block by a rotating pressure with a tool such as a small dapping punch or a repoussé tool. (The round depression is made where a completely spheroid ball is wanted. If a ball with one side flattened is wanted, place the metal on a flat surface. Balls with one flat surface are easy to place on a flat sheet and will not roll.) The metal is painted with borax flux to prevent oxidation of the surface of the shot and allow the formation of a perfectly round ball. A torch flame is then turned on the metal and allowed to play on it till it becomes molten and automatically draws itself into a ball by capillary attraction and surface tension. Once the ball is formed, turn off the air in the torch slowly and reduce the flame gradually. If this is not possible, then slowly reduce the size of the flame. A reduction flame (more gas than oxygen) leaves the ball oxide-free and perfectly spheroid.

Balls can be used round, or they can be *flattened* into small discs by hammering them

Box of nickel silver with silver shot decoration on the lid, by John Prip. The texture created by tools has been deliberately retained on the surface.

on a steel plate with a planishing hammer. Do not force the flattening too quickly or cracks might form at the edges.

To keep shot in place for soldering, a mixture of gum and flux can be applied, the shot put in place, and the whole allowed to dry. It is also possible to make a small depression on a metal surface by striking the spot with a small rounded tool and place the shot in the depression. Balls can first be soldered to each other in groups, and then soldered *as groups* onto a background. Such groups are of course more easily handled than individual balls of shot. When soldering shot, do not use more solder than is necessary. One small piece placed leaning against a ball of shot is probably enough. Too much solder on small shot causes malformation of the roundness of the ball; the solder runs over the surface and becomes a part of the ball, giving it a clumsy look.

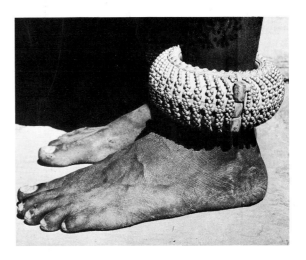

Gold ring with ruby, by Jean Claude Champagnat, Paris. The basic form was made first and was then completely covered with soldered shot of various sizes. *Photo by Del Bocca.*

BELOW: Gold ear ornament, front view, Nasca, Peru. Height: 2 inches. Balls of shot have been liberally used to delineate the main design elements. *Museum of the American Indian, Heye Foundation, New York.*

Woman's silver ankle bracelet from Madhya Pradesh, India, decorated with balls of shot. *Photo by Oppi.*

METAL TECHNIQUES THAT REQUIRE SOLDERING   209

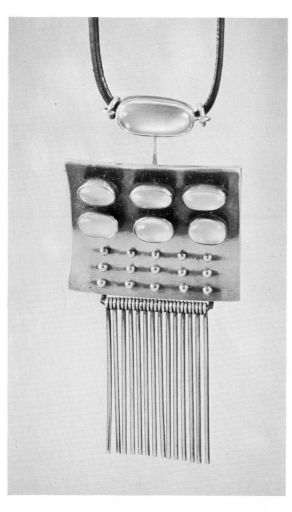

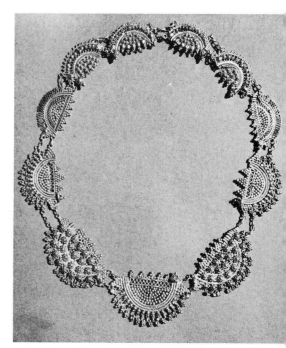

Silver necklace, thought to have been made in India. The construction is entirely of shot and wire in a variety of arrangements. *Photo by Oppi.*

ABOVE LEFT: Pendant of silver and gold with moonstones and regularly spaced balls of shot, by John Prip.

BELOW LEFT: Contemporary silver brooches from Israel. The designs were made with wire decorations, semi-precious stones, and shot often filed so that it presents a flat surface. *Photo by Oppi.*

BELOW AND OPPOSITE: Two contemporary silver rings, from Patna, Bihar, India. They utilize shot in round, flattened, embossed, and stamped forms for decorative effect. *Photos by Lex Tice.*

Contemporary silver necklace with silver and red glass beads, made in Yemen. Shot has been liberally used as a decorative element in the design. *Photo by Oppi.*

BELOW: Contemporary link necklace, from Israel. Decorated with flattened and stamped discs of shot that have been soldered to create link units. *Photo by Oppi.*

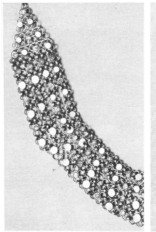
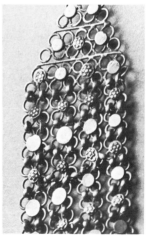

METAL TECHNIQUES THAT REQUIRE SOLDERING   211

Combining Metals with Nonmetallic Materials

Nonmetallic materials often make handsome combinations with metal, the metal playing either a dominant or a secondary role. Such material as wood, tortoise shell, ivory, bone, cloth, leather, and stone have been used in the past and offer decorative possibilities for the metal craftsman today. Combinations of plastic and metal, with the metal pieces used as inclusions in liquid or sheet plastic, can produce pleasant results if used with taste and imagination.

Metal Inlay in Wood

The use of wood as a background into which metal plates or wire are inlaid is an old technique, still utilized in Poland and in the Near and Far East. It is finding applications today among Western craftsmen as well. Tabletops, mirror and picture frames, bowls, furniture, doors, and faceplates are all articles of wood which can be embellished with metals.

Contemporary shisham wood tray inlaid with brass wire. Length: approximately 20 inches. Made by craftsmen in Ajmer, Rajasthan, India, where this technique is known as *tarkashi* work. *Photo by Oppi.*

RIGHT: Silver fork with wood handle inlaid with silver wire in lines and circlets, seventeenth century. *Museum of Decorative Art, Copenhagen.*

Inlay of brass wire in wood, in preparation for tarkashi work. The flat wire is cut from a sheet of hammered brass with a hand snips. The height of the wire is between 1/16 and 1/32 inch. *Photo by Oppi.*

BELOW: Contemporary wood box, from Zokopane and Nowy Targ, South Poland. Carved and inlaid with brass wire (called *inkrustacja*). *Cepelia, New York. Photo by Oppi.*

Tarkashi Work

In India, a form of brass wire inlay in wood known as *tarkashi* work is practiced. It can be described as "damascene" on wood. Craftsmen in Lucknow, Mainpuri, and other places produce boxes, screens, trays, tables, and other kinds of cabinet furniture decorated in this technique. The method is as follows.

A well-seasoned hardwood is used, and ordinarily the article is decorated when finished, though parts may be decorated and assembled later. The design is drawn on the wood with a pencil and usually consists of arabesques derived from plant forms, or of geometric pat-

terns. The design is then gone over with a sharp knife having a thin blade. The cut is made perpendicularly into the wood surface. In this way the wood is prepared to receive the metal inlay.

The brass wire used is flat, about 1/16″ wide. It is placed into the cut in the wood *edgewise* and hammered into the grooves with a flat-faced hammer till it is level with the wood surface. The wire is snipped off even with the ends of the cut before the ends are reached by the wire as it is driven into the wood. The wood is then finished by filing the whole surface if necessary, in the direction of the grain, or by rubbing it with steel wool, and finally

it is coated with oil or wax well rubbed in. No glue is used to hold the metal, as the pressure of the metal in the grooves, following the curves and angles of the design, holds it in place. The contrast between dark wood and bright metal is attractive.

This technique can be employed for articles of jewelry. Close-grained exotic hardwoods such as rosewood or ebony could be used, and gold or silver wire, as wire of the thickness called for is relatively inexpensive. Solid circular *dots* or spots of wire can be made a part of the design by drilling a hole of the same diameter as the *round* wire used in this case, and then cutting the wire and hammering it in.

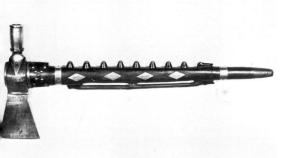

Kickapoo Indian ceremonial pipe tomahawk, with wood handle inlaid with steel rivets and diamond-shaped engraved ornaments. Length: 19 inches. *Museum of the American Indian, Heye Foundation, New York.*

OPPOSITE: An assortment of tie tacks, made by Hermine Milch. The largest is approximately ⅜ inch in diameter. Ebony wood in powder form was mixed with an epoxy cement and filled into the spaces between the silver parts. Then, after hardening, the surface was polished. *Photo by Oppi.*

RIGHT: French Sudan wooden dance mask. Decorated with brass ornaments stamped with patterns and mounted, by nailing, on the wood base. *The Olsen Foundation, Collection of Fred and Florence Olsen. Photo from the University Museum, University of Pennsylvania.*

BELOW: Silver cuff links with palisander wood, by Bertel Gardberg, Finland. *Photo by Studio Wendt, Helsinki.*

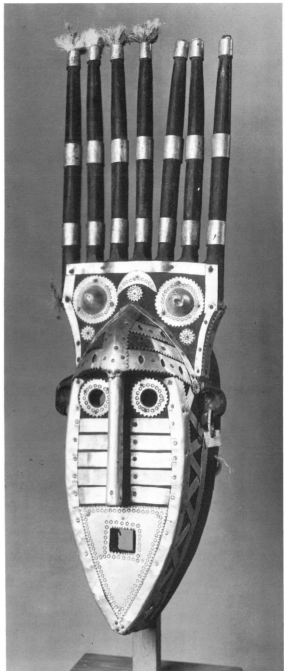

Wood as a Filler

Wood in the form of a powder or sawdust made by filing or sanding it with a tough abrasive paper can be mixed with a binder such as an epoxy rosin with the aid of a small spatula. The resulting paste can be used to fill in depressions in metal jewelry or shapes made with wire such as cloison wire in enamel work.

When it is dry, the surface can be filed and polished like ordinary wood, except that the paste has no grain and can be smoothed from any direction. The finished article resembles a well-fitting wood inlay. Designs can be developed with points of metal (wires of various cross sections soldered on end and projecting upward), surrounded by wood filler, and level with it. (See photo opposite, page 214.)

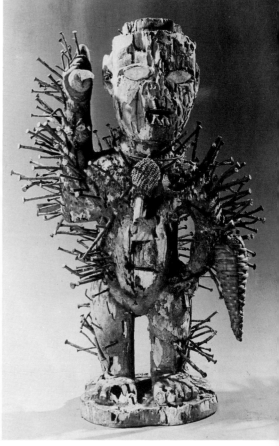

Rice measuring bowls (*kunkei* or *pai*) from Suri, West Bengal. Total height: about 3 feet. These bowls, in graduated sizes, are made of coconut wood and ornamented with chased brass, which is riveted to the wood with brass nails. *Collection of the Art in Industry Museum, Calcutta. Photo by Oppi.*

ABOVE RIGHT: Maté (tea) cup bombilla and accompanying silver spoon-straw for drinking, from Chile, South America. The maté cup bombilla is made of a coconut mounted in silver, with chased decorations. *Museum of Fine Arts, Boston.*

RIGHT: Lukula, Mayombe, magic ritual wood statue with nails. Height: 544 mm. *Musée Royal de L'Afrique Centrale, Tervuren, Belgium.*

ABOVE RIGHT: Rice measuring container (*para*), made of palmyra wood and decorated with riveted brass ornaments. Made in Ottapalam, Kerala, India. *Photo by Oppi.*

ABOVE LEFT: Sterling silver beverage pitcher with ebony handle, made by Frederick Miller. Because of its insulating qualities, as well as its decorative appearance, wood has been used for centuries for the handles of containers that might hold hot liquids. *Photo by John Paul Miller.*

LEFT: Silver coffee pot designed by Jørgen Bager, second half of the eighteenth century. The rosewood finial on the lid and the rosewood handle are not only practical but also heighten the drama of the design. *Museum of Decorative Art, Copenhagen. Georg Jensen Silversmiths, Ltd.*

ABOVE: Salad serving utensils with silver handles and ebony, made by Georg Jensen, Copenhagen. *Georg Jensen Silversmiths, Ltd.*

Tortoise Shell and Piqué Work

The use of tortoise shell as a background or as an adjunct to metal has old as well as new applications. In Victorian England, a process known as *piqué work* (piqué means *pricked* in French) was commonly used on small boxes, cigarette cases, watch cases, jewelry, combs, and other articles made of tortoise shell. Minute, round wire of fine gold or fine silver was hammered or inlaid, usually in geometric patterns, into the tortoise shell, much like miniature rivets, except that they did not pierce the shell.

The tortoise shell used then and still used today for many articles comes from the epidermic plates covering the bony carapace of the hawksbill turtle (*Eretmochelys imbricata*) which is the smallest of the sea turtles. It has thirteen plates on its back, five in the center and four on each side, which overlap about one-third, and are often eight by thirteen inches in size, weighing up to nine ounces each. These are the commercially desirable ones, though it has others, and their value on the market depends on their color and mottled pattern. The hawksbill lives in most tropical waters, but the best shell comes from the Eastern Archipelago, the West Indies, and Brazil. These plates of tortoise shell are a horny substance, but though harder, less fibrous, and more brittle than horn, they can be worked in the same manner as horn.

The plates are separated from the skeleton by heat. It is said that in some places, the captive turtle is laid on a hot fire and its plates fall off, after which it is returned to the sea to grow more. When they are removed, they are warped and irregular and are heated and flattened by pressure, after which irregularities are removed with a rasp file. To increase thickness or size, the surfaces to be joined are cleaned and rasped and the plates are put in boiling water. The heat softens the scale and liquefies the surface so that when the two parts are brought together and placed under pressure, they make a perfect union. Too high a temperature will cause the shell to become opaque and dark, therefore as low a heat as is practical is used. Heat is also used to mold the shell into forms under pressure. It can be cut into shapes with heated dies as was done in forming basic comb shapes. It will take and retain a high polish applied with buffs on a buffing wheel.

Silver necklace with twin serpent pendant, made by William Spratling, Taxco, Mexico. Tortoise shell employed to make the spots of inlay on one serpent is used in reverse on the other to delineate the body. The tortoise shell is held in position by cement and riveting. *Photo by Oppi.*

BELOW: Silver "Jaguar" pin and earrings, made by William Spratling, Taxco, Mexico. They are decorated with tortoise shell that has been cemented and riveted in position. *Photo by Oppi.*

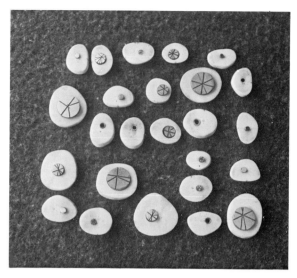

English Victorian watchcase made of tortoise shell, decorated with gold wire rivets and pierced-work medallions in a form of decoration known as "piqué" work. *Victoria and Albert Museum, London.*

BELOW: Necklace in ivory, 18-karat gold, and turquoise, by Mario Buccellati of Italy, whose jewelry often employs combinations of a variety of materials. Both the ivory parts and the turquoises are set in "modelato"-carved bezels that were ornamented in

Bone buttons set with silver, by Alvin Pine. Diameters: ¾ to ⅜ inch. *Photo by Pine.*

relief with engraver's burins. The turquoise bezels are pegged and cemented into the ivory, which exhibits the translucent grain characteristic of African and Indian ivory, unlike the fibrous one-color appearance of bone. *Mario Buccellati, New York. Photo by Irving Kaufman.*

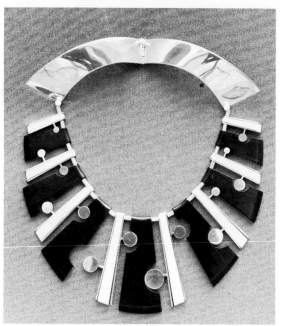

Back of an Hispano-Moresque (Cordoba) ivory casket, early eleventh century. The engraved silver mounts were probably made in the seventeenth or eighteenth century. Many small, intricately carved panels, limited in size because of the nature of the material, are harmoniously unified with a relatively simple metalwork construction. *Victoria and Albert Museum, London.*

LEFT: Silver necklace with ivory and ebony units, by Byron Wilson. Ivory can be cut, pierced, and otherwise treated in the same manner in which hardwoods are worked. *American Craftsmen's Council.*

OPPOSITE: Silver Madonna, by Matilde Eugenia Poulat, Mexico, 1962. A variety of decorative treatments, including piercing, chasing, and wirework with some repoussé, have been used to create a rich surface. Carved ivory, turquoise, and amethyst add color to the metalwork. *Photo by Oppi.*

Piqué Work with Tortoise Shell, Horn, Ivory, and Bone

Piqué work is a form of metal inlay somewhat resembling the damascene procedure but involving a nonmetallic material as a base into which the metal is inlaid. Bone, horn, tortoise shell, ivory, plastic, and other materials are used. These can be purchased in bulk and shaped into desired forms by sawing, turning, carving, or stamping with the usual tools, and smoothed by filing, rubbing with abrasive cloths, motor buffing with abrasives and polishing materials, or by hand processes. Some materials, such as ivory and bone, can be dyed with aniline dyes. Articles made for piqué decoration can be made in parts and then assembled after the application of the wire design. Joining can be done with rivets or glues appropriate to the material. Epoxy cements are eminently suited to most of these bases.

THE PIQUÉ PROCESS

The simplest form of piqué decoration consists of arranging pieces of round wire in patterns of dots in the material. Designs can be geometric, as in Victorian times, or in any pattern desired. Holes are drilled into the base of the same diameter as the gauge of the wire. If possible, a uniform depth should be maintained that does not penetrate the base. Short lengths of wire, either of fine gold or fine silver, as they are most malleable, are then driven into the holes with a lightweight hammer. If the article's base material is thin, it should be supported during this operation on an appropriately shaped metal surface such as an anvil. The projecting ends of wire are then nipped off with a hand nipper and the wire is again lightly hammered. When all the wires have been thus inlaid, the entire surface is filed smooth and polished by hand or mechanically with abrasives and polishes.

It is also possible to inlay small patterns of metal cut out by hand or with dies and stamps on such material as tortoise shell, horn, and plastic. In die stamping, a sheet of metal is held over an end grain of hardwood or on a

ABOVE: Silver brooch inlaid with ebony and ivory, by Earl B. Pardon. *American Craftsmen's Council.*
LEFT: Silver commemorative cup, mid-nineteenth century. Decorated with "staves" of alternating ivory and ebony wood. An inscription is engraved on the hoop. *Cooper Union Museum for the Arts of Decoration.*

Silver gilded goblet, with mother of pearl and enamel decoration, Germany, seventeenth century. Height: 16 cm.; diameter: 11 cm. Bequeathed by Salomon de Rothschild, 1922, to the Cluny Museum, Paris. *Archives Photographiques, Caisse Nationale des Monuments Historiques, Paris.*

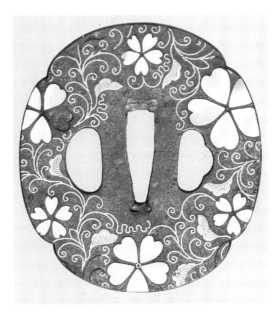

Japanese steel sword guard (*tsuba*), decorated with gold wire inlay and mother of pearl. Size: 3 inches by 2¾ inches. Bequest of Mrs. H. O. Havemeyer, 1929, The H. O. Havemeyer Collection. *Metropolitan Museum of Art, New York.*

lead block and the die is hammered through the metal. If necessary, the pieces cut out should be flattened with a mallet. The stamped-out pieces are then held in position upon the base material, and a heated soldering copper or a spatula heated over an alcohol lamp is held on the stamped unit till the base melts and the unit sinks in place. (The various base materials require differing amounts of heat, and experiments on a scrap is recommended.) The metal is then filed level with the surface and polished, burnished, or left slightly raised in the manner of rivet heads.

All sorts of articles can be decorated by piqué, such as the wood, bone, or ivory handles of knives, forks, and spoons, small boxes, combs, buttons, jewelry, napkin rings, mirror and picture frames, and other decorative accessories and toilet articles. Plastic can be substituted for tortoise shell.

New applications of tortoise shell are used today in Mexico on jewelry and other silver objects. The tortoise shell pieces are held in place with rivets aided by cements. Holes are drilled through the tortoise shell and the base metal and a wire rivet in silver is hammered in so that both materials are held together. Similar use can be made of polished ivory or bone of some thickness. Ivory can be studded with rivets of gold or silver. The end of a wire may first be melted to form a rounded head and the wire inserted into any of these materials. Needless to say, the materials cannot be subjected to any but normal heat used in forming them, or they will be destroyed.

Silver stir pitcher with ivory handle, by Frederick Miller. The handle is held in place by rivets. *Photo by John Paul Miller.*

Gold tunic, Peru, Chimu Period, twelfth century A.D. This ceremonial tunic, which was used in ritual feasts, is composed of 30,000 small plates of gold sewn to a cloth ground that is more than three feet long. The tunic is also decorated with symbolic, repousséd figure heads. *Collection of Miguel Mujica Gallo, Peru.*

Leather and Cloth

Metal has been used in conjunction with leather or cloth in the form of metallic yarn embroidery. Metallic yarns are still drawn by hand in India and other countries. Sometimes they are wound around silk supporting threads for strength or, if heavy enough, are used plain. When using metallic yarns for leather embroidery, to prevent the yarn from tearing, first pierce the leather with a sharp-pointed tool at the place where the needle is to draw the thread through. Besides metallic yarn embroidery, leather and cloth articles such as belts and purses can be decorated with metal medallions or studs. If the medallion has small holes at intervals near its edge, it can easily be sewn to the supporting material. Studs can be attached to leather by soldering a thin

Persian leather belt, eighteenth–nineteenth century. Decorated with metal ornaments and bosses. The purse and container strings have hanging metal "tassels." *Metropolitan Museum of Art, New York. Bequest of Edward C. Moore, 1891.*

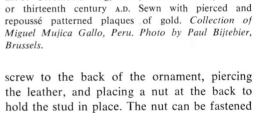

LEFT: Ceremonial bag, Peru, Chimu Period, twelfth or thirteenth century A.D. Sewn with pierced and repoussé patterned plaques of gold. *Collection of Miguel Mujica Gallo, Peru. Photo by Paul Bijtebier, Brussels.*

screw to the back of the ornament, piercing the leather, and placing a nut at the back to hold the stud in place. The nut can be fastened permanently by melting a little soft solder over it with a soldering copper. Bifurcated rivets are commonly used to hold metal ornaments to any surface, even metal, in North Africa and the East. The split rivet head is soldered to the back of the ornament, a hole is made through the base material, the rivet pushed through, and the two parts of the stem are spread and flattened. This is enough to hold any ornament in place. Rivets have the advantage of being removable should their replacement be necessary or the supporting material wear out.

Thin metal plates as a form of decoration on cloth have been used by the American Indians and the Incas. The Incas decorated whole garments with small square plates of polished pure gold, which were sewn in overlapping fish scale-like paillons.

Spanish leather Koran case embroidered in silver wire. It bears the device of the Kings of Granada, "God alone is Conqueror," and probably belonged to Mohammed Abu Abdullah (Boabdil), the last Moorish King of Granada (1486–92). *Metropolitan Museum of Art, New York. Rogers Fund, 1904.*

Evening bag, decorated by the Ganeshi Lal and Sons *zari* manufactory in Agra, India. The decoration was done in a form of embroidery that employs metallic gold and silver threads. Practiced in India, it is called *zari* work. *Photo by Oppi.*

Stones

Metal has been combined with gemstones since primitive times. A discussion of gemstones properly belongs in a book devoted to their use in jewelry and other articles, and is outside the scope of this volume. Several references are listed in the bibliography.

Stones can be combined with metals in other ways. Stone mosaics in which metals play a major or minor role are being made today. Terrazzo, a kind of material made with marble chips combined with cement and widely used for flooring, is distributed usually between brass dividers which can be decoratively ar-

ranged and later polished level with the terrazzo. Insertions of metal shapes in the terrazzo is also possible.

Essentially, this system is used in Mexico today by the Castillo brothers in Taxco to create door pulls, drawer pulls, escutcheons, and other articles.

The system used in Mexico is as follows. The metalwork is either cast or in one piece, or joined by soldering. Depressions in the surface, or walls of metal are filled with colored stone, and the effect somewhat resembles champlevé or cloisonné work in enameling. The space that is to contain the stone is first filled somewhat short of level with the retaining wall with pitch, or sealing wax, into which the stones are set. Heating the metal from below (a hotplate can be used) softens the pitch sufficiently to hold the stones in place. Colored cement prepared to match the color of the stone is then used as a grout in the spaces between them. Cements can be colored with powdered dyes when they are mixed.

The surface is then ground level with a carborundum stone and brought to the same height as the retaining metal wall. This leaves it dull and rough-looking. The final polish is applied with a buffing wheel loaded with tin oxide mixed with water. The wheel must be kept constantly wet. If desired, the metal surface after polishing can be gold-plated in any plating solution which does not require high heat. The plating process will not affect the stones, wax, or cement.

Silver ring with turquoises, designed for the middle finger, by Saara Hopea Untracht. Produced by Kultasepänliike Ossian Hopea, Porvoo, Finland. *Photo by Siren.*

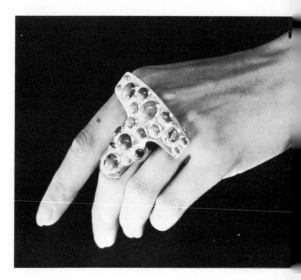

Jain shrine of cast brass, with crystal image of Parvanatha, the twenty-third Tirthankara. Made in Jaipur, Rajasthan, India, 1572. Height: approximately 10 inches. *Victoria and Albert Museum, London.*

Gold (22 karat) repoussé funeral mask of the Egyptian Pharaoh Tutenkhamon (less the beard). The funeral mask hooded the mummy of the king, which was inside the third inner coffin. The coffin was also of solid gold (about ⅛ inch thick). The mask, which is 1 foot 7⅞ inches high, is encrusted with lapis lazuli blue glass paste, carnelian, lapis lazuli, and green feldspar; it has calcite eyes and obsidian pupils. Stone encrustation in metal was widely practiced in Dynastic Egypt and resembled the cloisonné process of enameling that developed later in the history of art. Collection of the Cairo Museum. *Photo by Harry Burton, Metropolitan Museum of Art, New York.*

RIGHT: Contemporary silver bracelet, from Cairo, Egypt. The woven band holds a turquoise-encrusted medallion with stamped bosses and added wire ornaments. *Photo by Oppi.*

228   METAL DECORATIVE TECHNIQUES

Mr. and Mrs. Homer Vacit, Zuñi Indian silversmiths, in their Pueblo, New Mexico workshop. They are setting turquoise stones in jewelry. The raw stone material and stones mounted on shellac sticks ready for polishing are visible. In the center of the table is a simple alcohol flame, made of a covered jar and a string wick that emerges from a hole in the cover. It is used to heat and melt the shellac or sealing wax that holds the stones. *Photo by Josef Muench.*

Zuñi Indian (New Mexico) squashblossom necklace and brooch set with clusters of turquoise stones in silver. *Photo by Josef Muench.*

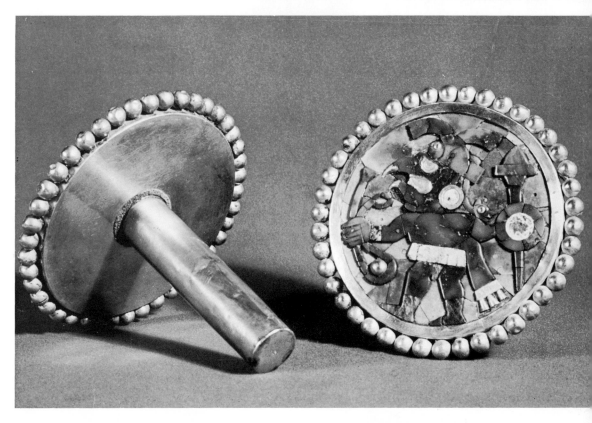

Gold ear ornaments with mosaic inlay of turquoise, crysacola, shell, pyrite, gypsum, and an unidentified mineral. Made in Peru during the Mochica Period. *American Museum of Natural History, New York.*

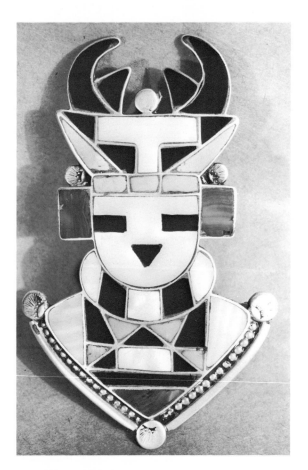

Eighteen-karat gold ring with smoky quartz, by Bertel Gardberg, Finland. The stone is fastened in only three places. *Photo by Studio Wendt, Helsinki.*

LEFT: Zuñi Indian (New Mexico) silver brooch representing an antelope dancer mask. Inlaid with turquoise, jet, and shell. Height: 3⅜ inches. *Museum of the American Indian, Heye Foundation, New York.*

A JEWELED ELEPHANT BEING SET WITH GEMS.

1. LEFT: The part of the surface that is otherwise decorated is covered with stick lac to protect it while the stone setting is taking place. Strips of soft, pure gold (as seen in the lower left) are cut and, once the stone is in place, forced into the space around the gem. This is called *Khundun* work. Several applications may be necessary. The metal is then burnished to hold the gem in place. *Photo by Oppi.*

2. BELOW LEFT: An enameled and jeweled elephant made in Jaipur, Rajasthan, India, whose gemmed eyes and decorations have been set in the manner just described. A final going over with the burnisher to insure the gem's fastness, followed by the removal of the lac with hot water, completes the piece. *Photo by Oppi.*

BELOW RIGHT: Jade ornament from India, made in the Moghul Period. The ornament is encrusted with precious stones in a process that is unique to Indian craftsmen. The depressions for the stones were carved in the jade and then the stones were cemented in place. The bezel of fine gold outlining each stone was made by forcing "ribbons" of fine gold into the remaining space and building the bezel up with repeated applications and burnishing. *Archives Photographiques, Caisse Nationale des Monuments Historiques, Paris.*

French *Book of the Gospels* cover, c. twelfth century. Length: 10 inches; width: 8¾ inches. The cover is made of oak covered with small panels and borders of gold. It is decorated with repoussé, wirework, and semi-precious stones. The metalwork is nailed to the underlying wood. *Victoria and Albert Museum, London.*

OPPOSITE: Silver-gilt ikon from Nepal, nineteenth century. Buddha seated on a lotus throne is hailed by angels (*apsaras*). The birth of Buddha while Maya, his mother, holds onto the sacred Bo tree (lower right), and worshipers are also seen. The entire panel is made of wire and bezels holding semi-precious coral, jade, shell, turquoise, pearls, and brilliants, with many of the stones carved. This kind of work, known as *jadau*, is still done in Nepal. Height: 14½ inches; width: 12¼ inches. *Metropolitan Museum of Art, New York. Kennedy Fund, 1915.*

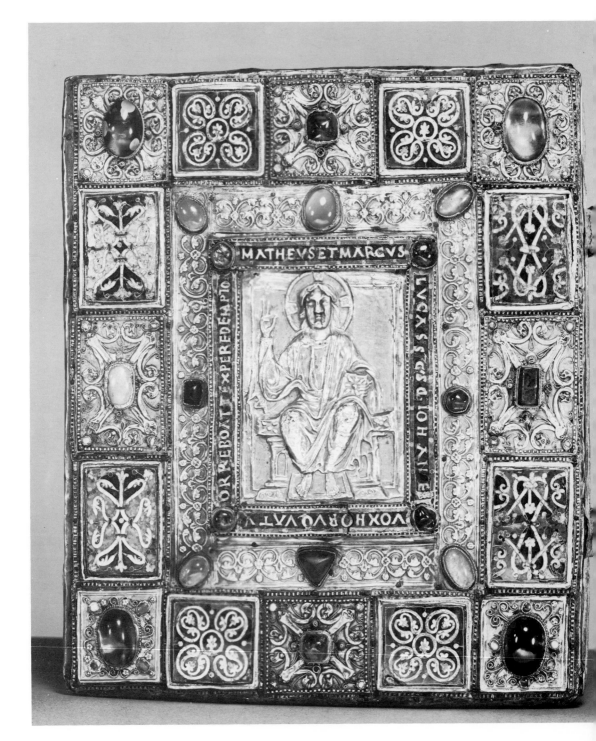

Gold reliquary statue of St. Foy in the treasury of the Cathedral of Conques, Aveyron, France, tenth–eleventh century. Encrusted with cabochon gems and crystal, this early medieval masterpiece is 85 cm. in height. *Archives Photographiques, Caisse Nationale des Monuments Historiques, Paris, France.*

OPPOSITE: Detail of the head, left side.

BELOW: Right side detail of the statue of St. Foy.

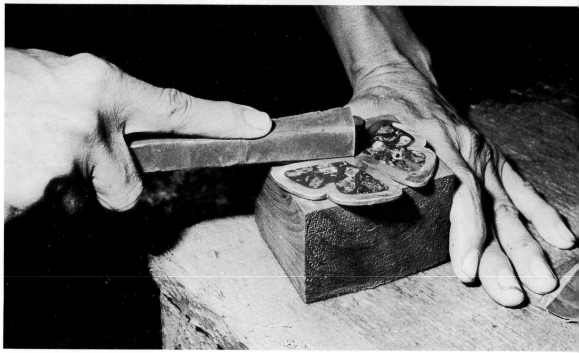

Decorative door escutcheon by Los Castillo made of brass and inlaid with semi-precious stone material that is cemented in depressions in the metal. Length: about 18 inches. The form was inspired by Aztec Indian designs. *Photo by Oppi.*

Abalone Shell Inlay

The Castillo brothers have developed the use of abalone shel!, which is beautifully iridescent and takes polishing well on articles of jewelry and others such as trays, plates, pitchers, and vases. Pieces of shell are cut, polished, and matched in color for the article on which they will be used. They are then carefully cemented into place, and either polished level or left irregular.

Door pull made of brass inlaid with a mosaic of a green stone material, by Los Castillo Plateros, Taxco, Mexico. *Photo by Oppi.*

RIGHT: Epergne in bronze and glass, executed by the Marinha Grande glass factory in Lisbon, Portugal, and designed by Nepir Ltd., New York. The molten glass bubble is blown directly into the metal form and is then trimmed to size. *Photo by Sam Meinhold.*

STONE INLAY WORK.

1. OPPOSITE ABOVE: The process, photographed by the author, was developed by Los Castillo Plateros of Taxco, Mexico. Pieces of abalone shell are being ground to fit the flower shape of the brass disc door escutcheon. The raised ridges are filled with a colored adhesive into which the shell fragments are embedded. To keep the shell pieces cool and prevent their fragmentation from the heat of friction caused by grinding, water is allowed to drip continually on the abrasive disc that is mounted on the motor.

2. BELOW: After the adhesive has hardened, the mosaic is leveled by placing the piece on a slab of soft wood, which absorbs shock, and then smoothing the surface with a carborundum stick.

French Lotharingian pricket candlestick of bronze-
gilt with ornamental crystal ball, mid-twelfth century.
Height: 8⅜ inches. *Metropolitan Museum of Art,
New York. Rogers Fund, 1950.*

Part Three

METHODS OF METAL FABRICATION

Silversmithing

Silversmithing, or the art of raising or shaping sheet metals into forms by the use of hammers, anvils, and other tools, is an ancient art that derives its name from the use of the metal silver, which is widely employed in this process. Other metals such as gold, copper, brass, aluminum, and iron can be handled in the same manner, with modifications.

There are two basic methods of shaping metals by the use of hammers. One is by *compressing* methods such as raising, crimping, and Dutch raising. The other method is by *stretching* the metal to form it and includes sandbag shaping, blocking in a mold, and pressing.

Raising a shape is a method of forming holloware by which a flat sheet of metal by *compression* can be made into a hollow form of almost any contour. By slow stages the metal is shaped into the desired form by hammering it on anvils to effect this compression. The blows are directed mainly at the *convex* surface of the form. The majority of raised shapes are seamless, or made of seamless units joined by soldering. Basically, they consist of variations of cylinder, cone, or free-form shapes, all capable of holding a volume. They may be shallow or deep.

Essentially a *stretching* process, *sinking* a form to create a volume consists of forcing the metal from the *concave* side into a mold or sandbag or by hammering it directly on a metal surface. As it is a stretching process, a thicker sheet of metal is used for sinking than for raising, which by compression thickens the metal. Combinations of shaping processes are common. It is possible to *begin* a form by sinking or blocking the metal into its basic shape, and to *complete* the form by crimping or other raising processes. A whole form can also be created by using one method only.

Metals Used in Forming Processes

The process utilized in forming an object determines to a degree the kind of metal used in its creation. For raising, the most suitable metal thicknesses are 14, 16, and 18 B. & S. gauges. Thicker and thinner gauges are used for special situations. For sinking, which is a stretching process, thicker gauges of metal are necessary (14 B. & S. gauge or thicker). In the making of a bowl by sinking, the size of the metal remains almost the same in diameter as the original metal disc size. In the making of a bowl by raising, the size of the metal disc is determined by adding the depth of the form to its widest diameter. This can be measured from the working design that is drawn on paper.

To cut a disc from a sheet in preparation for making a cylindrical or conical form, normally, the first step is to cut an accurate square, large enough to contain the diameter of the disc with a minimum of waste. A metal rule is then placed diagonally across the square, from corner to corner, and a short line is enscribed lightly in the near center, using any pointed tool. The same is done for the other two corners, so that a second line crosses the first. The point at which the lines cross is the exact mathematical center of the square, and this is then marked with a center punch and a hammer. The point is a useful future reference in making measurements, and is left on the *outside, bottom* of the finished piece. Leaving this mark intact is a tradition among holloware craftsmen.

Centered on the punch-marked center, a circle of the desired diameter is enscribed with a dividers. The disc is then carefully cut out with a straight-bladed shears if the disc is large, or a curved one if the disc is small. A bench shears can also be used if available. The line is followed slightly *outside* the circle diameter to make sure that, after the cut is finished, the full dimension remains. Excess metal and rough edges, if any, are filed away with a double-cut, medium file, *without removing the enscribed disc line,* which is a useful reference.

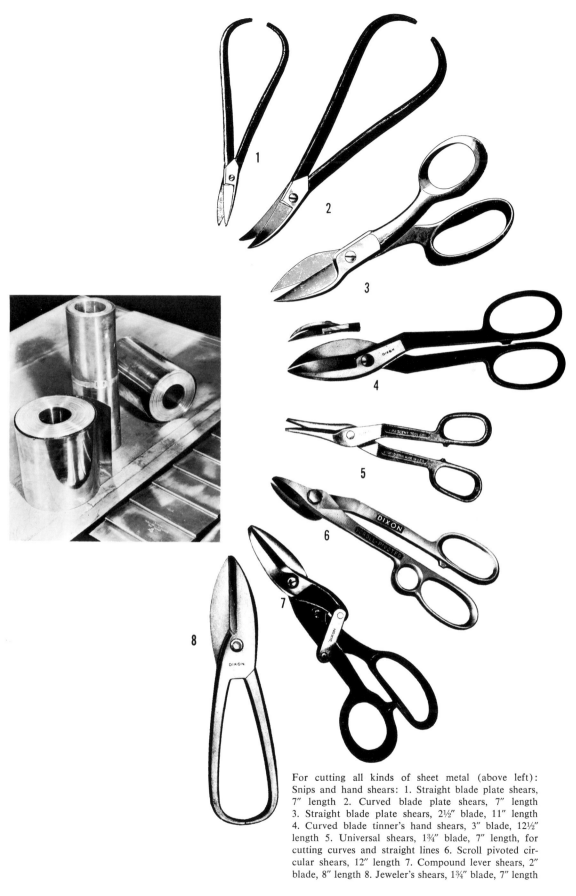

For cutting all kinds of sheet metal (above left): Snips and hand shears: 1. Straight blade plate shears, 7″ length 2. Curved blade plate shears, 7″ length 3. Straight blade plate shears, 2½″ blade, 11″ length 4. Curved blade tinner's hand shears, 3″ blade, 12½″ length 5. Universal shears, 1¾″ blade, 7″ length, for cutting curves and straight lines 6. Scroll pivoted circular shears, 12″ length 7. Compound lever shears, 2″ blade, 8″ length 8. Jeweler's shears, 1¾″ blade, 7″ length

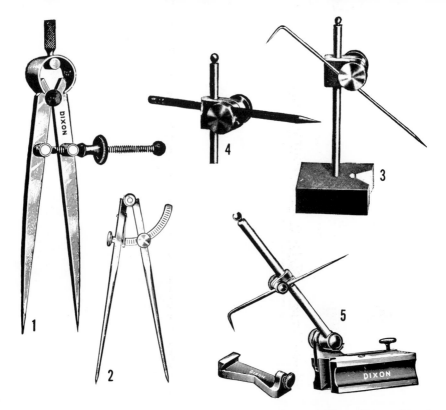

1. Spring dividers, available in 3″, 4″, 5″, 6″ lengths
2. Wing dividers, 6″, hardened points 3. Surface gauge used to mark a level for truing edges on a raised bowl or other form 4. Surface gauge in use with a lead pencil

5. Surface gauge with auxiliary guide clamped to the base. The work is set against the scriber point and turned, or the whole gauge can be moved against the work held on a level bench pin block.

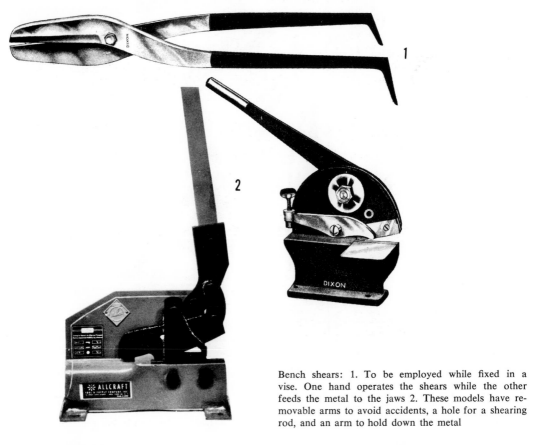

Bench shears: 1. To be employed while fixed in a vise. One hand operates the shears while the other feeds the metal to the jaws 2. These models have removable arms to avoid accidents, a hole for a shearing rod, and an arm to hold down the metal

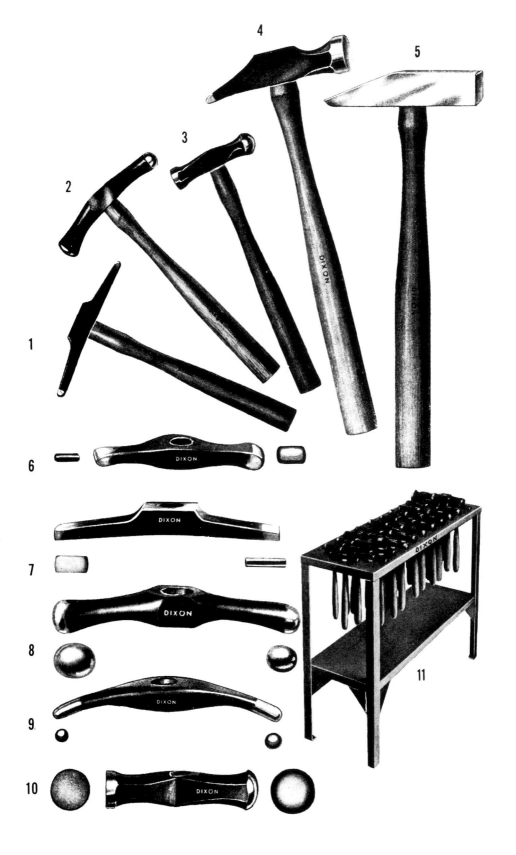

Raising hammers: 1. Embossing hammer 2. Raising hammer 3. Planishing hammer 4. Spotting hammer (a form of planishing hammer) 5. Setting hammer 6. Narrow-faced raising hammer 7. Raising hammer 8. Doming and embossing hammer 9. Narrow embossing hammer 10. Planishing hammer 11. Hammer rack

Use of the Hammer when Raising

Hammers used for raising are available in weights and shapes varying from a few ounces to about eight pounds. (See hand tools and their uses for a description of the various kinds of hammers used in raising, page 433.) To avoid fatigue when raising a form, and to insure maximum efficiency, it is essential to hold the hammer correctly and to use the body muscles to advantage. The worker can either sit or stand before the *anvil* or *stake,* the forming tool used in conjunction with the

hammer in raising. The metal is held in the left hand (for right-handed persons), and the hammer in the right, with the level of the anvil at the striking point in line with the level of the elbow. The fingers should grip the hammer handle firmly at the butt end for correct balance and maximum leverage, not near the head. When a blow is delivered, the handle is held in line with the forearm and the wrist is stiff, but not rigidly tense. The weight of the blow is directed by the muscles of the forearm, chest, and shoulder, with the feet placed apart and the body facing the anvil.

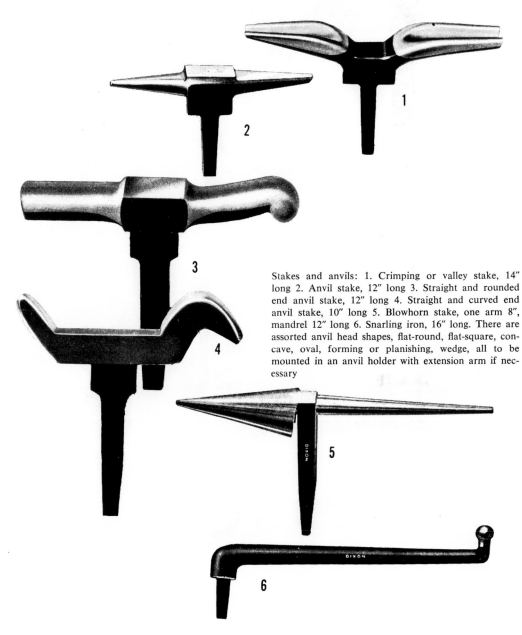

Stakes and anvils: 1. Crimping or valley stake, 14″ long 2. Anvil stake, 12″ long 3. Straight and rounded end anvil stake, 12″ long 4. Straight and curved end anvil stake, 10″ long 5. Blowhorn stake, one arm 8″, mandrel 12″ long 6. Snarling iron, 16″ long. There are assorted anvil head shapes, flat-round, flat-square, concave, oval, forming or planishing, wedge, all to be mounted in an anvil holder with extension arm if necessary

Stakes: 1. Round head mushroom stake 2. Ball 3. Half dome 4. Curved head 5. Round head, slightly flat- tened 6. Circular flat head 7. Spoon stake 8. Spoon stake 9. Angular head, oval face 10. Half moon 11. Hatchet stake

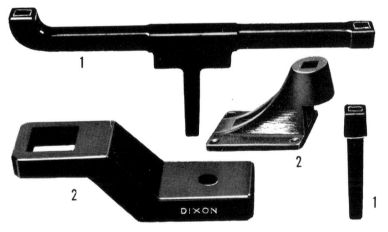

Anvil and Stake: 1. Extension arms 2. Holding devices

STAKES AND ANVILS

There are a great number of stakes and anvils (the terms are often used interchange- ably) designed for general and specific func- tions. Some of them have names indicating their function, and others have names which are derived from their appearance. Almost all stakes have a tapered tang end or shank which is used to hold them in a stake block per- manently fixed on a working bench, or they can be held in a sturdy vise which can take the impact of the hammer blows. Some craftsmen make a depression in the end grain of a hardwood tree stump of suitable height, and place the stake shank in it. Stake holders and extension arms are available to increase the usefulness of a beginner's few, well-chosen stake shapes. A few shapes are essential to basic forming situations. The T stake with one straight and one curved end, a stake with raised, curved ends, a crimping stake, an anvil-shaped stake with a tapered end, a bottoming stake, a mushroom stake, and a planishing stake are probably basic. The choice of stake depends on the function to be performed. With time the silversmith can collect those forms which he finds most useful for the kind of work he is interested in doing.

Annealing or Softening Work-Hardened Metal

During the forming process, the metal becomes hard from the compression of its molecular structure under repeated blows of the hammer. If this condition were allowed to continue, the metal would crack either at the edges or on the surface. Cracks are difficult to repair, and if bad enough they might necessitate a change in the design. To avoid excessive hardening and restore the metal to a favorable working condition, annealing is necessary. Annealing is the process of heating the metal for a certain length of time to soften it by making a change in its structure. Stresses built up in the metal during the working are released.

Metal is ready for annealing when it has become hard and stiff and does not move in reaction to hammer blows. An indication of this condition is the change in the sound of the hammering which is dull when the metal is in a working condition, and high-pitched when it needs annealing. Unless the metal is known to be annealed when purchased, it is best to begin any work by annealing the metal. The only danger that exists in annealing is from overheating. *Metals need not be heated to redness to anneal them.* Overheating often destroys a metal's working qualities. Every metal has a proper annealing temperature, and annealing is a function of time and temperature. In any case, the temperature is considerably short of the melting point. After annealing, some metals can be allowed to air-cool, and others must be immediately quenched to retain their softness. This information may be found under discussions of particular metals.

Annealing Temperatures of Some Metals

Aluminum (wrought)	640–670° F
Britannia Metal	No annealing required
Copper	700–1200° F
Gilding Metal	800–1450° F
Red Brass	800–1350° F
Muntz Metal	800–1100° F
Forging Brass	800–1100° F
Architectural Bronze	800–1100° F
Phosphor Bronze	900–1250° F
Nickel	1500–1700° F
Nickel Silver	1100–1500° F
Monel Metal	1500–1700° F
Pure Gold	No annealing required
Yellow, Red, and Green Gold	1200–1300° F (649–704° C)
Pure Silver	572° F (300° C)
Sterling Silver	1200° F (649° C)

The average craftsman has no technical facilities for temperature measurement, and other means must be employed. Color judgment is one method. To judge the color of heated metal, the metal should be heated in a darkened area, away from strong natural or artificial light. Another way to judge annealing temperature is to paint fluxes on the metal surface which fuse at known temperatures. Fluxes at the same time prevent the formation of firescale caused by the oxidation of metals under heat.

The article to be annealed should be placed in an annealing pan or tray filled with lump pumice or other refractory material capable of retaining and distributing heat. Ideally, all annealing should be done under a ventilation hood provided with an exhaust fan to draw off harmful fumes.

Use of the Annealing Torch

When a torch for annealing is used, a large, soft, neutral flame is called for. This type of flame is so balanced that the mixture of oxygen and gas is about equal, and the gas is consumed completely. Excess oxygen flames will cause the buildup of firescale on the metal.

The flame should be entirely blue, with a small inner air cone of greenish blue. Some yellow at the tip is not objectionable. The greatest heat exists at a point beyond the inner air cone.

When using a propane torch, where gas and air are mixed automatically, adjust the flame slowly till the air intake valve allows a bluish flame with a minimum of yellow at the tip. When using an air-gas torch, turn on the gas alone, and ignite the gas with a hand friction flint lighter. A large, yellow flame will be produced. Turn on the air slowly, and adjust the amount of air till the flame just loses its yellow tinge. After annealing, turn off the torch by turning off the air first and then the gas. Propane gas should also be turned off slowly.

While annealing, direct the flame onto the piece at an angle slightly less than ninety degrees to allow deflection of the flame, but not at too great an angle, for this will result in needless heat loss. In the annealing process, *maximum heat* is brought to bear on the metal *at once.* The flame is moved slowly over the entire surface to avoid excessive warpage. Observe the color change in the metal by occasionally removing the flame for a second. Sterling silver is annealed when the color is a dull cherry red and a yellowish-green flame is deflected from the surface.

Some decorating techniques, such as repoussé and stamping, may require partial or spot annealing in the area being worked. This can be done by using a smaller torch and concentrating the flame directly on the desired place.

Quenching Annealed Metals

Sometimes metals can be air-quenched (allowed to cool in air at a natural rate), but most often it is desirable to quench immediately after heating, either in water or in a dilute pickle bath. In water quenching, the annealed metal is held with iron tongs under running water or in a bath. If quenching is done in an acid pickle, copper or bronze tongs are used to avoid contaminating the acid. Quenching in acid has the double advantage of cleaning and quenching the metal simultaneously. When inserting hot metals in pickle solutions, stand well back to avoid inhaling fumes or being spattered by the acid.

To remove firescale from metals that have been allowed to air-cool, the metal can be placed in the acid pickle, which can be heated, if it is in a Pyrex glass container, to hasten the acid action. Copper pickle pans can be used for small articles such as pieces of jewelry. All acid-quenched or acid-cleaned articles should be rinsed thoroughly under running water. Acid residue may harm the skin, and it can be detected on the metal the next time it is heated, because it will produce a greenish deflected flame.

Compressed Metal Forming Methods

METAL RAISING

The ultimate objective of all metal-raising processes is to create a three-dimensional form from a flat sheet of metal. Raising a shape includes a cycle of *hammering* with various hammers designed to perform particular forming functions and *bouging,* a term derived from the French verb *bouger,* meaning "to move." Bouging consists of smoothing the worked metal shape with a leather, horn, or wood mallet. Finally, there follows a *planishing* or finishing of the piece to remove raising-hammer tool marks and to impart the characteristic texture to the surface that is associated with hand-raised pieces. Raising processes require various smoothly polished steel stakes (anvils) designed to conform to various contours and perform various functions.

ANGLE RAISING

A process known as *angle raising* is a basic technique. It derives its name from the fact that the form is created by hammering it on a stake into *a series of angles* and arriving *by stages* at the angle called for in the final piece. The angles are then rounded out by bouging. In this process, the metal disc is worked from the bottom base mark previously made with a dividers and measured from the center punch mark.

To illustrate this method, we will follow the creation of a simple bowl form. To create the first angle, the metal is held against a T stake with the base line at the point of contact. A cross-peen raising hammer weighing between twelve and twenty-four ounces is used, depending on the thickness and size of the metal being formed. Heavier hammers are used for the first course or angle, and lighter ones thereafter. The metal is struck slightly above the enscribed bottom line and rotated

Gold footed goblet, Egyptian, Eighteenth Dynasty, Thebes. Height: 3⁵⁄₁₆ inches. The goblet is engraved with the cartouche of the wife of Thutmose III and the epithet of the King. *Metropolitan Museum of Art, New York. Funds from Various Donors, 1958.*

Silver covered bonbonnière, oval-shaped, designed by Henning Koppel. *Georg Jensen Silversmiths, Ltd.*

Gold bowl of Darius I or II, Hamadan Province, Iran (Achaemenian Period) (522–404 B.C.). Height: 4½ inches; diameter: 7¾ inches. The simplicity of the fluted form ending in tear-shaped bosses gives this small object a feeling of monumentality. *Metropolitan Museum of Art, New York. Dick Fund, 1954.*

constantly after each stroke. The *same angle relationship* must always be maintained between the metal and the anvil surface to insure uniform shaping. The metal is continually rotated as each completed round of blows advances toward the edge of the disc, finally arriving at a point about one-quarter of an inch from the edge. The whole form is then bouged, and the metal, which has probably become work-hardened at this point, is annealed. The edge should at this time be *thickened,* as thickening should begin from the first stages in forming a bowl. (See description of edge thickening below.)

After annealing, the procedure is repeated, the only difference being that the angle of metal to stake is increased so that, when this second course is completed, the bowl assumes a steeper angle than before. The second angle, however, does not have to start at the base line, but might begin where the ultimate shape of the bowl makes a decided *change* in direction. The metal is bouged and annealed again, and a third, fourth, or as many angles as necessary are created to arrive at the final shape. Edge thickening is done after each completion of a course. Finally a vertical, mushroom-shaped anvil and heavy rawhide hammer are used to eliminate all the sharp angle changes where the courses have changed direction, till a smooth curve is achieved. Soft mallets or hammers of nonmetallic material do not mar but only move the metal.

EDGE THICKENING

Edge thickening, also known as *upsetting* or *swaging,* is desirable on a raised piece such as a bowl for several reasons. It helps the piece to retain its shape by rendering it more rigid and therefore more resistant to shock. Also a visually more satisfying appearance is created when a thick edge is seen than a thin edge. As a substitute for edge thickening, a wire is sometimes soldered to the edge of a bowl, but this is just an application of metal, whereas a thickened edge is an organic part of the bowl, formed in the process of its creation.

Thickening, because it follows each step in the raising process, is built up gradually. It is done by placing the object on a sandbag and striking the edge with a lightweight collet hammer with light, overlapping blows delivered directly against the edge at a *right angle* to the face of the hammer.

Sterling silver vase by Mitsuko Kambe Soellner, U.S.A. A die has been formed of masonite with concave hollows of exactly the desired shape. A sheet of metal previously curved to the general conformity of the die is clamped onto it and the metal is hammered into the depression, sinking it to the desired depth. The two sides formed in this way are then soldered together.

PLANISHING

After the piece is finally shaped, the entire surface can then be finished by *planishing* with a light, half-pound planishing hammer, which has a highly polished, slightly convex face and a springy handle. The piece must be held as flat as possible against the anvil used. Maximum metal-to-anvil contact is necessary to avoid misshaping the piece which is already in its final form. The anvil thereby supports the metal. Planishing of a bowl is done over a vertical mushroom stake, while curved T stakes, spout stakes, cow's-tongue stakes, or curved horse stakes are used for deeper forms such as vases and coffee or tea pots. The choice of anvil depends on the shape of the work. (See page 251.)

Planishing should be done slowly and steadily, with rhythmic blows starting from the bottom line and working toward the edge. Each planishing mark should slightly overlap the previous one as the piece is slowly rotated.

SQUARING A BOTTOM

To square the flat bottom of a form, a vertical bottoming stake is used. If the anvil is not long enough to reach the bottom of a deep form, a vertical extension arm can be inserted first into the holder, and the anvil then inserted. This circular, flat anvil is used with a flat-faced planishing hammer. First a series of blows are made following the edge and then a slow spiral, arriving at the center. The center punch mark, traditionally, is left visible on hand-raised pieces and should not be obliterated.

DUTCH RAISING

Dutch raising is a process for shaping open pieces such as bowls. The work progresses from the *outer edge* of the disc on the *convex side* in spiraling blows toward the center of the piece. A heavy cross-peen hammer is used, followed by a heavy rawhide mallet to help form the piece and even out irregularities. Instead of a series of angles being pursued, as is done in angle raising, the piece is annealed, bouged, and shaped directly in several stages. The final smoothing is done on a mushroom anvil, followed by planishing.

CRIMPING

Crimping is a raising process by which a form may be raised rapidly. A special crimping hammer or a rounded cross-peen hammer may be used in conjunction with a special valley stake which has a tapered, longitudinal groove designed for this method of forming. The metal is placed over the groove in the stake with the narrowing taper pointing toward the base line.

The finished pitcher, Kande №992, designed by Henning Koppel and executed by the craftsmen of Georg Jensen Silversmiths, Ltd., Copenhagen. This kind of asymmetrical form fully exploits the possibilities of the hand-raising process.

A groove is formed by hammering the metal into the depression. It is a good idea to alternate the grooves on opposite sides of the metal disc, so that the metal is balanced in its groove distortion. When the *crimp* is started, the groove may be formed by hammering either from the outer edge of the metal or from the inner surface. Once the shaping has begun, any further crimping that is necessary should start from the outer edge of the disc. The metal will need frequent annealing, as it stiffens quickly after crimping.

The crimped metal is held at an angle of about forty-five degrees against a T stake, and starting from the *base line,* it is hammered with a crimping hammer or a heavy cross-peen hammer. The work is rotated and hammered till the outer edge is nearly reached. It is then annealed, crimped again, then hammered and bouged into the desired form. When a steep angle is made, the crimped groove should extend only partly down the form into the area needing the accented angle. A crimped raised piece is finished in the same manner as described in other methods.

Crimping is often used in the beginning to raise a form quickly, especially with tall pieces. It can then be followed by other shaping methods.

Crimping can also be done on a hardwood form cut with a tapering groove which substitutes for a valley stake.

CREATING THE FORM BY RAISING.

This series of photographs shows the construction of a pitcher (Kande #992) in sterling silver, designed in 1952 by Henning Koppel, one of the outstanding designers for the Georg Jensen company. *Photos courtesy Georg Jensen Silversmiths, Ltd., Copenhagen.*

1

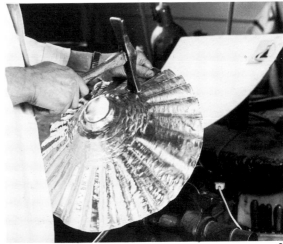

2

3

4

1. ABOVE LEFT: The metal required for the form is cut into disc shape. It is marked to establish a center and base line, and then the sides are crimped with a crimping hammer on a wood crimping form. Valley or crimping stakes are also used for this purpose.

2. ABOVE RIGHT: Starting at the base line and using a raising hammer on a straight anvil with a curved end, the first course is worked by slowly rotating the metal while keeping it at a constant angle to the anvil.

3. CENTER: The form is alternately crimped and raised in a series of courses until it approaches the desired shape.

4. BELOW: As the form evolves, the anvil shape used is chosen according to the conformation of the shape that is worked. Usually this also means that the hammer size becomes lighter as the work progresses.

5. When working on the neck, the metal must be compressed as the diameter decreases. The hammer shape becomes broader, and the strokes are placed closer together. Frequent annealing is necessary so that the work-hardened metal will again become malleable.

5

6. Dimensions are taken with the aid of calipers and the form is refined to its ultimate shape. Here we see a planishing hammer, with an anvil shape that comes closest to the curve of the form, being used to smooth out hammer marks from previous operations.

6

7

7. Whenever it is necessary, where a part of the object cannot be reached *directly* with a hammer, an anvil called a *snarling iron* is used to alter a form from the *inside* by stretching the metal. A heavy hammer is applied to the exposed end of the snarling iron, causing the end inside the form to kick. With proper control and placement, the result is very much like that of a peen hammer.

CREATING THE HANDLE
BY SHAPING.

8. The pattern for the pitcher handle is traced on the sheet metal and sawed out with a jeweler's saw.

8

9. The handle is formed on a wood shaping block with collet and raising hammers.

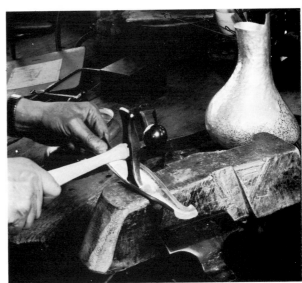

9

10. The handle is shaped into a hollow, tubular form. The seam is hard soldered, using stick solder that is held with a tongs and fed when it stops running along the joint.

11. After final shaping, the points of contact on the handle and pitcher are cleaned. Flux is applied and the two parts are firmly bound together with a heavy gauge iron binding wire jig. This keeps them in contact during the heating for soldering, when the form has a tendency to expand and change shape.

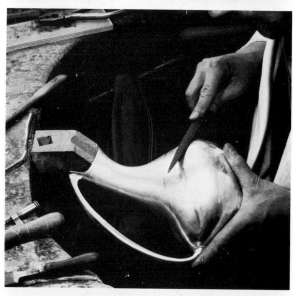

12

FINISHING THE PITCHER.

12. The surface of the pitcher is finished. In this case, irregularities are removed with a fine, double cut file. Silver filings are caught in a leather apron that is always slung under any work; they are eventually gathered for reclaiming.

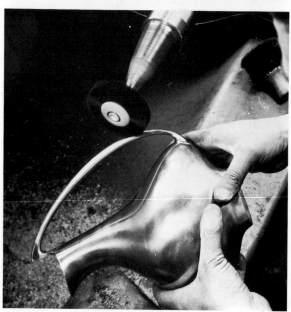

13. The pitcher is polished or finished on a buffing motor, using various abrasives and polishing materials until the object reaches the desired finish. In this case, a bristle brush wheel is being used to create a satin finish surface.

Stretched Metal Forming Methods

Creating a form such as a bowl by stretching is relatively simpler than by compressing, but can be used only for fairly simple, open shapes. The metal is thicker than that used for raising by compression. Metal of 14–16 gauge is not too thick, though 18 gauge can also be used if the form is not going to be too deep. Three basic methods are used: forming on a *sandbag; blocking,* which is shaping a piece by using either a wood or metal mold or a depression in the end grain of a log of wood; and *pressing,* the oldest method of raising, which consists of raising a form from an ingot.

SANDBAG

The annealed metal disc is held over a sand-bag that has been sprinkled with water or oil to reduce the dust raised by pounding. The form is depressed by being worked with a 1½-pound embossing hammer from the center (marked with a center punch) outward toward the edge. The outer edge is reached in a spiraling succession of blows. In the beginning stages, the metal quickly becomes misshapen. This necessitates frequent annealing, followed by bouging with a rawhide or wood mallet over a vertical mushroom anvil to restore and help form the shape. It is important to place the blows methodically, in a regular pattern, and to not strike the metal at random. Once the desired depth and form have been reached, the surface is finished by planishing. Edge thickening can be carried out at intervals during the shaping, in the manner already described.

BLOCKING

Blocking is sometimes done as the beginning step to accelerate the forming of large and deep pieces, but it can also be followed as a method by itself to create smaller ones. As a sole method, it is, strictly speaking, limited to the mechanical reproduction of the mold form that is used. This may be an advantage, however, when several repeats of the same shape are desired.

In blocking over a tree stump depression (often used as a working surface) more freedom is involved, as the metal can be manipulated easily. Usually the edge of the metal is

Forming molds: 1. Wood forming block 2. Metal forming plate 3. Aluminum tray, round form, duplex—may be used on either side 4. Aluminum tray, square form, duplex 5. Sandbag 6. Surface plate and surface gauge

BELOW: Stretched sterling silver pipkin (gravy bowl), by Adda Husted-Andersen. Formed by stretching from 10-gauge metal. The size and shape of the outer edge are the same as that of the original sheet metal used. All-over length: 6½ inches; height of bowl: 2¾ inches. Base is made of square wire applied to sheet metal.

turned up first before continuing toward the center, which is forced downward. Alternate bouging over an appropriate vertical anvil and blocking on the stump is conventional. The metal must, of course, be annealed intermittently to render it workable.

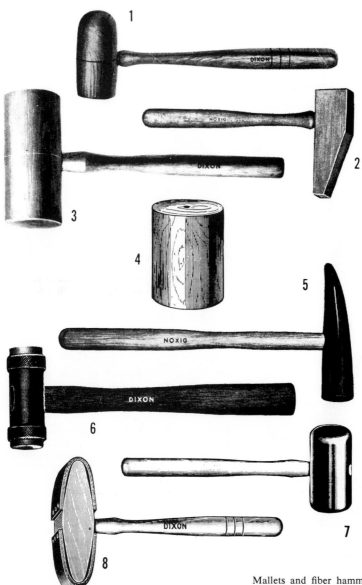

Mallets and fiber hammers: 1. Wood mallet, flat and round face 2. Wood mallet, square and wedge face 3. Wood mallet, flat faces 4. Tree stump 5. Horn mallet 6. Fiber head, flat face mallet 7. Composition fiber mallet 8. Leather tipped mallet

When a metal mold is employed, the disc size is selected to fit the mold, and the hammering starts from the center and works outward. Frequent annealing is necessary, but no bouging, as the form is completely controlled by the shape of the mold. The metal is alternately hammered and annealed till all surfaces are in contact with the mold form.

PRESSING

Pressing is a form of raising that begins with the ingot. The metal is prepared by melting it in a crucible and pouring it onto a cold steel plate to form a "cookie." In Santa Clara del Cobre, Mexico, a town where many metal craftsmen live who work in copper, this forming method is still widely used. There, the metal is poured onto a thick stone boulder and hammered while still red hot with repeated blows of a sledge hammer to stretch and flatten the ingot. When it becomes work-hardened, it is returned to the forge for annealing. The form is then shaped on a flat steel slab, starting from the center and spiraling outward to the edge if it is a simple shape. More complex shapes can then be developed on anvils after the beginning stages have been completed on the flat steel slab.

Here the planishing hammer is used to smooth the metal surface uniformly. Hand-raised pieces are often left with the finish that results from using this tool. *Georg Jensen Silversmiths, Ltd.*

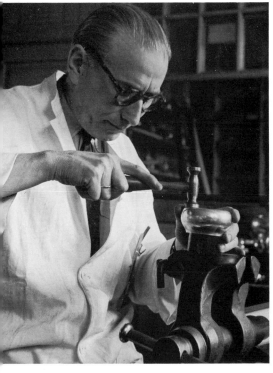

The bottoming hammer is used along with a bottoming stake to stiffen and make rigid surface on which an object rests. *Georg Jensen Silversmiths, Ltd.*

Silver one-gallon coffee urn on a stand with spirit heater, designed and executed by Robert Welch, London, 1960. The handle, base, and knob are made of rosewood. Commissioned for presentation to Churchill College, Cambridge, England. *Worshipful Company of Goldsmiths, London.*

ABOVE LEFT: Silver parcel-gilt chalice, North European, signed by F. Bertinus, 1222. Height: 7½ inches; diameter: 5⅜ inches. *Metropolitan Museum of Art, New York. The Cloisters Collection, Purchase, 1947.*

ABOVE: Silver altar chalice, designed by Georg Jensen in 1933. *Georg Jensen Silversmiths, Ltd.*

Lapland spoons with raised bowls, brass on the left, silver on the right, given by a Lappish man to his chosen woman as a gift when proposing marriage. The form and the engraved patterns on the handles are based on those found on old spoons made of reindeer horn formerly used for this purpose. Manufactured by Kalevala Koru, Helsinki, Finland. *Photo by Pietinen.*

Silver candelabrum, designed by Georg Jensen, 1919. *Metropolitan Museum of Art Collection, New York. Georg Jensen Silversmiths, Ltd.*

Brass candlesticks, designed and executed by David Mellor, 1961, for the altar of St. Giles Church, Sheffield, England. *Worshipful Company of Goldsmiths, London.*

Silver and gold wine ewer, Korea, eleventh century.
Surmounted by a Phoenix finial on a lotus base, this
elegant ewer is decorated with engraved floral and
geometric patterns. *Museum of Fine Arts, Boston.*

Brass coffee pot, tin-lined, from Italy. *Bonniers, New York.*

Silver teapot made by the late Hans Hansen, Jr., when completing his apprenticeship as a silversmith in Denmark. The horn handle is attached to the top of the lid which latches into a flange in the body of the pot. Height including the handle is 7.1 inches. *Photo by Lundgaard Andersen, courtesy of Hans Hansen Sølvsmedie A/S Copenhagen.*

Silver punch set designed by Tapio Wirkkala and manufactured by Hopeakeskus Oy, Hämeenlinna, Finland. The surfaces are left rough in the texture that occurs naturally in the process of raising the shapes with raising hammers. (See page 251, illustration 4) *Photo by Kalevi Pekkonen.*

Frederick Miller: Sterling silver bottle hand raised from one flat sheet of metal. The most difficult process in raising is to constrict the form after it has first been brought to a bowl form. By slow stages, utilizing the process of crimping, the upper section is gradually closed to form the upper portion and neck which here also flares out at the top. The smallest diameter of constriction is at the neck and this must be worked with special anvils. The neck is decorated with pellets of 23 karat gold. *Photo by John Paul Miller.*

Pewter: Britannia Metal

Melting point:
244° C (471° F), solidus temperature
295° C (563° F), liquidus temperature

The temperatures given above apply to the contemporary alloy known as *britannia metal,* generally the present form of pewter. In ancient times, pewter, which was used extensively in the Orient and throughout the Roman Empire, contained a large percentage of lead. Today, the pewter substitute, britannia metal, is predominantly a tin alloy and contains no lead.

The tin mines of Cornwall and Devon in England made Britain the center of pewter production in medieval Europe and later supplied the raw material to Colonial America. The widespread use of pewter for daily utensils was due primarily to its low melting point, which made it easy to recast damaged articles. The "golden age" of pewter in America was 1700–1850, when the British tradition of form and craftsmanship was the model. Old pieces were shaped by casting and hammering from sheets, and rarely spun. Today, stamping, casting, and spinning are the usual forming methods, though raising is also done.

During the second half of the eighteenth century, the pewter industry was threatened by the widespread acceptance of inexpensive porcelain for household utensils. At this time, the metal industry in Sheffield, England, developed a new pewter substitute, known today as britannia metal. Old pewter, because of its lead content, became dull and grayish, and undesirable as a container for food. The new britannia metal alloy was more silvery, resonant, and strong, retained its luster and polish longer, and was leadless. It was hoped that the improvement would answer the threat of porcelain, but gradually pewter lost favor for daily use, and now it is generally used for decorative articles and for the casting of sculpture.

Britannia metal is an alloy of 91 per cent tin, 7 per cent antimony, and 2 per cent copper. The tin gives it sheen, resistance to corrosion, and ductility, and prevents excessive oxidation in casting. The antimony hardens and whitens the metal, and because it has the additional property of expanding on cooling, it results in castings that have sharp, clear impressions from the mold. Copper is added for ductility and hardness. The proportions of antimony and copper vary slightly, but the alloy contains no lead whatsoever. The terms britannia metal and pewter are used synonymously by craftsmen, though they are actually different alloys.

In the preparation of pewter, the copper, which has the highest melting point, is placed first in the crucible, with a percentage of the tin added to lower the melting point. The antimony and the remaining tin are then added. When all the metals have been thoroughly combined, the alloy is poured into iron molds that produce slabs. These are ready for rolling to the desired gauge in rolling mills.

Pewter is available in sheets of 10 to 30 B. & S. gauge and up to twenty-four by thirty-six inches, in disc sizes of many diameters, in pigs and bars for casting, in wire of various gauges, and in round and square tubing.

The Forming of Pewter

Annealing of sheet pewter is not necessary, as the metal does not harden under working with tools. When a piece is raised, sandbags made of leather or canvas, with the usual hammers, mallets, anvils, and stakes are employed. The metal can also be beaten down or stretched into a mold to be formed. Because the metal is soft, it will fill and clog a file. Coarser float files, cleaned frequently with a *file card,* or filled first with chalk, are more efficient.

English pewter platter, 1662. Engraved with sun, tulips, Tudor Rose, oak leaves, and acorns. The central design is the British royal crest. An inscription reads: *Vicat Rex Carolus Secundus.* The initials of the maker (G T A) are framed in a laurel wreath at the bottom of the platter. *Victoria and Albert Museum, London.*

Soldering Pewter

Pewter is very easily soldered. The metal contains a large percentage of tin, one of the main constituents of *soft solder,* which is used to join pewter and for which it therefore has a great affinity. When the joints fit properly, the soldered seam is so complete that its detection is almost impossible.

The solders used must have a melting and flow point below that of the pewter. Pewter itself may be used, but it is necessary to work with great care or the piece will melt. The following solders are appropriate:

Soft solders	Liquidus
62 tin, 38 lead	
(eutectic alloy)	361° F
60 tin, 40 lead	
(most widely used on pewter)	368° F
50 tin, 50 lead	
(used for the first of a series of joints)	421° F

All these have the same melting point of 361° F but varying liquidus points.

16 tin, 32 lead, 52 bismuth

45 tin, 27.5 lead, 27.5 bismuth

50 tin, 25 lead, 25 cadmium

50 tin, 25 antimony, 25 cadmium

These solders all melt below 300° F and are safe for soldering pewter, when it is necessary to take the utmost caution.

Fluxes especially designed for use with pewter are sold by supply houses. A pewter flux may be prepared by adding ten drops of hydrochloric acid to one ounce of glycerine. Flux should be applied liberally to the entire cleaned joint.

In soldering, it is sometimes necessary to assemble parts and hold them in position with binding wire. Soft iron wire in gauges 18–24 are suitable. Other forms of jigs can be used.

The heat source utilized in soldering pewter can be a Bunsen burner, alcohol torch, or candle, all of which must be used with a mouth-type blowpipe. A small gas torch is also satisfactory, but care must be taken not to overheat the metal, because of the low melting point of pewter. *Never* use a soldering iron or copper; the heat is not easily controlled, and there is great danger of melting a hole upon contact with the pewter. It is helpful to place the work on an asbestos pad

mounted on a turntable; the flame can then be directed at all parts of the object. The flame should be kept moving constantly or the metal will melt. Remember that solder runs toward the hottest part of the metal.

The piece should remain in place after soldering till it is cool enough to be touched. Binding wire can then be removed, and excess solder, if any, can be filed away with a second-cut file or with fine emery cloth, 00 grade.

If a second soldering sequence is necessary, it is possible to avoid overheating joints already soldered by immersing the joints in sand or, if the piece is hollow, by filling it with sand.

ABOVE: Colonial American pewter nursing bottle. Old, used pewter often acquires an extremely pleasant patina and texture, which are unique to this metal. *Museum of Fine Arts, Boston.*

LEFT: Low-temperature metal melting furnace. *Johnson Gas Appliance Co.*

Polishing Pewter

Steel wool, medium grade, will smooth away file marks. Final removal of undesirable marks on the surface may be done with a cloth buffer and tripoli, followed by a color polish with rouge on a cotton wheel. A soft matte finish is achieved with a nickel wire brush.

Decorative Treatments for Pewter: Appliqué

Units of cut-out pewter to add ornamental levels can be applied to pewter itself and to other metals such as copper and brass. The units are joined to the metal with soft solder by sweat soldering. The back of the unit is entirely "tinned" with solder to within an eighth of an inch of the edge. The area where the appliqué is to be placed is likewise treated. Flux is then applied to the surface of both parts, and the parts are then fastened together with clips or clamps, binding wire, or any other device. Advantage should be taken of the force of gravity, both in holding the parts and in allowing the solder to flow properly. The heat is then applied till a slight settling movement indicates the flow of solder, which appears at the joint as a thin bright line. Close observation is needed so that the whole unit is held in place and overheating does not occur. The parts should be held together till they are really cool. Excess solder can be scraped away and the piece finished as described.

OTHER DECORATIVE POSSIBILITIES

For sawing or piercing pewter, a jeweler's saw frame and blades are used, with blades #1, 2, 3, or, most suitable, #4. Pewter can be chased and engraved in the same manner as other metals, with the object held on a pitch block or bowl. Since the metal is soft, it is not necessary to exert as much pressure with the tools as on other metals. Embossing can also be done, with a pitch bowl or lead block to support the metal. Pewter is etched with a so-

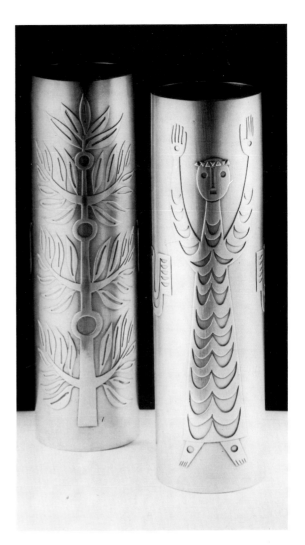

ABOVE: Pair of matching pewter vases, designed by Arne Jon Jutrem and executed by Mons Omvik, both of Oslo, Norway. Height: 18 cm. The designs on both sides of the vases, the Trinity (left) and Christ and Doves (right partially visible), consists of cut-out units applied to the base. *Photo by Kjell Munch.*

RIGHT: Detail of one of the doves from the same vase by Mons Omvik. When applying soldered units on pewter, great care must be taken not to overheat and melt the metal. This requires even heating and close observation of the melting solder. *Photo by Kjell Munch.*

Pewter cigarette box and ashtray, designed by Ferdinand Aars and executed by Mons Omvik, both of Oslo, Norway. *Photo by Kjell Munch.*

BELOW: Pewter bottle with stopper, by Lawrence G. Copeland. The linear pattern is made of brass wire soldered to the surface. *American Craftsmen's Council.*

lution of 20 per cent nitric acid and water. *Always add the acid to the water.* The areas that are to resist the acid can be protected with the usual resists (see etching of metals, page 126). The surface should be cleaned prior to etching, because grease will weaken adhesion of the resist material.

Casting Pewter

The low melting temperature and the ease with which pewter flows makes the alloy ideally suited to small castings. Pewter can be cast in permanent bronze molds, first heated to the melting temperature of pewter (471° F) to insure a successful casting. Such molds are used in production work. More usual for the craftsman are the molds made of plaster or by sand casting. For a description of these methods, see the sections on casting of metals, pages 325 and 330. The method of casting pewter with plaster casts has many possibilities. Inserts of a different metal, such as brass, can be included in the mold before casting the pewter; they are painted with flux to receive the pewter and assure its adhesion. The molten pewter can then be poured into the mold, and when the mold is removed, the inserts are permanently joined with the pewter. The combination of pewter and brass was popular with craftsmen in old China, and is done today in Hong Kong by appliquéing units.

The methods of casting with pewter can be used for casting other low-melting metals such as lead, zinc, white metal, type metal, and those mentioned below:

Low-melting metals	Melting point
White metal:	
92% tin, 8% antimony	475° F
Foundry type metal:	
62% lead, 13% tin, 25% antimony	617° F
Linotype metal:	
86% lead, 3% tin, 11% antimony	477° F
Babbitt metal (one of many):	
75% lead, 10% tin, 15% antimony	464° F

SLUSH CASTING OF PEWTER

Hollow castings of pewter can be made by pouring molten pewter into a chilled bronze mold. After a few seconds are allowed for the metal that makes contact with the mold wall to freeze, the mold is inverted and the still-liquid molten metal in the center of the mold space is poured out into a ladle or container. A thin, hollow casting is left behind. This system can be used for spouts, hollow handles, knobs, and similar objects.

Pewter boxes, designed by Mrs. Estrid Ericson, Svenskt Tenn, Stockholm, Sweden. The left box has a loose lid, a hand-engraved pattern, and brass edging on the lid and bottom. Its height is 5⅛ inches. The middle box has a polished surface with an antique jade ring handle. It is 4¼ inches in diameter and 3 inches high. The right box has a hinged lid and relief stripes; its diameter is 5¾ inches and its height 4⅞ inches. *Courtesy: Mrs. Estrid Ericson. Photo by Atelje Uggla AB.*

BELOW LEFT: Cast pewter salad set, from David Andersen, Oslo, Norway. *Norsk, New York.*

BELOW RIGHT: Eternal Light of spun pewter with cast inscription, by Stanley Lechtzin.

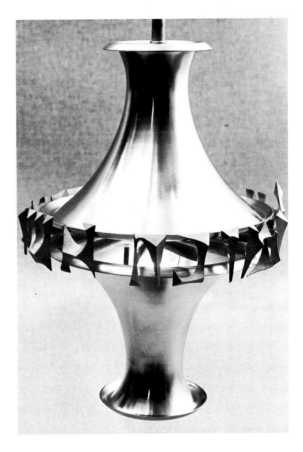

Forged-metal craftsman Stanislaw Skura at his anvil in Warsaw, Poland. *Cepelia, New York. Photo by J. Czecz.*

Forging

Hot forging in metal-forming processes has a history that goes back to at least 5500 B.C., when the Egyptians are known to have hot-forged copper and bronze by primitive methods to make tools.

Forging is a process of working metals with intermittent sharp blows from a hammer or other tools while the metal is from white to red hot and most malleable and plastic, or after the metal is annealed and cool. Forging is done primarily with iron and steel, but other malleable metals such as copper and bronze can also be forged. Forging of annealed precious metals for small work such as jewelry and ornamental objects is finding favor among craftsmen today, but this is generally a cold-forging process. Regardless of the metal employed, the procedures in shaping by forging techniques are relatively the same whether the metal is hot or cold. "Forged" has somehow come to be almost synonymous among some craftsmen with the word "wrought," though the latter is only a general term referring to metals beaten into shape with tools, while forging is a specific process.

Wrought Iron

Melting point: 2750° F
Pickle in 4–5 per cent sulphuric acid solution heated to 160–170° F.

Wrought iron is the metal traditionally used for forging and is still manufactured today for use in hand and machine forming methods. Wrought iron is a form of low carbon and manganese iron (less than 0.1 per cent of each) and contains 1 or 2 per cent generally but sometimes up to 4 per cent of *slag*. The slag consists of acid and basic and neutral oxides added for fusibility. It is mixed with the iron in a special manufacturing process called puddling, formerly a hand process but now mechanized. During manufacture, the iron is allowed to solidify partly, so as to retain the slag *without* complete fusion. The slag is therefore minutely and uniformly distributed in the metal, giving it its characteristics of being very tough, fibrous, malleable, ductile, relatively soft, and easily worked while hot. At white heat, two pieces can be joined or welded together permanently by simply hammering them together. The reason for this ease in welding is the relative purity of the metal, and the siliceous slag content, which gives the metal a self-fluxing quality allowing uniform, strong welds rapidly accomplished. The same characteristics make it easily weldable by oxy-acetylene torch welding.

Wrought iron has great tensile strength and high resistance to corrosion. Its resistance to progressive corrosion is due to the slag content. When exposed to the elements, the metal becomes coated with an oxide, or rust, which remains securely fixed to the surface and, because of the slag filaments, does not penetrate further. This characteristic has been known and appreciated in the past by the creators of ornamental wrought-iron work such as the elaborate gates, balcony railings, lanterns, and other objects which since their creation hundreds of years ago have withstood exposure to atmospheric conditions with relatively little effect.

Wrought iron is available in hammered bars of several forms, sheets, and wire.

German wrought-iron lamp hook, seventeenth century. Length: 6 feet; width: 3 feet. This object illustrates all the main treatments available to the wrought-iron worker: splitting, tapering, twisting, welding, etc. *Victoria and Albert Museum, London.*

Wrought iron candlestick No. 18, by Albert Paley. The four separate iron parts made by hot forging, tapering, bending, twisting, and wrapping techniques are structurally supported by a scrolled brass rod to which they have been riveted. Ornamented with inlaid copper; 28″ in height. *Photo by Roger B. Smith.*

X-Chair, wrought iron with leather seat sling and crystal hand grasps, French, c. 1400, *Philadelphia Museum of Art.*

Wrought-iron crosses, which are mounted on roof peaks in the area around San Cristobal de las Casas, Chiapas, Mexico. From the collection of Gertrude Duby-Blom and the late Franz Blom. *Photo by Oppi.*

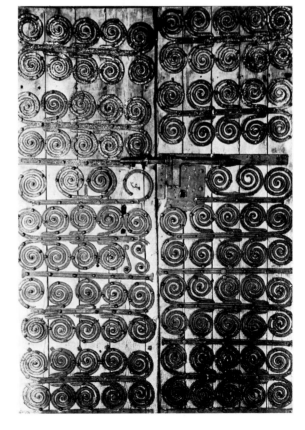

Wrought-iron decoration on wood door, French, Canton de Thuir, thirteenth century. *Philadelphia Museum of Art.*

Wrought-iron hardware for doors and closets, contemporary, made by Tridex, Madrid, Spain.

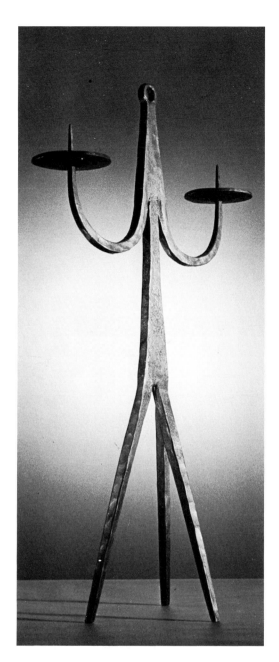

RIGHT: Gothic, Renaissance, and Baroque wrought-iron keys. From the Yale Lock Collection. *The Yale & Towne Manufacturing Company.*

ABOVE: Wrought-iron candlestick holder, by Stanislaw Skura, Warsaw, Poland, which illustrates the technique of splitting, as the arms and legs are made from one common stock. *Cepelia, New York. Photo by J. Czecz.*

ABOVE RIGHT: Wrought-iron andirons used to support burning logs. The vertical, decorated portion, called the *stauke,* prevents the log from falling forward out of the hearth, while the *billet bar* holds the logs. Andirons almost always have three legs for maximum stability. Contemporary, made by Tridex, Madrid, Spain.

Forge furnace. Built of steel and hard firebrick, with a large firebox and a front panel for gas and air adjustment. The furnace is equipped with four burners and two end burners that can be shut off when fewer are needed; a blower; a swinging, adjustable refractory lid; and a solenoid safety valve that insures positive gas shutoff in the event of electrical failure. The firebox is 4¾ inches wide, 7 inches deep, and 27 inches long. Over-all height: 30 inches; BTU input: 425,000 per hour maximum. Forge furnace ⚹133. *Johnson Gas Appliance Co.*

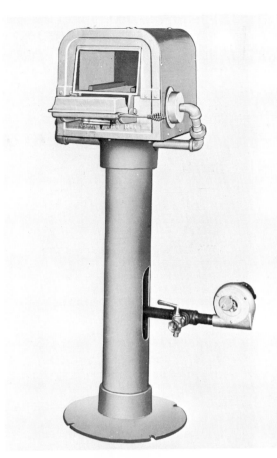

Gas-operated, high-speed heat furnace. It can be equipped with a special, hard refractory hearth which makes it possible to heat-treat and forge high-speed and carbon steels in the same unit. The firebox is 5 inches high, 7¾ inches wide, and 13½ inches deep. Temperature range to 2400° F, achieves 1500° F in 5 minutes and near maximum in 30 minutes. BTU input: 120,000 per hour maximum. Blower: ¹⁄₂₅ HP, 110 volts. *Johnson Gas Appliance Co.*

Forging Wrought Iron and Steel

Forged metals are generally worked hot, being first heated in a forge fire and then hammered on a flat, polished steel surface such as an anvil. The forge is made of brick, mild steel, or cast iron, with a depression in the center and a bottom opening for the tuyères or pipe nozzles. Through their small openings an air blast is forced to the fire mechanically by an electric fan, or by a foot bellows (discontinued for the most part), to elevate the temperature of the fire when necessary to heat the metal. Coke or bituminous coal in small pieces is the fuel generally used, and a good draught, hood, and chimney are necessary to take away fumes, unless forging is done out of doors. The forge should not be made too high from ground level to avoid unnecessary lifting. A furnace that can be heated to 1500–2200° F may also be used but it has limitations, such as size. A forge fire has the advantage of being able to heat only a part of the metal being worked. A quenching tank or trough filled with water should be near the forge.

Mild steel widely used today for forging can be worked in three kinds of heat: white heat for welding, yellow heat for easy working, and cherry-red heat for finishing the metal. High carbon steel must be cherry red. Wrought iron can be worked at all temperatures. Do not overheat the metal, however, as prolonged overheating will enlarge the grain structure, causing open spaces called "burning," which weakens the metal. Forged metals should be worked uniformly, to reduce residual stresses which might otherwise cause cracking.

Forging Tools

The *anvil* is the basic tool used in forging as the surface on which metals are shaped in conjunction with hammers. Large anvils consist of the main central part called the body, the horn or bick which is the pointed, rounded end used for forming curves and rings, and a

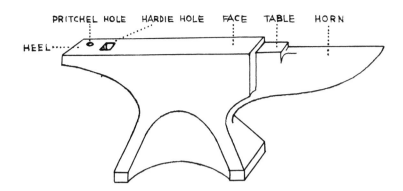

Forging anvil

Forging hammers and swages: 1. Cross peen forging hammer 2. Smith's hand hammer or fuller 3. Sledge hammer 4. Flatter 5. Top and bottom swage for rounding, tapering and setting down, with a withy handle 6. Hot set chisel and hardie 7. Top and bottom swage for angular shapes 8. Top and bottom swage for oval forms

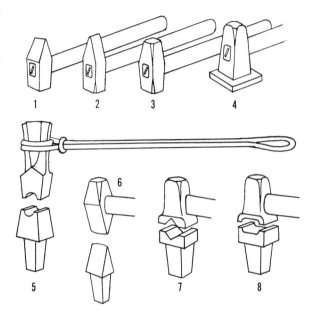

flat surface or face that has holes at the tail or heel end, called the hardie and pritchel holes. The flat surface is the main working area and is made of a blister-steel hardened plate welded to the upper surface. The hardie hole is used to hold tools called hardies, set chisels, and swage blocks, and the round pritchel hole is used during punching operations, forming operations, and to hold round shank tools. The anvil should be fixed in position at convenient working height (its face about two feet from the ground), near the forge, a water supply, and a bench vise. Anvils are usually set on a suitably heavy tree trunk stump (end grain up) which provides spring to its working surface.

The *hardie* is a wedge-shaped tool placed in the hardie hole of the anvil and used for cutting hot or cold metal of small size from underneath. The metal is placed on the hardie edge, hammered, reversed, hammered again, and then easily broken at the scored line with a hammer.

Hammers. Several hammers are used for forging. The *sledge hammer* is a heavy hammer about ten to twenty pounds in weight, has a handle about thirty inches in length, and is used for forming operations that require the greatest force. The sledge can be used directly on metal and in conjunction with other tools such as swages, fullers, flatters, hot and cold set chisels, round and square punches. Its weight makes necessary the assistance of *a second person* who strikes the other tool with the sledge while that tool is held in place by the smith. Swages, fullers, flatters, and punches are held with a wood or wire *withy* wrapped around the tool and held in place with a wire coupling. (These tools are also made with permanent wood handles.) Smaller hammers are used by the smith unassisted by helpers. A smith's hand hammer is two to seven pounds in weight with a handle of twelve to sixteen inches in length. A 1½-pound hammer is suitable for the forging of metals up to ⅝ inch in thickness; beyond that, heavier hammers are needed. The hardwood handles placed in hammers are positioned in the hole made at the point of balance between the ends.

In the forging of precious metals, some of the same hammers that are used for raising can be used. Cross peen, ball peen, and dome-faced forging hammers are suitable, depending on the function needed.

The *set hammer* is a flat-faced hammer employed when a depression to be worked is too small for a flatter. It is held in position by the

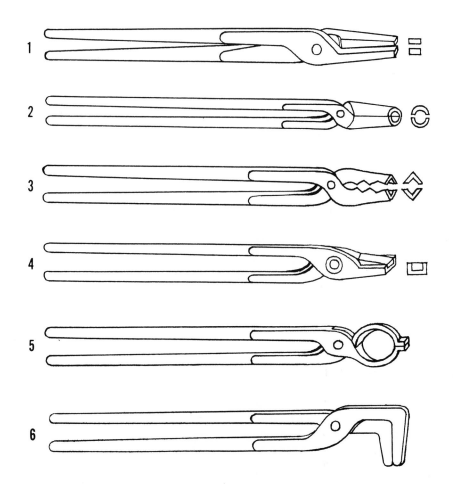

Forging tongs: 1. Flat nose, open mouth 2. Round, hollow bit 3. Square, hollow bit 4. Forming bit 5. Large hollow bit 6. Bent tip

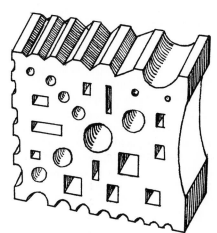

Swage block

smith and struck with a sledge by an assistant.

The *flatter* is a flat-faced tool used for flattening, smoothing, or spreading metal.

The *fuller* is a form of set hammer for making a longitudinal half round depression or groove in metal. The fuller can be placed in position and struck with a hammer or used with a bottom fuller in the hardie to form shoulders or hollows. Fullers are used for grooving, fluting, spreading metals, or making *concave* shapes.

The *swage* is a grooved rounding tool made in various sizes, diameters, and shapes for reducing the thickness of metal rods in *convex* shapes. A top and bottom swage can be used in conjunction with each other, the bottom one being placed in the hardie while the top one is held over the metal being shaped. The bottom swage can be used alone in conjunction with a hammer if only one side of a bar is being shaped.

The *swage block* is a perforated and grooved block of cast iron or steel made with grooves and depressions of various sizes and shapes on its face and sides. The cross-section shapes of rod can be formed or altered in these grooves in the same manner that swages are used.

Hot set and *cold set chisels* are used with handles, and those without are simply called hot or cold chisels. *Hot set chisels* are sharp chisels made exclusively for use on hot metals. Thinner than cold chisels, they are capable of cutting all the way through metal of considerable thickness. *Cold set chisels* are short, broad chisels of cast steel, with a sixty-degree cutting angle, held by a withy, and struck with a sledge hammer to notch, chip, gouge, or shear hot or cold worked metal. Metal can be broken by notching with a cold set chisel and then placing the metal on an anvil edge and administering a sharp blow. Notching can also be used for decorative effect. Cold chisels in lengths of three to eight inches can be used by holding them without a withy.

Tongs of many shapes and sizes are made to hold both hot and cold work. Several are designed for specific situations typical of forging work. Tong jaws are called *chaps,* and the handles are known as *reins.* Closed mouth (for thin metal), open mouth (for flat, thicker metal), hollow bit (to hold round or square metal), rivet (to hold rivets at right angles to the tongs), and bent tip (to hold metal parallel to tongs) are some of the tongs made. Others are grooved inside their jaws to aid in holding metal of small cross section. If they become hot while working, they can be quenched in water to allow them to be handled with comfort.

Vises strong enough to withstand heavy blows are constantly in use. The strongest is the leg vise, which has an extension to the floor which helps it to withstand heavy hammering impact. A smaller vise of cast steel is useful for small work. Serrated vise jaws should be lined with sheet copper to avoid marking hot metal which is held between them.

Several other tools are also used by the smith such as a two-foot steel rule, calipers, compasses, dividers, and scribers used in laying out forged work, and drills, bench shears, hand snips, and hacksaws. Various wrenches are used to bend and twist metal. Files of all kinds are used on cold metal and only *rasps* can be used on hot metal. C clamps and other types of clamps are in constant use to hold metal while forming.

Steel throwing knife, Uele Zande. Length: 470 mm. These knives are frequently decorated with chased designs. *Musée Royal de L'Afrique Centrale, Tervuren, Belgium.*

Pokers, shovels, and *rakes* are used to maintain the forge fire.

Forging Operations

Forging can be divided into two areas: *forged work* where the metal is worked hot, and *bench work* in which it is worked cold.

Rounding up, Roughing, or Cogging These are beginning operations in the preparation of the metal that are performed on the ingot or blank and are meant to rearrange the surface of the metal's structure and condense the central part of the metal.

Roughing Breaking down the ingot to a rough shape.

Cogging Consolidating metal structure by hammering ingots into blooms or billets. A *bloom* (from Old English *bloma,* a lump) or a billet is a semiworked ingot intended for conversion into strip, rod, wire, or sheet, the forms in which most craftsmen purchase their metal.

Cutting or Slicing Bringing the metal down to the desired size by the use of hot or cold chisels and a sledge hammer.

Drawing Out or Forging Down This common operation consists of *uniformly decreasing* the cross-section thickness while increasing the length.

Tapering Tapering, a form of drawing down, can be done in the *round* or *flat* (as in tapering a chisel point). In round tapering, the metal is

first shaped square till the cross section approximates the desired size. The corners of the square edge are then hammered to form an octagonal cross-section shape, and finally the work is rounded by swaging or rolling. The same procedure is used when reducing uniformly round cross sections.

Upsetting The opposite of drawing down, upsetting involves compressing, or changing the angle of the forging action by ninety degrees. A bar is hammered at the end to thicken it, an edge can be thickened, or a rivet head can be formed by upsetting.

Swaging Shaping metal against grooved swage tools or a swage block. The metal is rotated while being hammered.

the stock with a hacksaw or chisels, and close the ring. The ring can be formed on the horn of the anvil or on a mandrel.

Twisting Square or rectangular stock displays the twist best. After heating in the forge, one end of the metal is held in a vise while the other end is twisted the desired amount with tongs, *in one operation.* A twist wrench can also be used. Insert the stock into the wrench, heat the portion to be twisted, place the other end in a vise, and turn the wrench. To form a sharp twist, heat the metal in a concentrated area; that part will twist more easily. For a gradual twist, heat the entire length uniformly. For a twist in a part of a rod length, heat only the area to be twisted. Many variations are possible, depending on the composition of the stock being twisted and the shape of the cross section.

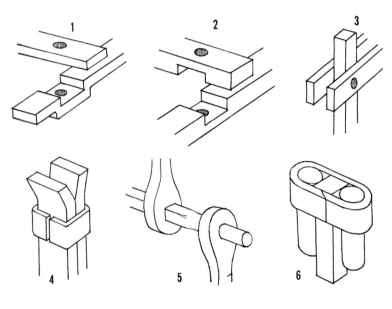

Types of joints:
1. Lap joint, rivet held
2. Interlocking joint, rivet held
3. Pinned bar, rivet or bolt held
4. Collar joint, square
5. Pierced joint, square, round
6. Collar joint, oval

Setting Down Reducing the thickness or cross section of *a part* of the metal being forged.

Bending A bar or the thickness of metal cannot ordinarily be bent to a right angle in one operation, especially if it is quite heavy, without cracking. First bend to *half* the distance, and return to the forge. Remove, upset both the end and the side edge, and complete the bend. To form a ring, estimate the amount of metal to be used, and bend that length from the stock *at a right angle first.* Reheat and start forming the curve *from the end,* gradually, reheating when necessary. When the circle is completed, cut away the formed ring from

Punching or Coring In punching, a cold punch is used to pierce the white-hot metal. When it is about to emerge from the other side, the metal is moved to a position above the hardie hole in the anvil to allow the tool to enter and thereby avoid dulling the tool or scarring the anvil surface. The metal is then reheated, reversed, and the opening increased by working from the opposite direction to that of the first operation. There is no loss of metal, because this is in effect a stretching operation. Work should proceed slowly to avoid cracking the metal. In *coring,* a *hollow punch* is used, and a section of the metal is removed to make a hole. It may be necessary to return the metal to the forge to reheat it before completing the opening.

Hollow Forging on Mandrels To make hollow cylinders or rings, a cylindrical mandrel is inserted in a punched or cored opening, and the metal is hammered or forged down. Sheet metal can be formed into a cylinder by heating, placing it over a swage block groove of suitable depth, placing a mandrel over the metal, and hammering the metal into the depression. The upstanding edges are then hammered over the mandrel form to complete the cylinder shape. The mandrel should be oiled before use to facilitate removal of the cylinder after forming.

Forge Welding

Forge welding is the oldest welding process. Wrought iron and mild steel can be welded in forging by heating the parts to be joined till they are brilliant white-hot and emitting sparks. The metal at this point has reached a condition of surface plasticity. The parts are then brought into contact quickly, on top of each other, and hammered together. They fuse into one unit. Butt joints can be welded by first upsetting the ends to be joined, to thicken them, then reheating the ends to welding temperature, placing them together, and hammering them. The original thickness is maintained. If the metal is absolutely clean, free of oil or cinder, *no flux is necessary,* because the slag in wrought iron acts as a flux. The force to be exerted by the hammer depends on the mass and size of the parts being joined.

Other Joining Methods

Riveting Metal parts can be joined by rivets which are inserted into drilled, punched, or cored holes. The fit should be tight, and the length of the rivet stem only long enough to form heads at both ends. See page 311 for information on types of rivets and their use.

Pinning A flat, wedge-shaped pin can be hammered into a preformed hole made with punches and tapered in shape. This is a strong way of joining parts and has the advantage of being removable. There are cases where units must be taken apart and reassembled when pins are of value.

Collaring When two or more parts are to be held together at one point, a collar made of half round or flat bar metal is formed to encircle the parts and is then hammered around them. This is a commonly used joining method.

Screwing In some cases a screw is the best joint. The hole to contain the screw is first drilled and then the threads are cut with taps. See page 314 for information on screws.

Bolting Ordinary or decorative-headed bolts with nuts can be used to join parts. This is a simple joining method, but not in favor with most wrought-iron workers. A hole of the proper dimension is drilled, the bolt inserted, and a nut tightened on the back with a wrench.

1. Scroll wrench 2. Scroll former 3. Twist wrench 4. Twisted bar made with a twist wrench

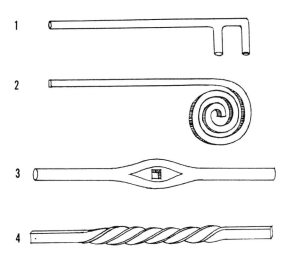

General Considerations in Forging

Forging designs which require accuracy means working from full-scale working drawings. To work the metal, first place the hammer to be used on the anvil so that no time is lost after removing the metal from the heat. Place the metal in the heat of the forge, pat the coke around it, and apply the heat with the help of the fan or bellows till the metal is yellow-hot. If the metal is long enough· to be held without danger of burning, lift it with the left hand and place it on the nearby anvil. Tap the metal against the anvil a few times or hit it with the hammer to remove any adhering cinders or scale which might otherwise be hammered into

Altar cross of cast and forged silver with a large piece of raw quartz crystal mounted in the foot, designed and made by Louis Osman, 1959. *Worshipful Company of Goldsmiths, London.*

Detail of the altar cross foot, showing the mounted
natural quartz crystal.

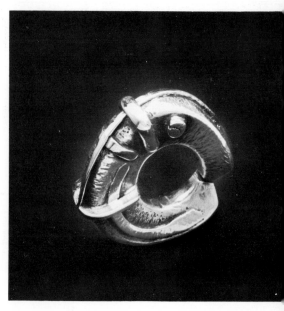

Bronze container with wrought silver ornament mounted on the lid, by John Prip, 1959.

Ring, by Oppi Untracht. The ring was forged from an ingot of fine silver and then decorated with heavy gold wire. It is designed to be worn on the small finger, with the design running around the outside of the hand. *Photo by Lex Tice.*

Pin No. 119 by Albert Paley. Forged and fabricated in silver (later oxidized) and gold, with three opals, inlays of mother of pearl and ivory, with a mounted ivory; 8″ by 6½″. *Photo by Roger B. Smith.*

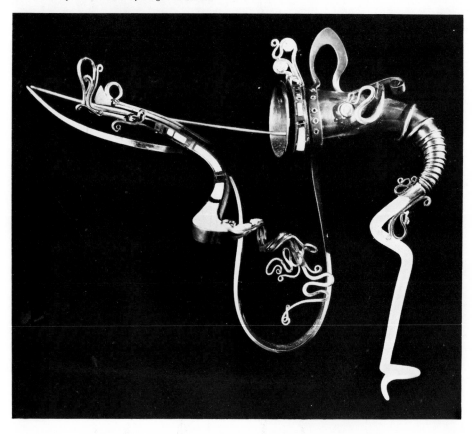

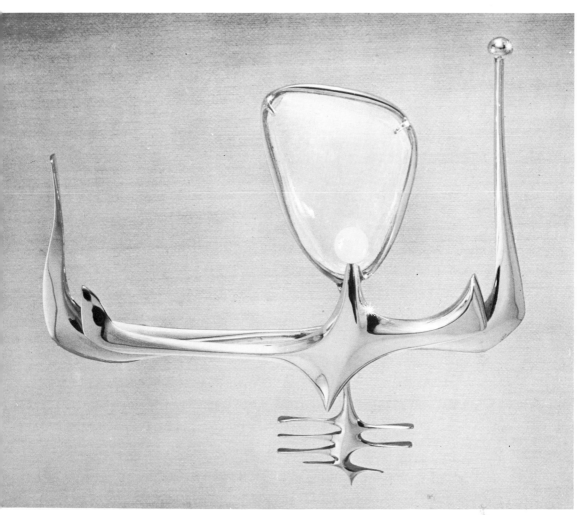

Gold pin, with a pearl mounted before an opal, by Ruth Radakovich. The process was forging, followed by filing to refine the forms.

the surface in working. Proceed to hammer the metal with the right hand. Exert enough force in hammering so that the entire metal is worked *in depth* and not merely on the surface. The metal should be worked at the temperature correct for its forming and for the operation involved. Yellow heat is used in major forming operations and cherry-red heat for finishing. Dampening the anvil surface during finishing stages produces a smoother metal surface. The metal should always be in contact with the surface or tool being used to form it. Return the metal to the fire (or anneal) as soon as it shows signs of resistance to working. Continued work beyond this point may cause cracking. Quench all tools when they become hot from contact with hot metal.

Cold Forging

Cold forging as a method of working on silver, gold, and nonferrous metals opens results to the craftsman that are unique in character. The tool marks left on the metal create a pleasing surface that is often a relief from the usual highly finished surfaces and gives the work a feeling of integrity. Forging can be especially appreciated on work where variations in metal thicknesses are visible, as in spoons and other flatware, jewelry, articles for religious use, and candelabra. There is no method of work that legitimately duplicates the forged metal look.

Oxyacetylene Fusion Welding

The development of welding metal by high temperature flame such as can be produced by an oxyacetylene torch did not come into existence till 1901. The cutting of metal by means of this fuel became commercially feasible in 1905.

Equipment

Of the several methods of fusion welding that exist, oxyacetylene welding is the most suitable to the craftsman's use and requires only a moderate amount of equipment:

An oxygen tank and an acetylene tank
Oxygen and acetylene regulators
Welding torch and connecting hose: red for acetylene, green for oxygen
A cutting torch or cutting attachment
Gloves
Dark goggles or eye shield to protect the operator and make hot work visible
Friction-type lighter
Steel bench equipped with firebrick surface, or steel table with open grating top

Welding should be done in an area with a concrete or metal-covered floor. The work surface and floor may be covered instead with transite board, an asbestos cement composition.

Oxyacetylene welding produces the coalescence or fusion of metals with or without the use of metal filler rods. The heat source is a flame made by the combustion of acetylene and commercially pure oxygen. The high heat produced by this flame brings the metals into a molten state quickly and unites them in a strong, consolidated mass. The fusion is localized; only the area being joined is heated, and the remainder of the metal is relatively cold.

The oxygen is compressed in seamless tanks or cylinders, which are available in several sizes. The size most commonly used by craftsmen is 110 cubic feet, filled to 2000 psi (pounds per square inch) pressure. Gas volume is indicated in cubic feet and pounds. Acetylene, a chemical compound of 92.3 per cent carbon and 7.7 per cent hydrogen, is stored in the tank by dissolving acetylene in acetone under pressure. Acetylene also is available in tanks of various sizes. Generally the sizes of the acetylene and oxygen tanks are similar.

Two tanks are used, therefore, one containing oxygen, and the other acetylene. A hose leads from each of these to the torch-and-tip assembly, where oxygen and acetylene are combined. When the combination is ignited, a flame of 6300° F is produced, the highest temperature of any commercially available flame. This temperature is capable of melting most alloys, and welding is therefore possible.

The cylinders containing the gas are tested and maintained in accordance with specifications and regulations set by the Interstate Commerce Commission. Users are advised not to tamper with the tanks. Should any irregularity develop, the tank should be *immediately* taken out of doors and the supplier notified. *Acetylene is highly combustible.*

Regulators are used with each tank to reduce the pressure to a working condition. Two-stage and single-stage construction regulators are used; they are designed for the specific gas used. Acetylene should not be used at a pressure exceeding 15 psi. The hoses are specially constructed of fabric and rubber for the purpose, the red hose for acetylene, and the green hose for oxygen. These hoses have special fittings with reversed threads, so that they are not interchangeable, even by mistake. The right-hand thread is for oxygen, and the left-hand thread is for acetylene.

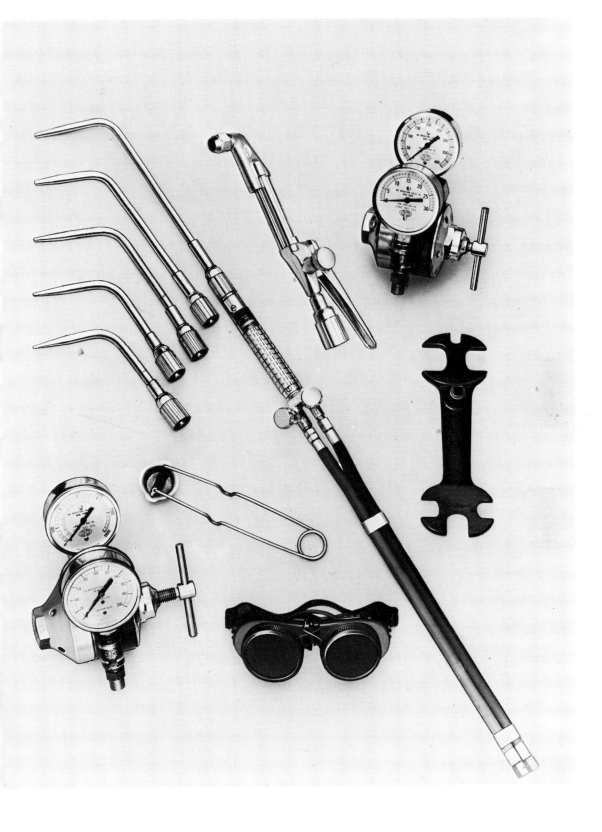

Welding equipment, without the tanks (acetylene and oxygen). Upper left to right: welding torch with tubing and different-sized interchangeable tips, cutting torch, oxygen tank gauge, and, below the gauge, a wrench. Lower left: acetylene gas gauge, flint flame lighter, and goggles. *The Air Reduction Company.*

"Star II," by Alvin Cooke. Welded steel sculpture with textures developed from the welding method and patina treatment from chemicals and heat. *Photo by Cooke.*

Procedural Preparations for Welding

The oxygen-valve cap is removed and the tank valve quickly opened and closed. This procedure, known as "cracking the tank," is intended to blow out any dirt or dust that might have accumulated in the valve. (Avoid directing the high-pressure oxygen stream toward a person or flame, for injury or fire might result.) The oxygen regulator is then connected to the tank valve and the collar tightened. The green

oxygen hose is tightly connected to the regulator. The same procedure is followed for the acetylene tank and regulator, and the red hose, which has a left-hand or counterclockwise tightening thread, is attached. The torch is connected to both the oxygen and acetylene hoses. The tip to be used is screwed into the torch nozzle, pointing correctly for convenient use when the handle of the torch is held.

ADJUSTING THE REGULATORS FOR PRESSURE

A gloved hand should be held before the gauge glass when the pressure is turned on,

Welded steel chair, constructed almost exclusively from welding rods, by Oppi Untracht.

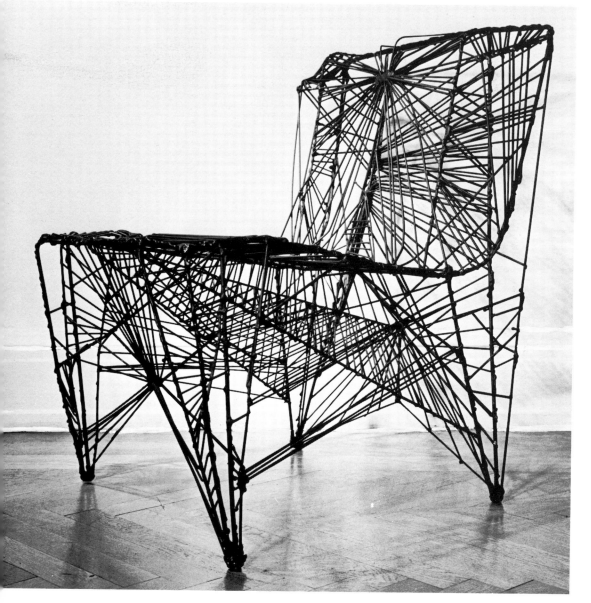

in the event some regulator or gauge defect causes the glass to shatter.

Oxygen The regulator adjusting screw should be screwed out, free of tension. The tank valve is fully opened, and tightened in the open position to avoid leaks during operation. The adjusting screw is turned clockwise till the proper pressure for the tip that is being used is registered on the gauge. For most tips, a working pressure of five psi is usual; the manufacturer's instructions should be followed. The working pressure is set with the oxygen torch valve slightly opened, after which it is shut, or it is set with the valve shut. It is more important to set the pressure with the valve opened when small, single-stage regulators are employed.

Acetylene The adjusting valve is completely released from tension. The acetylene tank valve is opened one-quarter to one-half turn, till the pressure registers on the tank gauge. The working pressure is controlled by screwing the adjusting screw clockwise till the pressure is registered on the acetylene gauge—usually five psi, but always according to the manufacturer's instructions. During this operation the acetylene torch valve may be left slightly open, after which it is closed; or with the torch closed, as above.

THE TORCH

The torch or blowpipe is a complicated mechanism and the complete assembly includes the handle (with needle valves), mixing head, and tip. It is designed to allow complete control of the flame by the welder and to produce a rapid, localized heating and melting of the base metal to produce a continuous piece. Torches should be kept away from grease or oil, for these interfere dangerously with torch function. A blowpipe has six to twelve different-sized tips, each producing a different-sized flame. The proper tip size must be selected for the particular task at hand. The diameter of the flame can vary from a pin size to ³⁄₁₆ inch by the use of interchangeable tips.

Regulating the Flame The torch is lighted best with a friction-type flint lighter or a pilot flame. First the acetylene is lighted and then the oxygen is introduced. There are three basic types of flame, each with its special character and use.

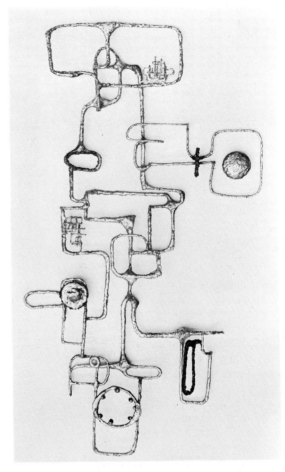

Door knob and welded wire escutcheon, by Ibram Lassaw. Height: 4 feet. The welded wire construction is brazed in gold- and silver-colored alloys. *The Yale & Towne Manufacturing Company.*

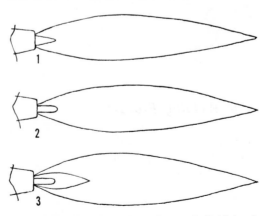

Types of oxyacetylene welding flames: 1. Oxidizing 2. Neutral 3. Carburizing or reducing

1. The *neutral* flame (5850° F at cone, 3800° F at envelope, 2300° F at tip of envelope) occurs when *equal volumes* of oxygen and acetylene are burned. Actually, an additional 1½ volumes of oxygen is necessary for complete combustion of the acetylene, but

this comes from the air surrounding the flame. The neutral flame is easiest to obtain by first producing an excess-acetylene flame, recognizable by the "feather" extension of the inner cone. A neutral flame is obtained while the oxygen is being increased and just as the feather disappears. The highest temperature exists at the tip of the inner cone, while the outer envelope produces a reducing atmosphere that protects the molten metal from oxidation during the welding. A neutral flame is recommended for most welding situations, but a slightly reducing or oxidizing flame is desirable on some metals and under certain conditions.

2. The *reducing* or carburizing flame (5700° F at the cone), an excess-acetylene flame, is made by allowing slightly more acetylene than oxygen to emerge, causing a carburization. A reducing flame has a large acetylene feather extending from the inner cone, making a flame of three zones. If the feather is twice as long as the cone, the flame is called 2X, and if it is three times as long, 3X. These special flames are used according to specifications in certain welding procedures. The reducing flame is used in welding low-alloy types of welding rods to weld steel, and in welding certain steel alloys.

3. The *oxydizing* flame (6300° F just below the cone) is an excess-oxygen flame used only in the welding of copper, bronze, and copper-based alloys such as the brasses. The inner cone is shorter and more pointed than the neutral flame. An oxidizing flame is made by first establishing a neutral flame and then increasing the oxygen or decreasing the acetylene. A highly oxidizing flame is the hottest.

The Welding Process

Whenever welding is done, even before the flame is lighted or regulated, the welder must protect his eyes from excessive glare by wearing dark glasses, goggles, or an eyeshield. With darkened eye coverings, the puddle of the welded material is easily seen and therefore better controlled. Gloves of asbestos or other heat-resistant material are an added safety precaution. Welding should be done in a well-ventilated room with an exhaust fan, to avoid the inhalation of harmful metal fumes.

When joining two pieces in setting up the work, the seam should widen slightly as it goes away from the beginning point, because contraction of the welded metal draws the opening together as the weld progresses. Assume a straight seam weld, with the metal placed on the work table. The metal is heated at the beginning of the seam till it forms a puddle, and the two parts hold in what is called a "tack" weld. The tip of the neutral flame is brought into contact with the metal to make the tack weld. Tacks should occur at either end of the seam and at intervals of six to eight inches, depending on the thickness of the metal. The welding rod or filler rod, if one is used, is then brought into the flame.

Oxyacetylene welding is done in one of two basic techniques when a welding or filler rod is used: forehand or backhand. In forehand welding, which is recommended for welding up to ⅛ inch in thickness, the torch points ahead in the direction of the welding, and the filler rod precedes the torch. (For right-handed welders, the torch is held in the right hand, and welding starts at the right and moves to the left.) In backhand welding, the torch points back toward the completed welding, and the rod is placed between the torch and the welded joint. (For the right-handed welder, welding starts at the left and moves to the right.) This method allows for an easier distribution of heat and better control of the puddle and the molten metal. Generally, backhand welding proceeds faster than forehand and is considered to pro-

Basic welding joints: 1. Butt joint 2. Lap joint 3. T-joint 4. Corner joint 5. Edge joint

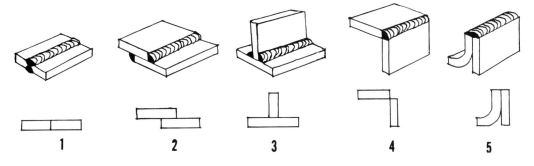

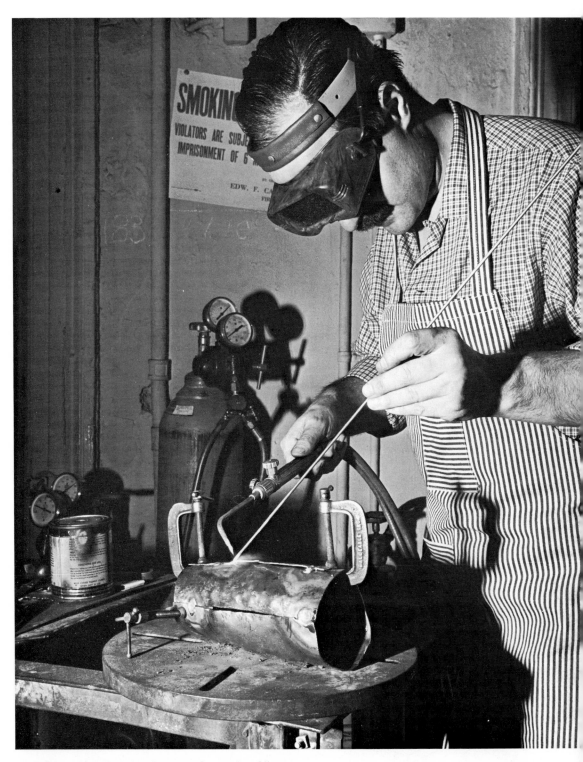

Robert Pinart demonstrating one of several welding positions for the torch and welding rod. *Photo by Oppi.*

OPPOSITE: Wild boar, by Jean-Vincent de Crozals, Vence, France. Height: 68 cm.; length: 80 cm. The boar is made of welded steel parts and was washed with a zinc bath in a galvanizing factory, as described in the picture caption on page 299.

duce a higher quality weld. It is also commonly used for metal over ⅛ inch in thickness.

A good weld is produced by first making a puddle with the torch, touching the welding rod to the metal, and allowing just enough to melt to fill the seam or make a *fillet* (in the case of joining a vertical piece of metal to a horizontal piece), and proceeding to the next puddle, distributing an equal amount of metal in a regular sequence. On flat seams, the added welding rod material should not stand up as a high ridge but should be almost level with the metal itself. Care should be taken not to overheat the welding metal, for this will cause carburization and a porous, weak weld.

WELDING RODS

The metal to be welded should be cleaned along the joint and on both sides unless the metal is known to be clean. Grease and dirt interfere with welding. It is advisable when using filler rods to use those that have mechanical properties similar to those of the base metal. This results in a joint that is of like character to that of the base metal and, in a carefully made weld, is stronger than the base metal itself.

Steel welding rods are used on iron and steel and are made in varying tensile strength and ductility and in various thicknesses. In high-quality welding, GA 60 welding rods are correct. No flux is needed for steel welding.

Welding rods are available for various metals, such as nickel (no flux needed) and its special alloys. Stainless steel must be welded

with flux and a neutral flame. Though all aluminum welding is difficult, some aluminum is weldable with the aid of special welding fluxes. Aluminum of 2S, 3S, and 61S are weldable with their own welding rods and fluxes. Flux must be applied to the rod, the top, the bottom, and the edges of the joint. In lead welding no fluxes are needed, but lead rods are necessary.

Fluxes may be used dry, in powder form, or, in some cases, in paste form. With dry flux, the filler rod is heated and touched while hot to the powdered flux. Flux will adhere on the rod up to the depth to which it is inserted in the powder. When this portion is used up, the process is repeated. Paste flux is painted on the metal and the filler rod with a brush. Filler rods are available already coated with a suitable flux. Flux residue should be removed after welding with hot water and a stiff brush or by abrasion with a wire brush attached to a flexible shaft. Fluxes might attack and corrode the underlying metal if not removed.

Dissimilar metals can be welded or brazed to each other with the aid of fluxes. Copper, brass, nickel, and nickel alloys can be welded to low carbon steel and cast iron or to each other. Carbon steels can be welded to stainless steels. Aluminum cannot be welded to other metals. Brass (yellow bronze) filler rods, nickel silver rods, and silicon bronze rods are usable with their corresponding metals or in brazing.

During the welding of wrought iron or mild steel, the slag contained in the metal rises to the surface at a low temperature. This is not an indication of fusion, and the heating must be continued till the base metal forms a deep puddle. A neutral flame and a low-carbon filler rod are called for.

BRAZE OR BRONZE WELDING

Braze welding can be performed for covering a metal surface to produce color and textural interest and to join metals. It can be applied to any metals that melt at temperatures higher than those of the rods used.

As practiced today, braze welding is done with a brass filler rod made of 60 per cent copper and 40 per cent zinc, with inclusions of small quantities of iron, tin, manganese, and silicon, which improve its flowing qualities. A suitable flux is applied by heating the rod and dipping it into the container with the flux powder. This is repeated as the fluxed portion of the rod is consumed. Already-coated fluxed filler rods are available. Flux tanks are made that can be connected to the torch, and combine flux with the flame automatically, at the same time minimizing metal oxidation.

The rod should not boil or spark excessively, but should be deposited smoothly. Slanting the surface off the horizontal will help in the coating of a surface entirely with filler rod material for texture. (Begin at the higher point.) When the metal melts, the filler rod metal and the base metal are joined or bonded to each other under heat by three forces that act simultaneously. These are tinning (coating of the surface), alloying, and intergranular penetration. The bond produced by tinning occurs as the cleaned, heated metal surface is coated with a thin film of the filler rod alloy; the bond results from low surface tension and the action

of atomic forces between the alloy and the base metal. Alloying occurs as the filler alloy and the base metal diffuse into each other where they make contact. Intergranular penetration takes place under heat as the crystal grain structure of the base metal and the alloy unite.

One advantage of braze welding is that the low temperature necessary to bond the filler rod alloy minimizes the distortion of the base

BELOW LEFT: Welded sculpture of bronze and chrome, by Harry Bertoia. The surfaces of the units have been brazed by puddling brass and other alloys, which produces the characteristic roughened texture. Remnants of flux must be removed with a crimped wire brush. *United States Information Service, New Delhi.*

BELOW: Detail of a free-standing screen of brazed, welded steel, done for the First National Bank of Miami, Florida, by Harry Bertoia. The irregular texture of the surface is the characteristic result of applying the brazing rods in molten puddles.

OPPOSITE: Welded steel candlestick, by Saara Hopea Untracht. Height: 11¼ inches. After the welding was completed, the entire surface was brazed with brass alloy brazing rods. *Photo by Oppi.*

Welded stairwell screen constructed with four metals and glass, done by John Rhoden for the Sheraton Hotel in Philadelphia. *United States Information Service, New Delhi.*

metal. The strength of the joint when brazing rod metal is used as a welding material for holding parts together is less than that of a fusion-welded joint. Surface colors of the metals used for texture can be varied by using alloys of different metals.

FLAME-CUTTING METAL

In the flame-cutting process, the metal is preheated to its ignition or kindling temperature and is then quickly oxidized by releasing an oxygen jet that comes from a special oxygen cutting torch. A special attachment can be added to a welding torch for the purpose, or a separate cutting torch can be used.

The torch is held at the edge of the metal at the beginning of the cutting line, which is called the drag line. Cutting is ordinarily done at a right angle to the metal surface, with the torch canted slightly toward the direction of the cut. (If a bevel cut is desired, the torch is held at the appropriate angle.) The end of the inner flame cone is held just above the metal, and as soon as a spot of red forms, indicating the arrival of kindling temperature, the oxygen jet is turned on by pressing a lever, and the cutting commences.

The torch is moved slowly but steadily along the drag line, and a kerf, or narrow slit having parallel smooth sides, is formed. There is some loss of metal, which is consumed by oxygen, and between 30 and 40 per cent remains as slag beads under the cut. A successful cutting operation should result in a clean break and produce a minimum of slag. An excess of slag is caused by moving the cutting torch across the metal too slowly, or unevenly. The same cutting tool can be used to make holes in metal or to cut the metal into any desired shape.

BELOW: Clock, by Jean-Vincent de Crozals, Vence, France. Height: 81 cm.; width: 55.5 cm. The clock is made of iron parts that were cut out, hammered into shapes, and welded together with an oxyacetylene torch. The finished piece was plunged into an acid bath for cleaning and was then washed and immersed in a liquid zinc bath at a galvanizing factory. To prevent deformation while in the zinc bath the form is constructed with a strong interior armature and care is taken to eliminate all liquid zinc as quickly as possible. The galvanization with zinc prevents future rusting and also allows the surface to be treated for a patina. The dial can be demounted for the installation of a mechanism and for repairing.

Welded iron "Madonna," contemporary, made by Tridex, Madrid, Spain.

Lathe-turned brass and nickel silver tower stands by Wendy Ramshaw, London, designed to hold sets of independent rings of 18 karat white and yellow gold, set with various semi-precious stones. The tower mounts can be separated to allow the placement and removal of the rings. The rings can be arranged in any sequence the wearer desires, thus making possible a variety of combinations. When not in use, the rings and stands serve as a decorative sculpture in miniature. *Photo by Bob Cramp, London, courtesy the Worshipful Company of Goldsmiths, London.*

Cold Metal Spinning

Cold metal spinning was introduced to the United States about 1840, though it has an old history. It is a process of metal forming on a lathe on which is mounted a wood or metal form called a *chuck*. Over this, while spinning, the metal is shaped by compression, with the aid of blunt tools, to form a seamless object. This method of forming is employed to make circular or cylindrical shapes, usually where several repeats of the same form (or *shell,* as it is sometimes called) are desired. The spinning lathe for metal is similar to a wood-turning lathe but is more powerful, because the exertion of more pressure is necessary in the spinning of metal than in the turning of wood. Some lathes may be used for both wood turning and metal spinning. Unless ready-made wood or steel chucks are purchased, the spinner must first turn the wood chuck. (See bibliography for book on wood turning.)

Almost any ductile metal can be spun, some metals offering more and others less resistance. The soft metals are gold, silver, copper, brass, aluminum, zinc, and pewter. Gold and silver harden faster than the others and must be annealed to make deep draws. The semi-hard metals are nickel, nickel-silver alloys, and Monel Metal. The hardest to spin is steel. Spinning work-hardens most metals, and when this occurs, annealing is necessary to restore them to ductility. (See page 302.)

General Considerations

Copper, brass, and Monel Metal should be plunged into cold water after annealing, but steel should be allowed to cool slowly. Brass work-hardens more readily than copper and must be annealed more often. All metals have a tendency to become stretched at the edges and ragged during spinning and may have to be trimmed at intervals. Care should be taken not to overheat or "burn" metals during deep draw operations when it is thought that several annealings will be necessary. Stop when the metal resists, and anneal. Steel and Monel should not be annealed too often, for structural changes will occur that make spinning difficult. Stainless steel is ductile and requires annealing during intermediate operations. Low-carbon steel can be spun deeper than stainless.

Lubrication

Lubrication is important in successful spinning. The friction produced causes heat, and lubricants reduce friction and thereby the danger of damage to the metal, which could otherwise become scratched, scarred, or torn. The lubricant must be viscous enough to adhere to the metal while it revolves at high speeds. It is usually applied with a swab of rolled-up cloth while the metal rotates. In addition to the lubricants mentioned in the table, yellow naphtha soap, hard cup grease, petroleum jelly, beeswax, paraffin, or beef tallow may be used, either singly or in combinations, according to the suggestions of the metal supplier.

Spinning Lathes

Spinning lathes are made exclusively for spinning, but a heavy-duty wood lathe with a variable-speed motor can also be used. Speeds should range from 300 rpm to about 1800 rpm in about four stages. Commercial spinners work at speeds up to 3000 rpm, but these are for experienced spinners only. The lathe should

Metal	Annealing Temperature (Fahrenheit)	Lubricant for Spinning (Apply often, in small amounts)
Gold and Silver Platinum	Paint with flux of known melting point of about 1200° F and anneal to dull red if necessary	Tallow candle
Copper (start with cold rolled, annealed)	Heat till dull red, 1000° F	Soap and oil, tallow candle, soft soap
Brass	1000° F till dull red	Same as copper
Aluminum (2SO or 3SO)	650° F Anneal only when necessary	Tallow and oil mixture, tallow candle, heavy oil
Zinc	212–375° F Put in boiling water, remove, and spin while hot	Tallow candle, tallow and oil
Pewter	No annealing required	Soap and oil mixture, tallow candle
Lead	No annealing required	Same as zinc
Monel	1700° F Bright yellow	Sheep's tallow
Steel (Cold rolled, deep-drawing quality)	1200° F Cherry red	Sheep's tallow, laundry soap

Spun pewter vase, from A. J. Van Dugteren & Sons, The Netherlands. *Netherlands Information Service.*

Contemporary brass water pot (*kalsi*), typical of those used in Calcutta, India. Height: one foot. The pot is first formed by casting and then finished with scraping tools and polished while on the lathe. Also while on the lathe, the lines of the design are inscribed with a sharp, pointed cutting tool. *Photo by Oppi.*

be equipped with a sliding spindle and cam lever for rapid adjustment of the tailstock. Metal discs can then be easily inserted, and finished forms removed. Also, it is possible to make deep forms. The tailpiece must have a live center for the pin and block. A gap bed lathe allows the spinning of forms of larger diameter which a continuous bed lathe would otherwise limit.

The tool or spinning rest should have vertical holes bored at intervals of ½ inch to accommodate a steel pin called the *fulcrum pin*, against which the tool presses during the spinning. The fulcrum pin should be easily removable, because it must be moved toward the head of the lathe as the spinning progresses.

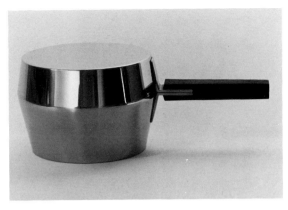

Spun stainless steel casserole, designed by Magnus Stephensen. *Georg Jensen Silversmiths, Ltd.*

Spinning lathe tools: 1. Metal spinning lathe, overall length: 78″; center to center: 60″. Can be placed on a floor stand. Requires ½ H.P. motor for metal spinning. Swing or clearance: 17″ diameter over 11″ gap bed. 4 Step cone pulley for variable speed. Spindle diameter 1″, self lubricating sealed ball bearings 2. Top to bottom: All purpose tongue tool: used for breaking down and rounding 3. Round nose tool: used to bring the disc to the chuck in the first steps, and for smaller radii 4. Ball tool: used for hard metals such as steel, brass and copper, but not for finishing 5. Diamond tool: used to trim edges 6. Beading wheel tool: used to turn an edge and make a beaded lip 7. Lubricating stick 8. Metal discs, two spinning face plates used to hold wood chucks; ball bearing back centers 9. Spinning tool rest with holes to change the location of the fulcrum

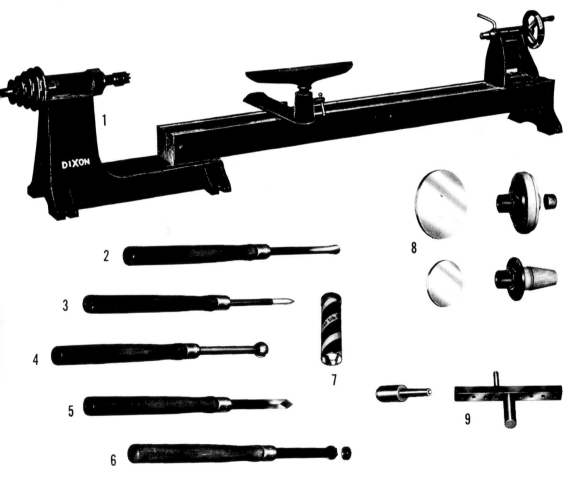

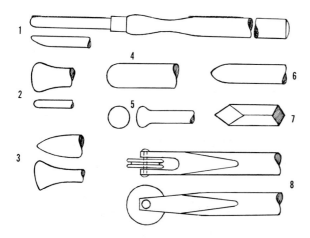

Metal spinning tools: 1. Tongue tool 2. Planisher (2 views) 3. Smoothing tool (2 views) 4. Tongue tool 5. Ball tool 6. Round nose 7. Diamond 8. Beading wheel (2 views)

Spinning Tools and Their Functions

Spinning tools are not standardized, and many spinners make their own tools. There are, however, three main groups: blunt tools, beading tools, and cutting tools. The blunt tools are the most numerous and are used most often. A few of these, plus one or two cutting tools, are all that is necessary for a beginner. Tools are made of forged steel, with the working end hardened and polished. Aluminum or phosphor bronze tools are used for spinning steel and other hard metals.

The tongue tool is designed for breaking down the disc at the start of the spinning operation and for final compressing and smoothing of the metal at the end of the spinning. The round-nose tool is intended for all shaping and finishing. The planishing tool has two tapered, flattened surfaces, and is applied to remove marks left by other tools. The beading tool serves to turn a bead or edge when necessary. A backstick twelve to fourteen inches long is a piece of wood used to support the pressure of a tool while shaping the metal and to prevent wrinkling of the metal during spinning. All these tools are applied *below the center* of the work. The diamond-point tool, rectangular and of hard tool steel, kept sharp, is the only instrument used directly on the edge of the metal; its purpose is to trim and true the disc.

Spinning tools are about two feet long and fitted with a handle about eighteen inches long. Length is necessary because of the great pres-

sure needed. Leverage is exerted during spinning by holding the handle under the arm and pivoting the tool end against the fulcrum pin, described later. Blunt tools should be kept hardened and polished—although they will stay hard under normal use. Polishing can be done by honing (clean and without oil) on a piece of shoe-sole leather sprinkled with putty powder.

THE CHUCK:
THE SPINNING FORM

The chuck is commonly made of a hardwood such as maple, cured and kiln-dried, and sometimes of the even harder lignum vitae. One-inch-thick strips of maple are also used; they are laminated together in layers with the grain running in alternate directions. Chucks are sometimes made of solid or laminated masonite. Metal chucks are turned from solid steel or brass blocks and are also made from castings. They are very expensive compared with wood chucks and are required only for precision work or very large runs of a form. Simple forms with no returns or undercuts can be made with one chuck. Deep forms and more intricate shapes are produced with a series of chucks known as "progressive" or "drawing up" chucks. Sectional chucks are used for forms that turn in beyond the largest diameter, such as vases, and are designed in parts or sections that fit together to make the whole form. After the spinning is completed, and the metal encloses the chuck, the sections are removed, being small enough to be taken out, one section at a time, through the opening in the form.

Wood chucks are made with wood-turning tools and should be smoothly finished on the lathe on which they are to be used, to assure their running true. Though an ordinary metal faceplate can suffice to secure a wood chuck, it is preferable to bore a hole in the chuck and cut a screw thread in the bore to correspond with the lathe spindle. The chuck can then be screwed directly onto the lathe. This should be done on the blank before it is finally shaped.

Basic Spun Shapes

The plate is the simplest spun shape, for the angle at which it meets the chuck is small, and the metal is not subject to severe strain while

Wood chucks of various forms and sizes used for spinning. The woods used are hard and close-grained. Sometimes wood chucks are screwed to a faceplate, which is subsequently attached to the lathe. It is more common in industry to cut an inside thread directly into the chuck and thereby eliminate the faceplate. The chuck can then be screwed right onto the lathe spindle of the spinning lathe. *Photo by Oppi at the Arrow Metal Spinning Company.*

Solid cast-iron and steel chucks. Metal chucks last longer than those of wood and are used where exact tolerances and greater accuracy and uniformity of results are required. They are finished while on the lathe to insure their running true. On the center shelf there is a sphere-shaped, eight-part, sectional steel chuck that is used for creating spheroid shapes. After spinning, the chuck is removed part by part, starting with the key piece. Steel chucks take more abuse than those of cast iron. *Photo by Oppi.*

it is being spun to its depth. The hemisphere or bowl is more difficult after the first easy stages. Generally speaking, the metal becomes more compressed as the angle becomes steeper, and it is therefore more difficult to force back onto the chuck. Making cylinders exposes the metal to the greatest strain.

Methods have recently been developed for hot spinning, which is done by heating the metal with an oxyacetylene torch while it revolves. This method has been employed especially in the spinning of tubing. It is not advised for any but the most skilled spinners.

THE TECHNIQUE OF SPINNING

Before the disc is in motion The blank metal disc is inserted between the chuck and the friction unit. A tail block or follower (a wood disc the same size as the base of the spun shape) is placed between the friction unit and the metal, and the unit is tightened with enough pressure to hold the metal and tail block in place. When the disc is being centered, it is sometimes necessary to allow a certain amount of looseness while it is rotated at slow speed, but beware of too much looseness, which might allow the metal to escape. The backstick or other board is used to center the disc by gently but firmly pressing the stick against the edge of the disc till it runs true. The pressure is then tightened to hold it firmly in place. The metal is lubricated with a thin coating of the proper lubricant. The toolrest is placed so that the disc edge clears its inside edge. A fulcrum pin is then inserted into the toolrest, slightly to the *right* of the disc edge.

HAND LATHE SPINNING.

Leonard Billings, proprietor and craftsman of the Arrow Metal Spinning Company, New York, is shown spinning a bowl form or shell. *Photos by Oppi.*

1. Starting from the left is the lathe tailstock, which revolves to tighten the metal in place—and to loosen it as well. Resting on the lathe are the common tools used in spinning: a centering stick, a point tool, a ball tool, a tongue tool or planisher, and a diamond point cutting tool. In the top center are the toolrest and fulcrum pin, and below them the friction unit or livecenter. To the right is the wood chuck, already screwed on the spindle. The lower center shows the sheet of coated abrasive cloth for smoothing the edge of the shell, a sample of the shell made from the chuck (6¾ inches in diameter), and a disc of the size required for the bowl. The friction disc unit or block and a piece of solid soap (Octagon) lubricant are to the left.

After the disc is in motion Start at low speed, because too fast a speed will work against the tool's force. Place the handle of the spinner's tool under the right arm, close to the body. Hold the tool with the right hand halfway down the wood handle and the left hand on the metal end, where it enters the wood handle. Stand slightly to the right of the disc. Place the tongue tool on the spinner's rest, to the *left,* but up against the fulcrum pin. Bring the point of the tool in contact with the disc at a point a little below the horizontal center of the chuck and as near the tail block as possible. Exert pressure, moving the tool back and forth quickly in short radii, till the metal fits firmly against the *base* of the chuck. At least one-half inch of the metal should be firmly against the chuck before proceeding to the rest of the disc. This is done to "lock" the metal in position.

Not just the tool but the whole body is used to exert pressure against the metal. The pressure is applied in several slow stages, advancing toward the edge of the disc till the entire disc assumes the shape of the form of the chuck. The fulcrum pin is moved further along the tool rest holes toward the edge of the shell as the work progresses. The tool is occasionally worked *back* over the area completed to compensate for the tendency of the metal to become stretched.

If the metal should buckle or wrinkle because of excessive pressure or work-hardening, stop the lathe, remove the metal, and anneal it. The wrinkles can then be hammered out with a wood mallet by placing the metal on an appropriate anvil or stake. To prevent wrinkling in the beginning stages, a backstick can be used. It is held in the left hand, on the left side of the metal, between the metal and the

 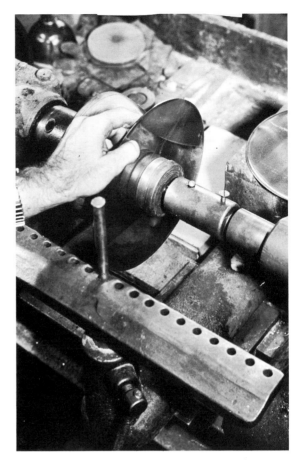

2. The wood chuck is placed on the spindle by holding it from below and engaging the spindle threads with the chuck threads while rotating the spindle. It must be made fairly tight. The friction block is placed in the friction unit or livecenter, which is then moved toward the chuck by turning the tailstock. A small space is left for the insertion of the metal disc that is to be spun.

3. The disc is inserted and centered as far as possible visually. The tailstock is tightened only sufficiently to hold the disc in place. True centering will follow with the aid of a centering stick.

chuck, while the lathe rotates. This supports the pressure of the spinning tool as it is drawn along *opposite* the tool.

Trimming Just before the final one-quarter inch of the shell is laid down, the edge of the metal must be finally trimmed with the diamond-point trimming or cutting tool. The edge should be at a *right angle,* pointing away from the chuck directly at the cutting tool. The trimming will then be at a right angle to the edge of the metal. The toolrest is brought close to the metal, and the diamond-point tool rested on it. Bring the cutting edge to the metal at an angle. Do not try to remove too much at once. A firm grip on the tool is needed to keep it from chattering and to assure its cutting cleanly. Stand to one side of the flying chips, and if it seems necessary, wear a face guard or goggles. On deep draws, the metal is

trimmed as required during the various steps or successive chucks to keep it even. After trimming, the edge is laid down to the chuck with a tongue tool. This enlarges the form slightly and allows for its easy removal from the chuck. Should the form seem too tight to remove, go over the entire form once with a tongue tool, starting from the base and continuing in one movement, if possible, to the edge. It should then be simple to remove.

Spinning "in air" is sometimes done to reduce the size of the opening of a form. This is a practice *not recommended* for any but skilled spinners, for there is some danger involved. A smaller chuck than the one that was used for forming the piece is inserted, and the shell tightened in place. A lubricated pair of curved pliers is then used to grip the edge, and while the metal rotates the pliers are gradually turned inward. Spinning in air is not a method

4. The lathe is put into motion. The wood centering stick is then placed almost below the spinning disc and, while resting against the toolrest, is brought into contact with the disc. The tailstock is loosened *slightly* and pressure is exerted to force the disc into a centered position between the chuck and the friction block. When this occurs, the tailstock is tightened enough to hold the metal in place. Lathes *always* rotate *toward* the spinner.

of changing a form drastically but only for making moderate changes such as turning in an edge.

GENERAL CONSIDERATIONS

Holding the tool too long in one place will cause that area to become hardened and will necessitate annealing. Work in short, sweeping strokes to reduce the need for annealing to a minimum. Avoid exerting excessive pressure at one time, and bring up the form slowly. This will help to avoid wrinkling and excessive vibration, which, if continued, would cause the metal to crack.

There is no way to measure exactly the size of the blank to be used. It is a better practice to choose a disc that seems to be close to the desired size, spin the form, see the result, and modify the size of the blank accordingly. The size chosen should allow enough metal for waste trimming of the edge.

5. The disc is lubricated. The first spinning tool used depends on both the spinner's preference and the circumstances. In this case, the point tool is used first. It is placed in position on the tool rest, to the *left* of the fulcrum pin. The point—below center and against the metal near the friction block—is at what will be the base of the shell. In order to begin compressing the metal against the chuck, pressure is brought to bear against the metal in short, radial movements while the lathe spins. Since the metal should grip the chuck, it is important to force the metal against the chuck at the base from the start.

6. OPPOSITE ABOVE LEFT: Another view of the beginning stages of spinning. The sequence, starting from the left, is: the spindle, the chuck, the disc, the friction block, the livecenter friction spindle, and a part of the tailstock. Below are the tool rest, the fulcrum pin, and the tool in use.

7. OPPOSITE ABOVE RIGHT: As the spinning progresses, the disc is brought almost entirely against the chuck. The last half inch is left away from the chuck to allow for the final trimming of the shell. Here a diamond-point cutting tool is brought against the edge of the spinning shell, and shavings of the metal are removed from the shell at approximately a right angle to the edge.

8. BELOW LEFT: Any sharpness of the edge of the shell should then be removed by applying an abrasive cloth.

9. BELOW RIGHT: At the very beginning and at intermittent stages in the spinning process, the disc must be lubricated to facilitate the action of the tool without excessive friction. Here a lubricant applicator, made of rolled-up cloth bound with wire and dipped into the lubricant (spinning grease), is brought against the shell before its final planishing.

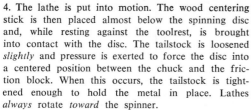

10. ABOVE LEFT: The final compression of the metal against the chuck must be accomplished with as sweeping and continuous an application of tool pressure as possible. The tool is started at the base line and brought smoothly to the edge.

11. ABOVE RIGHT: Seen from another view, the planishing tool compresses the shell against the chuck. A smooth operation will produce a shell without any ridges or obvious evidence of tool marks.

12. LEFT: The finished shell is removed from the chuck by releasing the tailstock pressure.

Joining with Rivets, Nails, and Screws

Riveting

A rivet might be described as a permanent bolt with head, body, and nut forming one piece. Riveting is one of the simplest and the oldest methods of joining sheet metals. It antedates the development of hollow casting. Rivets, besides serving a functional purpose, can be used decoratively on metals.

Rivets are used in several areas of metalwork, and special types have been designed for particular functions. All rivets can make a permanent joint, provided the size and style, relation to the hole size, metal thickness, spacing, and the form of the head are correct, and a permanent joint is desired.

Rivets are available in various metals, among them copper, brass, aluminum, and iron, and in solid, tubular, and bifurcated forms. Types of solid rivet are usually named after the shape of the head: mushroom head, countersunk, flat head, snap head, cone head, and pan head. The most frequently used rivethead shapes are the snap head and countersunk.

The most common methods of securing rivets to sheet metal are by *impact* (applying a succession of blows with a hammer), *compression* (squeezing the rivet with hand-operated or power tools), and a combination of both.

CHOOSING THE RIVET

The choice of rivet depends on its appearance, use, and location. For example, where a flush surface is desired, a countersunk rivet would be selected; where there is tension on the rivet, a high-headed rivet would be called for. Prior to use, all rivets should be annealed with a torch or in a furnace or kiln to soften the metal and make it more malleable, important considerations in the shaping of the head.

The rivet should have a *diameter* equal to twice the thickness of the metal being riveted. The *length* of the rivet stem depends on the shape of the head to be formed and the thickness of the metals to be joined. A flush countersunk rivet head requires that a length equal to three-quarters of the rivet diameter project past the surface of the metal. For a snap-head rivet, one and a half times the diameter projecting past the plate is sufficient. If the rivet is too long, the stem will bend, and if it is too short, it will not be possible to form the head at the opposite end from the preformed head.

If it should happen that rivets in precious metals are not available, they may be made by taking a wire of the necessary diameter and forming the head shape with hammers by upsetting. The length is cut to the necessary dimension, and the riveting process described below can be followed. It is important to start with the wire used cut accurately at a right angle to the stem or the head will not be evenly formed.

THE RIVETING PROCESS

The hole through the metals to be joined is made first. It is safer to drill the hole rather than punch it, because a drilled hole is cleaner than a punched one and more accurate. A punched hole may buckle the metal or leave a burr (which should be removed if this method of hole-making is employed and the metal hammered flat). The hole diameter should be accurate enough to allow the rivet stem to pass through *tightly*.

While forming the head opposite the preformed head, the latter can be supported in a depression that fits it in size and shape, such as the depressions in a dapping block. A rivet set (a tool with a semicircular depression at

Three rings in silver by Bertel Gardberg, Finland, using riveting in the design and construction. Top, silver with copper rivets; right, silver with ivory; left, silver with wood.

LEFT: "Man," riveted brass sculpture, by Ilya Schor, 1959. Rivets were used exclusively as the joining technique. *Courtesy: Mrs. Schor. Photo by J. J. Breit.*

OPPOSITE: Detail of four panels on the right door, showing scenes from the Life of Christ. Upper left: the lion-headed door pull; upper right: the Scourge of Christ; lower left: the Crucifixion; lower right: the visit of the Three Magi at the Birth of Christ. *Photo by Oppi.*

Bronze doors of a church in Novgorod, U.S.S.R., which were brought from Mecklenburg, Germany, as a war trophy in the thirteenth century. Each panel is made in repousséd units and depicts a scene from the Old or New Testament. The panels are riveted to the wood door beneath with cloverleaf-headed rivets. *Photo by Oppi.*

Rivet head forms: 1. Countersunk head 2. Flat head 3. Cone head 4. Pan head 5. Steeple head 6. Double radius head 7. Button head 8. Pan head. Conventional types of rivet joints: 9. Lap joint, single riveted 10. Lap joint, double zig-zag riveted 11. Butt joint, single riveted with plate above and below

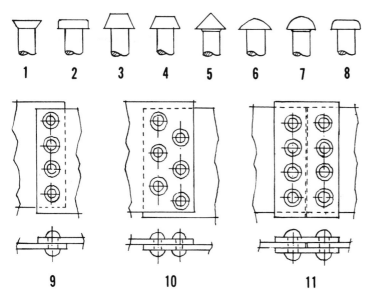

one end slightly wider than the diameter of the rivet head) or a properly shaped repoussé or dapping tool, or hollow punch, applied to the tail of the rivet and hammered will bulge the rivet tail and secure it in place. A flat, small-headed riveting hammer is then applied directly to the rivet in a series of taps in a circular direction around the rivet to shape the rivet roughly to the desired form. A rivet set of the correct head size, shape, and depression depth is then used to give final shape to the rivet head. There should be no movement between the sheets being riveted once the rivet is set, unless the rivet is being used deliberately as a pivotal point to hold two parts together and allow movement.

HOW TO AVOID RIVETING FAULTS

1. The holes in the two plates being joined should be in line with each other, or the rivet will be off-center and weakened, and the head will possibly shear off if it is under tension.

2. A rivet stem that is too long will bend and cause the head to be formed off center.

3. Hammering a rivet head too much will cause it to spread and become thin-headed and therefore weak.

4. Rivets placed too close to each other will cause the metal between them to split.

5. Rivets placed too near the edge of a piece of metal will cause the metal to break between the rivet and the edge.

JOINING WITH RIVETS, NAILS, AND SCREWS   313

6. Do not try to form a rivet head too quickly or with too much pressure at once. If the metal hardens during working, take the time to anneal it to render it soft again.

RIVETING WIRE FOR JEWELRY FINDINGS

A form of riveting for pure function is the use of a special nickel-silver rivet wire to hold

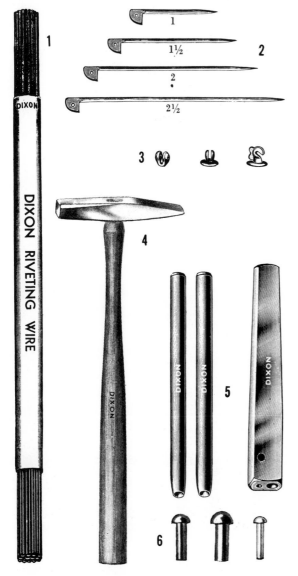

1. Rivet wire for findings, joints, and other uses 2. Pinstems 3. Joint, joint on patch, safety catch on patch. Pinstem and joint are held together with tightly fitting rivet wire 4. Riveting hammer 5. Rivet setting and heading tools. The combination rivet set and heading tool is used first to hold the rivet stem vertically in position while it is placed (head in a dolly held in a vise, or in a depression of a dapping block), and the heading depression is used *after* the head is basically shaped with a hammer, to make the final form 6. Buttonhead rivets

pinstems for joints on the backs of brooches, jewelry, and hinged articles. The procedure is basically the same as for all riveting. A piece of rivet wire is cut a little longer than the hinge joint. The joint is assembled, with the rivet wire in place. A head is formed by placing the wire on end over a polished steel block and hammering it with a small riveting hammer. Both ends of the wire are alternately hammered to mushroom the ends and hold it firmly in position. The rivet should not be hammered too tight, however, because this will inhibit the easy movement of the pinstem.

This wire can be purchased in bundles or packages of assorted B. & S. wire gauges from 14 to 21.

RIVET WIRE USED TO HOLD PIERCED STONES

Stones that are pierced through in the manner of a bead can be held to metal surfaces by rivets with great decorative effect. This system of embellishment has been used for centuries on jewel boxes, holy book covers, reliquaries, and candelabra.

Stones can be joined by first forming a rivet head on a wire of suitable gauge, placing the rivet through the stone, and setting the head of the rivet into a dapping block depression of suitable size. The other end of the rivet can then be carefully hammered from the back of the metal to which the stone is being applied. A bifurcated rivet can also be used in the same way, the two parts of the rivet being spread at the back by inserting a steel knife blade and bending the rivet legs back. Rivet heads can be decorated with ornaments of small metal plates or shot, and the rivet joined in the usual way to hold them. This system of joining metal ornaments or stones to metal is still common in the Orient.

Nails

Nails of various metals such as silver, copper, brass, and iron may be used to join metal plates to solid or hollow wood cores. Sometimes nails with decorated heads can be used. In the making of nails, after the head is joined the stem should be work-hardened by hammering to give it sufficient strength to be driven into the base material without bending.

Joining with Screws

Another method for joining metal parts, either temporarily or permanently, is by the use of screws—either those that are held in pressure

Silver ring with riveted white coral ornament, by Saara Hopea Untracht. The rivet was made by soldering the wire on end to the base, placing the bead, and then forming the rivet head. Produced by Kultasepänliike Ossian Hopea, Porvoo, Finland. *Photo by Pietinen.*

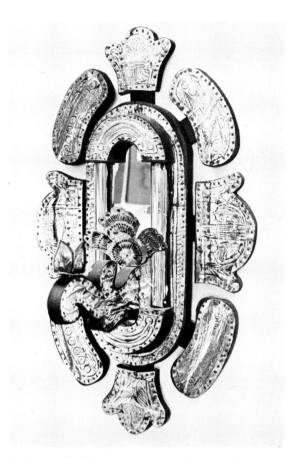

Bracket candlestick or sconce whose plaque contains a mirror. Protruding parts and surfaces are covered with stamped sheets of brass that are nailed to the wooden core. Made by Seppo Tamminen, Helsinki.

Silver-gilt reliquary head from Basle Cathedral, early thirteenth century. Height: 13⅝ inches. The shaped metal plates are nailed onto the wooden core. *British Museum, London.*

Brass and white metal bridal dowry chest (*petara*), made in Mahua, Saurashtra, India. Height: 12 inches; length: 20 inches. The metal is first stamped with patterns and then riveted to the wood box underneath. These boxes, mounted on wheels, are made in various sizes, are mainly quite large, and are used to hold the bride's dowry. *Photo by Oppi.*

on the metal with a nut, or those that can be screwed into the metal itself and held there without the aid of a nut. Of the two main kinds of screws are those that have parallel sides and are mainly held in position by a nut (these are called bolts), and those that taper and are designed to enter soft materials such as wood or soft metals. There are many situations where ornaments or parts can be fitted

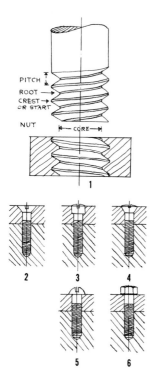

1. Screw thread and nut nomenclature: Types of American Standard machine screws and cap screws (same head, smaller size) 2. Flat head countersunk 3. Fillister head 4. Oval head 5. Button head 6. Hexagon head

There are several different types of screw threads, and each one is standardized. The strongest and most common threads in general use are the V thread (International) and the United States Standard thread which have a V-shaped groove with an angle of sixty degrees. The various types of screw thread are the following:

Types of Screw Thread	Angle between the Grooves
Acme	29°
American National	60°
British Association Thread	47.5°
V Thread (International)	60°
Whitworth Thread	55°
Worm Thread	29°

The vocabulary of screws and bolts includes:

The *pitch,* which is the distance between the crests of adjacent threads. The *lead,* which is the distance the screw moves axially in one revolution. The *start,* which is the name given to the thread along which the screw moves. Some screws have a single start; others have a double or triple start, which moves the screw twice or three times as fast as a single-start thread. The number of starts on a bolt can

This masterpiece of African art was brought to France at the end of the last century along with other pieces from the palace of King Behanzin at Abomey, capital of Dahomey, Africa. The lion, made of wood, is covered with sheets of silver and stands on a wood base that is covered with sheets of brass. All metals are held to the wood by nails, which are both functional and decorative. *Collection of Charles Ratton, Paris. Courtesy: Charles Ratton.*

together with screws and not by methods that require either excessive heat or pressure. Screws have been used in ornamental metalwork for many centuries. They are usually concealed in the work as in the gold cup by Benvenuto Cellini in the Metropolitan Museum of Art in New York which is held together by a system of gold screws. They can also be exposed with decorative effect.

be observed by looking at the end and counting the beginnings, or starts, of the threads.

The *core* is the solid central part of the screw, not including the threads.

Types of Fit between screw and threaded parts:

Wrench fit: Interference of metal requires the use of a wrench or other tool to tighten

Close fit: No interference of metal, the fit is tight and considered perfect
Medium fit: Can be assembled with the fingers
Free fit: Finger-assembled fastening screws
Loose fit: Deliberate allowance is left for speed and ease in assembly

Head Shapes: Cap, round, half round, countersunk, cheesehead, grub (headless).

Screw threads can be made by hand with *taps* and *dies* or on a lathe. The hand process is described here.

THE FEMALE THREAD

Screws are made of wire or rod and are cylindrical. The wire or rod is converted into screws with *dies.* If the screw is to be held by a nut, usually the nut is made *first,* then the screw, to assure a good fit. The thread in the nut is made with *taps.* Taps and dies are of high-carbon tempered steel and are available in many sizes, ranging from the very small ones used by watchmakers to the large ones used by machinists.

To make the *internal* or female thread either in a nut or in the metal into which the screw is placed, it is necessary to begin by making a hole. The hole is made with a drill (sometimes called a tapping drill, though ordinary drills of the proper size may be used) *equal to the diameter of the core* of the screw to be used. Into this hole, a *tap* will be inserted that will form the thread. There are three kinds of tap: the *taper* tap, the *intermediate* tap, and the *bottoming* or *plug* tap. These three comprise a set, though for smaller threads only the first and last are used, and for very fine threads a single tap and a *screw-plate.* The taper tap is used to begin the thread; the intermediate tap continues the thread when a thread of some depth is necessary, and the bottoming or plug tap completes the thread and is the most accurate of the three. The taper tap can be used alone when holes are cut right through the metal, but the plug tap assures accuracy. Plug taps are used to thread holes (known as *blind* holes) that do *not* pierce the metal. Deep holes might require all three taps, ending with the plug tap—also called the bottoming tap, because it allows completion of the threads down to the very bottom of blind holes.

To make the thread, the metal being tapped is first secured in a vise. The tap is held in the tap wrench. It is important that the tap be held *vertically, perpendicular* to the metal, and to check this, it is necessary to hold a square in several positions against the tap in the beginning. In the case of blind holes, reversing the tap and removing it at intervals during the operation to clear the hole of metal cuttings is necessary to avoid breaking the tap or stripping the threads. All metals except cast iron and brass need a lubricant of oil when a thread is being made. The tap is turned clockwise twice and reversed to eliminate loose chips. The tap must not be forced, because it is brittle and easily broken. Screwing the tap and reversing it, in slow stages, ends with the metal being pierced through, and the tap moving freely in the fully threaded hole.

THE MALE THREAD

The male or *external* thread is made on the outside of wire, screw, rod, tube, or pipe with a *die.* There are several kinds, but the *circular* die, used for diameters up to one inch, and the *two-piece* or *split* die, used for larger diameters, are the most common. The die is numbered to correspond with the tap, so that female and male threads will match. The *outside diameter* of the metal being threaded should be *slightly larger* than the outside diameter of the tap thread being made. The part to be threaded should be securely held, vertically, in a vise. The die is inserted into the *stock,* which has two handles, and it rests on an internal shoulder, where it is fixed in place with screws. The die is tapered slightly to allow the rod being threaded to be admitted easily into the die. It must be operated with the wider end toward the work or the pressure might cause the die to be forced out of the stock if it is in a reversed position. The rod end should be cut squarely and held at a right angle plane to the die so that, after threading, it will fit properly into the nut. The die is placed over the rod and turned clockwise (for right-handed threading). As many threads are made as are needed to fit the nut or blind hole. Fewer than three threads in either the male or female unit will not make a secure enough screw and nut.

TWO-PIECE DIES

Two-piece adjustable dies are used for *large diameters* and require several cuts to produce a full thread. The dies are assembled in the stock with their numbers corresponding with the numbers stamped on the stock. The dies are loosened and placed in a right-angle plane

Silver plated candlesticks, by Robert Welch, 1962. Height: 12 inches. Commissioned for the Church of the Ascension, Chelmsford, Essex. The supporting rods are threaded and bolted into the base. *Courtesy: Robert Welch.*

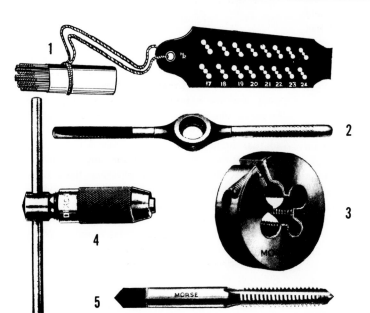

1. Double notched screw plate with taps 2. Die holder for round screw dies 3. Adjustable round split die 4. Adjustable tap wrench which will hold reamers, drills, hand turned tools 5. Machine screw tap

with the end of the trued bar, and then tightened. The work is lubricated and is screwed to make the first, shallow thread. A half turn forward is made, with great care, and a partial return, to assure that the thread begins properly. The stock is then unscrewed back to the beginning of the rod, and the dies are retightened and rescrewed. The thread should then be tested with a nut so that excessive cutting will not produce a loose thread or possibly remove or strip the entire thread.

Screw tap and die sets complete with die and tap holders are used mainly by watchmakers and jewelers and are made in sets of 15–18 dies ranging in metric sizes from 0.30 to 1.94 mm sizes.

Screwplates, flat steel plates having eight to sixty single- or double-notched holes numbered in graduated sizes, are designated for cutting fine threads (sampling of sizes listed below) for jewelry and watchmaking. The screwplates substitute for small-sized dies and are sold with matching taps to correspond with the screwplate thread sizes. This numbering system does not correspond with any common measuring system.

Screw rivets, which screw in place and are then *hammered* over, are available. Once in place, they are permanent.

Number of plate:	−6	−1	4	8	10	13	17
Approx. mm size:	4.0	2.15	1.46	1.11	0.95	0.74	0.47
Approx. inch size:	.158	.085	.058	.044	.037	.029	.019

Casting

Casting, one of the least expensive methods of forming metals, is an ancient process and among the first to have been developed by many cultures. Casting seems to have started shortly after man realized that metal had the property of being able to be melted into a mass. The next step was to control the shape of the mass as it solidified, and from this interest the making of molds developed.

None of the complex casting methods practiced today would be possible if the material —metal—did not have the character of *fluidity*. Metal can be heated till it becomes liquid, after which it can be made to flow freely and evenly into a mold and, before freezing, completely fill a cavity.

Metals do not adhere to mold surfaces, because they do not "wet" them. The surface tension of the metal and the formation of gases between metal and mold wall prevent adhesion. Molten metal often is prevented from making any contact at all with a mold surface by the thin cushion of gas that forms. The surface tension of metals increases as their melting point and their temperature increases. It is surface tension that prevents metal from flowing along narrow channels.

Many materials have been used for molds. The main requirement if a reasonably accurate casting is to be made is that the mold be able to withstand the thermal shock of the molten metal without damage. Clay and soft stone molds have been excavated at the sites of ancient cultures. Today a variety of materials are used for molds: paper (in the printing industry), wood, sand, plaster, bronze, steel, and other metals. The material chosen depends on the method of using the mold, the temperature of the molten metal, the kind of metal used, the complexity of the pattern, the number of castings to be made from the same mold, and the degree of accuracy desired.

The first step in the manufacture of any metal object, even before the craftsman can obtain his sheet metal or wire, is to form the metal into an ingot.

Casting an Ingot

The word *ingot* is derived from the Anglo-Saxon past participle of *geotan,* meaning to pour—*in+goten*=poured. Casting an ingot is a basic procedure. It is useful in the recovering of scrap metal once sufficient scrap of one kind has accumulated. Alloys can also be made and cast into ingot form before use. Casting is, of course, the first step in the preparation of metal for rolling through a mill, passing through a drawplate, forging, carving, or otherwise shaping with tools. When metal of more than usual thickness is needed, casting an ingot that approximates this thickness takes less time than building the thickness by other methods.

Simple bronze spoon mold used in the eighteenth century for casting pewter spoons. Length: 8⅛ inches. *Metropolitan Museum of Art, New York. Gift of Frederick S. Wait, 1907.*

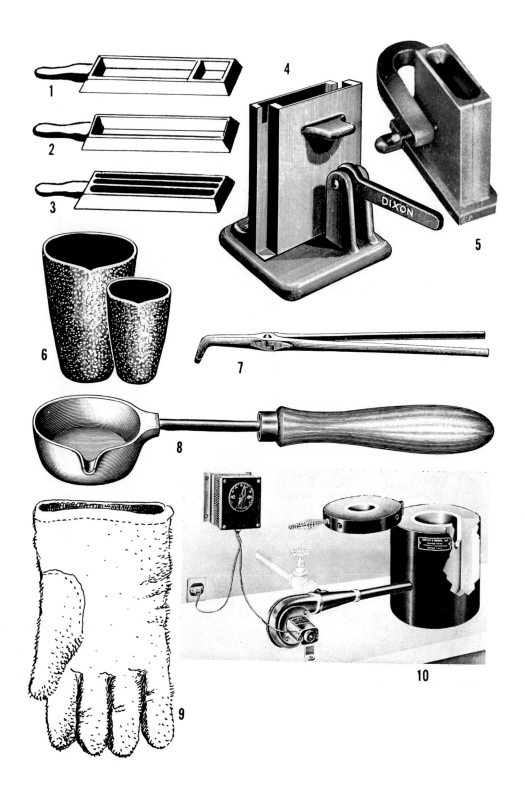

1. Ingot mold 2. Ingot mold 3. Wire ingot mold 4. Sliding, adjustable size ingot mold. Inside surfaces are milled smooth for easy removal of ingot, 5⅝″ high, 2¾″ wide, ³⁄₁₆″ thick 5. Vertical ingot mold 6. Crucibles 7. Crucible tongs 8. Melting and pouring ladle for low temperature melting point metals 9. Asbestos glove

10. Heavy duty electric metal melting furnace, reaches melting heat in 7½ minutes, from that time: 3½ minutes for 11 dwt 10 karat gold, 5 minutes for 1000 dwt 10 karat gold. Blower is attached to gas line, temperature control rheostat is plugged in. 27″ by 12″, maximum temperature: 2624° F

Several upright, sliding, adjustable models of ingot molds are available that create an ingot of 3″, 4½″, or 6″ in height and ⅛″, 3⁄16″, or ¼″ in thickness. These molds can be adjusted to smaller measurements to cast narrow bars or wide, flat ingots up to a maximum or 2¾″ in width. Before rolling an ingot through a rolling mill to reduce its thickness, file away all fins and projections.

Horizontal, open-wire ingot molds that form ingots of 6″, 6¼″, 9″, 11¾″, and 15¾″ in length and 3⁄8″ × ¼″, to 1 15⁄16″ × 1 1⁄16″ grooves are made for the casting of ingot bars. There usually are several parallel grooves of increasing dimensions in one mold. The bars can be treated in many ways, and they often are used after an end has first been tapered for making wire by drawing through a drawplate.

To prepare the metal for the casting of an ingot, the metal is placed in a graphite or sand crucible made for metals that require high melting temperatures. Low-melting metals can be placed in an iron melting ladle. The crucible can be placed in an electric melting or muffle furnace or heated with a torch after being placed in an annealing pan. For low-melting metals such as pewter, a torch played under the melting ladle is sufficient. Pewter readiness can be tested by touching the pewter with a pine stick, which will become slightly charred. For silver or gold, the metal while being melted is sprinkled with dry flux, which prevents the formation of oxide on the surface. The metal is stirred occasionally with a heated steel rod or a graphite stick while melting.

The inner surfaces of the ingot or wire mold are coated with soot or carbon by passing a candle flame under the mold. The carbon helps to form a smooth casting, and by preventing the metal from adhering to the mold (it is a parting agent) enables it to be ejected easily. Machine oil or fat can also be used for this purpose. The mold is then heated by playing a torch over the whole mold to prepare it for receiving the molten metal. Do not overheat the metal, but bring it to a temperature slightly above the liquidus, and pour quickly. Wear asbestos gloves, hold the crucible with crucible tongs, and pour the metal in one continuous stream into the mold. Allow the metal to cool and freeze. The ingot can then be released from the mold and processed.

Casting a Lead Block

A simple form of *open casting* can be used to produce a lead block that is useful for forming processes such as doming, dapping, and repoussé work. A battered old lead block can be easily restored by recasting. Fill a wood or heavy cardboard box with casting sand. Cut a piece of wood to the size of the block desired and hammer a nail partly into it to serve as a lifting device later. Press the block into the sand to a depth equal to the thickness wanted in the lead block. Lift the wood block out by the projecting nail. Dust the depression with parting powder. Heat the lead in an iron ladle and, when it is molten, pour it into the depression in the sand. Allow the metal to cool, and remove.

Vocabulary of Casting

Sprue: The vertical channel that connects the pouring gate with the runner to the mold cavity. This whole assembly is called the "gate."

Pouring Gate or Basin: The widened cup-shaped opening or depression into which the molten metal is first poured. It is located at the top of the assembly.

The Runner: The channel through which the molten metal passes to the casting, also called the *downgate*. In large castings, there may be several runners leading from the main runner to other parts of the casting.

Vent: Narrow openings in closed molds used to lead gases, which form in casting, away from the mold cavity via the riser. All vents are connected to a common riser (or risers) which comes to the top of the mold at one or either side of the sprue cup.

Riser: A channel meant to permit the escape of gas and air during the pour. Risers are sometimes joined to *shrinkage lumps* or *balls* which are joined to the riser near the heavier parts of the casting. As the mold cools some of this additional reservoir of metal is drawn into the casting to compensate for shrinkage. The ball is also called a *feeder head*.

Metal Casting: The process of pouring molten metal into a mold. Also the name given to the resulting object. Casting can also refer to the plaster reproduction of a model.

Burnout: The process of melting the wax out of the plaster mold and removing excess moisture from the plaster when used as a mold in preparation for pouring the metal.

Core: A mass of material such as sand, plaster, or clay used to fill a cavity in a mold

"Dancing Siva" (*Siva Nataraj*), cast bronze, from Tanjore, India, fourteenth century. Height: 33½ inches. *William Rockhill Nelson Gallery of Art, Kansas City. United States Information Service, New Delhi.*

to make a hollow casting. It is placed there in the process of making the mold and is usually removed completely or partially after casting. Metal spikes about three to five inches long and finishing nails are used to support a core. Cores can also be left intact in a casting when access to them for removal is impossible. They still serve their function, which is to make lighter the total weight of the casting.

Cheeks: Sections in a flask (used in making a sand or plaster mold) that are held between the cope and the drag parts, where the shape of the pattern makes it impossible to use a simple two-part mold. The necessity for more than one parting line is solved by the creation of these sections, which eliminate the problem of undercuts.

Cold Shut: In casting, when two streams of molten metal fail to join because one surface has been allowed to cool, the line at the joining of the two is called a cold shut. It appears on the surface of the casting as a line, which actually is a crack.

Crucible: A receptacle made of clay, graphite and clay, or other refractory material, cast iron, cast or wrought steel, or other material to contain metal to be melted and poured into a mold.

False Core: A separate removable part of a sand cast mold.

Fin: In lost-wax casting a fin is caused by a crack in the mold, usually irregular in direction, and is removed from the result after casting by chasing. In sand casting a fin is a thin projection of metal that forms at the parting line in a mold casting, caused by the imperfect joining of the mold parts. Fins can also be removed when small by filing.

Flux: The silica burn or melt which forms on the gate assembly after pouring the mold and is allowed to remain as it acts as a flux when remelting the used metal in preparation for pouring.

Gated Pattern: Two or more patterns joined by connecting channels to produce more than one casting in the same mold. This procedure is practiced in centrifugal and other casting, but in art foundry casting it is usual to cast only one model in a mold.

Holding Furnace: A small furnace used to maintain molten metal at a proper temperature for casting till it is ready to be poured.

Loam: A strongly bonded coarse sand used for making sand casting molds.

Lute: A mixture of refractory fire clay used to seal crucible covers prior to heating.

Mold Wash: A water-soluble emulsion prepared to coat the inside surface of plaster molds prior to casting to insure good definition and easy separation from the mold. Silica flour, graphite, carbon, and other substances are used.

Parting Line: The line on a casting indicating the position of the separation between the cope and the drag of a sand mold. It can also refer to the line which follows the parts of a casting from a multiple part plaster mold. This line is removed from castings by finishing processes such as chasing and filing.

Parting Sand: Finely ground or powdered sand that is dusted on surfaces of a sand mold that are intended to be separated.

Pattern: The form, often made of wood around which the sand for the creation of a sand mold is packed and which is later removed to create the mold cavity into which the metal will flow. Other materials besides wood are used.

Pig: An ingot of virgin or secondary metal that is remelted in a furnace or crucible for casting.

Pinhole Porosity: The condition of cast metals characterized by a sprinkling of small holes in a casting due to the evolution of gas in the metal during shrinkage.

Plumbago: Powdered graphite, from which, with the combination of clay, crucibles for melting metals are made.

Porosity: The condition of cast metals containing blowholes and cavities caused by shrinkage and trapped gas, or gas in the molten metal, which occurs with improper melting, improper venting, or overheating.

Run: In order for the metal to run or flow into the mold hollow, the wax of the model must be at least $\frac{1}{8}$ inch in thickness or the molten metal will cool off. In these parts of a model, extra gates are added to lead the molten metal.

Sand Burning: The hard surface resulting from the contact between molten metal and the sand mold surface.

Scale: A combination of oxide and silica glass which forms on the surface of a casting caused by the heat of molten metal coming in contact with the silica in the plaster mold. This is removed by placing the casting in a pickle bath of sulphuric acid (sixty parts water to one part acid) and allowing the casting to remain in the pickle overnight.

Spalling, Shift Spalling, or Drop: The collapse of an inner part of the plaster mold which falls into the casting during the pouring

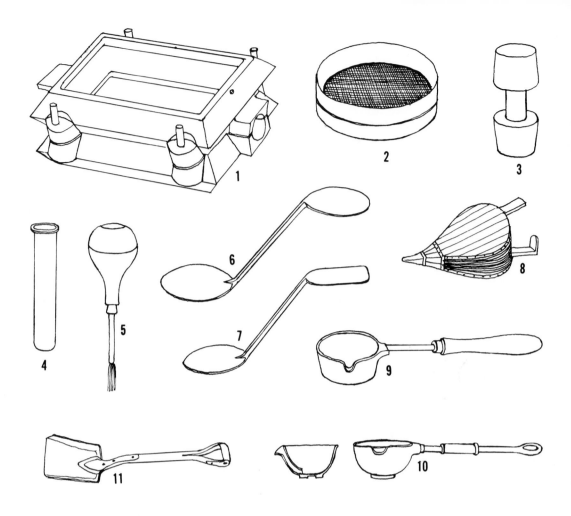

Sand casting materials: 1. Sand casting flask 2. Foundry riddle, 18″ diameter, galvanized wire screen 3. Wood sand rammer 4. Brass sprue cutter 5. Bulb sponge with camel hair brush 6. Slick and oval, used for finishing sand molds or for repair work 7. Slick and square 8. Molder's bellows, 10″ 9. Melting and pouring ladle for low temperature metals 10. Bottom pour ladle with sliding sleeve for handle length adjustment. Eliminates necessity to skim metal 11. Square point molder's shovel

of the metal. This can be a serious defect.

Shake-out: A term for the removal of castings from a mold. In art foundry casting, *break-out* or *break-up* are also used.

Skimmer: A tool used to remove dross or scum from the surface of molten metal or to prevent the slag from running over with the molten metal into the mold.

Skull: A thin film of metal or dross that remains in the crucible or ladle after the metal is poured. In art foundry casting, excess metal is poured off into pig molds for future use. A small amount is left to solidify *while the crucible is in a tilted position* with half the bottom exposed. If this is not done there is a risk of the crucible breaking when a new pouring of molten metal enters it due to unequal pressures at the bottom.

(In soldering the same term indicates visible solder remains after the solder flows.)

Slush Casting is done with a metal alloy having a low melting point and a wide freezing range. The mold is allowed to cool, and the metal is poured into it and allowed to make contact with all surfaces. The metal that touches the mold freezes, forming an inner shell, and the rest of the metal, still liquid, is then poured out, leaving a hollow casting. For hollow castings of white metal, rubber molds with high heat resistance are used.

Undercuts: A portion of a model which, if allowed to remain as it is, would prevent the

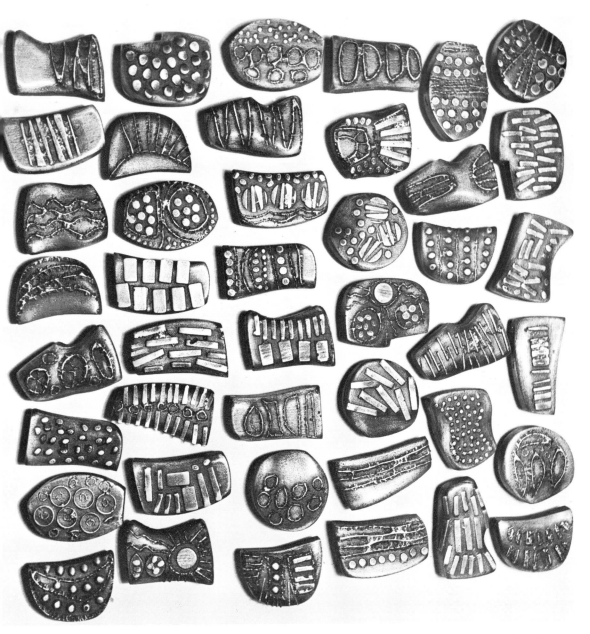

Forty-three cast aluminum door handles, by Don Drumm. Drumm's cast aluminum pieces often have highly textured surfaces. They are produced by sand casting, with the pattern carved directly into the sand mold. For smaller craft objects, when a series of similar shapes or their variations are wanted (such as casseroles, where a smooth inner surface is desired), a pattern is first made in wood, clay, or plaster. The mold is made from this pattern and then the surface is reworked directly in the sand for addi-

tional surface design and texture. Drumm enjoys the flexibility of design offered by direct carving. For larger works, such as sculpture, fountains, and screens, cast units are arc welded together, so that size limitations do not exist. After casting, the article is sand blasted both for finishing and to prepare the surface for patina treatment with chemicals. Drumm feels that the low melting temperature, light weight, and resistance to corrosion characteristic of aluminum well suit it to architectural application.

Sand Casting

(For a discussion of casting the bidri alloy, a process similar to the one described below, see page 138.)

In sand casting, a cast iron flask or frame is used to contain the sand that forms the mold. The flask is made in two parts resem-

easy separation of the mold parts without the destruction of that impeding part of the model in the mold. This condition should be avoided when using two-part molds, but can be solved if unavoidable by the use of multiple-part molds, or reverting to one-piece molds meant for unique castings. (Art foundry quote: this is what keeps us in business.)

bling open frames. When horizontal, the upper part is called the *cope,* and the lower part, the *drag.* The flask parts are keyed so that they will fit together perfectly without movement. There is usually one or more openings at one end called the sprue opening, through which the molten metal is normally poured, though the opening can also occur in the side of the sand itself.

CASTING SAND

Special casting sand is available that is treated so that it does not need any further processing, does not dry out, and can be used repeatedly. *Foundry sand,* a special mixture of silica and clay, is refractory, has enough bond (clay) to hold it together, and is sometimes called "brass sand." It is controlled for fineness (to produce an accurate, sharp, detailed casting), green strength (strength enough while hot to allow it to stand up to the heat stresses of the molten metal), permeability (to allow the escape of gases and steam), and moisture content (to allow adhesion). These characteristics produce castings free of such defects as *blows* (holes formed in a casting where trapped gas or steam has failed to escape), *scabs* (blemishes on a casting caused by gas eruption), and *veins* (unevenness in the surface due to irregularities in the crystallization of the metal).

Sand purchased dry for casting can be prepared or "tempered," with a little experience, by adding water to the outside of the sand pile, cutting the pile, and mixing it with a shovel. The sand is ready when it forms a firm ball when grasped in the hand. A lump when broken should show distinct, sharp corners. A *minimum of water* should be used, for an excess will cause steam and a faulty casting or at worst, an explosion, and possible injury from flying metal.

Generally speaking, for the craftsman sand casting is best suited to more or less symmetrical patterns, or patterns where the parting line is not too irregular and separation of the mold parts can be easily accomplished. In industry, highly skilled mold makers can solve unusual problems of multiple-part sand molds, but this takes years of training. The craftsman must choose the method of casting that best meets his particular circumstances.

PREPARING THE MOLD

(See the section "Materials for Patterns" on page 331 for a discussion of pattern materials.)

Depending on the shape of the pattern to be cast, the method of mold-making varies. Assuming that the pattern is without any unusual problems—it is symmetrical or can be divided into equal parts *without undercuts,* the procedure is as follows. Lay the pattern *half section* down on a flat surface, such as a board, steel slab, or plate glass. A board is most often used. Remember that the largest dimension of the pattern half-section is facing *downward.* Place the *drag* or *bottom* part of the mold, *bottom up* over the pattern, centering the pattern from side to side, but allowing space at the sprue end of the drag for the formation of a sprue opening later. Riddle (sift) enough "tempered" sand or prepared sand over the surface of the pattern to cover it to a depth of about one inch. Pack the sand firmly around the pattern with the fingers. Before adding more sand, roughen the surface. This must be done to *key* the sand so that the additional sand will adhere. Finish filling the drag with sand and pack it down firmly with a *rammer* or a wood mallet applied with light blows. If still more sand is needed to fill the drag, remember to roughen the already packed sand again before adding more. Strike off the excess sand by scraping across the surface with a straight board or metal bar, such as a metal rule.

Place a *molding board* on top of the drag, and if a board has been used under the drag, turn it over, holding both boards tightly with the drag between, to preserve the mold. Remove the top board. If necessary, cut back the sand to the midline or parting line should there be any small undercuts that at this point would prevent the removal of the half pattern. Gently remove the half pattern. Remove any loose particles of sand which may appear in the pattern cavity with a soft brush or with a hand bellows. Dust the exposed surface of the sand in the pattern cavity and the remaining area with a parting compound such as talc to allow the easy separation of the two parts of the mold after casting. Replace the half pattern, place the second half exactly over the first (facilitated if they have been keyed to each other), and dust with parting compound. Place the *cope* or top part of the mold on top of the drag. With a riddle (a round wood frame fitted with a coarse bottom wire screen), sift in enough sand to cover the complete pattern and then add more sand to fill the cope, wedging it in tightly with a rammer or mallet. Level the sand with a wood or metal strike bar.

To form a sprue opening, use a piece of brass tubing of appropriate diameter (or any tube with *thin* walls). Press the tube gently through one of the sprue openings in the flask frame till it comes in contact with the pattern. Remove it gently, and the sand will come with it, leaving a smooth hole. Enlarge the hole slightly at the top opening to form a cup that will facilitate the pouring of the metal.

Another method for forming a sprue opening is to place a tapered sprue former upright into the drag, alongside the pattern. Then place the cope and fill it with sand. The sprue former protrudes through the *side* of the cope sand. Remove it and separate the cope from the drag. Make a connection channel to connect the mold cavity in the cope with the sprue channel. With this method, the molten metal is poured through the sprue opening in the *side* sand of the cope and not through the mold frame. The flask is held together by weights, to prevent the force of the molten metal from separating the parts of the flask after pouring.

To return to the original method being described, lift up the cope and set it aside, mold cavity up. Dampen the surface *slightly* around the pattern, which is still in the drag, with a bulb syringe. If the pattern is made of wood, drive a sharp pin into it and rap it lightly in all directions to loosen the pattern, and then lift it carefully upward out of the mold. Patterns made of other material can be lifted out by pressing a wad of sticky modeling wax, or a special "stick-all plastic," preferably at *two* separate locations. It is sometimes possible to reverse the drag and allow the pattern to fall out, but there is less control in this procedure, and injury to the mold may occur.

Vents leading from the mold cavity to the same end as the main pouring sprue or to an edge must then be made if needed. Vents are made to lead gases away from areas where they may form. These small openings allow the escape of steam and gases generated during the pouring of the molten metal. Without them, a faulty casting may result, and the work of mold preparation be wasted. When cutting vents in a sand mold, a sharp knife point may be used, or a U-shaped wire clay modeling tool. A thin piece of wire or sheet metal bent into a U will also serve the purpose. Always cut *from* the mold cavity *outward* when making vents, to prevent particles of loose sand from falling into the cavity. Loose

sand can, however, be blown away with a hand bellows or brushed away with a soft brush. To avoid having particles of sand fall into the mold when pouring, pack down the sand in sprues and vents. If it is possible, draw the vents to the large sprue, but if the pattern does not allow this, bring the mold vents (which are small) to the *outer edge* of the mold, so that the gases can escape. Inspect the mold for loose particles, and replace the cope on the drag.

The assembled flask can then be backed on *both sides* with a board large enough to cover the sand, and tied together, held together with clamps, or placed in a bench vise.

PREPARING THE METAL

Sufficient metal to fill the cavity and the sprues and vents is prepared in a crucible. The melting can take place in a gas *melting furnace* (used to melt gold, silver, copper, brass, and bronze, which require high temperatures) in combination with air blast from a blower or a foot bellows. A forge fire or an open charcoal pit fire brought to high heat

Cast aluminum door escutcheon, by Don Drumm.

with a bellows or blower will also serve. Aluminum, too, requires melting in a crucible, although its melting point is below that of the metals named above.

Low-melting metals such as lead, pewter, type metal, and white metal can be prepared in a cast iron or wrought-steel ladle, which ordinarily needs no special preparation. The metal can be heated from below or over an ordinary Bunsen burner gas flame.

Small amounts of metal can be stirred with a graphite rod held by tongs.

Metals should not be overheated. Pouring overheated metal can cause an excess of steam to generate and destroy the mold. The metal should be poured at the *lowest possible temperature suited to the particular metal,* to reduce the time needed for solidification and prevent the possible development of cracks and porosity in the casting.

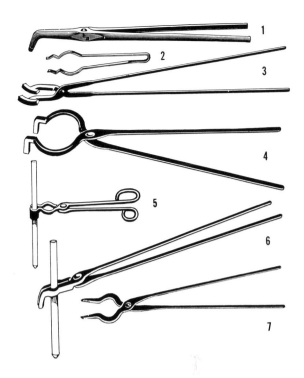

1. Hollow tongs for small crucibles 2. Flask tongs for loading 3. Safety tongs for equal wall pressure on crucible 4. Ring tongs for small crucibles and flasks 5. Scissor handle stirring rod tongs 6. Bent nose crucible and stirring rod and lifting tongs 7. Ribbed jaw tongs

POURING THE METAL

Prepare for pouring by wearing *asbestos gloves* and *tinted goggles.* When the metal is judged ready, bring the crucible with tongs to the mold, keeping this distance short. Some metals must be skimmed of dross and others should be dusted with borax. *Tilt* the mold to allow gases to escape, at the start of the pour, and move it to an upright position toward the end (this will require the assistance of another person, who should also wear asbestos gloves). Hold the crucible as close to the sprue opening as possible, to make contact with the air minimal. Pour as steadily as possible, directly into the center of the sprue opening, with a minimum agitation of the metal. Pouring too fast may cause agitation, which produces trapped slag and dross in the casting. Pouring too slowly may cause the metal to freeze and create "cold shuts," which would result in incompletely filling the mold cavity. When the metal has reached and filled the mold to the sprue cup, stop the pour and allow the metal to cool. Pour remaining metal in the crucible into an ingot mold or out on the floor or on any surface that will take the heat, so that the crucible is cleared for the next use. If the metal leaves a "skull" or trace behind, the crucible should be used for that metal exclusively the next time to avoid contamination of a new metal.

Sand molds cool quickly, and when the metal has hardened in the sprue cup, small castings can then be removed. Larger castings must be allowed to stand longer, and if there is any doubt about whether the metal has solidified, allow the mold to stand. Sand molds can be used only once under ordinary circumstances, but careful handling may allow for more than one use with a possible reduction in accuracy due to sand burning and shrinkage.

FINISHING THE CASTING

Wash the casting and brush it clean of sand after removing it from the mold. Remove the sprues, risers, vents, and "fins" (thin ridges that may occur at the parting line between the cope and the drag), with hacksaws, jeweler's saw, file, abrasive wheel, or knife, depending on the hardness, thickness, and position of the casting metal.

Many treatments of castings are possible. They are often detailed with chasing or engraving tools; chisels, abrasives, and files can

Cast aluminum casseroles, by Don Drumm, 1963. Top two: diameter, 8 inches; height, 4 inches. Bottom: diameter, 10 inches; height, 3 inches.

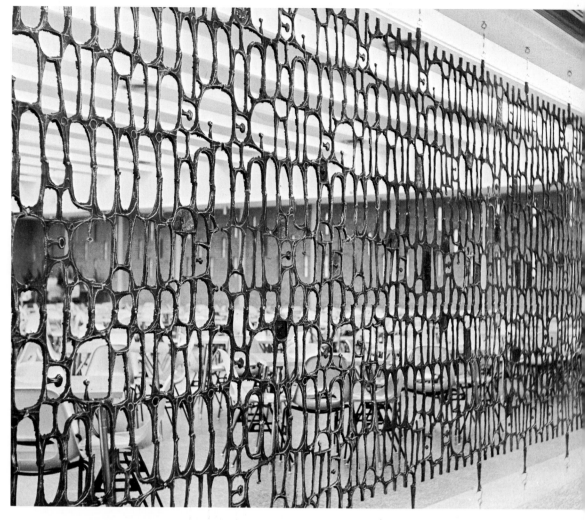

Cast aluminum screen, done for Firestone High School, Akron, Ohio, by Don Drumm, 1962. Length: 26 feet; height: 7½ feet. The screen has inserts of colored polyester plastic and was finished mainly by sand blasting, followed by chemical coloring.

create interest in surface texture, and finally, they can be polished partially or completely and given a coloring process or patina.

Metal Casting with Two-Part Plaster Molds

Plaster molds employing the cope and drag assembly system are a refinement of sand casting. Special plaster compositions suitable for making molds for the casting of non-ferrous metals and alloys are manufactured by the United States Gypsum Co. They are designed for making molds of low permeability, permitting fine, intricate detail, accurate surface reproduction, and accuracy in cast-to-size dimensions, and necessitating little or no

finishing of the casting. The refractory ingredients in the mold material, besides giving greater strength to the mold, allow a slow cooling of the metal, a casting of low residual stress, and the casting of thin sections.

Some of these plasters are made especially for use in two-part molds, and they each possess special characteristics. *Matchplate plaster* is used for matchplate sets (metal plates for mounting two-part molds that are split along a parting line and mounted with a gating system, back to back, to form one complete unit) and cope and drag sets (which, when assembled, are called flasks). This plaster can also be used for one-piece, closed plaster molds if the model is properly vented and gated. *Metal-casting plaster* is used for aluminum, one-piece, and brass castings and can also be used for matchplate casting. A *nonferrous in-*

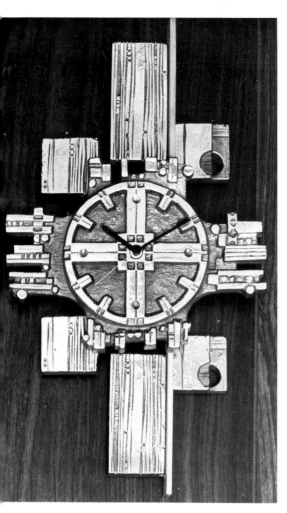

Cast 18/8 stainless-steel, battery-operated wall clock, 11.5″ by 19.75″, weight 11 pounds. Designed by Olav Jolf, produced by Polaris, Sandness, Norway. *Photo by Kaada Nor-Hansen, Stavanger.*

vestment plaster is made for easy separation from two-part mold patterns; in lost-wax casting, it absorbs a minimum of wax. A product called *Kastical* is designed for *open-face molds,* particularly for the casting of zinc alloys, and is outstanding in conductivity.

These materials can be carved directly for open-face casting. Larger open-face castings can easily be turned into two-part molds by backing the open casting with a thick slab of the same casting plaster and binding them together. This system might be used for making relief castings with flat backs.

MATERIALS FOR PATTERNS

Patterns for casting molds can be made of several materials. Some rigid materials that can be used are wax, laquered gypsum cement, polished metal, wood, tooling plastics, clay, and soap. Flexible materials can also be used, such as rubber compositions, Koroseal, cold molding compounds, and agar-agar (a gelatinous substance obtained from certain seaweeds). Synthetic materials such as Styrofoam, or any material which will be completely consumed in the burnout without leaving an ash, have been recently used in one-piece unique molds. In all cases, the resulting surface quality is an exact reproduction of the material used for the model—a factor that might influence the choice of pattern material.

Symmetrical wood-turned patterns should be turned from wood that has first been divided and glued in two parts, longitudinally, separated by a sheet of glued paper to facilitate splitting or separating the parts later. Fitting one part with *short pins* (projecting dowels), and the other with holes into which the pins fit, makes possible an easy matching or keying of the two parts of the pattern when a mold is being made.

PARTING COMPOUNDS

Parting compounds are used to allow the separation, after casting, of the two parts of the mold. The parting compound is brushed, dusted, or sprayed in some cases both on the pattern itself and the mold just prior to pouring the molten metal. Parting compounds for plaster are soft soap, stearine, wax in a suitable solvent, and emulsified or light oils. Only a thin layer of parting compound should be used, as too thick a coat will cause a loss of detail or will impregnate the plaster and result in a porous surface casting. Some procedures call for a parting compound of carbon, made with a candle or gas flame, which helps to promote a smooth casting.

PREPARING THE PLASTER

For maximum strength, the preparation of plaster should be carefully controlled. The plaster-water ratio should be that recommended by the plaster manufacturer. For the U. S. Gypsum Co. plasters, the ratios on the following page are recommended.

The weighed plaster is sifted manually into the proper amount of water at 72–80° F. It is allowed to soak from one to three minutes, till all the dry plaster disappears. It is then

Matchplate:	120–160	parts water per 100 parts plaster by weight
Metal Casting:	120–160	parts water per 100 parts plaster by weight
Nonferrous:	79–95	parts water per 100 parts plaster by weight
Kastical	60–100	parts water per 100 parts plaster by weight

mixed with the hands, and the lumps are broken by squeezing with the fingers. This should be done *below* the plaster surface, to avoid the introduction of excess air into the mixture. The mixing continues five to eight minutes till the plaster starts to cream; the resulting *slurry* should be uniform and free of lumps.

PLACING THE PATTERN: SYMMETRICAL SHAPE

There are several ways in which the pattern may be placed, depending on the shape. If it is half of a symmetrical shape or a shape with no undercuts, the procedure is as follows:

The half pattern, lightly greased, waxed, or painted with liquid soap or shellac, depending on the material from which it is made, is placed flat side down on a clean slab of plate glass, about four inches wider and longer than the mold dimension. If a cast iron cope and drag frame system is used, the drag is placed, parting line down, on the glass, with the pattern centered. Cope and drag frames made of wood can also be used. For lack of these, wood boards of suitable height or strips of tin or galvanized iron can be made to form a wall to contain the plaster. They must be sufficiently wide to accommodate the depth of half the pattern, plus an allowance of at least one inch for the plaster wall thickness at the thinnest point. To support such a wall and to prevent the liquid plaster slurry from escaping when poured, the seams and corners are sealed or luted with plasticene clay or soft modeling wax outside the wall material. The plaster is then poured into the mold container, and before it sets it is jarred slightly to make it settle level and bring air bubbles, if any, to the surface.

SETTING OF THE PLASTER

Plaster is gypsum ground to a fine powder and consists of the hemihydrate of calcium sulphate, made by calcining (heating) gypsum till it is partly dehydrated. To this, magnesium silicate (fine-fiber asbestos) or long-fiber talc is added to complete the composition. The plaster powder in dry form consists of small particles surrounded by air. When the powder is added to water, the air is replaced by the water, which penetrates the plaster pores and fills the spaces between the grains, producing a mass that cannot be poured. When more water is present and mixing commenced, the water and plaster become supersaturated and form a slurry that can be poured. Air is most easily removed at this time by sharply rapping the container, after which the plaster is usually poured. On being allowed to stand, the gypsum then precipitates and forms crystals that grow into larger needlelike forms, interlocking and cohering to each other; within twenty-five to thirty minutes, the plaster has "set," forming a solid mass and releasing heat in the process. If an excess of water is used, the crystals form with spaces between them, resulting, when the plaster is dry, in a weaker, more porous mass. This is why the proper ratio of water to plaster is important.

After the plaster sets, the surface may be screed off (smoothed) level with a metal straight edge; the drag is then turned face up. The sprue hole through which the molten metal will flow is then made by cutting with a small, sharp knife a V-shaped groove leading from the model's highest or heaviest part to the sprue hole at the end of the flask. If no flask is used, but only the plaster mold, the runner can lead to whichever side is most convenient (choose the shortest distance between sprue and mold cavity). It is also possible to use a rod or tube of suitable diameter, making it a part of the pattern before the plaster is poured. In this case, the rod or tube must be coated with parting compound the same as the rest of the pattern and is removed.

Several vents or small passages can be carved into the plaster with the point of a knife, leading from the model's heavier parts where there is a chance that gases will form that cannot otherwise escape. If the vents are not made, the trapped gases might cause incomplete castings. The vents are tapered and small enough in diameter so that the molten metal cannot pass through them, and they should reach the outer edge of the plaster mold. Vents can also be made by laying in a wire on the drag; after the cope is made and removed, the wire is also removed, leaving narrow openings.

More complex forms require a *riser,* an opening larger than a vent that leads from a heavier part of the pattern to the same side as the sprue opening, but separate from it. When the metal is poured through the runner or sprue hole during casting, its appearance at the riser opening is an indication that the mold is full. The riser allows the escape of air and gases.

Keys or register grooves can be cut in the edge of the drag, so that when the cope is formed it will have projecting parts that will exactly fit the negative grooves of the drag and insure an accurate match of the mold parts. Cast iron flask frames are already keyed to each other by projecting flanges with holes on one part into which rods on the other part will fit.

After the sprues, risers, and vents have been formed, the first half of the mold is treated with parting compound, and the second half of the pattern is placed exactly on top of the first, which is still in place. The cope, or the wood or metal frame, is then placed to retain the plaster, and the prepared plaster is poured. After being allowed to stand for about thirty minutes, the two parts of the mold can be carefully separated. The parting compound should allow this to be done quite easily. The pattern is then removed. Sprues, vents, and risers are then cleared in the second part of the mold. Should there be any difficulty in removing the pattern, or in separating the parts of the mold, a thin wire can be inserted at the parting line of the mold through to the pattern and removed. Into this opening, a compressed air jet is directed. Gently striking the cope frame upward with a mallet will help in stubborn situations.

In plaster casting, sprues and runners can be made smaller than those needed in sand mold casting, because of the insulating quality of the plaster, which also contains refractory material. This same insulating nature of the material makes it necessary to allow the metal to cool in the mold longer before removing the casting, as the heat loss is gradual.

DRYING THE MOLD

A mold that has not been allowed to dry properly contains moisture which, if allowed to come into contact with hot metal while it is poured, will result in the formation of steam, causing incomplete casting or porosity. All free water and a large part of the combined water is driven off during *drying.* After the pattern is removed, the reassembled mold is allowed to dry for twenty to thirty hours at about 400° F. This can be accomplished in an ordinary stove or atop a heated boiler. Some shrinkage and warpage may occur, but with careful, slow drying this is minimal.

When the mold is dry, the inner surfaces are treated with a parting compound, and the mold assembled. The parts should be *tied together* with wire or *clamped* in a vise. *The procedure already discussed under sand casting is followed for plaster mold casting.*

With care, plaster molds can be used several times before they are discarded.

CASTING AN IRREGULARLY SHAPED PATTERN

The procedure described above is for a two-part mold with a symmetrical pattern. When an irregular pattern is to be cast, the method is slightly different. The pattern should first be marked with a parting line that roughly divides it in half, following the *widest dimensions* of the pattern so that there are no *undercuts.* Undercuts make it impossible to separate the two parts of a mold. If the pattern cannot be made in two parts without avoiding undercuts, there are several choices. A more complex, multipart mold with additional *cheeks* or extra sections between the two parts can be made (this requires skill). A *one-piece,* expendable mold can be made. The undercuts in the pattern can be filled in with pattern material and circumvented, and the casting later finished or modified to restore the change. Assuming that a two-part mold is still possible, even though the pattern is irregular, the procedure is as follows.

Prepare the drag on a glass sheet or a level, true, metal plate. This is more important for the tight fitting of the flask walls or containing-mold walls than it is for the fitting of the pattern. The plaster is prepared and poured into the lower half of the mold. The pattern, coated with parting compound, is then pressed into the soft plaster, *up to the previously drawn parting line.* It is allowed to remain till the plaster sets. After setting, it may be necessary to carve away some portions of the plaster to expose a part of the parting line that has dipped below the center level. The lower mold is then keyed, sprued, and vented and covered with parting compound, and the upper part of the mold is placed. The pattern is still in place. Prepared plaster is poured into the upper part, and when it sets, the two parts are separated, the pattern is removed, and the mold dried and make ready for use as described.

CHANNEL-WORK TUFA CASTING.

For approximately the last one hundred years, the Navajo American Indians have been using a natural, porous, lightweight, and highly refractory stone known as *tuff* or *tufa,* to make molds for casting silver ornaments. Tufa is a porous rock (of which there are many varieties) composed of the finer kinds of detritus, or worn away, disintegrated rock particles. It is formed as a deposit from streams in various states of consolidation, more or less stratified. The Indians quarry it in blocks and use it in the manner to be described. The following series of photographs shows the late outstanding Navajo craftsman, Tom Burnsides, at work. *Photos by Western Ways Features.*

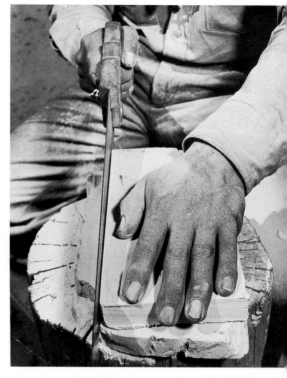

1. RIGHT: The tufa stone is cut into two flat slabs large enough to accommodate the size of the object to be cast. Only two part molds are made. Tufa material is soft enough to cut with an ordinary saw. Other materials, such as investment plaster or plaster mixed with powdered refractory material, could be substituted for tufa in this casting method.

4. The drawing of the article is carefully put on the tufa, and then the design is carved into the stone, frequently in "V"-shaped grooves or channels, which gives this work its name: channel-work casting. Provision must be made for the metal to run into the mold, so a runner is carved leading from the casting cavity to one end of the mold. For large pieces, small scratches are made, radiating from the heaviest areas. These are meant to carry off gases that might otherwise prevent a successful casting.

5. BELOW: The two parts of the mold are tied tightly together so there will be no leaking of hot metal. Since the back of this work is simply flat, it is not necessary to line up the two pieces of tufa in any special way. The metal is heated and melted in a small crucible, using a plumber's blowtorch. It is then poured into the uprighted mold, which is tilted slightly to one side, in a gravity pour, with the flame of the plumber's torch playing on the metal to keep it liquid and prevent cold shuts.

2. The flat surfaces of the tufa are filed level with a coarse file. It is important that the two surfaces of the mold be level and true.

3. To insure the proper fitting of the contacting surfaces, the two parts of the mold are rubbed together carefully. Irregularities wear away as powder.

7. To remove the sprue, the najahe casting is placed on a steel surface and the sprue is hammered through with a cold chisel.

6. After casting and cooling, the two-part tufa mold is separated. We see here the resulting casting, a pendant form known among the Navajo as a *najahe*. The fins that occur at the juncture of the two-part mold appear along the edge as a rough irregularity. Both fins and sprue must be removed.

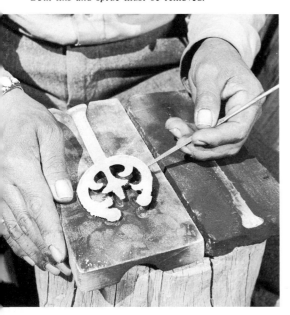

8. The surface of the najahe is finished by filing with needle files, and the opening is made by which the najahe will be suspended.

Core Casting

The method so far described results in a solid casting. In objects of relatively small size, solid castings are usual. Large objects or objects for which lesser weight is desired are cast hollow. This also reduces expense by decreasing the amount of metal needed and lessens the chances of fractures due to uneven cooling. Hollow casting necessitates the use of a *core* that almost fills the void in the mold cavity but allows space for the wall thickness of the casting. Cores should be readily removable after casting, but sometimes they are allowed to remain inside the casting. Cores are used in sand-mold, plaster-mold, and lost-wax casting.

CREATING THE CORE

The core must be supported in the mold cavity without being allowed to touch the mold wall. There are several methods by which a core can be made. For low-melting metals, a cardboard tube covered with newspaper and tied with string will serve. Over this, a layer of casting sand can be formed to approximate closely the shape of the mold cavity without touching it at any point. This can be tested by placing the core carefully in the mold and scraping away any part that is too close to the walls. The core is dipped in or dusted with talc, graphite, or mica to make the surface impenetrable to metal but still allow gases to escape.

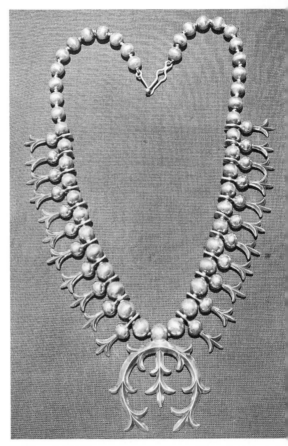

9. A completed squash blossom necklace with a najahe pendant similar to the one shown in the casting sequence. The hollow beads are formed by hammering a disc into a die or dapping block to make a half circle or dome. A hole through which the cord will pass is then punched outward from within. The holes also permit the escape of gas during soldering. Two such domes are soldered together to form the bead. Cast additions are often attached to these beads to make what is thought to be a conventionalized squash or pomegranate blossom, from which this kind of necklace derives its name. The najahe form, the crescent shape, is an amulet believed to carry auspicious implications. It is thought by experts to have been acquired from the Moors by the Spanish, who brought it to America.

It is then placed in the sand mold with the ends of the tube resting in hollows cut to fit their shape at the extremities past the mold cavity.

Another method provides for the suspension of the core by wires in smaller castings, and nails and rods in larger ones. The ends of the wires, nails, or rods are anchored to the sides of the opened parts of the mold in such a way that they can be removed easily. Cutting grooves in the edge of the mold where they rest is the usual method. The cavity of the mold is then filled with casting sand with the wires in position. The two parts are assembled, and an impression of the mold is made. The impression is then removed and *pared down* by an amount equal to the intended thickness of the metal. The core is carefully replaced, with the wires, nails, or rods fitted back into the grooves made to support them. The parts of the mold are assembled, and the casting proceeds.

Another method, *used for one-piece molds,* requires careful construction of the pattern, *beginning with the core.* The basic form is made with casting sand or some other refractory material over a wire armature; some of the wires, or nails which will support the pattern in the mold, are allowed to protrude. The form is made to approximate the size of the pattern *less* the metal thickness. This thickness is built up with wax, with which the whole core is covered. The final modeling is completed in the wax, and a mold made of the pattern in one of the usual ways. The wires, nails, or rods that protrude through the wax become embedded in the walls of the mold. The wax is melted out, leaving the core suspended inside the mold, supported by the wires, nails, or rods. After the casting is completed, the core can be removed wholly or in part. Holes that remain where the wires, nails, and rods pierce the outer metal can be filled with matching metal plugs soldered into place, or, as is done in the West, they can be filled by welding similar metal. Large bells are cast in this manner.

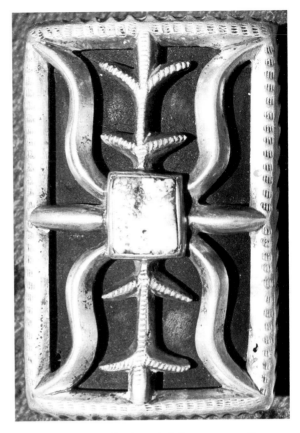

The wrist guard, or *ketoh,* as it is known among the Navajo, is designed to protect the wearer from the recoil of the bowstring against the inner surface of the wrist after the discharge of an arrow. Though once functional as well as decorative, they continue to be worn today mainly for their decorative value. The silver cast ketoh shown here has the customary central turquoise and radiating leaf forms with a border of stamped designs. Often parts were cast separately and joined by soldering. *Photo by Western Ways Features.*

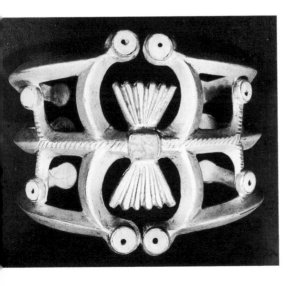

Navajo Indian cast silver bracelet, mounted with turquoise beads. Width: 2⅝ inches. The "V"-shaped form, which is triangular in cross section and commonly seen in cast bracelets and other Indian ornaments, is easily produced when carving the tufa stone mold. Carving a channel of this type presents a minimum of difficulty because the tufa stone used for molds is easily friable. Bracelets of this type are cast flat first. After being finished flat with files and abrasives, they are heated or annealed to soften the metal. Then they are curved to fit the wrist by hammering, which must be done carefully to avoid cracking, a common occurrence when shaping cast pieces because of the brittle structure of cast metal. *Museum of the American Indian, Heye Foundation, New York.*

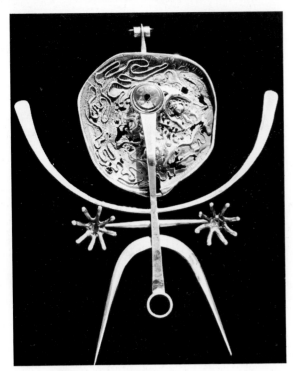

Pendant by Bob Winston. The upper, circular form was created by a type of casting called "core" casting (carving directly in the investment, then casting) and is decorated with forged wire elements.

Lost-wax cast gold pendant of a crocodile god, from Panama. Height: 4¼ inches. *Museum of Primitive Art, New York. Photo by Charles Uht.*

Lost-Wax Casting

Creating metal objects by the process called lost-wax casting is also known as *cire perdue* (French for "lost" or "waste" wax). It is practiced all over the world and known by various names in various places. The process has been known for many centuries and has changed very little. Basically, it consists of constructing

a model in wax or a wax-rosin combination of suitable thickness and forming a mold over the outside of the work to be cast. The wax is then drained or "lost" by heating the entire mold, which is left with a hollow space formerly occupied by the wax. Into this space the molten metal is poured until it fills the void completely. After cooling, the mold is removed (usually destroyed) and the casting is finished with tools, if finishing is necessary.

In the more than four thousand years in which this technique has been practiced, variations have been followed in widely dispersed areas of the world. Craftsmen in ancient India and Egypt were probably the earliest practitioners. The Shang, Chou, and Han Dynasties of China, the makers of the great bronzes of Nara and Kamakura in Japan, Greece's Golden Age, Imperial Rome, Renaissance Italy, the cast-gold workers of Central and South America, the creators of the bronzes of Ife and Benin in Africa, and the deities cast in Nepal and Tibet—all these have certainly been among man's outstanding aesthetic and technical producers.

In the lost-wax process, there are several methods for the construction of the model, the investment of the casting mold, and the introduction of the metal. The method employed depends greatly on the size of the object and on the metal. Techniques also vary with the availability of materials, the level of technical skills, and the presence of mechanical aids.

BENIN BRONZE CASTING:
PRIMITIVE LOST-WAX CASTING

Benin bronzes were discovered in 1897, when a British punitive expedition captured Benin City in present-day Nigeria. In this town, enormous quantities of bronze castings and carvings in ivory and wood were found. Though the Bini had contact with Europeans (Portuguese, Dutch, French, and British) beginning in 1485, their casting technique is believed to have originated from Ife, 110 miles northwest. Benin City had at least four wards with whole streets of blacksmiths, and the casters lived in a special ward. Some casting is still done today. The bronze plaques, which had ritual, ceremonial, and historical significance, were cast in the lost-wax process.

The general process begins with making a clay core roughly approximating the desired form. Wax is rolled out on a board and parts are cut off with a knife, applied to the core, and modeled with the fingers. New wax that is added is joined by applying a heated knife.

Cast bronze plaque from Benin, Nigeria, 15¾ inches
high, showing an Øba or chieftain and four attendants.
University of Pennsylvania Museum, Philadelphia.

Sculptor Jacques Lipchitz at work on a large model in wax at the Modern Art Foundry in Corona, New York. He is using a heated tool to create surface texture. *Photo by Oppi.*

RIGHT: Waxes that are being stored while still "in process" at the Modern Art Foundry. They are floating in a vat of cold water to prevent heat distortion. *Photo by Oppi.*

Forms are modeled with bone or wood spatulas and joined. After wax runners and a pouring cup are formed, the completed model is covered with a very smooth clay coating. The model is dried and another layer of clay is added. Bands of thin sheet iron are tied around the mold for reinforcement and then the bands are enclosed by additional layers of clay.

The dry mold is placed over a hole in the ground, with the pouring cup down. A fire is made over the mold and the wax is allowed to run out into the earth. The wax-free mold is removed from the pit and rubbed with wet earth to seal possible cracks. It is then returned to the hole, again with the opening down, and heated with a slow fire to insure complete penetration of the heat in preparation for casting.

Meanwhile, the metal is placed in a crucible and heated in a charcoal forge fire. When mold and metal are judged ready for pouring, the mold is removed from the fire with tongs and stood upright in soft earth. The crucible is removed from the forge fire with tongs, and the metal is poured until the mold is filled. Several molds are poured at one time. Any remains of metal in the crucible are poured off on the earth and salvaged for future casting.

After a short cooling period, the molds are placed on their side. To shake out the casting, the mold is initially and subsequently sprinkled with water, which also helps to cool it. The outer layers up to the metal bands are removed by knocking them off with a flat, heavy bar. The bands are pried off. The rest of the mold is removed in the same manner, until the softer, black inner layer is reached. The final mold remains are scraped away with an old saw blade. The sprues are cut away, any fins are filed off, and the surface is chiseled, chased, and polished.

LOST-WAX CASTING OF SCULPTURE:
USING ONE-PIECE, ENCLOSED PLASTER MOLDS

The method described here is *one* of those used at the Modern Art Foundry in Long Island City, New York.

Small, Solid Castings The finished model, made in wax, is ready for casting. It must then be *sprued* with wax tubes or rods no smaller in diameter than ¼ inch, in more or less vertical channels which in the mold will ultimately become the openings or *runners* through which the molten metal will flow. The runners lead to all the necessary points in the mold cavity that are going to receive the metal, especially to the heavier parts of the model and the extremes. All runners join and meet *above* the model. Here a *cup* or *pouring basin* is formed in wax to facilitate the later pouring of the metal. In addition (depending on the size of the model) a few *risers* are also made in wax. These are tubes *not connected* with the runners; starting from the model, they lead from the heaviest sections of the model and generally join before appearing at one or two points above the model at one or both sides of the sprue cup. On the finished mold they are level with the sprue cup at the top. The risers are meant to carry off the air and gases from the hollow of the mold when the molten metal is poured. At points where

they are needed, additional *wax balls* are added to the risers to provide an extra reservoir of metal which may be drawn into the casting as it shrinks on cooling. Without these wax balls, on large castings cavities might form on the surface of the casting. (During the pouring of the metal, it first appears at the openings at the top of the mold which are the outlets of the risers. This occurs just before the metal fills the sprue cup and is an indication that the metal has filled the mold cavity and that the pouring is nearly completed.) Vents are also made leading from heavier parts and joining the risers where necessary. The *whole assembly*—the pouring basin, sprues, runners, vents, and risers—is called the *gate assembly*.

Making the Mold There are several methods by which a mold can be made. One way is to start by spreading a thick layer (four to six inches) of *luto* plaster on a board large enough to accommodate the model and a wall of plaster about four inches thick which will be built up around it. The luto plaster for this wall is made by mixing two parts of new plaster of Paris with one part of used plaster ground up coarsely from old molds. These are combined and added slowly into a pan containing the necessary amount of water when the mixture is stirred with the hand, breaking up lumps, till it thickens into a slurry. With handfuls of thick slurry the wall is slowly built up, making sure that the space which it surrounds is large enough to accommodate the wax model *with its gate assembly*, to be placed later. Depending upon the height of the wall, it may be necessary to wait to allow the lower parts to harden somewhat so that the upper levels can be supported. The wall is built to the height of the sprue cup and riser ends.

A second, finer mixture of plaster of Paris (two parts), silica (one and a half parts), and water is prepared. This mixture is finer because it is intended to create an accurate reproduction of the surface texture of the model. The plaster acts as a binder medium for the silica, which by itself would not stay suspended or set. Before the mixture is poured, the whole model is placed into the center of the walled enclosure and held in place. The plaster is then poured while the model is held to avoid doing it any damage. Enough plaster should be made to fill the wall to the sprue cup (or top) in *one* pouring as joinings of hardened plaster and new added plaster might become actual cracks on the metal surface. Another method is to

1. The process begins once the wax has been properly gated. The sprue cup is in the center, and a riser comes to each side. In this photograph, the retaining wall has been built up and a liquid plaster slurry is being poured to fill the lower portion of the mold.

5. The burnout kilns are temporary constructions of refractory brick, heated with oil or gas burners. They are built high enough to accommodate one or a group of molds, depending on their size, and are covered with a clay and sand mixture to retain the heat. Since the open end of the mold is placed down, provision is made to funnel the melting wax to a container outside the kiln. This reclaimed wax may be reused.

ONE-PIECE-MOLD CASTING.

This sequence, taken by the author at the Modern Art Foundry in Long Island City, New York, shows how a unique one-piece mold is made from a wax model.

2. The wall is built up gradually so that it will support itself. Liquid slurry is flipped over the wax.

6. The molten metal is heated in a tilt furnace containing a large crucible. When the pour is ready, the metal is decanted into a smaller crucible that is large enough to contain the metal necessary for one complete pour. The smaller crucible is held by a two-man pouring shank.

3. Once the plaster has set, it is bound with a heavy gauge iron wire that reinforces and adds strength to the mold. The binding wire is covered with another application of plaster, which is roughened with the fingers to provide a better gripping surface for the final, smooth layer of plaster that finishes the mold. 7. The molds are made ready for the pour by placing them in a wood container and ramming earth between and around them. The earth supports the mold's position and helps minimize the danger of leaks of hot metal if a faulty pour or mold failure should occur.

4. A group of finished molds ready for the burnout furnace where the wax will be eliminated. Their scale is indicated by the size of the soft-drink bottle.

pour the necessary plaster into the wall and then slowly immerse the model till it reaches the bottom. In both cases, the model is held erect for three or four minutes till the plaster sets enough for it to remain in place without support.

After setting completely, the whole outside of the mold is then wound with a steel wire which has been anchored by inserting its beginning in the plaster. The wire, wound from top to bottom in one continuous length, serves to reinforce the mold. On very heavy castings, iron pipe is joined for reinforcement to the outside of the mold and covered with plaster. Additional rough plaster slurry or luto is added in handfuls, with a backhand flipping motion, over the entire mold, covering the

CASTING   343

wire. While it is still in a semi-soft state, it is smoothed with the palm of the hand to its final, smooth shape.

Larger models are made without the initial thick coating of the board with a layer of plaster. The wax model instead touches the board directly. It is turned upside down and additional wax sprues and runners are added to what will be *below* the model in order to insure the filling of the bottom of the mold. The wall is extended and plaster added to enclose the added sprues, but an opening is left at the bottom. In this case, the mold has two openings, and can be placed upright in the burnout kiln when the wax is drained. This is done to insure complete drainage of the wax on large pieces. After the burnout, this bottom opening is plugged with a mixture of clay and sand, so that only the sprue cup opening at the top remains.

The Burnout Kiln The mold can then be allowed to cure to reduce some of its moisture, or it can be placed directly into the wax melting kiln. This process is known as the *burnout*. A specially constructed *temporary,* oil-heated, beehive kiln made of refractory brick covered with clay and topped with corrugated metal covered with still more clay is used. The kiln is built around a group of molds (or one large one) and encloses them completely. The molds are placed *upside down,* that is, with the sprue cup pointing *down* (except for those having a bottom opening as mentioned), so that the wax of the model can drain out easily as the kiln is heated and run into a metal trough; this leads it to a pan placed outside the kiln. The gathered wax can be used again for gates and risers, but new wax is preferred for model construction. The kiln is heated to about 1000° F till all the wax is either drained or vaporized by burning out. The length of time needed to accomplish this depends on the size and thickness of the mold; small pieces take at least twenty-four to forty-eight hours, and large pieces of perhaps seven feet may take up to one week of continuous heating to do the job.

Pouring the Mold Once all the wax is "lost," the oven is partially opened and the molds are allowed to cool to an above room temperature so that they may be handled with gloves. They are then removed from the kiln and brought to the pouring room near the melting furnace. Here they are placed *upright,* that is, with the

pouring cup *up,* in a square, wood-reinforced enclosure called the *flask* or *box* which can contain several molds, or one mold if it is large. Earth is then rammed tightly around the molds to secure them in position and give them additional strength to resist the pressure of the molten metal during the pouring.

Prior to this time, the metal has been made ready for pouring so that the mold will not cool off too much. A special electric *tilt furnace* (so called because it is tilted for pouring) requires about two hours to melt bronze. The

Crucible melting furnace for melting high temperature metals for casting, with blower. *Johnson Gas Appliance Company.*

interior of the furnace contains a *fixed crucible* with a pouring spout, and its capacity is about three hundred pounds. It is used repeatedly for the *same metal* till replacement is necessary. (In the case of pouring a large piece, several melting furnaces can be used to make a total of fourteen hundred pounds of metal which is all poured into *one* crucible, which is then handled by an overhead crane.) When the metal is ready, the furnace is opened and tilted, and the metal is poured at specific temperatures (1950° F for bronze) into the crucible that will contain all the metal needed for filling the mold completely. The mold must be filled in *one continuous pouring.*

When pouring up to three hundred pounds of metal, the receiving crucible is centered in the middle ring of a *two-man pouring shank.* One man holds the end which is forked to allow it to be manipulated, in tilting, to pour the metal, and the second man supports the other single, straight rod end. The crucible is carried close to the pouring cup of the mold and poured in a slow, steady stream till the metal appears at the riser openings (there are two openings, one on either side of the cup when the casting weighs over twenty-five

SMALL-FOUNDRY CASTING.

This sequence shows William Underhill at work in the foundry he organized at Highlands University, Las Vegas, New Mexico.

1. The metal melting furnace was made of a 50-gallon steel drum lined with refractory material. The furnace was also equipped with an automatic blower. The crucible inside the furnace is being loaded with scrap metal for melting.

2. The furnace is lighted and the blower adjusted. The lid is then replaced.

3. The condition of the metal is tested by inserting a steel rod and observing the action of the heat. If it melts, the metal is judged ready for the pour. The lid is constructed with two welded loops through which a length of pipe can be inserted to facilitate a two-man lift.

4. The molds are being lifted from the ceramic firing kiln in which the burnout took place. Another kind of burnout kiln was made of lightweight firebrick (seen in another photograph) stacked loose. Any enclosure capable of being heated to 1200° F can be utilized for this purpose.

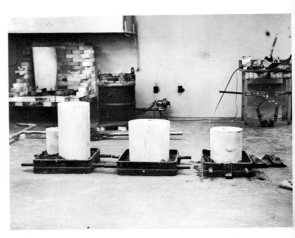

5. The burned-out molds are prepared for the pour by placing sections of sand mold flasks on the concrete floor, partially filling them with sand, placing a mold in each, and then adding some additional sand, the purpose of which is to support the mold during the pour and to contain any leakage of hot metal.

6. The molds ready for the pour. Also seen in the background are the partially dismantled burnout kiln under the hood, the metal melting furnace and blower, and, at the right, the crucible lifting tongs.

7. Once the cover of the furnace has been removed, the crucible is lifted from it with a two-man lifting tongs. It is then put into a two-man pouring shank.

8. The metal is poured into the mold.

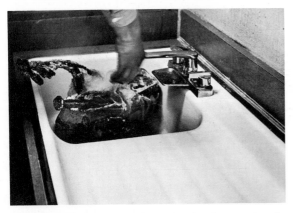

9. After *shaking out* the mold—that is, removing the investment material—remains of investment are washed from the mold with cold water.

Lost-wax cast bronze bowl, by William Underhill. Diameter: 7 inches.

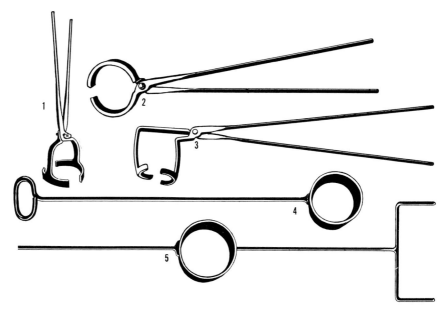

Foundry tongs: 1. Vertical lift tongs 2. Casting or pouring tongs 3. Top lift pickup tongs 4. Single handle spade type pouring shank 5. Two-man pouring shank

Lost-wax cast aluminum bronze bowl, by William Underhill. Diameter: 7 inches. The patina was created with a liver of sulphur solution.

Chinese cast bronze ceremonial wine vessel, called a *Yo*, Chou Dynasty (5th century B.C.). *Museum of Fine Arts, Boston.*

pounds). The pour is continued till it slightly overflows the sprue cup. A slow pouring, without producing laps and cold shuts, requires skill and experience. The gases escape from the mold through the risers, and to some extent through the plaster itself. Good ventilation is essential to draw off these possibly harmful fumes and gases. Metal should not be poured too hot or an undesirable surface will result, and not too cold or it will not run properly

and fill the mold, resulting in an imperfect casting which is a total loss. With most metals there is a leeway of about 150° F in which a pouring can be successfully completed. Experience allows the pourer to judge the metal temperature by color appearance.

The metal is allowed to cool sufficiently for the mold to be handled. The one-piece plaster

Lost-wax cast lidded bronze bowl with yellow-brown patina, by William Underhill. Diameter: 12 inches.

mold can be used only once. In the *shaking out* operation, the casting is removed and the mold is destroyed with a hammer and tools. The used plaster is saved for use in making luto for future molds.

Finishing the Casting The waste metal gated assembly—runners, risers, etc.—is removed with heavy-duty clippers, hacksaws, and me-chanical saws. Remaining projections are cleaned away with abrasive discs, mounted on a rotary flexible shaft, and with rotary files. The waste metal is also saved; it comprises about one-third of the metal used in future castings.

The casting is then cleaned by sand blasting followed by an acid bath and a scrubbing with stiff stainless steel brushes and abrasives if necessary. Should any cracks or openings have

Lost-wax cast bronze wine jug, hollow, with top opening and narrow spout. The jug is used by tribal people in Orissa State, India, for ceremonial occasions, when it is held in the hand while the wine emerges from the spout in a continuous stream into the mouth without touching the lips. *Photo by Oppi.*

Chinese cast bronze crouching tiger, Middle Chou Dynasty. Height to top of tail: 5⁹⁄₁₆ inches; length: 9 inches. *Fogg Museum, Cambridge, Massachusetts.*

Persian cast bronze ewer from Khurasan, end of the twelfth century. Height: 7½ inches. Engraved decoration partially inlaid with silver. *Metropolitan Museum of Art, New York. Rogers Fund, 1933.*

Cast bronze openwork belt buckle, Koban region of Georgia or the Caucasus, Scythian, c. fifth century B.C. Length: 5⅗ inches. *British Museum, London.*

developed in the casting, they can be repaired by welding with a welding rod of metal similar to the metal of the casting. Welded places can be chased to match the surface texture of the piece and take coloring, so that they are completely invisible. If desired, details can be added by chasing. The surface of bronze is malleable enough to be treated successfully with chasing tools.

In core casting (see page 336), the core is held in position during the process with steel rods, heavy spikes, or nails, which are so placed as to pierce the wax through the core to keep the core in place. After casting, the rods or nails project from the casting. They are removed, leaving holes in the casting which are filled in with matching metal by welding.

The coloring or patina is next and is produced mainly by chemicals. (See the section on coloring of metals, page 415.) After coloring, a bronze is treated with a coating of clear, natural-colored paste wax to give it a sheen and to help preserve the patina.

Chinese cast bronze statuette of a Mongolian youth with jade birds, Warring States, 481–221 B.C. *Museum of Fine Arts, Boston.*

Centrifugal Investment Casting

This method of lost-wax expendable-mold casting requires a *centrifugal casting machine.* The basic principle is that the metal is forced into the revolving mold by centrifugal action and pressure, filling the mold cavity. The special casting-plaster-mold materials that have been developed have made possible dense, accurate castings, with the possibility of thin sections and great detail. The size of the casting depends on the capacity of the flask and the centrifugal machine. Usually, the capacity is relatively small; the outside diameters of the flask, which contains the mold, range from 2½ to 5 inches and a height of 2½ to 9 inches is most common, though larger flask sizes are used in industry. The size limitation allows this method of casting to be used for small sculpture and jewelry pieces.

Flasks are of stainless steel for nonferrous metals and of special high-temperature nickel alloy for platinum and other high-melting-point alloys and metals. Because the wax patterns must clear the walls by at least ½ inch (less on smaller flasks), the maximum size possible is less than the diameter of the flask used. One can, of course, join and combine separately cast pieces to make larger units.

Because of the fineness of the wax and the casting material, great accuracy in detail and texture is possible in reproducing the wax model in metal, and little finishing is necessary. The high finish that can be achieved in the wax model eliminates hours of filing and surfacing. A well-prepared wax model needs only to have the sprue removed and the polishing done. The method is used for the casting of precious metals (gold, silver, platinum, palladium), but other metals such as bronze, brass, and aluminum can also be cast centrifugally.

Cast bronze toy horse and rider with copper wheels, from Rajasthan, India. Height: approximately 14 inches. *Collection of the Art in Industry Museum, Calcutta. Photo by Oppi.*

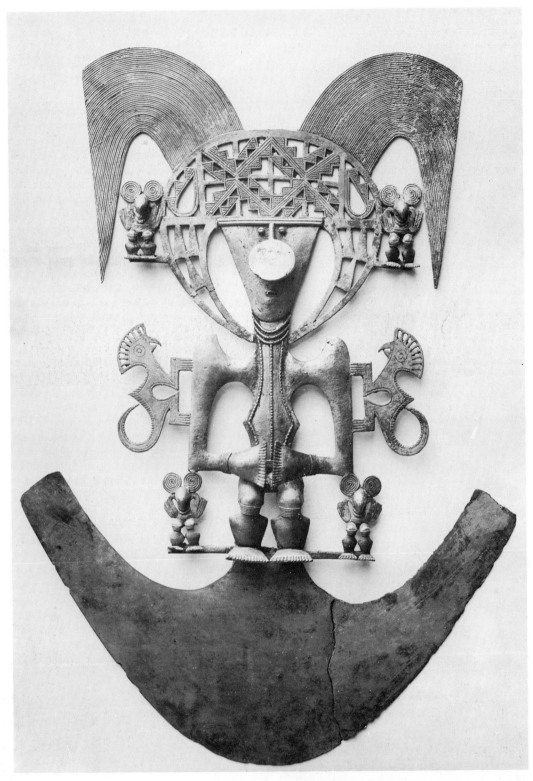

Lost-wax-cast pectoral in gold, from Quimbaya, Colombia, pre-sixteenth century. This masterpiece of technique and design shows outstanding skill in the handling of the initial wax model, the casting process, and the subsequent engraving of patterns in the headdress and flanking lizards. Height: Approximately 11½ inches. *British Museum, London.*

Cast bronze mask, Senufo, Ivory Coast, Africa. Height: 8¼ inches. *The Museum of Primitive Art, New York. Photo by Charles Uht.*

Contemporary cast brass head of the Goddess Lakshmi, used in worship in Rajasthan, India. Height: 5 inches. *Photo by Oppi.*

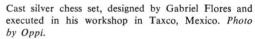

Cast silver chess set, designed by Gabriel Flores and executed in his workshop in Taxco, Mexico. *Photo by Oppi.*

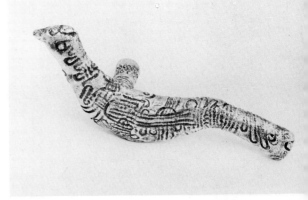

Bird-form lever door handle in cast bronze, by Mirko, silver plated, oxidized, and polished by hand. Commissioned by The Yale & Towne Manufacturing Company. *The Yale & Towne Manufacturing Company.*

Floral-form lever door handle in cast bronze, antique finish, by Mirko, Italy, for The Yale & Towne Manufacturing Company.

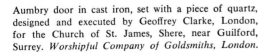

Cast aluminum bell, by Don Drumm, 1963. Total length: 15 inches.

Aumbry door in cast iron, set with a piece of quartz, designed and executed by Geoffrey Clarke, London, for the Church of St. James, Shere, near Guilford, Surrey. *Worshipful Company of Goldsmiths, London.*

"Mission," cast aluminum sculpture, by Jan de Swart. *Photo by de Swart.*

"The Cinema," cast bronze (lost-wax process) sculpture, by A. Van Kleeck. Height: 2 feet; width: 4 feet. The surface is finished bright with patches of purple patina. *Photo by Ron Partridge.*

Silver-gilt brooch, designed by Robert Adams, England, and executed by H. J. Company, Ltd., London. The brooch was made from one piece of wax that was formed into a curvilinear pattern while the wax was under warm water. *Worshipful Company of Goldsmiths, London. Photo by Peter Parkinson.*

Silver bird, 2½ inches high, by Florence Nach, New York, made entirely of investment casting wax rods or wire, cast by centrifugal lost-wax casting. *Photo by Nach.*

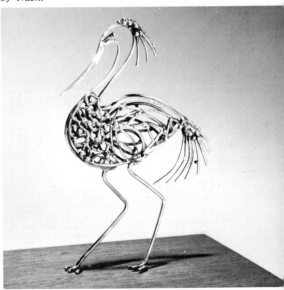

Natural waxes exist in a variety of textures and consistencies—hard, tough, soft, flexible, plastic, elastic, and brittle. The various surface qualities are sticky, dry, tacky, oily, fatty, and slippery. Special combinations are designed to obtain particular surface characteristics.

Besides their adaptability to casting, waxes are used in adhesives, buffing compounds, binding agents, dental waxes, emulsions, finishing, heat sealing, linings for containers of acid and other liquids, lubricants and lubricating greases, metal etching, modeling, masking, polishes, precision casting, rust and corrosion prevention, sealing compounds, sizings, varnishes, water repellents, and wax/rosin blends.

The waxes employed in the creation of models for casting are derived from three main sources: animal and insect, mineral and petroleum, and vegetable. Synthetic waxes are also manufactured, but natural waxes have superior work qualities. Melting points and flash points (the temperature at which a given wax will burst into flame) are factors that must be considered in the combining of waxes. The flash point is a criterion in testing wax quality. Specific gravity is useful in measuring the weight of metal equivalents needed for the casting.

Beeswax

Melting point: 142–149° F (61–65° C)
Flash point: 468–482° F
Specific gravity: (all given at 25° C), 0.950–0.960

Beeswax is an insect wax excreted by the honeybee to construct the honeycomb. Color depends on the flower upon which the bee feeds and on the age of the hive. Refined beeswax is made by remelting and filtering crude wax; white beeswax is bleached. It is compatible with almost all other waxes and oils, is plastic when warm, and is used for precision castings.

Spermaceti

Melting point: 113–120° F (45–49° C)
Flash point: 470–480° F
Specific gravity: 0.935–0.946

Spermaceti, an animal wax also called Cetin, is obtained from the head cavities and blubber of the sperm whale. It is purified and freed of oils by hydraulic pressure. It is quite brittle and is free of taste or odor.

Ozokerite

Melting point: 145–182° F (63–83° C)
Flash point: 500–580° F
Specific gravity: 0.950–0.960

Ozokerite is a bituminous coal product used in blends to produce a dry type of wax.

Ceresine

Melting point: 128–185° F (53.3–85° C)
Flash point: 400–500° F
Specific gravity: 0.880–0.935

Ceresine is a group of mineral waxes derived from refined and bleached ozokerite; it is used in combination with paraffins to make combinations that vary from hard to soft, depending on the additives. Used in casting, as a lubricant in mold release, and in die stamping, it is sometimes known as "cherry wax."

Petroleum waxes are petroleum industry byproducts, derived from crude oil by distillation. The main types, all hydrocarbons, are the paraffins, petrolatums, and microcrystallines. Hardness depends on the crystal character, freedom from oil, and melting point.

Paraffin

Melting point: 118–165° F (48–74° C)
Flash point: 400–470° F
Specific gravity: 0.880–0.920

A hard, dry, solid, chemically inert wax, paraffin is used for liners on gutta-percha bottles for containing hydrofluoric acid.

Petrolatum

Melting point: 106–145° F (41–63° C)
Flash point: 640° F maximum
Specific gravity: 0.815–0.865 (at 65° C)

Soft to medium-hard, without taste or odor, petrolatum is also made in a semi-solid form called petroleum jelly.

Microcrystalline

Melting point: 140–200° F (60–93° C)
Flash point: 500–580° F
Specific gravity: 0.915–0.935

Microcrystalline ranges from sticky and plastic to hard, dry solid. An oxidized variety melts at 180–200° F and is a hard solid.

VEGETABLE WAXES

Bayberry Wax

Melting point: 116–120° F (46–49° C)
Flash point: 470–490° F
Specific gravity: 0.977–0.982

Wax from the berry of the bayberry bush is mainly imported from Colombia. The berry's wax coating is removed by boiling in water and skimming off and straining the wax. Compatible with all vegetable, animal, and mineral waxes, it is used in buffing compounds. It is fragrant and green.

Japan Wax

Melting point: 122–133° F (50–56° C)
Flash point: 385–400° F
Specific gravity: 0.975–0.984

Gummy in feel, resembling a fat more than a wax, Japan wax is derived from the protective coating on sumac tree berries, which grow in Japan. The wax is extracted by pressure, melted, filtered, and bleached. It is compatible with beeswax and used in buffing compounds and metal lubricants.

Candelilla Wax

Melting point: 156–163° F (69–73° C)
Flash point: 465–490° F
Specific gravity: 0.982–0.993

Candelilla wax is found in the form of scales covering a reedlike wild plant found in northwestern Mexico and southern Texas. The plant is immersed in boiling water containing some sulphuric acid, and the wax is skimmed off and strained. Hard, brittle, slightly tacky, and lustrous, it combines well with all vegetable and animal waxes. It is used for precision casting.

Carnauba Wax

Melting point: 180–187° F (82.5–86° C)
Flash point: 570° F minimum
Specific gravity: 0.996–0.998

Carnauba wax is exuded by the leaves of the northern and northeastern Brazilian "Tree of Life," the carnauba palm, to conserve its moisture. The wax is removed from dried leaves by beating. The fine, powdery wax is melted and strained. It is brittle, hard, nontacky, and lustrous and has a great many uses in precision casting, lubricants, and varnishes.

WAX ADDITIVES

Waxes are usually combined with other materials, called additives, to produce specific characteristics revolving on hardness, softness, suitability for carving, tackyness or stickyness, use in blending, melting temperature, accuracy in reproduction, and low rate of thermal expansion in the mold. Depending on their composition, their melting range is roughly from 100 to 200° F. To create the wide variety of characteristics mentioned, rosins are added. Soft rosins such as mastic (a rosin exuded from a kind of pistachio tree) and damar (a neutral rosin derived from a Far Eastern evergreen fir tree), and hard rosins such as copal (derived from trees, plants, and fossils) and amber (a fossil rosin derived from trees) are used. Japan wax and Chinese tallow remain sticky even in ordinary temperatures. For sculpture casting wax, mutton tallow and beef tallow are added to waxes. They result in a characteristically unpleasant odor when volatilized. Waxes for sculpture are available in bulk and in sheet form.

No matter what the wax contains, it must burn out completely and leave no residue, which would result in an incomplete or porous casting.

CENTRIFUGAL CASTING WAXES

Centrifugal casting waxes were developed for the dental industry, where precision is essential. They are more refined than waxes used for large cast-sculpture models, and their characteristics and uses are more specifically restricted and controlled. Generally speaking, they must solidify rapidly, be relatively strong enough to retain their shape under handling, be easy to manipulate, shrink minimally, run out of the investment mold easily at a moderate temperature, and burn out cleanly.

Most waxes are colored by the manufacturer for identification but they also are left in their natural color. They are sold in strips, bars, rods, sheets, half rounds, sticks, wires, and solid pastes. Sheet and wire waxes are available in gauge numbers corresponding to the Brown and Sharpe gauge scale and are usually boxed. Shrinkage allowance of 5 to 10 per cent must be made when accuracy of size is a factor, as in making a ring. In connection with shrinkage, the investment material and the metal used are also factors in shrinkage; they both shrink slightly in casting.

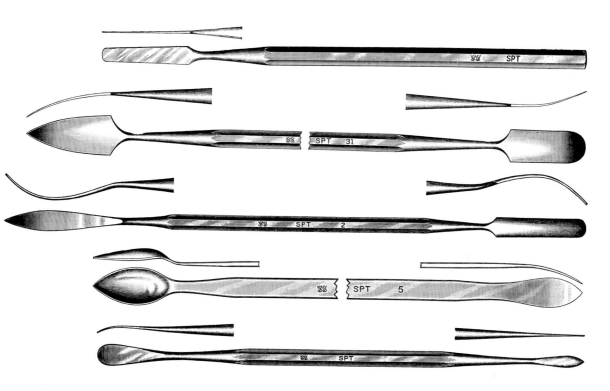

Wax forming spatulas

Wax carving instruments

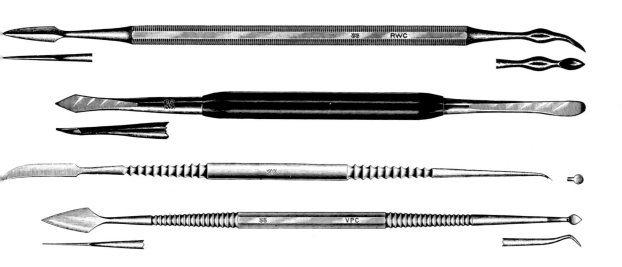

TOOLS FOR SHAPING WAX

The tools used in shaping wax can be few and simple. Heat in some form is necessary and can be provided by a Bunsen burner (gas or electric) or an alcohol lamp. A spatula, old dental tools with various ends such as carvers, scalers, patching tools made of carbon or stainless steel, and a pointed knife such as a small surgical tool are useful. Metal tools can be improvised, but when used with heat, they must be long enough or provided with an insulating handle. Linoleum-cutting tools, penknives, metal modeling tools, needles to make small holes, and some engraving tools might be helpful, depending on the desired effect. Warm water (below the melting point of the wax) is needed to soften waxes and allow them to be shaped or bent with minimal surface change.

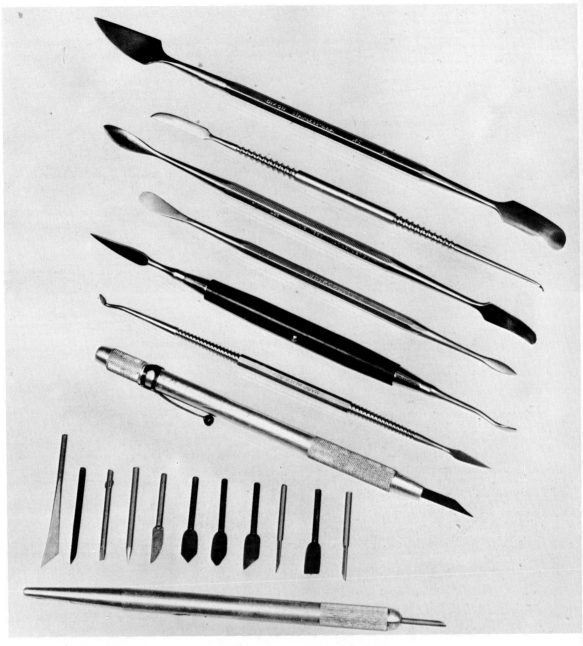

A variety of tools is available for shaping, carving, and forming wax models for investment casting. Small spatulas and dental tools are most common, but many others can be improvised. Shown here are some dental spatulas and cutting tools, all of which satisfy the main requirement of wax-forming tools: they can be heated and held while shaping the wax. *The Kerr Dental Manufacturing Co.*

The flame itself is, of course, also a tool, which can be used to melt wax, shape pieces, and help in other operations.

Cutting tools are used to make basic shapes and openings, and spatulas to add wax and develop a design. The tool is held over the heat for three or four seconds and then placed against the wax, which melts. This action can serve either to join parts or to add wax in a liquid state by holding it in the spoonlike de-pression of a spatula and trailing it onto other wax. The same spatula can be employed to cut wax, make holes, and develop an infinite number of surface textures.

To a certain extent, what is possible with the tool depends on the characteristics of the wax. The user should know waxes and exploit their possibilities. For the beginner, the time given to free exploration with waxes to see what they can do is by no means wasted. The range of

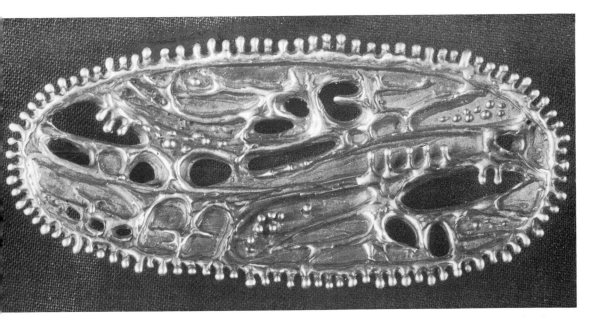

ABOVE: Robert Dhaemers' cast silver brooch, polished and completed. Its creation is shown in the following sequence.

CENTRIFUGAL INVESTMENT CASTING.

Robert Dhaemers, the artist-craftsman, demonstrates his method for the construction of a silver pin, from its formation in wax to its investment, casting, and completion. *Photos by Margaret Dhaemers.*

ABOVE: Robert Dhaemers' cast silver brooch, polished and completed. Its creation is shown in the following sequence.

1. The materials for creating the wax model, which are shown here, are: pink sheet wax ⚹16 (Kerr), sprue wax and thicker purple hard wax, spatula, old dental tools and knife, and gas burner (other heat sources could be used).

2. The oval shape of the brooch is cut out from the pink wax with a knife blade.

3. The cut-out wax is heated over the flame to soften it and allow it to be shaped. Just passing it over the flame is sufficient.

6. The wax trailing continues and the design develops in complexity.

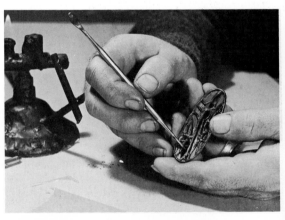

7. Openings are made in the base pink wax by heating the smaller end of the spatula in the flame and then pushing the heated end through the wax. The spatula is moved around to create the desired shape and reheated when necessary.

plasticity, hardness, strength, adhesiveness, brittleness, and other characteristics is great and, once known, can be utilized. Some waxes are hard enough to be carved and then polished by rubbing with a piece of soft cotton or soft brush under cold running water. A smooth piece of worn chamois leather can also be used dry for this purpose. The more finished the model, the less work there is in finishing the casting. Models can also be finished smooth by passing them lightly and quickly over the flame.

SPRUING THE MODEL

Once the model is completed, it is ready to be "sprued." The wax sprue, after the wax has been melted away in the investment later, will become the hole through which the metal is to flow into the mold cavity. Additional runners are added *to help bring the metal to heavier parts of the model.* These runners are made with 12- or 14-gauge wax wire, or thinner if the piece being cast is delicate or small. As few runners are used as are really necessary.

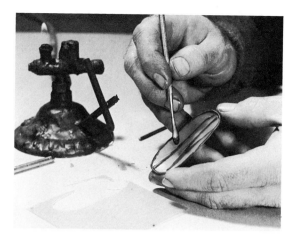

4. The spatula is heated over the flame and some purple, hard wax is allowed to melt on it. The spatula is passed over the flame again and then the wax is trailed along the edge of the pink brooch shape before it cools.

5. Additional wax is trailed over the form, dividing it into spaces as the design develops.

8. Using the small end of the spatula, a decorative outer edge is added to the form. To do this, #16 sprue wax is melted onto the form and is joined by touching both it and the form simultaneously with a heated spatula at the point of juncture. The wax is cut off at the desired length with a hot spatula.

9. Sprues (#16 sprue wax) are added to the back of the form to prepare it for casting. The sprues are placed about ½ inch apart and all join at a central point.

They should be as *short* as possible, and no closer to each other than a half inch. The number depends on the size and design of the piece. A heavy ring probably needs only one runner besides the sprue. In the casting of larger models, a runner can lead to the extremity or to the heavier parts. These heavier parts require more metal, they *freeze last,* and extra metal has to be drawn into this area from the runner because of shrinkage.

All runner wires should converge from the model upon one point above it, which will become the sprue opening. At the point at which the wires *touch the model,* a small amount of additional wax can be added; after melting, this will make the opening larger at that point and facilitate the entrance of the metal into the mold. Air vents to allow gases to escape are generally not necessary in investment casting, as they are in other forms of casting; this is mainly because of the small size of centrifugal castings and because gases escape through the pores of the investment material itself.

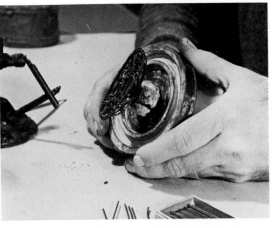

10. Once the sprues are completed, the sprue former, in this case made of rubber, is filled with hard wax in the *concave* central portion. Some craftsmen insert a sprue pin made of metal at this point. The wax form is then attached to the wax (which is in the opening in the center of the sprue former) at the apex of the sprues. The wax form is completely brushed with a debubblizer (a wetting agent) to break the surface tension and allowed to dry for about 15 minutes.

11. The cristobalite investment mixture is prepared according to manufacturer's instructions. Here it is being mixed with a hand spatula, but a manually operated mixing cover could also be used.

EQUIPMENT FOR INVESTMENT CASTING.

From left to right: a vibrator, a measuring glass graduate, a cannister of the investment material, two flexible rubber mixing bowls, a hand-operated mixing cover made in sizes to fit particular bowls, a spatula, and a brush. *The Kerr Dental Manufacturing Co.*

12. The investment mixture, now with a consistency similar to whipped cream, is applied over the entire object with a brush. Care must be taken not to trap any air bubbles, since air bubbles will cast as solid forms.

13. The investment covering the wax is allowed to set, which takes about 20 minutes. An asbestos-lined flask is then placed around the form, contacting the sprue former. The purpose of the asbestos liner is to allow for the expansion of the investment during the burnout.

14. The investment needed to fill the flask and make the mold is then prepared and placed on a vibrator to remove any bubbles. It now has the consistency of thick cream.

15. The flask is placed on the vibrator platform and the investment is poured into and fills the flask. The asbestos liner is visible here. Once the flask is filled, the vibrator is turned on again to bring any air bubbles to the surface.

MOUNTING THE MODEL

The model must then be mounted on a *sprue former*. The sprue former should first be covered with a thin layer of wax or oil to facilitate its removal later. Sprue formers are made of metal or rubber in various sizes to match the size of the flask used, or they may simply be a cone without a flange. There is either a cone shape or a rounded bulge in the center, which has a small central opening. This cone forms the depression that will later lead the molten metal to the sprue opening at the time of casting. The concave space of the sprue former is filled with hard or tacky wax to provide a point at which the wax sprues can be joined to the sprue former. The model is then mounted on the opening at the apex of the cone, with all the converging runners joining at the sprue former opening. This joining is done by touching both points with a heated spatula while the wax is soft. The sprue former automatically centers the sprue opening so that it lines up with the crucible opening. The joint should be secure, or there will be danger of the model breaking away later when the investment material is placed on a vibrator to remove air pockets and bubbles.

If there is any reason to doubt the strength of this joint, a *metal sprue pin* can be inserted through the cone opening into the model. The cone depression can in this case be filled with plasticene instead of wax, or the pin can be heated and inserted through the wax. *The pin must be removed later,* after the investment material has been cast and hardened and before the sprue former is removed.

Nonhardening plastic clays can also be used for forming the sprue depression if sprue formers are not available. They can be shaped into the form of a conical base and mounted on an asbestos pad or a sheet of glass, and a sprue pin added, after which the flask is placed.

POSITIONING THE MODEL

Most models need no other consideration in mounting than to be sure that they clear the flask wall and base by at least one-quarter inch for small flasks and one-half inch, the most common clearance, for normal-sized flasks. Very large flasks need up to one inch clearance, to accommodate the *liner* of asbestos and to assure the presence of enough investment material to give strength to the mold during the burnout of the wax and under the stresses of the molten metal caused by the centrifugal force of casting. Some special considerations are, however, necessary.

When the model surface facing the sprue opening is *flat,* the model should be tilted from the horizontal to allow the metal to flow into the mold more easily. If a portion of the model extends below the juncture of any runner or below the opening in the cone (when held with the cone pointing *upward*), there is danger of an air pocket forming and insufficient metal flowing to that part. In such a case,

it is necessary to attach a riser to the part leading to the cone formed by the sprue former, in other words, to the top of the investment. The wax can then be drained from that area easily, and the metal will flow there through the separate opening riser thus formed.

It is possible to mount several models in one flask for simultaneous casting (called *ganging*) as long as there is room for them, they do not touch each other, and the flask can take the amount of metal required. A few examples of flask capacity might serve as a guide. A flask 3½ inches in diameter by four inches high will take up to seven ounces of gold, depending on the size of the *crucible* used and the arm length of the centrifugal machine. A machine with a twenty-four-inch arm that accommodates a flask four inches in diameter and six inches high will take up to twenty-five ounces of gold and perhaps thirteen ounces of silver. The difference in the weights of metal in relation to their bulk depends on the specific gravity of the metal. For purposes of economy and minimum burnout time, the *smallest* flask needed for the model is the one to use.

DEBUBBLIZING THE WAX MODEL

To permit the investment material to flow uniformly around and make perfect contact with the model's surface, thus insuring an accurate and *nodule-free* casting (nodules occur when air bubbles form and cling to the wax surface of the model), the surface tension must be broken. This is done with a commercial debubblizing or wax-painting solution, which contains a wetting agent. The entire surface of the wax model is carefully painted with a brush, or else the model can be dipped several times into the solution. The excess liquid is blown away. Green soap mixed with some hydrogen peroxide can also be used for this purpose.

THE INVESTMENT MATERIAL

The most commonly used commercially available and reliable investment material contains cristobalite (so called because it comes from Cerro San Cristobal, Pachuca, Mexico; it is a silica, SiO_4 in white octahedra). Silica flour, also used, and cristobalite allow the investment to withstand extreme heating and cooling without cracking or breaking. Gypsum, a mineral of hydrous calcium sulphate from which plaster of Paris is made, is used to keep the silica in suspension; otherwise it would settle. The gypsum is the actual binder; in the form of plaster of Paris it also contains additives that control the viscosity and setting time of the mixture. The hardening or set of the material is the result of the formation of interlocking crystals when water and plaster are combined, and of the absorption of free water in the additives. Gypsum does not contain any acid-producing or corrosive ingredients that might attack flasks, castings, or furnace.

Mixing the investment must be done carefully to provide maximum working time before setting and proper consistency to insure accuracy. This is a critical step in casting. The equipment needed is a rubber mixing bowl, a spatula or large spoon (for hand mixing, but a mechanical, hand-operated mixer is available), a 100 cc. glass with graduated markings to measure water, a measuring cup to measure the investment, a vibrator (to remove air bubbles in the investment), and a paint brush with soft hair.

PREPARING THE INVESTMENT

The recommended proportion of water and cristobalite powder is 2.2 parts of cristobalite to one part water. Sample ratios, depending on flask capacity, are as follows:

Cristobalite (cup)	Water (cc.)
$\frac{1}{3}$	25
$\frac{2}{3}$	50
$1\frac{1}{2}$	110
$3\frac{1}{2}$	255

Water drawn from the faucet is satisfactory. If it is left to stand one hour some of the air will dissipate, and the temperature will stabilize at the acceptable range of 70–80° F. Colder water will retard the setting time of the investment and warmer water will accelerate it. The investment material should also be within this temperature range. The setting time is roughly eight to fifteen minutes, depending on the mixture.

Small amounts can be mixed in a small rubber mixing bowl, and large bowls will accommodate mixtures intended for large-flask capacity. More investment material should be mixed than necessary, to make sure that there is enough to fill the flask completely. The water is measured and placed in the bowl. The measured amount of cristobalite is added gradually while the mixture is stirred with the spatula or large spoon. The investment material is designed to mix easily and smoothly, without lumps, into a creamy slurry; this should be spatulated for one to four minutes. Further

removal of air bubbles is accomplished by placing and holding down the rubber mixing bowl, with its contents, on the vibrator. This is an electrically operated machine that can be regulated to variable speeds. It has a platform that vibrates, and air bubbles rise to the surface of the slurry, where they can easily be broken with the spatula. After this treatment, the investment is ready to be used for application with a brush or to be poured.

It is advisable to accept the recommendations of manufacturers concerning the ratio of water to investment powder for the most efficient results. If the proportion of water is increased, the investment slurry becomes thin and weak; it may separate on standing and become porous on setting, thus producing a rough surface in the casting. Water separation due to the settling of particles will not occur if the time between pouring the investment and setting is kept as short as possible. Globules of dry powder remaining because of incomplete mixture will show up later as bubbles with dents in them. Humidity is a factor that can affect the water-investment ratio, but if the investment container, once opened, is stored tightly closed in a dry place, this problem is minimal under normal conditions.

PREPARING THE ASBESTOS FLASK LINER

It is now necessary to backtrack to the point where the wax model has been painted with the debubblizing solution and allowed to dry. As it dries, the flask can be prepared by measuring its circumference with a string and allowing ⅛ inch extra. The added measurement allows for the 1/16-inch-thick sheet asbestos used as a liner in the flask. The height or width of the asbestos should be one-half inch less than the height of the flask, allowing one-quarter inch shortness at top and bottom. The liner acts as a cushion to the expansion of the investment material during burnout and casting. The investment expands twice as much as the flask metal during heating, and this extra expansion is taken up by the asbestos, which compresses easily. Dipping the asbestos liner once quickly into water will allow it to be pressed tightly against the inner flask wall. Also the small amount of water prevents it from absorbing too much of the moisture in the investment mixture when this is poured.

APPLYING THE INVESTMENT, AND POURING

After the debubblizer has been applied and is dry, the investment is applied with a small soft brush to precoat all parts of the wax model which has already been mounted on the sprue former. Great care must be taken to cover the model and sprues completely and to avoid trapping air bubbles; if these are allowed to remain, they will become a part of the casting *in solid form*. Sufficient investment is applied to make a solid cover over the entire model and sprues, and about twenty minutes is allowed for drying. The model is placed into the flask with the sprue former in contact with a sheet of plate glass. A coil of plasticene can be placed around the outside of the flask and pressed into place to cover the joint between the sides of the flask and the sprue former, so that no investment material leaks out after pouring. The supporting glass can then be safely tilted as the investment slurry is poured into the side of the flask. The slurry should be almost level with the top. The tilted position allows the air to escape and not become trapped under the model. The glass is then made level again and investment is added to completely fill the flask. The whole assembly is then placed on the vibrator, which is set to a *low cycle* to avoid breaking off the model at the sprue opening joint. Vibration removes the residual bubbles and packs the investment around the precoated model. If, in settling, additional investment is needed to bring the level to the top of the flask again, it can be added before the initial set begins.

Removal of air is sometimes done with a *vacuum pump unit*. A vacuum unit eliminates the need to precoat the model, because it removes all air, though it might be painted with debubblizing solution for safety. In this case, the flask is not filled to the top. The flask is placed under the bell jar and the pump turned on. The pump should run till the accelerated boiling of the investment becomes a steady bubbling (thirty seconds to one minute). The spring-mounted plate, which is covered with a rubber mat, can be jiggled automatically before and after releasing the vacuum, to allow the investment to flow back around the model. The remainder of the flask can then be filled with investment, which should be in place before the initial set begins.

THE BURNOUT

The flask is allowed to stand till the air set begins. The time will vary from one to three hours, depending on the size of the flask and the amount of investment material. After setting has begun, the investment at the top can

16. The investment is allowed to set, which takes from 15 to 30 minutes or longer, depending on the flask size. If necessary, excess investment can be screed off level with the flask.

19. The next step is the burnout, the purpose of which is to remove all moisture from the investment and to burn out all traces of the wax model. The burnout will leave a clean cavity into which the molten metal will flow, completely replacing the wax model. Dhaemers allows a minimum of three hours, and more usually four to six hours, depending on the size of the object being cast. The mold is ready for casting when all traces of carbon are gone and the investment looks bone white.

be screed level with a flat metal edge; excess flow over the sides should also be removed. The rubber mixing bowl should be cleaned out with paper and the excess investment not allowed to run down drains, where it can accumulate and cause clogging.

Once the airset has occurred, the investment shows no sign of external moisture. At this time, the sprue former can be removed. If it has been lightly coated with wax or petroleum, as suggested, removal is simple. Take the

17. The sprue former is then separated from the flask. In this case, the sprue former is rubber and therefore flexible. If a sprue pin has been used, it must be removed prior to this operation. The wax in the sprue cup breaks contact with the sprues in the mold.

18. When the sprue former is removed (left), a depression is left in the mold (right). It is in this depression that the molten metal will flow. Dhaemers scrapes this area smooth to allow unobstructed access of the metal into the mold cavity.

20. This photograph is not a part of this series but is inserted to illustrate the appearance of a partially completed burnout. The dark areas on the investment are carbon deposits that have not had sufficient time to be consumed by the heat. *The Kerr Dental Manufacturing Co.*

plasticene off the glass and lift the flask. Remove the sprue pin, if one has been used, by gently prying it loose with a pair of pliers. To separate the sprue former, insert a spatula edge between the metal former and the investment and push the former away with a little pressure. If the former is of rubber, it can be loosened with the fingers. A break will occur between the wax in the former cone and the sprues where they join at the opening. Once the sprue former is removed, the sprue is visible in the center of the investment. To insure a smooth flow of metal, the depression made by the sprue former may be scraped out with a knife. It is possible to set the mold aside for

a while if the casting for some reason cannot be continued immediately, but not for too long, because the investment may become too dry; *some* moisture aids the elimination of wax during the burnout.

Warning: do not drop or shock the investment material. This would cause visible cracks in the finished casting and perhaps destroy it. Burnout should not begin too early, for the too-rapid evaporation of moisture at elevated temperatures might cause the investment material to expand too fast, crack, or be destroyed completely. Cracks in the investment appear in the casting as "fins" or as finlike metal projections on the surface. These can be removed, but they might appear in a critical position and blemish a design or surface. Splintering of the inner mold surface, called "spalling," is another danger in too-rapid burnout at the beginning stages. The splinters, chips, or crumbs that might break away from the inner mold cavity become inclusions in the molten metal after it solidifies. Erosion of detail by too-rapid wax movement is also possible.

The purpose of the burnout is to remove all traces of wax in the mold, to eliminate gradually the chemical moisture in the investment material (which might otherwise cause a porous casting), and to bring the temperature of the investment up to the proper degree to receive the molten metal. During the burnout, the following things happen. The heat attacks the wax and the investment material. The outer layer of the wax penetrates into the investment pores, aided by steam from the moisture in the investment. In this way the wax pattern expands without the excessive pressure that might cause the investment to crack. Wax expands at a greater rate than the investment, causing stress, pressure, and strain on the investment, and it is therefore important not to have the temperature too high initially. During the first two hours of burnout, once the initial wax has been consumed by the heat there may still be a carbon residue; this also must be eliminated. The carbon shows on the outer surface of the investment as a black discoloration and is an indication of insufficient burnout. Continued burnout at the higher temperature recommended will eliminate all carbon and leave the investment material a clean, bone white.

If the wax is not eliminated entirely and the carbon residue is allowed to fill the pores, the displaced air and the gases formed by the molten metal when it flows will not be able to escape through the pores of the investment, and they will cause it to crack or suffer injury in other ways.

The ideal burnout condition allows the flask to be heated from the bottom; the wax then drains through the sprue first (the flask has been placed with sprue opening down) and progressively upward, allowing the pattern wax to follow and so reduce the pressure quickly. The best burnout kiln is of the gas-heated muffle type, heated from below and vented to allow gases to escape. Electric burnout kilns with a bottom element are good, but the element should be protected with a refractory shelf to avoid direct contact with the wax. The wax melts out, sizzles, burns, and smokes—all of which affects the longevity of the element. If neither kiln is available, a ceramic or enameling kiln that has heat control is satisfactory. In this case, it might be advisable to reverse the position of the flask after the first hour (during which it has been in the kiln with the sprue opening down), set the flask on a Nichrome wire trivet, and, an hour later, reverse it again. Metal tongs should be used to handle the hot flask, and asbestos gloves worn.

The time for burnout varies with the size of the flask and the amount of pattern wax in the model. Small flasks with delicate models may take only two hours, while larger flasks require from three to six hours and sometimes more. The color of the investment is a good indicator of burnout completion.

Recommended Burnout Cycle A wax-eliminating furnace or a kiln with an accurate pyrometer will assure the best control. Whatever the ultimate heat peak or time schedule, the whole process should be gradual and possible to follow by an accurate observation of the temperature. A slow beginning at 200° F for one hour, increased to 300° F for the second hour, and slowly to 600° F is advisable. From 600° F onward, the heating may be more rapid till it reaches 1200° F at the sixth hour. This is an adequate time cycle for most hand-operated crucibles and for normal flask capacity. If there is a large amount of wax to be eliminated, the length of time should be increased to eight hours, but in any case the temperature should not go beyond 1200° F or the investment will start to break down and the mold be lost.

The investment must then be cooled to 700–900° F (371 to 482° C), or to a temperature suitable for receiving the particular molten metal being used. Generally speaking, this temperature is about 200 to 500° F below the melting point of the metal. This heat reduction is necessary because too hot an investment will keep the poured molten metal in a liquid state too long before it solidifies, causing shrinkage and high porosity. At the other extreme, too cold an investment will cause the molten metal to freeze and solidify too quickly in the mold after pouring and might result in an incomplete casting. For sterling silver, a temperature of 700° F is sufficient, and for gold, a range of 800 to 950° F, depending on the kind of gold used. Low-karat gold requires a lower temperature than high-karat.

Thermal expansion of cristobalite investment is about 1.2 per cent from room temperature to 400° C (752° F), and 1.4 per cent to 700° C (1292° F). This rate of expansion is enough to compensate for the normal shrinkage of precious molten metals at the time of cooling, so that the casting result is almost equal to the wax model in size.

MEASURING THE METAL

Before the model wax has been mounted on the sprue former, it must be weighed, *with the sprues attached,* to arrive at a wax-metal ratio. If *sterling silver* is used, the wax is weighed and the weight multiplied by 10 to arrive at the weight of metal needed for casting. To this, one-quarter to one-half ounce is added, depending on the size of the *button* needed for the model. The button is the extra metal that acts as a reservoir from which metal can be drawn during cooling into the cavity of the mold if it is needed. For rings, one-quarter ounce is sufficient, and for larger pieces, add one-half ounce.

The wax model can also be weighed in a marked, graduated flask filled with water and its *displacement* noted. Place the wax in the water and mark the height on the graduated indicator. If the wax floats, push it under with a wire. Remove the wax and place sufficient metal in the flask to bring the water to the same level as marked. To this amount, add sufficient metal to fill the part of the mold which is the sprues and button.

Weighing for gold and other metals can be done by the same method as described for silver. A rough equivalent for 14K gold is to weigh the wax model and multiply the result by 12; for 18K gold, multiply by 18; for platinum, multiply by 18.

When weighing waxes, remember that some waxes are denser than others, and it is therefore better to allow one-quarter to one-half pennyweight of extra metal to compensate for the difference. A little extra metal can always be used in the next casting; also it gives the extra push, in casting, to fill the mold.

THE CENTRIFUGAL CASTING MACHINE

The centrifugal casting machine is an apparatus having two balanced arm extensions projecting from a central ball-bearing-mounted support. The extensions usually rotate on a horizontal plane. One arm carries the flask containing the mold and, next to it, the crucible carriage, which holds the crucible containing the molten metal. The other arm holds counterweights that are adjusted to balance the weight of the other arm. The machine is operated by an oversized, heavy-duty flat spring, which is wound and held by raising a stop rod pin; the pin is later allowed to drop to release the arms. Once the arms are released, the spring drives them in a rotating motion with great speed, forcing the molten metal to flow by centrifugal force from the mounted crucible into the adjacent flask containing the mold. The casting is thereby formed.

There are several varieties of centrifugal machines. Some are hand-driven, some motor-driven; some operate in a vertical plane. The spring-driven horizontal one described above is best suited to the craftsman and his needs.

Complete centrifugal casting outfit (without spatter shield). Center, centrifugal casting machine; left, flask tongs and flask cradles; below, a crucible; right, a sprue former, additional weights, and two other sprue formers; above them are investment flasks of various sizes. Note the raised stop rod pin resting against the crucible carriage. *The Kerr Dental Manufacturing Co.*

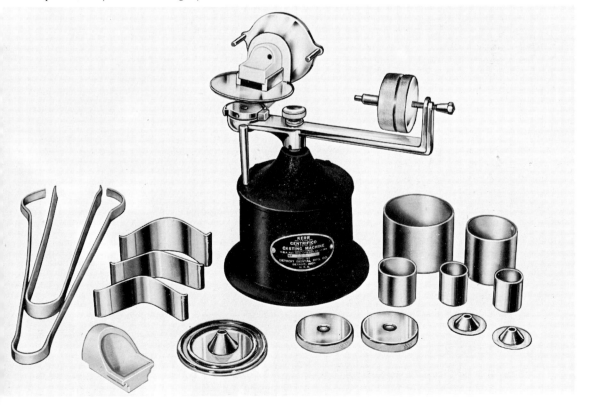

The centrifugal machine should be level and bolted securely in position. A metal shield placed around it (a sheet of galvanized iron or a large washtub is suitable) to prevent miscast metal from spattering is a worthwhile safety precaution. It should operate smoothly (oil before each casting operation) and should be without vibration, which could cause a miscasting.

To prepare the machine for casting, it is wound clockwise three to five times (follow manufacturer's instructions), depending on the pressure-tension force needed, which in turn depends on the size of the casting. The arm is locked in position, with the counterweight end in front of the operator, by raising the stop rod pin in the base and allowing the arm to press against it. The stop rod should be to the left of the operator when he is in the operating position in front of the machine. It is released later, when the casting is about to begin, by moving the arm *manually* until the pin falls back into the base.

The machine should have the proper-sized flask cradle to correspond with the flask number, so that it will hold and automatically *center* the crucible, which is snapped in place. The crucible carrier and the crucible are next, close up against the flask cradle. The crucible itself can be lined with asbestos, cut to shape. If this is made wet, it can be pressed into place. The asbestos liner helps to keep the crucible clean and prevents contamination from other metals if the crucible has been used for them. It is advisable, however, to reserve a special crucible for one metal only; in this case, a liner is probably not necessary.

Before the flask is heated for burnout, the arm must be weighted to counterbalance the weight of the flask. On some models, the counterweight is the one stamped with the corresponding number on the flask. The model described here is the Kerr Centrifico. Place the *invested flask* in casting position. Loosen the center retaining nut till the arm rocks. Set the secondary arm in line with the weight arm, and hold it there by inserting a matchstick at the arm junction. Move the weights in or out toward the center until the whole arm balances. If necessary, add extra weights. Lock the weights against each other. Tighten the center nut. Remove matchstick.

HEATING THE METAL

The metal used in casting may be an ingot, large shot, scrap, or a combination of these.

21. In preparation for casting, the metal must be weighed. Dhaemers calculates the amount of metal necessary by multiplying the weight of the wax form by 13 (for rings) and then adding ¼ to ½ ounce (for pins). The metal is heated with a little flux while it is in the crucible on the casting machine. This occurs just before the flask mold is ready to be removed from the kiln. When ready, the flask is placed in the flask cradle (upper left) behind the crucible. The flask-crucible arm and the arm with weights are then balanced. The machine, which operates on spring tension, is wound three times. The arm is held in tension by pulling up a pin from the base.

It must be clean. Before it is placed in the crucible for melting, it should be freed of contaminating oxides or grease by annealing, pickling, and washing. The melting of the metal should be *timed with the burnout* so that flask and metal are ready simultaneously. It is possible to melt the metal *first,* so that it forms a solid mass, and then to reheat it just before placing the flask. Sprinkle the asbestos with a flux, such as boric acid. Add flux at intervals during heating. To keep porosity of the casting to a minimum, the metal should be covered at all times during the melting with a *reducing flame.* This prevents oxidation of the metal, which makes it porous. A reducing flame in an acetylene torch is marked by a tinge of yellow in the part of the flame from the torch mouth to the center; in an oxygen-gas flame, add just enough gas to a neutral flame to turn the flame from blue to slightly yellow.

Put on asbestos gloves, remove the flask from the burnout furnace or kiln with a pair of large *flask tongs,* gripping it firmly, and place it in the flask cradle, on its side, *with the sprue hole pointing toward the crucible* and the bottom resting against the back of the arm. Push the crucible up against the flask with the tongs. The crucible should be in a position facing you at the other side of the retaining nut. The metal is in the crucible.

22. By this time, the metal has solidified and must be reheated to a liquid after being sprinkled with some commercial casting flux. The arm of the machine is pulled back and the holding pin is allowed to drop back into the base. The arm is then released and the spring pressure whirls it around at great speed. The centrifugal force causes the molten metal to flow through the crucible opening directly into the sprue openings in the mold, completely filling the mold cavity.

23. After the metal has lost its redness and the mold has cooled off, the flask is placed under running cold water. This dissolves the investment and exposes the casting.

24. The casting recovered from the mold, with sprues and "button" attached. Both of these are removed with either snips or saw and can be incorporated along with new metal in the next casting.

25. Any investment material not removed in the water can be eliminated by heating the metal and putting the whole object into a 10–1 solution of sulphuric acid and plain water. The article is then finished in the usual way.

Sprinkle the metal with some flux and apply the reducing flame. If any impurities or foreign particles appear on the surface of the molten metal, they can be picked up with a carbon stirring rod, a graphite rod, or a slate pencil. Keep the metal covered at all times with the reducing part of the flame, and as soon as it begins to melt, sprinkle it with a little flux. When the metal has formed a ball, continue heating it to bring the temperature up even higher and insure complete and rapid filling of the mold cavity. *Do not overheat* the metal to the point where it seems to boil. Add a bit of flux just before releasing the metal into the mold. With the left hand, move the counterweight arm of the crucible slightly clockwise, and allow the stop rod to drop. Then *release the arm* (simply let it go) and remove the flame, simultaneously. The arm will spin from the spring pressure and should be allowed to continue to do so till it stops, at which point the metal has solidified. If there is no vibration or oscillation, there is no danger of hot flying metal.

Cast sterling silver cuff links, by Jean Claude Champagnat, Paris. An imprint from the purchaser's fingers was made in the wax and then cast. *Photo by Jacqueline Guillot, Connaissance des Arts.*

Ring of 18-karat gold, by Jean Claude Champagnat, Paris. The casting process is capable of reproducing almost any natural, dimensional form in nature. In this ring, a natural plant has been electroplated first, then cast in separate parts, arranged, and soldered. *Photo by Del Bocca.*

Cast 18-karat gold ring with diamond, by Jean Claude Champagnat, Paris. The surface was treated with chisels to achieve the texture. *Photo by Del Bocca.*

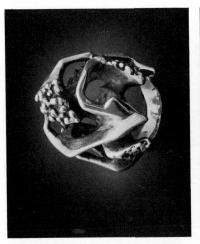

OPPOSITE: Pin, 16-karat gold, by Ruth Radakovich, Encinitas, California. Lost-wax cast section of a yucca seed pod burned out. Two black opal doublets. *Photo: Ferdinand Boesch.*

Cast silver ring, by Oppi Untracht. Concave surface forms were used as a light-catching device. *Photo by Lex Tice.*

Side view of the same ring.

REMOVING INVESTMENT AND SPRUES

Allow the flask to cool after the redness has gone out of the metal (visible at the sprue opening). This usually takes about five minutes for sterling and twice that for gold. Do not rush the cooling, because quenching the metal too quickly may crack the casting. When it is cool, hold the flask under cold running water with tongs, or immerse it in cold water. Most of the investment material will disintegrate. Observe the color of the investment. It should be bone white. If it is discolored, the deduction is that insufficient time was allowed for the burnout and there is a carbonaceous residue from the wax. This may cause a porous casting. Should some investment remain on the casting, it can be removed by heating it with a torch and dropping it into water or by boiling it in a 10 to 1 solution of sulphuric acid.

The sprues are removed by sawing them off with a jeweler's saw or by using a pair of nippers, if they are thin enough. The remaining points are filed or ground off with a grinding disc on a flexible shaft.

Finishing treatment is done in the usual way.

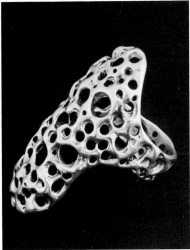

Cast gold ring, by Henri Leighton. The textural emphasis was heightened by oxidizing the background and polishing the raised surfaces. *Photo by Lex Tice.*

Cast gold ring, by Henri Leighton. The openwork texture was created in the original wax by inserting a heated tool and forming the holes. *Photo by Lex Tice.*

Cast gold ring with topaz, by Henri Leighton. The stone setting prongs are a part of the casting and were carefully forced over the stone to secure it in place. *Photo by Lex Tice.*

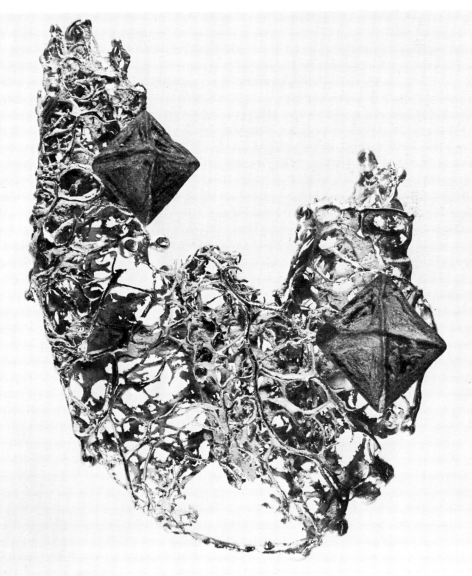

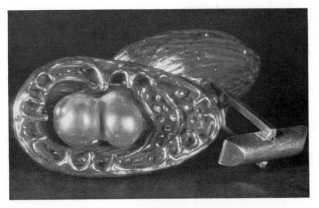

Investment cast silver cuff links with twin pearls, by Robert Dhaemers. *Photo by Margaret Dhaemers.*

RIGHT: Cast bronze bracelet, from Benin, Africa. The double rows of "buttons" between the figures represent cowrie shells. The alternately inverted male figures show Portuguese influence. *American Museum of Natural History, New York.*

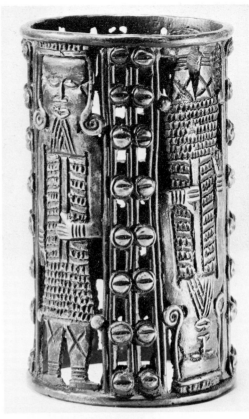

BELOW: Cast silver necklace, by Robert Dhaemers. *Photo by Margaret Dhaemers.*

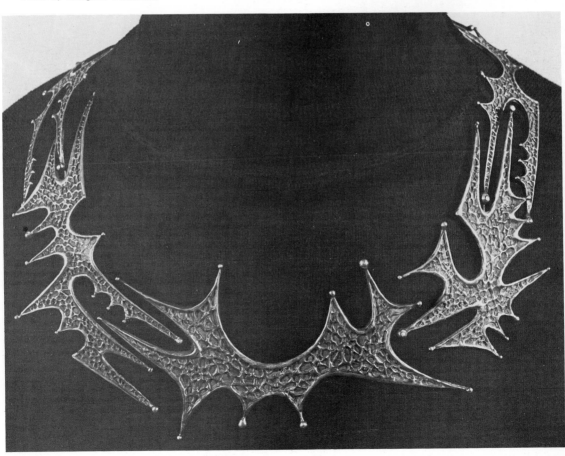

Cast gold pin with pearl, by Robert Dhaemers. The pearl is held in the setting by forcing the cast, round-ended "prongs" over onto the gem. This must be done carefully to prevent their breaking. *Photo by Margaret Dhaemers.*

Cast silver cuff link, by Jean Claude Champagnat, Paris. The form was inspired by the spiral core of a seashell and is "wound" into the cloth. *Photo by Del Bocca.*

Cast gold necklace, from Ashanti, Ghana, Africa. Length: approximately 15½ inches. *Museum of Primitive Art, New York. Photo by Charles Uht.*

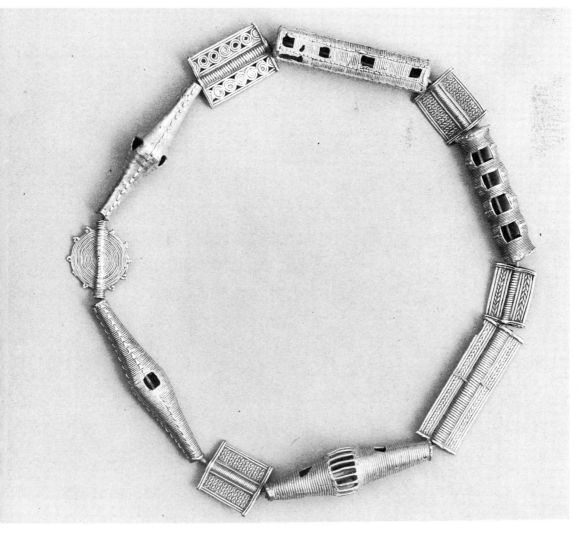

1. A piece of the investment material of a size that a flask can accommodate is shaped and carved with a design. Various cutting and scraping tools can be used and an endless variety of textures created. The wax is applied directly to the carved investment up to the thickness desired for the casting; it is then covered with investment and centrifugally cast as usual.

3. The casting shown from the front, with the formerly carved intaglio design now seen in relief. The sprues are removed and the pin is finished in the usual way.

CARVED-CORE CASTING.

Robert Winston demonstrates the method of creating a pin by the use of a carved core.

2. The back of the pin, shown here with sprues still attached after casting, can also be treated with any design or textural decoration desired.

Pin in double cast gold and bronze, by Robert Winston. The center of the pin is core cast in bronze. A second investment for gold is made over this bronze casting, thus permanently joining the two metals, one cast upon the other. After finishing, the bronze is chemically treated to create a greenish-blue patina that contrasts with the polished gold.

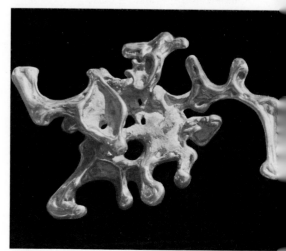

Electroplating and Electroforming

The principles involved in electroplating and electroforming were discovered and established by Michael Faraday in 1833. His two *laws* established the chemical and electrical relations that exist in electrochemical or electrolytic reactions. This knowledge has developed into an enormous store of information about the behavior of metals under such conditions through the work of others, and the growth of the large electrochemical metal plating industry. The processes which in industry make large, expensive installations necessary can be scaled down to their essentials and with a relative minimum of equipment can be practiced by the craftsman. Large areas of surface treatment and forming are possible by these means that the craftsman would not otherwise have at his disposal.

Electroplating, of which electroforming is an application, is a method of covering an article with a thin coat of metal, called a *plating,* by *electrodeposition.* Electroforming is a process of reproducing or creating a metal object through the use of a model, metallic or nonmetallic; permanent or temporary; by the electrical deposition of metal upon the model while it is suspended in a *metal salt* plus *acid* bath, a *neutral* bath, or an *alkaline* bath. The time needed for sufficient deposits to occur in electroforming is much greater than that needed for electroplating. Besides using the electroforming process to create or reproduce entire models, it can also be used to build up surfaces and create surface textures on existing metal objects. In their creative approach to this industrial process, the work of Stanley Lechtzin and June Schwarcz have pointed directions in each area which offer challenging possibilities for the craftsman.

The Electroplating Process

In simple terms, the process of electroplating and electroforming consists of allowing an electric current from a dry cell, a storage battery, a direct current generator, or the terminals of a rectifier, to flow through a solution between two metal or electric conducting material units placed in the solution at the positive and negative terminals of a *direct current circuit.* The current flow in this circuit results in the release of charged metal particles called *ions* into the solution. They pass from the *positive* terminal (or *electrode*) known as the *anode,* through the solution, and become deposited on the *negative* terminal (or electrode) called the *cathode.* The solutions or baths are called *electrolytes* as they are the conductors of the electric current. The battery or rectifier (the electrical source) forces the direct current through the anode to the electrolyte and deposits the positively charged ions on the negatively charged cathode. A metal bar or plate (gold, silver, copper, etc.) hung or suspended in the solution is the anode and slowly dissolves metal ions into the solution while the current acts on it. Attached to the cathode wire is the article upon which the metal is being deposited, making the article itself the cathode. (If the article is made of a nonmetallic material and is therefore nonconductive, it must be treated to make it so.) Insoluble anodes are also used, made of stainless steel and platinum, and in this case, the metal source is the contents of the electrolyte which ultimately become depleted and must be replenished. Besides the soluble compound of the metal to be deposited, the plating bath can contain additional agents to brighten, increase the conductivity, or the *throwing power* of the metal (its ability to cover all areas of the model).

The basic equipment for electroplating and electroforming are the same. The difference occurs in the concentration of the electrolyte solution, the time in the bath, the voltage, and the temperature used.

Pin by Stanley Lechtzin, electroformed in silver over copper foil, then gold plated. Set with smoky quartz.

Electroplating and electroforming equipment: a simplified arrangement for small scale use by craftsmen: 1. Selinium rectifier 2. Anode and cathode wire 3. Electrician's clips 4. Bus bars 5. Wood bus bar rack 6. Electric hotplate, two burner 7. Pyrex glass beakers: the first contains the article suspended from the anode bus bar for cleaning, the second is for rinsing, the third is the plating beaker with the anode plate and the article suspended from the cathode bar to be plated

ELECTRIC POWER

The electric current used for most plating and forming operations is between one-half to twelve volts, *Direct Current* (DC). Since most available electricity is produced at either 110 or at 220 volts, and *Alternating Current* (AC), the voltage must be reduced and the current changed to DC. For this purpose a motor generator or a rectifier are used, with or without rheostatic controls. These pieces of equipment are relatively expensive but are necessary for extensive use. For small work it is possible to use a dry cell battery or a six-volt 100-ampere-hour automobile storage battery which can be converted to make it suitable, and can be recharged when necessary. The voltage must be reduced to avoid burning the plating. To do this, since the battery consists of three two-volt cells in series to produce six volts, the connections between the cells are cut with a hacksaw. The three positive terminals are then connected to *one common conductor,* and the three negative terminals are connected to another conductor. Since the cells are now parallel, they are capable of producing a higher current at a lower voltage. The battery now produces two volts, and triple its former ampere-hour capacity. A voltmeter, used to measure the amount of current pressure (the voltage), an ammeter that measures the amperage or amount of current being used, and a rheostat, used to adjust current density, can be added to the circuit. If only one solution is used at a time (usual with craftsmen), no rheostat is needed as the surface area of the piece being plated raises the amperage automatically.

ELECTROPLATING AND
ELECTROFORMING EQUIPMENT

Electroplating Selinium Rectifier Of the several types of rectifiers, the selinium rectifier is recommended as best suited to the craftsman's needs. Smaller and larger units are available (10 amps, 10 volts; 25 amps, 6 volts; 50 amps, 6 volts), but the 25-amp or 50-amp model is recommended. The rectifier operates on 110 volts, single phase, 60 cycle, and converts the current from AC to DC, necessary for plating. Allowing the anode and cathode wires to touch, or overloading the rectifier will cause the fuse to burn out. It can be replaced with a 5-amp radio or auto fuse by unscrewing the fuse holder. Extra fuses should be kept in preparation for such an event. When the rectifier is not in use, it should be turned off, and if the period of nonuse is extensive, it should be turned on for an hour or two at least once a month. This is done to avoid the accumulation of moisture between the rectifier plates which could incapacitate it. Storage of a rectifier should be in a dry place.

Copper wire capable of carrying a 25-ampere or 50-ampere load, depending on the rectifier amperage, is used to carry the current from the rectifier to the copper anode bus bar or rod, and complete the circuit from the copper cathode bus bar or rod to the rectifier.

Copper bus bars or rods made of rigid copper of suitable length are suspended above the electric or gas hotplate at a height which allows sufficient clearance for the size of the beakers or tanks used to contain the electrolyte solution. A supporting rack made of wood, transite, or any insulating material can be made to hold the bars a distance of at least three inches apart to avoid contact between them. If the electroplating setup is permanent, the wire connecting the cathode bar to the rectifier can be permanently attached. The anode wire can terminate in an electrician's alligator or a battery clip to allow it to be easily changed to the two-, six-, or eight-volt terminals of the rectifier as required.

Thin copper wire (20 gauge) is needed to connect the anodic copper bus bar to the anode plate which is suspended from the bar to hang along the inside of the beaker or tank. Another wire is attached to the cathode bar and is attached to the article being plated which is the cathode. Electrician's clips can be used to facilitate these connections, or the wires can simply be wrapped securely around the bar. Do not use clips on anode plate or cathode object.

Pyrex beakers with covers, one quart capacity or larger depending on the size of the object being processed, are used to contain the electrolyte solution. Flat objects such as a plaque which is being electroplated or electroformed can be placed in a flat, Pyrex glass tray deep enough to submerge the article completely. Glass containers are breakable and should be handled with care. If a gas burner is used to heat the solution, a metal mesh, grill, or plate should be placed beneath the glass container. The temperatures used for plating are relatively high. As a safety factor, it might be advisable to use porcelain enamel containers or stainless steel tanks. Porcelain enamel containers are recommended for electrocleaning. If stainless steel containers are used over the element of an electric hotplate they may become electric conductors and interfere with normal electroplating processes. To avoid this, place a thin asbestos pad for insulation between the hotplate element and the stainless steel container. When using Pyrex glass beakers, a recommended procedure for added safety is to place the beaker in a stainless steel or porcelain enameled container holding water, which makes a double boiler arrangement. This is a precaution which allows the solution to be caught should the glass container break.

A *two-burner electric hotplate stove,* AC-DC, with on and off switches or a gas burner is used as the heat source for solutions. Above the burner and the containers for the solutions the two copper bus bars are arranged on a rack.

Anode plates, soluble when the current is on in electroplating solutions, theoretically are supposed to keep the metal content of solutions constant. Most of them work at high efficiency, but with some it is necessary to replenish the solution with soluble salts or an addition of the concentrated solution if commercially prepared solutions are used. In this case, follow the instructions which come with the solutions. Soluble anode plates are available in fine gold, fine silver, pure copper, and pure nickel. Platinum clad anodes and stainless steel anodes are nonsoluble, and in these cases the metal comes from the solution.

Stop-off lacquer is used to prevent areas of the metal or other surfaces from being plated while in the solution. Lacquer thinner can be used to dilute lacquer, and is also used to clean the brush with which the lacquer is applied. With the use of stop-off lacquer, it is possible to produce multicolored metal platings by exposing only a portion of the metal at a time to different metal baths. The thinner is also used to remove lacquer which is no longer wanted on the metal. The stop-off lacquer must be of a type that will withstand the heat of the plating solution without damage.

Plating solutions can be prepared by the plater from formulas, or they can be purchased already prepared from suppliers such as Hoover and Strong, Inc. According to the metal desired, the following are available. Gold (pure, yellow, pink, red, 14 karat, 18 karat, dark green, antique), silver, copper, nickel, and rhodium. Also available are electrocleaning solutions and electrostripping solutions. These instructions are recommended for products prepared by Hoover and Strong:

Temperature control is not highly critical, but the suggested temperatures are designed to produce the best results.

Used plating solutions should be kept in separate, labeled containers. These should be covered to avoid contamination from dust and to prevent evaporation. A container of known capacity can be used to indicate the evaporation of water from the solution while it was in use. Distilled water can then be added in the amount necessary to replenish the solution to its original amount. Any solution in which the presence of dust or dirt is apparent should be filtered to prevent the settling of particles on the plated surface which would cause imperfections.

Floating thermometer, or dial thermometer as used in photography.

Ribbed glass funnel to help pour electrolyte solutions into or from containers.

Paper filters used with a funnel to remove dust and dirt or sludge from solutions.

Asbestos insulating pad to act as an insulation between metal containers and electric hotplate elements.

Running water source near the plating bench area.

Rubber gloves to protect the hands against harmful chemicals. They should be rinsed in clear water before storage.

Plater fuses of the amperage needed kept near the rectifier in case of need.

Plating bench or table, and an exhaust fan or hood.

Electrician's alligator clips or battery clips to facilitate connections.

An electromagnetic stirrer can be used in electroforming to help agitate the solution which increases the speed of the metal deposit.

Solution	Temperature (Fahrenheit)	Solution parts	Water parts	Voltage	Maximum covering area in square inches
Gold (all colors)	180°	1	Use straight	6	80
Silver	70°	1	3	2	238
Copper	100°	1	3	6	39
Nickel	70°	1	Use straight	2	48
Rhodium	110°	1	Use straight	6	39
Electrocleaner	180°	1	3	6	40
Electrostripper	180°	1	3	6	40

Electroplating and Electroforming Procedures

The procedure described here is the simplest possible for electroplating and electroforming. The objective in electroplating is the formation of smooth, thin, highly polished coatings of metal with a minimum of necessary post-plating polishing. Platings of short duration produce only very thin thicknesses of metal which do not have good wearing qualities. The most important factor in achieving a smooth, bright plate is the condition of the surface *before* plating, and a state of *absolute cleanliness of the surface.* Polishing procedures and finishes are discussed in the section on Metal Finishing, page 394. Two additional methods of preparing the metal for electroplating are at the disposal of the plater. These are *electrocleaning* and *electrostripping.*

Metal models prepared for electrodeposition must be absolutely clean, free of grease, oxides, or sulphides. If these are not removed they would impede and impair plating and produce an imperfect result. Electrocleaning is a method designed to do a part of this job—the removal of all adhering dirt and greases.

ELECTROCLEANING

A 20-gauge copper wire is attached to the article and then to the anode bus bar. A stainless steel pot is made the cathode by attaching it to the cathode bar with a wire which is clipped to the edge of the pot. A prepared electrocleaning solution made according to instructions is placed in the pot and heated to 180° F. A six-volt current is then turned on and the article with wire attached is immersed into the solution.

An alkaline solution for an electrocleaning bath can be prepared by mixing one ounce of Oakite to one quart of water.

Formerly, the anode and cathode were reversed on object and pot, but now it is believed that though the cathode produces twice the amount of hydrogen as the anode produces oxygen, the anode plating-off of dirt is more efficient. The hydrogen and oxygen vigorously agitate the solution and dislodge dirt while the alkaline solution which contains a wetting agent (most are salts of organic sulfonic acids) emulsifies and saponifies greases and oils.

After a twenty-second immersion, the article is removed, washed in cold water, and dipped into a standard cold pickle solution of sulphuric acid which is intended to remove oxides which the cleaning solution will not do. It is then removed while held by the wire, thoroughly rinsed in cold water, and is ready for plating. It can, however, then be put into a bright dip acid solution and again rinsed before immersion into the plating solution. *DO NOT TOUCH THE METAL SURFACE* at any point, as dirt thus deposited will defeat the whole purpose of electrocleaning. If it must be handled, this should be done with clean copper tongs.

A test of whether the electrocleaner has done its work is to observe the surface of the metal while it is being washed under running water after it is taken from the electrocleaner. Should there be any *waterbreak,* that is, places where the water runs off and will not adhere, this is an indication of the presence of oil or grease. In this case, the metal should be returned to the electrocleaner and processed again.

ELECTROSTRIPPING

Electrostripping is the opposite function of electroplating. The metal on the surface of the article is *removed* electrolytically to produce a bright, clean surface, and clean places which are otherwise inaccessible, to prepare the metal for plating. The article is made the anode by suspending it from the anode bar by a copper wire, and a piece of brass is used as the cathode. Upon this the stripped metal is deposited and can later be reclaimed. The solution used is specially prepared for electrostripping and is usually a cyanide solution. Should the article become dark during this process, it can be polished with a scratch brush, returned to the solution, and submerged till the desired bright condition is attained. Old plating can be removed in this way in preparation for replating an article. After stripping, rinse the article thoroughly in cold water and commence with the plating bath. Any articles that have a protecting coat of lacquer must have this removed with lacquer thinner prior to electrostripping.

ELECTROLYTIC PLATING SOLUTIONS

It is probably more convenient to purchase ready-made solutions for electroplating and electroforming to which only distilled water need be added to prepare them for use, but some knowledge of their contents is necessary to an understanding of the plating process.

Gold Baths Gold baths consist of dilute cyanide solutions, most of which are alkaline in nature. Because of the high cost of gold, thin deposits are very often made on other base metals. A deposit of 0.0001 inch has good wearing qualities. Gold plating may be done on lower gold karat articles to give them the appearance of a higher quality of gold, or simply to heighten the color. It is also done on gold-filled objects to cover those parts which expose the other metal. Silver articles are often plated with gold to render them impervious to oxidation, as even alloyed gold does not oxidize very quickly in air, and when pure, hardly at all.

To avoid the necessity for polishing after plating which would in effect result in the removal of the very gold which has been plated, the article should be highly polished *before* plating. Besides the usual cleaning operations already described, it might be necessary to bright-dip the article. Brass, copper, nickel, and silver are all easily gold-plated. Insoluble anodes such as stainless steel, Nichrome, or hard carbon are frequently used, but a pure gold anode is also used. When the anodes are insoluble, the metal comes from the solution which must be replenished when necessary. Prepared solutions are available in several different colors of gold. The contents of only one is given here.

Gold Plating Bath
(fine gold, 24 karat color)

Water	1 gallon
Sodium *or*	½ ounce
Potassium gold cyanide	
(use either one)	
Sodium cyanide	½ to 1 ounce
Disodium phosphate	½ to 2 ounces
Sodium ferrocyanide	¼ ounce
(heightens color)	(approximately)

Insoluble anode of stainless steel, cathode-current density 1 to 5 amperes per square foot, 2½ to 6 volts. Flash deposits (thin coats) are possible in fifteen to twenty seconds. For longer, thicker deposits, the article may have to be removed, buffed to smooth any roughness, and reimmersed. Wash immediately after plating in cold clean water, then hot water to avoid water staining or spotting. Dry in a warmed container of clean hardwood sawdust or crushed corncob.

Gold Immersion Bath
(without electric current)

Water	1 gallon
Sodium cyanide	3 ounces
Sodium *or*	½ ounce
potassium gold cyanide	
Sodium bisulfite	2 ounces
Caustic potash	2 ounces

Heat the solution to 180° F and maintain this heat while plating. Immerse the article suspended by a thin copper wire. Only a few seconds of immersion are necessary as a prolonged immersion would not add thickness to the deposit. Once the article is covered with a thin gold plating, it acts as a solid gold article and the deposit ends. Gold immersion deposits are very thin and not as durable as those of regular gold plating baths.

As the gold in these plating and immersion baths formulas comes from the sodium or potassium gold cyanide in the solution, it is gradually diminished in use and needs replenishing. Some amount is removed with the article each time one is taken from the bath. This is called *drag-out*. The loss, which can become expensive, can be reduced by dipping the article immediately after removal into a container of clean distilled water kept for this purpose. This water can be saved and used to replenish the bath when necessary, thereby returning to the solution what it has lost.

Silver Baths Silver baths contain dissolved silver cyanide in a potassium cyanide solution. Silver has strong throwing power and therefore comes out of the solution with a dull surface which must be polished to attain luster. Brighteners such as carbon disulfide are added to form bright deposits. The solution does not have to be heated but can operate at room temperature or about 70° F.

Silver Strike Bath. To promote adhesion in the electroplating of silver, an extra bath known as a "strike" bath is sometimes used to quickly deposit a thin metal plate. This is especially used when silver electroplating is to be done on nonferrous base metals. To insure good adhesion (this is true in all cases) the model must be in contact electrically *before* immersion. The copper contact wire from the cathode to the model should make contact at a point where it will not be noticed later. Striking is done at a high current density and is done to prevent the formation of a very thin plate of nonadherent metal called an *immersion deposit* that *might* occur in an ordinary bath. This solution contains a low concentration of metal ions and a high cyanide concentration. A strike bath of thirty seconds is enough, after which the model can be placed immediately into the silver bath.

Silver Strike Bath

Silver (metal)	0.4 to 0.6 troy ounces per gallon
Free sodium cyanide	8 to 12 ounces per gallon
Sodium carbonate	1 to 4 ounces per gallon

Silver Bath

Silver (metal)	2 to 3.5 troy ounces per gallon
Silver cyanide	2.5 to 4.3 troy ounces per gallon
Potassium carbonate	5 to 15 avoirdupois
Potassium cyanide, free	4 to 7 avoirdupois
Brightener, fresh solution	⅛ fluid ounce per gallon

For plating, the article remains in the solution for fifteen to thirty seconds. The model can remain in the solution from fifteen minutes to more than twelve hours for electroforming, depending on the desired thickness, but a four-hour bath is sufficient for most purposes.

The brightener is made by mixing a quart of strike solution with a few ounces of carbon disulfide, letting the mixture stand for a few days, stirring it occasionally. A small amount of the clear liquid formed is added to the bath, the exact amount determined only by experiment and observation of the results.

Copper Baths Copper baths mainly contain acid sulfate and alkaline cyanide. The main contents of copper acid baths are copper sulfate and sulphuric acid along with other added agents. Cyanide baths contain cuprous cyanide and potassium or sodium cyanide. These combine to form complex cyanides.

Copper Bath (Acid)

Copper sulfate,
20 to 33 ounces per gallon of water (24 recommended)
Sulphuric acid,
6 to 13 ounces per gallon (6 recommended)

Anode: Rolled, cast, or electrolytic copper, about equal in area to the cathode area.
Cathode current density: 28 to 56 amperes per square foot of plating surface.

Copper Bath (Cyanide)

Copper cyanide,	3 ounces per gallon
Sodium cyanide,	4.5 ounces per gallon
Sodium carbonate,	2 ounces per gallon

Cathode current density: 40 to 50 amperes per square foot.
Temperature: 120° F to 175° F.

For use as a bath prior to silver plating and electroforming, immersion for two to five minutes produces a sufficient deposit of copper. Rinse thoroughly prior to immersion in the silver bath.

Nickel Baths Nickel baths contain nickel sulfate, nickel chloride, and boric acid, and are used mainly to plate metals before a final chromium plating, as it is possible to produce very bright nickel platings. It is also used as a plating prior to making one of rhodium, as its denseness allows it to be polished to a high luster, thus giving brilliance to the rhodium plate.

Rhodium Baths Rhodium belongs to the platinum metals group of which platinum, palladium, and rhodium are used in electroplating. It is used mainly for decorative purposes, especially over white gold jewelry, particularly those which contain nickel in the alloy which discolors after a short time in use. Rhodium plating produces a hard, brilliant, blue-white color, is easily applied, has good throwing power, and does not demand critical current conditions.

Rhodium baths contain rhodium sulfate dissolved in dilute sulphuric or phosphoric acid. Rhodium plating solutions are sold in concentrated solutions. If the article plated has been properly polished before plating, polishing the rhodium after plating is not necessary. Except in the case of plating platinum and white gold alloys, it is standard practice to precede the rhodium plating with a nickel plating. It is used with an insoluble platinum anode, so that replenishing the plating solution becomes necessary. If rhodium replenisher syrup is used, the bath is first brought to its original volume by adding distilled water, and then the syrup is added a drop at a time to bring the solution to its original amber color.

Chromium Baths Chromium baths because of the difficulties and dangers in their use are not recommended to any but the experienced plater.

CAUTION: All cyanide-containing solutions and solids are *highly poisonous.* Avoid contact with or touching any part of the skin or face, or contacting foods without thoroughly washing the hands. Use rubber gloves when handling these chemicals. Work in a well-ventilated area, preferably in the presence of an exhaust fan or under an exhaust hood. Breathing the vapors of electroplating solutions is unhealthy.

Electroforming on Metal Models

Electroforming is an application of electroplating. In industry it is practiced mainly to make articles from a model when the intention is to make an exact reproduction. Master records, fountain pen tubings, and articles of jewelry are some of the commercial products of electroforming. Generally a much thicker deposit of metal is produced than in electroplating. Though perfection of surface and reproduction is the main concern of the *commercial* electroplater, the new interest among craftsmen in this process is in a totally different direction. Utilizing the technical knowledge of commerce, the craftsman has begun to create with this process in ways that would be considered undesirable by commercial electroplaters. The use of excessive current, high-temperature solutions, and extended immersions to make the metal "grow" and create interesting surface effects which the craftsman interprets as having aesthetic qualities would certainly be termed unsuccessful results by the average electroformer.

As *all* electrodeposits of metal are crystalline in nature, *extended immersions* in the baths often produce a rough, coarse, crystalline-looking surface as the metal is built up. Such a result is sometimes due to nodular growth which occurs around nuclei as the crystals form radially from impurities in the metal. Other factors influencing the growth of crystals are *current density, temperature of the electrolyte, degree of agitation, the structure of the base metal,* and the *composition of the solution.* Variations in any of these will produce different results. A coarse, columnlike structure can best be made to form on copper in acid solutions. Decreased current density and low throwing power results in the growth of grain size. A higher solution temperature and agitation usually results in an increase in the size of crystals. The size and disposition of crystals on the *base metal* have an influence on the size of the crystals of the electrodeposit, as they often are an extension of the crystals of the base. Holes, projections, pits, scratches, and cracks in the base metal also affect the orientation of crystal growth. Some-

Copper bowl 5½ inches in diameter, by June Schwarcz, Sausalito, California. The inner surface is enameled, the outer surface and edge is built up by electroforming to create texture and dimension, interspersed with enameled areas. *Photo by Ruth Bernhard.*

"Rock Lines," copper panel 10 inches by 7⅞ inches, by June Schwarcz. The surface was etched and enameled, and the textured lines of exposed metal areas were allowed to "grow" by the electroforming process. The resists used can be stop-off lacquer, asphaltum varnish, rosin, wax, or a combination of these. *Collection of Dr. and Mrs. Elliot Lasser. Photo by Jerry Sharp.*

times vertical growth is faster than horizontal growth, producing peaklike columns or conical extensions. Other metals which form coarse structures in simple solutions are cadmium, lead, nickel, tin, silver, and zinc.

As mentioned, it is possible to electrodeposit metal on metal forms both flat or dimensional. Metal will be deposited in an electrolyte on any exposed, clean, metal surface. Whole areas can be covered, or only parts. Textured areas can be created, or only lines and ridges. Should it be desirable for some areas on a metal model *not* to be built up or deposited with metal (such as the back of a plaque or parts of the visible surface in the design), those areas must be protected with a nonconductive material. Stop-out lacquer, any nonmetallic lacquer (there are metallic lacquers meant to act as conductors, and metallic powders can be mixed with lacquers to deliberately make them conductive), varnish, rosin, wax, or asphaltum which must all be allowed to dry completely in order to function properly, can be used. The temperature used in the electrolyte is a determining factor in the choice of stop-out material.

NONMETALLIC MODELS

The object upon which the electrodeposit of metal will occur is variously called the model, mold, mandrel, or matrix. Metal models are naturally attractive and conductive to the deposition of metal. Many nonmetallic materials can also be used if after forming they are made *surface-conductive,* which is a relatively simple matter. (See page 388.)

The ease in creating a model from a nonmetallic material plus the possibility of speed and economy make it attractive. Asbestos, asphalt, cloth, fired ceramic, gelatin, glass, leather, papier-mâché, plaster, plastic, rubber, styrofoam, wax, and wood are all possible materials for making electroforming models. Models are formed by whatever means and tools are suited to the material from which they are made. Nonmetallic models are ordinarily temporary as they are usually made to be used only once and are destroyed after the completion of the deposition of metal.

Some materials such as plastic, rubber, and glass can be used indefinitely, as they are in industry, depending of whether the design allows the easy removal of the reproduction after electroforming. Low-relief electroformed pieces made on carved, plastic sheet can be "popped off" by flexing the plastic if the back was nonconductive and therefore without metal, and if there were no undercuts in the design. In some cases the metal can also be freed or cut away from the mold and reassembled afterward by soldering. If an electroformed model is to be deliberately rendered removable, the original model, depending on its substance, can be treated with a film of graphite, sulfide, oxide, or chromate before electroforming. It can then be separated easily from the model after forming. The model is made surface-conductive by spraying it with a surface-conductive material (see page 389).

Other materials for expendable models such as asphalt, gelatin, papier-mâché, styrofoam, wax, and wood can be heated after electroforming till they either run out or are reduced to an ash. Models made of highly porous materials such as cloth, leather, ceramic, papier-mâché, and wood should be sprayed with a clear lacquer to seal the surface before treating them with a surface-conductive material.

When using styrofoam, parts or pieces can be joined with glue or by heat. Styrofoam is more easily carved with a manually or mechanically heated tool. Where the model is completely enclosed, if provision has not been previously made to allow for the removal of any residue or an escape of gases while burning out the model material, an opening must be made in the electroformed result before the burnout, or expansion of the model material might cause damage to the piece.

SOLID OR HOLLOW OBJECTS

In cases such as jewelry where lightness in weight is desirable, and the thickness of the deposit is sufficient to resist normal use, pieces can be left hollow. Where the weight of the model is not detrimental to the function of the object, it may be left intact within. Where thin deposits need support, hollow cores can be filled with a lightweight material such as sealing wax or shellac. Larger hollow pieces such as sculpture which might require weight can be filled solid with a low-melting alloy of bismuth, cadmium, lead, or tin. The model can be used as a slush mold and the metal poured out before solidifying completely. In a reverse procedure, when electroforming with a high-melting metal such as copper or silver, if it should be desirable to create a hollow *after* electroforming, the model can be heated to a temperature necessary for the melting point of the interior metal which is much lower than that for the surface electroformed metal, and melted out.

PREPARING A NONMETALLIC MODEL.

The electroforming process is demonstrated by Stanley
Lechtzin of Philadelphia.

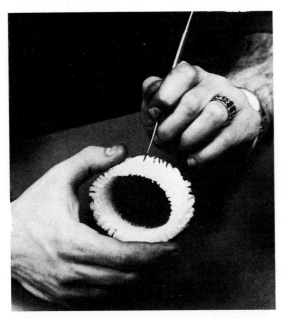

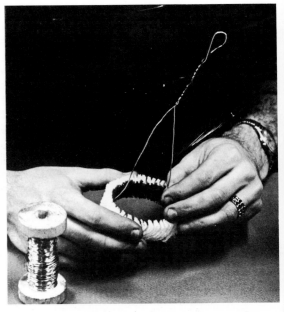

1. A bracelet is carved in Styrofoam by Stanley
Lechtzin. Heating the carving tool helps to make
the cuts more easily. An electrically heated tool can
also be used.

2. The completed model is prepared by attaching
a copper wire to it which will make it a part of the
electroforming circuit.

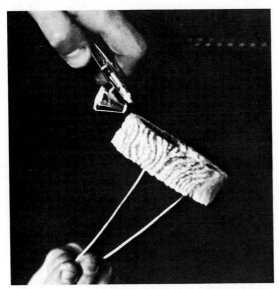

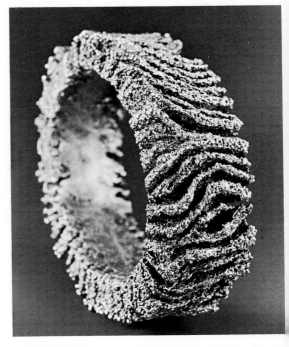

3. The model is sprayed with an ammoniacal silver
nitrate solution to make the surface of the Styrofoam
electroconductive, after which it goes through the
electroforming procedure.

4. The completed silver electroformed bracelet by
Stanley Lechtzin.

Models made of nonconductive material must have their surfaces made electroconductive before they can be electroformed. To do this, the easiest method is to dilute ½ ounce of clear lacquer with an equal amount of lacquer thinner. Add one ounce of finely divided dry copper metal powder (available at most paint stores) and stir together. Be sure that the powder is copper and not a substitute which may not be electroconductive, and that it contains no oil. The mixture is sprayed onto, can be dipped into, or painted with a brush over the model. It should contain only enough lacquer to hold the metallic powder, or the lacquer might become a current inhibitor. An indication of the right amount of metallic powder is the frosty look of the surface when dry. If the surface looks "glassy," too much lacquer was used, and more thinner should be added plus more powder and reapplied. Two coats may be necessary.

The clean model can also be prepared in the same way as a mirror is made. It is painted with a stannous chloride powder which is adsorbed into the surface and the excess is brushed away. Then it is sprayed with an ammoniacal silver nitrate solution followed by a dip into or a spraying with a reducing agent such as formaldehyde. The ammoniacal silver nitrate and the formaldehyde can be sprayed on simultaneously. The result looks like the *back* of a mirror, dull and frosty; the shining surface is actually on the inner surface, and not seen. This process makes the surface electroconductive.

A copper wire, 20 gauge, is attached to the model and then to the cathode. The current is turned on and the model is placed in a copper depositing solution at *low-current density* for two to five minutes to allow the formation of a film of copper thick enough to fix the plating and to allow the use of higher current to increase the deposit. The current is then increased to the desired voltage and the model remains in the solution till the desired thickness is reached. If only copper is to be deposited, that article remains in the solution for the time needed to make the thickness of deposit wanted, which may take as much as twelve hours or more.

If the ultimate deposit is to be silver, the model is allowed to remain in the copper electrolyte for forty to seventy minutes to build up the copper deposit from about 0.007 inch

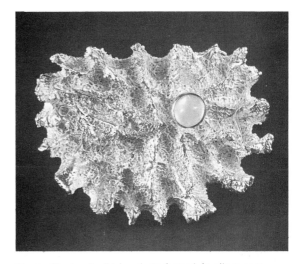

Pin by Stanley Lechtzin, electroformed in silver over a Styrofoam model, set with a moonstone.

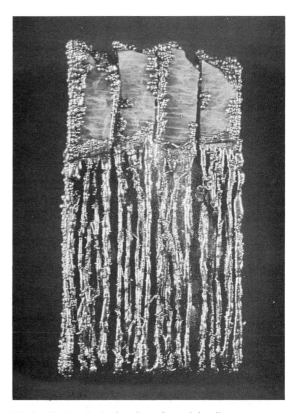

Pin by Stanley Lechtzin, electroformed in silver over a Styrofoam model, set with Amazonites. The stones were placed in position in the Styrofoam and the metal allowed to form in nodules around them, thus forming a setting.

to 0.015 inch to give the form a thick enough base. It is then removed, thoroughly rinsed in cold water and hot water, and deposited in the silver bath. Here it remains till the desired thickness of silver is reached.

ELECTROPLATING AND ELECTROFORMING   389

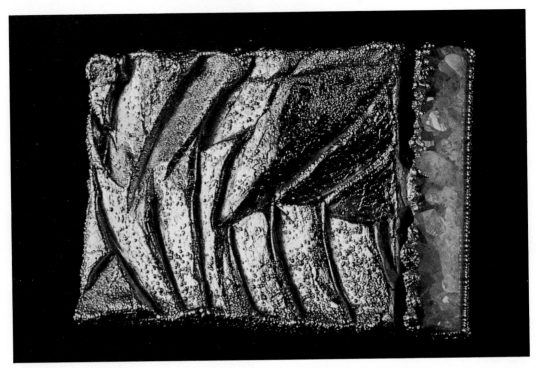

Pin by Stanley Lechtzin, electroformed in silver over a wax model, then gold plated. Set with agate crystals.

Upon removal from the silver bath the surface will be dull and cloudy, and after any further processing, such as the removal of the model material, the electroformed article can be polished. Some model materials (such as styrofoam) leave the surface rather rough and must be smoothed down with abrasives such as tripoli, followed by the usual polishing methods. If the surface must be cleaned and contains inaccessible areas, it may be bright-dipped. The article can also be gold-plated, if desired.

Plating Miscellany

Plating manufacturers make a gold antique plating solution and a dark green solution which produce a *smut finish,* dull and spongy in appearance, brown to blackish or green in color. In ordinary plating practice, this kind of surface is undesirable, but an interesting surface texture is produced. The high points of a piece so plated can be polished bright while the depressions are left dark.

Electroplating can be done while gem stones are already mounted in jewelry without damage to the stone if it can withstand the temperatures and chemicals necessary for the process. Turquoise, opals, natural and cultured pearls, and some synthetic stones cannot be placed in solutions without their destruction. When plating an article containing such stones, they must first be removed and replaced after plating.

Electroforming can be used as a method of making a "setting" for hard stones. The stone is placed in the model material *before* electroforming, and nodules of the electroforming metal are allowed to develop around their edge, thus holding them in place.

Metal enamels can be fired on electroformed surfaces after electroforming, provided that they are heavy enough to withstand the heat needed to fuse enamels (1400° F to 1600° F). Pieces containing enamel already fused to their surface can also be electroplated and electroformed, but the enameled areas should first be protected from chemical action by coating them with stop-off lacquer.

Some articles are more conveniently held in plating and forming solutions by a plating hook or suspended by a sling made of copper wire with which they come into contact.

To plate articles containing soft solder, or made of white metal, lead, or iron, they should be plated first with copper, and can then be plated with other metals.

Stainless steel can be plated by first placing it in a solution of stainless steel conditioner, at room temperature, six volts, with a nickel anode for six minutes for a nickel plating, after which it can be plated with gold or other metals.

The inside of silver articles, such as a water pitcher, teapot, sugar bowl, and creamer, can be gold-plated by pouring the gold plating solution *into* the article as high as it will go without overflowing. Put the article in a tray to catch any solution, and remove any solution which might contact the outside of the piece. Do not turn on the current or start the plating procedure till the article is filled. Suspend the gold anode *inside* the solution, and attach the cathode to the *outside*, possibly to the handle of the piece. Plating continues normally. To cover the edge or exposed areas that are not covered by the solution, mount a sponge on an anode with a copper wire, dip the sponge into the solution, and swab the areas to be plated.

Large areas can be plated without submersion by attaching them to the cathode. At the anode, a copper wire is wrapped around a brush with an end extending into the bristles to make contact with the solution and complete the circuit. The brush is dipped into the solution and applied to the areas to be plated. To avoid contamination of the plating solution, do not allow the metal ferule of the brush to contact the solution, and rinse the brush occasionally in water if more time is needed.

Gold bracelet, made by Arnaldo and Giorgio Pomodoro, Italy. Contrasting decoration of natural and mechanical forms. *Worshipful Company of Goldsmiths, London. Photo by Peter Parkinson.*

High-speed buffing motors are used by the A. Mickelson Silversmith Company of Copenhagen, Denmark, to finish a silver candelabra. The article is dipped from time to time in a vat (seen directly below the cone-shaped cotton buffer), which is filled with a soapy solution designed to remove accumulations that occur while buffing. The buffing is done *wet* for high gloss. *Photo by Oppi.*

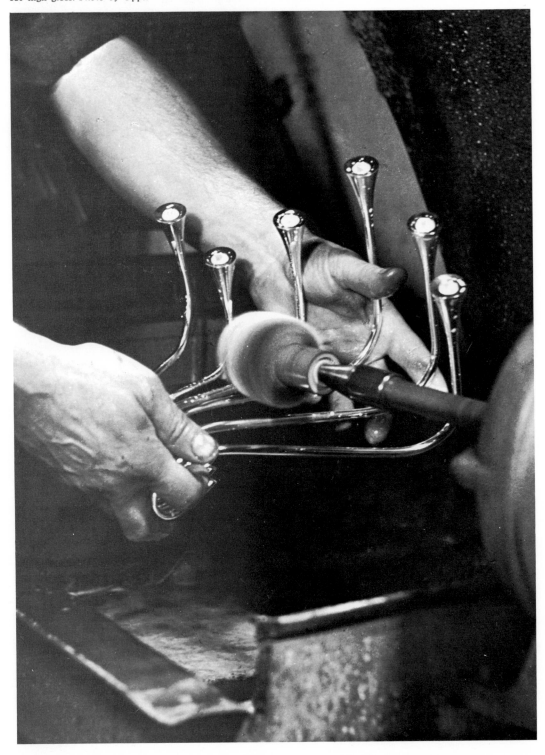

Part Four

METAL FINISHING

Polishing and Grinding

Polishing

Polishing is a method of producing a desired surface on metal by the removal of a certain amount of the surface through subjecting it to various kinds of abrasives. The abrasive material can be applied by hand with a cloth, or by the use of various types of buffing wheels mounted on a buffing motor. The technique chosen and the materials used depend on many variable factors, among which are the condition of the surface of the piece in relation to the desired surface, the method of polishing, that is, whether by hand or machine, the speed of the motor, the size and the material of the buffing wheel, and the abrasive used. Technically, *buffing follows polishing,* and involves very little removal of metal (already accomplished by polishing), its purpose being to bring the condition of the metal to its *final* surface appearance.

HAND POLISHING

The metal polisher has at his disposal hundreds of polishing materials. His biggest problem is deciding on which of them or a combination will be the most efficient, easiest, and most economical method of achieving the desired result.

For hand polishing, when this is necessary or desirable, several *polishing cloths* are available. Abrasive cloths impregnated electrolytically with abrasive grains such as aluminum oxide (which can be bent around objects without cracking), emery cloth of various coarsenesses (there are nine grades, 4/0, 3/0, 2/0, 1/0, 1/2, 1, 1½, 2, and 3, with the number increasing as the grain becomes finer, used on more or less flat work), crocus papers (used to remove scratches), sand or flint papers (used to create uniform texture), rouge cloths (used to impart a high luster to metal), chamois skins (used for cleaning and polishing with the addition of an applied abrasive or polishing agent), and several polishing cloths with commercial names, impregnated with chemical polishing agents (used to remove tarnish and restore luster without scratching), are available. A soft flannel cloth impregnated with rouge is a good final polisher.

A *polishing cloth* can be made of nonlinting canton flannel by immersing it in a hot solution of the following ingredients for one-half hour and then drying it.

Water	1 gallon
Diglycol-stearate	2 pounds
Pearlite Chalk	½ pound
Magnesium carbonate	½ pound
Red lead oxide	¼ pound
A water soluble wetting agent	2 ounces

Hand polishing cloths are often used in place of machine buffers, especially where delicate articles, such as chains and beads, must be polished. A double cloth is shown here polishing Mexican silver beads. The dark side is impregnated with rouge and is used first; the light side, chemically treated, is used for the final luster. *Photo by Oppi.*

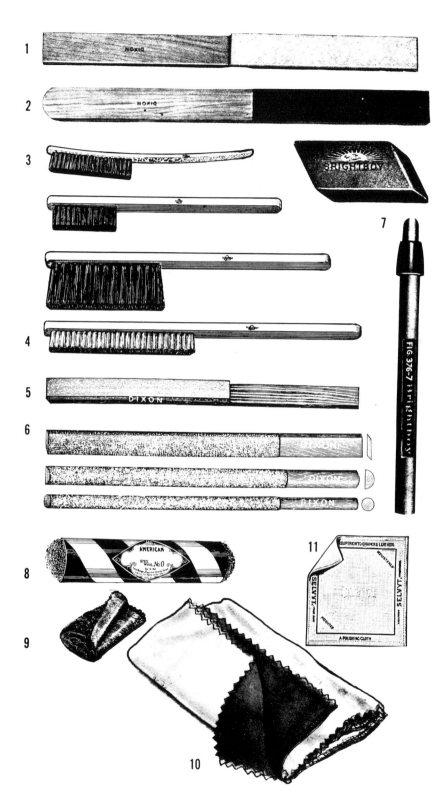

Hand polishing tools: 1. Felt flat hand polishing stick 2. Emery cloth stick 3. Three stiff bristle brushes, extra stiff, stiff, half hard 4. Brass metal wire brush 5. Buckskin or chamois flat hand buff 6. Hand emery buffs, flat, half round, round 7. Brightboy composition stick and eraser 8. Steel wool 9. Steel wool pad 10. Rouge polishing and cleaning cloth 11. Selvyt hand polishing cloth

In addition, there are flat stick hand buffs mounted with felt, buckskin, or chamois, which are used, with the addition of abrasives or polishing compounds, and flat stick buffs mounted with various coarsenesses of emery paper. These are used when polishing motors are not available, or on work which cannot be polished with a wheel.

Inaccessible inner surfaces of small settings or pierced work can be polished by *thrumming*. A cord held at one end in a vise is loaded with a polishing compound and threaded through the piece. The other end is held tight while the work is moved up and back on the cord.

Steel wool is used for a semi-matte finish, but will not remove deep scratches. It is made in various grades from 0000 (the finest) to 3 (the coarsest). The most commonly used grades are 000, 0, and 1. For uniform appearance, steel wool should be rubbed in one direction on the metal.

MOTOR POLISHING

The greatest variety of abrasive and polishing materials are made available for use on various wheels mounted on a polishing motor. This motor should be capable of rotating at 3450 rpm, the speed used for most polishing conditions. Some motors are made with variable speeds ranging from 1740 rpm (the speed usually used for grinding, but also used for some polishing situations such as polishing chain and wire), to 3450 rpm (sometimes with intermediate positions). In the United States, the motors are 110 or 220 volts, 60-cycle, one-phase, AC or DC with ⅓ or ½ hp, with sealed, lubricated ball bearings recommended. Some are mounted with tapered spindles marked R or L for use on the right or left side (do not interchange them or the wheel used will not stay tight, and might fly off), and others have a straight arbor for grinding or polishing. The same motor can be used for both polishing and grinding if it can be adjusted to the proper speed, and fitted interchangeably with tapered spindles or straight arbors (used for grinding). Straight arbors are also made for use on either the right- or left-side motor shaft, and are *not* interchangeable. The ½-inch shaft with a flat side, used for tightening set screws, is the most common, and most materials are easily available for this shaft size, but a ⅜-inch tapered shaft is also usable, though less desirable. The motor shaft should always *rotate toward the polisher*. The on-off switch should be conveniently placed and easily operated.

If a polishing motor with spindles is not available, any suitable motor can be utilized by connecting it with a belt to a bench-mounted *polishing* and *grinding head* onto which spindles and arbors can be mounted. The motor, of course, must be capable of the recommended speeds. (See page 398.)

Buffing wheels can also be mounted on a drill press, a lathe, or a flexible shaft where no other mechanical means of polishing is available. Flexible shafts with 1/10- or 1/15-hp motors can be used with small dental polishing brushes mounted on 3/32-inch arbors or other size depending on the collet capacity, made of bristle or metal wire. These small brushes, miniature buffs, and felt wheels are especially suited to working on small pieces or in otherwise inaccessible areas.

If the motor used cannot be speed-regulated, a compromise can be effected by the *choice of wheel size*. The ultimate wheel speed which is important is the *peripheral speed*, that is, the speed of the edge or outer perimeter of the wheel used. The peripheral speed in feet per minute of a wheel in relation to the wheel diameter and speed of the motor can be calculated from the table on page 399.

For larger diameters, multiply the diameter by the surface speed numbers listed in the one-inch-diameter column.

On a motor with a fixed speed of 3450 rpm, for instance, small diameter grinding wheels can be used. On a motor with a slower speed of 1740 rpm, polishing can be done by using the largest possible wheel to increase surface speed.

OPPOSITE: Motor polishing and buffing equipment: 1. Small buffing motor, 1/10 to ⅛ hp, 110 volts, 60 cycle, to 3500 rpm 2. Buffing and grinding motor, ⅙ to ½ hp, 110–220 volts, 60 cycle, 1750–3500 rpm 3. Heavy duty buffing motor, *not* for tapered spindles; buffs and grinding wheels are mounted between flanges, ⅓ to 1 hp, 1725–3450 rpm, shaft diameter: ½″ to ⅞″, 115–230 volts 4. Tapered buffing spindle 5. Buffing and grinding attachment 6. Drill chuck attachment 7. Lathe splasher to protect the operator against spattering by polishing compounds, and catch lint and grindings 8. Polishing bench with polishing motor, lighted lathe splashers, and suction exhaust

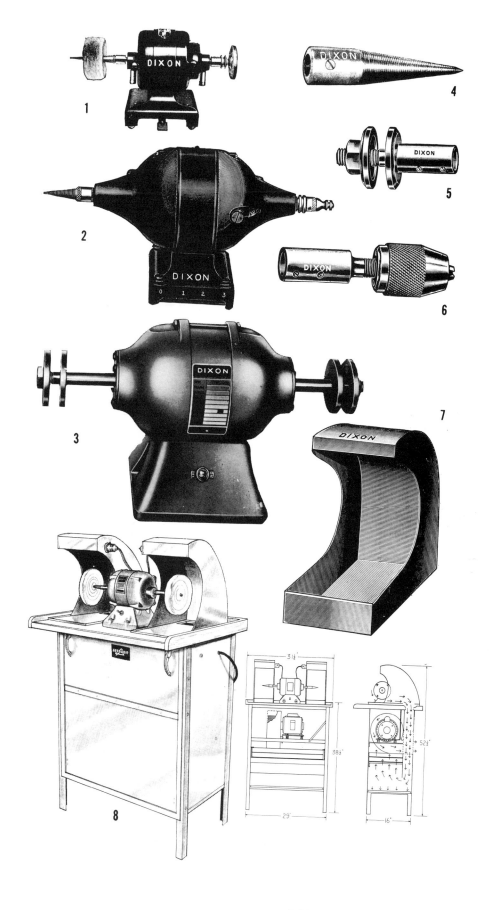

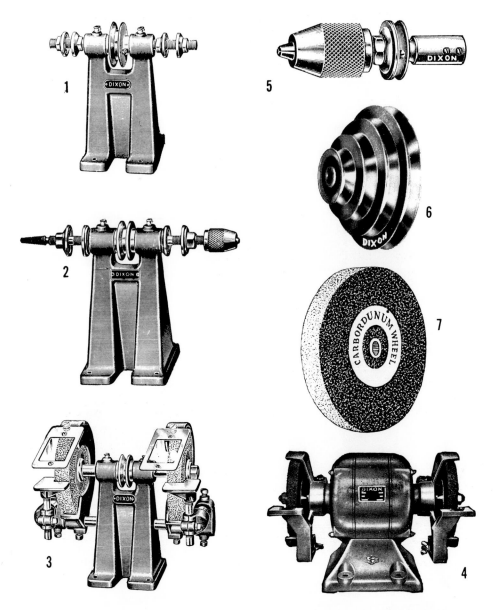

Polishing and grinding heads: 1. Grinding head, 6″ high, 4⅛″ by 4⅛″ base, 5¼ pounds, ½″ diameter spindle, 4″ wheel diameter with ½″ hole 2. Polishing head with chuck, 7½″ high, 5″ by 5″ base, 9 pounds, ¾″ spindle 3. Grinding head with adjustable work rests, wheel guards, spark guards, 1⅜″ flanges, 6″ wheels ½″ hole, 25 pounds 4. Bench grinding motor, ¼ hp, 110–220 volts, AC, 60 cycle, 1 phase 5. Chuck with pully groove 6. V belt pulley, ½″ center hold, 4 step speeds are reduced or accelerated by pulleys of different sizes by changing to the larger for slow speed, and smaller for higher speed 7. Carborundum grinding wheel

POLISHING COMPOUNDS

There are two main groups of polishing compounds: those which *cut the metal* to remove scratches and imperfections, and those which *bring out its color* with luster. There are some compounds which do both simultaneously, called cut and color compounds.

Basically, polishing compounds are abrasives in cake form held together with a bonding agent such as tallow, oil, wax, or other substances. Besides holding the abrasives together, the bonding agent acts as a lubricant during polishing.

Abrasives There are two main groups of abrasives used in polishing compounds, in grinding wheels, and on coated abrasives (cloth- or paper-backed abrasive belts, discs,

Table of Surface Speed (Peripheral Speed in Feet per Minute)

RPM	1" Diameter	4" Diameter	6" Diameter	8" Diameter
900	235	950	1400	1900
1150	300	1200	1800	2400
1200	315	1250	1900	2500
1500	400	1550	2350	3150
1750	450	1800	2750	3650
2000	525	2100	3100	4200
2400	625	2500	3800	5000
2800	730	2900	4400	5850
3000	785	3100	4700	6300
3200	840	3350	5000	6700
3450	900	3600	5400	7200
3750	980	3900	5900	7800
4000	1045	4200	6300	8400
4500	1180	4700	7200	9400
5000	1310	5200	7800	10500
5400	1410	5600	8500	11300
6000	1570	6300	9400	12500

etc. used mounted on portable or stationary rotary power tools). They are the *natural abrasives,* that is, those found in nature, and the *artificial abrasives,* that is, those which are man-made.

THE NATURAL ABRASIVES

Garnet, the most widely used natural abrasive, is a fairly hard mineral used as a coated abrasive in two of its seven known forms, Almandite and Rhodolite. It is mounted on garnet papers and cloths, and maintains its sharpness by fracturing sharply in use so that new, sharp points are constantly being exposed.

Emery, known as an abrasive for centuries, was mined in Turkey and in the Greek islands, taking its name from Cape Emeri on the island of Naxos. It is deep black in color, containing corundum and about 40 per cent iron oxide in the form of magnetite or hematite, which make it a better polishing agent than a cutter. It is used mounted on cloth, paper, and in powder form to remove file marks and scratches from metal. A strip or emery cloth inserted into the slot of a wood ring stick and

Garnet grain, magnified. *The Norton Company.*

Emery grain, magnified. *The Norton Company.*

Flint grain, magnified. *The Norton Company.*

Aluminum oxide grain, magnified. *The Norton Company.*

Silicon carbide grain, magnified. *The Norton Company.*

wrapped around it is used on a buffing spindle to polish the inside of rings.

Flint is the oldest and most commonly known abrasive, and was used by primitive man for striking sparks to make fire and for cutting tools. It is a form of quartz, commonly found everywhere, which breaks with a conchoidal (semicircular cavity) fracture with a sharp edge. It lacks durability, however, as compared to other abrasives, and has a short-lived cutting action. It is used mainly on sandpapers.

Tripoli occurs in schistose deposits of silica, as a pulverized powder. It is a common ingredient in a cutting compound mixed with a grease to form bars and used on a buffing wheel to remove surface scratches.

Lime is calcium oxide containing alumina, iron oxide, and silica, and is used for polishing in powder form.

Whiting is chalk, a form of calcium carbonate used in an impalpable powder form for fine hand polishing, especially after chemically "antiquing" metals, when it is rubbed on the metal with the fingers previously dipped in water.

Pumice is a form of volcanic glass that in its usual hardened glass froth form is full of minute air holes and very light. In the form of powder, it is used for cleaning and polishing.

THE ARTIFICIAL ABRASIVES

Aluminum Oxide, developed in 1897, is the toughest and most durable of all abrasives, and is made by the fusion of the mineral bauxite (an aluminous clay) with a small amount of coke and iron filings in electric furnaces at very high temperatures. Though it is not as hard as silicon carbide, its rugged toughness makes it ideal for use on hard as well as soft metals. It is widely used for coated abrasives.

Silicon Carbide is the hardest and sharpest of artificial abrasives. It was developed in 1891 in a search for a method of producing artificial diamonds, and has a hardness almost as great as the diamond. It is produced by the fusion of silica and coke at high temperatures. Like aluminum oxide, it fractures readily while in use, thus exposing new cutting points as old ones break off. It is used for grinding nonferrous soft metals, glass, enamels, ceramics, and plastics. Its most common form is in coated abrasives.

Coated Abrasives are abrasives which are *glued to various backings* such as paper, cloth, paper-cloth combinations, fiber, and fiber-cloth combinations. Paper backings are used where strength is not needed such as in hand abrading operations. Cloth backings are used where greater strength and flexibility are needed. Paper-cloth combinations have greater resistance to tearing than cloth, but are not as flexible as cloth. Fiber and fiber-cloth combinations are exceptional in durability and strength, and are stiff, suited to use on portable grinders.

Abrasives are glued to backings to form drums, belts, sheet, or discs in a great variety of sizes. The grains of abrasives are placed *on end* electrostatically, which makes them fully exposed, and therefore usable for high-speed work. To separate the grit or grain into various coarsenesses, they are passed through wire or silk screens of various meshes in sizes ranging from 6 to 240. Beyond 240 mesh, fine grain up to 600 is graded by a water flotation system.

The adhesives which hold the abrasive to the backing are hide glue, synthetic rosins, and modifications of each. Hide glue is used in dry polishing or grinding operations where severe grinding heat does not occur. Synthetic rosins

The more commonly used forms of coated abrasives include sheets, rolls, belts, discs, etc. *Behr-Manning Company, a division of the Norton Company, Troy, New York.*

are used when intensive heat is generated. They do not melt or become soft, and they hold the abrasive firmly in place. Waterproof-coated abrasives are made with a rosin bond, and are used when heat generated by tough cutting jobs must be reduced by water-cooling, as the water acts as a lubricant. Modified adhesives have outstanding grit anchorage, and are long-lasting.

Greaseless Compounds are basically glue combined with a sharp abrasive, combined in a stick form. They are applied to a rotating wheel (used exclusively for the particular compound), and dry there, forming a quick-cutting, greaseless surface with a matte effect.

Cutting Compounds are used to remove scratches and prepare the surface for polishing and coloring. Some of the more common kinds are listed here.

Tripoli: Used on all metals. Clean metal after use in a hot water and soap solution to which a few drops of ammonia is added.

Bobbing: Used on all metals, applied to a small solid felt or leather bobbing wheel made with rounded edges.

Aluminum oxide-coated abrasive specialties shown here include cones, discs, bands, pencils, and spira-points. *Behr-Manning Company.*

This photograph shows the manner in which, in certain situations, strips of coated abrasive cloths may be used manually to smooth metal surfaces, such as a bar or edge. *Behr-Manning Company.*

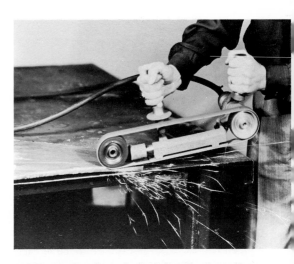

Portable hand units are suited for abrasive actions, such as deburring thick sheets of metal. The unit shown here is mounted with an aluminum oxide belt that is 3 inches by 36 inches. *Behr-Manning Company.*

Platinum: Used for platinum and white gold exclusively to avoid contamination from other metals.

Brown: For use on softer metals.

White Diamond: A fast cutting cut and color composition used on brass, copper, and aluminum. A typical cut and color composition might contain white silica powder and tripoli.

Crocus Composition: Used for fast cutting on copper, brass, and aluminum.

Greaseless Composition: Leaves a matte finish on copper, brass, aluminum, stainless steel, and chrome.

Coloring Compositions are used to bring metals to a final high luster.

Standard Red Rouge: Made of red iron oxide powder bonded with grease and stearic acid. Stearic acid is a white, crystalline, fatty acid made from the saponification of hard fats or tallow. Commercial stearine is a mixture of stearic and palmitic acids. The grease content

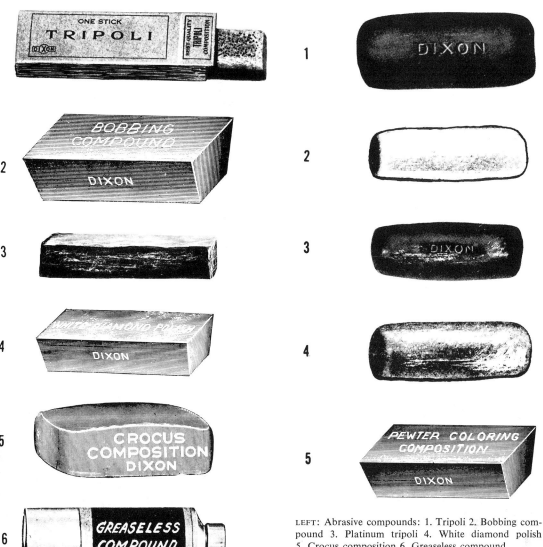

LEFT: Abrasive compounds: 1. Tripoli 2. Bobbing compound 3. Platinum tripoli 4. White diamond polish 5. Crocus composition 6. Greaseless compound

ABOVE: Polishing compounds: 1. Red rouge 2. White rouge 3. Green rouge 4. Porcelain rouge 5. Pewter coloring composition

in rouge is the reason that scrubbing with soap and a brush is necessary after buffing with rouge; the grease must be saponified as it is not water soluble.

White Rouge: For use on white gold and platinum.

Porcelain Rouge: Fast mirror finish on metals which require red rouge, except high karat golds.

White, Pink, Green, and Gray Compounds: Cut and color most metals. Some are designed for use on particular metals. (Green is used on stainless steel, chrome, and platinum for very bright finishes.)

Chrome Buffing Composition: Made for polishing chrome and aluminum.

Pewter Coloring Composition: Used specifically for pewter.

Mirror Lapping Compounds: Used in the lapping-polishing process when large, flat surfaces must be polished and sharp corners retained.

GENERAL POLISHING AND BUFFING CONSIDERATIONS

In most cases, it is considered good practice to confine the use of a particular polishing or buffing compound to a particular buff for maximum efficiency, and to avoid contamination. Should it be necessary to change the use of a buff to another agent, it can be thoroughly cleaned with a *wheel rake,* if the buff is of a soft material. The rake is held against

Wheels which become overloaded with an abrasive or polishing compound are reduced in efficiency, and must be cleaned. Overloaded wheels will leave a black deposit of abrasive or polishing compound on the surface of the metal being treated. Both should be applied sparingly, as repeated small applications are more efficient than large doses at one time.

POLISHING AND BUFFING WHEELS

Polishing wheels and buffing wheels are made in a wide variety of materials, diameters, thicknesses, and construction. Polishing wheels are constructed of muslin, cotton flannel, canton flannel, canvas, felt, and various leathers. Generally speaking, buffing wheels are more flexible and softer than polishing wheels, but there is some overlapping in the case of stitched wheels. Muslin buffs are extensively used for buffing, though loose sewn wool cloth buffs, loose string buffs with no cross threads, and loose disc sheepskin buffs are used, especially under conditions which demand high flexibility.

Generally speaking, close-stitched, hard buffs are used for cutting compounds, while cotton and unstitched buffs of soft materials, wool and chamois are used for coloring to high luster and mirror finish. The hardest wheels are those in which the layers of canvas discs have been cemented together. For general polishing, cotton fabric wheels such as muslin, sewn together, are most versatile. Both polishing and buffing wheels are stitched spirally, radially, concentrically, loose sewn, or crescent curved to the edge. The closer the sewing, the more rigid the wheel. Spiral sewn wheels are most commonly used. High count muslin sheet is used for heavy work, and low count is used for coloring operations. For heavy, cut down polishing, 84×92 count muslin is generally used, and for coloring, 64×68 count is common.

Pressed felt wheels are available in several densities from extra soft to rock hard. They are used where the face of the wheel must be kept uniform and true, in combination with fine abrasive grit. Felt wheel faces can be easily contoured to fit special shapes.

Rubber wheels are made mixed with emery for use on buffing wheels or flexible shafts. Good for removing scratches, they can be dressed to shape by holding a file against them while they rotate. Besides the usual buffs, there are buffs used for special purposes such as goblet string buffs (used for areas inaccessible

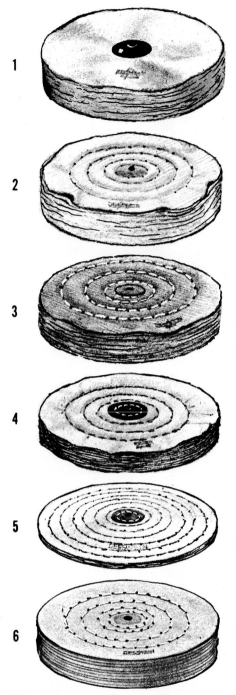

Polishing buffs: 1. Lead center muslin buff 2. Canton flannel buff 3. Wool cloth buff 4. Reinforced leather center muslin buff 5. Razor edge corner buff 6. Sheepskin hard edge buff

the face of the wheel while it rotates, and is moved back and forth till only a clean surface is seen on the face, or till the wheel has the desired shape. An old hacksaw blade can be substituted for this purpose if a wheel rake is not available. Wheel rakes are also used to *shape* buffs if necessary in special situations.

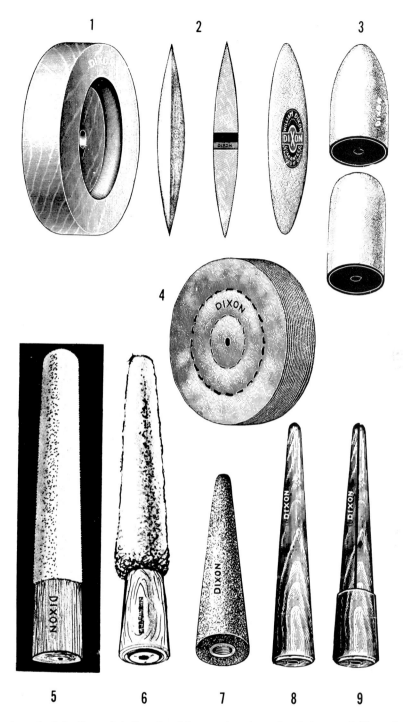

1. Wood lapping wheel 2. Tapered knife edge felt wheels 3. Felt cones, pointed, round 4. Stitched chamois wheel 5. Felt ring buff 6. Cotton ring buff 7. Solid grit carborundum lathe cone 8. Tapered wood ring lap 9. Split wood emery paper ring lathe buff

for ordinary buffs such as the insides of bowls, vases, and deep forms), felt ring buffs (for polishing the insides of rings), and pointed and blunt felt cones (used to get to difficult areas), to mention a few.

POLISHING AND BUFFING PRACTICE

When polishing or buffing with a buffing motor, apply a *downward* slight pressure in the direction of the rotation of the wheel (the wheel should *always rotate toward the oper-*

Cotton buffs: 1. Cotton string polishing wheel, wood center 2. Cotton string goblet buffs 3. Tapered cotton buff 4. Cotton goblet buff 5. Cotton cylinder buff

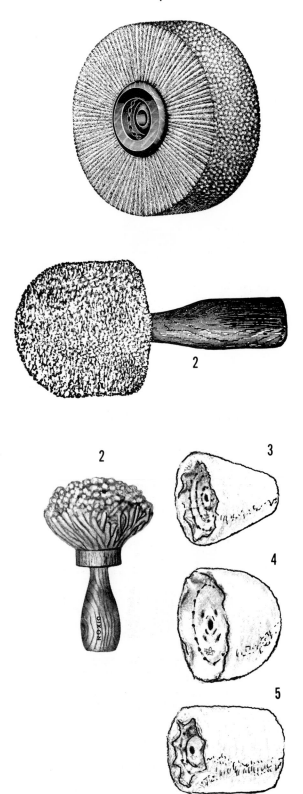

ator). Place the metal being buffed *below the center* of the wheel for safety, or the work might be torn out of the hands with injury to the operator and the work. *Avoid* placing metal *edges against* the direction of the wheel's motion as again, the work might be caught and thrown from the hand. *Do not hold articles with a cloth* (*it might become entangled*), *and keep loose hair, ties, or garments from proximity to the wheel.*

Usually an excess of pressure is not necessary in any buffing situation. If the wheel and compound do not seem to be working, there are several possible causes for the failure: the wheel speed may be too slow (change to a larger wheel or a higher speed), the wheel may be overloaded with the compound being used (clean with a metal rake and apply less compound than formerly), or the wrong compound is being used for the desired result. Judgment is required in every polishing and buffing situation to choose the correct compound, wheel type, and speed to get the desired result. With the wide range of materials available, this may sometimes become a problem, but experience will soon dictate procedures.

Small pieces should be supported on a block of soft, rounded edge wood while polishing. Chain polishing by machine is potentially *dangerous,* but should it be done, the chain should be held tightly against and wrapped around a wood support, with only a small area of chain exposed at one time. One end of the chain can be nailed to the back of the supporting wood. Wire bracelets and other delicate wire work must also be handled carefully. Once polished, small pieces should be handled with paper to avoid fingerprints. Large surfaces should be polished in overlapping strokes. Small pieces should be cross polished, changing the direction in which the wheel passes over the surface to achieve a uniform surface.

To retain a mirror finish on precious metals

Polishing and finishing bristle brushes: 1. Converging shape stiff bristle 2. Saucer shape extra stiff bristle 3. Cup shape stiff bristle 4. End bristle 5. Spiral or flue tapered bristle scratch brush 6. Lathe goblet brush, long hub 7. Lathe goblet brush, short hub 8. Drum shape bristle

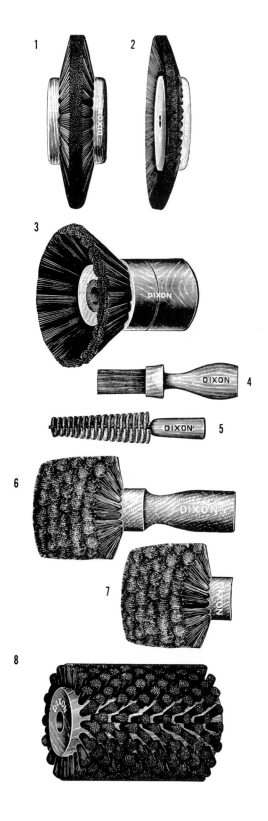

and their alloys, after buffing, wash the piece with warm water and soap. Dry the piece by tumbling in the sawdust of true mahogany, boxwood, maple wood, or crushed corn cob. Other woods may tarnish the metal due to the soluble minerals they contain. Fingerprints on highly polished metal surfaces may be removed by rubbing Venetian lime on the surface with a canton-flannel cloth which will absorb the grease without scratching the surface.

BRISTLE BRUSHES

Brushes or wheels made with hog hair, horse hair, Tampico fiber, or nylon are used for several special purposes. Their important characteristic is that they do not change the basic dimensions of the metal but impart a surface or texture. Because they are so flexible (the flexibility varying with the length of the bristle and density), they can be used to get at *irregular surfaces* easily. They are used to eliminate scratch and tool marks, to remove burrs and round edges. Since they run cooler than cloth buffs, they are used on light metal pieces where overheating the metal is to be avoided. Bristle brushes are used with grease-bonded compounds as these adhere to the brush easily. Emery compounds are used to create satin and butler finishes. For polishing delicate filigree and wirework, they are used with a paste of lime or whiting. Pumice and water pastes can be used for cleaning operations. They can be used with rouge for polishing decorated surfaces such as engraved or chased pieces, as they are flexible and do not remove metal and therefore will not obliterate or wear away the design.

WIRE BRUSHES

Crimped or straight wire brushes are made for many functions. The purpose of *crimped* wire in brushes is to provide an even distribu-

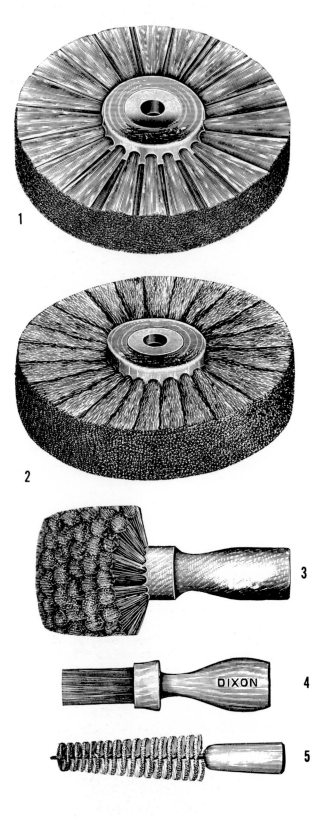

tion of wire in the wheel while it is in motion. The crimp in adjacent wires support each other so that the wheel becomes rigid in motion, and the wires are less susceptible to fatigue. Crimped wire provides better finish and control of tip action. The *trim length* refers to the length of the wire protruding past the diameter of the center plate or wire-holding material. Short trim length means a stiffer brush, while long trim length provides flexible action especially useful against irregular surfaces. *Fill density* refers to the amount of wire material in a given area. An increase in density means more wire ends are coming in contact with the metal and results in a better finish, more quickly achieved. Reducing the fill increases the flexibility and produces the same result as a longer trim length brush. Trim length and fill density are the two most important deciding factors in choosing a wire brush (and a bristle brush) for a particular job.

The Washburn and Moen Wire Gauge Standard is universally used in wire brush manufacture. Coarse wire brushes, 35 gauge (.0095) to 18 gauge (.0475), are used to scratch brush large castings such as sculpture, to finish the surface, remove sand from castings, firescale from heat-treated metals and forgings, and to prepare the surface for coloring operations.

Fine wire brushes, 50 gauge (.0044) to 36 gauge (.0090), are used in creating surface texture, for cleaning metal, elimination of scratches and pits, burr removal, blending irregularities, and in preparing the metal for plating and coloring operations. There is no dimensional change in the metal when using wire brushes, as the brush alters the surface without removing metal. The effect achieved depends on the rotating speed of the brush, the size of the wire, and the pressure used against the metal. When using wire brushes, do not exert too much pressure as the *ends* of the wire do the work, and if they are bent by excess pressure they will merely skim the metal and not function properly. The spindle speed should not be faster than 1750 rpm. The most efficient brushing is done at the highest possible speed with the lightest pressure. Steel, brass, or nickel wire brushes are used for the creation of matte, satin, or brush finishes, used dry. Crimped steel or nickel wire brushes give a matte finish to silver, aluminum, and pewter. Crimped soft brass wire (.003 inch diameter) is used for a softer effect on most metals. Stainless steel wire brushes should be used on Monel Metal, stainless steel, and aluminum.

Wire brushes: 1. Straight wire, brass, steel, nickel silver 2. Crimped wire, brass, steel, nickel silver 3. Goblet shape wire brush 4. End scratch brush 5. Spiral or flue tapered metal scratch brush

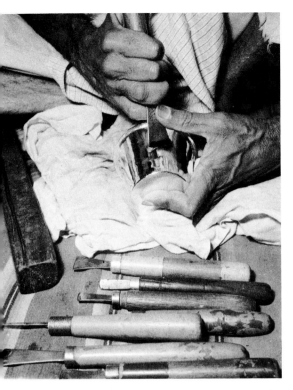

Craftsmen in India practice hand burnishing with hard-steel, highly polished burnishers of various forms that are made to fit the conformity of many surfaces. Sometimes agate-tipped burnishers are used. Several burnishers are shown in the foreground of this photograph, which also illustrates the method of holding and directing the movements of the tool— *away* from the worker. *Photo by Oppi.*

A hard-steel, polished burnisher is being used here on a repoussé-constructed, silver Jain deity, made in Palitana, Saurashtra, India. The burnisher compresses the silver surface and renders it brilliant and lastingly lustrous. *Photo by Oppi.*

Wire brushes can also be run wet to produce matte finishes with an application of pumice and water. An old-time silversmith's practice is to clean metal in preparation for soldering, plating, or coloring by dousing the work and the brush with stale beer or ale.

The life of a brush is increased if it is *reversed* occasionally in its direction of rotation on the buffing motor.

BURNISHING

Polishing by burnishing is a method still widely employed on silver, gold, and delicate pierced and wire work. Special burnishers made of hardened, highly polished steel can be used first and followed by curved or rounded agate or bloodstone burnishers. The lubricant varies with different metals, but generally a neutral (nonalkaline or acid) soap with water is used (saliva is a good lubricant for gold). The entire metal surface is worked over, a small area at a time, compressing the metal till it shines with high luster. Sometimes burnishing is followed by mirror finish buffing.

COMMON POLISHING AND BUFFING SITUATIONS

Polishing to Cut Metal Surface Muslin buff, 6 to 8 inches in diameter. Apply tripoli while buff rotates, avoid overloading. Buff below horizontal center of the wheel, taking care to avoid edges of the metal from catching and being pulled from the hands. Spindle speed: 1750 to 3450 rpm, depending on the condition of the metal and the amount to be removed. Used on most metals.

Rouge or Color Buffing Follows cutting polishing. Cotton buff 64×68 weave, flannel or chamois buff, 4 to 8 inches diameter. Spindle speed: 3450 rpm. Compound: red rouge, greasy, or dry type. Used on gold, silver, copper, brass, etc. Do not overload wheel. Apply article to the buff below the horizontal center, and lift away from the wheel in a motion continuing *downward* along with the direction of the movement of the wheel.

POLISHING AND GRINDING   409

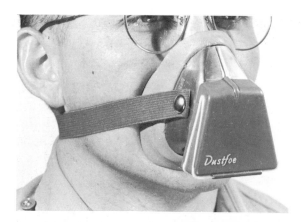

Dustfoe "66" respirator mask with replaceable, electrostatic filter that provides respiratory protection against all dust concentrations, fibrous-producing dusts, toxic dusts, and mists. Manufactured by the Mine Safety Appliances Co. and approved by the United States Bureau of Mines.

Platinum and Palladium Use separate wheels for these metals to avoid contamination from other metals or transference onto their surface: a cutting buff charged with tripoli, followed by cleaning with hot water containing ammonia and soap; and then white or green rouge on a loose cotton buff, and washing as above. Avoid red rouge.

Brushing Used on irregular surfaces. Bristle brushes, 3½ inches diameter. Spindle speed: 3450 rpm. Compound: red rouge, greasy type.

Butler Finish By wheel: cotton buffs 64×68 weave, 2 to 8 inches diameter. Spindle speed: 1750 rpm. Compound: greaseless cut and color compounds. By hand: either 240 or 320 grit emery cloth. The surface becomes deadened. A satin sheen can also be achieved with a soft brass wire brush.

Scratch Brushing Karat Gold and Sterling Silver Nickel silver, steel or brass wire brush, 2½ inches diameter, ¼ to ¾ inch long wire Spindle speed: 1750 rpm. Lubricant: warm water or soapbark solution.

Lapping Wood wheel, ¼ inch wide, 6 to 10 inches diameter. Spindle speed: 2000 to 3450 rpm, tripoli compound or rouge.

Lapping is a polishing term referring to polishing done by a nonyielding surface such as a stiff felt wheel, or, more commonly, a wood wheel made of a close-grained wood such as poplar. It is done when flat, smooth surfaces with sharp corners must be polished to a high luster. Wood wheels can be dressed to special shapes by holding wood-turning tools or an old, broad chisel against them while they rotate. Most lapping is done against the side of the wheel which is usually wedge-shaped and has flat or slightly convex sides—the lapping wheel can be charged with tripoli for polishing or rouge for buffing. Mirror lapping refers to lapping with tin or steel wheels with special compounds to produce a bright, mirrorlike finish.

POLISHING HAZARDS AND PRECAUTIONS

Polishing with abrasive and polishing agents sometimes presents certain hazards which must be considered and steps taken to avoid them. The main hazard is from *dust,* which is breathed in and which can affect the eyes. Ideally, polishing and buffing should be done near an exhaust fan which draws off dust. For lack of a fan, even a simple *splash pan* with some water in the bottom will help to catch dust. *Dust-collecting systems* are efficient but expensive, and are used to collect dust when working a great deal with precious metals when dust becomes a valuable source for reclaimed metal. Splash pans are made with installed electric lights at the top, switch outside, for better vision while buffing.

For those who are affected by the breathing of dusts, a Bureau of Mines Approved *dust respirator mask* which removes harmful dust and mist particles from inhaled air is essential. For those who react to polishing agents with skin dermatitis conditions, a doctor's advice and the use of protective ointments is needed. Danger from flying particles and irritation to eyes can be partially avoided by the use of goggles with fine screen or plastic side shields, or by the use of face shields with a plastic window, mounted on a pivoting headgear, which protects the entire face area.

Grinding and Abrasives

Abrasives or cutting agents are used in a number of ways by the metal craftsman. They are prepared in the form of papers, cloths, belts, sticks, wheels, cones, discs, and shells. They can be used by hand, or in conjunction with a wheel, mounted on a grinding motor. Each form has its special function, depending on the specific need. Wheel-mounted abrasives are used for reshaping and grinding tools, remov-

Abrasive wheels are manufactured in a wide range of coarsenesses, bonding agents, and forms designed for specific situations. *The Norton Company.*

ing excess metal, creating shapes, making patterns or textures, and other uses.

Hand grinding on abrasive papers stretched on hard, flat wood blocks or metal surfaces is accomplished by moving the article back and forth over the abrasive paper. It is a long and tedious process, but has the advantage of not overheating the metal or distorting its shape.

GRINDING WHEELS

Most grinding is done on grinding wheels mounted on an arbor attached to a grinding or buffing motor, and is used at slow speeds below 1750 rpm, as high speeds do not produce the best results and do not expedite the process. Three natural abrasives are used in wheels: corundum (aluminum oxide), emery (aluminum oxide plus abrasive iron oxide), and diamond, the hardest known substance. These abrasives or cutting agents are manufactured in various grain sizes and are combined with a bond or binder material that will hold the grain together and form the wheel. The grade of the wheel is measured by the strength of the bond plus the porosity or grain structure.

Artificially made abrasives such as silicon carbide (stamped symbol C on the wheel) is used for grinding brittle hard metals such as hard alloys, brass, soft bronze, copper, aluminum, gray iron, and other materials such as marble, other stones, and ceramics. Aluminum oxide is used for materials which have high tensile strength such as wrought iron, and high-speed steels of which tools are made.

The bonds used to hold the abrasive grain together in wheels are of several types:

Silicate of soda: Symbol S, a baked bond known as "water glass," used where the heat generated by grinding must be held to a minimum.

Vitrified: Symbol V, baked clay, not affected by acids, oils, water, or ordinary temperature conditions.

Shellac: Symbol E.

Rubber: Symbol R, a strong, dense material used for thin wheels.

Resinoid: Symbol B, can be run at high speeds and cuts cool.

Grain sizes:

Coarse: 6, 8, 10, 12, 14, 16, 20, 24.
Medium: 30, 36, 46, 54, 60.
Fine: 70, 80, 90, 100, 120, 150, 180, 220, 240, 280, 320, 400, 500, 600

Grades are designated by letters:

Very Soft: C–G
Soft: H–K
Medium: L–O
Hard: P–S
Very Hard: T–Z

Abrasive wheels are used to sharpen or reshape steel tools. The tools are placed firmly on the tool rest, in the manner shown, and drawn slowly from side to side across the face of the wheel. *Behr-Manning Company.*

When hand-sharpening metal cutting tools, such as chisels, engravers, knives, etc., a small amount of oil suitable for oilstones is applied to the sharpening stone. The tool is held firmly at a constant angle to the stone and is drawn over the stone in a figure-eight motion, as illustrated. *Behr-Manning Company.*

The standard marking system for grinding wheels is to mention these qualities in the following order: Abrasive type, grain size, grade, bond type. Example: A=36=L=V means a grinding wheel made of aluminum oxide (A), of medium grain (36), medium on the soft-to-hard scale (L), and of the bond type Vitrified (V).

TOOL MAINTENANCE

Tools must be kept in excellent, sharp condition to function best. The time and care taken to maintain tools is well worth the trouble. A cold chisel which has developed a mushroom head or a broken or nicked cutting edge can be fully restored to working condition.

When using a motor-driven grinding wheel to recondition tools or grind metals, *always wear goggles to protect the eyes against flying particles.* Many grinding motors have protecting glass shields mounted on the motor, but goggles are an added precaution. If the motor in use is not of the sealed ball bearing, permanently lubricated type, an occasional oiling with a light motor oil will prolong its life. The grinding wheel on a grinding motor turns *toward* the operator.

The preferred grinding wheel is one of soft emery. The tool being ground is supported on a tool rest before the grinding wheel, and is moved slowly back and forth across the revolving wheel face. A grinder which has more of a gap than 1/16 inch between the tool rest and the wheel face should first be trued and dressed before use. To do this, a *grinding wheel dresser* which has cutters of 1¼ inch

in diameter for large wheels, or an abrasive stick dresser for small diameter wheels is used. The wheel dresser is supported on the tool rest, held firmly, and moved *straight across* the rotating wheel face. The tool is then held against the wheel at the correct angle and moved back and forth to avoid overheating. The edge being cut should be dipped into cold water during grinding to keep it cool. Do not press too hard against the grinding wheel to avoid burning the metal, and grind *away* from the cutting edge and not toward it. Retemper the tool after grinding if necessary.

SHARPENING STONES

Both natural and artificial sharpening stones are used to put a last sharpness on tool edges after grinding and shaping. A small amount of a clear, thin oil is put on the stone to float away particles of metal removed from the tool during this operation, and prevent the stone from becoming glazed or clogged, which would reduce its efficiency. If the stone becomes dark in use, it is too hard for the work. This darkening is caused by oxidation of the metal. If the stone remains light, it is probably too soft. The correct hardness will show *some* discoloration after a period of time.

JUDGING STEEL COMPOSITION BY SPARK OBSERVATION

Judging steel content from the sparks which occur during grinding operations can only be an approximation for the amateur, but professional observers can make accurate judgments. When steel (such as a tool being reshaped or sharpened) is held against a rotating, high-speed (at least 4500 rpm peripheral speed) grinding wheel, sparks are emitted. This occurs when small particles of metal are torn loose, thrown into the air, and burn with incandescence. Goggles should be worn during this procedure to protect the eyes. The burning occurs while the carbon in the particle is in contact with air oxygen and is burned to carbon dioxide. The greater the carbon content in the steel, the greater is the intensity of the burst.

Spark testing should be done in shadow, away from natural or artificial light, against a dark ground. To observe the spark, focus the eyes at a distance of about one-third from the tail end of the spark stream, and only observe the sparks which cross the path of vision. A mental vision of the spark develops. Sparks are divided into wheel sparks, center area sparks, and tail sparks, each taking about one-third of the total length.

Elements in steel are identifiable by the pattern and brightness of the sparks, and the distance they travel.

Sparks from steel with 0.15 per cent carbon have a simple forking effect.

Steel with 0.45 per cent carbon has a fine secondary burst.

Steel with 1.0 per cent carbon has sparks with intense bursts.

Steel with molybdenum has a detached spearhead.

Silicon makes a short spark and ends abruptly with a white flash.

Nickel makes sparks with tiny, brilliant, white light.

If properly interpreted, sparks that occur during the grinding of steel can indicate the composition of the steel. *Mine Safety Appliance Co. Photo by Tom Walczak.*

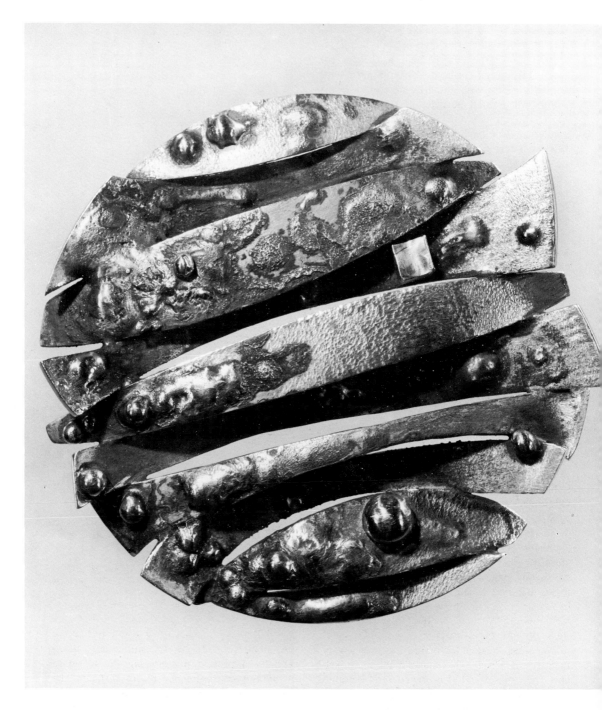

Silver coat pin, by Patrick F. Maher, 1962. Diameter: 2 inches. The basic metal, silver, was shaped by cutting and hammering. The units of the design consist of colored metals: bronze, brass, or gold. The units were hard soldered on the surface, which was then flooded in places with a low-alloy silver solder, such as Silvaloy, containing a high percentage of copper. The piece was then pickled in acid in the presence of iron, which acted to copper plate the areas flooded with the low-alloy solder. The copper plating was attacked with nitric acid, resulting in a yellow metal relief of gold, brass, or bronze shapes; silver in the areas not covered with the low-alloy solder; and a patina of copper plate. Finishing was done with a soft brush or a flexible shaft-mounted wire brush, which cut the surface to expose the desired metal color. *Photo by Ed Gilliland.*

Coloring Metals

Coloring of metals should follow buffing as it is the *last* step in finishing a piece. The main purpose in coloring metals is to produce an effect in its appearance in a short time which might ordinarily occur in nature, but would take much longer and might require special conditions. The natural discoloration of metal surfaces after an exposure to air, moisture, and gases is actually a combination of corrosion and oxidation which completely alters the composition of the metal surface, mainly because of the oxidation process which occurs. The development of this color change is called the acquiring of a *patina,* and in most cases it is the artificial acquisition of a patina which is the purpose of coloring.

Coloring is done as a *last* process after all soldering and polishing have been completed. Good ventilation is essential in all chemical coloring processes, and should be done near an exhaust fan or, if possible, in the open air.

Coloring can be done by various methods: chemical, heat, and electrochemical. Mechanical processes which require the use of lacquers, paints, and varnishes are not included here as these materials do not form chemical combinations with the metals, and therefore remain essentially surface effects which have little to do with the properties of the metal itself.

There are certain factors in the coloring of metals which make it less than an exact science, and these should be taken into account. The composition of the metal is one factor. Especially in the case of alloys, the reactions of the metals to the chemical agents will vary with the alloy composition. The temperature range at which the chemical is applied, the time allowed for the change, whether the metal is wrought or cast (cast metals are more difficult to color), and the purity of the chemicals used are all factors which influence the effect.

For coloring large pieces, stoneware crocks protected against thermal or mechanical shock by placing them into wood boxes or containers are used. Glass containers such as Pyrex (used where heat is recommended or necessary) should be similarly protected with wood. A wood slat grid placed in the bottom of such containers, weighted with stones, is a worthwhile precaution against breakage should a heavy piece being colored fall into the container. Special wood tanks for coloring are also used, and in some cases, vinyl plastic is possible.

Heat generally hastens the action of chemicals, but often coloring at normal temperatures produces longer-lasting effects. Large pieces wholly submerged in hot solutions are more easily colored uniformly, as the entire surface is heated and attacked simultaneously. Where this is not possible, the chemical can be poured over the piece and the liquid caught in a container placed underneath. Chemicals can also be applied with cloth swabs, natural sponges, or brushes if the piece is too large to manage for dipping.

Cleaning the Metal before Coloring

Whether the piece being colored is large or small, it must be *absolutely clean* to receive the chemicals properly. Cleaning metal is essentially a process of *reducing the adhesion or affinity of substances to its surface.* The metal to be colored should be free of adhering grease, dirt, or any oxide which may have formed on its surface from heating or exposure. Cleaned metal surfaces *should not be handled,* and *should not be exposed to air* for any length of time, but should be processed immediately. Most metal coloring failures are due to incomplete or improper cleaning.

Dirt can be removed by pumice and water mixed into a paste and applied briskly with a cloth, when all the surfaces are accessible. Organic and mineral greases can be removed by boiling in a solution of caustic soda or soda ash (sodium carbonate), or potash (potassium carbonate) in water. These are the least expensive cleaners, and a strong solution may be stored for future use. The usual mixture requires one pound added to a gallon of water. These materials produce alkalinity in the cleaning bath which causes the oils and fats to saponify, and mineral oils and greases to emulsify and float away. Copper, brass, bronze, iron, and zinc may be cleaned this way; the last two should be immersed for a short time only. A final rinse with plain water prepares the piece for coloring. As an alternative to the above, a vigorous scrubbing with a brush and a strong detergent may work, if it is repeated a few times. In some cases a greaseless abrasive can be applied to the metal with a buffing wheel.

Oxided surfaces on copper and its alloys, silver, and nickel silver can be removed (*after they have been degreased if necessary*), by immersing them in an ordinary pickle bath. Oxides can usually be removed by heating metal to a dull redness, and then immersing it into a weak pickle solution. This is not advised for cast articles of any size which might run the danger of cracking under the shock of cooling rapidly in the pickle.

When dipping small articles in pickle for cleaning, attach a wire *of the same metal* to the article to be able to insert and remove the article. This avoids contamination of the pickle. Acid solutions which have been used for metals containing copper have copper in solution, and are not suited to the cleaning of lead, zinc, or tin, as the copper will form a deposit on the surface which will be difficult to remove. Such a plating (better done by electroplating) *could* be used in a coloring process, however, which takes advantage of the possibilities of treating copper for coloring.

All metals should be thoroughly rinsed in running water after cleaning in acid. Zinc must be placed under water for storage if there is any delay in its coloring as it oxidizes rapidly in air. Iron and steel are cleaned in a weak solution (20 to 1) of sulphuric acid, after which they can be brushed with a steel scratch brush. If iron or steel must wait to be colored, oxidation may be prevented by immersing them in lime water. Lead and tin alloys are ready for coloring after being cleaned in a caustic soda solution.

Scratch brushing is another method for cleaning metals and can be done with a brush mounted on a buffing motor, or by hand. Wire brushes and their uses have been described under polishing. Scratch brushing often follows the first treatment in coloring metals, and the article is then retreated to greater effect. Should the first application of chemicals not produce the desired effect, scratch brushing and a reapplication of chemicals will probably work.

The *prior condition* of a metal surface *before coloring* has a direct bearing on the final appearance of a patina. Highly polished metals after coloring take a glossy finish of a similar polished look. Surfaces which are dull before coloring will also look dull or matte after coloring. *This is an important basic fact in coloring.*

Chemical Coloring

There are hundreds of coloring solutions available to the metalworker. Some of these require complicated procedures or chemicals which may be difficult to find. Formulas requiring *common chemicals* are given here. The same chemical agent can often be used to produce greatly varying effects, and the time element is another factor. Immersion for a short or a longer time in the solution will produce different results. Chemically created colors generally cannot be dissolved or removed easily unless they are attacked with additional chemicals or high heat.

FORMULAS FOR CHEMICAL COLORING

Gold, Silver, Copper: Black, Brown These metals are colored mainly by the creation of oxides or sulphides on the surface through the application of oxygen and sulphur compounds. Copper develops cuprous oxides or sulphides, and silver develops a layer of silver sulphide. It is mainly the copper content in karat golds which reacts to the coloring processes. The oldest coloring method with results ranging from brown to black is effected by the use of alkaline impure potassium sulphides in salt form, commonly known as "liver of sulphur." Sodium, barium, potassium, ammonium sulphides or polysulphides in a liquid state are also used today. They must be diluted with water to weaken the solution to produce slowly built up, more permanent, denser films. Used strong, the oxides created may just peel off.

Browns To prepare small amounts of liver of sulphur, dilute enough of a particle of the solid salt cake in water to produce a deep yellow color. The dilution may be hastened by heating but not boiling the water. Stir till all the liver of sulphur is dissolved. When coloring copper, immerse the clean metal into the solution and allow it to remain till the color begins. Remove it at intervals for inspection till the desired depth of color is attained. Wash in cold running water first, then in hot water to stop the action, and dry. This will color the entire article. If only *parts* are to be colored, the solution can be applied *locally* to the areas to be colored. If the color is uneven, repeat the process, increase the strength of the solution, or scratch brush the surface and repeat. The same procedure is followed for sterling silver (which contains copper), and can be made to appear gray if the procedure is arrested before the color has deepened too much. Gold can be colored black if it is heated first and immersed into the solution hot.

Black If a dark black is desired, the following modification is recommended:

Liver of Sulphur	2 ounces
Aqua Ammonia (Sp. gr. 0.89)	¼ ounce
Water	1 gallon

Use at room temperature.

This solution is quite effective to completely blacken a part of an object or the entire object. It can be applied locally with a brush. The same procedure as above is followed.

Bluish-Black

Barium sulphide	10 grains
Water	5 ounces

Used hot, this solution will produce a deep bluish-black. Reducing the barium sulphide to five ounces in five ounces of water will produce a pale to deep gold tint on silver, using the solution cold, and removing the metal from the solution as soon as the desired depth of color is reached.

To partially remove excess color or to create gradually shaded effects, the piece can be rubbed with the fingers or a soft cloth dipped into a paste of fine pumice or whiting, or by using some greaseless compound in the same way.

Rich Reddish-Brown on Copper and Brass

Copper sulphate	120 grains
Water	½ pint

Boil the water till the copper sulphate dissolves, neutralize the mixture with sodium nitrate, then add 150 grains of red iron oxide. The article is immersed in this solution and watched till the color change begins. Then remove it and heat it on a hotplate which will deepen the color. Still further darkening is possible by repeating the procedure till the desired color is reached. Castings take a lighter tone.

Antique Green on Copper and Brass

Copper nitrate	4 ounces
Calcium carbonate	4 ounces
Ammonium chloride	4 ounces
Water	1 gallon

Warm the article as well as the solution. Stipple it on the metal with a cloth or sponge. The color varies according to the alloy. For color variation, immerse in clean boiling water after the antique green has developed.

Blue on Brass and Highly Polished High Carbon Steel

Lead acetate	2–4 ounces
Sodium thiosulphate	8 ounces
Acetic acid	4 ounces
Water	1 gallon
Temperature	180° F

This color must be laquered for permanence.

Crystallized Brass or Bronze

Copper sulphate	8 ounces
Ammonium chloride	4 ounces
Water	1 gallon

Apply cold or warm.

Yellowish-Green on Brass and Copper

Copper nitrate	48 grains
Ammonium chloride	48 grains
Calcium chloride	48 grains
Water	3 ounces

This solution produces a uniform green patina, applied with a brush and allowed to dry, repeated in three applications.

Yellow to Bright Red on Brass

Copper carbonate	2 parts
Caustic soda	1 part
Water	10 parts

Dip till the desired color appears, then wash in water.

Rose, Violet, Blue on Brass

Sulphate of copper	435 grains
Hyposulphate of soda	300 grains
Cream of tartar	150 parts
(potassium hydrogen tartrate)	
Water	1 pint

Bronzing Copper

Copper sulphate	400 grains
Water	2 ounces

Use warm, immerse two or three times, scratch brushing between immersions. Depending on the purity of the copper, the color may be light brown, terra cotta, purplish, or dark brown.

Blue-Black on Brass

Copper sulphate	2 ounces

Water, enough to dissolve the above and redissolve the precipitate which forms. Ammonia, a small amount to neutralize and make the solution slightly alkaline. Immerse in this heated solution.

Black on Steel Highly polished steel can be colored a smooth black by dipping into the following solution:

Water	1 gallon
Nitric Acid	¾ ounce
Copper sulphate	1½ ounces
Selenious acid	1 ounce

Bluing Steel Chemically

Mercuric chloride	4 parts
Potassium chlorate	3 parts
Alcohol	8 parts
Water	85 parts

Use at room temperature.

or

Sodium hyposulphite	8 ounces
Lead acetate	2 ounces
Water	1 gallon

Use boiling.

Black on Zinc

Copper sulphate	30 parts
Potassium chloride	30 parts
Water	400 parts

Article must be absolutely clean. At room temperature, immerse the article in the solution, or paint large pieces with a brush dipped in solution. Allow to stand till the color forms, then wash in water and dry. Can be rubbed to get bluish cast. Wax or oil coating makes it black.

Coloring Lead Artificial patinas on lead are not as durable as the natural patina which develops on lead exposed to the atmosphere. When an article can be placed in a protected environment, patinas for lead are possible.

The surface must be prepared by removing any existing film by scraping, wire brushing, buffing, or rubbing down with steel wool. If the object presents surfaces which cannot be readily reached, it can be cleaned with a weak solution of nitric acid followed by a thorough washing with water. A solution of two ounces each of trisodium phosphate and sodium carbonate per gallon of water can also be used.

Jet Black The cleaned lead is heated and brushed with an application of warm muriatic acid (HCl) mixed with some lampblack. The lead is heated again with a torch, taking care not to overheat and melt it. After the surface turns black, it can be waxed, and the article used out of doors as well as indoors.

Green To one gallon of water add:

Ammonium chloride	4 ounces
Copper nitrate	8 ounces
Chromic acid	1 ounce
Acetic acid	4 ounces

Heat the solution and dip the lead in it or apply with a brush or swab. Rinse and dry, and spray with lacquer.

Several colors, depending on the time in which they are submerged, can be achieved with the following solution:

Aluminum chloride	1 ounce
Ammonium molybdate	½ ounce

Add to one gallon of water, heat, and dip lead. In order of appearance, the colors are golden yellow, green, crimson, blue, brown, and black.

Coloring Low-Karat Gold The purpose of the process described here is to give the color of *fine gold* to gold objects of a *lower, alloyed* karat gold (18K to 12K). The base metal in the surface of the article is dissolved out, leaving a pure coating of gold. This is done after the article is completely finished and polished.

Saltpeter (Potassium nitrate)	4 parts
Alum	2 parts
Common salt	2 parts

Add enough water to make a thin paste. Place in a crucible and boil. Insert the article attached to a silver wire into the mixture for ten to twenty minutes. Rinse with hot water and scratch brush with brass wire brush, and return to solution. Rinse in hot water again, scratch brush, wash with soap and hot water, rinse in hot water, and dry in sawdust.

Water Gilding Gilding by simple immersion on brass and copper.

Gold Chloride	1½ parts
Hydrogen potassium carbonate	60 parts
Water	200 parts

Boil in a Pyrex glass container for two hours while the solution turns yellow and then green, when it is ready. Dip brass and copper articles in hot solution for one-half minute. Nickel silver articles can also be gilded in this manner by putting them in contact with a copper or zinc wire.

Coloring by Heat

Heat can be used alone to color metals.

Bluing Steel by Heat This process is known as tempering when it is applied to the hardening of tools made of steel. Clean the steel, and polish it brightly as the colors are best seen on polished steel. Heat it in air over a charcoal or another evenly applied heat source. The color change which appears depends on the temperature and the composition of the alloy.

Stop the process immediately when the desired color has appeared by quenching the article in water or oil immediately.

Color	Temperature (Fahrenheit)
Light Yellow	410°
Straw	440°
Bronze	510°
Light Blue	560°
Dark Blue	610°

Oil Blackening of Steel Heat the steel in a steel box packed with charcoal to prevent oxidation prior to quenching. When red hot, remove and plunge into a bath of sperm oil.

Gold Low-karat gold containing copper can be oxidized by slow heating till the copper rises to the surface, oxidizes, and becomes black. The outer layers of this oxide are black and the inner ones are red. This can be deliberately partially removed to get variations in exposed underlayers of the oxide, when cleaning the piece. Cast pieces are easily colored in this way.

Coloring Copper by Heat The coloring of copper by heat can be easily accomplished, but is not always permanent. When copper is heated, it passes through the following color changes: pale yellow, red, violet, during which time cuprous oxide (Cu_2O) is being formed. If the heating continues, the metal becomes black as at this time cupric oxide (CuO) builds up and thickens. To build up permanent layers of oxide a slow heat is advised; in some cases, plunging the copper into oil after allowing it to cool off somewhat, but while it is still hot, produces a deeper color. Overheating will often cause the oxide to scale off in patches which will also occur if the metal is suddenly quenched in water immediately after heating. Most such patinas are not permanent.

Tools are generally extensions of the functions of the hands, but in some cultures, of the feet as well. We in the West deprive ourselves of the use of our feet in work for the sake of comfort, immobilizing them in stockings and shoes. Wherever metalsmiths work in India, they use their feet to hold, guide, manipulate, and support large objects under work, as naturally as they use their feet for standing and walking. Shown here is a brass worker (*thathera*) from Pemberti, Andhra Pradesh, in South India, planishing a brass water pot with hand and hammer, at the same time using one foot to guide its movement over the earth-anchored anvil, and the other to help keep it in position to receive the regular rain of blows over its surface. *Photo by Oppi.*

Part Five

HAND TOOLS AND THEIR USES

Basic Tool Groups

A certain number of basic tools are necessary for the craftsman involved in the particular areas of work mentioned in the headings below. Some are indispensable for elementary work, and others are optional. For beginning craftsmen, tools should be acquired *as the need for them arises*. By normal progress, ultimately the equipment necessary to pursue the particular interest of the craftsman will accumulate.

BASIC METALWORK AND JEWELRY-MAKING TOOLS

Jeweler's saw frame, 2" to 5" deep
2 dozen jeweler's saw blades, No. 5 and No. 0
V board and bench pin
Jeweler's snips, 7" long, 1¾" cut
12" steel rule
Center punch, 4" long
Scriber
Dividers, 3"
Tweezer, pointed
Tweezer, cross lock, blunt tip
Hand drill for drills up to 5⁄32" diameter
Twist drills, 1⁄16", 5⁄64", 3⁄32", 7⁄64", 1⁄8", 9⁄64"
Flat nose pliers, smooth jaws, 5"
Round nose pliers, 5"
End cutting nipper, 4½"
Side cutting nipper, 4½"
Set of needle files, 16 cm. long, No. 2 cut
Half round file, Swiss pattern, 6", No. 1 cut, with handle
Flat file, and tri-square, same as above
Ball peen hammer, 8-ounce
Rawhide or wood mallet, round end, flat end
Ring mandrel, size marked
Hand ring clamp

DECORATIVE METALWORK TOOLS

Repoussé tools
Pitch bowl, pitch
Chasing tools
Engraving tools
Engraving liners
Eye loupe, 4" focus
Matting tools
Stamping tools
Solid and hollow punch tools

Dapping die block
Die cutting tools
Hammers, planishing, riveting, chasing
Cold chisels
Files, needle
Hand drill with twist drills
Drawplate and draw tongs
Rolling mill
Hand vise
Pin vise
Engraver's block
Shellac mounting stick
Bezel setter
Burnisher
Flexible shaft, with burrs, grinders, wheels, etc.

BASIC SOLDERING TOOLS AND EQUIPMENT

Hard Soldering
Torch and tank, or torch and gas supply
Set of different-sized torch tips
Blowpipe and alcohol lamp
Friction lighter
Asbestos block, 12" × 12", ½" thick
Charcoal block, 3¼" × 2¼" by 2"
Borax slate
Borax brushes
Cone or powdered borax or liquid hard soldering flux, 3-oz. bottle
Scraper, 2½" blade
Steel wool, No. 0
Silver Solder: IT, hard, medium, easy, easy flo
Solder snips
Cross-locking tweezer, blunt point
Pointed tweezer
Copper tongs
Copper pickle pan
Binding wire
Pumice powder
Yellow ochre or rouge powder
Small stiff brush
Emery cloth, medium

Soft Soldering
Soft solder, roll, stick or sheet
Solder flux, paste or liquid
Steel wool, No. 0
Soldering coppers
Torch
Solder snips

A basic metalworker's collection of tools, mainly suited to jewelry making and small metalwork. *Craftool, Inc.*

BASIC FORMING AND RAISING TOOLS

Anvils and stakes
    T-stake, 10½″ over-all length, cylinder arm, squared top, flat arm
    Domed head or mushroom stake
    Bottoming stake
    Curved end stake
    Crimping stake
Bench anvil, 50 lbs.
Bench block, hardened steel, 4″ square, 1½″ thick
Bench vise, steel jaws, swivel base, 6½″ opening
Hammers
    3 raising hammers, 8 oz., 12 oz., 1⅛ lb.
    planishing hammer, 12 oz.
    ball peen hammer, 12 oz.
    2 rawhide or hardwood mallets, round end, flat end, and wedge shape
Universal metal cutting shears, 7″ long
Flat file with handle, 10″, bastard cut, 00
Half round file with handle, 8″, bastard cut, 00
Tongs, bent nose, for annealing, 17″ long
Steel Rule, 12″
Center punch
Spring dividers, 6″
Surface gauge
Tree stump, hardwood, end grain up, with self-made hollows as needed
Sandbag

The Hand Tools

The hand tools discussed below have been grouped as far as possible according to their function. Additional information may be found where some tools are discussed under the section describing a technique requiring their use.

MARKING AND MEASURING TOOLS AND MATERIALS

Steel Rules The steel rule is a strip of hardened steel whose width, length, and flexibility varies. One or both sides may be marked with inch (and millimeter) measurements, further divided into fractional measurements. Besides its use for measuring straight line dimensions which are often then enscribed with a scriber, it can be used to check straightness of edges and surfaces. It is also used for setting measurements of calipers and dividers. (See page 55.)

Squares and Right Angles Squares are used primarily for checking right angles, but some are marked for use in measuring as well. There are several types: the solid square (has no markings), the steel square (has one edge marked), the double square (has an adjustable handle and sometimes a leveling device in the handle), and the combination square (used for 45° angles and as a leveler). (See page 55.)

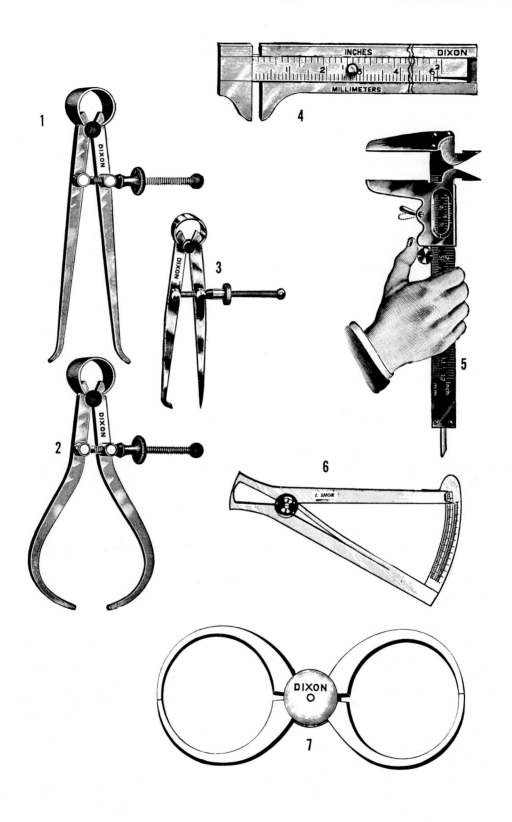

Measuring tools: 1. Inside spring calipers 2. Outside spring calipers 3. Hermaphrodite spring calipers 4. Vest pocket slide calipers for outside measurements of drills, rods, and tubing, 6″ length, graduated in millimeters and 16ths 5. Vernier caliper, 6″ length, graduated in millimeters and 16ths 6. Degree spring gauge, measures in douzièmes and tenths of millimeters 7. Circle calipers

Metal Gauge for Sheet Metal and Wire The American Standard Wire and Sheet Metal Gauge, also known as the Brown & Sharpe gauge, has slits on the edges which are used to measure the thickness of sheet metal and wire. One side is usually stamped with the gauge numbers, and the other side with their decimal equivalents. This gauge is used for the measurements of gold, silver, copper, brass, aluminum, and other nonferrous metals and usually is used for wire gauge sizes ranging from ⌗0 to ⌗36 (.289″ to .005″). (See page 47.)

Twist Drill Gauges A high alloy steel perforated plate used to measure twist drills, sizes ⌗1 to ⌗80, with decimal equivalents and other information usually stamped on the sheet surface. It is also used to measure steel wire. (See page 72.)

Prick Punch A small fine steel point hardened tool used with a lightweight hammer to mark centers and other points for use as a measuring reference. This mark is also visible when the metal is hot. Also known as a *center punch*. It can be purchased made with a spring mechanism which is built in, and of adjustable pressure designed to automatically strike a blow where desired, once in position. The mark made is also used as a depression for starting a small drill to prevent the point from wandering when the drilling begins. (See page 72.)

Scratch Awl or Scriber A steel, point-hardened tool in many different forms used with a steel rule or other straight edge to mark a line on metal. An *engraver's marker* is a special tool used for engraver's markings. Cant the tool away from the rule to assure accuracy. (See page 55.)

Spring Dividers Spring dividers are made for measuring and transferring measurements from rules to metal, and for enscribing circles or arcs. The legs are made with sharp, hardened points, and the spring at the top provides the pressure to maintain the distance measured. This distance can be controlled by releasing or tightening a knurled nut on the side. When used to mark circles, one leg is placed firmly in the mark made by the center punch while the other leg is rotated. When taking a measurement from a steel rule, place one leg into the stamped mark on the rule, and adjust the other leg. Tighten the knurled nut to hold the dividers in this position. The sharp points of the dividers should be protected by inserting

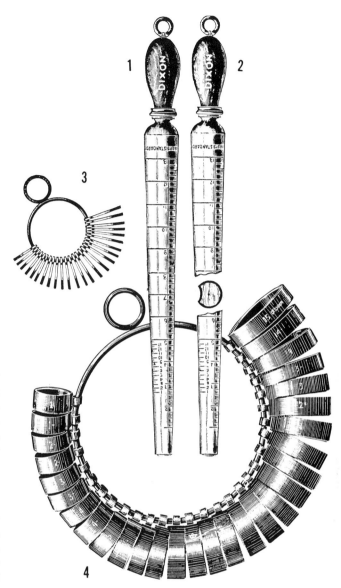

Ring sizing tools: 1. Plain ring mandrel marked with ring sizes, used for sizing only 2. Ring mandrel marked with sizes, with groove for rings containing center mounted stones, for sizing only, not for working 3. Ring sizes, narrow band or shank 4. Ring sizes, wide band, including half sizes from No. 1 to No. 15, guaranteed accurate within .1003″ as recommended by the U. S. Bureau of Standards on September 4, 1951

them into small corks when they are not in use. (See page 242.)

Calipers Two basic types of spring calipers are made, one to measure the distances between *outside* surfaces, and the other for *inside* surface measurements. Adjustments should be made carefully and slowly when measuring. Once the measurement is taken, the calipers are placed against a steel rule, and the reading

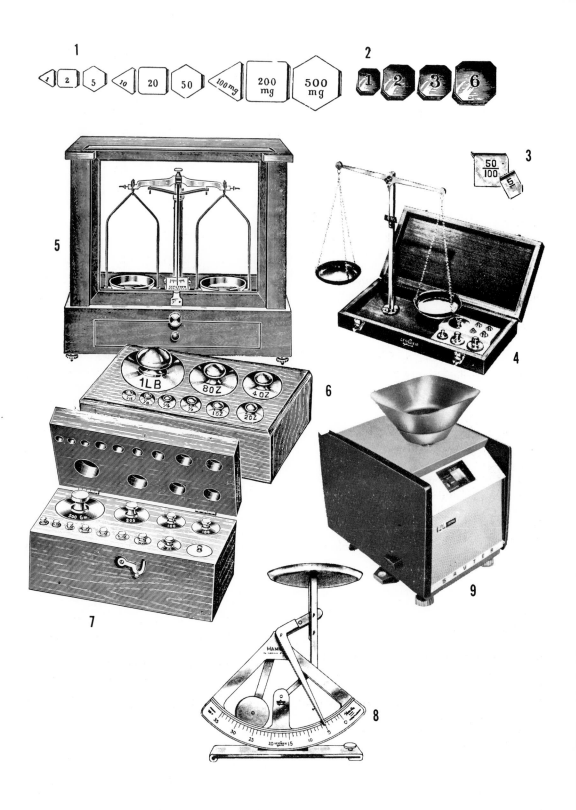

Scales and weights for precious metals: 1. Milligram weights, 1 to 500 mg 2. Grain weights, ½ to 12 grains 3. Metric diamond weights 4. Portable gold scale, 2 ounce capacity 5. Gold weight scale, glass enclosed protector from dust 6. Weight set, ¹⁄₁₆ ounce to 1 pound 7. Weight set, ¼ gram to 500 grams 8. Penny-weight scale, up to 35 dwt 9. Automatic, high speed, AC electric gold scale. Two models: ¹⁄₁₀th dwt to 1000 dwt, 1 grain to 14000 dwt is taken. Inside calipers can be compressed after being adjusted for a measurement, and once withdrawn, they will spring back to exact size. There are special kinds of calipers such as slide calipers marked with millimeters and Vernier readings, used in the jewelry industry for very fine adjustments (invented by Pierre Vernier, a French mathematician, 1580–1637). (See page 424.)

Micrometer Micrometers are precision instruments used for measuring distances of zero to one inch, and larger ones which measure up to twenty-four inches. Two kinds are made, one for outside measurements and another for inside measurements. Detailed instructions for their use are available with the purchase of a micrometer for reading and interpreting micrometer scale findings. (See page 47.)

Ring Stick Ring sticks or gauges, U. S. Standard, are not used for forming processes, but only to measure ring sizes. Some are grooved so that they can measure rings with stones set in them. They are made in marked graduations on a metal sheath over a wood core, in solid aluminum, and plastic. (See page 175.)

Ring Sizers A series of marked, U. S. Standard ring sizes held in graduated half sizes from 1 to 15, stamped on a steel ring, they are used for taking measurements from fingers for ring sizes. They are available for measuring for normal ring widths or wide, and also for rings of the following cross section: regular flat, square, and half round. (See page 425.)

Steel Stamps for Quality Marking Stamps (or punches) made for impressing the word "sterling," karat quality, or other words or identifying symbols on articles made of precious metals can be purchased upon presentation of qualifications from supply houses for the trade. Curved stamps are made in various sizes to fit the inside of rings, and flat stamps are available in various sizes to mark flat surfaces. The stamp can be ordered to produce raised or recessed letters. (See page 89.)

Balances and Scales Balances and scales are made for the weight measurement of precious metals and precious stones. Gold balances are made which measure from 0 to 300 troy ounces of metal. The weighing of metals is necessary when preparing metal for casting, in recording metal sent for refining, and in the recording of the actual weight used on an article for purposes of accurate pricing. Graduated weights made to U. S. Bureau of Standards tolerances are usually sold with the scale when purchased, but may also be purchased separately. (See page 426.)

Graduate A marked Pyrex glass container used for the measurement and preparation of liquids, especially acids.

CUTTING AND PIERCING TOOLS AND MATERIALS

Metal Snips, and Shears Shears are used for cutting sheet metal and wire by hand. Snips are used for cutting solder, wire, and thin-gauge metals. Always hold the metal at right angles to the cutting blades, and push the metal far back in the jaws. Some shears are designed to cut along only straight lines and outside curves, others are designed for curved cuts, and the universal shears cuts both straight and curved lines. Every cut should be one-half to three-quarters of the blade length, the blades are then opened slowly, and the metal is pushed into the jaws so that the cut can continue in the same line, without the occurrence of sharp spurs. (See page 241.)

A great variety of shears and snips are made for special uses. Metals heavier than 14 gauge should probably be cut with a hacksaw, a bench shears, or a jeweler's saw frame. For additional leverage force, the lower handle of a hand shears can be held either against a workbench or in a bench vise, while the upper handle alone is operated. (See page 242.)

Bench Shears Bench shears used for cutting metal are permanently fastened to a workbench or held by a bench vise. They are much more powerful than hand shears and have blades of high-grade tool steel. Many models have an arrangement which allows the cutting of rods as well as sheet metal.

Cutting Nippers Nippers are a form of pliers with hardened and tempered cutting edges. They are designed with side cutting, end cutting, and diagonal cutting blades. They are used mostly for cutting wire, but are adaptable for cutting small sections of thinner sheet metals. (See page 202.)

Hand Hacksaws Hacksaws are used to cut heavy-gauge metals, rods, bars, and tubing. The metal being cut is firmly placed in the

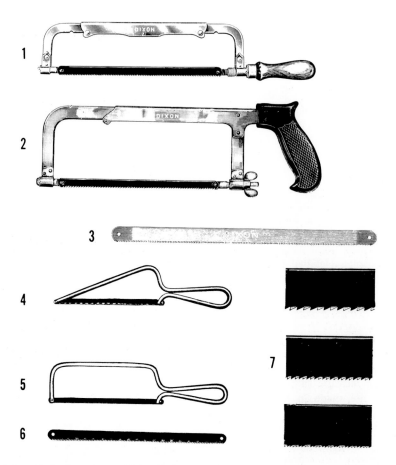

Hacksaws: 1. Adjustable hacksaw frame, 8"–12" blade, 2½" depth 2. Adjustable hacksaw frame, pistol grip handle, 8"–12" blade, 2½" depth 3. Hacksaw blade, 12" 4. Pointed nose midget hacksaw, non-adjustable 6" blade, 1⅞" deep at handle 5. Square midget hacksaw, non-adjustable, 6" blade, 1⅞" deep 6. 6" blade 7. Hacksaw blade teeth: regular, fine, tubing

jaws of a bench vise, protected from scarring by the jaws, if necessary by sheets of paper or cardboard. Hacksaw frames are made solid for a particular size blade, or adjustable. The blade is attached to the frame by inserting the frame pins through the end holes in the blade, and then tightening the wing nuts. Some blades are completely hardened and therefore brittle, while others are teeth-hardened only and more flexible. The teeth are made "set," meaning they point alternately outward to the blade sides, and thereby prevent the blade from binding in the groove. "Wave" set teeth cut a wider groove than regular set teeth. The cutting stroke of the blade occurs on the *push* stroke; therefore the teeth of the blade should point *away* from the handle. Full, long strokes are recommended for maximum, efficient cutting action. Blades are made in varying tooth fineness depending on the number of teeth per inch (14, 18, 24, 32), the finest being used to cut tubing.

Jeweler's Saw Frame The jeweler's saw frame is an adjustable frame which holds a blade under spring tension and is available in varying depths (2¼" to 8") to permit shallow or deep cutting; the most commonly used depth is three inches. The jeweler's saw frame is designed primarily for cutting nonferrous metals. For a discussion of the frame and its use, see The Use of Basic Tools in Metalwork, page 56; also page 66.

Jeweler's Saw Blades Jeweler's saw blades are used with the jeweler's saw frame for cutting and piercing metals. They are made in graduated sizes from ⌗8/0 to ⌗14 (finest to coarsest). The finer the blade, the narrower it is in width and depth. Blades must be inserted in the frame with the teeth pointing *downward,* and out, pointing away from the back of the frame. As the cutting stroke is the downward one only, slightly more pressure is exerted on this stroke. Numbers 1/0, 1, or 2 are recommended for sawing 18- or 20-gauge metal. Narrower blades are used for greatly curving cuts. When sawing tubing, little pressure is exerted until the halfway mark is reached. (See page 459.)

Beeswax Refined beeswax, available in one-ounce cakes and larger bars, is used as a lubricant on jeweler's saw blades. Before beginning to cut, run the blade *once* through the wax cake. Do not overload, and renew when the blade seems to be getting "tight."

V Board and Bench Pin A board of hardwood usually with a "V"-shaped notch which is fastened to the workbench, and is used to support metal during sawing and filing operations. There are several types, some made for insertion in an individual workbench, and others can be secured to the bench with clamps or screws. One is available combined with a small anvil surface. (See page 67.)

Cold Chisels Large, flat-shaped cold chisels ground to wedge shape with hardened and tempered cutting ends are used with the aid of a 1 to 1½-pound hammer to cut metal too thick to be cut with hand shears. The metal to be cut is placed on a steel block or anvil, the flat chisel is placed on the cutting line, and one sharp blow is administered. The next blow is applied to the chisel after it has moved along the line, slightly overlapping the last cut. Flat chisels can also be used to shear thick metal by placing the sheet in a vise, with the cutting line just emerging from the jaws. The chisel is placed at the beginning of the metal about 30° above the horizontal, and moved along the vise jaw, blow after blow, till the metal is severed. Some misshaping of the metal occurs which can be corrected by placing it on a flat surface and hammering with a mallet.

Smaller chisels are used for piercing, splitting, and carving, discussed elsewhere. (See page 74.)

The Hand Drill The most common hand drill designed to hold twist drills which are used for the purpose of making holes has a chuck which accommodates twist drills up to ¼" shank diameter. Larger chucks on hand drills are available, but a power-operated drill would most likely be used with twist drills beyond ¼". Always hold the drill perpendicularly to the metal being drilled. The breast drill is a

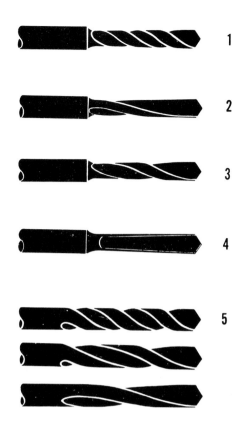

High speed small drills are sensitive to excessively high speeds, and should be run at a speed lower than conventional large drills 1. Flat helix type for tough metals, tool steel, stainless steel, copper and aluminum 2. Slow cutting for brass 3. Medium helix for general use on mild steel and soft brass 4. Flat pivot drill which makes precise, straight holes without first making a center 5. Three straight shank drills with shank diameter equal to the drill size, used for making deep holes

larger drill with a large mushroom head against which pressure can be comfortably exerted in cases where this is necessary. Larger sizes of twist drills are used. (See page 73.)

Twist Drills Twist drills consist of two parts, the *shank* (gripped by the self-centering chuck of the hand drill), and the body or *flutes* (which perform the cutting action). They are made of carbon steel for ordinary hand use, and of a special high-speed steel designed to withstand heat and friction while maintaining sharpness when used with power tools. The tip end or point of the drill does the cutting, removing chips from the metal as it advances. The metal being cut should be held securely in place with clamps or nails hammered into a scrap of wood, placed to hold the metal in a position which *counteracts* the rotating force of the drill. The diameters of twist drills are

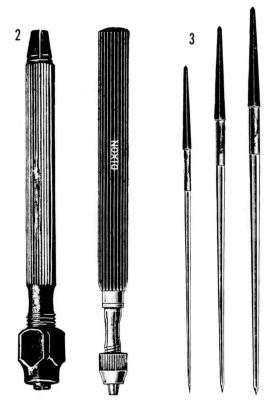

1. Hand reamer or broach for enlarging holes 2. Hand pin vises used to hold miniature reamers 3. Miniature hand reamers

is intended. Apply a little light machine oil to the drill tip.

Reamers or Broaches For holes which must be made larger, this long, tapered hand tool with five cutting edges is used. The reamer can be secured in a hollow-handled holder or pin vise, is then inserted in the opening, and rotated in alternate directions till the desired amount of metal is removed.

Center Punch This is a hard-pointed steel tool used to mark the centers of holes before drilling operations and for use in measurements. Its use in drilling prevents the drill from wandering at the beginning of the drilling operation. (See page 72.)

Solid- and Hollow-Punch Tools Small holes may be made in metal by the use of small solid punches, and larger ones up to three inches in diameter are made with hollow punches. The metal is placed on a lead block or an end grain hardwood block. The tool is placed on the metal and hammered with a heavy hammer till it cuts through the metal into the block. Holes can be made with punches when two or more sheets of metal are being joined by riveting, but if any misshaping of the metal occurs, it should be flattened after the holes are made by placing the metal on a flat steel sheet, and applying a mallet. (See page 81.)

measured in wire gauge numbers, letters, fractions, and decimals of an inch. (See page 460.) The sizes are stamped on the twist drill where the shank joins the flutes, but if their markings are not clear, they can be checked by using a *wire* or *twist drill gauge*. Simply insert the drill into the tightest opening and take a reading. (See page 72.)

When hand drilling, make sure that the metal is resting securely on a scrap hardwood block. When drilling holes larger than ⅜ inch, start by first making a smaller hole. When drilling holes into metals other than brass, bronze, or cast iron, the cutting action is increased by using a little machine oil as a lubricant. Drills should be placed as deeply into the chuck as possible. This gives them maximum rigidity and prevents the formation of oversized or irregularly shaped holes.

Drill Press Many electrically operated drill presses with varying chuck capacity and speeds are available, depending on the needs of the craftsman. With mechanically operated presses, always use the drill at the speed for which it

FORMING TOOLS AND MATERIALS

General Files Files made of chrome or other hard steel are used for the shaping and finishing of metals, and to remove burrs from edges. The length of a file is its *cutting* surface from the point to the tang (the narrow, long end which can be fastened to a handle). The most common lengths for general files are six, eight, or ten inches. All files are designed to remove small amounts of metal when pushed in a *forward-moving stroke;* therefore the pressure is eased on the return stroke. While the metal is being filed, it should be securely fixed in a holding device, or held up against a bench pin. Long, sweeping strokes are more efficient than repeated short ones.

There are four main classifications of files: general, rasp, needle, and riffle. The teeth or ridges which form the cutting edges of the file, called the *cut,* are made mechanically with

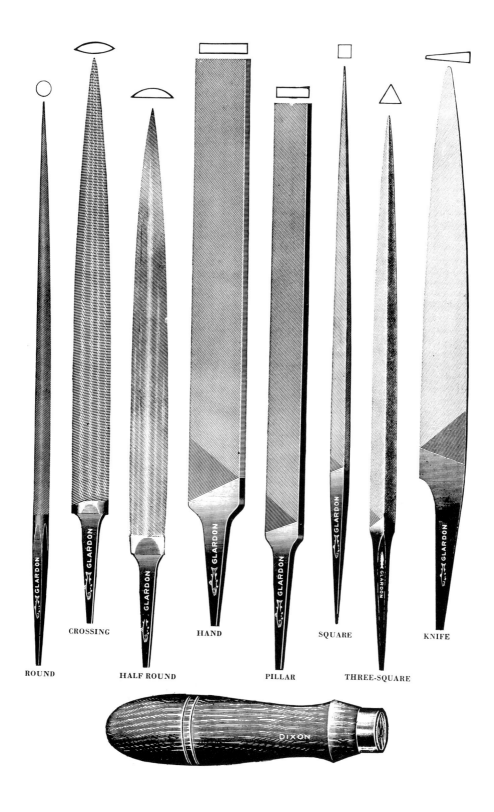

ROUND

CROSSING

HALF ROUND

HAND

PILLAR

SQUARE

THREE-SQUARE

KNIFE

DIXON

Swiss hand files, tempered, 4″ to 8″ length with wood handle

BASIC TOOL GROUPS   431

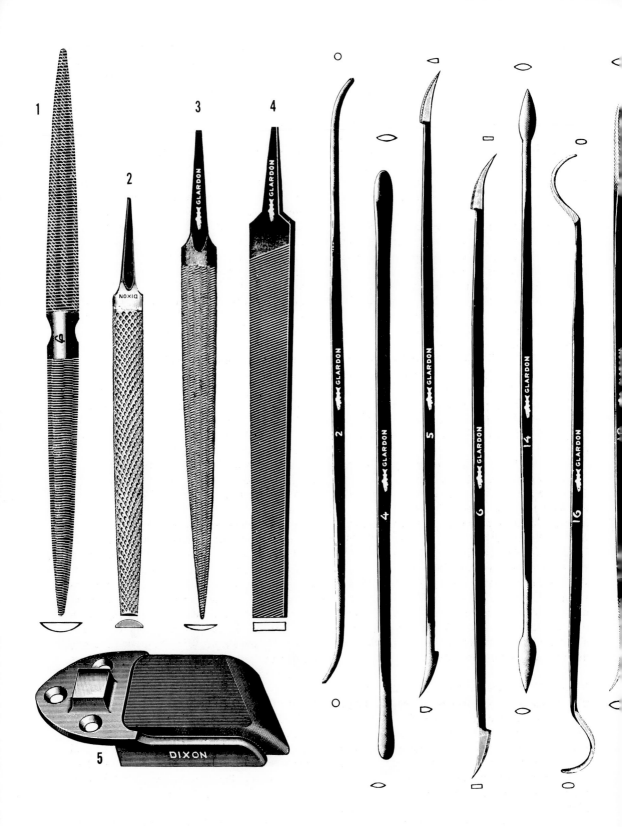

Coarse files for work on soft materials: 1. Vulcanite file, for shaping wax 2. Rasp, for soft metals and wood 3. Float file, half round, for soft metals 4. Float file, flat, for soft metals 5. Bench filing block with rubber rest for supporting work without marking it

Jeweler's riffle files or die sinker riffle files

chisels in degrees of roughness ranging from coarse to smooth. These cutting edges are the basis for the grading of files. When ordering files, it is necessary to mention length, shape, and cut.

The grades of coarseness or cut of foreign, so-called Swiss files, range from 00 (the coarsest) to 8 (the finest). American file equivalents: 00 is called a rough file, 0 is a bastard, 1 a second cut, and 2 a smooth cut, with any beyond this called supersmooth or deadsmooth. *Single cut* files have a series of parallel cuts at an angle of about 25° to the length of the file. They cut slowly, and are generally used for finishing. *Double cut or crosscut* files have two crossing series of cuts which form teeth. The first cut is at about a 25° angle, and the second, which is finer, is between 45 and 50°. Double cut files generally remove more metal than single cut files, and are used for rougher work, but the degree of coarseness is also a factor. *Circular cut* files usually have teeth at a radius of about 1½ inches, and are used for soft metals. *Rasps* are coarse files with distinct projecting points which are made with a sharp punch instead of a chisel as on true files, and are available in rough to smooth coarseness.

Files are also classified according to *cross-section shape*. Flat, round, square, triangular (three square), half round, rattail, knife, oval, and safe edge (one side is left smooth so that it does not act on a finished surface) are some of the common shapes.

Files are also classified according to their *special* function: saw file (for filing saw teeth), slot file, needle files (used by jewelers and silversmiths), and float files (single cut, made for use on soft metals) are some of them. New files should be used on softer, nonferrous metals first, till they are worn, and then on harder metals such as iron and steel.

Needle Files Needle files are fine, narrow files about 4 to 7¾ inches in length, single cut, smooth, and are used generally for jewelry making. The teeth are scraped on by a toothed cutter in an operation called "combing." They are usually made in 0 to 6 cut (#2 cut is the most commonly used one). All needle files have round handles, except those called *escapement* files which have square handles. A greater variety of cross-sectional shapes are available in needle files than in general files. When ordering, it is usually understood that the length referred to is the *cutting* length and not the over-all length.

Rifflers Rifflers are special files with curved and shaped ends of various cross section, used for getting into depressions and angles which are inaccessible with ordinary shaped files. They are available in small, medium, and large 0 to 6 cuts. (See page 434.)

File Cleaners In use, files may become clogged with metal particles called *pins,* which scratch the metal being worked. Oil and grease also clog files and reduce their efficiency; therefore *only clean surfaces* should be filed. Files should be cleaned occasionally to keep them in optimum working condition. To clean a file, a tool called a *file card,* with or without a brush, is passed *across the width* and *not* the length of the file. Pins can also be scratched out with a pointed brass, copper, or soft iron wire. File cards are made of soft brass or steel wire. (See page 435.)

File Handles Wood handles with a hole at one end usually reinforced with a metal ferule are designed to be used with files, and are made in sizes to suit all file sizes. The tang end of the file can be forced into the file handle enough to hold, with just manual pressure. If more pressure is needed, a few taps with a wood mallet on the handle, holding small files in the hand, and resting larger files on a wood surface, will suffice. (See page 431.)

Hammers Hammers of forged steel with polished heads of various weights which are fixed to a wood handle, exist in great variety, each designed to suit various functions. They are used in conjunction with other tools (such as chasing and riveting hammers), or by themselves against the metal directly in conjunction with resisting surfaces (raising hammers and anvils), in the shaping of metals, and, at times, against the metal alone "in air." Usually, faces are hardened by tempering.

Silversmith Hammers Used in the beginning operations of raising a shape. Made in various weights ranging from three ounces to two pounds (or more), they have rounded or oval faces shaped in a variety of depth-of-face curves to suit the contour of the work as it progresses. (See page 243.)

Raising Hammers Used on the outside surfaces of metals in the early forming stages. They are generally wide, rectangular, edge-rounded faces which cut the metal less than narrow ones.

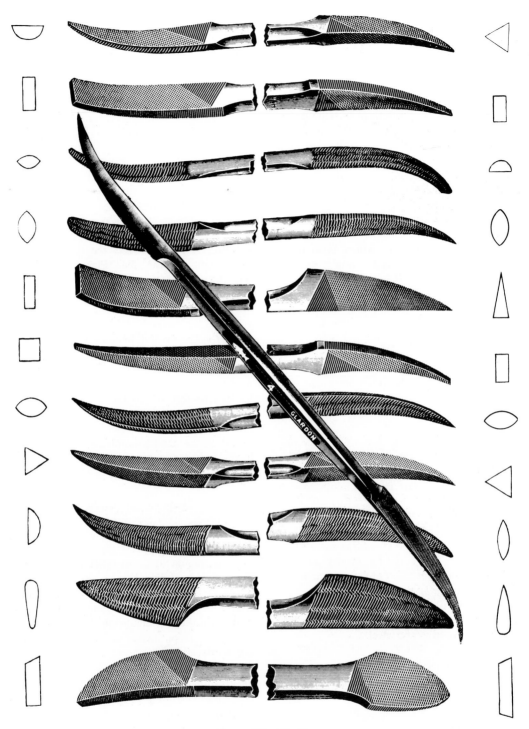

Silversmith's riffle files

Embossing Hammers Generally driven against the *inner* surfaces of work being shaped, to raise contours while the work rests on a sandbag or pitch bowl, these hammers have smooth, rounded ends.

Blocking Hammer Large hook-shaped hammer used for reaching surfaces inside deep forms.

Collet Hammer A narrow-faced hammer used in raising, suited to forming deep curves.

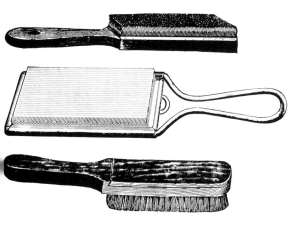

File cards or file cleaners

Planishing Hammer A hammer with two flat faces weighing about ¾ pound, used to surface forms and smooth out irregularities after the above-mentioned hammers have done their work. Usually, the surface created with this hammer is the final one.

Pein (Peen or Pane) Hammers These hammers have a head with one flat face, and one rounded, hemispherical, or thin end (cross pein), opposite the flat face called the *pein*. The *ball pein* or hemispherical pein-ended hammer is also known as the machinist's hammer. This is an all-purpose tool used on center punches, cold chisels, for flattening rivet heads, and sometimes for doming operations. It is made in weights from two ounces to four pounds.

Riveting Hammer Slightly concave-faced hammer used to round out rivet heads.

Forging Hammer A heavy hammer (about six pounds) used in forging operations. (See page 279.)

Chasing Hammers Used in conjunction with chasing and repoussé tools. (See page 97.)

Mallets Mallets are used in the preliminary shaping stages of objects being raised, and during forming operations when a minimum of surface marking is desired. They are made of a great variety of materials: wood, fiber, buckskin, horn (sometimes lead-weighted), rawhide, plastic, lignum vitae, rubber, and nylon, in a great many shapes suited to specific functions. Mallet ends can be flat-faced, rounded (for bossing or rounding out), flat-

tapered, tapered wedge (used for raising), and others. Mallets are sometimes used exclusively in the forming of soft metals such as pewter and lead. (See page 256.)

Stakes and Anvils A great variety of stakes and anvils are available to the metalworker, some with special functions, and others made for use in a variety of functions. Terminology is not standardized, and often confusing, with the same shaped stake having a different name among manufacturers and users. An attempt is made here to group them according to *function* or *shape,* though the vast number of stakes and anvils prevents the list from being comprehensive.

Regardless of the shape of the stake, it must be firmly secured in position before use. The most functional level is usually elbow level, held in an anvil base or stake holder which is secured to a heavy bench; an appropriate hole in the end grain of a log or tree stump; a heavy vise; or in the set chisel or hardie hole of a large, bolted-down forging anvil.

Though some stakes defy classification, basically, most stakes can be grouped into the following divisions: T-stakes, mushroom and flat-topped stakes, anvil heads, mandrels, plate and tray stakes, and surface blocks or plates. All are made of a tough steel, and working surfaces are highly polished. (See page 244.)

T-Stakes T-stakes take their name from the general conformation of the stake shape: two working ends joined perpendicularly, with an extension which is placed in the stake holder. They are used for standard raising, forming, and planishing operations, and all working surfaces are highly polished. They are made with varying straight, tapered, and curved ends for general use. Some special T-stake shapes are the valley, fluting, or crimping stake as it is variously called (used for crimping or fluting operations), the cow's tongue stake which has upward curving, arched, tapered ends (used for forming and planishing to fit varying curved contours), curved knob end stakes (used for forming small and highly raised objects), and others. The choice of stake used depends on the desired form of the object being made.

Mushroom and Flat-Topped Stakes Mushroom stakes fit vertically into stake holders, have many curved conformations, from the semicircular or ball shape to the slightly domed, and have diameters ranging from 10 inches down to 1½ inches. Oval shapes for

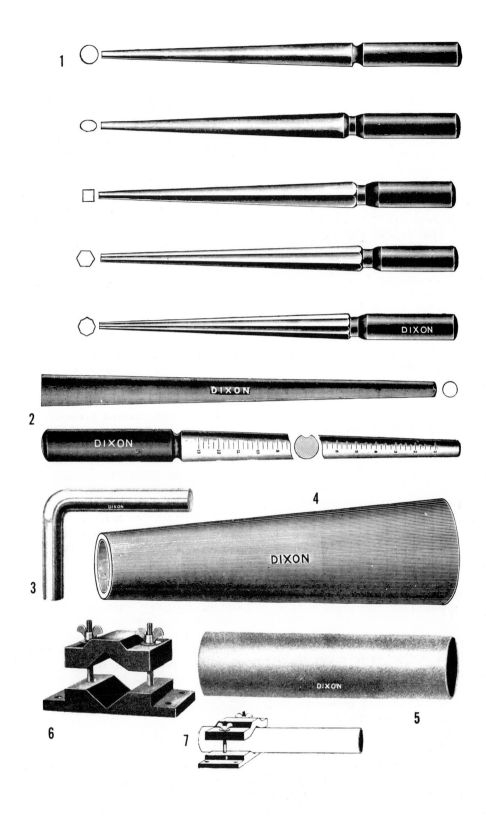

Mandrels: 1. Bezel making mandrels 2. Ring mandrels, unmarked, ring size marked, can be used for working 3. Bent mandrel 4. Bracelet mandrel, tapered, oval 5. Straight silversmith's mandrel 6. Bench mandrel holder 7. Holder in use

use in making flatware are also available. They are used for shaping and planishing operations.

Flat-topped stakes are made in a variety of diameters, and are also called *bottoming* stakes. They are used in conjunction with a planishing hammer to true the bottom of a raised form. Extension devices added to the stake holder permit the "bottoming" of deep forms.

Anvil Heads Anvil heads of a great variety of forms to suit special and general purposes of forming and planishing are made with short bases, and must therefore be used held in a vise, or by insertion in an extension arm (straight, curved, or right angle). Besides the regular geometric shapes, grooved, sloping, triangular, oval, and other shapes are available.

Mandrels Starting with the smallest, mandrels of long, tapered, conical section are used for the shaping of bezels, rings, bracelets, and holloware. They are held in a vise, or when heavy enough, they can be used directly on a workbench.

Plate and Tray Stakes These plates have a step-down depression which is used in the shaping of plate and tray rims, and are designed to be held in a bench vise.

Surface Blocks and Plates These are used when the need arises for a flat, polished, true surface in shaping and planishing operations. They are held in a vise or when quite heavy, free standing on a workbench.

SPECIAL STAKES

Snarling Iron A long, narrow, curved stake, usually with a rounded or peen end which is inserted into narrow or long-necked holloware to aid in forming. The work proceeds by hammering the end of the tool near the vise holding it. The reacting kick of the peen end which is *inside* the article strikes the inside of the metal form. The article must be positioned so that the resulting blow will fall where desired.

Wood and Metal Forms or Blocks Forms and blocks made of hardwood and metal are used in forming a piece by the stretching method (described in the Silversmithing section). Wood blocks with V-shaped grooves are sometimes used for crimping in place of the valley or crimping stake. (See page 255.)

A simple, thick steel plate is a useful tool in itself. It is suitable for truing or flattening forms (as shown) and also as a surface against which raising by stretching processes can be worked. *Photo taken by the author at Los Costillo Plateros, Taxco, Mexico.*

Sandbags Made of canvas and filled with sand, they are used for forming and embossing operations. Sandbags may also be used to support a pitchbowl while it is in use.

Lead Block Used in the shaping of small raised design units in holloware and jewelry. The usual size is three inches square by one inch in thickness. It may be used as a dapping block substitute. Adhering particles of lead must be cleaned from the metal being worked before any heating operations, as the lead melts at a low temperature and will eat into and pit the other metal. (See page 321.)

Repoussé tools, *chasing* tools, *engraving* tools, and *matting* tools are all described under the section dealing with the process in which they are used. *Pitch bowls* and their uses will be found in the same sections. (See pages 96 and 112.)

Pliers There are two groups of pliers, those whose jaws pivot around a rivet, and those whose jaws remain parallel when open. Rivet-pivoted pliers may be constructed with cross-lap or box joints.

Many kinds of pliers are made for special purposes, usually of cast steel, between 5 and 10 inches graduated in half-inch lengths. Inside box construction jaws may be *serrated* for easy gripping, or *smooth,* which leaves the metal unmarked. Pliers are used in a variety

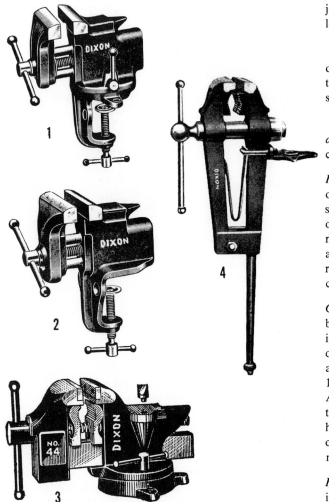

jeweler's pliers can be changed by filing followed by smoothing with emery cloth.

Drawplates and *tongs* used to change the diameter or cross-section shape of wire, and the *rolling mill* used to reduce the thickness of sheet metal, are discussed elsewhere.

Die cutting, die stamping, dapping blocks, dapping punches, and *dapping dies* are all discussed in other sections. (See pages 81–84.)

Hollow Punches These are classified as a form of dapping die punch. The cutting edge is very sharp, and the punch is hollow. With the aid of a hammer, the punch is forced through the metal while it is being held on a softer metal and produces a circular disc (if the die is round, or another shape depending on the contour of the die). (See page 81.)

Circle Cutters A tool made of two steel blocks with a space between them for the insertion of the metal sheet, pierced with holes of various sizes (⅛″, 3⁄16″, ¼″, 5⁄16″, ⅜″, 7⁄16″, and ½″). Some models will cut metals up to 16 gauge, and others up to ⅝″ in thickness. After the metal is inserted in the slot space, the positive die punch made to match the hole size being cut is placed in the correct opening, and hammered lightly through the metal to produce a disc. (See page 81.)

Hole Punch A tool used to make small holes in metal which operates on a similar principle as the one above, except that the hole maker is forced through the metal in a screwing motion. (See page 81.)

Spinning lathes and *tools* and *casting tools* and *apparatus* are discussed in separate sections. (See pages 301 and 320–24.)

HOLDING TOOLS AND MATERIALS

Bench Vise Bench vises of varying jaw width (5″ to 3½″ are the most commonly used for general purposes), and jaw opening width capacity (4″ to 6″), some with tempered, replaceable jaws and others with permanent jaws, are an essential craftsman's tool. A positive locking swivel base to allow work to be rotated without removal is an additional convenience.

Clamp-on Vise A lightweight vise of swivel and stationary type opening to 2¼″ jaws, can be clamped to any worktable.

Bench vises: 1. Swivel vise, 2½″ jaw width, 2¼″ jaw opening, 2 pounds 2. Bench vise, 1½″ jaw width, 2¼″ jaw opening, 3½ pounds 3. Utility bench vise, swivel base, 4″ jaw width, 4½″ jaw opening, 28 pounds 4. Blacksmith's leg vise, removable pipe jaws, jaw width 4¼″, jaw opening 4½″, 50 pounds, used to hold stakes and anvils

of ways, for bending and shaping wire and thin sheet metal, forming bezels, small rivet setting, and handling hot articles, to mention a few uses. The cross section of the pliers' nose or jaws are designed for specific functions: *chain nose* (for forming chain links, both jaws flat inside and round outside); *round nose* (both tapered jaws round); *half round* (one jaw flat, the other round); *flat nose* (both jaws flat); *combination* pliers (an inexpensive pliers with adjustable jaws used for general work and for holding hot metal). Still others have unique functions such as ring holding, chain loop closing, small tube cutting, and an extra long nosed series. The shape of the jaws of

Ring Vise or Clamp A rounded hardwood hand vise with leather-lined jaws used to hold small objects and rings while filing, polishing, or setting stones. A wood wedge is forced between the two parts opposite the jaw end to hold the object securely.

Hand Vise A small vise to be held in one hand with jaws controlled by tightening a wing nut. Used for holding objects inconvenient to hold in a fixed vise, or while drilling, and is also used to hold wire while twisting while the other end is clamped in a bench vise.

Pin Vise Used for holding small tools such as needles, fine drills, and reamers, also wire. Those equipped with chucks have collets which will admit tools up to 2 mm. diameter. Some have hollow stems to permit the entry of wire.

Engraver's Block or Ball Vise and Attachments Used by engravers to hold almost any shaped article with exposed edges rigidly in position while it is being engraved. A standard model has a diameter of 5 inches, a maximum jaw opening of 3 inches, and maximum jaw depth of 2¼ inches, which indicates the size limitation of the object. The ball weighs about fifteen pounds, and rests in a felt ring or leather pad which contacts the outside polished surface and can therefore be rotated easily and smoothly at slight pressure, an important factor in the engraving process. Attachments consisting of pins and holders of various shapes, ring holders, etc., are available for use held in the holes of the jaw face to hold objects of practically any shape which the jaw opening size will accommodate. Closing and tightening the jaws is controlled by a special key provided with the block. (See page 113.)

C-Clamp Made of forged steel or malleable iron, C-clamps of various openings and depth are used to hold metal down for other operations such as filing, drilling, and sawing. (See page 67.)

Tweezers Tweezers are used for picking up small objects such as solder snippets and placing them. Besides plain pointed tweezers, there are cross-locking tweezers which are spring constructed to automatically hold things without pressure, slide lock tweezers, and a great variety of differently shaped tweezers for special functions. Tweezers can be used to hold metal parts together during soldering.

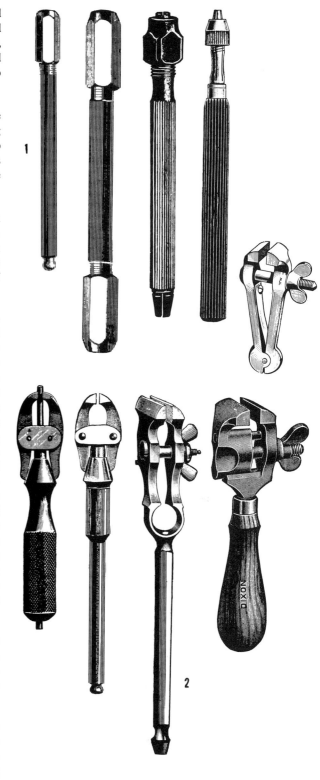

Holding tools for wire and small work: 1. Hand holding devices for needles and round tools 2. Thumb screw hand vises for holding work

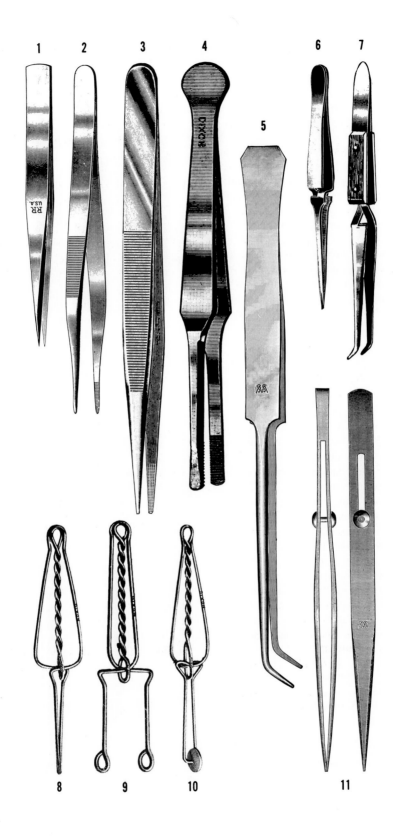

Tweezers: 1, 2. Pointed 3. Plain point 4. Flat point 5. Bent point 6. Self locking 7. Cross locking

Wire soldering tweezers: 8. Flat end 9. Round end 10. Disc style 11. Slide locking

Black Iron Binding Wire Soft iron or annealed binding wire is used to hold pieces together while they are being joined by soldering. It is available in spools in various thicknesses, depending on the need. Larger pieces require heavier gauges which will not burn through readily during heating. The common sizes, the gauge number given with the Stubbs Iron Wire decimal equivalent, are as follows: 16 (.063), 18 (.049), 20 (.035), 26 (.018), 28 (.014), 31 (.010). If the wire is coated with a mixture of ochre, rouge, or whiting and water, and applied with a brush before heating, the wire will be better protected from burning through. Do not twist the wire together too tightly or the expanding metal being held will be marked after heating operations. If no heavier wire is available, two strands of a finer gauge wire can be twisted together and used that way. (See page 171.)

Spatulas and Spreaders Small spatulas can be used to carry and place powders such as ground niello being prepared for firing, and for combining small amounts of powders and liquids on a glass surface. They are made in many shapes. Some *dental* spatulas are useful in metalwork for probing and scratching, and for use in shaping wax when making a wax model for casting.

Shellac Mounting Stick This tool consists of a wood disc with attached handle, with the disc covered by a layer of stick shellac. It is used to securely hold small metal objects in place while they are being engraved, chased, or otherwise worked on. The shellac is heated to soften it, and the metal is placed in position. Once it cools, it becomes firmly fixed. To be removed, heat it again, and pry it loose with a metal tool. The solvent for removing particles of shellac from the metal is alcohol. (See page 93.)

For a description of the use of *Chaser's Pitch* and *Burgundy Pitch* see page 94.

Gums, Glues, and Cements There are many new cements and glues available on the market, and newer ones are constantly being developed. The list given here is by no means complete, but contains the commonly used types.

Epoxy A form of which is called no-peg pearl cement, epoxy is a strong cement which holds wood, stone, or metal to metal. It is used in situations where soldering is impractical. Two tubes, one containing a catalyst for the other, must be mixed in equal amounts and then applied. Epoxy can be mixed with metal filings, applied to a metal surface, then sprinkled with more filings to make an interesting and permanent surface texture, not otherwise possible.

Gum Arabic and Gum Tragacanth Both of these organic gums, derived from a tree and a plant respectively, are used in several processes such as granulation, niello, and in some soldering situations. They completely volatilize under heat and leave no residue ash. They are water soluble.

Rubber Cement A non-curling paper cement used to glue patterns to metal in preparation for sawing out. Paper can be easily removed by peeling it off. The solvent is acetone.

Cutlery Cement A good cement for fixing knife blades into handles is made with the following formula:

Rosin	4 parts
Beeswax	1 part
Plaster of Paris or brickdust	1 part

Combine and while hot, pour the mixture into the handle. Insert the heated tang end of the blade into the cement while hot, and allow it to set.

Sealing Wax Used to fill in depressions at the back of thin metal repoussé work, also in hollow metal beads, to support the metal and help it retain its shape.

Shellac Mixed with some denatured alcohol, shellac can be used to cement many materials to each other, or to hold articles temporarily.

Jeweler's Cement

Lump rosin	6 parts
Plaster of Paris	4 parts

Heat the rosin slowly till it melts, and add the plaster slowly, stirring in a small amount at a time. Adjust the proportions for a harder or softer cement. Good as a temporary binder.

Cement Brasses This is a *tool* used when working on a lathe in special situations when the metal cannot be held in the usual way. It

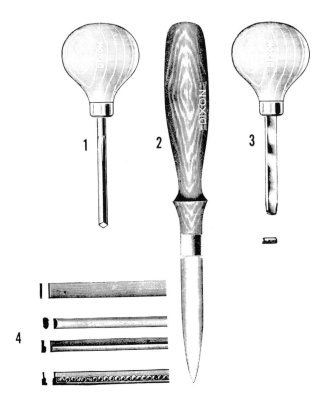

For setting stones: 1. Bezel pusher 2. Steel burnisher
3. Creaser 4. Bezel gallery wire

It should fit easily and not have to be forced, as on occasion it may have to be removed. (Stones which fit properly can be lifted out of bezels by touching them with a wad of sticky wax.) As bezels are usually made of fine silver which is softer than sterling, and since the bezel has been subjected to the heat of soldering, it is quite soft, and therefore can be easily compressed.

The bezel setting tool is placed at the base of the bezel and is pressed in a rolling motion from the base toward the stone surface till the metal touches the stone. To insure the centering of the stone, and an even flattening of the bezel, the tool is first applied to the cardinal points so that it is held in place, and then the rest of the bezel metal is pressed down.

Crown settings for faceted stones also employ a bezel stone setter for the same purpose. Each crown point or prong is pushed over the stone with the bezel setter till they all hold the stone in place.

In setting a stone, it is also possible to use a flat-ended repoussé tool. This can be handled by the use of a very lightweight hammer, as very little pressure is needed.

The Burnisher Burnishers are used for smoothing and polishing metal surfaces. They are made of polished, hard steel, and are oval in cross section, with tapered, straight, or curved blades. Some burnishers are used exclusively for *polish burnishing* employed as the final finishing process on metal. This type is usually made with an agate stone tip in a variety of shapes and sizes. (See page 409.)

Burnishers are used in the stone setting process after the bezel has been compressed into position with the bezel setter. The bezel is then smoothed by going over it with the burnisher in sweeping motions, using soapy water as a lubricant. If this does not smooth the bezel completely, it may be necessary to file some irregularities away, and then go over these portions again with the burnisher.

Soldering and *heating* tools, *casting* tools, and tools used for *acid processes* will be found discussed in the section dealing with the process.

can be held on this ridged lathe disc by the cement or shellac which is spread over the surface, by first heating the cement or shellac, and immediately placing the metal, then allowing it to cool. The disc has an attached projecting threaded rod which can be held by or screwed to the lathe chuck.

STONE-SETTING TOOLS

Bezel Setter When setting a stone in a bezel setting, the stone when finally placed in the formed bezel is made to remain permanently in position, held by the bezel, with the aid of a bezel setter. This tool resembles an engraving tool as it has a rounded wood handle and a short steel square rod about two inches in length which projects from the handle, and has a polished, squared-off end. Smoothing the bezel is usually done with a burnisher.

Setting a Stone: Cabochon Cut in a Bezel A general description for setting a bezel-held, cabochon-cut stone is as follows: The article, let us say a ring, is held firmly in a clamp, vise, or other holding device. The stone is placed in the bezel and pushed down securely.

THE FLEXIBLE SHAFT AND MOTOR

In a class by itself, this versatile tool can be used in so many ways it is becoming an "extra hand" for the craftsman, jeweler, and stone setter. The tool consists of a small motor

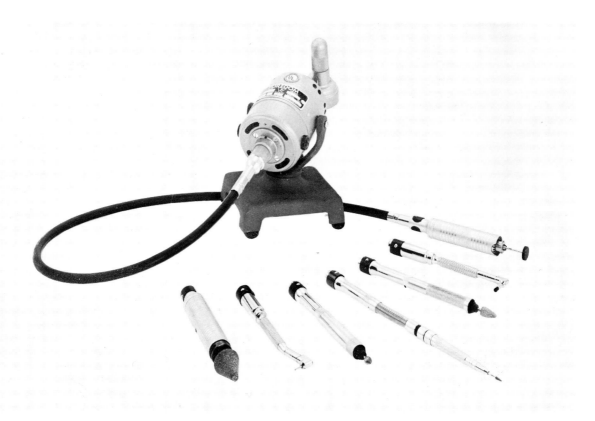

Universal flexible shaft with motor; a variety of handpieces suitable for different situations. *Craftool, Inc.*

of ⅒ or ⅕ hp (horsepower), 110 volts, 1.5 amperes, which can be suspended from a hook over a workbench or wall. The motor is usable with both AC and DC current, and is worked by applying pressure on a foot rheostat which regulates the speed from 1500 to 14,000 rpm (revolutions per minute), depending on the pressure exerted. A speed of at least 3500 rpm is recommended for cutting, and higher speeds are used for polishing.

The enclosed shaft which extends from the motor is quite flexible, and not counting the handpiece, is about 36 inches long. Some models can be attached to a ¼-inch capacity electric hand drill, drill press, or motor of ¼, ⅓, or ½ hp. When attaching the shaft to an electric hand drill or drill press, simply insert the projecting shaft chuck into the hand drill or drill press chuck, and tighten. For attachment to a motor, a special coupling is necessary.

The shaft ends in a handpiece 5 to 7 inches long which contains a collet designed to hold the mandrel of the accessory used. Collets are interchangeable up to a certain maximum capacity, depending on the model. The usual collet is capable of holding mandrels from 0 to ⅛ inch in diameter. Adapter chucks of larger sizes can be inserted into a small chuck to increase its capacity. Some handpieces have key chucks, and others are hand-adjusted for tightening.

Many accessories are available for use with a flexible shaft assembly. They often perform jobs which are otherwise difficult or time-consuming. These accessories are made already mounted permanently on mandrels of various diameters. Separate mandrels are available with removable mounting screws so that accessories can be attached, interchanged, or replaced when worn. When purchasing an accessory, keep in mind the *chuck capacity* of your particular model of flexible shaft, and get a mandrel size which will fit it, or use an *adapter collet.*

Accessories are available for various operations. For drilling, use high-speed jeweler's drills. For grinding, mounted or unmounted carborundum and aluminum oxide discs, made in a great variety of shapes. High-speed and tool steel burrs of various shapes, usable on all metals but steel, circular files, reamer burrs, and miniature abrasive belts are useful for shaping, grinding, and cutting metals. For abrasive action in the removal of scratches, pumice and brightboy wheels are used. For polishing, there are bristle and wire brushes, small mus-

1. Hanging flexible shaft motor with flexible hand piece and foot peddle rheostat starter 2. Floor model flexible shaft motor and rigid handpiece, heavy duty 3. Two kinds of flexible handpieces: for ³⁄₃₂″ shank capacity; for ¹⁄₃₂″ to ¹⁄₈″ capacity

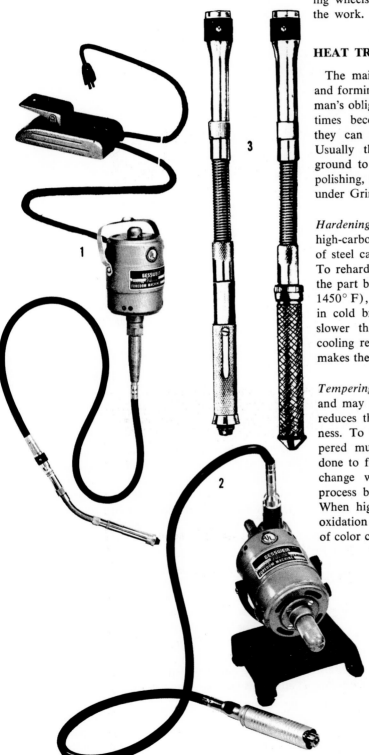

lin buffs made to fit spare mandrels, and square or knife-edge felt wheels. They are used with the usual polishing abrasives and compositions such as tripoli, rouge, and greaseless compounds, in situations where ordinary-sized buffing wheels are too large to reach portions of the work.

HEAT TREATMENT FOR SMALL TOOLS

The maintenance of tools used for cutting and forming is an important part of the craftsman's obligation to himself. Tools in use sometimes become dull or possibly broken, but they can usually be restored to usefulness. Usually this means the tool must first be ground to reshape it, followed by hardening, polishing, and tempering. Grinding is discussed under Grinding and Abrasives on page 410.

Hardening Many hand tools are made of high-carbon, plain, or alloy steel. These kinds of steel can be easily hardened and tempered. To reharden an edge or point, it is heated till the part becomes a medium cherry red (about 1450° F), and then it is rapidly quenched in cold brine water or oil. An oil quench is slower than water quenching. The quickest cooling results in the hardest steel. Quenching makes the steel structure fine-grained and hard.

Tempering The steel is now too hard for use, and may be brittle. The process of tempering reduces this hardness and increases its toughness. To temper a tool, the end being tempered must first be *highly polished*. This is done to facilitate the observation of the color change which occurs during the tempering process by which temper readiness is judged. When high-carbon steel is slowly heated, the oxidation of the surface is visible by a series of color changes which follow in a set sequence and indicate a rise in temperature. The color changes are: straw yellow, golden yellow, purple, dark blue, pale blue. Tools of various uses need more or less tempering to function efficiently.

OPPOSITE: Accessories for flexible shafts: 1. Table of standard head sizes 2. Metal burs 3. White polishing points 4. Circular routers, saws, diamond discs, and files 5. Metal burs of various shapes 6. Fissure bur

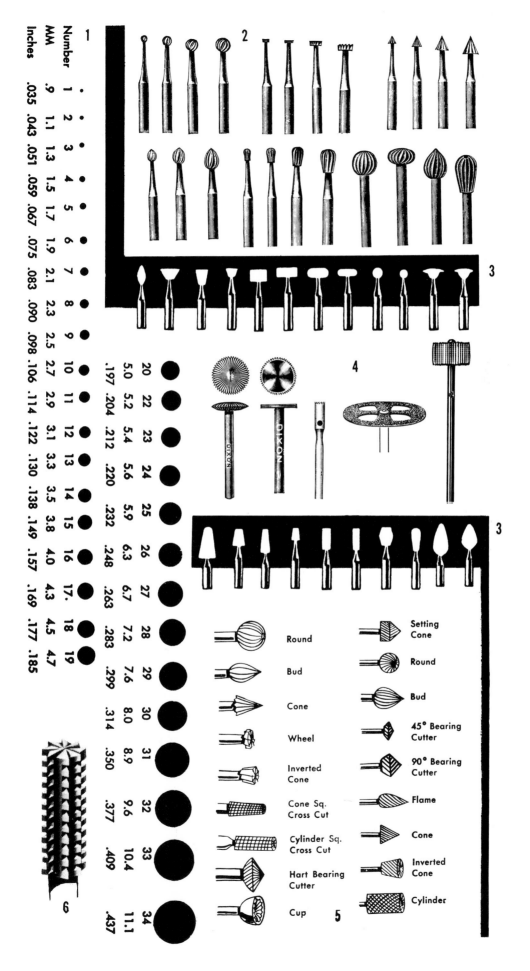

Number	Inches	MM
1	.035	.9
2	.043	1.1
3	.051	1.3
4	.059	1.5
5	.067	1.7
6	.075	1.9
7	.083	2.1
8	.090	2.3
9	.098	2.5
10	.106	2.7
11	.114	2.9
12	.122	3.1
13	.130	3.3
14	.138	3.5
15	.149	3.8
16	.157	4.0
17.	.169	4.3
18	.177	4.5
19	.185	4.7
20	.197	5.0
22	.204	5.2
23	.212	5.4
24	.220	5.6
25	.232	5.9
26	.248	6.3
27	.263	6.7
28	.283	7.2
29	.299	7.6
30	.314	8.0
31	.350	8.9
32	.377	9.6
33	.409	10.4
34	.437	11.1

Round
Bud
Cone
Wheel
Inverted Cone
Cone Sq. Cross Cut
Cylinder Sq. Cross Cut
Hart Bearing Cutter
Cup

Setting Cone
Round
Bud
45° Bearing Cutter
90° Bearing Cutter
Flame
Cone
Inverted Cone
Cylinder

1
2
3
4
5
6

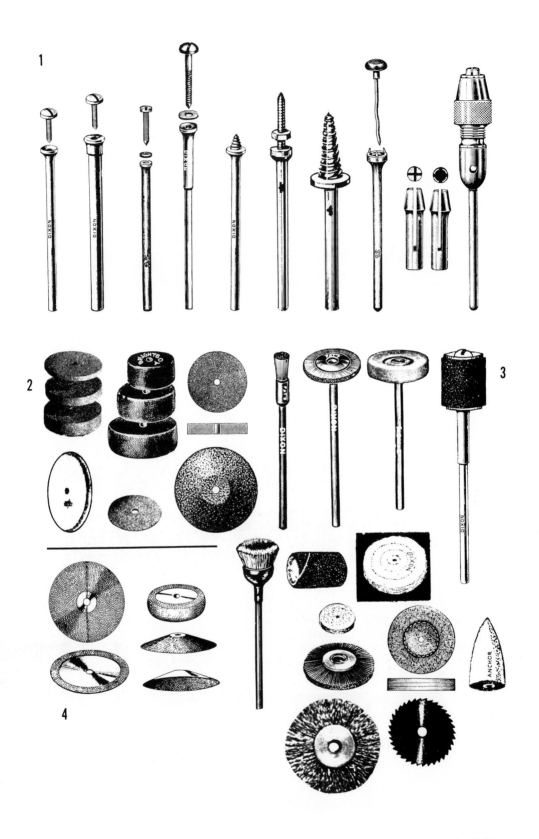

Accessories for flexible shafts: 1. Flexible shaft hand-piece mandrels and adaptor chucks 2. Abrasive discs (carborundum, brightboy, emery, rubber, pumice wheels, paper carborundum discs) 3. Brushes, muslin buffs, felt wheels, chamois wheel, pointed felt cone, bristle brush, wire brush, saw 4. Diamond wheels and cones

When tempering a tool, a Bunsen burner or a red-hot piece of steel can be used. The heat is applied to about one inch from the edge, but if possible directed away from the edge, point, or surface being tempered, and the color change is observed. As soon as the desired color is reached, quench the entire tool *immediately* or the temperature will continue past the desired heat. If a piece of red-hot steel is used, the tool is placed on the hot steel. The color must approach almost to the cutting edge of the tool. (See table below.)

Point or Edge Hardening When hardening and tempering is done in one operation, the process is called point hardening. The tool is heated to cherry red, and the point is dipped into the quenching liquid. While being held with tongs, the point is polished with a piece of emery cloth held on a piece of wood. As the remainder of the tool has retained its heat, the polished portion is watched till the desired tempering color has been reached. The whole tool is then quenched immediately. When dipping the tool into the quenching liquid the first time, do not hold it stationary, but move it vertically into and out of the liquid. This is done to avoid the formation of a *water line* which might cause the tool to crack at that point when the tempering heat approaches.

Tool Tempering Judged By Color

Color	Temperature	Tool
Straw yellow	428° F	Scrapers, light turning tools, lathe tools, twist drills, finishing tools
Golden yellow	469° F	Hammer faces, cold chisels
Purple	531° F	Bone cutting tools, shear blades, dies and punches, chasing tools, gouges
Dark blue	550° F	Dental and surgical tools, hot chisels
Pale blue	610° F	Needles, hacksaws, springs, screwdrivers

A caster from Brindaban, India, polishing a cast brass figure of Lord Krishna with powdered brick dust. *Photo by Oppi.*

PERIODIC TABLE OF ELEMENTS

The atomic number is given at the top of each square, then the symbol of the element, and the relative atomic weight below (Oxygen=15.999). The groups are arranged vertically, and the periods are arranged horizontally. The element names are given below the chart.

IA	IIA	IIIB	IVB	VB	VIB	VIIB	VIII	VIII	VIII	IB	IIB	IIIA	IVA	VA	VIA	VIIA	0
1 H 1.0080																	2 He 4.0026
3 Li 6.939	4 Be 9.012											5 B 10.81	6 C 12.011	7 N 14.007	8 O 15.999	9 F 18.998	10 Ne 20.183
11 Na 22.99	12 Mg 24.31											13 Al 26.98	14 Si 28.09	15 P 30.974	16 S 32.06	17 Cl 35.453	18 Ar 39.948
19 K 39.102	20 Ca 40.08	21 Sc 44.96	22 Ti 47.90	23 V 50.94	24 Cr 52.00	25 Mn 54.94	26 Fe 55.85	27 Co 58.93	28 Ni 58.71	29 Cu 63.54	30 Zn 65.37	31 Ga 69.72	32 Ge 72.59	33 As 74.92	34 Se 78.96	35 Br 79.909	36 Kr 83.80
37 Rb 85.47	38 Sr 87.62	39 Y 88.90	40 Zr 91.22	41 Nb 92.91	42 Mo 95.94	43 Tc (99)	44 Ru 101.07	45 Rh 102.90	46 Pd 106.4	47 Ag 107.87	48 Cd 112.40	49 In 114.82	50 Sn 118.69	51 Sb 121.75	52 Te 127.60	53 I 126.90	54 Xe 131.30
55 Cs 132.90	56 Ba 137.34	57 *La 138.91	72 Hf 178.49	73 Ta 180.95	74 W 183.85	75 Re 186.2	76 Os 190.2	77 Ir 192.2	78 Pt 195.09	79 Au 196.97	80 Hg 200.59	81 Tl 204.37	82 Pb 207.19	83 Bi 208.98	84 Po (210)	85 At (210)	86 Rn (222)
87 Fr (223)	88 Ra (226)	89 †Ac (227)															

* LANTHANIDE SERIES

58 Ce 140.12	59 Pr 140.91	60 Nd 144.24	61 Pm (145)	62 Sm 150.35	63 Eu 151.96	64 Gd 157.25	65 Tb 158.92	66 Dy 162.50	67 Ho 164.93	68 Er 167.26	69 Tm 168.93	70 Yb 173.04	71 Lu 174.97

† ACTINIDE SERIES

90 Th 232.04	91 Pa (231)	92 U 238.03	93 Np (237)	94 Pu (244)	95 Am (243)	96 Cm (245)	97 Bk (247)	98 Cf (249)	99 Es (254)	100 Fm (252)	101 Md (256)	102 No (254)	103 Lw (257)

Atomic weights are based on carbon¹² = 12. In several cases, the weights are rounded to four or five significant figures. Electron configurations taken from *Theoretical Inorganic Chemistry* by M. Clyde Day and Joel Selbin, Reinhold Publishing Corporation.

* Numbers in parentheses indicate mass number of most stable known isotopes.

Atomic Number, Element Symbol and Name

1. H — Hydrogen	35. Br — Bromine	69. Tm — Thulium
2. He — Helium	36. Kr — Krypton	70. Yb — Ytterbium
3. Li — Lithium	37. Rb — Rubidium	71. Lu — Lutecium
4. Be — Beryllium	38. Sr — Strontium	72. Hf — Hafnium
5. B — Boron	39. Y — Yttrium	73. Ta — Tantalum
6. C — Carbon	40. Zr — Zirconium	74. W — Tungsten
7. N — Nitrogen	41. Nb — Niobium	75. Re — Rhenium
8. O — Oxygen	42. Mo — Molybdenum	76. Os — Osmium
9. F — Fluorine	43. Tc — Technetium	77. Ir — Iridium
10. Ne — Neon	44. Ru — Ruthenium	78. Pt — Platinum
11. Na — Sodium	45. Rh — Rhodium	79. Au — Gold
12. Mg — Magnesium	46. Pd — Palladium	80. Hg — Mercury
13. Al — Aluminum	47. Ag — Silver	81. Tl — Thallium
14. Si — Silicon	48. Cd — Cadmium	82. Pb — Lead
15. P — Phosphorus	49. In — Indium	83. Bi — Bismuth
16. S — Sulphur	50. Sn — Tin	84. Po — Polonium
17. Cl — Chlorine	51. Sb — Antimony	85. At — Astatine
18. A or Ar — Argon	52. Te — Tellurium	86. Rn — Radon
19. K — Potassium	53. I — Iodine	87. Fr — Francium
20. Ca — Calcium	54. Xe — Xenon	88. Ra — Radium
21. Sc — Scandium	55. Cs — Cesium	89. Ac — Actinium
22. Ti — Titanium	56. Ba — Barium	90. Th — Thorium
23. V — Vanadium	57. La — Lanthanum	91. Pa — Protoactinium
24. Cr — Chromium	58. Ce — Cerium	92. U — Uranium
25. Mn — Manganese	59. Pr — Praseodymium	93. Np — Neptunium
26. Fe — Iron	60. Nd — Neodymium	94. Pu — Plutonium
27. Co — Cobalt	61. Pm — Promethium	95. Am — Ammonium
28. Ni — Nickel	62. Sm — Samarium	96. Cm — Curium
29. Cu — Copper	63. Eu — Europium	97. Bk — Berkelium
30. Zn — Zinc	64. Gd — Gadolinium	98. Cf — Californium
31. Ga — Gallium	65. Tb — Terbium	99. E or Es — Einsteinium
32. Ge — Germanium	66. Dy — Dysprosium	100. Fm — Fermium
33. As — Arsenic	67. Ho — Holmium	101. Md or Mv — Mendelevium
34. Se — Selenium	68. Er — Erbium	102. No — Nobelium
		103. Lw — Lawrencium

Part Six

CHARTS AND TABLES

WEIGHTS AND MEASURES

(Dwts. Abbreviation for "Pennyweight")

1 Troy ounce = 31.103 Grams
1 Kilogram = 32.151 Troy ounces
1 Troy ounce = 1.10 Avoirdupois ounces
14.58 Troy ounces = 1 Avoirdupois pound

TROY WEIGHT

24 grains = 1 pennyweight
20 pennyweights = 1 ounce
12 ounces = 1 pound
    Used for weighing gold, silver, and jewels.

APOTHECARIES' WEIGHT

20 grains = 1 scruple   8 drams = 1 ounce
 3 scruples = 1 dram   12 ounces = 1 pound
    The ounce and pound in this are the same as in Troy weight.

AVOIRDUPOIS WEIGHT

27.343 grains = 1 dram
16 drams = 1 ounce
16 ounces = 1 pound   2,000 pounds = 1 short ton
28 pounds = 1 quarter   2,240 pounds = 1 long ton

LIQUID MEASURE

4 gills = 1 pint   31½ gallons = 1 barrel
2 pints = 1 quart   2 barrels = 1 hogshead
4 quarts = 1 gallon   1 quart = 57.75 cubic inches
1 gallon = 3.785 liters   1 gallon = 231 cubic inches
1 imperial gallon = 277.42 cubic inches = 4.543 liters
    The standard unit of liquid measure adopted by the U. S. Government is the Winchester wine gallon, which contains 231 cubic inches, and holds 8.339 pounds avoirdupois of distilled water, at its maximum density weighed in air, the barometer being at 30 inches.

The imperial gallon adopted by Great Britain contains 277.42 cubic inches, and equals 1.20094 U.S. gallons.

LONG MEASURE

12 inches = 1 foot   8 furlongs = 1 statute mile
 3 feet = 1 yard   5,280 feet = 1 mile
 5½ yards = 1 rod   3 nautical miles = 1 league
40 rods = 1 furlong

CUBIC MEASURE

1,728 cubic inches = 1 cubic foot
27 cubic feet = 1 cubic yard
40 cubic feet = 1 ton (shipping)
2,150.42 cubic inches = 1 standard bushel
268.8 cubic inches = 1 standard dry gallon
1 cubic foot = about four-fifths of a bushel

SQUARE MEASURE

144 square inches = 1 square foot   40 square rods = 1 rood
9 square feet = 1 square yard   4 roods = 1 acre
30¼ square yards = 1 square rod   640 acres = 1 square mile
A township is 6 miles square = 36 sections
A section is 1 mile square = 640 acres
¼ section is ½ mile square = 160 acres
1/16 section is ¼ mile square = 40 acres

MISCELLANEOUS

3 inches = 1 palm   18 inches = 1 cubit
4 inches = 1 hand
9 inches = 1 span
12 articles = 1 dozen   2 articles = 1 pair
12 dozen = 1 gross   20 articles = 1 score
12 gross = 1 great gross

EQUIVALENTS OF MEASURES

LENGTHS

1 meter, m = 10 decimeters, dm = 100 centimeters, cm = 1000 millimeters, mm.
1 meter, m = 0.1 decameter, dkm = 0.01 hectometer, hm = 0.001 kilometer, km.
1 meter, m = 39.37 in., U. S. Standard = 39.370113 in., British Standard.
1 millimeter, mm = 1000 microns, μ = 0.03937 in. = 39.37 mils.

Meters, m.	Inches, in.	Feet, ft.	Yards, yd.
1	39.37	3.28083	1.09361
0.02540	1	0.08333	0.02778
0.30480	12	1	0.33333
0.91440	36	3	1
5.02921	198	16.5	5.5
20.1168	792	66	22
1,609.35	63,367	5,280	1,760
1,853.27	72,962.5	6,080.27	2,026.73
1,000	39,370	3,280.83	1,093.61

COMPARISON OF STANDARD GAUGES   Thickness in decimals of an inch

No. of gauge	Birmingham wire (B.w.g.), also known as Stubbs iron wire	American wire or Brown & Sharpe	American Steel & Wire Co., formerly Washburn & Moen	Trenton Iron Co.	British Imperial Standard Wire (S.w.g.)	Standard Birmingham sheet and hoop (B.g.)	London or Old English	United States Standard	Gauge No.
0000000	.....	....	0.4900	......	0.500			.500	0000000
000000	.....	0.580000	0.4615	......	0.464			.46875	000000
00000	.....	0.516500	0.4305	0.450	0.432			.4375	00000
0000	0.454	0.460000	0.3938	0.400	0.400		.454	.40625	0000
000	0.425	0.409642	0.3625	0.360	0.372	0.5000	.425	.375	000
00	0.380	0.364796	0.3310	0.330	0.348	0.4452	.38	.34375	00
0	0.340	0.324861	0.3065	0.305	0.324	0.3964	.34	.3125	0
1	0.300	0.289297	0.2830	0.285	0.300	0.3532	.3	.28125	1
2	0.284	0.257627	0.2625	0.265	0.276	0.3147	.284	.265625	2
3	0.259	0.229423	0.2437	0.245	0.252	0.2804	.259	.25	3
4	0.238	0.204307	0.2253	0.225	0.232	0.2500	.238	.234375	4
5	0.220	0.181940	0.2070	0.205	0.212	0.2225	.22	.21875	5
6	0.203	0.162023	0.1920	0.190	0.192	0.1931	.203	.203125	6
7	0.180	0.144285	0.1770	0.175	0.176	0.1764	.18	.1875	7
8	0.165	0.128490	0.1620	0.160	0.160	0.1570	.165	.171875	8
9	0.148	0.114423	0.1483	0.145	0.144	0.1398	.148	.15625	9
10	0.134	0.101897	0.1350	0.130	0.128	0.1250	.134	.140625	10
11	0.120	0.090742	0.1205	0.1175	0.116	0.1113	.12	.125	11
12	0.109	0.080808	0.1055	0.105	0.104	0.0991	.109	.109375	12
13	0.095	0.071962	0.0915	0.0925	0.092	0.0882	.095	.09375	13
14	0.083	0.064084	0.0800	0.0806	0.080	0.0785	.083	.078125	14
15	0.072	0.057068	0.0720	0.070	0.072	0.0699	.072	.0703125	15
16	0.065	0.050821	0.0625	0.061	0.064	0.0625	.065	.0625	16
17	0.058	0.045257	0.0540	0.0525	0.056	0.0556	.058	.05625	17
18	0.049	0.040303	0.0475	0.045	0.048	0.0495	.049	.05	18
19	0.042	0.035890	0.0410	0.040	0.040	0.0440	.040	.04375	19
20	0.035	0.031961	0.0348	0.035	0.036	0.0392	.035	.0375	20
21	0.032	0.028462	0.03175	0.031	0.032	0.0349	.0315	.034375	21
22	0.028	0.025346	0.0286	0.028	0.028	0.03125	.0295	.03125	22
23	0.025	0.022572	0.0258	0.025	0.024	0.02782	.027	.028125	23
24	0.022	0.020101	0.0230	0.0225	0.022	0.02476	.025	.025	24
25	0.020	0.017900	0.0204	0.020	0.020	0.02204	.023	.021875	25
26	0.018	0.015941	0.0181	0.018	0.018	0.01961	.0205	.01875	26
27	0.016	0.014195	0.0173	0.017	0.0164	0.01745	.0187	.0171875	27
28	0.014	0.012641	0.0162	0.016	0.0148	0.015625	.0165	.015625	28
29	0.013	0.011257	0.0150	0.015	0.0136	0.0139	.0155	.0140625	29
30	0.012	0.010025	0.0140	0.014	0.0124	0.0123	.01372	.0125	30
31	0.010	0.008928	0.0132	0.013	0.0116	0.0110	.0122	.0109375	31
32	0.009	0.007950	0.0128	0.012	0.0108	0.0098	.0112	.01015625	32
33	0.008	0.007080	0.0118	0.011	0.0100	0.0087	.0102	.009375	33
34	0.007	0.006305	0.0104	0.010	0.0092	0.0077	.0095	.00859375	34
35	0.005	0.005615	0.0095	0.0095	0.0084	0.0069	.009	.0078125	35
36	0.004	0.005000	0.0090	0.009	0.0076	0.0061	.0075	.00703125	36
37	.....	0.004453	0.0085	0.0085	0.0068	0.0054	.0065	.006640625	37
38	.....	0.003965	0.0080	0.008	0.0060	0.0048	.0057	.00625	38
39	.....	0.003531	0.0075	0.0075	0.0052		.005		39
40	.....	0.003144	0.0070	0.007	0.0048		.0045		40

SHEET METAL

Weight Per Square Inch by B. & S. Gauge

B & S Gauge	Thick- ness in	Fine Silver	Sterling Silver	Coin Silver	Fine Gold	10K Yel. Gold	14K Yel. Gold	18K Yel. Gold	Plat- inum	Palla- dium
	Inches	Ozs.	Ozs.	Ozs.	Dwts.	Dwts.	Dwts.	Dwts.	Ozs.	Ozs.
1	.28930	1.60	1.58	1.58	58.9	35.3	39.8	47.5	3.27	1.83
2	.25763	1.42	1.41	1.40	52.5	31.4	35.5	42.3	2.91	1.63
3	.22942	1.26	1.25	1.25	46.7	28.0	31.6	37.7	2.59	1.45
4	.20431	1.12	1.12	1.11	41.6	24.9	28.1	33.6	2.31	1.29
5	.18194	1.00	.993	.988	37.0	22.2	25.1	29.9	2.06	1.15
6	.16202	.894	.884	.880	33.0	19.8	22.3	26.6	1.83	1.02
7	.14428	.796	.787	.783	29.4	17.6	19.9	23.7	1.63	.912
8	.12849	.709	.701	.697	26.2	15.7	17.7	21.1	1.45	.812
9	.11443	.631	.624	.622	23.3	14.0	15.8	18.8	1.29	.723
10	.10189	.562	.556	.553	20.8	12.4	14.0	16.7	1.15	.644
11	.09074	.500	.495	.494	18.5	11.1	12.5	14.9	1.03	.574
12	.08080	.446	.441	.439	16.5	9.85	11.1	13.3	.913	.511
13	.07196	.397	.392	.391	14.7	8.77	9.91	11.8	.813	.455
14	.06408	.354	.350	.348	13.1	7.81	8.82	10.5	.724	.405
15	.05706	.316	.311	.310	11.6	6.96	7.86	9.37	.645	.361
16	.05082	.281	.277	.276	10.4	6.21	7.00	8.35	.574	.321
17	.04525	.250	.247	.246	9.21	5.52	6.23	7.43	.511	.286
18	.04030	.223	.220	.219	8.20	4.91	5.55	6.62	.455	.255
19	.03589	.198	.196	.195	7.32	4.38	4.94	5.89	.406	.227
20	.03196	.176	.174	.173	6.51	3.90	4.40	5.25	.361	.202
21	.02846	.157	.155	.154	5.80	3.47	3.92	4.67	.322	.180
22	.02534	.140	.138	.138	5.16	3.09	3.49	4.16	.286	.160
23	.02257	.124	.123	.123	4.59	2.75	3.11	3.71	.255	.143
24	.02010	.111	.110	.110	4.09	2.45	2.77	3.30	.227	.127
25	.01790	.0988	.0976	.0973	3.64	2.18	2.46	2.94	.202	.113
26	.01594	.0879	.0870	.0866	3.24	1.94	2.19	2.62	.180	.101
27	.01419	.0783	.0774	.0770	2.88	1.73	1.95	2.33	.160	.0897
28	.01264	.0697	.0690	.0686	2.58	1.54	1.74	2.08	.143	.0799
29	.01125	.0620	.0614	.0611	2.29	1.37	1.55	1.85	.127	.0711
30	.01002	.0553	.0547	.0544	2.04	1.22	1.38	1.65	.113	.0633
31	.00892	.0492	.0487	.0484	1.82	1.09	1.23	1.46	.101	.0564
32	.00795	.0438	.0434	.0432	1.62	.969	1.09	1.31	.0898	.0503
33	.00708	.0391	.0386	.0385	1.44	.863	.975	1.16	.0800	.0448
34	.00630	.0348	.0344	.0342	1.29	.768	.868	1.03	.0712	.0398
35	.00561	.0310	.0306	.0305	1.14	.684	.772	.921	.0634	.0355
36	.00500	.0276	.0273	.0272	1.02	.610	.689	.821	.0565	.0316
37	.00445	.0246	.0243	.0242	.908	.543	.613	.731	.0503	.0281
38	.00396	.0219	.0216	.0215	.808	.483	.545	.650	.0448	.0250
39	.00353	.0195	.0193	.0191	.712	.430	.486	.580	.0399	.0223
40	.00314	.0173	.0172	.0171	.640	.383	.432	.516	.0355	.0199

ROUND WIRE

Weight in Pennyweights or Ounces Per Foot in B. & S. Gauge

B. & S. Gauge	Thick-ness in Inches	Fine Silver	Sterling Silver	Coin Silver	Fine Gold	10K Yel. Gold	14K Yel. Gold	18K Yel. Gold	Plat-inum	Palla-dium
		Ozs.	Ozs.	Ozs.	Dwts.	Dwts.	Dwts.	Dwts.	Ozs.	Ozs.
1	.28930	4.36	4.30	4.28	161.	96.2	109.	130.	8.91	4.99
2	.25763	3.45	3.41	3.40	128.	76.3	86.1	104.	7.07	3.94
3	.22942	2.74	2.71	2.69	101.	60.5	68.3	81.5	5.61	3.19
4	.20431	2.17	2.14	2.13	80.1	48.0	54.2	64.6	4.45	2.42
5	.18194	1.72	1.70	1.69	63.5	38.0	43.0	51.2	3.53	1.97
6	.16202	1.36	1.35	1.34	50.4	30.2	34.1	40.6	2.80	1.56
7	.14428	1.09	1.07	1.07	39.9	23.9	27.0	32.2	2.22	1.24
8	.12849	.859	.848	.844	31.6	19.0	21.4	25.6	1.76	.984
9	.11443	.682	.673	.670	25.2	15.1	17.0	20.3	1.39	.780
10	.10189	.541	.534	.530	20.0	11.9	13.5	16.1	1.11	.619
11	.09074	.429	.423	.421	15.8	9.46	10.7	12.7	.877	.491
12	.08080	.339	.335	.333	12.6	7.50	8.47	10.1	.695	.389
13	.07196	.270	.266	.265	9.94	5.95	6.72	8.01	.552	.309
14	.06408	.214	.211	.210	7.87	4.72	5.33	6.36	.437	.245
15	.05706	.169	.167	.166	6.25	3.74	4.23	5.04	.347	.194
16	.05082	.135	.132	.132	4.96	2.97	3.35	4.00	.275	.154
17	.04525	.107	.105	.105	3.93	2.35	2.66	3.17	.218	.122
18	.04030	.0846	.0835	.0834	3.11	1.87	2.11	2.51	.173	.0968
19	.03589	.0671	.0662	.0659	2.48	1.48	1.67	1.99	.137	.0767
20	.03196	.0532	.0525	.0522	1.96	1.17	1.33	1.58	.109	.0609
21	.02846	.0422	.0416	.0414	1.56	.931	1.05	1.25	.0863	.0483
22	.02534	.0335	.0330	.0328	1.23	.738	.833	.994	.0684	.0383
23	.02257	.0265	.0262	.0261	.977	.585	.661	.789	.0543	.0304
24	.02010	.0210	.0208	.0207	.775	.464	.524	.625	.0430	.0241
25	.01790	.0167	.0165	.0164	.615	.368	.416	.496	.0341	.0191
26	.01594	.0133	.0131	.01304	.488	.292	.330	.393	.0271	.0151
27	.01419	.0105	.0103	.0103	.386	.231	.261	.312	.0214	.0120
28	.01264	.00831	.00821	.00817	.306	.184	.207	.247	.0170	.00952
29	.01125	.00659	.00650	.00647	.243	.145	.164	.196	.0135	.00754
30	.01002	.00522	.00516	.00513	.193	.115	.130	.155	.0107	.00598
31	.00892	.00414	.00410	.00407	.153	.0914	.103	.123	.00847	.00474
32	.00795	.00328	.00325	.00323	.122	.0726	.0820	.0978	.00673	.00377
33	.00708	.00261	.00258	.00257	.0962	.0576	.0651	.0776	.00534	.00299
34	.00630	.00207	.00204	.00203	.0761	.0456	.0515	.0614	.00423	.00236
35	.00561	.00164	.00162	.00161	.0604	.0362	.0408	.0487	.00335	.00188
36	.00500	.00130	.00128	.00127	.0480	.0287	.0324	.0387	.00266	.00149
37	.00445	.00104	.00102	.00102	.0380	.0228	.0257	.0306	.00211	.00118
38	.00396	.000816	.000806	.000802	.0301	.0180	.0204	.0243	.00167	.000934
39	.00353	.000649	.000641	.000637	.0240	.0143	.0162	.0193	.00133	.000742
40	.00314	.000513	.000507	.000504	.0190	.0113	.0128	.0153	.00105	.000587

APPROXIMATE LENGTH PER TROY OUNCE OF STERLING SILVER WIRE

Nearest Fractional Size	RECTANGULAR B&S Gauge	Feet	SQUARE B&S Gauge	Feet	ROUND B&S Gauge	Feet	HALF ROUND B&S Gauge	Feet
5/16"							5/16" base	5 inches
5/32"							6 "	1½
1/8"			8	1	8	1¼	8 "	2½
					10	2	10 "	3¾
5/64"			12	2¼	12	3		
1/16"			14	3¾	14	4¾	14 "	9½
	4 x 16	1½	16	6	16	7½		
	6 x 18	2¼	18	9¼	18	12		
1/32"					20	19		
	8 x 22	4¾			22	30		
1/64"	8 x 26				24			
	14 x 30							
	14 x 32							

STERLING SILVER SQUARE AND HALF ROUND WIRE
Weight in Ounces per Foot

Gauge	Inches	Square	Half Round
26	.016	0.016	0.007
24	.020	0.027	0.011
22	.025	0.042	0.017
20	.032	0.067	0.027
18	.040	0.107	0.042
16	.051	0.170	0.067
14	.064	0.270	0.106
12	.081	0.430	0.169
10	.102	0.682	0.270
8	.128	1.082	0.426
6	.162	1.730	0.678
4	.204	2.730	1.075

STERLING SILVER SHEET WEIGHT IN TROY OUNCES PER SQUARE INCH

B&S Gauge	Weight
12	.443
14	.351
16	.278
18	.221
20	.175
22	.139
24	.110
26	.087

SILVER AND GOLD WIRE FORMS AVAILABLE IN STANDARD MILLIMETER SIZES

SQUARE WIRE	RECTANGULAR WIRE	HALF ROUND WIRE
4 x 4 mm	6 x 2 mm	6 x 2 mm
3 x 3 mm	5 x 2 mm	5 x 2 mm
2½ x 2½ mm	4 x 2 mm	4 x 2 mm
2 x 2 mm	6 x 1½ mm	6 x 1½ mm
1½ x 1½ mm	5 x 1½ mm	5 x 1½ mm
1 x 1 mm	4 x 1½ mm	4 x 1½ mm
	3 x 1½ mm	3 x 1½ mm
	2 x 1½ mm	2 x 1½ mm
	4 x 1 mm	1½ x 1 mm
	3 x 1 mm	
	2 x 1 mm	
	1½ x 1 mm	

STERLING SILVER SEAMLESS TUBING
Outside Diameter, Wall Thickness, Inside Diameter

O.D.	1″ Dia. × .025″	wall	O.D.	3⁄16″ Dia. × .070″	I.D.
O.D.	3⁄4″ Dia. × .025″	wall	O.D.	3⁄16″ Dia. × .032″	wall
O.D.	5⁄8″ Dia. × .036″	wall	O.D.	.150″ Dia. × .120″	I.D.
O.D.	1⁄2″ Dia. × .036″	wall	O.D.	1⁄8″ Dia. × .068″	I.D.
O.D.	3⁄8″ Dia. × .032″	wall	O.D.	3⁄32″ Dia. × .055″	I.D.
O.D.	1⁄4″ Dia. × .032″	wall	O.D.	.062″ Dia. × .040″	I.D.

CIRCLES AND SQUARES

Circumferences and Areas

Size Inches	Circumference of ○ in Inches	Area of ○ in Square Inches	Area of □ in Square Inches	Size Inches	Circumference of ○ in Inches	Area of ○ in Square Inches	Area of □ in Square Inches
				2	6.283	3.142	4.000
1⁄16	.1963	.0031	.0039	2 1⁄16	6.480	3.341	4.254
1⁄8	.3927	.0123	.0156	2 1⁄8	6.676	3.547	4.516
3⁄16	.5890	.0276	.0352	2 3⁄16	6.872	3.758	4.785
1⁄4	.7854	.0491	.0625	2 1⁄4	7.069	3.976	5.063
5⁄16	.9817	.0767	.0977	2 5⁄16	7.265	4.200	5.348
3⁄8	1.178	.1104	.1406	2 3⁄8	7.461	4.430	5.641
7⁄16	1.374	.1503	.1914	2 7⁄16	7.658	4.666	5.941
1⁄2	1.571	.1963	.2500	2 1⁄2	7.854	4.909	6.250
9⁄16	1.767	.2485	.3164	2 9⁄16	8.050	5.157	6.566
5⁄8	1.963	.3068	.3906	2 5⁄8	8.247	5.412	6.891
11⁄16	2.160	.3712	.4727	2 11⁄16	8.443	5.673	7.223
3⁄4	2.356	.4418	.5625	2 3⁄4	8.639	5.940	7.563
13⁄16	2.553	.5185	.6602	2 13⁄16	8.836	6.213	7.910
7⁄8	2.749	.6013	.7656	2 7⁄8	9.032	6.492	8.266
15⁄16	2.945	.6903	.8789	2 15⁄16	9.228	6.777	8.629
1	3.142	.7854	1.000	3	9.425	7.069	9.000
1 1⁄16	3.338	.8866	1.129	3 1⁄16	9.621	7.366	9.379
1 1⁄8	3.534	.9940	1.266	3 1⁄8	9.817	7.670	9.766
1 3⁄16	3.731	1.108	1.410	3 3⁄16	10.01	7.980	10.16
1 1⁄4	3.927	1.227	1.563	3 1⁄4	10.21	8.296	10.56
1 5⁄16	4.123	1.353	1.723	3 5⁄16	10.41	8.618	10.97
1 3⁄8	4.320	1.485	1.891	3 3⁄8	10.60	8.946	11.39
1 7⁄16	4.516	1.623	2.066	3 7⁄16	10.80	9.281	11.82
1 1⁄2	4.712	1.767	2.250	3 1⁄2	11.00	9.621	12.25
1 9⁄16	4.909	1.917	2.441	3 9⁄16	11.19	9.968	12.69
1 5⁄8	5.105	2.074	2.641	3 5⁄8	11.39	10.32	13.14
1 11⁄16	5.301	2.237	2.848	3 11⁄16	11.58	10.68	13.60
1 3⁄4	5.498	2.405	3.063	3 3⁄4	11.78	11.04	14.06
1 13⁄16	5.694	2.580	3.285	3 13⁄16	11.98	11.42	14.54
1 7⁄8	5.890	2.761	3.516	3 7⁄8	12.17	11.79	15.02
1 15⁄16	6.087	2.948	3.754	3 15⁄16	12.37	12.18	15.50

CIRCLES AND SQUARES

Circumferences and Areas

Size Inches	Circumference of ○ in Inches	Area of ○ in Square Inches	Area of □ in Square Inches	Size Inches	Circumference of ○ in Inches	Area of ○ in Square Inches	Area of □ in Square Inches
4	12.57	12.57	16.00	6⅝	20.81	34.47	43.89
4¹⁄₁₆	12.76	12.96	16.50	6¹¹⁄₁₆	21.01	35.13	44.72
4⅛	12.96	13.36	17.02	6¾	21.21	35.78	45.56
4³⁄₁₆	13.16	13.77	17.54	6¹³⁄₁₆	21.40	36.45	46.41
4¼	13.35	14.19	18.06	6⅞	21.60	37.12	47.27
4⁵⁄₁₆	13.55	14.61	18.60	6¹⁵⁄₁₆	21.79	37.80	48.13
4⅜	13.74	15.03	19.14	7	21.99	38.48	49.00
4⁷⁄₁₆	13.94	15.47	19.69	7¹⁄₁₆	22.19	39.17	49.88
4½	14.14	15.90	20.25	7⅛	22.38	39.87	50.77
4⁹⁄₁₆	14.33	16.35	20.82	7³⁄₁₆	22.58	40.57	51.66
4⅝	14.53	16.80	21.39	7¼	22.78	41.28	52.56
4¹¹⁄₁₆	14.73	16.80	21.39	7⁵⁄₁₆	22.97	42.00	53.47
4¾	14.92	17.72	22.56	7⅜	23.17	42.72	54.39
4¹³⁄₁₆	15.12	18.19	23.16	7⁷⁄₁₆	23.37	43.45	55.32
4⅞	15.32	18.67	23.77	7½	23.56	44.18	56.25
4¹⁵⁄₁₆	15.51	19.15	24.38	7⁹⁄₁₆	23.76	44.92	57.19
5	15.71	19.63	25.00	7⅝	23.95	45.66	58.14
5¹⁄₁₆	15.90	20.13	25.63	7¹¹⁄₁₆	24.15	46.42	59.10
5⅛	16.10	20.63	26.27	7¾	24.35	47.17	60.06
5³⁄₁₆	16.30	21.14	26.91	7¹³⁄₁₆	24.54	47.94	61.04
5¼	16.49	21.65	27.56	7⅞	24.74	48.71	62.02
5⁵⁄₁₆	16.69	22.17	28.22	7¹⁵⁄₁₆	24.94	49.48	63.00
5⅜	16.89	22.69	28.89	8	25.13	50.27	64.00
5⁷⁄₁₆	17.08	23.22	29.57	8¹⁄₁₆	25.33	51.05	65.00
5½	17.28	23.76	30.25	8⅛	25.53	51.85	66.02
5⁹⁄₁₆	17.48	24.30	30.94	8³⁄₁₆	25.72	52.65	67.04
5⅝	17.67	24.85	31.64	8¼	25.92	53.46	68.06
5¹¹⁄₁₆	17.87	25.41	32.35	8⁵⁄₁₆	26.11	54.27	69.10
5¾	18.06	15.97	33.06	8⅜	26.31	55.09	70.14
5¹³⁄₁₆	18.26	26.53	33.79	8⁷⁄₁₆	26.51	55.91	71.19
5⅞	18.46	27.11	34.52	8½	27.70	56.75	72.25
5¹⁵⁄₁₆	18.65	27.69	35.25	8⁹⁄₁₆	26.90	57.58	73.32
6	18.85	28.27	36.00	8⅝	27.10	58.43	74.39
6¹⁄₁₆	19.05	28.87	36.75	8¹¹⁄₁₆	27.29	59.28	75.47
6⅛	19.24	29.46	37.52	8¾	27.49	60.13	76.56
6³⁄₁₆	19.44	30.07	38.29	8¹³⁄₁₆	27.69	60.99	77.66
6¼	19.63	30.68	39.06	8⅞	27.88	61.86	78.77
6⁵⁄₁₆	19.83	31.30	39.85	8¹⁵⁄₁₆	28.08	62.74	79.88
6⅜	20.03	31.92	40.64	9	28.27	63.62	81.00
6⁷⁄₁₆	20.22	32.55	41.44	9¹⁄₁₆	28.47	64.50	82.13
6½	20.42	33.18	42.25	9⅛	28.67	65.40	83.27
6⁹⁄₁₆	20.62	33.82	43.07	9³⁄₁₆	28.86	66.30	84.41

Size Inches	Circumference of ○ in Inches	Area of ○ in Square Inches	Area of □ in Square Inches	Size Inches	Circumference of ○ in Inches	Area of ○ in Square Inches	Area of □ in Square Inches
9¼	29.06	67.20	85.56	10⅝	33.38	88.66	112.9
9⁵⁄₁₆	29.26	68.11	86.72	10¹¹⁄₁₆	33.58	89.71	114.2
9⅜	29.45	69.03	87.89	10¾	33.77	90.76	115.6
9⁷⁄₁₆	29.65	69.95	89.07	10¹³⁄₁₆	33.97	91.82	116.9
9½	29.85	70.88	90.25	10⅞	34.16	92.89	118.3
9⁹⁄₁₆	30.04	71.82	91.44	10¹⁵⁄₁₆	34.36	93.96	119.6
9⅝	30.24	72.76	92.64	11	34.56	95.03	121.0
9¹¹⁄₁₆	30.43	73.71	93.85	11¹⁄₁₆	34.75	96.12	122.4
9¾	30.63	74.66	95.06	11⅛	34.95	97.20	123.8
9¹³⁄₁₆	30.83	75.62	96.29	11³⁄₁₆	35.15	98.30	125.2
9⅞	31.02	76.59	97.52	11¼	35.34	99.40	126.6
9¹⁵⁄₁₆	31.22	77.56	98.75	11⁵⁄₁₆	35.54	100.5	128.0
10	31.42	78.54	100.0	11⅜	35.74	101.6	129.4
10¹⁄₁₆	31.61	79.52	101.3	11⁷⁄₁₆	35.93	102.7	130.8
10⅛	31.81	80.52	102.5	11½	36.13	103.9	132.3
10³⁄₁₆	32.00	81.51	103.8	11⁹⁄₁₆	36.32	105.0	133.7
10¼	32.20	82.52	105.1	11⅝	36.52	106.1	135.1
10⁵⁄₁₆	32.40	83.52	106.3	11¹¹⁄₁₆	36.72	107.3	136.6
10⅜	32.59	84.54	107.6	11¾	36.91	108.4	138.1
10⁷⁄₁₆	32.79	85.56	108.9	11¹³⁄₁₆	37.11	109.6	139.5
10½	32.99	86.59	110.3	11⅞	37.31	110.8	141.0
10⁹⁄₁₆	33.18	87.62	111.6	11¹⁵⁄₁₆	37.50	111.9	142.5

COMPARISON OF MEASUREMENTS

Inch	M/M	B. & S. Gauge	Stubbs Steel Wire	Drill No.	Inch	M/M	B. & S. Gauge	Stubbs Steel Wire	Drill No.	Inch	M/M	B. & S. Gauge	Stubbs Steel Wire	Drill No.
.0130	0.330	—	80	—	.0270	0.685	—	70	—	.0453	1.151	17	—	—
.0135	0.343	—	—	80	.0280	0.712	—	—	70	.0465	1.181	—	—	56
.0140	0.356	—	79	—	.0285	0.724	21	—	—	.0500	1.270	—	55	—
.0142	0.361	27	—	—	.0290	0.737	—	69	—	.0508	1.290	16	—	—
.0145	0.369	—	—	79	.02925	0.743	—	—	69	.0520	1.321	—	—	55
.0150	0.381	—	78	—	.0300	0.762	—	68	—	.0550	1.397	—	54	54
.0159	0.404	26	—	—	.0310	0.787	—	67	68	.0571	1.450	15	—	—
.0160	0.406	—	77	78	.0320	0.813	20	66	67	.0580	1.473	—	53	—
.0179	0.455	25	—	—	.0330	0.838	—	65	66	.0595	1.512	—	—	53
.0180	0.457	—	76	77	.0350	0.889	—	64	65	.0630	1.600	—	52	—
.0200	0.508	—	75	76	.0359	0.912	19	—	—	.0635	1.613	—	—	52
.0201	0.511	24	—	—	.0360	0.914	—	63	64	.0641	1.629	14	—	—
.0210	0.533	—	—	75	.0370	0.940	—	62	63	.0660	1.676	—	51	—
.0220	0.559	—	74	—	.0380	0.965	—	61	62	.0670	1.702	—	—	51
.0225	0.572	—	—	74	.0390	0.990	—	60	61	.0690	1.753	—	50	—
.0226	0.574	23	—	—	.0400	1.016	—	59	60	.0700	1.778	—	—	50
.0230	0.584	—	73	—	.0403	1.024	18	—	—	.0720	1.829	13	49	—
.0240	0.610	—	72	73	.0410	1.041	—	58	59	.0730	1.854	—	—	49
.0250	0.635	—	—	72	.0420	1.067	—	57	58	.0750	1.905	—	48	—
.0253	0.643	22	—	—	.0430	1.092	—	—	57	.0760	1.930	—	—	48
.0260	0.660	—	71	71	.0450	1.143	—	56	56	.0770	1.956	—	47	—

COMPARISON OF MEASUREMENTS

Inch	M/M	B. & S. Gauge	Stubbs Steel Wire	Drill No.	Inch	M/M	B. & S. Gauge	Stubbs Steel Wire	Drill No.	Inch	M/M	B. & S. Gauge	Stubbs Steel Wire	Drill No.
.0785	1.994	—	—	47	.1150	2.921	—	32	—	.1750	4.447	—	16	—
.0790	2.007	—	46	—	.1160	2.946	—	—	32	.1770	4.498	—	—	16
.0808	2.052	12	—	—	.1200	3.048	—	31	31	.1780	4.523	—	15	—
.0810	2.057	—	45	46	.1270	3.226	—	30	—	.1800	4.570	—	14	15
.0820	2.083	—	—	45	.1285	3.264	8	—	30	.1819	4.618	5	—	—
.0850	2.159	—	44	—	.1340	3.404	—	29	—	.1820	4.621	—	13	14
.0860	2.184	—	—	44	.1360	3.454	—	—	29	.1850	4.697	—	12	13
.0880	2.235	—	43	—	.1390	3.531	—	28	—	.1880	4.773	—	11	—
.0890	2.261	—	—	43	.1405	3.573	—	—	28	.1890	4.799	—	—	12
.0907	2.304	11	—	—	.1430	3.636	—	27	—	.1910	4.855	—	10	11
.0920	2.337	—	42	—	.1440	3.662	—	—	27	.1935	4.919	—	—	10
.0935	2.378	—	—	42	.1443	3.670	7	—	—	.1940	4.932	—	9	—
.0950	2.413	—	41	—	.1460	3.712	—	26	—	.1960	4.982	—	—	9
.0960	2.438	—	—	41	.1470	3.758	—	—	26	.1970	5.008	—	8	—
.0970	2.464	—	40	—	.1480	3.763	—	25	—	.1990	5.059	—	7	8
.0980	2.489	—	—	40	.1495	3.802	—	—	25	.2010	5.105	—	6	7
.0990	2.515	—	39	—	.1510	3.835	—	24	—	.2040	5.182	—	5	6
.0995	2.528	—	—	39	.1520	3.861	—	—	24	.2043	5.189	4	—	—
.1010	2.565	—	38	—	.1530	3.886	—	23	—	.2055	5.220	—	—	5
.1015	2.578	—	—	38	.1540	3.912	—	—	23	.2070	5.258	—	4	—
.1019	2.588	10	—	—	.1550	3.937	—	22	—	.2090	5.309	—	—	4
.1030	2.616	—	37	—	.1570	3.988	—	21	22	.2120	5.381	—	3	—
.1040	2.642	—	—	37	.1590	4.039	—	—	21	.2130	5.406	—	—	3
.1060	2.692	—	36	—	.1610	4.085	—	20	20	.2190	5.559	—	2	—
.1065	2.705	—	—	36	.1620	4.111	6	—	—	.2210	5.615	—	—	2
.1080	2.743	—	35	—	.1640	4.162	—	19	—	.2270	5.768	—	1	—
.1100	2.794	—	34	35	.1660	4.212	—	—	19	.2280	5.793	—	—	1
.1110	2.819	—	—	34	.1680	4.263	—	18	—	.2294	5.829	3	—	—
.1120	2.845	—	33	—	.1695	4.302	—	—	18	.2576	6.543	2	—	—
.1130	2.870	—	—	33	.1720	4.371	—	17	—	.2893	7.346	1	—	—
.1144	2.906	9	—	—	.1730	4.396	—	—	17					

FRACTIONAL, DECIMAL INCH, AND MILLIMETER EQUIVALENTS

Fractions	Inches	M/M	Fractions	Inches	M/M	Fractions	Inches	M/M	Fractions	Inches	M/M
1/64	.0156	0.3969	9/64	.1406	3.5718	17/64	.2656	6.7468	25/64	.3906	9.9217
1/32	.0313	0.7937	5/32	.1562	3.9687	9/32	.2812	7.1437	13/32	.4062	10.3186
3/64	.0469	1.1906	11/64	.1719	4.3656	19/64	.2969	7.5405	27/64	.4219	10.7155
1/16	.0625	1.5875	3/16	.1875	4.7624	5/16	.3125	7.9374	7/16	.4375	11.1124
5/64	.0781	1.9843	13/64	.2031	5.1593	21/64	.3281	8.3343	29/64	.4531	11.5092
3/32	.0937	2.3812	7/32	.2187	5.5562	11/32	.3438	8.7312	15/32	.4687	11.9061
7/64	.1094	2.7781	15/64	.2344	5.9530	23/64	.3594	9.1280	31/64	.4844	12.3030
1/8	.1250	3.1750	1/4	.2500	6.3499	3/8	.3750	9.5249	1/2	.5000	12.6999

COMPARISON OF
SAW BLADE SIZES AND DRILLS

No.	Thickness	Depth	Drill
8/0	.0060	.0130	80
7/0	.0065	.0135	80
6/0	.0070	.0140	79
5/0	.0080	.0150	78
4/0	.0085	.0170	77
3/0	.0095	.0190	76
2/0	.0100	.0200	75
0	.0110	.0230	73
1	.0115	.0250	71
1½	.0120	.0255	71
2	.0135	.0270	70
3	.0140	.0290	68
4	.0150	.0310	67
5	.0160	.0340	65
6	.0190	.0410	58
8	.0200	.0480	55
10	.0205	.0580	51
12	.0230	.0640	51
14	.0240	.0680	50

JEWELER'S SAW BLADES, THICKNESS AND WIDTH IN INCHES

JEWELER'S SAWS			BLADES	
Size	Thickness	Width	Saws Finer than 4/0 not Illustrated	
8/0	.0063	.0126		
7/0	.0067	.0130		
6/0	.007	.014		
5/0	.008	.0157		
4/0	.0086	.0175	4/0	
3/0	.0095	.019	3/0	
2/0	.0103	.0204	2/0	
1/0	.011	.022	1/0	
1	.012	.024	1	
1½	.0125	.025	1½	
2	.0134	.0276	2	
3	.014	.029	3	
4	.015	.0307	4	
5	.0158	.0331	5	
6	.0173	.0370	6	
7	.0189	.040		
8	.0197	.044	8	
10	.0215	.051	10	
12	.0236	.065	12	
14	.0236	.069	14	

STRAIGHT SHANK TWIST DRILLS, WIRE GAUGE SIZES

Wire gauge No.	Decimal diam, in.	Over-all length, in.	Flute length, in.	Wire gauge No.	Decimal diam, in.	Over-all length, in.	Flute length, in.
80	0.0135	¾	³⁄₁₆	39	0.0995	2⅜	1⅜
79	0.0145	¾	³⁄₁₆	38	0.1015	2½	1⁷⁄₁₆
78	0.016	⅞	³⁄₁₆	37	0.104	2½	1⁷⁄₁₆
77	0.018	⅞	³⁄₁₆	36	0.1065	2½	1⁷⁄₁₆
76	0.020	⅞	³⁄₁₆	35	0.110	2⅝	1½
75	0.021	1	¼	34	0.111	2⅝	1½
74	0.0225	1	¼	33	0.113	2⅝	1½
73	0.024	1⅛	⁵⁄₁₆	32	0.116	2¾	1⅝
72	0.025	1⅛	⁵⁄₁₆	31	0.120	2¾	1⅝
71	0.026	1¼	⅜	30	0.1285	2¾	1⅝
70	0.028	1¼	⅜	29	0.136	2⅞	1¾
69	0.0292	1⅜	½	28	0.1405	2⅞	1¾
68	0.031	1⅜	½	27	0.144	3	1⅞
67	0.032	1⅜	½	26	0.147	3	1⅞
66	0.033	1⅜	½	25	0.1495	3	1⅞
65	0.035	1½	⅝	24	0.152	3⅛	2
64	0.036	1½	⅝	23	0.154	3⅛	2
63	0.037	1½	⅝	22	0.157	3⅛	2
62	0.038	1½	⅝	21	0.159	3¼	2⅛
61	0.039	1⅝	¹¹⁄₁₆	20	0.161	3¼	2⅛
60	0.040	1⅝	¹¹⁄₁₆	19	0.166	3¼	2⅛
59	0.041	1⅝	¹¹⁄₁₆	18	0.1695	3¼	2⅛
58	0.042	1⅝	¹¹⁄₁₆	17	0.173	3⅜	2³⁄₁₆
57	0.043	1¾	¾	16	0.177	3⅜	2³⁄₁₆
56	0.0465	1¾	¾	15	0.180	3⅜	2³⁄₁₆
55	0.052	1⅞	⅞	14	0.182	3⅜	2³⁄₁₆
54	0.055	1⅞	⅞	13	0.185	3½	2⁵⁄₁₆
53	0.0595	1⅞	⅞	12	0.189	3½	2⁵⁄₁₆
52	0.0635	1⅞	⅞	11	0.191	3½	2⁵⁄₁₆
51	0.067	2	1	10	0.1935	3⅝	2⁷⁄₁₆
50	0.070	2	1	9	0.196	3⅝	2⁷⁄₁₆
49	0.073	2	1	8	0.199	3⅝	2⁷⁄₁₆
48	0.076	2	1	7	0.201	3⅝	2⁷⁄₁₆
47	0.0785	2	1	6	0.204	3¾	2½
46	0.081	2⅛	1⅛	5	0.2055	3¾	2½
45	0.082	2⅛	1⅛	4	0.209	3¾	2½
44	0.086	2⅛	1⅛	3	0.213	3¾	2½
43	0.089	2¼	1¼	2	0.221	3⅞	2⅝
42	0.0935	2¼	1¼	1	0.228	3⅞	2⅝
41	0.096	2⅜	1⅜				
40	0.098	2⅜	1⅜				

U. S. STANDARD RING SIZES, LENGTH AND DIAMETER IN INCHES

Size	Length	Diameter	Size	Length	Diameter	Size	Length	Diameter
0	1.429	.458	4	1.835	.586	9	2.35	.746
¼		.466	4½		.602	9½		.762
½		.474	5	1.943	.618	10	2.46	.778
¾		.482	5½		.634	10½		.794
1	1.528	.490	6	2.045	.650	11	2.56	.810
1½		.506	6½		.666	11½		.826
2	1.632	.522	7	2.15	.682	12	2.63	.842
2½		.538	7½		.698	12½		.858
3	1.735	.554	8	2.25	.714	13	2.76	.874
3½		.570	8½		.730	13½		.890

STANDARD COPPER SHEET THICKNESS

Rolled to Weight

Weight per Sq. Ft.		Thickness	Nearest Gauge No.		Nearest Fraction
Ounces	Pounds	Inches	B. & S.	Stubbs	
	16	.3456	00	00	11⁄32
	15	.3240	0	0	21⁄64+
	14	.3024	1	1	19⁄64—
	13	.2808	1	2	9⁄32
	12	.2592	2	3	¼ —
	11	.2376	3	4	15⁄64—
	10	.2160	4	5	7⁄32 +
	9½	.2052	4	6	13⁄64
	9	.1944	4	6	
	8½	.1836	5	7	3⁄16 +
	8	.1728	5	8	11⁄64
	7½	.1620	6	8	
	7	.1512	7	9	5⁄32 +
	6½	.1404	7	10	9⁄64
	6	.1296	8	10	⅛ —
	5½	.1188	9	11	
80	5	.1080	10	12	7⁄64 +
72	4½	.0972	10	13	3⁄32 —
64	4	.0864	11	14	
56	3½	.0756	13	15	5⁄64 +
48	3	.0648	14	16	1⁄16 —
44	2¾	.0594	15	17	
40	2½	.0540	15	17	
36	2¼	.0486	16	18	3⁄64 —
32	2	.0432	17	19	
28	1¾	.0378	19	20	
24	1½	.0324	20	21	1⁄32 —
20	1¼	.0270	21	22	
18	1⅛	.0243	22	23	
16	1	.0216	23	24	
14	⅞	.0189	25	26	
12	¾	.0162	26	27	1⁄64 —
10	⅝	.0135	27	29	
8	½	.0108	29	31	
6	⅜	.0081	32	33	
4	¼	.0054	35	35	
2	⅛	.0027			

The + sign shows that the size is more than 1 per cent. full.
The — sign shows that the size is more than 1 per cent. scant.

TEMPERATURE CONVERSION TABLES

FAHRENHEIT TO CENTIGRADE

°F	°C	°F	°C	°F	°C	°F	°C	°F	°C	°F	°C	°F	°C
32	0	660	349	960	516	1260	682	1560	849	1880	1026	2180	1193
212	100	680	360	980	527	1280	693	1580	860	1900	1038	2200	1204
400	204	700	371	1000	538	1300	704	1600	871	1920	1049	2220	1216
420	216	720	382	1020	549	1320	716	1620	882	1940	1060	2240	1227
440	227	740	393	1040	560	1340	727	1640	893	1960	1071	2260	1238
460	238	760	404	1060	571	1360	738	1660	904	1980	1082	2280	1249
480	249	780	416	1080	582	1380	749	1680	916	2000	1093	2300	1260
500	260	800	427	1100	593	1400	760	1700	927	2020	1105	2320	1271
520	271	820	438	1120	604	1420	771	1740	949	2940	1116	2340	1284
540	282	840	449	1140	616	1440	782	1760	960	2060	1127	2360	1293
560	293	860	460	1160	627	1460	793	1780	971	2080	1138	2380	1305
580	304	880	471	1180	638	1480	804	1800	982	2100	1149	2400	1316
600	316	900	482	1200	649	1500	816	1820	993	2120	1160		
620	327	920	493	1220	660	1520	827	1840	1004	2140	1171		
640	338	940	504	1240	671	1540	838	1860	1015	2160	1182		

CENTIGRADE TO FAHRENHEIT

°C	°F	°C	°F	°C	°F	°C	°F	°C	°F	°C	°F	°C	°F
0	32	330	626	480	896	630	1166	780	1436	930	1706	1080	1976
100	212	340	644	490	914	640	1184	790	1454	940	1724	1090	1994
200	392	350	662	500	932	650	1202	800	1472	950	1742	1100	2012
210	410	360	680	510	950	660	1220	810	1490	960	1760	1110	2030
220	428	370	698	520	968	670	1238	820	1508	970	1778	1120	2048
230	446	380	716	530	986	680	1256	830	1526	980	1796	1130	2066
240	464	390	734	540	1004	690	1274	840	1544	990	1814	1140	2084
250	482	400	752	550	1022	700	1292	850	1562	1000	1832	1150	2102
260	500	410	770	560	1040	710	1310	860	1580	1010	1850	1160	2120
270	518	420	788	570	1058	720	1328	870	1598	1020	1868	1170	2138
280	536	430	806	580	1076	730	1346	880	1616	1030	1886	1180	2156
290	545	440	824	590	1094	740	1364	890	1634	1040	1904	1190	2174
300	572	450	842	600	1112	750	1382	900	1652	1050	1922		
310	590	460	860	610	1130	760	1400	910	1670	1060	1940		
320	608	470	878	620	1148	770	1418	920	1688	1070	1958		

Comparison of Thermometers
Freezing point = 32° Fahrenheit = 0° centigrade · Boiling point = 212° Fahrenheit = 100° centigrade
Cent × ⅘ + 32° = Fahr · Fahr − 32° × ⅝ = cent

THE MELTING POINTS OF SELECTED METALS

Metal	Symbol	Atomic Number	Atomic Weight	Centigrade	Fahrenheit	Melting Points of Metals According to Centigrade Temperature (low to high)	
Aluminum	Al	13	26.9815	660.2	1220.4	Mercury ————	−38.85
Antimony	Sb	51	121.75	630.5	1166.9	Phosphorus ———	44.1
Bismuth	Bi	83	208.980	271.3	520.3	Tin ————————	231.9
Cadmium	Cd	48	112.40	320.0	1490	Bismuth ————	271.3
Carbon	C	6	12.01115	3500	6332	Cadmium ————	320.0
Chromium	Cr	24	51.996	1765	3209	Lead ———————	327.35
Cobalt	Co	27	58.9332	1480	2696	Zinc ———————	419.4
Copper	Cu	29	63.54	1083	1981.4	Antimony ———	630.5
Gold	Au	79	196.967	1063	1945.4	Magnesium ———	651.0
Iridium	Ir	77	192.2	2454	4449	Aluminum ———	660.2
Iron	Fe	26	55.847	1539	2802	Silver ———————	960.5
Lead	Pb	82	207.19	327.35	621.3	Gold ———————	1063.0
Magnesium	Mg	12	24.312	651	1204	Copper ————	1083.0
Manganese	Mn	25	54.9380	1260	2300	Manganese ———	1260.0
Mercury	Hg	80	200.59	−38.85	−37.67	Silicon ————	1420.0
Molybdenum	Mo	42	95.94	2620	4748	Nickel ————	1455.0
Nickel	Ni	28	58.71	1455	2651	Cobalt ————	1480.0
Osmium	Os	76	190.2	2700	4900	Iron ———————	1539.0
Palladium	Pd	46	106.4	1554	2829	Palladium ———	1554.0
Phosphorus	P	15	30.9738	44.1	111.4	Vanadium ———	1710.0
Platinum	Pt	78	195.09	1773.5	3224.3	Chromium ———	1765.0
Rhodium	Rh	45	109.905	1966	3571	Platinum ———	1773.5
Ruthenium	Ru	44	101.07	2500	4500	Rhodium ———	1966.0
Silicon	Si	14	28.086	1420	2588	Iridium ————	2454.0
Silver	Ag	47	107.870	960.5	1760.9	Ruthenium ———	2500.0
Tin	Sn	50	118.69	231.9	449.4	Molybdenum —	2620.0
Tungsten	W	74	183.85	3400	6152	Osmium ————	2700.0
Vanadium	V	23	50.942	1710	3110	Tungsten ———	3400.0
Zinc	Zn	30	65.37	419.4	787	Carbon ————	3500.0

COEFFICIENTS OF LINEAR EXPANSION OF METALS BETWEEN ROOM TEMPERATURE AND 100° C (212° F)

Metal	per ° C	per ° F	Metal	per ° C	per ° F
Aluminum	0.0000238	0.0000132	Iron, cast gray		
Brass (85% Cu)—			(3.1% C, 1.7% Si)	.0000084	.0000047
Cold Drawn	.0000177	.0000098	Iron, electrolytic	.0000120	.0000067
Brass (75% Cu)—			Lead	.0000291	.0000162
Cold Drawn	.0000184	.0000102	Magnesium	.0000260	.0000144
Brass (65% Cu)—			Nickel	.0000133	.0000074
Cold Drawn	.0000190	.0000105	Platinum	.0000090	.0000050
Bronze (4.2% Sn)—			Silver	.0000191	.0000106
Cold Drawn	.0000173	.0000096	Steels	.0000111 to	.0000062 to
Copper	.0000168	.0000094		.0000124	.0000069
Everdur-1010	.0000170	.0000094	Tin[1]	.0000270	.0000150
Gold	.0000143	.0000079	Zinc,[1] cast	.0000395	.0000219

[1] Anisotropic; coefficient of expansion varies with different samples. (See following pages.)

COEFFICIENTS OF LINEAR EXPANSION OF METALS

The coefficient of linear expansion of a body is the rate at which the unit of length changes, under constant pressure, with an increase of unit or one degree of temperature; the coefficient of expansion for areas is, approximately, two times, and the coefficient of cubical expansion three times the coefficient of linear expansion. A bar, if not fixed, undergoes a change in length = *ltn,* where *l* is the length of the bar, *t* the number of degrees, *n* the corresponding linear coefficient.

To find the increase of a bar due to an increase in temperature, multiply the length of the bar by the increase in degrees and by the coefficient from the table.

RELATIVE CHARACTERISTICS OF COMMON METALS

(Arranged in descending order for each property)

Malleability	Ductility	Tensile strength
Gold	Gold	Iron
Silver	Silver	Copper
Aluminum	Platinum	Platinum
Copper	Iron	Silver
Tin	Copper	Zinc
Platinum	Aluminum	Gold
Lead	Nickel	Aluminum
Zinc	Zinc	Tin
Iron	Tin	Lead
	Lead	

TABLE OF SPECIFIC GRAVITIES AND WEIGHTS OF METALS AND OTHER MATERIALS USED BY CRAFTSMEN

Substance	Specific gravity	Weight, lb per cu ft	Substance	Specific gravity	Weight, lb per cu ft
METALS, ALLOYS, ORES:			TIMBER, U. S. SEASONED:		
Aluminum, cast-hammered	2.55–2.75	165	Ash, white, red	0.60	40
Aluminum, bronze	7.7	481	Cedar, white, red	0.32–0.38	22
Antimony	6.62	416	Chestnut	0.39	41
Arsenic	5.73	358	Cypress	0.46	30
Bismuth	9.79	608	Fir, Douglas spruce	0.48	32
Brass, cast-rolled	8.4–8.7	534	Fir, eastern	0.40	25
Bronze, 7.9 to 14% Sn	7.4–8.9	509	Elm, white	0.50	45
Chromium	6.93	428	Hemlock	0.42–0.52	29
Cobalt	8.72–8.95	552	Hickory	0.72	49
Copper, cast-rolled	8.8–9.0	556	Locust	0.73	46
Copper, ore, pyrites	4.1–4.3	262	Maple, hard	0.63	43
Gold, cast-hammered	19.25–19.35	1205	Maple, white	0.45	33
Iron, cast, pig	7.2	450	Oak, chestnut	0.86	54
Iron, wrought	7.6–7.9	485	Oak, live	0.95	59
Iron, steel	7.8–7.9	490	Oak, red, black	0.63	41
Iron, spiegeleisen	7.5	468	Oak, white	0.68	46
Iron, ferrosilicon	6.7–7.3	437	Pine, Oregon	0.51	32
Iron, ore, hematite	5.2	325	Pine, red	0.48	30
Iron, ore, limonite	3.6–4.0	237	Pine, white	0.41	26
Iron, ore, magnetite	4.9–5.2	315	Pine, yellow, long-leaf	0.58	44
Iron, slag	2.5–3.0	172	Pine, yellow, short-leaf	0.51	38
Lead	11.28–11.35	706	Poplar	0.42	30
Lead ore, galena	7.3–7.6	465	Redwood, California	0.40	26
Magnesium	1.74	109	Spruce, white, black	0.40–0.46	27
Manganese	7.20–7.42	456	Walnut, black	0.55	38
Mercury	13.55	848	Walnut, white	0.41	26
Molybdenum	10.2	562	VARIOUS LIQUIDS:		
Nickel	8.57–8.90	545	Alcohol, 100%	0.79	49
Nickel monel metal	8.8–9.0	556	Acids, muriatic, 40%	1.20	75

TABLE OF SPECIFIC GRAVITIES AND WEIGHTS

Substance	Specific Gravity	Weight, lb per cu foot	Substance	Specific Gravity	Weight, lb. per cu foot
Platinum, cast-hammered	21.1–21.5	1330	Acids, nitric, 91%	1.50	94
Silver, cast-hammered	10.4–10.6	656	Acids, sulphuric, 87%	1.80	112
Tin, cast-hammered	7.2–7.5	459	Lye, soda, 66%	1.70	106
Tin, babbitt metal	7.1	443	Oils, vegetable	0.91–0.94	58
Tin, ore, cassiterite	6.4–7.0	418	Oils, mineral, lubricants	0.90–0.93	57
Tungsten	18.7–19.1	1180	Petroleum	0.88	55
Vanadium	5.5–5.7	350	Gasoline	0.66–0.69	42
Zinc, cast-rolled	6.9–7.2	440	Water, 4° C, max. density	1.0	62.428
Zinc, ore, blende	3.9–4.2	253	Water, 100° C	0.9584	59.830
VARIOUS SOLIDS:			Water, ice	0.88–0.92	56
Carbon, amorphous, graphitic	1.88–2.25	129	Water, snow, fresh fallen	0.125	8
Cork	0.24	15	Water, sea water	1.02–1.03	64
Ebony	1.22	76	GASES, AIR = 1:		
Fats	0.92–0.94	58	Air, 0° C, 760 mm	1.0	0.08071
Glass, common, plate	2.40–2.72	160	Ammonia	0.5920	0.0478
Glass, crystal	2.90–3.00	184	Carbon dioxide	1.5291	0.1234
Glass, flint	3.15–3.90	220	Carbon monoxide	0.9673	0.0781
Phosphorus, white	1.83	114	Gas, illuminating	0.35–0.45	0.028–0.036
Porcelain, china	2.30–2.50	150	Gas, natural	0.47–0.48	0.038–0.039
Resins, rosin, amber	1.07	67	Hydrogen	0.0693	0.00559
Rubber, caoutchouc	0.93	58	Nitrogen	0.9714	0.0784
Silicon	2.49	155	Oxygen	1.1056	0.0892
Sulphur, amorphous	2.05	128			
Wax	0.95–0.98	60			

The specific gravities of solids and liquids refer to water at 4° C; those of gases to air at 0° C and 760-mm pressure. The weights per cubic foot are derived from average specific gravities except where stated that weights are for bulk, heaped, or loose material, etc.

Craft supply houses, such as Allcraft Tool and Supply
Company of New York, shown here, are located in
many cities throughout the United States. (See the
Tools and Supplies listing.) They offer a wide variety
of materials and tools in one convenient center. This
ready availability of craft materials has been a major
factor in fostering the growth of interest on amateur
and professional levels today. *Photo by Oppi.*

Sources of Supply*

Precious Metals

LEACH AND GARNER CO.
608 Fifth Avenue
New York City
Gold, silver, gold-filled and -laminated metals

L. S. PLATE AND WIRE CORP.
70-17 51st Avenue
Woodside, N.Y.
Gold, and gold-filled and -laminated metal for
jewelry and industrial use

KEMETRADE, INC.
74 West 46th Street
New York City
Platinum, palladium, iridium, ruthenium

AMERICAN METAL CLIMAX, INC.
1270 Avenue of the Americas
New York City

HANDY AND HARMAN
850 Third Avenue
New York 22, N.Y.
All forms of precious metals

Branches:
Bridgeport 1, Conn.
845 Waterman Avenue
East Providence, R.I.
1900 West Kinzie Street
Chicago 22, Ill.
330 N. Gibson Road
El Monte, Los Angeles, Calif.
141 John Street
Toronto, Canada

Gold Leaf

GOLD LEAF AND METALLIC POWDERS, INC.
145 Nassau Street
New York City

RALPH W. GRAUERT, INC.
100 Gold Street
New York City

PEERLESS ROLL LEAF CO.
Division of Howe Sound Co.
4511 New York Avenue
Union City, N.J.

Copper, Brass, Bronze, Aluminum

MANHATTAN BRASS AND COPPER CO., INC.
150–156 Lafayette Street
New York 13, N.Y.

MANHATTAN ALUMINUM CORP.
150–156 Lafayette Street
New York 13, N.Y.

T. E. CONKLIN BRASS AND COPPER CO., INC.
113–115 Leonard Street
New York 13, N.Y.

REVERE COPPER AND BRASS, INC.
230 Park Avenue
New York 17, N.Y.

COPPER AND BRASS RESEARCH ASSOCIATION
420 Lexington Avenue
New York 17, N.Y.
Copper and brass information

BADGER ALUMINUM EXTRUSIONS CORP.
950 Georgia Avenue
Brooklyn 7, N.Y.

THE WILLIAM L. BONNELL CO., INC.
350 Fifth Avenue
New York City
Aluminum extrusions

OLIN MATHIESON CHEMICAL CORP.
Metals Division
400 Park Avenue
New York 22, N.Y.
Aluminum information

* Addresses change from time to time. Those given were correct at time of publication.

REYNOLDS METALS CO.
19 East 47th Street
New York City
Aluminum

STANDARD TINSMITH AND ROOFER SUPPLY CORP.
183 Chrystie Street
New York 2, N.Y.

STAN PAK PRODUCTS
Johnson Foil Division of
Standard Packaging Corp.
200 East 42nd Street
New York City
Aluminum, tin, lead, and composition foil products

White Metal, Pewter, Lead

ATLAS WHITE METAL CO.
77 Delevan
Brooklyn, N.Y.

BELMONT SMELTING AND REFINING WORKS
320 Belmont Avenue
Brooklyn, N.Y.

NATIONAL LEAD CO.
111 Broadway
New York City

STANDARD ROLLING MILLS
145 Jewell Street
Brooklyn, N.Y.
Pewter

WHITE METAL ROLLING AND STAMPING CORP.
80 Moultrie Street
Brooklyn, N.Y.
Pewter

LEAD INDUSTRIES ASSOCIATION
292 Madison Avenue
New York 17, N.Y.
Lead information

Alloys

BARTLETT-SNOW-PACIFIC, INC.
1270 Sixth Avenue
New York City
Stainless steel alloys

INTERNATIONAL NICKEL CO., INC.
67 Wall Street
New York City
Nickel alloys

VANADIUM CORPORATION OF AMERICA
420 Lexington Avenue
New York City
Ferro alloys of chromium, manganese, silicon, titanium, and vanadium

NATIONAL FOIL CO.
9 Rockefeller Plaza
New York City
Foils

AMERICAN ZINC INSTITUTE, INC.
292 Madison Avenue
New York 17, N.Y.
Zinc information

AMERICAN METALIZING CORP.
150 Bruckner Boulevard
New York 54, N.Y.
Processors of metalizing

METALIZING CO. OF AMERICA, INC.
431 East 75th Street
New York City
Metalizing equipment

EASTERN METALIZING CO.
113 Marine
Farmingdale, Long Island, New York
Spraying of metals

METAL POWDER PRODUCERS ASSOCIATION
60 East 42nd Street
New York 17, N.Y.
Metal powders information

CHARLES HARDY, INC.
420 Lexington Avenue
New York 17, N.Y.
Metal powders

UNITED STATES GYPSUM
415 Madison Avenue
New York City
Expanded metals

Eastern States
Other than New York City

COHN SIGMUND CORP.
121 Columbus Avenue
Mount Vernon, N.Y.
Precious metals

KAISER ALUMINUM AND CHEMICAL SALES, INC.
190 East Post Road
White Plains, N.Y.
Aluminum

THE J. M. NEY CO.
Bloomfield, Conn.
Precious metals

THE AMERICAN BRASS CO.
Waterbury, Conn.

REED AND BARTON
Taunton, Mass.
Pewter

AMERICAN JEWELRY CHAIN CO.
560 Atwells Avenue
Providence, R.I.

HOOVER AND STRONG, INC.
119 West Tupper Street
Buffalo 1, N.Y.
Gold

OTTO BERNG CO., INC.
Rochester 13, N.Y.
Metals

RIGIDIZED METALS CORP.
773 Ohio Street
Buffalo 3, N.Y.
Rigidized metals with stamped, patterned surfaces, ferrous, nonferrous

AMERICAN PLATINUM AND SILVER
(Division of Engelhard Industries, Inc.)
113 Astor
Newark, N.J.
Precious metals

ENGELHARD INDUSTRIES, INC.
429 Delancy
Newark, N.J.
Refining of precious metals

CHARLES MUNDT AND SONS
51–61 Fairmont Avenue
Jersey City 4, N.J.
Perforated metals, ferrous, nonferrous

T. B. HAGSTOZ & SON
709 Sansom Street
Philadelphia 6, Pa.
Precious metals

ERNEST W. BEISSINGER
402 Clark Building
Pittsburgh 22, Pa.
Metal suppliers

THE SCULP METAL CO.
701-C Investment Building
Pittsburgh 22, Pa.
Aluminum plastic compound material

ALUMINUM COMPANY OF AMERICA
Pittsburgh, Pa.
Aluminum

HASTINGS AND CO., INC.
2314 Market Street
Philadelphia 3, Pa.
Precious metal leaf

Branches:
43 West 16th Street,
New York 11, N.Y.

330 South Wells Street,
Chicago 6, Ill.

GOLDSMITH BROS. SMELTING AND REFINING CO.
111 N. Wabash Avenue
Chicago 2, Ill.
Metals, alloys, chemicals

AMERICAN METALCRAFT, INC.
4100 Belmont Avenue
Chicago 41, Ill.
Metals and findings

CHARLES WEIDINGER
625 West 54th Place
Chicago 9, Ill.
Silver, findings

A-1 CRAFT PRODUCTS CO.
11447 S. Michigan Avenue
Chicago 28, Ill.

ILLINOIS ZINC CO.
Chicago, Ill.

ILLINOIS BRONZE POWDER CORP.
2023 S. Clark Street
Chicago 16, Ill.

L. E. SIMMONS REFINING
440 North Orleans
Chicago 10, Ill.
Metals

GAR-ALLOY
BRODHEAD-GARRETT & CO.
4560 East 71st Street
Cleveland 5, O.
Zinc

I. MILLER, INC.
304 Colonial Arcade
Cleveland, O.
Metal, jeweler's supplies

IMMERMAN AND SONS
1924 Euclid Avenue
Cleveland 15, O.
Liquid lead

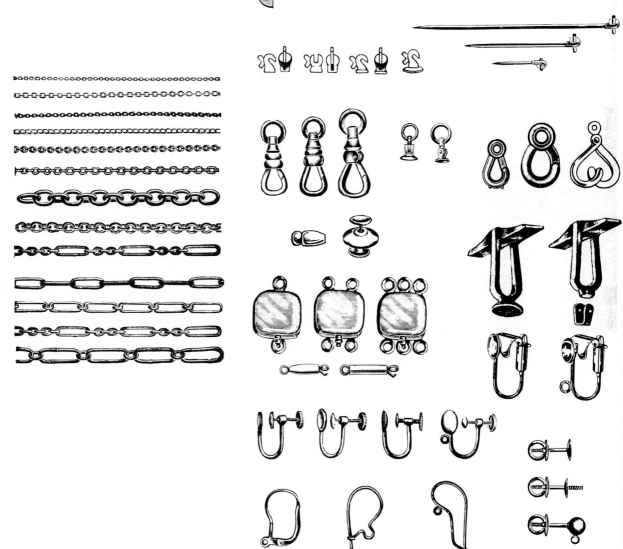

Ready made jeweler's chains
and jeweler's findings

A sidewalk jeweler's supply shop in Tiruchirapalli, South India. *Photo by Oppi.*

NATIONAL LEAD CO.
  659 Freeman Avenue
  Cincinnati, O.

CHASE BRASS AND COPPER
  222 Post Square
  Cincinnati 2, O.

WILLIAM WERKHAVEN AND SON
  2630 North High Street
  Columbus 2, O.
  Metal, stones and findings

HAUSER AND MILLER
  4011 Forest Park Boulevard
  St. Louis 8, Mo.
  Metals and metal supplies, smelters and refiners

METAL GOODS CORP.
  640 Rosedale Avenue
  St. Louis 12, Mo.

ANACONDA ALUMINUM CO.
  General Offices
  Louisville, Ky.

J. M. TULL METAL AND SUPPLY CO.
285 Mariett Street, N.W.
Atlanta 3, Ga.

CHASE BRASS AND COPPER CO., INC.
1000 S. Jefferson Davis Parkway
New Orleans, La.

SWEST, INC.
10803 Composite Drive
Dallas, Texas 75220
Metals and metal tools and supplies

METAL GOODS CORP.
1623 North 71st East Avenue
Tulsa 15, Okla.

WILDBERG BROS. SMELTING AND REFINING CO.
349 Butler Ave.
South San Francisco, Calif.
635 South Hill Street
Los Angeles 14, Calif.

PACIFIC METALS CO., LTD.
1900 Third Street
San Francisco, Calif.

ENGELHARD INDUSTRIES, INC.
760 Market Street
San Francisco, Calif.
Gold and silver refiners

AMERICAN BRASS AND COPPER
1920 Union Street
Oakland, Calif.

WESTERN GOLD AND PLATINUM CO.
525 Harbor Boulevard
Belmont, Calif.
Gold and silver refiners

DICK ELLS CO.
908 Venice Boulevard
Los Angeles 15, Calif.
Metals and metal supplies

SPEYERS SMELTING AND REFINING CO.
Medical-Dental Building
Seattle, Wash.
Metals

General Tools and Supplies (New York)

ALLCRAFT TOOL AND SUPPLY CO., INC.
15 West 45th Street
New York, New York 10036

ANCHOR TOOL CO.
12 John Street
New York, New York 10038

CRAFTOOL, INC.
396 Broadway
New York, New York

GAMZON BROS., INC.
21 West 46th Street
New York, New York 10036

PAUL H. GESSWEIN & CO., INC.
235 Park Avenue South
New York, New York 10003

I. SHOR CO., INC.
64 West 48th Street
New York, New York 10036

STANDARD DIAMOND TOOL CO., INC.
71 West 47th Street
New York City

JOHN SELLS AND SONS
66 West Broadway
New York City
Etching and engraving tools

Findings and Chains (See page 470.)

EASTERN FINDINGS CORP.
19 West 34th Street
New York, N.Y. 10001
Metal Jewelry findings and chains

METAL FINDINGS CORP.
152 West 22nd Street
New York, N.Y. 10011
Brass, sterling, gold, gold-filled, and nonferrous
findings
Minimum shipment: one gross

AMERICAN GOLD CHAIN CO.
7 West 45th Street
New York City

AMERICAN JEWELRY CHAIN CO., INC.
303 Fifth Avenue
New York City

AUTOMATIC CHAIN CO.
93 Nassau Street
New York City

ATLAS CHAIN CO.
47 West 34th Street
New York, New York 10001

UNIVERSAL CHAIN CO., INC.
110 West 34th Street
New York City
Specializing in fancy link chains

EASTERN CHAIN WORKS
309 East 22nd Street
New York City

Eastern States except New York

CRAFT SERVICE
337–341 University Avenue
Rochester, New York 14607
Tools and supplies

WILLIAM DIXON CO.
Carlstadt, New Jersey 07072

T. B. HAGSTOZ & SON
709 Sansom Street
Philadelphia, Pa. 19106

B. A. BALLOU AND CO., INC.
61 Peck Street
Providence, R.I.
Jewelry findings

CAPITOL TOOL AND FINDINGS CO., INC.
100 Delaine
Providence, R.I.

MANIN JEWELERS SUPPLY CO., INC.
373 Washington Street
Boston, Massachusetts

C. W. SOMERS CO.
387 Washington Street
Boston, Massachusetts 02108
Jewelers metalsmith's supplies

GENERAL FINDINGS, INC.
Attleboro, Massachusetts
Jewelry findings in all metals

MACMILLAN ARTS & CRAFTS, INC.
9520 Baltimore Avenue
College Park, Maryland 20740

Midwest and South

BRODHEAD GARRETT & CO.
4560 East 71st Street
Cleveland 5, O.
Tools and supplies

OHIO JEWELERS SUPPLY
1030 Euclid Avenue
Cleveland, Ohio 44115

SNAPVENT COMPANY
1107 West Cumberland Avenue
Knoxville, Tenn.
Tool and supplies

C. R. HILL CO.
2734 W. Eleven Mile Rd.
Berkley, Mich. 48072

BARTLETT & CO., INC.
5 South Wabash Avenue
Room 819
Chicago 3, Ill.
Small tools, and jewelry supplies

THE JEWELRY CRAFTSMAN CO.
139 North Wabash Avenue
Chicago 2, Ill.
Findings

ERNEST LINICK CO.
5 South Wabash Avenue
Chicago 3, Ill.
Jeweler's supplies

SAX CRAFTS
P. O. Box 2002
Milwaukee, Wisconsin 53201

GAGERS HANDICRAFT
1024 Nicollet Avenue
Minneapolis, Minn.
Tools

NORVELL MARCUM CO.
1609 S. Boston
P. O. Box 2887
Tulsa, Okla. 74119

NEW ORLEANS JEWELER'S SUPPLY CO.
208 Chartres Street
New Orleans, La.

West

NORDMAN & AURICH
657 Mission Street
San Francisco, Calif. 94105

J. J. JEWELCRAFT
2732 Colorado Boulevard
Los Angeles, Calif.

GRIEGER AND CO.
900 S. Arroyo Parkway
Pasadena, Calif. 91105
Tools and supplies, lapidary equipment

L. A. CLARK CO.
1417 4th Avenue
Seattle, Wash.

Electric Power Tools

BLACK AND DECKER MFG. CO.
701 E. Joppa Rd.
Towson, Md. 21204

MILWAUKEE ELECTRIC TOOL CORP.
(Pet Power Tools)
35-12 Crescent
Long Island City, N.Y.

THOR POWER TOOL CO.
(Thor Electric Tools)
950 Ashland Avenue
Folcroft, Pa. 19032

MAURICE S. DESSAU CO., INC.
400 Madison Avenue
New York, New York 10017
Diamond tools

J. K. SMIT & SONS, INC.
571 Central Avenue
Murray Hill, N.J. 07974

BURGESS VIBROCRAFTERS, INC.
Grayslake, Ill. 60030
Engraving tools and supplies

H. SERABIAN
71 West 47th Street
New York, New York
Flexible shaft machines and accessories

Polishing and Buffing

BENCE BUFFING AND POLISHING WHEEL MFG. CO.
93 Crosby
New York, N.Y.

DRACKETT PRODUCTS CO.
1 Rockefeller Plaza
New York City
Metal polish

FOURPOINT PRODUCTS
1123 Broadway
New York City
Jeweler's polishing cloths

J. HOLLAND AND SONS, INC.
475 Keap Street
Brooklyn, N.Y.
Buffing and polishing equipment and supplies

KING AND MALCOLM CO., INC.
57-10 Grand Avenue
Maspeth, N.Y.
Distributors, carborundum, pumice, rouge

THE BUCKEYE PRODUCTS CO.
7031 Vine Street
Cincinnati, Ohio 45216

SCHAFFNER MANUFACTURING CO., INC.
Schaffner Center
Emsworth, Pittsburgh, Pa. 15202
Polishing and buffing supplies

Abrasives

ABRASIVE SALES CO.
132 Lafayette Street
New York, New York

THE CARBORUNDUM CO.
Niagara Falls, New York
Grinding wheels, sharpening stones, etc.

Authorized Distributor:
U. S. GRINDING WHEEL CO.
180 Lafayette Street
New York, New York

BRIGHTBOY INDUSTRIAL
(Division of Weldon Roberts Rubber Co.)
351 Sixth Avenue
Newark, N.J.

UNITED MINERAL & CHEMICAL CORP.
129 Hudson Street
New York, New York 10013

THE BUCKEYE PRODUCTS CO.
7031 Vine Street
Cincinnati, Ohio 45216

THE LEA MANUFACTURING CO.
237 East Aurora Street
Waterbury, Connecticut 06720

CARTER PRODUCTS
P. O. Box 1924
Columbus, Ohio 43216

GRAPHIC CHEMICAL AND INK CO.
728 No. Yale Avenue—Box 27
Villa Park, Ill. 60181

FEDERATED SALES CO.
9852 Dupree St.
South El Monte, Calif. 91733

NICHOLSON FILE CO.
The Cooper Group
Providence, R.I.
Files and saws

NASCO
901 Janesville Ave.
Fort Atkinson, Wis. 53538

VAN WATERS & ROGERS
4300 Holly St.
Denver, Colo. 80217
3745 Bayshore Blvd.
Brisbane, Calif. 94005

SCIENTIFIC SUPPLIES CO.
600 Spokane Street
Seattle, Wash.

CANADIAN LABORATORY SUPPLIES, LTD.
403 St. Paul Street W.
Montreal, Quebec, Canada

Casting Supplies

Waxes

WILLIAM DIEHL AND CO.
120 East 56th Street
New York, New York 10022

SCULPTURE ASSOCIATES LTD.
114 East 25th Street
New York, New York 10010

Chemicals

ALLIED CHEMICAL CORP.
40 Rector Street
New York City

ALUMINIUM LTD. INC.
620 Fifth Avenue
New York City
Chemicals related to aluminum

AMERICAN CYANAMID CO.
30 Rockefeller Plaza
New York City

AIRCO, INC.
85 Chestnut Ridge Road
Montvale, New Jersey 07645

BERG CHEMICAL CO., INC.
441 West 37th Street
New York City

CITY CHEMICAL CORP.
132 West 22nd Street
New York, N.Y. 10011

DU PONT DE NEMOURS, E. I. & CO.
350 Fifth Avenue
New York City

NEW YORK LABORATORY SUPPLY CO.
78 Varick Street
New York 13, N.Y.

SEIDLER CHEMICAL & SUPPLY CO.
12–16 Orange Street
Newark, N.J.

BURELL CORP.
2223 Fifth Avenue
Pittsburgh 19, Pa.

WILL CORPORATION OF GEORGIA
P. O. Box 966
Atlanta, Ga.

E. H. SARGENT AND CO.
4647 West Foster Avenue
Chicago 30, Ill.

REGENT PRODUCTS CO.
251 East Grand Avenue
Chicago 11, Ill.

KANSAS CITY LABORATORY SUPPLY CO.
307 Westport Road
Kansas City 11, Mo.

F. W. STEADMAN CO., INC.
(Steadco Waxes)
59 Pearl Street
New York, New York

FRANK B. ROSS CO., INC.
(Ross Industrial Waxes)
6 Ash Street
Jersey City, N.J. 07304

THE S. S. WHITE DENTAL MFG. CO.
211–17 South 12th Street
Philadelphia, Pa. 19105

THE CLEVELAND DENTAL MFG. CO.
3307 Scranton Road
Cleveland, Ohio

KERR DENTAL MANUFACTURING CO.
6081–6095 12th Street
Detroit, Mich.

General Casting Supplies

ALEXANDER SAUNDERS AND CO.
95 Bedford Street
New York, New York 10014

WHITING CORP.
30 Church Street
New York, New York

CASTING SUPPLY HOUSE
62 West 47th Street
New York, New York 10036

LOUCKS DENTAL SUPPLY
  1506 East 15
  Tulsa, Okla.

Foundries

BEDI-MAKKY ART FOUNDRY
  227 India Street
  Brooklyn, New York 11222

MODERN ART FOUNDRY
  18–70 41st Avenue
  Long Island City, N.Y.

Miscellaneous

S. S. WHITE DENTAL MFG. CO.
  211–17 South 12th Street
  Philadelphia, Pa. 19105
  Silver amalgams, dental tools

JOHNSON GAS APPLIANCE CO.
  Cedar Rapids, Ia. 52405
  Forges, furnaces

Welding Supplies

APEX WELDING SUPPLIES, INC.
  1066 Tchoupitoulas St.
  New Orleans, La.

Authorized distributor:
  New York Welding Supply Co., Inc.
  133 Leroy Street
  New York, New York

EUTECTIC WELDING ALLOYS CORP.
  40–40 172nd Street
  Flushing, New York 11358
  Welding and brazing rods

LINDE CO.
  (Division of Union Carbide Corp.)
  270 Park Avenue
  New York, New York

T. W. SMITH WELDING SUPPLY CORP.
  545 West 59th Street
  New York, New York 10019

NATIONAL CYLINDER GAS
  (Division of Chemetron Corp.)
  2136 85th Street
  North Bergen, N.J.

NATIONAL WELDING EQUIPMENT
Distributor:
  Weldex Equipment Co., Inc.
  543 East 75th Street
  New York, New York

Adhesives

CHEMIONICS, DIVISION OF ADHESIVES, INC.
  20 Wagaraw Road
  Fair Lawn, N.J.

MANHATTAN ADHESIVES CORP.
  425 Greenpoint Avenue
  Brooklyn, N.Y.

Asbestos Products

JANES ASBESTOS CO.
  Box 67
  Carlton Hill
  East Rutherford, N.J.
  Gloves, board, cloth, etc.

Dust Collectors

CRAFTOOL, INC.
  396 Broadway
  New York, New York 10013

MINE SAFETY APPLIANCES CO.
  400 Penn Center Blvd.
  Pittsburgh, Pa. 15235

Hand Spinning

ARROW METAL SPINNING CO.
  Star Route
  Candia, New Hampshire 03034

Solvents

PHILLIPS MANUFACTURING CO.
  248 East 33rd Street
  New York, New York
  Degreasing solvents

Solders

ANCHOR ALLOYS, INC.
  966 Meeker Avenue
  Brooklyn, New York

KESTER SOLDER CO.
  88 Ferguson Street
  Newark, New Jersey

Wetting Agents

CHLORAL CHEMICAL CORP.
171 Lombardy Street
Brooklyn, New York

DOW CHEMICAL CO.
Midland, Mich.

General Metalcraft Suppliers

DON JER PRODUCTS CO.
55 Alder St., Unit D
West Babylon, N.Y. 11704

AURORA PLASTICS CORP.
44 Cherry Valley Road
West Hempstead, N.Y.

CRAFT SERVICE
337 University Avenue
Rochester 7, N.Y.

CRAFTSMAN'S SUPPLY HOUSE
35 Brown's Avenue
Scottsville, N.Y.

J. L. HAMMETT CO.
Hammett Place
Braintree, Mass. 02184

JEWELRY CRAFTSMAN CO.
139 North Wabash Avenue
Chicago, Ill. 60602

CHARLES A. BENNETT CO.
809 W. Detweiller Dr.
Peoria, Ill. 61614

DWINNELL ART & CRAFT SUPPLY
2312 National Road
Wheeling, W.Va.

HOUSE OF WOOD AND CRAFTS
3408 North Holton Street
Milwaukee, Wis.

THE HANDCRAFTERS
1 West Brown Street
Wapun, Wis. 53963

JERARTS HOUSE OF MANY CRAFTS
5744 Tujunga Avenue
North Hollywood, Calif. 91601

Stones, Gem Material, and Lapidary Equipment

INTERNATIONAL GEM CORP.
15 Maiden Lane
New York, New York

SAM KRAMER
29 West Eighth Street
New York, New York 10011

JOHN J. BARRY CO.
P. O. Box 15
Detroit, Mich.

B & I MANUFACTURING CO.
461 Washington Street
Burlington, Wis.

MATHESON'S STONE HOUSE
Joshua Green Building
Seattle, Wash.

FRANCIS J. SPERISEN
166 Geary Street
San Francisco, Calif. 94108

BELMONT LAPIDARY SUPPLY
749 El Camino Real
Belmont, Calif.

M.D.R. MANUFACTURING CO., INC.
4853 West Jefferson Blvd.
Los Angeles, Calif.

Wood

ALBERT CONSTANTINE & SON, INC.
2050 Eastchester Road
Bronx, New York 10461

J. H. MONTEATH CO.
2500 Park Avenue
Bronx, New York 10451

WILLIAM L. MARSHALL, LTD.
450 Park Avenue South
New York, New York 10016

ICHABOD T. WILLIAMS & SONS, INC.
11th Avenue and West 25th St.
New York, New York

CRAFTSMAN WOOD SERVICE
2727 South Mary Street
Chicago, Ill.

HAAS WOOD AND IVORY WORKS
64 Clementina Street
San Francisco, Calif. 94105

Plating

B & D POLISHING & PLATING CORP.
1575 York Avenue
New York, New York 10028
Gold and silver plating

HILL CROSS CO., INC.
393 Pearl Street
New York, New York 10038

HOOVER AND STRONG, INC.
111 West Tupper Street
Buffalo, New York
Electroplating

FRANKLIN PLATING AND POLISHING CO., INC.
630 South Sixth Street
Columbus, Ohio, 43206

Sources of Supply: Great Britain

London

JOHNSON MATTHEY & CO. LTD
73–83 Hatton Garden, London W1
Tel. 020 7269 8103
Tools and supplies

CECIL W. TYZACK LTD
79 Kingsland Road, London, E2
Tel. 020 7739 2630
Tools and machinery

SHESTO LTD
Unit 2, Sapcote Trading Centre
374 High Road
Willesden
London NW10 2DH
Tel. 020 8451 6188

Birmingham

A.J. REEVES & CO. (BIRMINGHAM) LTD
Holly Lane, Marston Lane
Birmingham B37 7AW
Tel. 0121 779 6831
Tools

EXCHANGE FINDINGS
81 Caroline Street
Hockley
Birmingham, B3 1UP
Tel. 0121 236 5211

H.S. WALSH & SONS LTD
(Birmingham Showroom)
1–2 Warstone Mews
Warstone Lane
Birmingham B18 6JB
Tel. 0121 236 9346
Lathe and machine tools

J.F. RATCLIFF (METALS) LTD
New Summer Street,
Birmingham, B19 3QN
Tel. 0121 359 5901

THOMAS SUTTON (BIRMINGHAM) LTD
37 Frederick Street
Birmingham B1 3HU
Tel. 0121 236 7139
Tools and supplies

Sheffield

JOHNSON MATTHEY METALS LTD
175 Arundel Gate Court
1 Froggatt Lane
Sheffield, S1 2NL
Tel. 0114 241 9400

WILLIAM ROWLAND LTD
9 Meadow Street, Sheffield
Tel. 0114 276 9421
Metals

Other Locations: Metals

AXMINSTER POWER TOOL CENTRE
Chard Street
Axminster
Devon EX13 5DZ
Tel. 01297 33656

H.S. WALSH & SONS LTD
243 Beckenham Road
Kent BR3 4TS
Tel. 020 8778 7061
Lathe and machine tools

PROOPS BROTHERS LTD
Technology House
34 Saddington Road
Fleckney
Leicester LE8 8AW
Tel. 0116 240 3400

Cast bronze Kuduo, Ashanti, Ghana, Africa. Height: 6½ inches. *Museum of Primitive Art, New York. Photo by Charles Uht.*

Persian silver rose water bottle, parcel-gilt, twelfth century. Decorated with chasing and niello. The design consists of roundels of quadrupeds and birks and Kufic inscriptions. Height: 9¹³⁄₁₆ inches; diameter: 4¾ inches. *Freer Gallery of Art, Washington, D.C.*

Glossary of Terms

abrasive blasting A wet or dry method of cleaning or finishing metals. Abrasive grain particles are blown against the metal surface by compressed air through a nozzle, making the metal chemically and mechanically clean.

abrasives Natural or synthetic materials used in powders of various grits; solids of various cross sections and forms or lengths, or mounted on papers and cloths, whose main purpose is to wear away metal surfaces, edges, etc.

age hardening A change in properties of a metal or alloy resulting in increased hardening and strength and reduced ductility which usually occurs after rapid cooling, more slowly in air.

alkaline cleaning The removal of soil from metal surfaces with alkaline cleaners such as detergents. The soil is removed by *detergency* rather than solvency—i.e., by displacement—and is distributed through the solution as an emulsion.

alloy A metal composed of a combination of two or more metals, or a metal and a chemical element.

amalgam A mercury-based alloy.

ampere Electrical current unit measurement of the passage of one coulomb per second.

annealing Heat-treating a metal to a temperature below its critical range, mainly to relieve residual stresses but also to render the metal soft for further cold working. After annealing, copper may be immediately quenched; iron and steel may be cooled in air; brass- and zinc-containing alloys must be slow cooled because the zinc in them, if subjected to sudden cooling, would cause cracks. Aluminum can be judged to be annealed when soap previously applied to its surface turns black under heat.

anode The positive pole of an electrolytic cell, usually the supply source of the metal being deposited.

anodizing A method of dyeing the surface of aluminum by coating the metal with an anodic film of aluminum oxide while it is in an acid bath; this is followed by washing and immersion in organic dyes, allowing the oxide film to absorb the dye, and a final washing, drying, and sealing with lanolin.

anvil A block of iron, formed in a characteristic shape and usually with a hardened steel face, against which a smith holds metal for forming by hammering or forging.

Aqua Fortis Nitric Acid.

Aqua Regia A combination of acids (known as "king's water") that will successfully bring the precious metals gold, silver, and platinum into solution.

asbestos A mineral unaffected by fire which is processed and used for gloves, boards, luting, plaster, yarn, and cloth and in other forms when heat or fire resistance is the function of the object. A silicate of calcium and magnesium with one or more other metals, it occurs in nature in long, delicate fibers or fibrous masses and seams of crystalline rock of a nonaluminous variety.

assaying The examination of a metal by chemical tests to determine the quantity of precious metal in its ingredients, in order to assess its compliance with a standard.

backstick A wooden stick used by the spinner to assist in the forming of spun metal shapes.

batter To hammer a piece of iron to compress, flatten, or spread it.

bellows A compressible container of leather and wood, spring-loaded, used to create an air blast to raise the temperature of a forge fire or to introduce oxygen into a torch flame.

bidri A form of decorative metalwork originating in India; silver is inlaid in a special zinc alloy base, which is finally blackened.

billet In nonferrous metals, a part of an ingot suited for extrusion, rolling, or forging. A casting suitable for rolling.

binding The use of iron binding wire to hold units while they are being soldered together. Any such device is called a soldering jig.

blank An unfinished, possibly stamped metal shape that must be processed further for finishing.

blocking The beginning stages of a method of forming metal shapes by hammering a disc or other shape of metal into a depression or mold to begin breaking the disc into a form with a third dimension.

bloom A ferrous-metal billet intended for conversion into bars, rods, wire, and sheet, or for shaping by forging.

blooming Subjecting jewelry of precious metal to a matte acid dip to produce a special matte surface.

blowhole A hole that occurs in casting when gas trapped during the pour fails to escape, is held in pockets, and creates an imperfection in the casting.

blue vitriol Copper sulphate.

bolster A hollow plate or ring placed on an anvil and used as a base for punching holes in metal to avoid scarring the anvil surface.

bossing Beating a sheet of metal from the back to a required form; also known as embossing.

bottoming The process of flattening and stiffening the bottom of a raised shape by placing it on a flat or slightly concave stake and hammering with a flat bottoming hammer.

bouging Removing irregularities, during intermediate stages, in a metal form that is being raised. The object is rounded or smoothed out while resting on an anvil or a flat metal surface; a nonmarking mallet made of wood, rawhide, plastic, or rubber is used.

brazing A form of hard soldering that involves the uses of a soldering spelter. Brazing is also a term used in welding, when brass alloy weld rods are melted onto other metal surfaces.

breakdown chuck A preliminary chuck or series of chucks used when making a deep or complex form that requires development through several stages of forming with intermittent annealings before the object is placed on the chuck that produces its final form.

bright annealing Annealing done in a controlled furnace atmosphere so that a minimum of surface oxidation occurs on the metal.

bright dip An acid solution that results in a bright, clean surface on metal after submersion and washing.

brittleness The tendency of metal to break without much deformation.

broaching Using a sharp, tapered tool called a broach to create or enlarge holes in metal.

buff A disc made of cotton, muslin, and other materials sewn together in layers and used in polishing and buffing metals.

burin An engraver's tool, also known as a graver or scorper.

burnishing A polishing process applied to metals by the use of a burnisher tool. Also used to shape metals, as in the case of setting a bezel. The burnisher may be of a variety of shapes and is made of steel, hematite, agate, or bloodstone.

burr A sharp or rough edge that occurs on the edge of metal, usually after cutting.

butt joint A joint made directly between two pieces of metal lying edge to edge in the same plane.

butt welding Joining two pieces of metal edge to edge by welding.

cabochon A stone made of a semi-precious material ground into a rounded or domed shape, usually with a flat back and not faceted.

capillarity A physical law of action by which a liquid (such as molten solder), when in contact with a solid (the metal being soldered), is attracted to the solid because the molecules of the liquid attract those of the solid. This accounts for the tendency of solder to flow or run in a well-fitting seam or joint.

carat A unit of measure used when referring to the weight of precious stones. Distinguished from karat. (See karat.)

casting The process of pouring molten metal into a mold. Also, the name given to the result. See page 321 for additional casting terms under Vocabulary of Casting.

casting strains Strains that occur in a casting after cooling, along with residual stresses.

cathode The negatively charged pole in an electrolytic cell on which the metal is deposited.

centrifugal casting A casting process in which the filling of the mold occurs during the rotation of the metal and mold while they are held in a centrifugal machine. The metal is forced into the mold by centrifugal force.

chaps Tong jaws.

chasing A decorative metal process involving surface modeling of metal from the front with the aid of various-shaped punches and a hammer.

chenier Metal tubing used in making hinges.

chuck A wood or metal solid, three-dimensional form with an inside thread used to attach it to a spinning lathe. Sheet metal discs are forced against this form with the aid of spinning tools in order to create a metal shell.

cladding A process of joining two slabs of metal, one on top of the other, and then reducing their thickness by rolling.

cogging Rolling or forging ferrous-metal ingots into blooms or billets.

coin silver A silver alloy containing 900 parts of silver and 100 parts of copper (U.S.A.).

cold shut A line that occurs on the surface of a casting because of two streams of metal failing to unite owing to an inconsistency in their temperatures while pouring.

collaring The joining of two or more pieces of metal with a collar.

coloring Applying a patina to metal by the use of chemicals, heat, paint, or lacquers, or by allowing natural oxidation.

cope The upper section of a two-part sand-casting flask.

core A unit of sand or other material used inside a pattern or mold hollow to create a hollow in the casting.

corrosion A gradual attack on metals, either chemical or electrochemical, that occurs when the metal is exposed to moisture, gas, atmosphere, or other conditions.

cotter pin In forging, a tapered, wedge-shaped pin with a head, used to join parts. In soldering, an elongated U-shaped pin used to hold metal parts together during soldering.

coursing A name sometimes given to raising a shape by hammering from the outside toward the edge in spirals and shaping the form by stages or "courses" to its final form.

covering agents Any resist material, such as lacquer, asphaltum, varnish, wax, soft and hard ground, used to protect metal from being attacked during exposure to acids.

crimping A beginning process in a method of raising a form that involves a special stake called a valley stake, or a wood form with a longitudinal depression, in conjunction with a crimping or narrow-faced hammer. Radiating grooves are made in the metal that are then smoothed out with the aid of hammers and stakes or anvils.

critical range The temperature at which the internal structure of a metal is altered.

crucible A refractory container for metal that is to be melted.

crystallization When a molten metal solidifies, the atoms assume definite positions and form crystals in a pattern characteristic of the particular metal. This process is crystallization.

cupellation A process of oxidizing fusion effected to remove silver or gold from lead.

damascene A metal-decorating process that involves the application of one metal on another by encrustation or inlay.

dapping block The cube-shaped metal tool, usually having varisized, semicircular depressions on all sides, used in conjunction with dapping punches for making small semicircular metal forms.

deep drawing Using a punch to force cup-shaped shells or articles into a die or over a chuck.

deposited metal Metal that has been added by a welding process.

die A metal form or forms, usually of a hard metal such as steel, bronze, or brass, into which sheet metal is forced so it will take on the conformation of the depression in the die.

die casting Using metal molds to cast shapes.

doré silver Silver that still contains a small amount of gold after the removal of lead by cupellation.

drag The lower portion of a two-part sand mold.

drawfiling Smoothing a roughly filed edge or metal surface by holding a file with two hands, sidewise on the surface, perpendicular to the direction of movement, and drawing it toward the operator until all marks from previous work are eliminated.

drawplate A flat steel plate pierced with rows of graduated openings through which wire is drawn with the aid of a draw tongs either to reduce its cross-section dimension or its shape.

drilling Using a pump drill, hand drill, breast drill, drill press, or flexible shaft installed with a twist drill to make a hole in metal.

drop forging The forming of metals, under impact by compression into dies, to produce a particular shape.

dross Metal oxides on or in molten metal.

ductility The ability of metal to be drawn into fine wire.

emulsion The nonsetting suspension of one liquid in another.

encrustation The application of metal units on a base of the same or a contrasting metal.

engraving The decorative process of making lines or textures on metal by the use of engraving tools called gravers, burins, or scorpers.

etching The process of corroding or removing metal by subjecting it to the action of acids. Various stop-out materials or covering agents are applied to the parts of the metal to be protected against the corrosion.

eutectic A binary or ternary alloy containing components in a specific proportion so that the melting point and the flowing point occur simultaneously at the same temperature.

extrusion Shaping metal into continuous forms, such as rods, tubing, or other cross-section shapes, by forcing it through a die while molten.

file card A file cleaner used to remove chips of wood or metal from clogged files.

filigree An open ornamental structure utilizing all forms of wire soldered together into small and large units.

filler metal The metal added in brazing or welding and melted by the flame to bind edges, fill empty places, or cover surfaces.

fillet weld A weld approximately triangular in cross section used in a lap joint, corner joint, or T joint, where two pieces of metal are joined at right angles to each other.

findings Mechanical fittings in a great variety of shapes, either commercially available or handmade, used to hold jewelry to clothing or the person.

fire-stain, fire-scale, or fire An oxide that forms below the surface of copper-bearing alloys such as sterling silver; when thick, the oxide is due mainly to overheating or unprotected heating. It is sometimes difficult to remove and can be avoided by painting the surface with flux before heating or by quick dipping, after subjection to heat, in a 50 per cent solution of nitric acid and water, followed by thorough rinsing in water.

flask A wood or metal frame in two parts, the upper called the cope and the lower the drag, employed to hold the sand used in sand-mold casting.

fluidity The ability of a molten metal to flow readily when heated to a certain temperature.

flux A chemical in liquid, paste, or powder form that assists in the flow of solder by dissolving, preventing, or hindering the formation of oxide and other foreign material that might impede the flow. Also used in casting to assist in the viscosity of molten metals. Depending on the condition, borax, saltpeter, sal ammoniac, ordinary salt, and sulphur are used as fluxes.

foil Sheet metal usually not more than 0.005 inch thick.

forging The process of forming or shaping metals while hot or cold by the use of hammers and anvils or other metal surfaces. Hot-forged metals should not be worked below an orange-red color. Cold-forged metal requires annealing if it becomes work-hardened.

ganging Mounting more than one wax model in a flask for simultaneous casting by centrifugal investment casting.

gangue The commercially undesirable portion of an ore that must be removed before it can be processed further.

gate The place where molten metal enters and passes into a mold cavity; it consists of an entire "assembly," including the pouring basin, sprues, runners.

gold leaf Gold that is beaten or rolled into extremely thin sheets. Other metals such as platinum and silver are also made into leaf for decorative uses.

granulation A form of metal decoration, used primarily in jewelry making, in which small balls of gold or silver are joined to a metal surface without the aid of solder.

gravity pour A pouring of the molten metal in casting that depends solely on gravity to fill the mold cavity.

grinding The removal of metal by holding it against a revolving device, such as motor-mounted abrasive wheels, bands, discs, or belts. Grinding is usually preliminary to future polishing and removes excess metal on weldings, castings, and forgings. It is also an operation in the reshaping of tools.

groove weld A weld made by depositing filler metal in a groove between two metal parts that are to be joined.

hard drawing Tempering wire, rod, or tubing by cold drawing.

hardening The process of making alloy, plain or high-carbon steel as hard as possible, often applied to the working end of a high-carbon steel tool. The metal is heated to a cherry red and quenched as quickly as possible in oil, water, or brine. In hardening, the metal is heated to a point beyond its "critical range" to obtain maximum hardness.

heading The process of forming a rivet head by upsetting.

hearth The furnace used to heat metals during forging.

heat treating A process of hardening, tempering, or annealing steel or other metals.

hot forming Working on metals that are heated above room temperature.

ingot A casting that is to be processed further by rolling, forging, or other methods of forming.

inlaying A generic term referring to any decorative process that involves cutting grooves or areas in a metal surface and forcing another metal into the sunken area. Damascene, bidri, and kuftgari are examples of metal-inlay work. The same term can be applied to the inlay of other materials, such as lacquer or niello into metal. Metal inlay into yet other materials such as wood, plastic, nylon, or shell can also be referred to as inlay.

karat A unit of measure indicating the content of gold in an alloy. Since there are twenty-four karats in pure gold, one karat equals one-twenty-fourth part of the alloy. Distinguished from carat.

kuftgari A form of damascene originating in India and consisting of the inlay of silver or gold wire into steel.

lamination The joining of several layers of metal of the same kind or different kinds.

lap joint A welded or soldered joint in which two overlapping parts are joined.

lemel Filings of precious scrap metal saved for reclaiming and refining. From the French *limaille,* filings.

liver of sulphur Mixed potassium sulphides used in a water solution to create a patina, or color, to oxidize or "antique" metal surfaces.

lost-wax casting A process of precision casting that involves making a pattern in wax, investing the model in a plaster or clay mold, and when dry, creating a cavity by melting out the wax and filling the cavity with molten metal.

lute A mixture made with fireclay or other suitable refractory material, used to seal the openings between the cover and a crucible when heat is to be applied. Mixtures of loam, rouge, tripoli, whiting, or fireclay with water applied to parts of a metal object to be protected during the soldering of other parts.

malleability The property of metal that allows it to be formed by hammering or rolling processes.

mandrel A metal rod of any cross section from small to large, used variously for the forming of chains, wire coiling, rings, bracelets, and the preparation of metal for tube drawing.

marking out Making a full-sized drawing on a flat surface for a forging job. Against this, the work may be measured and checked.

metal spraying A process of applying a fine spray of molten metal to coat a surface by the use of a special torch gun which feeds metal wire into an oxyacetylene blast and projects it against the surface being coated.

mold The form containing a hollow into which molten metal is poured to produce a casting.

muriatic acid Another name for hydrochloric acid.

niello A decorative process in which an approximately eutectic combination of the sulphides of silver, copper, and lead are fused into depressions on a metal surface to produce black areas or lines.

nugget A small mass of metal, such as gold or silver, found in a native state in nature.

ore A mineral found in nature from which a metal can be profitably extracted.

oxidizing flame A torch flame in which there is an excess of oxygen over gas.

paillon Another name for a solder snippet or a small piece of sheet metal used decoratively.

parcel-gilt Metal that has been completely or partially gold-plated either by applying an amalgam of gold and mercury or by electroplating.

parting line A line on a pattern where the cope and drag of a sand mold separate.

parting powder A powder sprinkled on the face surface of a mold before casting to facilitate the separation of the mold parts after casting. Also called parting compound.

patina The surface appearance that occurs on metal after aging or chemical treatment.

pattern A form of wood or other material around which the sand in sand-mold casting is packed to form the hollow in the mold; it is removed before casting. Patterns are also used in other forms of casting.

pickle An acid solution used for the removal of oxides or "flux glass" from metal surfaces, usually after soldering.

piercing Making holes in metal by the use of mechanical or hand-operated tools for functional and/or decorative effect.

pig A virgin or secondary metal ingot used for remelting.

pinhole porosity Extremely small holes scattered throughout a casting because of the incomplete release of gases during cooling or shrinkage.

planishing A smoothing process for finishing raised shapes by the use of special, slightly dome-faced planishing hammers and an anvil or stake; the entire surface is hammered systematically.

plating The deposit of a thin coat of metal on another metal surface by immersion in a solution containing ions of the plating metal.

point hardening A process of both hardening and tempering the point of a steel tool in one operation.

punch The movable part of a punch-and-die combination that forces the metal into the die. Also used in reference to chasing and repoussé tools.

pyrometer An instrument used for measuring high temperatures in kilns, furnaces, and annealing ovens.

quenching The rapid cooling of metals from high temperatures by bringing them in contact with liquids, solids, or gases to "set" desired qualities.

raising The process of making a hollow form from a flat sheet by bringing the sides up gradually in stages of hammering the metal on anvils.

ramming Forcing sand into a mold to pack it solidly, with the aid of a rammer.

red sear A crack that is the result of hammering an overheated piece of iron.

reducing flame A flame in a torch in which there is an excess of gas over oxygen.

refining The process of purifying crude metals.

refractory A nonmetallic material resistant to destruction by heat, used for furnace linings and other heat-retaining or -resisting purposes.

repoussé The decorative process of beating out the shape of metal, usually from the back, utilizing punches and hammers. The process is usually followed by chasing with chasing tools from the front of the metal for design definition and development.

residual stress Stress that forms in metal during uneven cold working or from drastic temperature changes during welding or quenching.

rheostat Fixed resistance elements in an assembly inserted in an electric circuit and controlled by a switch.

riddle A sieve used for uniformly distributing the first particles of sand directly on the pattern during the sand-casting process.

rifflers Files with variously curved ends used for reaching areas where straight files cannot be used.

rolling Passing sheet metal through the rollers of a rolling mill to decrease its thickness, or, in the case of wire, to reduce its cross section or shape.

runner The part of the gate assembly in casting that connects the downgate or sprue with the cavity in the mold.

runout Molten metal that escapes from a mold, melting furnace, or crucible.

sal ammoniac Ammonium chloride, so called because it was originally made from the soot of camel's dung at the temple of Jupiter Ammon in Africa. Used as a reagent in the etching of metals and as a flux in soft soldering.

sand burning The hard surface or crust formed on the sand by the heat of the molten metal that contacts the sand in a casting.

saponify To convert grease or oil into a soap, as when cleaning metals.

scalping Removing surface layers from billets, ingots, or slabs of metal before further processing.

scorpers Varishaped small chisels used for engraving metal.

scrap Metal unsuitable for direct use that can be reclaimed by smelting and refining.

sectional chuck A chuck used for spinning forms in metal when the opening is of a smaller diameter than the diameter at some other part of the shell. To allow its removal from the form after spinning, the chuck is made in sections, each of which is small enough to allow its removal through the opening, starting with the "key" piece.

shake-out The removal of a casting from a mold.

shift A defect in sand casting caused by the mismatching of the cope and drag of a flask.

shortness The quality of brittleness in metal.

sinking A method of raising a form by directing the blows of the hammer on the inner or concave surface of the metal while holding the metal over a sandbag, block of wood, or metal surface.

skull A thin film of metal that remains in a pouring vessel after pouring. Also the shadowy remains of a particle of hard solder after the particle has melted; sometimes called a "ghost."

smelting The process by which metal is separated from other metals or nonmetallic materials with which it is found in nature or in reclaiming.

soldering The joining of metals by the use of alloys that flow at a temperature lower than that of the metals being joined.

soldering jig Any device, such as binding wire, cotter pins, and tweezers, that is used to hold parts together while being soldered.

soldering mop A tangled mass of iron binding wire used for the support of small articles while they are being soldered.

spalling The splintering off of inner plaster casting mold surfaces that spoil the casting by becoming inclusions.

spelter solders Copper-zinc alloys with low melting points.

spinning The process of turning sheet metal into hollow shapes or shells by forcing it, while rotating on a spinning lathe, against a metal or wood form called a chuck.

spinning tools Tools used by the spinner in conjunction with a lathe to create spun metal forms.

splitting A method of dividing metal with chisels without any loss of metal.

sprue The part of each impression of a drop-forging die that receives the rough bar from which the forging is made. It connects the edge of the die block with the gate or flask.

stake A kind of anvil with a tang end used to secure it in a hardie hole, bench hole, bench vise, or stake holder. Metals are hammered against it for shaping.

stamping A process by which patterns are made on smooth metal surfaces with a punch. Embossing and blanking are other forms of stamping.

stretching A method of forming metal shapes that consists of shaping a thick piece of metal (disc or bar) by hammering it on a metal surface; in the case of circular or raised shapes, hammering starts from the center and spirals outward. Also known as pressing.

stripping A solution in which metals are dipped to remove surface metal without affecting the base metal; it is done either to color the surface or to prepare the metal for plating.

sweeps Table and floor sweepings containing precious metals, gathered in a workshop and saved for refining.

tang The end of a file, graver, or stake that is inserted into a handle or other holding device.

tapping Making screw threads by the use of taps and dies. Taps are used to cut the female thread in a nut or internal metal. Dies are used for cutting the male thread on the screws.

tarkashi The inlaying of wire in wood as practiced in India and Poland (called *inkrustacja*).

tarnish Surface discoloration of metal due to the formation of a thin film of oxide or sulphide when the metal is exposed to air or gases.

temper A condition produced in metal through heat treatment or working. *Annealed temper:* metal softened by heating. *Hard temper:* cold-worked metal. *Spring temper:* metal worked harder than cold-working temper. *Point tempering:* hardening the working end of a steel tool.

tempering Treating tools with a reheating process after hardening and then quenching at a point that is often judged by the color appearance of a polished surface on the metal. The procedure slightly reduces the hardness of the metal but makes it tougher and less brittle.

thrumming Polishing difficult-to-reach areas of metalwork with a strong cotton or nylon string coated with abrasive, or by drawing the metal through a cutting compound. The string is then threaded through an opening or around the section being reached, and while the object is held securely, it is pulled up and back.

tin cry The sound that occurs when one is bending pure tin.

tinning The process of coating metals with tin by hot coating, immersion, or electrodeposition.

T-joint A joint at the junction of two metal parts at approximately right angles to each other, in the form of a T.

torsion Metal that contains a strain due to twisting action.

toxicity The degree of poisonousness of metal when inhaled or absorbed through the skin in forms of dust or vapor.

truing In silversmithing, testing a symmetrical form's accuracy of curvature by the use of a template, calipers, or *surface gauge*. The gauge inscribes lines parallel with the base and is usually used to inscribe a trimming line on a completed piece, which is then cut away with shears or snips.

upsetting A forging process in which the metal is compressed, as when forming a rivet head or when edge-thickening a raised bowl, or in general when working a metal in a direction perpendicular to its longitudinal axis.

vents Narrow openings in closed molds to allow the escape of gases.

virgin metal Metal taken directly from ore and not previously used.

viscosity The ability of a substance to flow at a given temperature under definite conditions.

volatility The vaporization of a substance at a given temperature.

welding rod Filler metal in wire or rod form used in gas welding.

wetting agent A solution used to reduce the surface tension on an object and allow it to be "wetted" by the solution or material that follows, promoting intimate contact.

Bibliography

HISTORICAL

ADAIR, JOHN, *The Navajo and Pueblo Silversmiths.* University of Oklahoma Press, Norman, Okla. (1958).

AGRICOLA, GEORGIUS, *De Re Metallica.* Basle, 1556. Translated by Herbert Clark Hoover and Lou Hoover (1912). Republished: Dover Publications, New York (1950).

AITCHISON, LESLIE, *A History of Metals.* Two volumes; Interscience Publishers, Inc., New York (1960); Macdonald and Evans, London (1960).

ANDERSON, LAWRENCE, *The Art of the Silversmith in Mexico: 1519–1936.* Two volumes; Oxford University Press, New York (1941).

BANCO DE LA REPUBLICA, Bogotá, Colombia, *80 Masterpieces from the Gold Museum* (1954).

———, Barradas, José Perez de, *Orfebreria Prehispanica de Colombia* (1958).

BERGSØE, PAUL, *The Gilding Process and the Metallurgy of Copper and Lead among the Pre-Columbian Indians.* Translated by C. F. Reynolds; Danmarks Naturvidenskabelige Samfund, København (1938).

BERRY-HILL, HENRY and SIDNEY, *Antique Gold Boxes, Their Lore and Their Lure.* Abelard Press, New York (1953).

BHUSHAN, JAMILA BRIJ, *Indian Jewellery, Ornaments and Decorative Designs.* D. B. Taraporevala Sons and Co., Ltd., Bombay (1958). A general survey of Indian jewelry.

BIRINGUCCIO, VANNOCCIO, *The Pirotechnica* (De la Pirotechnica). Venice, 1540. English translation by Cyril Stanley Smith and Martha Teach Gnudi, The American Institute of Mining and Metallurgical Engineers, Inc. (1942). This is the first printed book dealing with the applied metal arts and the processes of ore reduction.

BONNIN, ALFRED, *Tutenag and Paktong.* Oxford University Press (1924). A history of Chinese nickel alloys.

BOYER, MARTHA, *Mongol Jewellery.* Nationalmuseets Skrifter, Etnografisk Roekke, V, I Kommission Hos, Gyldendalske Boghandel, Nordisk Forlag, København (1952).

BRADFORD, ERNLE DUSGATE SELBY, *Contemporary Jewellery and Silver Design.* Heywood and Co., London (1950).

———, *Four Centuries of European Jewellery.* Philosophical Library, New York (1953).

———, *English Victorian Jewellery.* Robert M. McBride Co., New York (1959).

BURGESS, FRED W., *Antique Jewelry and Trinkets.* Tudor Publishing Co., New York (1937).

CALVILLO, MADRIGAL S., *Plateria Mexicana.* Vol. 9 of Collección Anahuac De Arte Mexicano, Ediciones De Arte, Mexico (1948).

CARLI, ENZO, *Pre-Conquest Goldsmith's Work of Colombia.* William Heinemann, London (1957).

CELLINI, BENVENUTO, *Treatises on Goldsmithing and Sculpture.* Trans. by C. R. Ashbee (1898).

CENNINI, CENNINO D'ANDREA, *The Craftsman's Handbook.* Il Libro Dell' Arte, fifteenth century. Translated by Daniel V. Thompson Jr., Yale University Press (1933). New Edition: Dover Publications, New York (1963).

CHIKASHIGE, MASUMI, *Alchemy and Other Chemical Achievements of the Orient.* Tokyo (1936).

DAVIS, MARY L., and PACK, GRETA, *Mexican Jewelry.* University of Texas Press, Austin (1963). An excellent survey.

DE KERTESZ, M. WAGNER, *Historia Universal de las Joyas.* Ediciones Centurión, Buenos Aires (1947).

DE LA BORBOLLA, DR. DANIEL RUBIN, *Los Tesoros Artisticos del Peru.* Museo Nacional de Ciencias y Arte, Universidad Nacional Autonoma de Mexico, Mexico, D.F. (1961).

EVANS, JOAN, *A History of Jewellery, 1100–1870.* Pitman Publishing Corp., New York (1953).

FETTICH, NÁNDOR, *Archeologia Hungarica,* Archaologische Studien, Akademiai Kaido, Budapest (1951). A history of the late metal art of the Huns.

Finnish Kalevala Trinkets, Kalevalaisen Naisen Muistromerkkiyhdistys, r. y. Suomi, Helsinki (1939).

FLOWER, MARGARET, *Victorian Jewelry.* Duell, Sloan & Pearce, New York (1951).

FORMAN, W., *Swords and Daggers of Indonesia.* London. Photographs.

GEERLINGS, GERALD K., *Wrought Iron in Architecture.* Charles Scribner's Sons, New York (1929).

GOWLAND, W., *Metals and Metalworking in Old Japan*. Translated, Japan Society (1915).

HAMLYN, PAUL W., FORMAN, B., and DARK, PHILIP, *Benin Art*. Batchworth Press Ltd., Spring House, London (1960).

HOMMA, J., editor, *Masterpieces of Japanese Sword Guards*. Tokyo Society for the Preservation of Japanese Art Swords (1952). Text in Japanese and English. Folio of 159 plates.

HUGHES, GRAHAM, *Modern Jewelry*. Crown Publishers, New York (1963). A handsome book, profusely illustrated.

HUNT, W. BEN, *Indian Silversmithing*. Bruce Publishing Co., Milwaukee (1952).

JESSUP, RONALD F., *Anglo-Saxon Jewellery*. Frederick A. Praeger, New York (1953).

JOHNSON, ADA MARSHALL, *Hispanic Silverwork*. Hispanic Society of America, New York (1944).

KAYSER, STEPHEN S., *Jewish Ceremonial Art*. The Jewish Publication Society of America, Philadelphia (1959).

MANN, JAMES G., *The Etched Decoration of Armour*. Proc. British Academy (1942).

MCCARTHY, JAMES REMINGTON, *Rings through the Ages*. Harper & Brothers, New York (1945).

Lietuviu Liaudies Menas (Lithuanian Prehistoric Jewelry). Vilnius (1958). Russian and Lithuanian text, lavishly illustrated.

MERA, HARRY P., *Indian Silverwork of the Southwest*. Volume 1, Dale Stuart King, Globe, Arizona (1959). Illustrated.

PORTA, JOHN BAPTISTA, *Natural Magick*. A volume in the Collector's Series in Science, edited by Derek J. Price, The Smithsonian Institution. Basic Books, New York (1957).

RACZ, ISTVAN, *Kivikirves ja Hopearisti* (Stone Axe and Silver Cross). Helsingissa Kustannusosakeyhtio Otava, Helsinki (1962). Early Finnish "Kalevala" jewelry.

REIN, J. J., *The Industries of Japan*. London (1889).

RIVET, PAUL and ARSANDAUX, H., *La Metallurgie en Amerique Pre-Columbienne*. L'Institut d'Ethnologie, Paris (1946).

ROBINSON, B. W., *The Arts of the Japanese Sword*. Charles E. Tuttle Co., Rutland, Vt. (1961).

ROGERS, FRANCES, and BEARD, ALICE, *5000 Years of Gems and Jewelry*. J. B. Lippincott Co., Philadelphia (1947).

ROSSI, FILIPPO, *Italian Jeweled Arts*. Harry N. Abrams, Inc., New York (1954).

SAVILLE, MARSHALL H., *The Goldsmith's Art in Ancient Mexico*. Museum of the American Indian, Heye Foundation, New York (1920).

SISSONS, W., *Old Sheffield Plate*. Pawson and Brailsford, Sheffield.

SIVIERO, RODOLFO, *Gli Ori e Le Ambre del Museo Nazionale di Napoli* (Jewelry and Amber of the National Museum of Naples). Sotto L'Alto Patronato della Accademia Nazionale dei Lincei, Sansoni (1959).

STEINGRÄBER, ERICH, *Antique Jewelry*. Frederick A. Praeger, Inc., (1957).

The State Armoury Museum of the Moscow Kremlin. Moscow (1958); 381 pages of plates illustrating mainly metal objects in the collection.

THEOPHILUS PRESBYTER (Roger of Helmarshausen), *Schedula Diversarium Artium* (On Diverse Arts). A twelfth-century treatise, translated by John G. Hawthorne and Cyril Stanley Smith, The University of Chicago Press (1963). The earliest account, firsthand, of metalworking. Of special interest is Book III: The Art of the Metalworker (pp. 77–187).

UNDERWOOD, LEON, *Bronzes of West Africa*. Alec Tiranti Ltd., London (1949).

VASARI, GEORGIO, *Vasari on Technique,* 1550; translated by Louisa S. Maclehose (1907). Republished by Dover Publications, New York (1960).

WYLER, SEYMOUR B., *The Book of Sheffield Plate*. Crown Publishers, New York (1949).

———, *The Book of Old Silver, English, American, Foreign*. Crown Publishers, New York (1960).

BOOKS ON METAL CRAFTS

BOLAS, THOMAS, *Etching on Metals, Niello and Metal Inlay*. Articles from the Useful Arts and Handicrafts Series, No. 22, edited by Snowdon Ward; Dawbarn and Ward, London (about 1900).

BOLLINGER, JOSEPH WALTER, *Elementary Wrought Iron*. Bruce Publishing Co., Milwaukee (1930).

BOVIN, MURRAY, *Jewelry Making for Schools, Tradesmen and Craftsmen*. Published by the author, New York (1964).

BOWMAN, JOHN J., and HARDY, R. ALLEN, *The Jewelry Engraver's Manual*. D. Van Nostrand Company, Princeton, N.J. (1954).

CUZNER, BERNARD, *A Silversmith's Manual*. London (1958).

ELLACOTT, S. E., *Forge and Foundry*. Methuen's Outlines, Methuen, London (1955).

EMERSON, A. R., *Hand-Made Jewelry*. The Dryad Press, Leicester (1953).

EVANS, T. FRANKLIN, *Hammered Metalwork*. University of London Press, London (1936).

FEIRER, JOHN L., *General Metals*. McGraw-Hill Book Co., New York (1959).

FRANKE, LOIS E., *Handwrought Jewelry*. McKnight and McKnight Publishing Co., Bloomington, Ill. (1962).

GEE, GEORGE E., *The Goldsmith's and Silversmith's Handbook*. The Technical Press, Gloucester Road, Kingston Hill, Surrey (1952).

GOOGERTY, THOMAS F., *Hand Forging and Wrought Iron Ornamental Work*. Popular Mechanics, Chicago (1911).

HARDY, R. ALLEN, and BOWMAN, JOHN J., *The*

Jewelry Repair Manual. D. Van Nostrand Company, Princeton, N.J. (1956).

———, *The Jewelry Engraver's Manual.* D. Van Nostrand Company, Princeton, N.J. (1954).

HORTH, A. C., *Repoussé Metalwork.* Methuen and Co., London (1905). Art nouveau designs.

KRONQUIST, EMIL F., *Metalcraft and Jewelry.* The Charles A. Bennet Company, Peoria, Ill. (1926).

LILLICO, J. W., *Blacksmith's Manual, Illustrated.* Crosby Lockwood & Son, London (1930).

LINICK, LESLIE L., *Jeweler's Workshop Practices.* Henry Paulson and Co., Chicago (1948).

MARTIN, CHARLES J., with D'AMICO, VICTOR, *How to Make Modern Jewelry.* Museum of Modern Art, New York (1949). Distributed by Doubleday & Co., Inc., Garden City, N.Y.

MARYON, HERBERT, F.S.A., *Metalwork and Enamelling,* Third Edition. Dover Publications, New York (1955).

MILLER, JOHN G., *Metal Art Crafts.* D. Van Nostrand Company, Princeton, N.J. (1948).

PACK, GRETA, *Jewelry and Enameling.* D. Van Nostrand Company, Princeton, N.J. (1941).

———, *Chains and Beads.* D. Van Nostrand Company, Princeton, N.J. (1952).

PRUDEN, DUNSTAN, *Silversmithing, Its Principle and Practice in the Small Workshop.* St. Dominican Press, Sussex (1933).

ROOD, JOHN, *Sculpture with a Torch.* University of Minnesota Press, Minneapolis (1963).

RURAL INDUSTRIES BUREAU, *The Blacksmith's Craft* (Publication No. 54). Wimbeldon, England (1952).

———, *Wrought Ironwork* (Publication No. 55). Wimbeldon, England (1953).

SCHOENFELT, JOSEPH F., *Designing and Making Handwrought Jewelry.* McGraw-Hill Book Co., New York (1960).

SHIRLEY, A. J., and SHIRLEY, A. F., *Handcraft in Metal.* B. T. Batsford, London (1953).

SMITH, DONALD, *Metalwork.* B. T. Batsford, London (1948).

STOREY, MICKEY, *Centrifugal Casting as a Jewelry Process.* International Text Book (1963).

THOMAS, RICHARD, *Metalsmithing for the Artist-Craftsman.* Chilton Company, Book Division, New York (1960).

VON NEUMANN, ROBERT, *The Design and Creation of Jewelry.* Chilton Company, Book Division, New York (1961).

WATSON, JOHN, *Tables for the Use of Blacksmiths and Forgers.* Longman's, London (1906).

WEINER, LOUIS, *Hand Made Jewelry.* D. Van Nostrand Company, Princeton, N.J. (1948).

WILSON, H., *Silverwork and Jewellery.* Sir Isaac Pitman and Sons, London (1951). Includes sections done with Professor Unno Bisei of the Imperial Fine Art College, Tokyo, on Japanese Techniques.

WINEBRENNER, KENNETH D., *Jewelry Making as an Art Expression.* International Textbook Company, Scranton, Pa. (1955).

TECHNICAL

BLUM, WILLIAM, and HOGABOOM, GEORGE B., *Principles of Electroplating and Electroforming,* Third Edition. McGraw-Hill Book Co., New York (1949). Authoritative work on the subject.

BRANNT, WILLIAM T., editor, *Metal Worker's Handy Book of Receipts and Processes.* Hodder and Stoughton, London (1920).

BRAY, JOHN L., *Non-Ferrous Production Metallurgy,* Second Edition. John Wiley and Sons, New York; Chapman and Hall, London (1953).

FIELD, SAMUEL, and BONNEY, SAMUEL ROBERT, *The Chemical Coloring of Metals.* Chapman and Hall, London (1925).

FRASER, ROLAND R., *General Metal: Principles, Procedures and Projects.* Prentice-Hall, Englewood Cliffs, N.J. (1955).

Henley's Twentieth-Century Book of Formulas, Processes and Trade Secrets, edited by Gardner D. Hiscox, M.E.; 1944 revised and enlarged edition by Professor T. O'Conor Sloane,. A.B., A.M., E.M., Ph.D. The Norman W. Henley Publishing Co., New York.

HIORNS, ARTHUR H., *Metal Coloring and Bronzing.* Macmillan and Co., London (1920).

JOHNSON, CARL G., *Metallurgy,* Fourth Edition, Revised. American Technical Society, Chicago (1956).

Metal Finishing Guidebook-Directory for 1963, Thirty-first Annual Edition. Metals and Plastics Publications, New York.

Metals Handbook, 1948 Edition, prepared under the direction of the Metals Handbook Committee; edited by Taylor Lyman. American Society for Metals, Cleveland. Reprinted January 1954.

Metals Handbook, Volume 1: Properties and Selection of Metals, Eighth Edition. American Society for Metals, Metals Park, O. (1961).

1959 Minerals Yearbook, Volume III, Area Reports, prepared by the staff of the Bureau of Mines, Division of Minerals, United States Department of the Interior. United States Government Printing Office, Washington, D.C. (1960).

NIGHTINGALE, *Tin Solders.* Tin Research Institute, Birmingham Printers, London (1932).

The Oxy-Acetylene Handbook. Linde Company, Division of Union Carbide Corporation, New York (1960).

Oxyacetylene Welding, Fourth Edition, revised by Morgan H. Potter. American Technical Society, Chicago (1956).

REAGAN, JAMES E., and SMITH, EARL E., *Metal Spinning.* The Bruce Publishing Co., Milwaukee (1946).

SMITH, CYRIL STANLEY, *A History of Metallography.* University of Chicago Press (1960). The development of ideas on the structure of metals before 1890.

Tool Engineers Handbook, American Society of Tool Engineers, Detroit, Mich. McGraw-Hill Book Co., New York (1949).

WAGNER, CHARLES L. H., *Text Book of Gilding.* Wagner School of Sign and Commercial Art, Boston (1950).

Welding Handbook, Section Two, *Gas, Arc and Resistance Welding Processes,* Fourth Edition. American Welding Society, New York (1958).

MISCELLANEOUS

LYNCH, JOHN, *Metal Sculpture.* Studio-Crowell, New York (1957).

Marking Precious Metals
Commercial Standards published by the U. S. Department of Commerce, National Bureau of Standards; sold by Superintendent of Documents, Washington, D.C.

Commercial Standard CS66-38, Marking of Articles Made Wholly or in Part of Platinum

Commercial Standard CS67-38, Marking Articles Made of Karat Gold

Commercial Standard CS118-44, Marking of Jewelry and Novelties of Silver

Commercial Standard CS51-35, Marking Articles Made of Silver in Combination with Gold

Commercial Standard CS47-34, Marking of Gold-Filled and -Rolled Gold-plate Articles Other than Watchcases

The Marking of Precious Metals, A Guide to Markings and Descriptions Used in the Jewelry Trade. Jeweler's Vigilance Committee, 45 West 45th Street, New York City.

SPERISEN, FRANCIS J., *The Art of the Lapidary.* The Bruce Publishing Company, Milwaukee (1961).

UNTRACHT, OPPI, *Enameling on Metal.* Chilton Company, Book Division, Philadelphia and New York (1957).

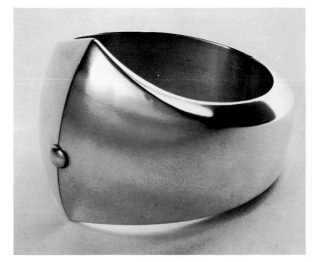

Hollow sterling silver bracelet, designed by Nanna and Jørgen Ditzel for Georg Jensen Silversmiths, Ltd., 1960. *Photo by Junior.*

Index

A-1 Craft Products Company, 469
Aars, Ferdinand, 268
Abalone shell, inlaid, 237
Abbott Laboratories, 475
Abomey, Dahomey (Africa), 286, 315, 316
Abrasive blasting, defined, 481
Abrasives, 394ff., 399–403, 404, 410–13, 446; defined, 481; sources, 474
Abrasive Sales Company, 474
Abyssinian silver armlet, 103
Acetic acid for coloring, 417, 418
Acetylene torches, 62, 63, 168, 170. *See also* Oxyacetylene welding; Torches
Acids (*See also* Etching; Fluxes; Pickling; specific acids): specific gravities, weights, 464–65
Adams, Robert, 356
Adhesives, 401, 441, 477
Adhesives, Inc., 477
African work: cast bronzes, 338–41, 353, 376, 420; cast gold, 377; chasing, 17, 281; filigree, 196; forged iron, 286; repoussé, 101; wood with metal, 87, 215, 216, 315, 316
Agar-agar, 331
Aging, age hardening, 13, 33; defined, 481
Agra, India, 226
Air, specific gravity, weight of, 465
Airbrasives, Inc., 474
Air-gas torches, 166, 169, 170, 247. *See also* Torches
Air Reduction Chemical and Carbide Company, 475
Air Reduction Company, 475, 476
Air Reduction Sales Company, 476
Ajmer, India, 212
Akron, Ohio, 330
Alams, 75
Albert, Gilbert, 14, 16, 51
Alchemists, and mercury, 31
Alcob Metals, Ltd., 479
Alcohol, specific gravity, weight of, 464
Alcohol lamps, 168
Ale for cleaning metal, 409
Algerian work, 11, 87
Alkaline cleaning, defined, 481
Allcraft Tool and Supply Company, 466, 471
Allied Chemical Corporation, 475
Alloys, 4, 7 (*See also* specific alloys, kinds, uses); defined, 481; sources of supply, 468–69; specific gravities, weights, 464–65
All-State Welding Alloys Company, Inc., 476
Alluvial (placer) gold, 3, 7
Almandite, 399
Alpaca, silver, 70
Alpha brasses, 18
Alum for coloring, 419
Aluminum, 4, 6, 7, 26–28, 32–33, 463, 464 (*See also* specific techniques); in alloys (*see* main compo-

nents; specific techniques, uses); articles made of (*see* specific objects, techniques); coefficient of linear expansion, 463; etching solution, 132; extruded, 49; ore, bauxite, 2, 26; sources of supply, 467, 468–69; temperature for annealing wrought, 246 (*see also* Annealing); toxicity, 51; welding, 295
Aluminum chloride for coloring, 418
Aluminum Company of America, 469
Aluminium Goods Ltd., 479
Aluminum Ltd., Inc., 475
Aluminum oxide, 400, 402, 411
Aluminium Wire & Cable Company, Ltd., 479
Amalgams, amalgamation, 7, 11, 31–32; defined, 481
Amber, 358, 465
Amenemhet III, 75
American Brass Company, The, 468
American Brass and Copper, 469
American Cyanamid Company, 475
American Gold Chain Company, 472
American Handicrafts Company (East Orange, New Jersey), 472
American Handicrafts Company, Inc. (New York City), 477
American Jewelry Chain Company, Inc., 468, 472
American Marietta Company, 474
American Metal Climax, Inc., 467
American Metalcraft, Inc., 469
American Metalizing Corporation, 468
American Platinum and Silver, 468
American Standard gauge. *See* Brown & Sharpe Standard gauge
American Steel & Wire Company gauges, 451. *See also* Washburn & Moen
American Wire Gauge. *See* Brown & Sharpe Standard gauge
American work (*See also* Indians, American; United States; specific craftsmen, places): copper, repoussé, 99; iron, 35; pewter, 264, 266; tin, 24, 86; wire, 201
American Zinc Institute, Inc., 468
Ames, Jean, 75
Ammeters, 381
Ammonia (*See also* Aqua ammonia): specific gravity, weight, 465
Ammonium chloride (sal ammoniac), 179, 180, 485; and casting lead, 21; for coloring, 147, 417, 418; for niello, 191
Ammonium molybdate for coloring, 418
Amozoc, Mexico, steel bluing in, 158
Ampere, defined, 481
Anaconda Aluminum Company, 469
Anchor Alloys, Inc., 477
Anchor Tool Company, 471
Andersen, David, 269
Andirons, wrought iron, 277
Angle raising, 247–48

Linick, Ernest, Company, 472
Linoleum: cutting tools for wax, 359; on plywood, for repoussé, 93, 95
Linotype metal, cutting, 268
Lions: aquamanile in form of, 109; wood with metal, 316
Lipchitz, Jacques, 339
Liquid measure, 450
Liquidus temperature, 4. See also specific metals
Lisbon, Portugal, 237
Lithium, 4
Liver of sulphur, 416–17, 484
Loam, 323. See also Yellow ochre
Lock and key, pierced and engraved, 76
London, 33, 87, 202 (See also specific craftsmen); sources of supply in, 479
London gauges, 451
London Metal Warehouses, Ltd., 479, 480
Lost-wax casting, 16, 205, 338–77; centrifugal, 351–74; defined, 484
Loucks Dental Supply, 476
Low-alloy steels. 36. See also Steel; specific techniques
Low-carbon (soft) steel, 6, 35–36 (See also Forging; Welding); cold spinning, 301
Low-zinc brasses, 18
Lubrication, 301. See also specific techniques
Lucknow, India, 75, 110
Lukula, Mayombe, 216
Luster, 5. See also Polishing and grinding
Lute, defined, 323, 484
Lye, specific gravity, weight of, 465

M. D. R. Manufacturing Company, Inc., 478
McCracken, R. S., and Sons, 476
McKinney Welding Supply Company, 476
Madhya Pradesh, India, 211
Madonnas: silver, Mexican, 220; welded iron, 299
Madrid, Spain, 276, 277, 299
Magnesium, 463, 464; alloys (see main components; specific techniques); soldering blocks, 170, 171
Magnetite, 33, 464
Magnifiers, optical, 114
Magnus Craft Materials, Inc., 477
Maher, Patrick F., 414
Mahua, India, 315
Malay Peninsula, Malaya, 22, 188
Malleability, 5–6, 464, 484. See also specific metals
Malleable iron, 33
Mallets, 256, 435
Mallory, D. N., 474
"Man" (sculpture), 312
Mandrels, 283, 425, 437, 484; examples of, 436, 446; for flexible shaft, 443, 446
Manganese, 463, 464; alloys (see main components; specific techniques); platinum's attraction for, 16; toxicity, 52
Manhattan Adhesives Corporation, 477
Manhattan Aluminum Corporation, 467
Manhattan Brass and Copper Company, Inc., 467
Mani, 103
Mani, P., 157
Manin Jewelers Supply Company, Inc., 472
"Man of War" (pendant-brooch), 207
Marggraf, Andreas, 26
Marinha Grande factory, 237
Marking and measuring tools and equipment, 425–27. See also specific equipment, uses
Marking out, defined, 484
Married metals, 184–86

Marshall, C. and E., Company, 473
Marshall, William L., Ltd., 478
Masks: French funerary, 103; for metal dust, 52, 438; Mexican tin, 23; Senufo cast bronze, 353; Sudanese metal on wood, 215
Mastic, 358
Matchplate plaster, 330, 332
Maté cup bombilla, 216
Matheson's Stone House, 478
Matte, 3
Matte finishes, 409 (See also Polishing and grinding); dips, 132
Matting tools, 84–85, 97, 99, 105; examples, 85, 96
Mayombe, 216
Meaker Company, The, 479
Measurements, measuring equipment, 55, 57, 59, 395–99, 450 (See also specific equipment, uses); comparison of, 457–58; equivalents of, 450
Medieval guilds, 87
Medieval times, lead in, 19
Medium-carbon steel, 36
Mellor, David, 259
Melting points, 4, 173, 463. See also specific metals
Mercer, William, 478
Mercuric chloride for coloring, 418
Mercuric sulphide, 31
Mercury, 4, 31–32, 463, 464; toxicity, 52
Meshed, Persia, 109
Mesopotamians, and pitch, 96–97
Metales casados, 184–86
Metal Findings Corporation, 472
Metal fume fever, 52
Metal Goods Corporation, 469, 478
Metalizing Company of America, Inc., 468
Metallurgy, 31–41
Metal Powder Producers Association, 468
Mexico, Mexican work, 22, 23 (See also Oaxaca; Taxco); bluing of steel in, 158; married metals, 184–86; and mercury, 31; piqué work, 218, 220, 223; polishing of silver beads, 394; pressing of metal, 256; wirework ring, 200; wrought iron crosses, 275
Miami, Florida, 296
Mica for soldering, 198–99
Michigan Buff Company, Inc., 474
Mickelson, A., Silversmith Company, 392
Microcrystalline, 357
Micrometers, 47, 48, 427
Middle East (See also specific countries): filigree, 196
Milan, Italy. See specific craftsmen, techniques
Milch, Hermine, 215
Mild steel. See Low-carbon steel
Miller, Frederick, 120, 217, 223
Miller, I., Inc., 469
Miller, John Paul, 202, 206, 207
Millers Falls Company, 473
Miller Tool and Supply Company, 473
Millimeter equivalents, 458
Milwaukee Electric Tool Corporation, 473
"Minerva" (bracelet), 50
Mine Safety Appliances Company, 410, 477
Minnesota Mining and Manufacturing Company, 474, 477
Miracle Adhesives Corporation, 477
Mirko, 354
Mirror, Etruscan bronze, 109
Mirror back, gold pierced work, 77
Mirror finish, 29, 407
Mirror lapping, 403, 410
"Mission" (cast aluminum sculpture), 355
Mixtec gold wirework ring, 200

Stakes, 244–46ff., 435–37, 486. *See also* specific uses

Stamps, stamping, 96, 486 (*See also* Dies; Punches, punchwork; Stamps, stamping, quality); examples of, 85–93 *passim,* 103, 108, 111, 152, 215, 228; production and assembly of ring, 80–81

Stamps, stamping, quality, 9, 12, 16, 85–89, 427; on decanter, 90; tools for, 89, 427

Standard Birmingham gauges, 451

Standard Diamond Tool Company, Inc., 472

Standard Rolling Mills, 468

Standard Tinsmith & Roofer Supply Corporation, 467

Stanley Works, The (Stanley Electric Tools), 473

Stannous chloride, 24, 389

Stan Pak Products, 467

"Star II" (sculpture), 290

"Starfish" (silver with granules), 204

Statues (*See also* specific subjects, techniques): Mayombe ritual, wood with nails, 216; reliquary, of St. Foy, 234; Tibetan gilded bronze, 30

Steadco Waxes, 475

Steadman, F. W., Company, Inc., 475

Stearic acid, 402

Stearin fluxes, 179

Steel, 6, 7, 35–37 (*See also* specific techniques); alloys (*see* Stainless steel; main components); articles of (*see* specific objects, techniques); coefficient of linear expansion, 463; coloring, 158, 417, 418, 419; etching solutions, 132; extruded, 49; gauges for, 47–48 (*see also* Gauges; specific gauges); plating of, 22, 23 (*see also* Plating; specific metals); spark observation in grinding, 412–13; tools (*see* specific tools); toxicity of cadmium-plated, 51; zinc-coating, 26

Steel blocks, 93

Steel wool, 160, 395, 396

Stephensen, Magnus, 262, 303

Sterling silver, 12–13, 14, 173, 246, 247, 452, 453, 454; articles made of (*see* specific objects, techniques); centrifugal casting of, 370; manufacturing of sheet metal, 38–42; scratch brushing, 410; testing for, 13; tubing, measurements of, 454

Stevens, Ronald, 120

Stick solder. *See* Soldering

Stirrers, electromagnetic, 382

Stirring rods for niello, 187, 188

Stirring rod tongs, 187, 329

Stockholm, Sweden, 269

Stone(s) (*See also* Encrustation; Inlay): black testing, for gold, 10; and electroforming, 390; metal with, 226–38, 442 (*see also* specific metals, objects, techniques); oilstones, 114, 115, 412; relief modeling, 82; riveting wire for, 314; sources of supply, 478

Stone Age, 17

Stoneware crocks, 131, 415

Stove, Franklin, 35

Strength, 6

Stress equalization annealing, 50

Stretching, 486. *See also* Silversmithing

Stripping, 126, 182, 382, 383, 486

Strips, 40

"Structure 14B," 41

Stubbs gauges, 47–48, 441, 451, 457–58

Studs on leather, 224–25

Stumps, tree, 246, 255, 256

Styrofoam, 331, 387, 388, 389, 390

Sudanese dance mask, 215

Sudbury, Ontario, 29

Sugar bowls, plated, 196

Sugar castor, engraved, 120

Sulphates (*See also* specific sulphates): for plating, 385

Sulphide ores, 3

Sulphides, 29 (*See also* specific sulphides); tarnish, 13 (*see also* Corrosion)

Sulphur, 3, 465 (*See also* Corrosion); iron ore, 33; in Monel Metal, 30; for niello, 188, 191

Sulphuric acid, 465; to anodize aluminum, 26; as by-product of zinc purification, 26; for copper baths, 385; for etching, 131, 132; for finishing dips, 132; for layout dye, 55; for pickling (*see* Pickling); to remove investment material, 373, 374; for swami work (*see* Swami work)

Sunbeam Equipment Corporation, 476

Superior Gems and Materials, 478

Supply, sources of, 467–80

Surface blocks and plates, 72, 255, 437

Surfaces. *See* Finishing

Surface speeds, 399

Suri, India, 216

Sutton, Thomas, Ltd., 480

Sutton-Hoo, England, 191

Swage blocks, 280–81

Swages, 279, 280

Swaging, 248, 282; example of edge thickening, 249

Swart, Jan de, 28, 355

Sweat soldering, 180, 267

Sweden: iron ore, 33; pewter boxes from, 269; silver beaker from, 119

Sweeps, defined, 486

Swiss files, 431, 433

Switzerland. *See* specific craftsmen

Sword guards, Japanese, 182, 223

Syrian canteen, 150

T-joint, defined, 486

T-stakes, 435. *See also* Stakes

Tallow, 22, 42, 179; as casting additive, 358; as spinning lubricant, 301, 302

Tang, defined, 486

T'ang Dynasty, 77

Tanjore, India, 134–38, 322

Tankard, coin-appliquéed, 138

Tanks, welding, 63, 298

Tapemeasure, 55

"Tapering," 281–82

Taps, tapping, 317, 318, 486

Tarkashi work, 213–14, 486

Tarnish, 486. *See also* Corrosion; specific metals

Taxco, Mexico, 23, 218, 353. *See also* Costillo brothers

Teapots: engraved silver, 119; planished silver, xiv; silver with horn handle, 262

Technical Adhesives, Inc., 477

Technical books, 489–90

Technicraft Lapidaries Corporation, 478

Teke tribe, chief's collar by, 17

Tellurium, copper alloy with, 18

Temper (*See also* Tempering): defined, 486

Temper annealing, 50

Temperature conversion tables, 462

Tempering, 115, 444–47, 486

Tensile strength, 6, 464

Tepping Studio Supply Company, 473

Ternary alloys, 7, 159

Terrazzo, 226; strip, 26

Testing. *See* Assaying

Thailand: and niello, 186; silver-gilt bowl, 111